第二届中国—中东欧国家
文化遗产论坛文集

Papers from the 2nd China–CEEC
Cultural Heritage Forum

国家文物局办公室（外事联络司）
中国文化遗产研究院   编

Department of Foreign Affairs of National Cultural Heritage Administration

Chinese Academy of Cultural Heritage

文物出版社

图书在版编目（CIP）数据

第二届中国—中东欧国家文化遗产论坛文集：汉英
对照／国家文物局办公室（外事联络司），中国文化遗
产研究院编 . —北京：文物出版社，2020.10
 ISBN 978－7－5010－6667－4

Ⅰ. ①第…　Ⅱ. ①国…②中…　Ⅲ. ①文化遗产－保
护－中国－文集－汉、英②文化遗产－保护－欧洲－文集
－汉、英　Ⅳ. ①K203－53②K500.3－53

中国版本图书馆 CIP 数据核字（2020）第 047530 号

第二届中国—中东欧国家文化遗产论坛文集

编　　者：国家文物局办公室（外事联络司）　中国文化遗产研究院
　　　　　Department of Foreign Affairs of National Cultural Heritage Administration
　　　　　Chinese Academy of Cultural Heritage

责任编辑：李　睿
封面设计：王文娴
责任印制：苏　林

出版发行：文物出版社
社　　址：北京市东直门内北小街 2 号楼
邮　　编：100007
网　　址：http：//www.wenwu.com
邮　　箱：web@ wenwu.com
经　　销：新华书店
印　　刷：北京京都六环印刷厂
开　　本：889mm×1194mm　1/16
印　　张：30
版　　次：2020 年 10 月第 1 版
印　　次：2020 年 10 月第 1 次印刷
书　　号：ISBN 978－7－5010－6667－4
定　　价：400.00 元

CONTENTS 目录

02 目录

考古研究与实践

开幕式致辞

在第二届中国—中东欧国家文化遗产论坛上的致辞

河南省委常委、洛阳市委书记 李 亚

（2019年4月10日·洛阳）

尊敬的波黑民政部扎菲奇副部长，

尊敬的国家文物局刘玉珠局长，

尊敬的各位嘉宾，女士们、先生们，朋友们：

大家上午好！值此春满河洛、牡丹盛开的美好时节，大家相聚洛阳，出席第二届中国—中东欧国家文化遗产论坛。我代表中共洛阳市委、洛阳市人民政府，对本次论坛的举办表示热烈的祝贺！对大家的到来表示诚挚的欢迎！

文化遗产是全人类的宝贵财富。中国共产党和中国政府高度重视文化遗产的保护利用工作，主张在构建人类命运共同体中加强各国间的人文交流与合作。中共中央总书记、中国国家主席习近平同志指出，要"像爱惜生命一样保护好历史文化遗产"，特别强调"文明交流互鉴是增进各国人民友谊的桥梁、推动人类社会进步的动力、维护世界和平的纽带"。中国—中东欧国家合作机制自2012年建立以来，人文领域一直是各国交流与合作的重要领域。举办中国—中东欧国家文化遗产论坛，对于促进人类文化遗产保护利用工作，对于深化中国—中东欧国家人文等领域交流与合作，都是大事、喜事、盛事。

洛阳是中华文明的重要发祥地，有5000多年文明史、4000多年城市史、1500多年建都史，是十三朝古都、丝绸之路的东方起点。现有世界文化遗产3项6处、全国重点文物保护单位43处、各类博物馆68家、馆藏文物40多万件。历史上，自丝绸之路开辟后，洛阳就与中东欧国家有着密切交往，深受欧洲人民喜爱的中国瓷器、丝绸、茶叶，就是从洛阳出发来到欧洲的。近年来，洛阳坚定文化自信、坚持守正出新，以建设国际文化旅游名城为抓手，扎实做好文化遗产保护利用工作，努力把优秀传统文化的精神标识提炼出来、展示出来，把优秀传统文化中具有当代价值、世界意义的文化精髓提炼出来、展示出来，保护固态、传承活态、发展业态，让洛阳厚重的历史文化"走出去"，致力让世界了解洛阳、让洛阳走向世界。在此过程中，洛阳与中东欧国家的人文交流日益密切。2017年12月至2018年3月在波兰卢布林省举办的《洛阳唐三彩艺术展》获得巨大成功，就是我们深化对外人文交流的一个缩影。

城市承载着人类文明的精华，文化是一座城市的"根"与"魂"。第二届中国—中东欧国家文化遗产论坛以"文化遗产与城市发展"为主题，共同探讨新时代文化遗产与城市发展的努力方向，这对于进一步推动文化遗产的科学保护、永续传承和合理利用，充分发挥文化遗产对城市发展的促进作用，深化中国—中东欧国家的人文交流、并带动形成全方位多层次宽领域的开放合作格局，都具有十分重要的意义。期待大家集思广益、畅所欲言，分享文化遗产保护利用工作成果，共商人文交流与合作路线图！期待大家对洛阳文化遗产保护利用工作多提宝贵意见！洛阳将以自美其美的底气、美人之美的胸怀、与人共美的合作，与大家携起手来，为做好文化遗产保护利用工作贡献智慧和力量！

北宋大文豪欧阳修有句诗，"洛阳地脉花最宜，牡丹尤为天下奇"。洛阳正在举办第 37 届牡丹文化节，诚邀大家在洛阳多走走、多看看，赏国色天香、品古都神韵，留下美好而深刻的印象。

预祝第二届中国—中东欧国家文化遗产论坛圆满成功！祝各位嘉宾身体健康、工作顺利！

谢谢大家！

Speech at the 2nd China–CEEC Cultural Heritage Forum

Li Ya

Member of Henan Provincial Committee of the CPC, Party Secretary of Luoyang City

(10 April 2019, in Luoyang City)

Honorable Mr. Suvad Dzafic, Assistant Minister of Civil Affairs of Bosnia and Herzegovina,

Honorable Mr. Liu Yuzhu, Administrator of the China's National Cultural Heritage Administration,

Distinguished guests,

Ladies and gentlemen,

Dear friends,

Good morning. In this beautiful season of spring when the land of the Yellow River and the Luo River is full of green and peony blossoms, we are very pleased to be here with you all in the city of Luoyang to celebrate the 2nd China-CEEC Cultural Heritage Forum. On behalf of the Municipal Party Committee and People's Government of Luoyang, I would like to extend warm congratulations on the forum and sincere welcome to you all.

Cultural heritage is the valuable asset of all humanity. The Chinese Communist Party and Government attach vital importance to the conservation and utilization of cultural heritage, calling for increasing people-to-people exchanges and cooperation among all countries through the building of a community of shared future for mankind. General Secretary and President Xi Jinping noted that "We should preserve and protect historical and cultural heritage just like we do to our own lives" and "Exchanges and mutual learning among civilizations serve as bridges enhancing friendship among people of all nations, driving forces facilitating progress of human society, and bonds safeguarding world peace". Since the establishment of the China-CEEC cooperation mechanism in 2012, people-to-people exchanges has remained an important front of cooperation. The China-CEEC Cultural Heritage Forum is a major, good and great event for promoting the conservation and utilization of cultural heritage for all humanity and increasing China-CEEC cultural exchanges and cooperation.

Luoyang is a major birthplace of Chinese civilization. It has a history of 5,000 years as a civilization center, 4,000 years as a city, and 1,500 years as a capital. It is the seat of capital for 13 dynasties and the eastern starting point of the Silk Road. Luoyang boasts 3 World Cultural Heritage sites (6 components in total) , 43 State Priority Protected Sites, and 68 museums with a collection totaling 40 pieces. After the Silk Road was pioneered, Luoyang maintained close contacts with CEE nations and Chinese silk, porcelain and tea that were favored by Europeans were exported to Europe via Luoyang. In recent years, Luoyang people have endeavored to consolidate confidence in Chinese culture, protect their traditions while making innovations, preserve and utilize cultural heritage for the purpose of building Luoyang into an international city of culture and tourism, develop and present the best of the traditional culture that bears contemporary values and universal significance, protect tangible heritage, continue intangible heritage, and develop cultural industries, so as to make the rich and profound culture and history of Luoyang known to the rest of the world. In this process, cultural exchanges between Luoyang and CEE countries have continued to increase. For example, the Exhibition of Tang Tri-colored Potteries of Luoyang, held in Lublin, Poland from December 2017 to March 2018, was a great success demonstrating ever-increasing cultural exchanges between Luoyang and the rest of the world.

Cities bear the essence of human civilization and culture carries the root and soul of a city. The 2nd China-CEEC Cultural Heritage Forum, featuring the theme of "cultural heritage and urban development", is aimed at discussing trends and orientations for cultural heritage and urban development in the new era. It is of great importance for facilitating scientific conservation, sustainable continuation and reasonable utilization of cultural heritage, giving full play to the role of cultural heritage in promoting urban development, increasing China-CEEC cultural exchanges, and contributing to all-round openness and cooperation in various fields and at various levels. We hope that participants would share their achievements in cultural heritage conservation and utilization, offer their advice and insights, and jointly propose a road map for deepening cultural exchanges and cooperation. We are looking forward to your valuable comments on Luoyang's work in the conservation and utilization of cultural heritage. With its confidence, vision and aspiration for collaboration, Luoyang is ready to work together with you and contribute its wisdom and strength to better conservation and utilization of cultural heritage.

Ouyang Xiu, a famous poet of the Northern Song Dynasty (960–1127) once remarked in his poem, "Flowers flourishing in Luoyang, with its ideal geographical position, where grow the finest peonies of the nation". The 37th Peony Culture Festival is ongoing in Luoyang. I sincerely invite you to travel around Luoyang to appreciate the national flower of peony and enjoy the appeal of the ancient capital. I hope you could have a good and unforgettable impression on Luoyang.

Last but not the least, I wish the 2nd China-CEEC Cultural Heritage Forum a great success and I wish you good health and all the best!

Thank you!

在第二届中国—中东欧国家文化遗产论坛上的致辞

河南省人民政府副省长　霍金花

（2019年4月10日·洛阳）

尊敬的各位来宾，女士们、先生们：

大家上午好！

在这满目葱茏、生机盎然的美好时节，我们相聚在古都洛阳，共同庆祝第二届中国—中东欧国家文化遗产论坛隆重开幕，共商文化遗产保护利用大计。在此，我谨代表河南省人民政府，向远道而来的各位嘉宾表示诚挚的欢迎！向长期以来关心支持河南文化遗产保护利用工作的海内外各界朋友表示衷心的感谢！

河南历史悠久、文化厚重，是中华民族和华夏文明的重要发祥地，在5000年中华文明史中，作为国家政治、经济、文化中心长达3000多年，世界华人的人文始祖黄帝诞生在这里，最古老汉字甲骨文在这里发现，少林武术和太极拳均发源于此，中国古代四大发明均源自河南。河南区位优越、交通便利，四通八达的"米"字形高速铁路网加快建设，从郑州机场起飞2小时内就可以到达中国大部分城市，高速公路网覆盖全省所有县城，连通境内外、辐射东中西的物流通道枢纽正在形成。河南经济体量大、发展后劲足，市场广阔，人力资源丰富，是中国重要的人口大省、经济大省、农业大省、新兴工业大省和内陆开放大省，郑州航空港经济综合实验区、郑洛新国家自主创新示范区、中国（河南）自由贸易试验区、中国（郑州）跨境电子商务综合试验区等加快建设，基础设施日益完备，与世界的联系越来越密切、交流越来越频繁。

文化遗产承载着珍贵的历史记忆，是一个国家和地区的"金色名片"。近年来，河南省高度重视文化遗产保护利用工作，坚持"保护为主、抢救第一、合理利用、加强管理"的工作方针，在保护中发展、在发展中保护，紧紧围绕打造华夏历史文明传承创新区和构筑全国重要的文化高地，持续加大投入，创新体制机制，强化世界文化遗产申报管理，大力推进创造性转化、创新性发展，着力让收藏在博物馆里的文物、陈列在广阔大地上的遗产、书写在古籍里的文字都活起来，加快实现由文化资源大省向文化强省的跨越。

相知无远近，万里尚为邻。2100多年前，中国汉代张骞肩负着和平友好的使命，两次出使中亚，开辟出一条连接欧亚的丝绸之路。洛阳是古丝绸之路的东方起点。千百年来，在这条古老的丝绸之路上，伴随着清脆悠扬的驼铃声，河南同沿线国家和地区的经贸往来、人文交流绵延不绝，留下了厚重的历史记忆。进入新时代，河南积极融入"一带一路"建设，搭建联接世界的空中、陆上、网上、海上丝绸之路，同中东欧国家的交流合作不断拓展。本届论坛围绕文化遗产与城市发展的主题，将就文化遗产领域的相关问题深入交流探讨，必将对河南加强文化遗产保护利用、深化同中东欧国家的交流合作产生有力推动作用。我们将以此次论坛为契机，积极借鉴国内外文化遗产保护利用的好经验好做法，进一步加快华夏历史文明传承创新区建设，促进中原文化大发展、大繁荣，为传承弘扬中华优秀传统文化、扩大中外文明交流互鉴贡献力量！

最后，祝愿第二届中国—中东欧国家文化遗产论坛取得圆满成功！祝各位来宾身体健康、万事如意！

谢谢大家！

Speech at the 2nd China-CEEC Cultural Heritage Forum

Huo Jinhua

Vice Governor of the People's Government of Henan Province

(10 April 2019, in Luoyang City)

Distinguished guests,

Ladies and gentlemen,

Good morning. In this beautiful season full of green and vitality, we are here together to celebrate the opening of the 2nd China-CEEC Cultural Heritage Forum, with the aim of discussing strategy for the conservation and utilization of cultural heritage. On behalf of the People's Government of Henan Province, I would like to extend warm welcome to all the guests travelling from afar and express heartfelt thanks to all the friends at home and from abroad who have long supported the conservation and utilization of cultural heritage in Henan.

Henan is a major birthplace of Chinese nation and civilization, with time-honored history and rich culture. Over the course of Chinese civilization for 5,000 years, Henan served as the nation's political, economic and cultural center for more than 3,000 years. It bears witness to the birth of the Yellow Emperor known as the founding ancestor of Chinese people, the oracle bone script as the most ancient system of Chinese writing, and Shaolin Kung Fu and Taichi Boxing. All the four great inventions of ancient China were made in Henan. Today, Henan enjoys a favorable geographical and transport conditions, with a star-shaped high-speed railway network. A flight from the airport of Zhengzhou, Henan's capital, can take passengers to a majority of cities across the country within two hours. Its expressway network covers all counties around the province. A logistics hub is taking shape in Henan, accessing the country's eastern and middle regions and connecting China with the rest of the world. Henan is a big economy, with a strong capacity for future growth, a huge market and rich human resources. It is one of the most populous provinces in the country, playing a significant role in the country's economic, agricultural and industrial sectors. It is also an exemplar inland province in implementing the policy of opening up. Zhengzhou Airport Economic Zone, Zhengzhou-Luoyang New

National Pilot Zone for Innovation, China Henan Free Trade Pilot Zone, and China Zhengzhou Cross-border E-commerce Pilot Zone are under construction. With ever-improving infrastructure, Henan sees ever-closer ties and ever-increasing exchanges with the rest of the world.

Cultural heritage bears valuable historical memories and establishes itself as a shining name card for projecting national or regional images. In recent years, Henan has attached vital importance to the conservation and utilization of cultural heritage. By following the guideline of "preservation with timely rescue, utilization under strict control", emphasis has been placed on both conservation and development, with the aim of building Henan into an innovative area to continue Chinese civilization and a major cultural highland across the country. Funds have been increased, systems and mechanisms innovated, nomination and management of World Cultural Heritage sites improved, and innovative transformation and development promoted, with the aim of revitalizing cultural objects collected in museums, monuments and sites distributed over vast territories and contents documented in historical literatures and speeding up the progress of Henan from a culturally-rich province to a culturally-strong province.

As an old Chinese saying goes, "We can know each other well no matter how far away, just like we can still be neighbors ten thousand kilometers away from each other." 2,100 years ago, Zhang Qian as an envoy of the Han Dynasty was dispatched to take a mission of peace and friendship to Central Asia, pioneering the Silk Road connecting Asia and Europe. Luoyang is the eastern starting point of the Silk Road. For hundreds of years, camel caravans passed through the trade route to link countries and regions along the Silk Road with Henan, through constant trade contacts and cultural exchanges, which left behind rich and diverse historical memories in this land. In the new era, Henan is working actively to participate in the Belt and Road Initiative, build aerial, land, maritime and online Silk Roads, and increase exchanges and cooperation with CEEC countries. This forum, featuring the theme of "cultural heritage and urban development", is aimed at conducting in-depth discussion about issues involving cultural heritage. It will surely facilitate the conservation and utilization of cultural heritage in Henan and deepen its exchanges and cooperation with CEE countries. We will take this forum as an opportunity to draw from good experiences and practices in protecting and utilizing cultural heritage so as to speed up the construction of the innovative area for continuing Chinese civilization, promote the development of Central Plain culture, and make new contribution to continuing and promoting the best of Chinese culture and enhancing exchanges and mutual learning between Chinese and foreign civilizations.

Last but not the least, I wish the 2nd China-CEEC Cultural Heritage Forum a great success and I wish you good health and all the best!

Thank you for your attention!

在第二届中国—中东欧国家文化遗产论坛上的致辞

波黑民政部副部长　苏瓦德·扎菲奇

（2019年4月10日·洛阳）

尊敬的各位女士、先生：

我谨代表波黑民政部向大家致以诚挚的问候。今天我很荣幸来到洛阳。作为中国四大古都之一，洛阳有着悠久而丰富的历史。我们相聚在这里，是为了加强文化领域的成功合作。借此机会，我谨对东道主的邀请表示感谢，并祝第二届中国—中东欧国家文化遗产论坛圆满成功。

"16+1合作"很重要，这是波黑在国际文化合作框架内的首要任务之一。我想强调的是，我们将更加重视文化遗产，这至关重要，同时也将形成归属感，并为投资县域可持续发展提供灵感和创造力。

中国和中东欧国家拥有丰富的文化遗产，我们将重点加强在共同的、有价值的历史遗产保护领域的合作，促进文化遗产保护、修复和利用等方面的交流及合作。

我相信，不久的将来，我们肯定能成功合作，一起为推动中国和中东欧国家的文化遗产建设贡献力量。

我很高兴受邀来洛阳参加这次论坛。此刻，李克强总理正在我国访问。中国正在向世界发出一个明确的信号，那就是发展和深化中欧战略合作。李克强总理将对克罗地亚进行正式访问，并出席在著名世界遗址地杜布罗夫尼克市中心举行的第八次中国—中东欧国家领导人会晤。

欧洲和中国是重要的贸易伙伴，现在，贸易和经济质量上升了新台阶，国家最高领导人也赋予我们新的任务，落实细化会议内容，也就是把工作落到实处。我建议通过此次论坛成立专家组，制定共同的行动规划。内容包括：通过专家交流互访的方式进行协调、修复等工作，指定一些我们可以共同开展的项目，以及与联合国教科文组织和其他世界遗产机构和组织展开合作。这表明，通过双方深入合作可以开发出新的文化模式，这种交流和行动规划也将促进双方在文化旅游产业和经济领域的发展。同时加强在教育、文化、文化遗产、旅游等方面的人文交流，增进两国人民之间的相互了解。

我们地处不同经常面临共同的问题，甚至危机和战争，因此有必要分享价值观、经验、知识和项目，加强合作。

中国是我们伟大的合作伙伴，也可以成为我们伟大的老师。中国已经建立了自己的文明。现在，中国正在向世界展示如何保护、传承其历史悠久的文明。感谢中国政府。非常感谢洛阳市及市领导。期待我们的合作。

Speach at the 2nd China-CEEC Cultural Heritage Forum

Suvad Dzafic

Assistant Minister of Ministry of Civil Affairs of BiH

(10 April 2019, in Luoyang City)

Dear Ladies and Gentlemen,

Allow me to greet you on behalf of the Ministry of Civil Affairs of Bosnia and Herzegovina. It is my great pleasure to be here today in Luoyang, in the city of long and rich history, the city which represents one of the Four Great Ancient Capitals of China, the city where we have gathered together in order to make our cooperation in the field of culture even stronger and more successful. I would like to use this opportunity to thank our host for the invitation as well as to congratulate for the excellent organization of the second Cultural Heritage Forum of China and Central Eastern European Countries.

Considering the cooperation of the "16+1" to be of great importance, it represents one of the priorities of Bosnia and Herzegovina in the framework of international cultural cooperation. I would like to emphasize that we will give more importance to the cultural heritage, which is essential and at the same time provides a sense of belonging on the one hand, and on the other, inspiration and creativity for investing in the sustainable development of the counties.

China and Central and Eastern European Countries have a rich cultural heritage, so our efforts will be focused on further cooperation and protection of common valuable historical heritage by facilitating exchange and cooperation in the area of conservation, restoration and utilization of cultural heritage.

I am convinced that we will have successful cooperation in the upcoming period as well as that we will provide a common contribution to the promotion of China and Central and Eastern European Countries heritage.

It is really exciting to actively take part in this forum here in Luoyang. At the same time, Prime Minister Li Keqiang touched down at the Bosnia Airport. China is sending a clear signal to the world of growing and deepening strategic cooperation between China and European nations. Primer will make official visits to

Croatia and attend the 8th meeting of China and Central and Eastern European Countries in the central city of Dubrovnik, great and famous UNESCO site.

Europe and China are big trading partners, but now in the time that trading and economy could get new quality, our highest state officials gave us the task to concretize and specify these formal gathering and speeches. I propose that we on this forum create expert group which will make common action plan. That action plan can include exchanging experts for coordination, restoration etc., appointing some projects we can work on together, and joint work in UNESCO and other global heritage institutions and organizations. That demonstrates that new cultural modes can be developed with the cooperation of both sides. This exchange and this action plan will also increase the promotion of cultural tourism industry and economic ties from both sides. People to people exchanges including education, culture, cultural heritage and tourism should also be strengthened to improve mutual understanding between our people.

We from the region often shared mutual problems, even crises and wars, therefore sharing values, experience, knowledge and projects and strengthening cooperation are necessary.

China is our great partner, but China can be also our great teacher. China has built their own civilization. Now China is showing the world how to preserve it and keep it for the future. Thanks to the Chinese government. Thank you very much indeed for the City of Luoyang and its leaders. I am looking forward for our common future projects.

在第二届中国—中东欧国家文化遗产论坛上的致辞

中国国家文物局局长　刘玉珠

（2019年4月10日·洛阳）

尊敬的苏瓦德·扎菲奇副部长和来自中东欧国家的同行们，

尊敬的李亚书记、霍金花副省长，

女士们、先生们、朋友们：

在牡丹花开的美好时节，很高兴与各位新老朋友相聚丝绸之路的东方节点——古都洛阳，共同出席第二届中国—中东欧国家文化遗产论坛。我谨代表中国国家文物局，对论坛的开幕表示热烈祝贺！对远道而来的中东欧各国嘉宾表示诚挚欢迎！对长期以来致力于中国—中东欧国家文化遗产交流合作的各界人士表示崇高敬意！对精心筹办这次论坛的河南省人民政府、洛阳市人民政府及有关方面表示衷心感谢！

友好和合作始终是中国与中东欧国家关系发展主旋律。即使远隔千山万水，早在2000多年前，"丝绸之路"就把我们连在一起。2013年中国提出"一带一路"倡议，获得了中东欧各国的积极响应，16国均与中国签署了"一带一路"合作文件。在"一带一路"倡议的持续引领和"16+1"合作机制的不断推动下，中国—中东欧文化遗产交流合作呈现稳中有进的良好态势。

——文物展览更加活跃，不断成为"16+1"合作"金名片"。中国赴中东欧国家6年累计举办12个中国文物精品展；中国文物大展首次亮相捷克、拉脱维亚，成为纪念中捷建交65周年、中拉建交25周年的文化盛事；捷克、波兰、匈牙利、罗马尼亚来华举办6个文物精品展，展出地域不断拓展，策展模式不断创新，以文明交流丰富文化外交，以文明互鉴促进民心相通。

——人员交往更加密切，不断成为"16+1"合作新窗口。中国—中东欧国家文化遗产领域高层互访日渐增多，工作交流和学术研讨日渐深入，"朋友圈"持续扩大，在交往中拉近了心与心的距离，在交流中凝聚了更多合作共识。成功举办首届中国—中东欧国家文化遗产论坛，为"16+1"人文交流搭建了新平台。中国国家文物局局长首访匈牙利、塞尔维亚；爱沙尼亚、塞尔维亚、波黑高级官员来华访问，就深化合作达成重要共识。

——机制建设实现突破，不断成为"16+1"合作新亮点。中国与塞尔维亚签署关于促进文化遗产领域交流与合作的谅解备忘录，中国文化遗产研究院启动塞尔维亚巴契遗址申报世界遗产合作项目；

中国与罗马尼亚就签署关于防止盗窃、盗掘和非法进出境文化财产协定达成一致，这是中塞、中罗合作务实性的充分体现，具有示范性的引领意义。中国—中东欧国家文化合作协调中心在马其顿设立，中国—中东欧国家文创产业交流合作中心落户中国成都，为"16+1"文化遗产合作注入了新动能。

"一带一路"倡议正在成为当今世界规模最大的国际合作平台和最受欢迎的国际公共产品，今年4月第二届"一带一路"国际合作高峰论坛即将在北京举行。文化遗产国际合作是"一带一路"建设的重要组成部分，更是促进中外人文交流的"动车组"。伴随中华民族的复兴征程，古老丝路焕发勃勃生机，"16+1"文化遗产合作正当其势、大有可为。中方愿同中东欧国家一道，秉持共商共建共享的原则，搭乘"一带一路"合作的快车、便车，共同推动"16+1"文化遗产合作相向而行、行稳致远。

一是加强统筹规划。"16+1"文化遗产合作尚在起步期，我们要聚焦重点、精雕细琢，共同绘制好精谨细腻的"工笔画"。要在"一带一路"框架下，以更开放的胸襟、更包容的心态、更宽广的视角，对接各国发展战略和人民美好生活需要，对接各国文化遗产资源禀赋和文化遗产保护利用规划，对接中外人文交流行动计划和文化遗产领域双边协议，尊重彼此利益和重要关切，做好顶层设计、整体布局、项目规划和政策衔接，为"16+1"文化遗产合作确定大方向和路线图，为文化遗产管理部门和保护机构务实合作带来更多利好。在新一轮国家机构改革中，中国新设了国家国际发展合作署，充分体现了中国政府对国际发展合作的高度重视。中方正在积极推动将文化遗产国际合作整体纳入中国国际发展合作体系，完善中国文化遗产国际合作多部门协调、各地区联动的长效机制，为"16+1"文化遗产合作提供支撑和便利。

二是做大对话平台。更好借力"一带一路"、中国—中东欧、中欧多边合作机制，推动将文化遗产国际合作纳入"一带一路"参与国和"16+1"高级别人文交流机制，推动更多文化遗产合作项目和成果纳入国事访问成果清单。更好依托"一带一路"国际合作高峰论坛、丝绸之路文化遗产国际论坛、丝绸之路国际博物馆联盟、中国—中东欧国家文化合作部长论坛和文化遗产论坛，把对话当作"黄金法则"用起来，把文化遗产论坛办成跨国家跨区域对话协商和友好合作的创新典范。

三是聚焦务实合作。"16+1合作"的主基调是务实合作。中方已在海外开展了10个文化遗产保护修复合作项目和40个中外联合考古项目，涉及亚洲、非洲、欧洲、南美洲的24个国家。中方乐见与有需求有意愿的中东欧国家在文物保护修复和联合考古项目的策划、遴选和试点上加强沟通、有序推进、尽早落地。紧扣重大活动、重大事件、重要会议、重要展会和国家文化年、文化节，举办有影响有分量的文化遗产领域人文交流系列活动。坚持有来有往，实施文化遗产外展精品工程，打造文化遗产外交品牌，促进双方人民尤其是青年一代相互了解、加深友谊。以信息共享、智能应用、体验服务和跨界创意为重点，建设"一带一路"文化遗产智慧网络，联合打造具有丝绸之路特色的文化遗产旅游产品和保护品牌。中方愿意推动双方在人力资源培训领域的合作，推动文化遗产领域高等院校、科研机构和文博单位的交流，邀请更多中东欧国家的文化遗产官员和技术人员来华培训，鼓励文化遗产科技人员的交流。鼓励双方友好省市发挥优势，带动文化遗产领域地方合作。中方倡议适时举办中国—中东欧国家中学生文化遗产暑期课堂和大学生中华历史文化研习营活动，促进双方文化遗产青年学者间交流往来，让中国—中东欧国家友谊薪火相传。

四是协同国际行动。中国已与21国签署关于防止盗窃、盗掘和非法进出境的文化财产双边协定；今年美国、意大利政府相继向中国返还流失海外文物艺术品1157件/套。中方希望与更多中东欧国家签署防止盗窃盗掘和非法进出境文化财产双边协定、文化遗产领域政府部门间合作谅解备忘录，构建稳定多维的政府间文化遗产国际合作网络。中方愿同更多中东欧国家积极参与文化遗产领域全球治理和公共产品供给，加强在文化遗产国际组织事务上的协调合作，支持武装冲突地区濒危文化遗产保护国际行动，共同防范打击非法劫掠、盗窃、盗掘及走私文物行为。推动各方提升文化遗产国际合作便利化程度，促进政策、规则、标准的联通，多做行动派、实干家，将我们的合作愿景转化为实际行动。

"积力之所举，则无不胜也；众智之所为，则无不成也。"中国—中东欧国家文化遗产论坛是中国与中东欧各国共同创建的合作平台，是"16+1"合作深化拓展的创新举措。中方高度重视这一跨区域合作平台，愿与中东欧国家共同努力，使之不断完善机制、日益走向成熟，为"16+1"合作、中欧合作做出更大贡献。今年，中国—中东欧国家文化遗产论坛首次来到中国，各方嘉宾齐聚一堂，围绕"世界文化遗产申报与管理、考古研究和文物保护"主题，深入交流、共享经验、共襄合作。期待与会嘉宾畅所欲言、分享真知灼见，期待本次论坛就如何规划好未来"16+1"文化遗产合作的基本理念、整体布局、项目安排和制度设计出谋划策、贡献智慧，用文化遗产促进思想交流、文明对话、民心相通，推动形成平等、包容、互惠、活跃的"16+1"文化遗产国际合作向好态势。

预祝第二届中国—中东欧国家文化遗产论坛圆满成功！

谨祝中东欧各国嘉宾在华期间工作顺利、身体健康！

谢谢大家！

Speech at the 2ⁿᵈ China-CEEC Cultural Heritage Forum

Liu Yuzhu

Adminiatrator of the National Cultural Heritage Administration of China

(10 April 2019, in Luoyang City)

Honorable Mr. Suvad Dzafic, Assistant Minister of Civil Affairs of Bosnia and Herzegovina,

Colleagues from CEEC,

Honorable Party Secretary Li Ya,

Honorable Vice Governor Huo Jinhua,

Ladies and gentlemen,

Dear friends,

In the beautiful season with peony blossoms, I am delighted to meet the old and new friends in Luoyang, the ancient capital of China and the ancient node of the Silk Road, for celebrating the 2ⁿᵈ China-CEEC Cultural Heritage Forum. On behalf of the China's National Cultural Heritage Administration, I would like to extend my sincere congratulations to the opening of the forum and my warm welcome to guests from CEEC. I would like to pay tribute to people from all walks of life who have been committed to China-CEEC cultural heritage exchanges. My thanks also go to the People's Government of Henan Province, the Luoyang Municipal People's Government and relevant parties for organizing this forum.

Friendship and cooperation have always been the main theme of China-CEEC relations. Though distant geographically, the Silk Road brought us together as early as more than 2,000 years ago. In 2013, China put forward the Belt and Road Initiative, which received positive responses from CEEC, with 16 countries signing the Belt and Road Initiative cooperation documents with China. Under the continuous guidance of the Belt and Road Initiative and the promotion of the "16+1" cooperation mechanism, China-CEEC exchange and cooperation of cultural heritage have maintained steady progress.

Frequent cultural relics exhibitions have become the golden business card of "16+1" cooperation. China has hosted 12 Chinese cultural relics exhibitions in CEEC in the last six years. The China cultural relics exhibition debuted in the Czech Republic and Latvia, serving as a cultural event to commemorate the 65th anniversary of the establishment of diplomatic relations between China and Czech Republic and the 25th anniversary of the establishment of diplomatic relations between China and Latvia. The Czech Republic, Poland, Hungary and Romania held 6 cultural relics exhibitions in China. There are more places holding the exhibition and new curatorial models keep emerging. Cultural exchanges have enriched cultural diplomacy. Mutual learning between culture has promoted people-to-people connectivity.

Personnel exchanges have become a new window for "16+1" cooperation. China-CEEC exchange of high-level visits in the field of cultural heritage is increasing. Work communication and academic discussions are deepening. The circle of friends continues to expand. Our people get closer and more cooperation and consensus have been reached through exchanges. The success of the 1st China-CEEC Cultural Heritage Forum set up a new platform for "16+1" people-to-people exchanges. The Administrator of the China's National Cultural Heritage Administration visited Hungary and Serbia. Officials of Estonia, Serbia and Bosnia and Herzegovina visited China and reached important consensus on deepening cooperation.

The breakthrough in mechanism construction has become a new highlight of "16+1" cooperation. China and Serbia signed an MOU on promoting exchanges and cooperation in the field of cultural heritage, and the Chinese Academy of Cultural Heritage launched a cooperative project for Bač's bid to become a UNESCO World Heritage site in Serbia. China and Romania reached an agreement on the prevention of theft, excavation and illegal entry and exit of cultural property. These are a leading manifestation of the practical cooperation between China and Serbia and China and Romania. The China-CEEC Coordination Center for Cultural Cooperation has been established in Macedonia. The China-CEEC Cultural Innovation Industry Exchange and Cooperation Center has been located in Chengdu, China. These have injected new impetus into the "16+1" cultural heritage cooperation.

The Belt and Road Initiative is becoming the largest international cooperation platform and the most popular international public goods. The Second Belt and Road Forum for International Cooperation will be held in Beijing in April this year. International cooperation in cultural heritage is an important part of the Belt and Road construction and cultural exchanges between China and foreign countries. With the revival of the Chinese nation, the ancient Silk Road is full of vitality and the "16+1" cultural heritage cooperation is promising. The Chinese side is willing to work with CEEC to uphold the principle of extensive consultation, joint contribution and shared benefits, take advantage of the Belt and Road cooperation and jointly promote the "16+1" cultural heritage cooperation.

First, strengthen overall planning. The "16+1" cultural heritage cooperation is still in its infancy. We must focus on the key areas for result-oriented cooperation. Under the framework of the Belt and Road and with a more inclusive mindset, we will align the development strategies of all countries, people's needs for a better life, cultural heritage resources, cultural heritage protection and utilization plans, Chinese and foreign people-to-people exchange action plans and bilateral agreements in the field of cultural heritage. We respect the interests and important concerns of each other. Through top-level design, overall layout, project planning and policy linkage, we will charter the course for the "16+1" cultural heritage cooperation, benefiting the pragmatic cooperation between the heritage management departments and the protection agencies. In the new round of state institution reform, China International Development Cooperation Agency has been established, which fully reflects the importance the Chinese government attaches to international development and cooperation. China is promoting the integration of international cultural heritage into its international development and cooperation system, improving the multi-sectoral and cross-regional coordination mechanism of international cooperation in China's cultural heritage and providing support and convenience for "16+1" cultural heritage cooperation.

Second, expand the dialogue platform. We should leverage the Belt and Road and China-CEEC and China-EU multilateral cooperation mechanisms to integrate the international cooperation of cultural heritage into the Belt and Road participating countries and the "16+1" high-level people-to-people exchange mechanism. Therefore, more projects and results of cultural heritage cooperation will be included in the list of results of the state visits. Relying on the Belt and Road Forum for International Cooperation, the Silk Road Cultural Heritage International Forum, the International Alliance of Museums of the Silk Road, the China-CEEC Cultural Cooperation Forum and the China-CEEC Cultural Heritage Forum, we should cherish dialogue as a "golden rule". We need to make China-CEEC Cultural Heritage Forum an innovative model of cross-national dialogue, consultation and friendly cooperation.

Third, focus on pragmatic cooperation. The "16+1" cooperation pays attention to pragmatic cooperation. China has carried out 10 cultural heritage protection and restoration cooperation projects and 40 joint archaeological projects overseas, covering 24 countries in Asia, Africa, Europe and South America. The Chinese side is pleased to strengthen communication on the planning, selection and pilot of cultural relics restoration and joint archaeological projects in CEEC. We should organize a series of influential cultural exchange activities such as major events, important meetings, important exhibitions, national cultural years and cultural festivals. Exchanges require implementing cultural heritage outreach projects, building cultural heritage diplomatic brands and promoting mutual understanding and friendship between the two peoples, especially the younger generation. Focusing on information sharing, intelligent application, experience service and cross-border creativity, we will build a smart Belt and Road cultural heritage network and jointly create cultural heritage tourism products and protection brands with the characteristics of the Silk Road. China is willing to promote cooperation in the field of human resources training and exchanges between institutions of higher learning, scientific research institutions and cultural and museum institutions. More cultural heritage officials and technicians from CEEC will be invited to train in China and exchanges of cultural heritage and scientific personnel will be encouraged. The friendly provinces and cities should leverage their advantages and promote local cooperation in the field of cultural heritage. The Chinese side advocates the timely holding of the China-CEEC Cultural Heritage Summer Class for Middle School Students and the Chinese History and Culture Camp for Undergraduates, strengthening exchanges between young scholars of cultural heritage and China-CEEC friendship.

Fourth, coordinate international action. China has signed bilateral agreements with 21 countries on the prevention of theft, excavation and illegal entry and exit of cultural property. This year, the US and Italian governments have returned to China 1,157 pieces/sets of lost Chinese cultural relics. China hopes to sign bilateral agreements on the prevention of theft, excavation and illegal entry and exit of cultural property with CEEC and to see the MOUs on cooperation between government departments in the field of cultural heritage so as to build a stable and multidimensional intergovernmental cooperation network of cultural heritage. China is ready to work with CEEC to participate in the global governance and supply of public goods in the field of cultural heritage, strengthen coordination and cooperation in the affairs of international organizations of cultural heritage, support international actions in the protection of endangered cultural heritage in armed conflict areas and jointly prevent against illegal looting, theft, excavation and smuggling of cultural relics. We can help all parties enhance international cooperation and facilitation of cultural heritage, promote the integration of policies, rules and standards and adopt concrete actions.

It is joint efforts that count. The China-CEEC Cultural Heritage Forum is a cooperation platform jointly established by China and CEEC. It shows the deepening of "16+1" cooperation. China attaches great importance to this cross-regional cooperation platform and is willing to work with CEEC to improve the mechanism and make greater contributions to the "16+1" cooperation and China-Europe cooperation. This year, the China-CEEC Cultural Heritage Forum is held in China for the first time. The guests are gathered together to exchange ideas, share experiences and cooperate in the theme of World Cultural Heritage Nomination and Management, Archaeological Research and Cultural Relics Protection. I look forward to hearing your insights. I expect your ideas on how to plan the basic concept, overall layout, project arrangement and system design of the future "16+1" cultural heritage cooperation. I hope we can promote cultural exchanges and dialogues and people-to-people connectivity through cultural heritage, forming an equal, inclusive, mutually beneficial and active "16+1" cultural heritage cooperation.

I wish the 2nd China-CEEC Cultural Heritage Forum a complete success!

I wish the guests of CEEC successful career and good health during your stay in China!

Thank you!

主旨发言

中国世界文化遗产保护实践与展望

中国国家文物局副局长　胡　冰

（2019年4月10日·洛阳）

尊敬的各位来宾，各位朋友：

最美人间四月天，很高兴此时与大家相聚在洛阳，分享中国世界文化遗产保护、管理、利用的实践经验。

1972年，联合国教科文组织通过《保护世界文化和自然遗产公约》，旨在对全人类具有突出普遍价值的文化和自然遗产进行保护。

30多年前，1985年12月12日，中国成为《保护世界文化和自然遗产公约》的缔约国，中国的世界文化遗产事业正式扬帆起航。1987年12月11日，在联合国教科文组织世界遗产委员会第11届会议上，北京故宫、秦始皇陵、敦煌莫高窟、周口店"北京人"遗址、长城、泰山等6项遗产列入世界遗产名录，成为中国首批世界遗产。这6项遗产在世界范围内早已享有盛名，突出反映了中国历史文化特征和古代文明辉煌成就，为中国世界文化遗产事业迎来了成功开局，也为中国文化遗产事业的发展奠定了坚实基础。

30多年来，中国的世界文化遗产从无到有，由少变多，发展迅速。目前，中国已有53项世界遗产，其中文化遗产36项，自然遗产13项，文化与自然双遗产4项，总数仅次于意大利，居世界第二位。

30多年来，中国政府始终信守对国际社会作出的庄严承诺，坚持不懈开展世界遗产保护、管理和申报工作，不断深入发掘、阐释和展示遗产内涵，使世界遗产的突出普遍价值、真实性与完整性得以传承，对中华文明进行全景式呈现。

下面，我将从中国世界文化遗产保护的实践经验，中国世界文化遗产事业展望，中国—中东欧国家文化遗产合作愿景三方面进行阐述。

一、中国世界文化遗产保护的实践经验

近年来，中国世界文化遗产在增强文化自信和国家认同、改善遗产地生态环境和民生、推动遗产

地经济社会发展、服务"一带一路"倡议和大运河文化带建设等方面的能力日渐提升，逐步探索出一条符合国情的世界文化遗产保护之路，主要呈现出六大特点：

（一）**申报类型日趋多样**。中国世界文化遗产类型丰富，分布地域广泛，时间跨度宏大，文化内涵多元。既有人类征服自然的杰作，也有人与自然和谐共生的产物；既有单点遗产，也有跨区域跨国境文化线路。这是中国人民对世界文明的丰厚贡献。

20 世纪 90 年代后，世界遗产申报在世界范围内呈现出新的发展趋势，从关注人类历史和人类文明的伟大遗迹，转向关注人类文化多样性和人类文化交流的重要遗存。中国顺应这种趋势，近年来申报项目侧重于文化景观、文化线路等新型遗产，譬如 2013 年列入世界遗产名录的红河哈尼梯田文化景观，2014 年的丝绸之路：长安—天山廊道的路网、大运河等。并在预备名单中逐步增加了近现代遗产、少数民族文化遗产、活态遗产等新类型。

（二）**法律法规体系不断完善**。中国逐步建立起以《文物保护法》为核心、地方性法规为补充的中国特色世界文化遗产保护管理法律制度体系，不断与世界遗产公约等国际规则有效衔接，并将世界遗产保护管理要求融入国家法律法规之中。2006 年，中国政府颁布了第一部世界文化遗产专项法规《长城保护条例》；同年，文化部颁布了《世界文化遗产保护管理办法》；2012 年又出台了《大运河遗产保护管理办法》；截至目前，各地共颁布地方性法规规章 72 件，其中，洛阳市早在 1999 年就颁布实施了《龙门石窟保护管理条例》。这些法律法规为中国世界文化遗产提供了有效的立法保护。

（三）**管理体制及协调机制日益健全**。中国世界文化遗产保护管理实施分级负责体制。国家文物局全面统筹世界文化遗产工作，省级文物主管部门负责业务指导，遗产地人民政府按照属地管理原则承担保护管理责任，遗产地均设立专门保护管理机构负责日常管理。

我们建立了国内部门间协调机制。如大运河申遗期间，由文化部、国家文物局牵头，13 个相关部委及大运河沿线 8 省、市人民政府共同组成大运河保护和申遗省部际会商小组。大运河成功列入世界遗产名录后，沿线 35 个城市又成立大运河沿线保护城市联盟，在联盟的机制下协调做好大运河全线遗产的保护管理工作。

我们还建立了跨国议事协调机制。在中国与哈萨克斯坦、吉尔吉斯斯坦跨国联合申报的"丝绸之路：长安—天山廊道的路网"项目中，中国主动承担国际协商协调任务，承办相关国际协调会议 14 次。2014 年，该项目成功列入《世界遗产名录》，成为联合国教科文组织倡导的世界遗产国际合作典范。

（四）**保护状况显著改善**。中国对世界文化遗产实行"规划先行"策略，通过保护规划协调各利益相关方的诉求，统筹保护管理与展示利用。尤其是针对长城、大运河等巨型文化遗产，中国政府相继颁布《长城保护总体规划》《大运河文化保护传承利用规划纲要》。

20 世纪 80 年代以来，中国投入大量资金，实施长城、故宫、布达拉宫等一批世界文化遗产保护修复项目。近年来，国家文物局又着力推动完成了长城保护工程、平安故宫工程、承德避暑山及周围寺庙、大足石刻千手观音等一批保护修复项目。这些项目的实施切实改善了文化遗产保护状况，让遗产更有尊严，也大幅提升了遗产地人居环境。

（五）监测预警系统日臻完善。世界文化遗产监测是世界遗产公约及其操作指南的刚性要求。国家文物局出台了《中国世界文化遗产监测巡视管理办法》，建立了重大干预活动监测、反应性监测、定期报告等监测预警工作制度，确立了监测管理框架体系，颁布了系列监测标准规范，搭建了监测预警系统平台，并在北京故宫、敦煌莫高窟、苏州古典园林、杭州西湖文化景观等遗产地建立了遗产监测系统。

（六）国际交流与合作日益深化。中国于 1991 年、1999 年、2007 年、2017 年四度担任世界遗产委员会委员国，中国专家在国际古迹遗址理事会（ICOMOS）、国际文化财产保护与修复中心（ICCROM）等国际组织中担任重要职务，直接深度参与世界遗产国际事务。

中国先后举办了第 28 届世界遗产委员会会议（2004 年）、ICOMOS 第 15 届大会（2005 年）等系列重要国际会议，形成了《苏州决议》《西安宣言》《北京文件》等重要国际文件。

2016 年、2017 年、2018 年，国家文物局与 ICCROM 共同举办了世界文化遗产监测培训班，系统性地对中国的世界文化遗产监测体系进行国际推介。

二、中国世界文化遗产事业展望

中国世界文化遗产事业快速发展的进程中，保护管理也面临诸多挑战，突出体现在妥善处理遗产保护与社会经济发展之间的矛盾，保护世界文化遗产的突出普遍价值及其真实性与完整性，发挥世界文化遗产的国际性和公益性等方面。

近年来，习近平主席就文化遗产保护，特别是世界文化遗产的申报、保护、展示和传承，作出了一系列重要指示和部署。他要求，要让"让收藏在博物馆里的文物、陈列在广阔大地上的遗产、书写在古籍里的文字都活起来，让中华文明同世界各国人民创造的丰富多彩的文明一道，为人类提供正确的精神指引和强大的精神动力"，成为我们今后努力的方向。

（一）坚持"三个有利于"，持续推进世界文化遗产申报。我们将坚持有利于突出中华文明历史文化价值、有利于体现中华民族精神追求、有利于展示全面真实的古代中国和现代中国的工作原则，着力传播中华优秀传统文化，科学制定世界文化遗产申报策略，有序推进良渚遗址、海上丝绸之路等申遗工作。

（二）推进现代科技与遗产监测相结合，不断提升保护管理水平。现代科学技术的发展为提升中国世界文化遗产监测预警水平提供了新机遇。我们将健全反应性监测机制，落实巡视巡查，推广无人机、监测云等现代科技手段，科学监测遗产及其周边环境变化，及时发现潜在风险，积极采取因应措施，防患于未然。

（三）大力倡导遗产与民生协调发展，努力提高公共文化服务水平。鼓励公众，尤其是遗产地社区居民，参与遗产保护活动，提升人民群众的参与感、获得感和认同感，增强社会凝聚力。世界遗产是世界的，是缔约国的，但首先是世代栖息于此的居民们的生活家园。社区居民作为直接利益相关方，应全面参与世界文化遗产成果的保护与共享。同时，通过世界文化遗产进校园、进社区等展示宣传活动，努力提高全社会特别是青少年的世界文化遗产保护意识。推动世界遗产"5C"战略（可信度、保护、能力建设、宣传、社区），引入现代技术，提升遗产展示阐释和展示水平。

（四）加速推动文化和旅游融合发展，创新世界文化遗产保护利用手段，实现经济社会可持续发展。我们将以文旅融合为目标，面向社会探索遗产酒店、国家公园、国家文化公园和国家遗产线路等文化遗产保护利用形式，形成具有特定开放性空间的文化载体，实现遗产保护与和科学研究、文化教育、公共服务、旅游观光、休闲娱乐协调发展。我们将依托世界文化遗产资源，运用互联网技术，开发兼顾艺术性和实用性的文化创意产品，拓展遗产价值传播途径和方式，创造更多文化品牌，使文化遗产成为经济社会可持续发展的重要组成部分。

三、中国—中东欧国家文化遗产合作愿景

五年前，习近平主席在联合国教科文组织总部向世界发表了历史性演讲，提出文明交流互鉴是推动人类文明进步和世界和平发展的重要动力。五年来，我们与柬埔寨、乌兹别克斯坦、吉尔吉斯斯坦、尼泊尔、缅甸等"一带一路"沿线国家深度合作，共同推进文物古迹保护修复工作，得到了遗产所在国家和世界遗产专家的充分肯定；我们与塞尔维亚密切对接，共同推进巴契遗址的申遗规划、方案制定和人员培训；我们支持中国文化遗产研究院、中国社会科学院考古研究所、故宫博物院、中国国家博物馆、敦煌研究院以及河南考古研究院等考古专业机构，与20多个国家合作开展40余项考古项目；我们加强与文化遗产国际组织的互动合作，与21个国家签署政府间关于防止盗窃、盗掘和非法进出境文化财产的双边协议，成功实现文物返还1000余件；我们累计举办近300个文物进出境展览，波兰、匈牙利、捷克、罗马尼亚、拉脱维亚、塞尔维亚等中东欧国家的文博机构都是我们长期的合作伙伴。

2017年，在中国—中东欧"16+1"合作框架下，我们在塞尔维亚举办了首届中国—中东欧国家文化遗产论坛，开启了中国—中东欧国家文化遗产领域全面合作的"首班车"。今天，我们又欢聚一堂，共商合作设想。刚才刘玉珠局长已经对未来"16+1"文化遗产合作提出加强统筹规划、做大对话平台、聚焦务实合作、协同国际行动的建议，在此，我愿继续呼吁：

中东欧同行与中国一道，共同完善文化遗产国际协调联络机制，打造中国—中东欧国家人文交流"推进器"，推动中国—中东欧国家文化遗产论坛在"16+1"的合作框架下，更好发挥文化遗产在文明交流互鉴中的积极作用，使文化遗产论坛成为跨国家跨区域对话协商和友好合作的创新典范。

让我们携起手来，共同构建稳定多维的政府间文化遗产合作网络，建设中国—中东欧国家文化遗产合作"共同体"，强化在文化遗产国际组织的协调互动，共同支持武装冲突地区濒危文化遗产保护国

际行动，共同防范和打击非法劫掠、盗窃、盗掘及走私文物行为。

让我们加强合作，共同寻找中国—中东欧国家政府间合作新亮点，除世界文化遗产领域外，在博物馆管理、联合考古、文物科技、人员培训、防止文物走私等方面开展全方位、多维度务实合作，使文化遗产合作成为提升中国—中东欧国家政府间合作的"催化剂"。

女士们、先生们：

中国与中东欧国家历史交往密切、传统友谊深厚。从贝尔格莱德到洛阳，中国与中东欧国家文化遗产合作逐渐驶入快车道，迸发出勃勃生机，正展现出广阔前景。我们愿继续同中东欧国家一道，通过务实合作，共同推进人类文化遗产的保护与传承，为构建人类命运共同体贡献力量！

谢谢！

Actual Practice and Looking Ahead Conservation of World Cultural Heritage in China

Hu Bing

Deputy Administrator of the National Cultural Heritage Administration of China

(10 April 2019, in Luoyang City)

Honorable Guests,

Dear Friends,

It's a great pleasure to have all of you here in this beautiful April of Luoyang to share our actual practice and experience in conservation, management and use of World Cultural Heritage in China.

In 1972, the United Nations Educational, Scientific and Cultural Organization (UNESCO) adopted the *Convention Concerning the Protection of the World Cultural and Natural Heritage* with an aim to preserve the cultural or natural heritage of outstanding universal value as part of the world heritage of mankind as a whole.

More than 30 years ago on December 12, 1985, China became a state party to the *Convention Concerning the Protection of World Cultural and Natural Heritage*. From that date, China set sail to assure the conservation and protection of World Cultural Heritage in China. On December 11, 1987, at the eleventh session of the UNESCO World Heritage Committee, China's six heritage properties-Imperial Palace of the Ming and Qing Dynasties in Beijing, Mausoleum of the First Qin Emperor, Mogao Caves, Peking Men Site at Zhoukoudian, The Great Wall and Mount Taishan, were inscribed on the World Heritage List and became the first batch of World Heritage in China. These six sites are already well-known at home and abroad. They specifically highlight Chinese history and culture, and the glorious civilization of ancient China. They successfully kick-off and lay a solid foundation for all forces to conserve and protect the World Cultural Heritage in China.

Over the course of more than three decades, World Cultural Heritage in China started from scratch and grew significantly. Today, China has 36 cultural properties, 13 natural properties, 4 mixed properties, 53 World Heritage properties in all, next to Italy's and ranking World No.2.

During this period of more than three decades, China government is committed to fulfilling her promise to international community, relentlessly pursuing her efforts in conservation, management and nomination of World Heritage, in discovering, interpretation and presentation of heritage properties, so that the Outstanding Universal Value, authenticity and integrity of World Heritage are preserved and passed on to future generations, the glory of Chinese civilization is presented panoramically.

Next, I will talk about three areas. First is actual practice and experience in the conservation of China's World Heritage properties, second is looking ahead in this endeavor, and the third, the prospect of China-Central/Eastern Europe working together in national cultural heritage.

I. Actual Practice and Experience in Conservation of World Cultural Heritage in China

In recent years, regarding World Cultural Heritage, China is gathering force, from strengthening cultural self-confidence to national affinity, from improvement of ecological setting, people's livelihood to socio-economic development in heritage sites, from serving "the Belt and Road Initiative" to Grand Canal Culture Belt. China is finding a way in line with own situation to protect the World Heritage properties in the country, which are characterized by the following six features:

(I) **More diverse and varied nominations.** World Heritage properties in China are varied, spanning wide area and time period and have a variety of cultures. They can be masterpiece of mankind conquering nature or living in harmony with nature, one single site or trans-regional/national cultural routes. These are impressive contributions to world civilization by Chinese people.

Since the 1990s, new trends appear in World Heritage nominations around the world. Instead of focusing on majestic monuments/sites concerning mankind history and civilization, the focus is shifted to important ruins related to cultural diversity and cultural exchange. Riding along with this trend, in recent years China emphasizes new types of heritage properties to nominate such as cultural landscape, cultural routes. For instance, the Cultural Landscape of Honghe Hani Rice Terraces inscribed on the World Heritage List, Silk Roads: The Routes Network of Chang'an-Tianshan Corridor, the Grand Canal inscribed in 2014. On the tentative list, more new types of heritage are included, such as near-modern sites, ethnic minority cultural heritage, living heritage.

(II) **Well-developed legal framework.** To protect World Cultural Heritage, China has set up a framework with Chinese characteristics referencing *Law of the People's Republic of China on Protection of Cultural Relics*, supplemented by regional regulations and connecting to World Heritage Convention effectively. Conservation and management of World Heritage are incorporated into national laws and regulations. In 2006, China government announced *Regulations on Protection of Great Wall*, the first regulations specifically dealing with World Heritage properties. In the same year, the Ministry of Culture promulgated *Measures for Conservation* and Management of World Cultural Heritage and Measures for Conservation and Management of The Grand Canal in 2012. As of today, there are 72 regional charters. Among them, Luoyang enacted Regulations on Conservation and Management of Longmen Grottoes in 1999. All these laws and regulations provide effective legal instruments to protect World Cultural Heritage in China.

(III) Comprehensive management system and coordination mechanism. Conservation and management of World Cultural Heritage in China are enacted through several levels of responsibility. China's National Cultural Heritage Administration is overall in-charge, provincial culture departments provide guidance and instructions, People's governments at the heritage sites protect and manage according to management principles at the sties. All heritage sites have specific units to conduct day-to-day activities.

We have established a mechanism for coordination between ministry and departments. During the nomination of The Grand Canal, Ministry of Culture and China's National Cultural Heritage Administration took the lead to form an Inter-Provincial and Ministerial Consultation Group. The group was made up of 13 concerned committees and People's governments of the 8 provinces and municipalities along the canal. After the successful inscription of the Grand Canal, 35 cities along the canal set up City Alliance for Conservation of the Grand Canal. The coordination of the Grand Canal's conservation and management is now in the hands of this City Alliance.

We also established a transboundary coordinating mechanism. For the "Silk Roads: The Routes Network of Chang'an-Tianshan Corridor" jointly nominated by China, Kazakhstan and Kyrgyzstan, China took the initiative to coordinate between the three State Parties and organize 14 international collaboration meetings. In 2014, Silk Roads was successfully inscribed on the World Heritage List. UNESCO heralded the inscription as an example of international collaboration.

(IV) State of conservation obviously improved. In preserving World Cultural Heritage, China endorses "Plan First" strategy. Through conservation plan, consensus can be reached on the claims by all stakeholders, taking into account all matters related to conservation and management, presentation and utilization. In particular, large cultural properties such as Great Wall, Grand Canal, China government successively announced Master Plan for the Protection of Great Wall and Outline Plan for Conservation, Inheritance and Utilization of The Grand Canal Culture.

From 1980s onwards, China dedicates sufficient investment for conservation and restoration of World Cultural Heritage such as Great Wall, Imperial Palace of the Ming and Qing Dynasties, Potala Palace. During the past few years, China's National Cultural Heritage Administration has concentrated on several projects to protect and restore Great Wall, The Palace Museum, Chengde Mountain Resort and surrounding temples, Dazu Rock Cravings and Thousand Hand Bodhisattva (Goddess of Mercy) . Through the implementation of these projects, their states of conservation improve remarkably, they receive more respect, their environment also significantly improved for people to live and work.

(V) **Monitoring/early warning system getting better.** Monitoring World Heritage Sites is a mandatory requirement stated in World Heritage Convention and Operational Guidelines. The China's National Cultural Heritage Administration announced the *Principles for Monitoring, Inspection and Management of World Cultural Heritage in China* to form a monitoring/early warning system for important intervention, responsive monitoring, periodic reporting, to establish a monitoring management framework, to enforce monitoring standings, and to set up a monitoring/early warning platform. Monitoring systems have been set up accordingly for Imperial Palace of the Ming and Qing Dynasties in Beijing, Mogao Caves in Dunhuang, Classical Gardens of Suzhou and West Lake Cultural Landscape of Hangzhou.

(VI) **International exchange and collaboration intensified increasingly.** China is the host four times for World Heritage Committee meetings in 1991, 1999, 2007 and 2017. China experts take important positions in international organizations such as International Council on Monuments and Sites (ICOMOS) , International Centre for the Study of the Preservation and Restoration of Cultural Property (ICCROM) , and directly involve in World Heritage affairs.

China has hosted many large international conferences, namely, the 28th session of World Heritage Committee (2004) , the 15th General Assembly of ICOMOS (2005) , where important international documents-*Suzhou Resolution, Xi'an Declaration, Beijing Document*, have been announced.

In 2016, 2017, 2018, China's National Cultural Heritage Administration and ICCROM jointly held Workshop for the promotion of monitoring World Cultural Heritage in China worldwide.

II. Looking Ahead

While China gathering force in preserving World Cultural Heritage, yet there are numerous challenges in conservation and management. These challenges are specifically reflected in the settlement of conflicts between heritage conservation and socio-economic development, protection of World Heritage's Outstanding Universal Value, authenticity and integrity, and the international and well-being role played by World Heritage.

In recent years, President Xi Jinping delivered important instructions and deployment on protection of cultural heritage, especially the nomination, conservation, presentation and inheritance of World Cultural Heritage. President Xi stated: "Let all cultural relics collected in museum alive, all heritage displayed in wide open area alive, all words written in ancient books alive. Let Chinese civilization melts into Oneness with the richness of the civilization created by the people around the world. Let all these provide correct spiritual guidance and magnificent spiritual force for humankind". President Xi's statement becomes what we should achieve in our future endeavor.

(I) **Stay with "Three Favors" in driving World Heritage nominations.** We stay with the working principles that favor the historic and cultural value of Chinese civilization, favor the spiritual pursuit of Chinese people, favor the truly presentation of ancient China as well as modern China. We strive to spread the excellence of Chinese culture, to lay down nomination strategy on a scientific base, to proceed accordingly the nomination of the Archaeological Ruins of Liangzhu City and Maritime Silk Road.

(II) **Merging modern technology with heritage monitoring to improve conservation and management.** Modern science and technology provide new opportunities to improve the monitoring and early warning system for World Cultural Heritage in China. We will make sound mechanism for responsive monitoring, implement routine check-up and inspection and promote the use of modern technology and means such as unmanned aerial vehicles, monitoring cloud to monitor the heritage and changes in surrounding area. The aim of these precautionary approaches is to find out potential risks and take responsive measures timely.

(III) **Intensively advocate heritage to develop with people's livelihood, improve standard of public services.** The public, especially community and residents living in the heritage site, are encouraged to join the efforts to protect the heritage so that they can participate more, make them feel engaged and accepted to strengthen social cohesiveness. World Heritage belongs to the world, to State Parties, but first of all, World Heritage is home to those living here for generations. Community and residents are direct stakeholders. They have the right to participate in conservation effort and share the achievement. Besides, through promotion and presentation, World Cultural Heritage is making inroads into campus, community, with an aim to increase the awareness of the public, especially the young generation, to protect World Cultural Heritage. By launching World Heritage "5C" Strategy (Credibility, Conservation, Capacity-building, Communication, Community) and introduction of modern technology, interpretation and presentation can be significantly improved.

(IV) **Speed up the co-development of heritage and tourism, create new ways to protect and use World Cultural Heritage to achieve socio-economic sustainable development.** Our focus is cultural tourism, exploring new ways to protect and use cultural properties which include heritage hotel, national park, national culture park and national heritage route. They are specific open cultural space for integrated development between heritage preservation and scientific study, culture education, public services, tourism/sightseeing, leisure/recreation. We will leverage World Cultural Heritage resource and internet technology to launch creative, artistic and practical culture products, to expand means and methods for spreading the value of heritage, to create more culture brands so that cultural properties become an important component of socio-economic sustainable development.

III. China-Central/Eastern Europe Cooperation in National Cultural Heritage

Five years ago, President Xi delivered his historic speech at the UNESCO headquarter, stating that exchange and learning other countries' civilization is an important force to drive mankind progress, civilization and world peace. Since then, we have in-depth cooperation with Cambodia, Uzbekistan, Kyrgyzstan, Nepal, Myanmar, countries along the "the Belt and Road Initiative", to promote the conservation and restoration of cultural monuments and sites together. We receive full recognition from countries of heritage residence and World Heritage experts. We have close relationship with Serbia to nominate Cultural Landscape of Bač and Its Surroundings, draft plans and train staff. We support archaeological institutions including Chinese Academy of Cultural Heritage, Institute of Archaeology at the Chines Academy of Social Sciences, The Palace Museum, National Museum of China, Dunhuang Academy and Henan Institute of Archaeology to work with more than 20 countries on 40+ archaeological projects. We strengthen our force in working with international cultural heritage organizations. We conclude intergovernmental bilateral agreements with 21 countries on the prevention of theft, excavation and illegal import and export of cultural property. More than 1000 cultural objects have been successfully returned to China. We have organized a total of nearly 300 exhibitions involving the transport of cultural objects in and out of China. Many countries in Central and Eastern Europe such as Poland, Hungary, Czech, Romania, Latvia and Serbia, their cultural museums are long-term partners of us.

In 2017, we hosted the First China-Central/Eastern Europe National Cultural Heritage Forum in Serbia under the "16+1" Cooperation Framework. The Forum marked the "first train" working together for China-Central/Eastern Europe National Cultural Heritage. Today, we gather again to discuss further cooperation. Just now, Administrator Liu Yuzhu has mentioned more collaboration efforts recommended for the future "16+1" Cultural Heritage Cooperation, involving overall planning, expansion of dialogue platform and focusing on practice and coordinated international initiatives. Here, I continue call for:

Heritage colleagues from Central/Eastern Europe and China join together to form international collaboration, a "propellant" for the launch of China-Central/Eastern Europe National Cultural Heritage Forum under the "16+1" Cooperation Framework, so that cultural heritage can play an even more active role in exchange and learning other countries' civilization, the Forum can be a creative example of trans-boundary/regional dialogue and friendly cooperation.

Let us join hands to establish a stable, multi-dimensional intergovernmental network for cultural heritage cooperation, to form China-Central/Eastern Europe National Cultural Heritage Cooperation "Community", to strengthen the coordination and interaction with cultural heritage international organizations, to support international initiatives for the protection of cultural heritage in danger in armed conflict regions, to prevent and stop looting, theft, excavation and illicit trafficking of cultural objects.

Let us get together for greater cooperation, seeking new spotlight in China-Central/Eastern Europe intergovernmental cooperation. Besides World Cultural Heritage, we can launch comprehensive, multi-dimensional cooperation in many other areas such as museum management, joint archaeology, heritage science and technology, staff training and prevention of illicit smuggling of cultural property. Let cultural heritage cooperation becomes a "catalyst" to elevate the intergovernmental cooperation between China and Central/ Eastern Europe.

Ladies and Gentlemen:

China and Central/Eastern European countries have close ties in history and deep friendship in tradition. From Belgrade to Luoyang, collaboration between China and Central European countries in cultural heritage is moving on a fast track, vibrant, exotic, offering great promise ahead. We wish to continue cooperation with countries in Central/Eastern Europe. Through working together, we move the cooperation forward to protect and inherit cultural heritage for mankind, to contribute to the Community of Common Destiny!

Thank You!

世界文化遗产保护管理

基于价值的敦煌莫高窟保护利用平衡发展模式的探索与实践

中国　敦煌研究院　王旭东[①]

摘要：

莫高窟因其为现存规模最宏大、延续时间最长、内容最丰富、保存最完整的佛教石窟群，被誉为"沙漠中的美术馆"和"墙壁上的博物馆"，具有不可替代的历史、艺术和科技价值，1961 年，莫高窟被列为第一批全国重点文物保护单位。1987 年，因符合世界文化遗产全部六条标准，被列入世界文化遗产名录。

75 年来，敦煌研究院一代又一代专家学者始终围绕敦煌文化遗产"保护、研究、弘扬"任务，以真实完整地保护，并负责任的传承利用莫高窟的文化价值为使命，经过不断探索，总结出了符合敦煌石窟事业发展规律的"十位一体"事业发展模式和"基于价值完整性的平衡发展质量管理模式"，也逐步形成"用匠心呵护遗产，以文化滋养社会"的质量文化。未来的敦煌研究院，将始终坚持"保护是基础、研究是核心、传承弘扬是目的"的历史担当，将真实完整的莫高窟传给我们的下一代，同时也将不遗余力地让敦煌走向世界，让世界走近敦煌。

关键词：世界文化遗产，敦煌莫高窟，平衡发展，保护利用模式

一、莫高窟的价值

敦煌，是古丝绸之路上的"咽喉之地"。在漫长的历史长河中，不同民族，不同种族，多种宗教，多元文化在敦煌地区交流、碰撞、融合、发展，汇聚了中国文化、印度文化、波斯文化、希腊文化，

[①] 王旭东，男，生于 1967 年。敦煌研究院研究馆员、工学博士。1991—2019 年在敦煌研究院工作，历任敦煌研究院副所长、所长，副院长、院长，兼任国家古代壁画与土遗址保护工程技术研究中心主任，兰州大学、西北大学和牛津大学兼职教授、博士生导师，2019 年 4 月任故宫博物院院长。主要社会任职有国际岩石力学与岩石工程学会古遗址保护专业委员会主席、中国古迹遗址保护协会副主席、中国岩石力学与工程学会古遗址保护与加固工程专业委员会主任委员等。主要从事石窟、古代壁画和土遗址保护，文化遗产监测预警与预防性保护等方面的研究。1991 年开始文物保护工作以来，主持完成全国重点文物保护单位保护维修工程 60 余项，承担国家及省部级课题 20 余项，主持或作为主要参与人完成与美国、日本、英国、澳大利亚等国相关文化遗产保护和管理机构开展的国际合作项目 10 余项。

图 1 远眺莫高窟

图 2 莫高窟第 45 窟—西龛—彩塑一铺（盛唐）

最终形成了多姿多彩、丰润厚重的敦煌文化。

　　莫高窟是多元文化交融发展的重要载体和结晶。公元4—14世纪，由于佛教的传播，古代艺术家在莫高窟陆续营建了大量的佛教洞窟，至今仍保存洞窟735个，其中有壁画和彩塑的洞窟492个，包括壁画45000平方米、彩塑2000多身、唐宋木构窟檐5座、文物建筑26座、以及从藏经洞出土的文物5万多件。

　　以百科全书式的莫高窟艺术和藏经洞文物为代表的敦煌文化遗产，不仅保存了千年间多元文化艺术的发展流变和不同时期的社会生活场景，而且记录了中古时期丝绸之路和敦煌地区广阔的历史，地理，宗教，哲学，政治，经济，文化，民族，科技，文学，艺术，中外文化交流等历史资料。这些文化遗存不仅对于考古和艺术研究、历史与地理研究、宗教研究、古代语言文学研究、科技研究、古代民族研究、中外文化交流研究、中华民族传统文化精神研究等学术研究具有不可替代的史料价值；而且对于当代世界文化、艺术的发展仍然具有重要的启示意义，对于传承中华民族优秀文化精神、增强社会凝聚力和国家软实力具有不可替代的文化价值，对于当代世界的多元文化和平共处，交流融合和文明互鉴具有十分重要的借鉴意义。

图3　莫高窟第158窟—西壁佛坛—释迦牟尼佛
　　　涅槃像局部（中唐）

图4　莫高窟第112窟—南壁东侧—观无量寿经变之
　　　乐队与反弹琵琶（中唐）

图5　敦煌文物研究所徒步进城的同志在城内办事处合影（1965年9月30日）

莫高窟因其现存规模最宏大、延续时间最长、内容最丰富、保存最完整的佛教石窟群，被誉为"沙漠中的美术馆"和"墙壁上的博物馆"，具有不可替代的历史、艺术和科技价值，1961 年，莫高窟被列为第一批全国重点文物保护单位。1987 年，因符合世界文化遗产全部六条标准，被列入世界文化遗产名录，充分说明莫高窟是一处具有全世界突出意义和普遍价值的文化遗产。

二、莫高窟面临的文物保护问题

在敦煌莫高窟目前存有壁画、彩塑的 492 个洞窟中，一半以上的壁画和彩塑出现过病害，在 4.5 万平方米的壁画中，有 20% 受到不同程度的损坏。造成珍贵文物损害的，主要有自然因素和人为因素。

（一）自然因素

敦煌石窟开凿于石质疏松的砾岩之上，无法精雕细刻，便采用了泥塑彩绘和壁画的艺术形式。经历上千年的时间，因自身材料逐渐老化和遭受诸如地震、集中式降雨、风沙等自然因素的威胁，洞窟围岩和壁画彩塑存在各种病害，极大地影响着石窟文物的完整保存。

（二）人为因素

1900 年敦煌莫高窟藏经洞被偶然发现，因清末时局动荡，在 1907 年至 1923 年期间，英、法、日、俄、美等国探险家先后抵达敦煌，通过贿买方式骗取莫高窟藏经洞珍贵写本、艺术品 3.9 万余件，大肆盗窃塑像及剥取壁画。并且由于莫高窟疏于管理，造成洞窟内遭到烟熏、刻画等人为破坏。

现如今，虽然人为破坏已不复存在，但自 1979 年莫高窟对公众开放以来，尤其是近年来随着游客接待量的急剧增加，洞窟微环境逐渐受到影响，对十分脆弱的壁画、彩塑带来潜在的威胁。

三、探索敦煌莫高窟文物保护利用的探索管理模式

敦煌研究院是负责世界文化遗产敦煌莫高窟、天水麦积山石窟、永靖炳灵寺石窟，全国重点文物保护单位瓜州榆林窟、敦煌西千佛洞、庆阳北石窟寺保护管理的综合性研究型事业单位，是我国拥有世界文化遗产数量最多、跨区域范围最广的文博管理机构，最大的敦煌学研究实体，国家古代壁画与土遗址保护工程技术研究中心，国家一级博物馆。

敦煌研究院，其前身是 1944 成立的国立敦煌艺术研究所。建院 75 年来，一代又一代莫高窟人始终围绕敦煌文化遗产"保护、研究、弘扬"任务，以真实完整地保护，并负责任的传承利用莫高窟的文化价值为使命，经过不断探索，总结出了符合敦煌石窟事业发展规律的"十位一体"事业发展模式和"基于价值完整性的平衡发展质量管理模式"，逐步形成了"坚守大漠、甘于奉献、勇于担当、开拓

进取"的莫高精神和"用匠心呵护遗产，以文化滋养社会"的质量文化。

基于价值完整性的平衡发展质量管理模式

遗产管理是一项复杂的、多层面、多维度、跨领域的开放式动态管理过程，涉及诸多物理的和人为的要素，整个管理过程平衡是相对的，不平衡是绝对的。实现莫高窟价值得到真实、完整、可持续地保护、研究、传承和弘扬是敦煌文物事业的终极目标；基于价值完整性的平衡发展质量管理模式是敦煌文物事业发展的关键所在；以莫高窟的价值吸引和留住人才，让人才在围绕莫高窟价值的工作中实现自我价值是敦煌文物事业发展的根本保证。

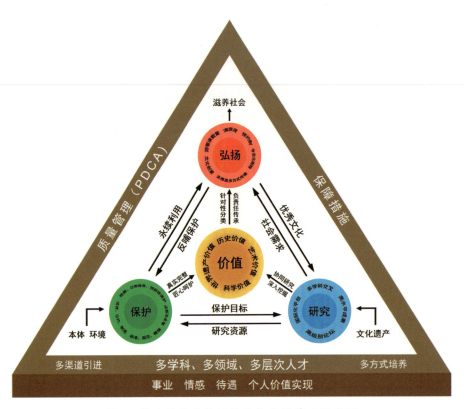

图 6　基于价值完整性的平衡发展管理模式图

基于价值完整性的平衡发展质量管理模式关键在于保障模式的立体性、系统性、整体性、关联性、等级结构性、动态平衡性和均衡创造动力。从表象上来看，保护是基础、研究是核心、弘扬是目的。但是这三者又是相互关联、互为表里，协同发展的整体性系统。通过研究和挖掘，明确了保护对象所蕴含的价值，为保护提出更高的要求，也为传承和弘扬提供了文化基础和精神内涵；通过保护，保证了研究和挖掘对象材料物理信息和文化信息的完整性，也为基于价值的传承和弘扬提供了基础条件和根本保证；通过基于价值的传承和弘扬，为基于价值的保护、研究和挖掘提供了持续发展的驱动力。

同时，保护、研究、弘扬工作又与莫高窟价值、人才培养等不同等级结构层面要素相互交叉，构成相互协同发展的立体式结构。莫高窟无与伦比的价值，吸引了越来越多的各类人才汇聚敦煌；保护、研究、弘扬事业平衡发展、稳步上升的良好局面为各类人才实现自我价值提供了良好的展示平台和发展空间。基于莫高窟价值和人才自我价值的实现，逐步形成了一支稳定的、高水平的，涉及人文学科与自然学科领域多学科交叉的队伍，成为莫高窟保护、研究和弘扬工作的基石。

在基于价值完整性的平衡发展质量管理模式统筹下，文化遗产的保护、研究、弘扬各有其规律和特点，没有统一的管理范式，因此我们针对其各自规律和特点采取不同管理方式，让其各自的动能和创造力得以有效释放；同时在其各自释放动能的过程中，强调莫高窟价值不断呈现和人才价值自我实现，以及保护、研究和弘扬事业之间相互驱动、相互协同和相互制约的逻辑关系，保障了莫高窟保护、研究和弘扬事业发展的均衡创造力，维持了莫高窟事业发展的动态平衡，实现了敦煌文物事业的持续创新发展。在此基础上，积极面对社会需求，勇于承担社会责任，妥善处理了外部需求与内部运行之间的平衡关系。

——保护方面：建立了基于"目标导向"的文物保护科学技术应用与评价管理体系

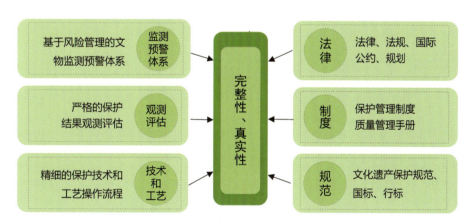

图 7　文物保护科学技术应用与评价管理体系

高质量的文物保护，就是要做到最小干预，保持文物本体及其赋存环境的真实性、完整性。

为了保持文物本体及其赋存环境的真实性、完整性，以安全性和有效性作为文物保护科技手段的测评目标。围绕这一目标，在文物保护领域建立起了集详细的莫高窟保护管理制度，基于风险管理的文物监测预警体系，标准的文化遗产保护规范，精细的保护技术和工艺操作流程，严格的保护结果观测评估为一体的文物保护科学技术应用与评价管理体系，对文物保护调查、科学研究、保护实践、保护结果监测评估等各个环节实施科学化、标准化、精细化的管理，确保用于保护文物的各项实践和科学技术的安全性、有效性。

——研究方面：建立基于莫高窟价值整合社会资源的"协同管理"研究体系

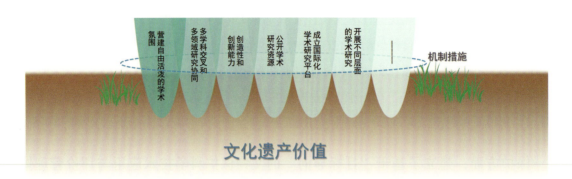

图8　基于莫高窟价值整合社会资源的研究体系

高质量的研究，就是要对博大精深的莫高窟文物价值及其相关问题展开深入的挖掘、广泛的研究。

基于莫高窟价值多元化、国际化特性，开展石窟考古、石窟艺术、历史地理、民族宗教等多个领域的学术研究；以莫高窟和敦煌学为研究核心，以图像、文献、文物为研究对象，开展从古至今、从国内到国外、从广度到深度等不同层次的学术研究；公开学术研究资源，搭建敦煌学国际化交流平台，完善访问学者招募机制，吸引国内外专家学者共同研究；鼓励人文科学同自然科学的几十个学科交叉研究和多领域协同研究。通过这样的"协同管理"体系，充分整合社会资源，形成了各方力量参与敦煌文化遗产研究的格局。

美术研究创立了以"复原临摹、整理临摹、现状临摹"为核心的临摹体系和方法论，并在古代绘画技法的基础上，积极开展岩彩画创作，努力构建敦煌画派体系。

通过不断努力，敦煌研究院以敦煌石窟、敦煌艺术研究为核心，结合敦煌文献研究的敦煌学学术研究体系，初步构建了包含考古学、历史学、宗教学、民族学等多学科结合的敦煌学学科体系。

——弘扬方面：建立基于观众类型的"针对性分类"弘扬管理体系

高质量的弘扬是让不同类型、不同背景、不同层次的社会大众能看得好、听得懂、记得住、讲得出。因此我们建立基于观众类型的"针对性分类"弘扬管理体系。

对于来莫高窟的游客，我们始终坚持负责任的文化旅游，本着对文物和游客高度负责的态度，在保护好文物的前提下充分拓展开放空间，增加游客体验；在充分满足游客需求的情况下，利用先进的科技和管理手段，不断加强文物保护，协调处理好二者之间的关系，使其平衡发展。在国内首次开展游客承载量方法研究，找到了既不影响石窟保护又能最大满足社会和游客需求的措施方法，建立了以

质量管理实践——弘扬

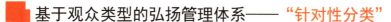
基于观众类型的弘扬管理体系——"针对性分类"

图9　基于观众类型的弘扬管理体系

"总量控制，网上预约，数字展示，实体洞窟参观"为特点的莫高窟旅游开放新模式。

在旅游特旺季，针对没有预约到门票的普通游客，适时启动应急参观模式；在旅游淡季，针对高端需求游客，开辟深度体验旅游模式。为了让莫高窟的价值惠及更多的当代人，对于没有来到莫高窟的公众，敦煌研究院利用实体文物、传统临摹艺术、数字敦煌资源、网络技术和数字展示技术、纸质出版物及新媒体平台，针对不同年龄段、不同知识结构、不同种族、不同民族、不同信仰的公众开展形式多样、丰富多彩的艺术传播形式。

四、基于价值完整性的平衡发展质量管理模式的实践

基于价值完整性的平衡发展质量管理模式通过多年实践被证实是行之有效的，有益保证了敦煌莫高窟保护、研究、弘扬的高质量发展，促使我们各项事业取得了良好的社会效益、品牌效益，和一定的经济效益。

——文物保护方面

在文物保护"真实性、完整性"理念和"不改变原状、最低限度干预"的保护原则指导下，采取多种技术手段和管理措施，真实、完整地保存莫高窟价值载体的物理信息和文化信息。以问题为导向，科学认识价值载体材料和制作技法，充分识别影响价值载体保存的各类要素，以科学试验为基础，深度解析病害机理，提出价值载体修复材料和工艺，建立了一整套文化遗产保护规范。

在规范的流程下实施精细化保护，并将监测与研究贯穿于保护过程的始终。不仅建立起了预防性保护和抢救性保护并重的科学保护体系，实现了对莫高窟文物的有效保护，成立了依托敦煌研究院科研平台的"国家古代壁画与土遗址保护工程技术研究中心"，还在西藏、新疆、宁夏、山西、山东、河北、河南等全国7个省（自治区）成立工作站，对全国多地区的文物实施保护，"国家古代壁画与土遗址保护工程技术研究中心"已成为行业标志性的品牌，"数字敦煌"项目实现敦煌石窟文物的"永久保存、永续利用"。

——人文社科研究方面

在"协同发展"理念的指导下，敦煌研究院持续引领敦煌石窟研究的发展方向，不断拓展敦煌石窟研究领域，从最初的壁画临摹与绘画技法研究，逐步扩展到敦煌石窟考古研究、敦煌石窟艺术研究、敦煌壁画图像研究、敦煌文献研究、敦煌历史文化研究、丝绸之路民族宗教研究，以及敦煌文化价值和精神内涵的系统解读，取得了丰硕的研究成果。

多年来，敦煌研究院在敦煌学研究领域先后出版学术专著500多部，发表学术论文3700余篇，40余项学术成果荣获国家和省级哲学社会科学优秀成果奖，其中由敦煌研究院历时多年、跨领域多学科交叉协作、院内外多家机构协同完成的《敦煌石窟全集》第一卷《莫高窟第266~275窟考古报告》，受到了国内外学术界的一致好评。饶宗颐先生评价此部考古报告为"既真且确，精致绝伦，敦煌学又进一境，佩服之至"；著名敦煌学者、英国伦敦大学名誉教授韦陀（R. Whitfield）先生称赞其具有从未有过的资料系统完整的科学性，将为中国其他石窟寺遗址的考古报告提供标准与模式。本书获甘肃省第十三次哲学社会科学优秀成果奖一等奖、中国人文社科领域最高奖项的第七届吴玉章人文社会科学奖优秀奖。

——文化弘扬方面

针对不同的公众，采用不同的文化弘扬和传播方式，取得了良好的社会效益和一定的经济效益，初步建立了敦煌研究院的品牌影响力。

自莫高窟对外开放以来，共接待来自100多个国家和地区的游客1600余万人次，近两年，每年接待游客达160万人次以上，在弘扬莫高窟价值的同时，为当地经济发展做出了重要贡献；先后在20多个国家（地区）和国内20多个省市举办100多场敦煌艺术展览；"数字敦煌"资源库第一期中英文2种版本于2016年、2017年先后上线，实现30个洞窟整窟高清图像的全球共享；积极拓展淡季旅游项目，开发系列研学品牌和体验课程，满足游客不同层次的需求，赢得了广泛的市场认可；积极开展文化遗产"六进"活动，组织甘肃省多地贫困学生开展"走进敦煌"交流体验活动，实现了文化弘扬的"大众化、普及化、多维化"，初步形成高质量的敦煌石窟文化传播体系，取得了良好的社会效果。

随着保护、研究和弘扬事业的平衡发展，不仅保障了敦煌文物事业的整体稳步提升，逐渐形成了基于价值完整性的平衡发展质量管理模式，而且得到了社会的广泛认可。在2017年，甘肃省政府将

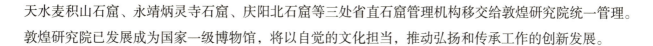

天水麦积山石窟、永靖炳灵寺石窟、庆阳北石窟等三处省直石窟管理机构移交给敦煌研究院统一管理。敦煌研究院已发展成为国家一级博物馆，将以自觉的文化担当，推动弘扬和传承工作的创新发展。

——品牌效益

敦煌研究院以多种方式培育品牌，并积极拓展品牌的价值、成果，在文物保护、学术研究、展览、文化创意、学术出版、公共教育等方面已经树立了良好的品牌形象，注册了120余项商标和50多个数字化洞窟的著作权登记，形成了"慈悲能承载，智慧能沟通，美能成就"意蕴的敦煌研究院品牌文化，打造了"敦煌研究""敦煌论坛""莫高讲堂"等学术品牌，"念念敦煌""如是敦煌"等文创品牌，"数字敦煌展""敦煌艺术大展""敦煌壁画艺术精品高校公益巡展"等展览品牌，"绝色敦煌之夜"文化展示品牌，"莫高小学堂""莫高驿——九色鹿星空夜话""霓裳佛国·摇曳唐风"等研学品牌，"敦煌岁时节令""敦煌说""敦煌壁画里的现代节日"等数字媒体品牌，"敦煌文化驿站""敦煌文化守望者"等公益品牌，取得了良好的品牌效益。

——社会效益

国家层面：落实"一带一路"倡议、国家软实力提升、促进民族团结；地方层面：促进地方经济社会发展；精神层面：满足人民精神文化需求、提升国民文化自信。

五、敦煌研究院的愿景

敦煌研究院将紧抓"一带一路"建设机遇，深入挖掘敦煌文化所蕴含的人文价值和精神内涵，不断加强人文交流，促进民心相通，致力于将莫高窟打造成为国际上文化遗产保护的典范、把敦煌研究院建成国际最具活力的敦煌学研究实体和国际最有影响力的敦煌文化展示与交流平台，让敦煌走向世界，让世界走近敦煌。我们也希望所有热爱敦煌的国内外朋友们以不同的方式加入保护、研究、弘扬敦煌文化的行动中来，为了敦煌文化遗产的长久保存和永续利用一起努力，将一个真实完整的莫高窟传给我们的下一代。

Explorations and Practices: A Model of Balanced Development for Value-based Conservation and Utilization of Mogao Caves in Dunhuang

Wang Xudong[①]

Dunhuang Academy China

Abstract:

Mogao Caves is known for its best-preserved Buddhist grottoes that contain the most diverse types of artworks created over the sweep of history. With indispensable historical, artistic and scientific values, it is hailed as an "art gallery in the desert" and a "museum on the wall". It was included on the First List of State Priority Protected Sites in 1961 and inscribed on the World Heritage List in 1987 on the basis of all the six criteria to justify a World Cultural Heritage site.

For 75 years, several generations of experts and scholars from Dunhuang Academy have made continued efforts to develop an institutional system of "Ten in One" and a quality management model that emphasizes balanced development based on value integrity and to foster an institutional philosophy of "caring the heritage with craftsmanship and nourishing the society with culture", by following the principle of "conservation, research and promotion" and by pursuing the mission of continuing and utilizing cultural values of Mogao

---

① Wang Xudong was born in 1967. Dr Wang is a research fellow of the Dunhuang Academy, and holds a PhD degree in Engineering. From 1991 to 2019, he successively served as vice director, director of the Department of Heritage Conservation and Research of the Dunhuang Academy, and vice director, director of the Dunhuang Academy, Director of the National Research Center for Conservation of Ancient Wall-paintings and Earthen sites, adjunct professor and PhD mentor of Lanzhou University, Northwest University and Oxford University.He is the director of the Palace Museum since April 2019. Dr. Wang is also the president of the Commission of Preservation of Ancient Sites of International Society for Rock Mechanics and Engineering, vice chairman of ICOMOS China, and chairman of the Commission of Conservation and Reinforcement of Ancient Sites of the Chinese Society for Rock Mechanics and Engineering. Dr Wang has been mainly engaged in the conservation of grottoes, ancient wall paintings and earthen sites, as well as the research of the monitoring, early warning, and preventive conservation of cultural heritage. Since 1991 when Dr. Wang began the conservation of cultural relics, he has presided more than 60 protection and maintenance projects of National Priority Protected Sites and undertaken more than 20 national or provincial projects. And as a host or main participant, Dr. Wang carried out more than 10 international projects related to cultural heritage conservation and management, with the international institutions from the United States, Japan, Britain, Australia and other countries.

Caves through conservation in an authentic and integral manner. In the future, Dunhuang Academy will as always bear in mind the principle of "conservation as the basis, research as the core, and continuation and promotion as the purpose" so as to hand down Mogao Caves in an authentic and integral state to future generations, while sparing no efforts to promote Dunhuang to the rest of the world.

Key words: World Cultural Heritage, Mogao Caves in Dunhuang, balanced development, model of conservation and utilization

1. Value of Mogao Caves

Dunhuang, the key junction of the ancient Silk Road, is a region where diverse peoples, races, religions and cultures exchanged, collided, merged and developed in the long course of history. Converging the cultures of China, India, Persia and Greece, the Dunhuang culture has been developed with richness and diversity.

Fig. 1   The Stunning View of Mogao Caves

One important carrier and crystallization of multicultural integration and development, Mogao Caves attracted numerous ancient artists to construct plenty of Buddhist caves by virtue of the transmission of Buddhism from the 4th century to 14th century. Today, 735 caves are still preserved, including 492 caves with frescoes and painted sculptures, where there are over 45,000 square meters of frescoes, over 2,000 painted sculptures, five wooden cave eaves in the Tang and Song dynasties, 26 historic buildings as well as more than 50,000 pieces of cultural relics unearthed from the Cave Library.

Represented by the art of encyclopedic Mogao Caves and the cultural relics unearthed from the Cave Library, the Dunhuang cultural heritage not only preserves the development and evolution of multicultural arts and social life scenes of different periods in the past thousand years, but also records the rich historical data about the history, geography, religion, philosophy, politics, economy, culture, nationality, science and technology, literature, art and cultural exchanges between China and other countries along the Silk Road and in the Dunhuang region during the ancient times. Cultural heritage like these is invaluable and significant

Fig. 2   Statues in the Main Niche, West Wall, Mogao Cave 45 (High Tang Dynasty)

Fig. 3   Statue of Buddha in Nirvāṇa, Mogao Cave 158 (Middle Tang Dynasty)

Fig. 4   Dancer Holding A Pipa Behind Her Back, Mogao Cave 112 (Middle Tang Dynasty)

Fig. 5   Researchers of the National Research Institute on Dunhuang Art (1965)

historical evidence for research on archaeology and art, history and geography, religion, ancient language and literature, science and technology, ancient ethnic studies, cultural exchanges between China and other countries, and the spirit of traditional Chinese culture. Furthermore, it is still of great enlightening significance for the development of contemporary world culture and art. In addition, it has irreplaceable value for inheriting the excellent cultural spirit of the Chinese nation, enhancing social cohesion and national soft power. It provides significant reference for the peaceful coexistence of diverse cultures, exchanges and integration, and mutual learning of civilizations in the contemporary world.

As the existing Buddhist grottoes with the grandest scale, longest duration, richest content and completest preservation, Mogao Caves have gained the reputation as "Art Gallery in the Desert" and "Museum on the Wall". In 1961, Mogao Caves, thanks to its irreplaceable historical, artistic and technological value, was included on the First List of State Priority Protected Sites. In 1987, it was inscribed on the World Heritage List by virtue of meeting all the six criteria, which fully demonstrated that Mogao Caves is a cultural heritage property with outstanding significance and universal value.

2. Challenges Facing the Preservation of the Cultural Relics in Mogao Caves

Among the existing frescoes and painted sculptures in the 492 caves, there have appeared cases of damage to half of them. 20% of 45,000 square meters of fresco has suffered from damage to varying degrees. Natural factors and human factors have been the main causes for damaging precious cultural relics.

(1) Natural Factors

Dunhuang Caves were initially built on loose conglomerate, where beautiful carvings could not be completed, and thus plenty of clay sculpture paintings and frescoes were created. Over thousands of years, there were various damages to the surrounding rock of caves, frescoes and painted sculptures because of the aging process of the original material. Moreover, the natural threats like earthquakes, centralized rainfalls and the sand blown by the wind have also greatly affected the integrated preservation of cultural relics in the grottoes.

(2) Human Factors

In 1900, the caves for preserving Buddhist sutra were discovered by accident. Because of the turbulent period in the late Qing Dynasty, particularly from 1907 to 1923, the explorers from Britain, France, Japan, Russia and America arrived there one after another and gained by cheating and bribery more than 39,000 precious hand-copied books and art works. The invaders also stole statues and frescoes in the same way. In addition, because of the neglect of management, there were many man-made damages like smoke and scrawl in the caves.

Currently, man-made damages have no longer existed. However, the micro-environment of the caves has been affected gradually since it was opened to public in 1979, especially the rapid increase of tourists in recent years. That poses a potential threat to the very fragile frescoes and painted sculptures.

3. Exploration of the Management Model for the Dunhuang Cultural Heritage

The Dunhuang Academy is a comprehensive research institution in charge of the protection and management of the World Cultural Heritage sites of Dunhuang Mogao Caves, Maijishan Grottoes (in Tianshui City) and Bingling Temple Grottoes (in Yongjing County), and the State Priority Protected Sites of Yulin Grottoes in Guazhou, Xiqianfo Cave in Dunhuang and North Grottoes Temple in Qingyang. With the largest number of World Cultural Heritage properties and the broadest cross-regional scope, Dunhuang Academy is the largest institution on Dunhuang Studies in China, a National Research Center for Conservation of ancient Wall-paintings and Earthen Sites, and a national first-class museum.

In 1944, the National Dunhuang Art Research Institute was established as the predecessor to the Dunhuang Academy. Since its establishment, generations of the researchers in Mogao Caves have centered around the task of the "Conservation, Research and Promotion" of the Dunhuang cultural heritage. With the mission of authentically and integrally protecting and responsibly inheriting the cultural value of Mogao Caves, the researchers have summed up the "Ten in One" development model and "the value-based balanced development quality management model", which have well conformed to the law of development in the Dunhuang Caces. Not only that, the Mogao Spirit of "keeping in dessert, devoting in will, undertaking in bravery and forging ahead in sustainability" and the quality culture of "preserving cultural heritage with originality and nourishing the society with culture" have also been formed gradually.

The Balanced Development Quality Management Model Based on Value Integrity

Heritage management is a complex, multifaceted, multidimensional, cross-disciplinary open dynamic management process, involving various physical and human factors, with relative balance and absolute imbalance in the process. The ultimate goal of the Dunhuang cultural relics undertaking is to realize the value of the Mogao Caves by authentically, integrally and sustainably protecting, researching, inheriting and carrying it forward; the key to the development of the Dunhuang cultural heritages undertaking is the balanced development quality management model based on value integrity; the fundamental guarantee for the development of the Dunhuang cultural relics undertaking is attracting talents and retaining them to achieve their self-value in the quest for realizing the value of the Mogao Caves.

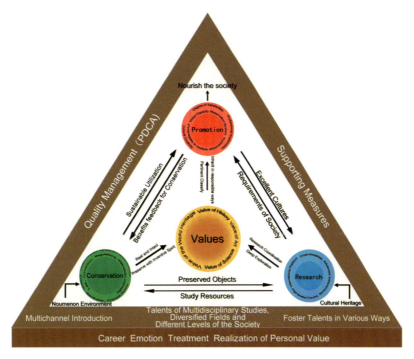

Fig. 6   The Balanced Development Quality Management Model Based on Value Integrity

The key to the balanced development quality management model based on value integrity lies in the multi-dimension, systematicness, integrity, relevance, hierarchical structure, dynamic equilibrium and balanced creation power of the protection model.

On the surface, protection is the foundation, research is the core and promotion is the purpose. However, the three of them are an integrated system of mutual correlation, mutual dependence and coordinated development. Through research and excavation, the value of the protected object can be defined, which puts forward higher requirements for protection and provides the cultural basis and spiritual connotation for inheritance and promotion. Through protection, the integrity of the physical and cultural information about the object we research and excavate can be guaranteed. Protection also provides the basic conditions and the fundamental guarantee for the inheritance and promotion based on value. Through value-based inheritance and promotion, the driving forces of the continuous development can be provided for the protection, research and excavation based on value.

Meanwhile, the protection, research and promotion work is intersected with different levels of structural dimensions such as the value of the Mogao Caves and personnel training, forming a multidimensional structure of coordinated development. A growing number of talents were attracted to gather in Dunhuang by the unparalleled value of the Mogao Grottoes. The balanced development and the steady rise of the protection, research and promotion undertakings provide a good display platform and development space for all kinds of talents to realize their self-value. Based on the realization of the value of the Mogao Caves and the self-value of talents, a stable and high-level team involved in the interdisciplinary field of humanities and natural sciences has gradually come into being, which has become the cornerstone of the conservation, research and promotion of the Mogao Caves.

Under the overall planning of the balanced development quality management model based on value integrity, we adopt different management methods in allusion to their respective laws and characteristics because the conservation, research and promotion of cultural heritage has no unified management paradigm due to their own laws and characteristics so that their respective momentum and creativity can be effectively released. During their respective release of momentum, we have not only stressed the continuous display of the value of the Mogao Caves and the self-realization of talents, but also emphasized the logical relationships of mutual driving, coordination and constraints among the conservation, research and promotion undertakings. In this way, the balanced creativity of the conservation, research and promotion of the cause of the Mogao Caves has been ensured, the dynamic balance of the development of the cause of the Mogao Caves has been maintained, and the sustainable and innovative development of the cause of Dunhuang cultural heritage has been achieved. On the basis of that, we have coped with the balance between external demand and internal operation by meeting the need of society positively and assuming social responsibility bravely.

Protection: The Establishment of "Goal-oriented" Management System in the Application and Evaluation of Science and Technology for Cultural Relics Protection

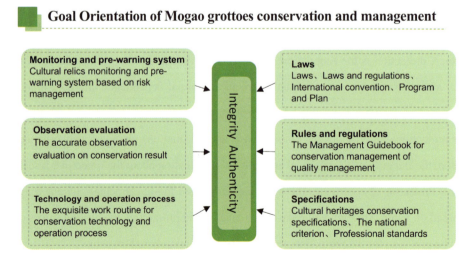

Fig. 7 "Goal-oriented" Management System

The high-quality protection of cultural relics, we always say, can be interpreted as the minimal intervention to maintain the authenticity and integrity of cultural heritage themselves and their existing environment.

For the sake of maintaining the authenticity and integrity of cultural heritage themselves and their existing environment, the safety and effectiveness of the scientific and technological means is taken as the evaluation target for cultural heritage protection. Centering on this target, we have set up and integrated detailed management regulations for the conservation of the Mogao Caves, the cultural heritage monitoring and early warning system based on risk management, standard norms for the protection of cultural heritage, the elaborate protection technology and operation process, the strict observation and evaluation of protection results and integrated all of them into the management system in the application and evaluation of science and technology for conservation of the cultural heritage. With this system, we have conducted the scientific, standardized, meticulous management of each stage, including the protection survey, scientific research, conservation practice, monitoring and evaluation of conservation results, etc. to ensure the safety and effectiveness of various practices and technologies for conservation of the cultural heritage.

Research: The Establishment of the "Coordinated Management" Research System of the Integrated Social Resources Based on the Value of the Mogao Caves

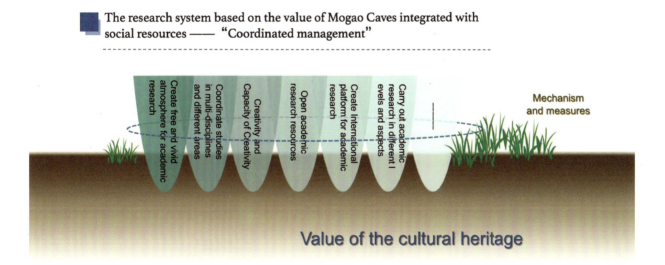

Fig. 8   Practice of Quality Management

The high-quality research, we always say, can be interpreted as the in-depth excavation and extensive research of the value of the broad and profound Mogao Caves and its related issues.

On account of the diversification and internationalization of the value of the Mogao Caves, the academic research in multiple fields like grotto archaeology, grotto art, history and geography, nationalities and religions has been conducted. And with the core of the Mogao Grottoes and Dunhuang Studies and on the basis of images, literature, cultural relics, different levels of academic research, from the ancient times to the present, from home to abroad and from breadth to depth have been carried out. We have also opened the academic research resources, set up an international exchange platform for Dunhuang Studies, improved the recruitment mechanism of visiting scholars, and attracted experts and scholars from home and abroad to study together. Finally, we have encouraged the cross-disciplinary study of dozens of disciplines in humanities and natural sciences as well as the collaborative research of multiple fields. Through the "collaborative management" system and the full integration of social resources, we have formed a pattern of the research of Dunhuang cultural heritage with various forces participating.

The facsimile system and methodology of the art research has established "restoration facsimile, arrangement facsimile, and current situation facsimile" as its core, and on the basis of the ancient painting techniques, we have carried out the creation of rock painting and strive to build the Dunhuang painting system.

Through continuous efforts, the Duhuang Academy, with the core of the Dunhuang Caves and the Dunhuang Art Research, combined with the Dunhuang Studies academic research system of Dunhuang literature studies, has preliminarily constructed the discipline system of Dunhuang Studies, which includes archaeology, history, religion, ethnology and so forth.

Promotion: The Establishment of the "Targeted Classification" Promotion Management System Based on Audience Types

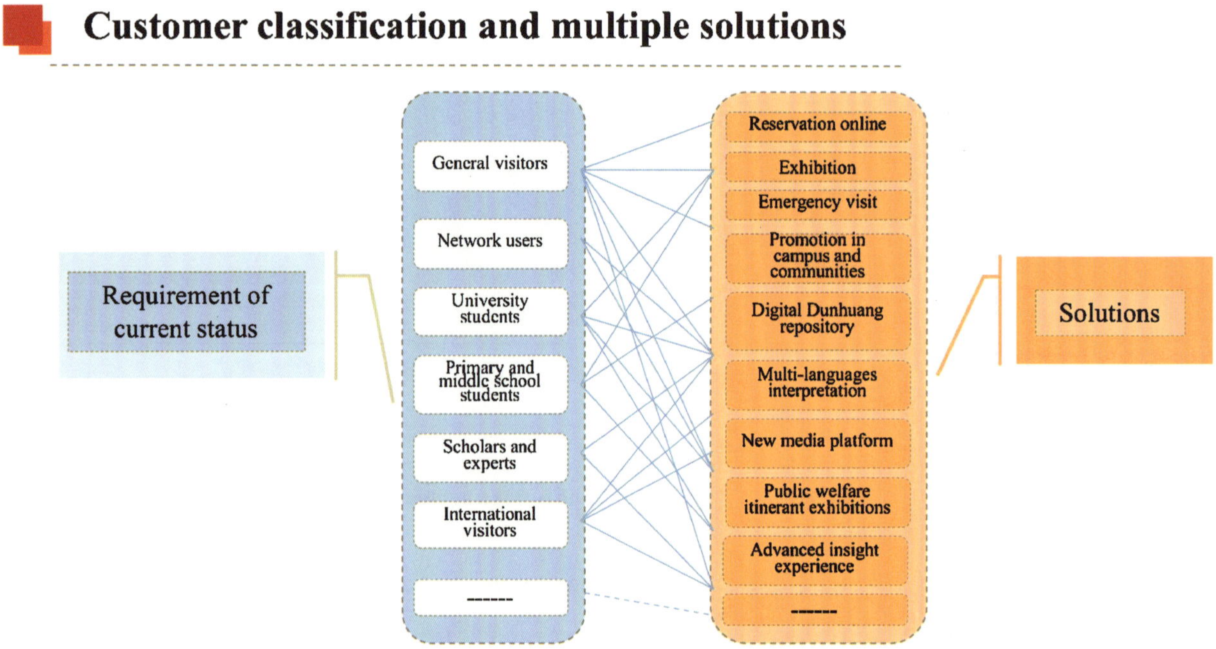

Customer classification and multiple solutions

Fig. 9   "Targeted Classification" Promotion Management System

The high-quality promotion means enabling the public of different backgrounds, types and levels to enjoy a good view of, understand, remember and talk about the cultural heritage. Therefore, we have set up the "targeted classification" promotion management system based on audience type.

For tourists to the Mogao Caves, we have always adhered to cultural tourism, take a high degree of responsibility for cultural heritage and tourists, and on the premise of protecting cultural heritage, fully expand the open space and enrich the tourists' experience. With the tourists' needs fully satisfied, we have adopted the advanced technology and management measures to reinforce the protection of cultural relics and coordinate the relationship between them and realize the balanced development. We have also carried out the first research on the tourist carrying capacity method for the first time in China, found out measures to avoid affecting the protection of grottoes and at the same time meet the needs of society and tourists to the largest extent, and established the new development mode of the Mogao Grottoes tourism, which features "Total Quantity Control, Online Reservation, Digital Display, Entity Cave Visit".

During the tourist peak season, emergency visiting mode is initiated duly for ordinary visitors who fail to book tickets in advance. In the tourist off-season, however, we open up the in-depth experience mode for tourists with high-end demand. To make the value of the Mogao Caves reach more people, for the public without the chance to visit the Mogao Grottoes in person, the Dunhuang Academy has utilized the entity cultural relics, traditional facsimile works, digital Dunhuang resources, network technology and digital display technology, paper publications and new media platform to conduct a wide range of artistic transmission forms aimed at different age groups, knowledge structures, races, nationalities and beliefs.

4. Practices of the Balanced Development Quality Management Model Based on Value Integrity

The balanced development quality management mode based on value integrity has proved to be effective over the years, which ensures the high quality development of the protection, research, promotion of the Mogao Caves, thus prompting our various undertakings to gain benefits from the social, brand and certain economic aspects.

Protection of Cultural Relics

Under the direction of the concept of "authenticity and integrity" and the principle of "no change of the original state and minimum intervention" in cultural relics protection, we have taken multiple technical means and management measures to authentically and integrally preserve the physical and cultural information of the value carriers in the Mogao Caves. We have taken a problem-oriented approach, gained a scientific understanding of the materials and manufacturing techniques of the value carriers and fully identified the various factors affecting the preservation of the value carriers. Moreover, on the basis of scientific experiments, we have made an in-depth analysis of damage mechanism, proposed the restoration materials and techniques of the value carriers and established a set of norms for the preservation of cultural heritage.

Fine Preservation has been implemented in a standardized process, with the supervision and research throughout the process of protection. Not only have we established the scientific protection system with an equal focus on both preventive protection and emergent protection, but also achieved the effective protection of the cultural relics in the Mogao Caves and set up the National Research Center for the Conservation of Ancient Wall-paintings and Earthen Sites, which is based on the scientific research platform of the Dunhuang Academy. Besides, to carry out the protection of cultural relics in other places across China, we have established seven provincial (autonomous regional) workstations in Tibet, Xinjiang, Ningxia, Shanxi, Shandong, Hebei, Henan have been established. Through the efforts, the National Research Center has become the iconic brand of the industry, and the "Digital Dunhuang" project has achieved the permanent preservation and utilization of the cultural relics in the Dunhuang Caves.

Research of Humanities and Social Science

Directed by the concept of "Coordinated Development", the Dunhuang Academy has consistently taken the lead in the research of the Mogao Caves, continuously expanded the research field from the original study of mural copying and painting techniques to the archaeological study of the Mogao Caves, the study of Dunhuang Grottoes art, the study of the Dunhuang mural images, the study of the Dunhuang literature, the study of the Dunhuang history and culture, the national religions on Silk Road as well as the interpretation of the cultural value and spiritual connotation in Dunhuang, bearing rich fruits.

Over the years, the Dunhuang Academy has published more than 500 academic monographs and announced over 3700 academic papers in the field of Dunhuang Studies, among which over 40 academic achievements were awarded as the Excellent Achievements in Philosophy and Social Sciences at the National and Provincial Levels, including the *Complete Set of the Dunhuang Grottoes Volume I: Archaeological Report of Caves 266-275 in the Mogao Grottoes*, with the collaboration among various institutions and throughout the interdisciplinary cooperation for years, has been well received in academic circles at home and abroad. Mr. Rao Zongyi praises this report as "realistic, accurate and exquisite, marking a higher level in Dunhuang Studies." R.Whitfield, a famous scholar of Dunhuang Studies and a honorary professor in University of London, thinks of the report as the standard and mode for the archaeological report on other grotto and temple sites in China with its unprecedented systematic integrity and scientificity. In addition, the report won the first prize of the 13ᵗʰ Outstanding Achievement Award of Philosophy and Social Sciences in Gansu Province and the Excellent Award of the 7ᵗʰ Wu Yuzhang Award for Humanities and Social Sciences, the China's highest award in the field of Humanities and Social Sciences.

Cultural Promotion

According to different audience, the diverse modes of cultural promotion and transmission have been adopted, thus gaining good social and economical benefits and beginning to set up the public brand perception of the Dunhuang Academy.

Since its opening-up to the outside world, the Mogao Cavess has received about 16 million tourists from more than 100 countries and regions, and particularly last year, the tourist accommodation has reached more than 1.95 million, making great contributions to the local economical development while carrying forward the value of the Mogao Caves. More than 100 Dunhuang art exhibitions have been held in more than 20 countries (regions) and more than 20 provinces and municipalities in China; the first-phase of "Digital Dunhuang" resource banks, in both Chinese and English versions, were launched online successively in 2016 and 2017 to realize the global sharing of high-definition images of 30 caves; off-season tourism projects, a series of research brands and experience courses have been actively developed and expanded to cater for the needs of tourists at different levels, winning extensive market recognition; "Six Entry" campaign on cultural heritage have been actively carried out and "Walking into Dunhuang" exchange and experience activities for the needy students from many places in Gansu Province have been organized. In this way, we have realized the "popularization, universalness, multi-dimension" of cultural promotion and initially formed the high-quality system of cultural transmission of the Dunhuang Caves, achieving good social results.

Along with the balanced development of conservation, research and promotion undertakings, the whole steady improvement of the Dunhuang cultural heritage has not only been guaranteed, gradually forming the balanced development quality management mode based on value integrity, but gained extensive social recognition. In 2017, three provincial grotto management organizations, namely the TianshuiMaijishan Grottoes, the YongjingBingling Temple Grottoes and the Qingyang North Grottoes were handed over to the Dunhuang Academy for the unified management by Gansu Provincial Government. Nowadays, the Dunhuang Academy has become the national first-class museum, and will consciously take on the cultural responsibility to promote the innovative development of carrying forward and inheriting the cultural heritage.

Brand Benefits

The Dunhuang Academy has set up a good brand image in many fields like cultural heritage protection, academic research, exhibition, cultural creativity, academic publishing, public education, etc. through various means of nurturing the brand and actively expanding the value and fruits from the brand. It has registered about 120 trademarks and the copyrights of more than 50 digital caves, and formed the brand culture specific to the Dunhuang Academy, which implies "compassion can be carried, wisdom can be communicated and beauty can be achieved." A variety of brands have been established: the academic brands such as "Dunhuang Research","Dunhuang Forum" and "Mogao Lecture"; the cultural creation brands such as "Echoing

Dunhuang" and "This is Dunhuang"; the exhibition brands such as "Digital Dunhuang Exhibition,""Dunhuang Art Exhibition" and "Dunhuang Fine Fresco Art Public Welfare Tour Exhibition at College"; the Cultural display brand of "The Colour Extravaganza of Dunhuang "; the research brands such as "Mogao Primary School,""Mogao Post:Nine-colored Deer Talking on Starry Nights" and "Buddhist Grace:The Style of the Tang Dynasty"; the digital media brands such as "Dunhuang Seasons," "On Dunhuang" and "Modern Festivals in Dunhuang Frescoes"; the public welfare brands such as "Dunhuang Cultural Post" and "Dunhuang Cultural Watchers". All of them have gained good brand benefits for the Academy.

Social Benefits

At the national level, the Belt and Road Initiative has been implemented, the national soft power has been strengthened boosted and the unity among various nationalities has been promoted. At the local level, the development of local economy has been improved markedly. At the spiritual level, the people's spiritual and cultural needs have been satisfiedand the national cultural self-confidence has been boosted.

5. Vision of Dunhuang Academy

Dunhuang Academy will grasp the opportunity of "the Belt and Road Initiative" construction, dig deeply into the humanistic value and spiritual connotation contained in the Dunhuang culture, continuously strengthen people-to-people exchanges and promote the common aspiration of people. We will devote ourselves to building the Mogao Caves as the international model on conservation of the world cultural heritage, and build the Dunhuang Academy as the most dynamic Dunhuang research entity and the most influential Dunhuang cultural exhibitions and exchanges platform in the world so as to make Dunhuang embrace the world and the world approaches Dunhuang. We also hope that all friends with love for Dunhuang can join us in the conservation, research and transmission of the Dunhuang culture in different ways, and make joint efforts for the permanent preservation and utilization so as to pass on the authentic and complete Mogao Caves to our next generation.

传承历史文脉 打造金色名片
加快建设独具魅力的国际文化旅游名城

中国 洛阳市人民政府 刘宛康

　　历史文化是城市的灵魂，是城市最独特、最宝贵的资源和优势。保护好、传承好、利用好历史文化遗产，是城市发展必须面对的重大课题。洛阳是华夏文明的重要发源地，国务院首批公布的历史文化名城和著名古都，拥有 5000 多年文明史、4000 多年城市史和 1500 多年建都史，先后有 13 个王朝100 多位帝王在此执政。丝绸之路和隋唐大运河在洛阳交汇转接，夏都二里头、偃师商城、东周王城、汉魏故城、隋唐洛阳城等五大都城遗址沿洛河一字排开、举世罕见。拥有龙门石窟等 3 项 6 处世界文化遗产，43 处全国重点文物保护单位、122 处省级文物保护单位、9000 多处不可移动文物。"河出图，洛出书，圣人则之"，礼乐典制成形于此，中国古代四大发明中的造纸术、印刷术、指南针都诞生于此。这些数不胜数的宝贵遗产向人们讲述着在长达 2500 多年的历史长河里，洛阳作为中国政治、经济、文化中心的沧桑变迁，成为从"最早的中国"到"强大的中国"的重要见证。

　　习近平总书记指出，"要像爱惜自己的生命一样保护好城市历史文化遗产"。近年来，洛阳市委、市政府围绕建设国际文化旅游名城、华夏历史文明传承创新区，坚持"保护固态、传承活态、发展业态"，在文化遗产保护与城市建设、产业升级、民生改善、融合发展方面进行了积极有益的探索与尝试，一幅城市发展与文化遗产保护互促共融的美好画卷正在河洛大地徐徐展开。

　　——注重规划引领，完善保护机制，留住历史文化根脉。坚持守土有责、保护第一，实现城市建设发展与文物保护利用的统筹协调，努力让古都文脉薪火相传、绵延不绝。20 世纪 50 年代，我们开创了"避开老城建新城"的洛阳模式。80 年代初，在全国率先建立了"城市建设必须先考古发掘、后动土施工"的文物保护模式，天子驾六、回洛仓等一大批重要文物得到了有效保护。进入新世纪、特别是"十三五"以来，我们科学编制了全市域文物保护与利用总体规划，划定文物保护"紫线"，实现文物保护与经济发展、城乡建设等"多规合一"。加强地方立法，为五大都城遗址和非物质文化遗产保护提供法律保障。我市荣膺中国文化遗产保护传承十佳城市，近五年的考古成果 4 次入选全国考古十大新发现。

　　——突出守正出新，展示厚重底蕴，擦亮古都金色名片。坚持真实性保护、整体性保护，注重点线面结合，实施了一大批保护展示工程。规划建设了隋唐洛阳城国家考古遗址公园，天堂明堂成为古都文化新地标，定鼎门遗址入选世界文化遗产，九洲池遗址公园一期落成开放，应天门主体完工，推动宫城区由景点到景区相互连通、连片发展，形成"四点一区"格局，实现城墙—城门—遗址大道—里坊—十字街等多个层次体系的展示，力求完整勾勒隋唐洛阳城历史轴线和47平方公里的都城轮廓，再现隋唐洛阳恢弘大气的帝都风貌。精心打造了69家各具特色、品类众多的博物馆，二里头夏都遗址博物馆将于10月对外开放，隋唐大运河遗址博物馆年内开工，"博物馆之都"初见成效，越来越多的宝贵遗产正从地下"走"到地上，焕发出新的光彩。

——**坚持保用结合，做好活化转化，推动文旅融合发展**。将文物保护与产业发展紧密结合，以文促旅、以旅彰文、文旅融合，打造了牡丹文化节、河洛文化旅游节等四季节会品牌，陆续推出了遗址游、研学游、博物馆游等一系列精品旅游线路。建设了洛邑古城、三彩小镇等重大文化产业园区。龙门石窟"互联网＋文物＋旅游"融合发展新模式，成为全国智慧旅游景区的新标杆。一批历史悠久、民俗古朴的传统村落焕发生机，孟津卫坡、伊滨倒盏游客盈门、人气爆棚。加强非遗传承保护，三彩制品、牡丹瓷、青铜器等"洛阳礼物"深受市场青睐。2018年接待游客1.32亿人次，旅游总收入1145亿元。古都洛阳正向着建设国际文化旅游名城的目标阔步前行，成为令人向往的"诗和远方"。

——**彰显古今辉映，提升文化品位，塑造城市独特魅力**。尊重历史、尊重自然，挖掘利用河洛文化、牡丹文化、隋唐文化等经典洛阳文化符号，抓好城市风貌、城市景观和建筑色彩的打造，因地制宜规划各个城区板块的建设风格，让古城古得经典、新区新得现代。在老城历史文化街区建设中，保留了"老城老街老巷子、老墙老院老房子、老门老户老名字、老号老店老铺子"，保存城市肌理，植入现代功能，留住老洛阳的"底片"，建好新洛阳的"客厅"。在每一处公共基础设施的细节中，注重融入历史文化元素，青瓦木檐的观景平台、古朴典雅的公交站亭、斗拱造型的路灯、道路桥梁的命名，都增添了古风古韵，彰显了历史文化名城特色。

——**体现山水交融，厚植生态优势，践行绿色惠民理念**。注重历史文化元素与生态自然特征相互协调，在隋唐城宫城核心区整治中，实施了和谐征迁，优化了周边环境、改善了居住条件。建成占地近3000亩的隋唐城遗址公园，将22平方公里的隋唐城洛南里坊区打造为城市"绿肺"。在洛河南岸规划建设了450多亩集休闲、娱乐、旅游、观光为一体的大型生态文博体育公园。沿大运河故道—洛河建成绵延20多公里的洛浦公园，再现城水相依、林水一脉的运河风光。兴洛湖公园、伊水游园生态良好、风景如画，150处别致的精品游园、111座典雅的城市书房星罗棋布、相得益彰，洛阳正在成为居者心怡、来者心悦的幸福之城。

——**促进融通互鉴，扩大开放合作，深化国际人文交流**。洛阳自古就是中西方文化交流的重要枢纽，罗马帝国与古代中国仅有的4次交往中有3次在汉魏洛阳城。早在1900多年前的东汉，班超自洛阳出使西域，重新打通了中东欧经贸、文化交流的通道。近年来，继续秉承开放理念，通过互建友好城市、互办艺术节、互设文化中心等形式，加强文物对外交流合作，筹办了丝绸之路上的中原文物展、丝绸之路音乐文物展等活动，促进中西文化合作交流，打造"一带一路"上的文化高地，让宝贵的文化遗产穿越时空、跨越国度，成为人文交流、文明对话的使者。去年4月，我们成功举办首届"世界古都论坛"，搭建了文化交流的新平台。

回望历史，我们挖掘文化内涵、厚植文化优势，实现了城市建设与遗产保护的互融互促。展望未来，我们将以新发展理念为引领，全面构建文化传承创新体系，让历史文化名城的"金字招牌"历久弥新，焕发更加璀璨夺目的时代光彩。

坚持守土尽责、保护传承。始终保持对历史文化遗产的敬畏之心，像爱惜生命一样守护历史文化遗产，建立全社会共同参与的保护体制机制，让宝贵的历史文化遗产世世代代传承下去。

坚持统筹协调、融合发展。主动融入"一带一路"和大运河文化带建设，统筹推进遗产保护和城市建设，有机结合、相互促进，让古今辉映、山环水润的城市魅力更加彰显。

坚持活化创新、塑造特色。围绕加快建设国际文化旅游名城，深入挖掘历史文化资源，设计特色鲜明的文化旅游产品，进一步完善产业链条，丰富产品供给，弘扬中华文化，讲好洛阳故事。

坚持开放包容、交流合作。发挥"一带一路"主要节点城市作用，依托中国—中东欧国家文化遗产论坛、世界古都论坛等平台，积极"走出去""请进来"，实现更宽领域、更高水平的开放合作。

坚持以人为本、惠民利民。坚持将惠民利民作为文化遗产保护利用的出发点和落脚点，让城市的每一处遗址、每一件文物，都成为人民群众共享的宝贵财富。

"志合者，不以山海为远"。第二届中国—中东欧国家文化遗产论坛在洛阳举办，将各国文化遗产保护领域的精英翘楚汇聚在洛阳，为我们提供了一次互学互鉴的宝贵机会，更打开了一扇认知中国、读懂河南、走进洛阳的沟通之窗。和而不同、美美与共。我们将以此为契机，进一步树立"多彩、平等、包容"的新型文明观，深化国际交流合作，与大家一道为文化遗产保护传承和人类文明发展进步作出新的贡献，让文明互鉴之光照亮城市发展未来。

Inheriting the History and Culture and Building a Distinct Brand Image for the Construction of an International City of Culture and Tourism

Liu Wankang

The People's Government of Luoyang China

History and culture carry the soul of a city. They are the most distinct and valuable resources and advantages for a city. Protecting, inheriting and utilizing cultural heritage in an appropriate way is on the top agenda of urban development. Luoyang is a major birthplace of Chinese civilization and a famous ancient capital inscribed on the First List of Historically and Culturally Famous Cities by the State Council of China. With a history of 5,000 years as a civilization, 4,000 years as a city and 1,500 years as a capital, Luoyang was the seat of government for over 100 monarchs from 13 dynasties. It witnesses the meeting of the Silk Road and the Sui-Tang Grand Canal and the existence of five major capital sites, including Erlitou as the capital of the Xia Dynasty, Yanshi as the capital of the Shang Dynasty, the capital of the Eastern Zhou Dynasty, the ancient city of Han and Wei, and Luoyang City of the Sui and Tang dynasties. Luoyang has three World Cultural Heritage properties (including six component sites) , 43 State Priority Protected Sites, 122 designated heritage properties under provincial-level protection, and up to 9,000 immoveable heritage properties. As an old Chinese saying goes, "The Diagram appears in the Yellow River and the Book in the Luo River. The Sage called Fu Xi later invented the Eight Diagrams based on the Diagram of the River and the Book of the Luo." Luoyang was the place where Chinese traditional ritual and music systems took shape and where three of the four great inventions of ancient China were created, including papermaking, printing and the compass. The numerous valuable heritage properties bear a testimony to the vicissitude of Luoyang as a political, economic and cultural center of ancient China for more than 2,500 years, witnessing the transformation from an "early China" to a "powerful China".

General Secretary Xi Jinping noted that "We should safeguard urban historical and cultural heritage like what we do for our own lives." In recent years, the Party and Government of Luoyang City have made active and effective explorations and trials in cultural heritage conservation, urban construction, industrial upgrading, improvement of people's livelihood and integrated development in order to develop an international city of culture and tourism and an innovative area for inheriting Chinese history and civilization, in line with the strategic guideline of "protecting tangible heritage, inheriting intangible heritage, and developing modern industries". As a result, a magnificent and beautiful scenario of harmony between urban development and cultural heritage conservation is unfolding.

Emphasis on urban planning as the guidance, improvement of conservation mechanisms and preservation of historical and cultural contexts. We did a diligent job in performing our assigned responsibilities and giving priority to heritage protection so as to achieve coordination between urban construction and heritage conservation and continue the culture of the ancient capital. In the 1950s, we developed the Luoyang Model that "A new city was built so as to preserve the old city". In the early 1980s, we pioneered the conservation model that "Archaeological excavation must be conducted prior to the implementation of construction projects". As a result, a large number of significant monuments and sites have been brought under effective preservation and protection, such as the Six-Horse Carriage for the Emperor and Huiluo Granary. In the new century, particular in the 13th Five-Year Plan period, we prepared a master plan for the city-wide protection and utilization of cultural heritage, demarcated a "purple line" for heritage conservation and integrated several different departmental regulations into one unified set of regulations for heritage conservation, economic development and urban and rural construction. Local legislation work has been strengthened so as to provide legal guarantees for the protection of the five major capital sites and the safeguarding of intangible cultural heritage. Luoyang was therefore honored with the title "Ten Best Cities of China in Inheriting and Protecting Cultural Heritage". Over the past five years, four archaeological findings in Luoyang were chosen as the Ten Archaeological Discoveries of the Year across the Country.

Following traditions and making innovations to showcase historical richness and build a brand new image for the ancient capital. A large number of conservation and presentation works have been carried out based on the principle of authenticity-oriented and integrated protection, with particular focus on the protection of both individual sites and historic areas. The National Archaeological Park of Luoyang City in the Sui and Tang Dynasties, along with its Hall of Heaven and Hall of Brightness, has become a new cultural landmark of the ancient capital. The Site of Dingding Gate was inscribed on the World Heritage List as a component site of the Silk Road. The first-phase Archaeological Park of Jiuzhouchi Site (lake of nine lands) was completed and opened to public. The main part of Yingtian Gate was completed. A layout of "one area outlined with four key sites" took shape, with individual sites connected with each other to form an entire scenic area of Palace City. Several ancient urban fabrics were restored, featuring city walls, city gates, Site Avenue, neighborhoods and Crossing Street, with an attempt to re-present the historic axis and 47 square kilometers capital boundary of Luoyang City in the Sui and Tang Dynasty. 69 museums with distinct characteristics and divers types of collection have been established. The Museum of the Xia Dynasty Capital Site of Erlitou will be opened to public in coming October. The construction of the Museum of the Site of the Sui-Tang Grand Canal will be started. The strategy of building Luoyang into a "Capital of Museums" is becoming a reality. More and more valuable heritage properties are being brought from underground to regain their vigor and splendor.

Integrating conservation with utilization, activating cultural heritage, and promoting integrated development of culture and tourism. An urban strategy for integrating cultural heritage conservation with industrial development has been developed, with the aim of promoting integrated development of culture and tourism. Four major festivals are launched in each of the four seasons a year, such as Peony Culture Festival and He & Luo Cultural Tourism Festival. A series of travelling routes were developed, such as tour of archaeological sites, tour of museums, and study tour. Several major cultural industry parks have been built, such as Luoyi Ancient City and Three Colors Town. An innovative model of integrated development featuring "Internet + cultural heritage + tourism" has been introduced to Longmen Grottoes which establishes itself as a new landmark of smart scenic area nationwide. A number of time-honored traditional villages have been revitalized and become popular tourist destinations, such as Weipo and Yibing villages. The safeguarding of intangible cultural heritage has been strengthened. Tri-colored pottery wares, porcelain wares with peony design, and bronze wares are popular Luoyang Gifts that are sold well. In 2018, Luoyang accommodated tourists totaling 132 million person times, with a total tourism revenue standing at 114.5 billion RMB yuan. The ancient capital of Luoyang is leaping forward towards the goal of building itself into an international city of culture and tourism and an admirable destination of poems and dreams.

Combining history with modernity and cultivating cultural taste so as to shape a city with unique harm. Based on the principle of respecting history and nature, efforts have been made to cultivate typical cultural symbols of Luoyang, such as He & Luo culture, peony culture and Sui-Tang culture, emphasize on design of urban scenarios, landscapes and building colors, develop distinct architectural styles for each of urban sections based on their specific conditions, with the aim of retaining classical features of the old city and building a modern new city. As regards historic and cultural quarters of the old city, old quarters, streets, alleys, walls, courtyards, houses, gates, names, brands and shops have been retained and original urban fabrics preserved, with modern functions introduced, so as to turn the old city into a new "living room" of the city. Historical and cultural elements have been integrated into details of public facilities. Landscape platforms decorated with black tiles and wooden eaves, historical and elegant bus stops, street lamps in the shape of Dougong bracket, and historical names of roads and bridges, all have added to the historical richness of the city and highlighted characteristics of Luoyang as a historically and culturally famous city.

Building an eco-friendly city for the people by taking advantage of mountain and river landscapes.

Emphasis has been placed on harmony between historical and cultural elements and natural and ecological characteristics. For the environmental enhancement of the core area of the Sui-Tang Palace City, relocation based on full consultation was carried out to beautify its surrounding environment and improve people's housing conditions. The Archaeological Park of the Site of Luoyang City in the Sui and Tang Dynasties has been completed, covering an area of nearly 3,000 mu. The Luonan neighborhood area in the site of ancient city, covering an area of 22 square kilometers, has been turned into a "green lung" of the city. A huge eco-park with cultural, museum and sport facilities has been planned and constructed on the southern bank of Luo River, providing leisure, recreational, sightseeing and travelling services. Luopu Park that extends for more than 20 kilometers along the ancient course of the Grand Canal and Luo River has been built to re-present Grand Canal landscapes that feature a combination of urban structures and forests with rivers. Xingluo Lake Park and Yishui Lake are picturesque gardens with good ecosystems. In addition, 150 beautiful gardens and 111 elegant city studies are dotted at every corner of the city. Luoyang is becoming a city of happiness that attracts both residents and tourists.

Promoting exchanges and mutual learning, increasing openness and cooperation, and deepening international cultural exchanges. Luoyang has long been an important hub for cultural encounters between East and West. Among the only four encounters between the Roman Empire and ancient China, three occurred in Luoyang during the Han and Wei period. More than 1,900 years ago in the Eastern Han Dynasty, Chinese envoy Ban Chao set out from Luoyang to embark on his mission to the Western Regions, re-opening the route for trade and cultural exchanges between China and Eastern Europe. In recent years, Luoyang has continued to increase international exchanges and cooperation in the field of cultural heritage based on the principle of openness. Cultural exchanges and cooperation have been promoted through the establishment of twin-sister cities and cultural centers and organization of arts festivals and exhibitions, such as the Exhibition of Silk Road Artifacts of the Central Plain and the Exhibition of Music Instrument Artifacts of the Silk Road. Luoyang has an ambition to build itself into a cultural highland along the Belt and Road and an envoy for promoting cultural exchanges and dialogue among civilizations and enabling worldwide access to its valuable cultural heritage. Last April, we successfully hosted the 1st Forum of World Ancient Capitals, a new platform for cultural exchanges with the rest of the world.

In retrospect, we have cultivated cultural richness and explored cultural resources so as to achieve coordinated development of urban construction and heritage conservation. Looking into the future, we will develop a comprehensive, innovative system for inheriting culture and history under the guidance of new development concepts, with the aim to revitalize the historically and culturally famous city.

First, fulfilling our due responsibilities for heritage conservation and continuation. We will always maintain respect for historical and cultural heritage and cherish them like what we do for our own lives. We will establish a conservation system and conservation mechanisms with participation of the whole society so as to hand down valuable cultural heritage to future generations.

Second, focusing on coordinated and integrated development. We will use active efforts to join in the Belt and Road Initiative and the construction of the Grand Canal Cultural Belt. We will work to coordinate and promote heritage conservation and urban construction so as to build a city that highlights a combination of history and modernity and an environment of mountains and rivers.

Third, emphasizing activation and innovation with focus on the development of characteristic products. We will speed up the construction of an international city of culture and tourism, cultivate historical and cultural resources, develop cultural and tourist products with distinct characteristics, and improve industrial chains with more supply of goods, with the aim of promoting Chinese culture and telling a good story about Luoyang.

Fourth, promoting exchanges and cooperation based on the principle of openness and inclusion. We will give full play to the role of Luoyang as a node city on the Belt and Road and make full use of such platforms as the China-CEEC Cultural Heritage Forum and the Forum of World Ancient Capitals so as to achieve greater openness and more cooperation in wider areas and at higher level.

Fifth, observing the people-oriented principle. Benefiting people will as always the fundamental purpose for our work to protect and utilize cultural heritage. We will use our utmost efforts to make each site and each artifact of the city shared and enjoyed by our people.

As an old Chinese saying goes, "Nothing, not even mountains and oceans, can separate people with shared goals and vision." The 2ⁿᵈ China-CEEC Cultural Heritage Forum has assembled elite conservationists from various countries here in Luoyang, providing us with a valuable opportunity for mutual learning and opening up a window for you to know about China, Henan and Luoyang. There are also Chinese mottoes like "unity in diversity" and "appreciating the culture and values of others as do to our own". We will take this opportunity to develop a new outlook on civilizations that features "diversity, equality and inclusion", increase international exchange and cooperation, and work together with you all to make new contribution to the conservation and continuation of cultural heritage and development and progress of human civilizations and to shed light of civilizations and mutual learning on urban development in the future.

科托尔自然和文化历史区的整体管理

黑山　文化部文化遗产总司　亚历山大·达吉科维奇 [①]

摘要：

本论文阐述了运用部分与整体方法来保持和稳定科托尔自然和文化历史区（1979 年列入联合国教科文组织世界遗产名录）价值的必要性，并运用威尔伯整体意识理论，即全现象全层次理论（AQAL），分析了造成该地区现状的原因、以及为实现可持续发展原则可能采取的措施。

现代公共行政机构在其关于战略结构的文件中，认为自然文化遗产是一种重要的发展资源，与此同时，他们发现公众对遗产的重要性和意义认识不足，各部分之间合作不足及缺乏整体方法。问题出现了：如何保护现存遗产并创造新的价值？如何为公众利益之目的保护这些遗产？如何减少遗产保护的负面影响？

关键词： 文化遗产，科托尔，全现象全层次理论（AQAL），整体保护

引言

为了紧紧跟上当代全球化战略的步伐，有必要对公共政策的理论、实践和文件进行修订；遗产的长期保护必然需要跨学科的方法。因此，在自然文化遗产的保护、管理和价值稳定等问题上，必须由不同部门和机构共同承担责任。文化遗产不仅仅对那些拥有它或者享受其文化价值好处的人有价值，遗产也会影响整个社会的福利和生活质量。它可以有效缓解文化全球化的影响，它还可以促进可持续发展。欧洲委员会在报告《让文化遗产为欧洲服务》中提出了文化遗产的目标。报告指出，欧盟应明确鼓励创新地利用文化遗产来促进经济增长、增加就业机会、加强社会凝聚力和促进生活环境的可持续发展。

1979 年，科托尔自然、文化和历史保护区基于前四项标准被列入世界遗产名录。过去十年科托尔地区出现了巨大的城市化压力，开展了众多建筑活动，对遗产的文化价值造成了负面影响，而正是这

---

① 亚历山大·达吉科维奇（Aleksandar Dajković），2015.11 至今，黑山文化部文化遗产总司司长，负责管理文化遗产总司的工作，并就执行该司范围内的任务，组织制定工作计划；2014.04—2015.11 黑山文化部独立顾问；2009.09—2014.04 采蒂涅皇家旧都规划设计、空间规划及环境部独立顾问；2018.09—2009.06 Maja Art & TO 公司专家；以色列 Giora Gur 建筑事务有限公司专家；英国谢菲尔德大学建筑学院专家。2016 至今塞尔维亚贝尔格莱德大学建筑学博士研究生；2010—2014 黑山大学建筑空间设计系建筑科学硕士。

些文化价值,使科托尔地区获得了在联合国教科文组织中的世界遗产地位。与此同时,这个国家试图建立相关机制来解决这种状况。《科托尔市自然和文化历史区保护法》的通过使得科托尔市的这一世界遗产地得到了更高层次的立法保护。除此之外,法律规定设立地区管理机构——科托尔自然、文化和历史保护区地区管理理事会。理事会由科托尔市长牵头,其作用是提升突出普遍价值的重要性。理事会负责协调起草、修订和实施管理计划,启动和监管管理规划所要求的活动,就建议、计划、项目及规划文件等提供意见,以确保其符合管理规划的规定。此外,理事会也对该区域的情况进行监测,并要求采取措施改善其状况。理事会还起草了关于执行政府管理规划的报告。理事会成员包括活跃在科托尔地区的国家代表、地方行政当局以及非政府组织代表。

科托尔地区突出普遍价值的保护

科托尔保护区是多个历史时期以来自然景观和人类活动互相影响而形成的。世界遗产地科托尔占地约 12,000 公顷,含 2,500 公顷海域面积。科托尔市大部分区域都位于保护区范围内。

除世界遗产外,科托尔还拥有不少已被确认登记的、和尚未登记的各类文化遗产,它们仅仅代表了该地区丰富多样文化遗产(不可移动遗产、可移动遗产及非物质遗存等)的一部分。这些数量丰富的不可移动文化遗产以及世界遗产地科托尔的突出普遍价值使我们有责任使用规划文件等工具来确保对遗产实施保护。其中之一是市政当局的城市空间总体规划。该规划旨在分析和明确长期的保护措施、稳定个别文化遗产的价值及文化景观作为一个整体的价值。所有这些手段的最终目的是确保对文化遗产的维护和保护,在现代生活中得到持续利用,见证现在及过去的时光,对现在及未来发挥作用。在这方面,保护该地区价值最重要的工具之一是研究保护文化遗产,这将为编制科托尔市政空间规划打下基础。除迄今为止已批准的文件(如文化遗产保护研究,其目的是帮助制定沿海地区特定目的空间规划和科托尔遗产影响评估)外,应将空间总体规划审批程序作为重中之重。2017 年初建设活动被暂停,这大大简化了该规划的编制和审批。

科托尔地区突出普遍价值属性及其制度和法律框架的分析

高质量的建筑(包括独立和复杂的建筑结构)、城市和定居点与海湾自然环境的有机融合、以及该地区在巴尔干半岛地中海文化传播方面所发挥的独特作用,都被认为是科托尔地区突出普遍价值的属性特征。另一个重要方面是在整个地理文化区域内东西方文化融合所造就的高质量的艺术和技艺。

十九世纪中叶至今,科托尔地区持续开展了专业的文化遗产保护工作。事实上,通过各种国家模式和制度方式,这些工作有效管理和保护了该地区最具重要意义的遗产形式。

二战以后,采蒂涅成立了文化和自然遗址保护局,后来改为共和国采蒂涅文化遗址保护局,主要监测科托尔地区的现状。直到二十世纪八十年代中期,科托尔文化古迹保护局成立,总部设在科托尔。

1992 年，该保护局成为位于科托尔的地区机构。众多来自国内外的专家学者和联合国教科文组织的专家曾经聚集于此，为 1979 年 4 月 15 日大地震之后科托尔地区的重建工作出谋划策[①]。

联合国教科文组织世界遗产委员会 1979 年通过的决议明确了科托尔地区的地位，认为它是最高级别自然及文化遗产的一部分。当年发生毁灭性大地震之后，黑山共和国启动了长期的国际性综合研究工作，并依据研究成果成功开展了多项历史结构复原工程，同时还制定了相关规划，旨在设计受保护区域。这些规划和战略以文件形式被纳入空间规划、总体规划和管理规划中，以实现对遗产的整体保护和可持续发展。

大部分科托尔地区相关法律规则的基本结构都很好，但有必要予以系统化实施，以确保对文化遗产保护的同时还能改善当地人民生活品质。有必要向公众介绍联合国教科文组织主管机构关于科托尔自然和文化历史区保护问题制定的相关程序、过程及结论，引导当地民众参与其中。

波卡科多斯卡（科托尔湾）地区文化遗产的法律保护主要有文化遗产保护法和科托尔自然和文化历史区保护法，其中明确界定了下述目标：保护突出普遍价值；永久保护原生态真实的自然、历史、城市、建筑、环境、美学和景观价值；确保有相应的条件实现可持续发展和利用，实现遗产展示并通过专业的、科学的方式维护遗产价值。科托尔地区的保护及保存相关事务由国家行政机构、科托尔市政部门、以及国家及市政当局设立的公共服务机构在其职权范围内进行。除上述机构，该地区的保护和保存也得到了邻近周边城市主管机构的支持。

2011 年，政府通过了科托尔自然和文化历史区管理规划，进一步界定了科托尔保护区的管理、保护、保存、利用和展示。该规划文件内容丰富，包括了科托尔自然和文化历史区 15 年间的管理战略、为实施战略制定的准则、活动方案、实现整体保护的机制、对计划内活动进行监测的方式等。目前该文件正在修订。

保护普遍价值面临的威胁和挑战

毫无疑问，国家和当地行政部门是制定和实施公共政策的主体，他们在科托尔地区突出普遍价值的保护和保存方面起到至关重要的作用。相关规划文件的质量以及管理规划的执行实施将在今后一段时间面临很多挑战。

在空间上已经确认了下述程序；同时还有其他系统化的、反映立法和专家结构的事项[②]：

> 根据 1969 年开始持续编制的空间文件，在科托尔自然和文化历史区域，城市化被认为是一个连续的过程

---

① 为科托尔空间计划之目的而开展文化遗产保护研究，黑山保护文化遗产理事会，采蒂涅，2017 年。为科托尔空间计划之目的而开展文化遗产保护研究，黑山保护文化遗产理事会，采蒂涅，2017。
② 科托尔自然和文化历史区遗产影响评估，黑山大学建筑系，波德戈里察，2017 年。

这一过程正急速展开，尤其是过去十年间的城市化发展

在这些过程和活动中，遗产保护和保存中的程序、过程和参与人员大多被界定、且被视为阻碍和壁垒，而非一个促进城市化发展的因素

长期不变的空间和规划文件结构类型和内容雷同，其结构方面存在问题

空间和规划文件中未将文化景观空间作为独立类别

建议采取下述措施改善现状：

采用在科托尔保护和管理规划研究基础上制定的科托尔市空间规划

对长期不变的空间和规划文件进行修订，并制定新的、较低层级的空间和规划文件

加强监察能力和监管次数

提升对联合国教科文组织遗产地重要性及重要意义的认知

非政府组织和市民积极参与当地遗产保护的所有环节

改进科托尔地区整体保护的必要性

科托尔自然和文化历史区的建设问题较为复杂，几乎可以肯定，这是由于缺乏整体保护方法造成的。尤其是，现在我们讨论的不是个别的历史文化或自然结构，而是一个覆盖重要区域和脆弱视觉轴线的地区。在某些情况下，建筑空间数量不足和密度不够是多方因素造成的，其中包括，现行法律法规之间出现不协调，未能遵守规划参数，规划师、设计师、市民的道德标准较低等。监管机构在考虑可持续发展、寻找保护和发展、保存和建设措施时需要具有特殊的敏感性。在进行整体保护和可持续发展时，必须将交通基础设施涵盖进来，并有特殊敏感度，重点关注自然景观的结构、进行保护的必要性以及开展视觉影响研究等，从而找到符合遗产突出普遍价值属性的高质量解决方案。如对上述问题考虑不周，将会影响遗产的普遍价值。

整体框架在研究课题的运用

如上所述，我们有必要采用整体的方法来讨论影响科托尔地区现状的复杂因素。为了更简便、更好地进行综述，我们运用威尔伯整体意识理论作为整体理论的基础框架[1]。

---

① 整体理论或全面理论试图将不同的思想和范式整合进同一个相互关联的体系中。其观点是利用所有的知识和经验，并将其展示在四象限网格里，即四个存在象限（国际、行为、文化和社会）、内部—外部关系和个别—集体关系中，具有连贯性特征。可运用该模式对如何使用综合的、广泛的和整体的方法研究最具影响力的意识和奋斗案例提供引导，逐步过渡到整体感知理论。

威尔伯整体意识理论（威尔伯 K.，2015）共展示了四个基本维度：内部 / 外部、个体 / 集体。左上象限代表个案的内部维度（个体意志、意识），左下象限则与个案的集体相关（文化、社会关系）。右上象限指个案的外部维度（行为），右下象限则代表集体案例的外部维度（社会体系）。

在科托尔这一具体案例中，我们从两个层面（国内和国际）创建了四个维度（见图 1）。

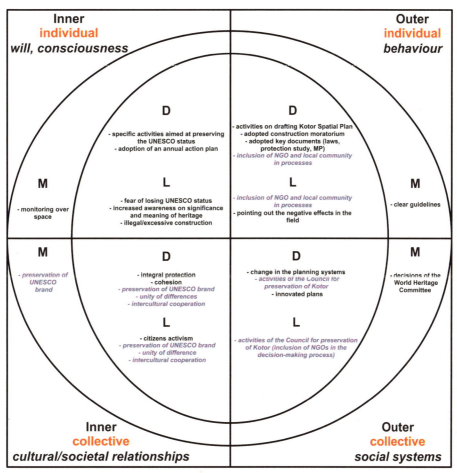

M—国际层面；D—国家 / 国内层面；L—当地层面

图 1　将整体框架应用于科托尔

该模式指出，国家在保护联合国教科文组织在特定地点的地位方面，有特殊的重要性，并承担相应责任。深化联合国教科文组织、非政府组织和当地社区间的合作十分有必要。另外还指出，这一必要性比较复杂，应开展相关活动确保这个拥有 12,000 公顷面积的遗产地留在世界遗产名录中。各级行动的唯一目的都是为了保护联合国教科文组织在科托尔地区的品牌。

结论

在全球化时代，遗产的可持续利用和管理势在必行，这也是当代政策所面临的挑战。发展的各个环节，无论经济层面还是文化层面，都应关注对自然和文化遗产价值、重要性及意义的理解。为了从系统化的角度开展系统行动以保护和维持遗产的价值，有必要使用整体的和跨学科的方法。毫无疑问，文化遗产对实现联合国和欧盟的战略目标、社区的可持续发展、以及对战略资源的理性和智慧运用都将产生重要影响。但是，如果不能协调开展上述明确设定的任务，那么遗产很可能会丧失其重要意义。为此科托尔地区在多个方面来说都是一个重要的案例，因为它集中反映了来自国际、国内和当地因素的影响，所有相关方的责任和需要开展的活动，以及未能采取整体方法可能带来的后果。

参考书目

1. 威尔伯 K.（1997），意识的整体理论，意识研究杂志

2. Rentchler M.（2006），*AQAL* 术语表，整体理论与实践杂志，第 1 卷

3. Grazuleviciute I.（2006），可持续发展框架下的文化遗产。环境研究、工程和管理

4. 希力 P.（2007），城市的复杂性和空间策略，伦敦：劳特利奇出版社

5. 布朗 B.（2006），可持续发展的四个世界，整体可持续发展中心

6. 宾利 I.（1999），城市转型：权力、人与城市设计，伦敦：劳特利奇出版社

7. 威尔伯 K.（2015），对"整体 2.0"及"AQAL 中没有'你'"的回应

8. Kocovic M., Đukic, V.（2015），伙伴关系作为实现最佳参与性治理和风险缓解的战略（文化和自然遗产），文化管理和政策的 ENCATC 杂志

9. Jokilehto J. 2005. 文化遗产的定义，历史文件的参考，国际文化遗产保护及修复中心遗产和社会工作组

10. 可持续发展框架下的文化遗产：https://www.researchgate.net/publication/228466259_Cultural_Heritage_in_the_Context_of_Sustainable_Development

11. 欧洲理事会 . 2005. 改变社会的行动 . 社会文化遗产价值框架公约 http://www.coe.int/t/dg4/culture heritage/heritage/identities/Faro-brochure_en.PDF

12. 为科托尔空间规划之目的保护文化遗产保护研究，黑山保护文化遗产理事会，采蒂涅，2017

13. 科托尔自然和文化历史区遗产影响评估，黑山大学建筑系，波德戈里察，2017

Integral Management of the Natural and Culturo-Historical Region of Kotor

Aleksandar Dajković[①]

Ministry of Culture of Montenegro

Abstract

The aim of the paper is to point out the necessity of an intersectoral and integral approach in the preservation and valorization of the values of the Natural and Cultural Historical Area of Kotor, which is on the UNESCO World Heritage List since 1979, analyzes the causes of the situation in the Region and potential measures in order to achieve the principles of sustainable development, using Wilber's Integral Theory of Consciousness, that is, the Four Quadrants of Reality (AQAL).

Modern public administrations in strategic structural documents recognize the aspect of cultural and natural heritage as an important resource for development, and concurrently with this, they find insufficient public awareness of the significance and meaning of heritage, and poor inter-sectoral cooperation and an integral approach. Questions arise: How to preserve the existing and create new values of heritage? How to manage the heritage, as good of public interest? How to reduce negative impacts on preservation of heritage?

Keywords: cultural heritage, Kotor, AQAL, integral protection

Introduction

In order to stay up to date with contemporary global strategies, it is necessary to amend theories, practices and documents of public policies; long term protection of heritage surly necessitates an interdisciplinary approach. Therefore, it is necessary to initiate joint responsibility of different sectors and bodies when it comes to subjects such

---

① ALEKSANDAR DAJKOVIC, 11/2019 present Director General of the Directorate for Protection of Cultural Heritage, Ministry of Culture, Montenegro, Manages the work of the Directorate for Cultural Heritage and performs organizing and programming the work on the execution of tasks within the scope of the Directorate; 04/2014-11/2015 Independent Adviser, Ministry of Culture, Montenegro; 11/2009-04/2014 Independent Adviser, Department for Planning and Spatial Planning and Environment, Old Royal capital Cetinje, Montenegro; 09/2009-06/2009 Expert, MajaArt & TO; Giora Gur & Partners Architects LTD, Israel; The University of Sheffield, School of Architecture, UK. 2016-present Student PHD of Architecture, University of Belgrade, Serbia; 2010-2014 Master of Science in Architecture, University of Montenegro, department Architectural design of space.

as protection, management and valorization of cultural and natural heritage. Cultural heritage is not valuable only for the individuals who own it or live in the benefits of cultural values, the heritage can also have an impact on the welfare and quality of life of the whole community, it can support mitigation of effects of cultural globalization and it can become a stimulus for sustainable development. Goals in cultural heritage have been given in the report *Getting Cultural Heritage to Work for Europe*, which is a document of the European Commission. The Report states that EU should expressly foster the innovative use of cultural heritage for economic growth and employment opportunities, social cohesion and sustainability of the living environment.

Culturo-Historical Region of Kotor has been inscribed in the World Heritage List in 1979, on the basis of the first four criteria. This past decade in the Region of Kotor has been characterized by extraordinary urbanistic pressure which resulted in construction that sometimes endangered the cultural values which recommended this property for the UNESCO status. Simultaneously, the State tried to establish a system that would resolve this situation. *Lex specialis* the Law on Protection of Natural and Culturo-Historical Region of Kotor has been adopted in order for this World Heritage Site to gain a higher level of legislative protection. Among other things, the Law prescribes establishment of a management body for this Region-Council for Management of the Natural and Culturo-Historical Region of Kotor, which is to be headed by the Mayor of Kotor Municipality, and whose role is to promote the significance of the OUV, coordinate drafting, revision and implementation of the Management Plan, initiate and monitor implementation of activities prescribed by the Management Plan, provide opinion on suggestions, programmes, projects and planning documents so as to ensure their compliance with the Management Plan. In addition, the Council performs the monitoring of the condition in the Region and requests measures for its improvement. It also drafts the Report on Implementation of the Management Plan for the Government. Membership in the Council consists of representatives of state and local administration as well as NGOs that are active in the Kotor Region.

Preservation of the Outstanding Universal Values of the Kotor Region

Protected Region of Kotor represents an example of intertwining of natural landscape and form of human activities forged through several historical epochs. Region of the World Heritage Site Kotor encompasses area of 12.000 hectares, of which 2.500 hectares are sea territory, while the most of Kotor Municipality territory is included in the scope of its protected surroundings.

In addition to World Heritage, the Municipality of Kotor also features a number of cultural properties, both registered and potential ones, that represent only a part of the rich and varied cultural heritage (immovable, movable and intangible) of this Region. Number of immovable cultural properties as well as the Outstanding Universal Value of the World Heritage Site Kotor bind us with an obligation to use planning documents, among which is the umbrella plan of the Municipality *Spatial Plan*, to examine and define long term measures of preservation and valorization of individual cultural properties and cultural landscape as a whole, in a manner that would ensure cultural properties have a purpose that can be sustained and used in contemporary flow of life and that should be of use to present and future generations as a testament to present and past times. In that regard, one of the most important instruments of protection of values of this Region is the Study on Protection of Cultural Properties, as a basis for drafting of the Spatial Plan of the Municipality of Kotor. In addition to the documents that were adopted so far, such as the Study on Protection of Cultural Properties for the purposes of the Special Purpose Spatial Plan for the Coastal Zone and Heritage Impact Assessment for Kotor, the process of adoption of the Spatial Plan as an umbrella local plan must be a priority, whose drafting and adoption has been significantly made easier through introduction of a construction moratorium in the beginning of 2017.

Attributes of the Outstanding Universal Value of the Kotor Region and Analysis of the Institutional and Legislative Frameworks

Quality architecture (both independent and complex structures) , successful unity of cities and settlements with natural environment of the Bay as well as unique testament to the role that the Region had in spreading the Mediterranean culture in Balkans were recognized as attributes of the OUV of the Kotor Region. Also significant is the quality of arts and crafts of the whole geo-cultural zone, forged through the merging of western and eastern cultures.

Professional protection of cultural properties in the Kotor Region has been active since mid XIX century and it has been continuously conducted to the present day. Truthfully, through different state models and institutional forms, it still managed to preserve the most significant forms in this Region.

Following World War II, Bureau for Protection of Cultural and Natural Monuments was established in Cetinje, and it later transformed into the Republic Bureau for Protection of Cultural Monuments Cetinje. The Bureau predominantly monitored the conditioon of the Kotor Region until mid 1980, when the Municipal Bureau for Protection of Cultural Monuments Kotor was established, with headquarters in Kotor. In 1992 it transformed into a regional institution seated in Kotor. Municipal Bureau Kotor represented a center point for numerous national and international experts as well as UNESCO professionals, who all gathered to work on the restoration of Kotor Region following the big earthquake of April 15th 1979.[①]

Decisions of the UNESCO World Heritage Committee adopted in 1979, established the status of the Kotor Region as a part of the natural and cultural heritage of the highest tier. Following the devastating earthquake that hit Montenegro that year, long term, international complex research was initiated, and it resulted in mostly

---

① Study on Protection of Cultural Properties for the purposes of the Spatial Plan of Kotor, Directorate for Protection of Cultural Properties of Montenegro, Cetinje, 2017.

successful projects of restoration of historical structures as well as preparation of plans that aimed to design the protected area. Those plans and strategies were incorporated in Spatial, General and Management plans as documents that serve to integrally protect the heritage and map out the sustainable development.

The basic structure of legislative regulations that pertains to the Kotor Region is mostly quality, but it is necessary for it to be systematically applied, as this is a condition for ensuring not only protection of the cultural property but also a betterment of the life quality. The public as a whole needs to be introduced to procedures and processes as well as conclusions of the competent bodies of UNESCO that pertain to the matter of protection of the Natural and Culturo-Historical Region of Kotor.

Protection of cultural properties in the area of BokaKotorska is regulated through the Law on Protection of Cultural Properties and the Law on Protection of the Natural and Culturo-Historical Region of Kotor, whose determined goals are the following: preservation of the OUV; permanent preservation of the authentic natural, historical, urbanistic, architectural, ambiental, aesthetic and landscape values; ensuring of conditions for sustainable development and usage, as well as presentation and professional and scientific valorization of the heritage. Affairs of protection and preservation of the Kotor Region are conducted by the bodies of state administration within their competencies, as well as bodies of the Kotor Municipality and public services established by the State and the Municipality. Protection and preservation of the protected area of the Kotor Region, in addition to aforementioned subjects, is also ensured by competent bodies of neighbouring municipalities.

Management, protection, preservation, usage and presentation of the protected area are further defined in the Management Plan of the Natural and Culturo-Historical Region of Kotor that has been adopted by the Government in 2011. This document contains a strategy of management of the Natural and Culturo-Historical Region of Kotor for the period of 15 years, guidelines for the implementation of said strategy, programme of activities, mechanisms for accomplishing integral protection, manner of conducting monitoring of planned activities and other things. Currently the revision of this document is ongoing.

Threats and Challenges to Preservation of the Universal Values

Undoubtedly the role of state and local administration is of great importance for the protection and preservation of the OUV of the Kotor Region, seeings as they are the bodies that establish and implement public policies. The matter of quality of planning documents and the Management Plan and implementation thereof shall represent a special challenge in the upcoming period.

The following processes were recognized in the space; there are also processes which are of systemic nature and represent an issue of legislation and expert structures[①]:

---

① Heritage Impact Assessment for the Natural and Culturo-Historical Region of Kotor, Faculty of Architecture of the University of Montenegro, Podgorica, 2017.

In the Natural and Culturo-Historical Region of Kotor the urbanization has been recognized as a continuous process suggested by the spatial documentation, prepared and managed consistently since 1969

Extreme speed with which the processes are unfolding, primarily urbanization in the past decade

Processes, procedures and participants in the affairs of protection and preservation of the heritage are mostly defined and seen as an obstruction and business obstacle, and not as a corrective factor in these procedures and activities

Problematic structure of standing spatial and planning documentation that includes their mutual structure types as well as their contents

The space of cultural landscape has not been treated as an individual category in the spatial and planning documents.

Suggestion of operative measures for improvement of the condition:

Adoption of the Spatial Plan of Kotor Municipality based on the Study on Protection and the Management Plan

Amendments to standing and drafting of new spatial and planning documents of the lower tier

Strengthening of inspection capacities and number of supervisions

Strengthening of awareness on significance and meaning of UNESCO Sites

Necessity of active local participation of NGOs and citizens in all processes.

Need for Improvement of Integral Protection of the Kotor Region

The matter of construction in the area of the Natural and Culturo-Historical Region of Kotor is complex and is certainly a result of non-existence of an integral approach. Especially since here we are not talking about an individual culturo-historical or natural structure, but about a region covering a significant area and with vulnerable visual axes. In certain cases, inadequate quantity and density of space under construction is a result of several factors, among others, unharmonized relation between standing legislation, failure to adhere to planning parameters, insufficient ethics of planners and designers as well as citizens. Special type of sensibility needs to be demonstrated when it comes to sustainable development and finding measures of protection and development, conservation and construction. Considerations on integral protection and sustainable development must include the segment of traffic infrastructure that requires special sensibility in order to take care of natural landscape structures, necessity of their preservation as well as implementation of visual impact studies in order to reach quality solutions that are adequate in regards to the OUV attributes. Insufficent consideration of the aforementioned could certainly lead to endaganderment of universal values.

Application of Integral Framework on the Research Subject

As already stated, when it comes to the complexity of factors that impact the condition of the Kotor Region, it is necessary to consider them in an integral manner. Due to easier and better overview, we used Wilber's AQAL model, as a basic framework of the Integral Theory.[①]

According to (Wilber K., 2015), four basic dimensions of the case are represented: inner/outer, individual/collective. Upper left quadrant refers to the inner dimension of the individual case (individual will, consciousness), while the lower left quadrant pertains to the collective side of the case (culture, societal relationships). Upper right quadrant refers to outer individual case (behaviour) while the lower right one refers to outer collective case (social systems).

In this specific case, through two levels (national and international), we can consider four dimensions of the Kotor case (Fig 1).

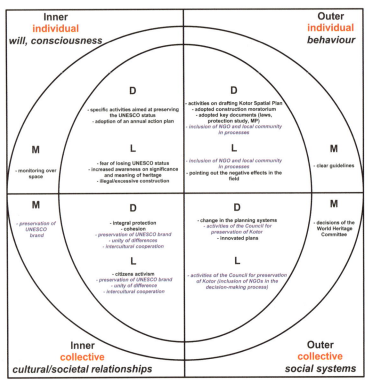

M—international; D—state/national; L—local level

Fig 1 Application of integral framework on Kotor

---

① Integral theory or theory of all is an attempt to connect different thoughts and paradigms into an interconnected system. The idea is to use all the knowledge and experience and to present it through a network of four quadrants, i.e. four quadrants of existence (international, behavioural, cultural and social), relations inner-outer and individual-collective, so that it may appear coherent.The model is used to point to ways of conducting a comprehensive synthesis and integration of the most impactful studies of consciousness and strivings towards the integral theory of consciousness.

This model points to the special importance and responsibility of the State in the preservation of the UNESCO status of a certain location, as well as necessity of deepening the cooperation between UNESCO, NGOs and local community. In addition, it points to the complexity of necessary and undertaken activities that would keep the area of 12.000 ha on the World Heritage List. The singular goal of all levels of action is preservation of UNESCO brand in Kotor.

Conclusion

In the time of globalization, sustainable usage and management of heritage is imperative and also a challenge of contemporary policies. Understanding of values, significance and meaning of cultural and natural heritage is focused on the developmental segment, both in economic and cultural sense. Due to the necessity of systemic and systematic action with an aim of protection and valorization of heritage, integral and interdisciplinary activities are needed. Cultural heritage can certainly contribute to fulfillment of strategic goals of UN and EU as well as sustainable development of communities and rational and smart usage of strategic resources; however, if there is no harmony in undertaking clearly set tasks, it (the heritage) may lose its significance. In that regard, the example of the Kotor Region is important in several aspects, because it serves to reflect impact of international, national and local factors, obligations and necessary activities of all actors as well as possible consequences of a failure to apply the integral approach.

References

1. Wilber K. (1997) , *An Integral Theory of Consciousness*, Journal of Consciousness Studies

2. Rentchler M. (2006) , *AQAL Glossary, Journal of Integral Theory and Practice, Vol. 1*

3. Grazuleviciute I. (2006) , *Cultural heritage in the context of sustainable development. Environmental research engineering and management*

4. Healey P. (2007) , *Urban Complexity and Spatial Strategies*, London: Routledge

5. Brown B. (2006) , *Four Worlds of Sustainability*, Integral Sustainability Center

6. Bentley I. (1999) , *Urban transformations: Power, people and urban design*, London: Routledge

7. Wilber K. (2015) , *Response to "Integral 2.0" and "There is No 'You' in AQAL"*

8. Kocovic M., Đukic, V. (2015) , "Partnership as a strategy to achieve optimal participatory governance and risk mitigation (of cultural and natural heritage) ", in *The ENCATC Journal of Cultural Management and Policy*

9. Jokilehto J. 2005. "Definition of Cultural Heritage, References to Documents in History", *ICCROM Working Group Heritage and Society*

10. Cultural Heritage in the Context of Sustainable Development: https://www.researchgate.net/publication/228466259_Cultural_Heritage_in_the_Context_of_Sustainable_Development

11. Council of Europe. 2005. Action for a changing society. Framework Convention on the value of cultural heritage for society http://www.coe.int/t/dg4/cultureheritage/heritage/identities/Faro-brochure_en.PDF

12. Study on Protection of Cultural Properties for the purposes of the Spatial Plan of Kotor, Directorate for Protection of Cultural Properties of Montenegro, Cetinje, 2017

13. Heritage Impact Assessment for the Natural and Culturo-Historical Region of Kotor, Faculty of Architecture of the University of Montenegro, Podgorica, 2017

世界遗产与可持续发展

清华大学　吕　舟[①]

1972 年，梅多斯（Donella Meadows）等人出版了《增长的极限》一书，反映了 20 世纪 60—70 年代人们对于当时人类社会的发展模式是否具有可持续性的反思。同年年底，教科文组织通过了《世界遗产公约》，提出要在人类社会发展的同时保护好文化和自然遗产。根据《世界遗产公约》，对文化和自然遗产的保护是"保护不论属于哪国人民的这类罕见且无法替代的财产，对全世界人民都很重要"，"考虑到部分文化或自然遗产具有突出的重要性，因而需作为全人类世界遗产的一部分加以保护"，"鉴于威胁这类遗产的新危险的规模和严重性，整个国际社会有责任通过提供集体性援助来参与保护具有突出的普遍价值的文化和自然遗产"。

对文化和自然遗产的保护同样是对工业社会（或现代主义时期）发展模式的反思。人类社会在经历了工业社会的发展之后，资源消耗、环境污染等问题促进了对工业时代发展模式的批判。工业社会促进的城市化发展极大的改变了原有城市的形态，改变了城市中原有的社会结构，更造成了对城市中原有建成环境的改变，对教科文组织而言，对以人类重要纪念性建筑、历史古迹进行保护是其自 1946 年成立之后始终关注的问题。1952 年教科文组织通过的《在武装冲突情况下保护文化财产的公约》以及之后推动的对埃及努比亚遗产、意大利威尼斯、印度尼西亚波罗浮屠的保护等都反映了对文化财产的保护在教科文组织工作中的重要地位。

一、文化和自然遗产的保护是可持续发展的基础步骤

对文化遗产的保护是 20 世纪后半期人类重要的普遍价值观。它不仅反映了人类对于认知自身历史的追求，反映了审美的延续性和普遍性，更反映了人类对文化认同的精神需求。人类知识的积累是社会的延续性的基础，相对于跳跃的发展更能满足人类稳定和持续发展的需要，而稳定和持续从发展的

[①] 吕舟，清华大学教授，是文化遗产领域的重要专家。吕舟教授主持、领导了大量重要文物保护单位的保护规划、维修设计，作为主要专家参与起草了《中国文物古迹保护准则 2015 版》的工作。吕舟教授主持的文化遗产保护项目曾两次获得"教科文组织亚太地区文化遗产保护奖"和中国文物保护项目的最高荣誉。作为 ICOMOS 和 ICCROM 专家，吕舟教授参与了大量世界遗产的相关工作和遗产保护的国际培训项目。由于他在文化遗产保护领域的杰出贡献，2013 年 ICCROM 授予吕舟教授 ICCROM Award。

角度更能够体现可持续的原则。

60—70 年代西方社会在进入到后现代社会之后，基于对于资源和环境问题的认识，特别是工业社会对不可再生资源的依赖和大规模使用，造成严重的环境和能源问题，促进了人们环境保护运动的发展。1962 年美国作家雷切尔·卡逊（Rachel Carson）出版了《寂静的春天》对人类大量使用化学药剂对生态环境造成的巨大危害做了生动的描述，并导致了一些国家对 DDT 等化学杀虫剂的禁用。梅多斯等人在《增长的极限》第一版的前言中提出"通过技术、文化和制度上重大、前瞻和社会性的创新来避免人类生态足迹的增加超出地球的承载能力"[1]。"我们希望这种反思将促使人类社会采取矫正行动以降低崩溃发生的可能。崩溃并不是什么诱人的未来。人口和经济急剧下降到地球自然系统不能够支撑的水平无疑将伴随着健康恶化、冲突、生态灾难以及严重的不平等。死亡率的迅速上升和消费水平的迅速下降将导致人类足迹走向无法控制的崩溃"[2]。"增长并不必然导致崩溃；但如果增长导致了过冲、导致了需求的扩张超出了地球资源所能维持的水平时，崩溃必然紧随而来"[3]。这些观念在 20 世纪 70 年代引发了广泛的讨论，这些讨论促进了重要国际组织包括联合国经社理事会（Economic and Social Council）等对环境问题的关注。1972 年在瑞典斯德哥尔摩召开的人类环境与发展大会上通过的《人类环境宣言（斯德哥尔摩宣言）》提出了保护自然资源、维护地球可以产生可再生能源的能力、保护野生动物、共享不可再生资源、把污染控制在环境可自我清理的程度等重要原则。

1972 年教科文组织在这样的背景下通过了《世界遗产公约》，促进对具有"突出普遍价值"的文化和自然遗产的保护，并"建立一个根据现代科学方法制定的永久性的有效制度"[4]。值得注意的是，这一制度的基本出发点是对这些具有突出普遍价值的文化和自然遗产加以保护。尽管这一时期关于环境问题的讨论已经引发了普遍的关注，但从世界遗产的层面则更强调"历史"的意义和对历史的记录。这种特征不仅反映在文化遗产的相关标准当中，同样也反映在关于自然遗产相关的标准当中。根据1977 年世界遗产委员会通过的《实施世界遗产公约的操作指南》，评价自然遗产是否具有突出普遍价值，《实施世界遗产公约的操作指南》提出了四条基本标准：

1. 是代表地球进化历史主要阶段的杰出例证；

2. 展现重要的正在进行过程中的地质过程、生物进化和人类与环境互动的杰出案例；

3. 包含独一无二的，罕见的或最高级的自然现象、组合或特征或具有杰出的自然美景的区域，如典型的案例是，对人类最重要的生态系统，自然要素（河流、山岳、瀑布），高密度的动物聚集区域，大面积自然植被覆盖区和独特的自然与文化要素的组合；

4. 稀有或濒危动植物物种的栖息地。

无论对文化还是自然遗产在《世界遗产公约》的初期都表现出了对于人类历史和地球演变历史的

---

① 梅多斯等著，增长的极限，李涛等译，机械工业出版社，2013。
② 同上。
③ 同上。
④ 教科文组织，世界遗产公约，1972。

关注。对于这些人类历史和自然演变历史的证据，这一时期最基本的要求是严格地进行保护。保护对于文化遗产而言必须符合真实性的标准，自然遗产则必须符合完整性的要求。从真实性的角度，文化遗产需要重点考虑原有的物质形态的遗存，包括设计、工艺、材料和地点，这种物质形态并非文化遗产瞬间的形态，而是其整个生命过程中能够体现其作为世界遗产的突出普遍价值的形态演变。对于自然遗产而言，采用"代表地球进化历史主要阶段的杰出例证"的标准申报的遗产项目，应当包含这一现象在自然的相互关系中所有或绝大部分相互关联和相互依存的关键因素；以"展现重要的正在进行过程中的地质过程、生物进化和人类与环境互动的杰出案例"标准申报的区域需要有足够的尺度，并包含展现这一进程关键方面能够延续的必要的要素；以"包含独一无二的，罕见的或最高级的自然现象、组合或特征或具有杰出的自然美景的区域"标准申报的遗产应当包括物种延续和保存所需要生态系统的各个组成部分；以"稀有或濒危动植物物种的栖息地"申报的遗产的完整性反映在是否拥有足够尺度的区域栖息足以延续这些物种的种群。

对于《世界遗产公约》而言，保护这些对人类具有突出的世界性价值的遗产是提出这一公约的根本目标，用保护来消除或减缓这些文化财产或自然环境、资源在人类发展及自然演进过程中的损耗成为这一公约号召各国政府参与的工作。为此公约还提出各国政府也应当在自己的国家建立相应的保护体系，保护文化和自然遗产。

二、遗产保护纳入发展的维度

经过20世纪70和80年代的发展，《世界遗产公约》已经成为"国际合作的重要工具"[1]，获得了国际社会的广泛关注。但在这一时期，无论是对于世界遗产的标准还是真实性和完整性的基本标准都还存在广泛的争议。这些争议集中在这些标准是否能够涵盖世界各个不同区域的遗产特征？关于真实性和完整性标准是基于哪些观念和实践的检验？这些讨论促进了从观念和实践不同的层面对于遗产的思考，也导致了遗产标准和真实性、完整性原则在90年代出现的变化。

需要注意的是20世纪80年代，冷战结束以后，世界进入了一个新的发展进程，对于发展的需求再次对文化和自然遗产的保护产生了巨大的压力。在这一时期，人们开始注意到世界遗产保护中发达国家和发展中国家的差异，如何理解、表达遗产的价值，如何理解和实施操作指南的相关要求在发达国家和发展中国家之间存在着明显的差异，甚至随着世界遗产名录的扩大这种差异不但没有消弭，甚至在一定程度上在不断扩大。这反映了处于不同发展阶段或经济地位的国家在保护遗产意义上认知的差异，也反映了保护能力的不平衡。

1980年，联合国大会特别会议通过了《联合国第三个发展十年的国际发展战略》针对世界经济、社会发展的不平衡性提出了，推动第三世界国家经济发展，及对第三世界国家的发展提供援助的目标

---

[1] UNESCO, activity-564-2. pdf, Léon Pressouyre.

要求。东亚和东南亚经济的发展也成为这一时期受到国际社会广泛关注的重要经验。民营化、市场自由化释放出了新的发展动力。在这种情况下，作为《世界遗产公约》创立者的教科文组织同样也关注到了文化和自然遗产的保护与公约各缔约国强烈的发展要求之间的关系。在 1988—1997 年联合国发起的"世界文化发展十年"（World Decade for Cultural Development）活动中，教科文组织强调了发展的文化维度。时任总干事马约尔（Federico Mayor）在《信使》杂志发文指出："过去 20 年的经验证明了文化不能与社会的发展相分离，无论是经济增长的水平或政治和经济的取向"[1]。马约尔强调"文化必将在经济活动上留下印记，并定义社会生产过程的优劣"[2]。"这些结论来自所有国家的经验和教训。每当一个国家在不参考其文化环境的情况下确定经济增长目标时，就会造成严重的经济和文化失衡，其创造潜力被严重削弱。真正的发展必须基于对社区人力资源和物质财富的最佳利用。因此，归根结底，必须在文化中找到发展的优先事项、动机和目标。但在过去，这显然被忽视了"[3]。马约尔特别提出世界文化发展十年是提高对文化紧迫性的认识，并培育一种新心态，以形成一种'整体的多样'、'融合的创造'和'充满自由的团结'的新的观念。在这种表述的背后不难看到 20 世纪 80—90 年代人们对于在趋同的经济发展模式影响下，人们对于文化多样性关注的觉醒，在于人们开始意识到文化多样性对于人类社会发展所具有的重要性。

教科文组织在 1984—1989 年的中期规划中在"文化与未来"的部分中，也特别强调了文化多样性的问题，并认为文化多样性应当是一个开放的系统，对文化多样性的认同意味着对所有文化多样性的尊重。这一观念一直是教科文组织关于文化多样性保护实践的基础。文化多样性观念的觉醒，与 20 世纪 70 年代环境保护意识的觉醒有极高的相似性。对文化多样性的尊重和保护在很大程度上影响了 20 世纪 90 年代以后世界遗产的发展方向。

在 1984—1989 年的中期规划中，教科文组织在关于文化的"行动战略"中，强调了 1982 年"世界文化政策大会"（World Conference on Cultural Policies）的宣言中所指出的"每一个人都有权利和义务发展自己的文化"，"通过丰富的变化和多样性，通过相互的影响，所有文化都是共同遗产的一部分"[4]，提出通过这种多样性创造性的更新文化发展的目标，以促进社会的发展。这一表述显示了这一时期教科文组织的文化发展观。

20 世纪 80—90 年代，既是一个世界各国寻求经济快速发展的时期，也是一个局部战争、冲突不断的时期。这种冲突从冷战时期两个阵营意识形态的对立转而呈现出更多的文明或文化间冲突的特征。亨廷顿（Samuel P. Huntington）1996 年出版的《文明的冲突与世界秩序的重建》把冷战之后世界上的各种冲突归结为文化的冲突。亨廷顿的观点引发了世界广泛的关注和讨论，并在一定程度上影响了教科文组织对于世界发展的判断。在教科文组织 1996 年—2001 年中期战略报告（Medium-Term

---

① UNESCO, The Courier, 1988/11, 5.
② 同上。
③ 同上。
④ UNESCO, 054611eb-MTP-1984-89, 11037.

Strategy）中就清晰地表明了这种情况。较之 1984—1989 年的中期规划对发展的强调，在 1996 年—2001 年中期战略报告中和平与安全成为了核心的内容。这一中期战略不仅再次强调了教科文组织组织法中提出的"在人之思想中筑起保卫和平之屏障"。通过发展来消除引发战争的根源也是这一中期战略提出的解决世界面临的冲突的威胁的方法："战争本身必须通过消除一切形式的经济贫困，社会不公正，政治压迫，歧视和排斥来摧毁，这些冲突的根源"①。而加强文化遗产、促进活态文化、鼓励创新（To enhance cultural heritage，promote living cultures and encourage creativity）成为促进发展、构建和平的重要途径。

在涉及《世界遗产公约》的内容中，1996 年—2001 年中期战略报告中提出"世界遗产名录中包含了具有"突出普遍价值"的纪念碑和遗址，必须更具代表性。在这方面，需要进一步考虑世界遗产的现实概念，除了传统的类别外，还应扩大到包括世界文化多样性的其他标志性的对象"②。文化景观被视为体现文化多样性的标志性对象。而"现实的概念"（actual concept）则把对遗产的保护与当代的发展和建设和平更为密切地联系在一起。

遗产的保护也不再仅仅是政府的工作，"保护世界遗产是一项巨大的任务，从长远来看，只有当地社区积极参与才能取得成功。必须在保护和遗产地维护方面制定新的方法，利用当地的传统，技术和知识"③。

"我们必须帮助确保遗产更充分地融入社区的经济和社会生活。教科文组织已经开始这一进程，为城市复兴项目提供援助，旨在使历史遗产重新融入城市的日常生活。在旅游业是许多国家重要收入来源的时候，保障政策需要更多地考虑到东道国人民的合理关注，以分享旅游业的经济利益。因此，教科文组织的战略是促进文化旅游的发展，尊重文化特征，鼓励加强国际理解，同时为长期的当地社区需求提供解决方案"④。在这一表述中，遗产已不再仅仅是静态的被保护的对象，而是活跃的、深度参与当代社会和经济发展的积极力量。基于教科文组织的立场，文化间的冲突，源于缺少文化间对话和相互尊重，因此建设和平的重要途径是鼓励文化间的交流和对话，保护和展现体现这种交流和对话的遗产项目作为历史的经验就成为遗产保护的重要目的。在 1996 年—2001 年中期战略中关于建设和平的战略中，"鼓励文化多样化和文化对话"是重要的组成部分："教科文组织一直致力于发展不同文化之间的对话，这是任何建设和平战略的基本要素。通过鼓励世界主要文化区域之间的交流，特别是东西方之间的交流，以及通过帮助新独立国家确认其文化特征，教科文组织帮助促进了教科文组织组织法所提到的多样性文化富有成果的的广泛认识。……在教科文组织的推动下发展起来的国际合作建立起了人类"共同遗产"的概念，使许多文化更好地相互了解……"⑤，"当我们面对人与人之间隔绝的屏障和可能引发'文明间冲突'的最坏结果的状况，我们相信以对话和开放的精神，建立一个无论文化

---

① UNESCO, 102501e-MTS-96-01, Foreword.
② UNESCO, 102501e-MTS-96-01, 125.
③ UNESCO, 102501e-MTS-96-01, 130.
④ UNESCO, 102501e-MTS-96-01, 131.
⑤ UNESCO, 102501e-MTS-96-01, 177.

身份如何人人都可以分享的价值观,奠定人类共同生活愿望的基础"①。

通过遗产,无论是可移动还是不可移动,无论是物质和非物质,无论是自然还是文化,形成一种开放和对话的精神,建立文化间相互尊重、包容的共同价值观,避免"文明间的冲突",建设和平,促进文化的发展和创造,这是教科文组织在这一阶段的中期战略中提出的基本观点。这种对遗产所具有的现实价值的理解已不同于 1972 年通过《世界遗产公约》时对遗产价值的理解,对遗产也不再仅仅关注于保护的问题,而开始关注如何让遗产在当代社会的建设和平和社会、经济、社区的发展中发挥作用。遗产保护则被教科文组织作为一种建立开放的文化价值观,促进建设和平与发展的工具,被更明确地纳入到发展的维度。

三、二十一世纪基于可持续发展的遗产保护

2000 年在第五十四届联合国大会上,与会的各国首脑通过了"联合国千年宣言",并指出:"我们今天面临的主要挑战是确保全球化成为一股有利于全世界所有人民的积极力量。因为尽管全球化带来了巨大机遇,但它所产生的惠益目前分配非常不均,各方付出的代价也不公平。我们认识到发展中国家和转型期经济国家为应付这一主要挑战而面临特殊的困难。因此,只有以我们人类共有的多样性为基础,通过广泛和持续的努力创造共同的未来,才能使全球化充分做到兼容并蓄,公平合理。这些努力还必须包括顾及发展中国家和转型期经济体的需要、并由这两者有效参与制订和执行的全球性政策和措施"②。

对于联合国和各国首脑而言,他们认为在 21 世纪来临之时,世界面临的挑战是全球化发展带来的不平衡和不公平,需要以人类共有的多样性为基础,实现全球化的兼容并蓄和公平发展。提出了包括自由、平等、团结、容忍、尊重大自然、共同承担责任在内的基本价值,提出了和平、安全与裁军,发展与消除贫困,保护共同环境,人权、民主和善政,保护易受伤害者,满足非洲的特殊需要,加强联合国的基本目标。并特别为减轻贫困确定了具体的目标:"在 2015 年年底前,使世界上每日收入低于一美元的人口比例和挨饿人口比例降低一半,并在同一日期之前,使无法得到或负担不起安全饮用水的人口比例降低一半;确保在同一日期之前,使世界各地的儿童,不论男女,都能上完小学全部课程,男女儿童都享有平等的机会,接受所有各级教育;在同一日期之前,将目前产妇死亡率降低四分之三,将目前五岁以下儿童死亡率减少三分之二;届时制止并开始扭转艾滋病毒 / 艾滋病的蔓延、消灭疟疾及其他折磨人类的主要疾病的祸害;向艾滋病毒 / 艾滋病孤儿提供特别援助;到 2020 年年底前,根据'无贫民窟城市'倡议,使至少一亿贫民窟居民的生活得到重大改善"③。

相对于这样一些全球性的挑战,世界遗产的保护也越来越强调对这样一些基本目标的贡献,各国

---

① UNESCO, 102501e-MTS-96-01, 180.
② https : //documents-dds-ny.un.org/doc/UNDOC/GEN/N00/559/50/PDF/N0055950.pdf ? OpenElement.
③ https : //documents-dds-ny.un.org/doc/UNDOC/GEN/N00/559/50/PDF/N0055950.pdf ? OpenElement.

政府也越来越关注于遗产保护对社会和经济发展的贡献与影响。这种情况进一步推高了各国对把自己的遗产项目列入世界遗产名录的诉求，也在一定程度上造成了受到非议的世界遗产的评审政治化倾向的发展。

把"联合国千年宣言"视为进入 21 世纪时人们对于未来挑战的共识的话，联合国针对这些挑战，提出了"千年发展目标"（The Millennium Development Goals-MDG），包括 8 个方面基本的目标：减轻贫困；普及初等教育；促进性别平等并赋予妇女权力；降低儿童死亡率；改善产妇健康；防治艾滋病毒 / 艾滋病、疟疾和其他疾病；确保环境可持续性；发展全球发展伙伴关系。针对这样一个涉及到经济、教育、健康、环境和全球参与的可持续发展的综合目标，世界遗产作为教科文组织的旗舰项目应当如何发挥作用，同样也是世界遗产保护领域应当面对和回答的重要问题。

2012 年教科文组织把纪念《世界遗产公约》40 周年活动的主题确定为"世界遗产与可持续发展：地方社区的作用"。促进以地方社区为核心的可持续发展成为世界遗产的重要议题，"这反映了人们越来越关注经济和社会发展之间的关系以及当地人民的参与对保护自然和文化遗产的日益重要"[1]。在庆祝活动期间，教科文组织及各缔约国政府组织了一系列的活动，都强调了世界遗产与可持续发展的关系，以及社区具有的重要作用。这些会议包括 2012 年 2 月在巴西召开的"世界遗产与可持续发展国际专家会议"，2012 年 5 月在挪威召开的"与世界遗产一起生活的地区间大会"，9 月在韩国召开的"让社区参与世界遗产保护：概念和行动国际会议"，9 月在丹麦召开的"世界遗产公约和土著人民国际专家讲习班"，9 月在南非召开的"在非洲与世界遗产共生国际会议"。2012 年 11 月世界遗产中心、日本文化厅和富山县政府联合在日本富山召开了"遗产与可持续发展：从原则到实践"的国际研讨会。会议通过了《遗产与可持续发展的富山提案》，提出自然与文化遗产的保护、管理，在可持续、平等和人类权利的基本原则下，应当为人类环境的可持续性、包容性社会发展、包容性经济发展以及和平与安全的核心方面发挥作用，做出贡献[2]。富山提案认为："有必要加深对遗产保护与可持续发展之间关系的理解，并尽可能确定表达遗产对可持续发展贡献的定量和定性指标"[3]，实现遗产保护对可持续发展做出贡献的基本途径是"将世界遗产的保护与管理纳入地方治理和政治进程，促进所有相关的参与方，地方官员、民众、旅游和其他商业部门及广泛的市民社会的能力建设"[4]。

通过对世界遗产与可持续发展关系的讨论，人们更多地注意到世界遗产对可持续发展的影响和促进作用，这种促进作用又更直接地作用于遗产地所在的社区。基于这种认识，世界遗产也呈现出从基于遗产价值的保护向以人为中心的促进可持续发展的方向的转变。这种转变反映了世界遗产在经历了 40 年的发展后已经成为影响人类社会发展的重要途径，另一方面这种发展和转变也使得世界遗产的保护不再仅仅是基于其遗产价值的技术性方法，而被赋予了更多的社会发展诉求，这不可避免的使世界

---

① UNESCO, activity-664-10, 1.

② UNESCO/whc/event-930-1.

③ 同上。

④ UNESCO/whc/event-930-1.

遗产被添加了更浓重的政治色彩,如何在现实需求的基础上,实现世界遗产在遗产价值的保护与促进社会可持续发展的需求之间新的平衡,同样是今天世界遗产面临的重要挑战。

在纪念《世界遗产公约》40周年活动通过的《京都愿景》提出:"世界遗产与当地社区之间的关系无疑是公约的核心,对于世界所有地区应对面临的人口增长和发展压力、全球金融危机和气候变化的挑战至关重要"[①]。《京都愿景》提出"公约的目标之一是'赋予遗产在社区生活中的作用'(第5条),那么社区的关注和愿望必须汇集在保护和管理工作中。只有在尊重文化和生物多样性的基础上,加强人与遗产之间的关系,将有形和无形两方面结合起来,面向可持续发展,才能实现'我们想要的未来'"[②],"除非将这种可持续发展的观点纳入世界遗产的管理之中,否则从长远来看,很难确保保护其突出的普遍价值"[③]。把社区作为保护世界遗产的基础,把通过遗产保护给社区带来的发展促进人类社会的可持续发展是21世纪前期世界遗产发展的基本取向。

世界遗产作为当代全球文化的一个重要标志,反映了当代文化的基本观念。2013年教科文组织和中国政府在杭州召开的"文化:可持续发展的关键"国际会议通过的《杭州宣言》提出:"文化应当视为可持续发展的根本推动者、意义和能量的来源、创新的源泉,以及应对挑战、寻找适当解决方案的自愿。当我们把以人为本、因地制宜的措施纳入发展计划和维和倡议时,文化在促成真正意义上可持续发展方面的超常力量将显得尤为突出","文化作为一项只是资本和活力产业,通过其对包容性社会文化经济发展、社会和谐、环境可持续性、和平与安全的特殊贡献,有望成为可持续发展的驱动者"。

《杭州宣言》提出了促进发挥文化在可持续发展中作用的九方面的行动:

> 把文化纳入所有发展政策和计划中;
> 推动文化发展和相互理解,促进和平与和解;
> 确保所有人都能获得文化权利,从而推动包容性社会发展;
> 推动文化对于减贫及包容性经济发展的作用;
> 发展文化以促进环境可持续性;
> 通过文化提升对灾害的适应能力,并与气候变化作斗争;
> 珍惜文化、保护文化,将文化带给子孙后代;
> 将文化作为实现城市可持续发展和管理的资源;
> 利用文化开展可持续的新型合作模式[④]。

《杭州宣言》表达了一个重要的认知——文化对于可持续发展的影响是整体、综合和全面的。世界

---

① UNESCO, activity–664–10, 11.
② 同上。
③ 同上。
④ UNESCO, CLT–2013/WS/14.

遗产对于可持续发展的意义也是如此。

教科文组织在 2014—2021 年中期战略中提出"在未来几年中，教科文组织将调动资源、发展相关思想观念和提出承诺，实现通过文化促进对和平与可持续发展的新认识。在多边层面上，利用最近的成果，通过加强文化的各个方面，促进文化为驱动的和平和可持续发展，实现基于以人为本的发展方针，得到可持续、包容和公平的结果。从整体上认识遗产，包括自然与文化，有形与无形的遗产，它们因社会价值和所体现的身份与归属的方式构成了继承自先人并希望传承给子孙后代的资产。这些资产应用于促进社会稳定、建设和平、从危机中恢复和发展的战略"[①]。

对教科文组织而言，世界遗产公约是建立在共同的价值观的基础上，同时尊重文化的多样性，通过世界遗产领域的合作与对话，尊重不同的文化观念，在人们的观念中消除冲突的思想基础，实现和平，为可持续发展创造条件。从这个角度，世界遗产对于可持续发展的贡献并不仅仅在于为遗产地提供了经济发展的可能性，更从思想的层面提供了共同的价值观，为文化之间的交流与对话提供了平台。世界遗产对于可持续发展的作用和影响是多方面和整体的，片面强调某一方面的作用，可能影响其发挥整体的作用。

2015 年第 20 届世界遗产公约缔约国大会通过了《将可持续发展观点纳入世界遗产公约进程的政策性文件》，认为"世界遗产公约是教科文组织促进公平的可持续发展及促进和平与安全的首要任务的组成部分"[②]，基于可持续发展的视角，世界遗产的保护、管理不仅是要保护其所具有的突出普遍价值，也要为当代和后代保持良好的状况；世界遗产的保护管理策略要基于联合国相关宪章和 2030 议程，特别是人权、平等、永续发展的观念；充分认识生物多样性与文化多样性的密切关联和相互依赖；可持续发展的所有维度；实现可持续发展可能需要超出世界遗产的尺度，应在更大的范围内考虑可持续发展的规划；把可持续发展的观念纳入世界遗产的保护和管理需要进行能力建设。这些基本原则表达了世界遗产的保护管理与可持续发展之间关系的基本认知。在这样的原则框架下，《将可持续发展观点纳入世界遗产公约进程的政策性文件》提出了可持续发展作用于世界遗产保护管理的几个基本维度：

> 环境的可持续性；
>
> 保护生物和文化多样性，维护生态系统和相关利益；
>
> 加强对自然灾害和气候变化的抵御能力；
>
> 包容性社会发展；
>
> 促进包容和公平；
>
> 提高生活质量和福利；
>
> 尊重、保护和促进人的权利；

---

① UNESCO, 227860e-MTS-14-21, 66.

② UNESCO, activity-834-5.1.

尊重、咨询和促进土著居民和当地社区的参与；

实现性别平等。[1]

结语

世界遗产的保护和管理，在经历了近 50 年的发展，从对自然和文化资源的以价值为基础的保护，发展为人类可持续发展的重要组成部分。这种发展反映了世界遗产公约所具有的广泛和巨大的影响力，反映了它所展现并促进其发展的价值观已成为人类社会的基本价值观之一。

世界遗产对可持续发展的促进作用，是整体性的作用，不仅体现在提供就业机会，产生经济利益的方面，更体现在促进文化交流与对话，建设和平，创造可持续发展的基础条件，促进文化自觉和文化身份的认知，提高社区凝聚力，促进能力建设，提供教育、培训等多个方面。

遗产地所在社区是遗产保护和管理促进可持续发展的基本单元，世界遗产的保护对社区可持续发展的作用同样是综合和总体的。社区参与遗产地的保护和管理是社区发展的重要途径，通过参与遗产的保护和管理，提高社区的教育水平，展现社区的文化特征，促进文化多样性与遗产地的融合，促进文化发展和创新，改善社区的生活水平也是世界遗产促进可持续发展的基本途径。

---

① UNESCO, activity-834-5.

The World Heritage and the Sustainable Development

Lyu Zhou[①]
China Tsinghua University

In 1972, *Donella Meadows* et al published the book of *Limits to Growth*, which reflected human's introspection on whether the development model of human society was sustainable in the 1960s and 1970s. In the same year, the UNESCO passed *The Convention Concerning the Protection of the World Cultural and Natural Heritage* at the end of 1972, proposing protecting the cultural and natural heritage well while maintaining the development of human society. According to *The Convention Concerning the Protection of the World Cultural and Natural Heritage*, the protection of the cultural and natural heritage is "for all the peoples of the world, of safeguarding this unique and irreplaceable property, to whatever people it may belong," "Considering that parts of the cultural or natural heritage are of outstanding interest and therefore need to be preserved as part of the world heritage of mankind as a whole" and "Considering that, in view of the magnitude and gravity of the new dangers threatening them, it is incumbent on the international community as a whole to participate in the protection of the cultural and natural heritage of outstanding universal value."

The preservation of the cultural and natural heritage is also a reflection on the development model of industrial society (or the period of modernism) . After the human society experienced the development of the industrial society, a lot of problems, such as the consumption of the natural resource,the environmental pollution promoted the criticism of the development model in the industrial age. The development of urbanization, which was driven by the industrial society greatly changed the original form of the city, the original social structure of the city, and even the original built environment in the city. For the UNESCO, the

---

① Professor Lyu Zhou, a distinguished professor at Tsinghua University, is well known for his expertise in the field of cultural heritage. He has played a key role in the conservation planning, design and maintenance for numerous heritage sites of national importance. He is also the leading expert involved in the drafting of Principles for the Conservation of Heritage Sites in China (2015) . Heritage conservation projects under his directorship were awarded "UNESCO Asia-Pacific Cultural Heritage Conservation Award" twice and Top Honor for China Cultural Heritage Conservation Project. As the expert in ICOMOS and ICCROM, Professor Lyu Zhou has a full agenda related to World Heritage and international training on heritage conservation. In 2013, ICCROM named Professor Lyu Zhou as the recipient of ICCROM Award in recognition of his extraordinary contribution to cultural heritage conservation.

protection of the important memorial buildings and historical sites of human beings had been a major concern since it was founded in 1946. *The Convention for the Protection of Cultural Property in the Context of Armed Conflict* passed by the UNESCO in 1952 and its subsequent promotion of the protections of the Nubian heritage in Egypt, Venice in Italy and Borobudur in Indonesia, among others, reflected that the protection of cultural property occupied an important position in the UNESCO's work.

The Protection of the Cultural and Natural Heritage is the Basic Step to the Sustainable Development

The protection of the cultural heritage was the important universal view of human beings in the second half of the 20ᵗʰ century. It not only reflected the human beings' pursuit of the cognition of their own history, the aesthetic continuity and universality, but also reflected the spiritual needs of cultural identity. The accumulation of human knowledge was the the basis of the social continuity and could meet the human needs of stability and sustainable development more easily compared with the leaping development, and stability and sustainable development can better embody the principles of sustainability from the perspective of development.

From the 1960s to the 1970s, after the Western World stepped into the postmodern society, the recognition of the issues of resources and the environment, especially the dependence on and large-scale use of the non-renewable resources in the industrial society, which led to serious environmental and energy problems, promoted the development of the environmental protection movements. In 1962, the American writer Rachel Carson published a book entitled *Silent Spring*, in which the great harmfulness to the ecological environment caused by the massive use of chemicals by human beings has been vividly described, leading to a ban on chemical pesticides such as DDT in some countries. In the foreword of the first edition of Limits to Growth, Meadows notes that "pleaded for profound, proactive, societal innovation through technological, cultural, and institutional change in order to avoid an increase in the ecological footprint of humanity beyond the carrying capacity of planet Earth" [1], "we hoped that such deliberation would lead society to take corrective actions to reduce the possibilities of collapse. Collapse is not an attractive future. The rapid decline of population and economy to levels that can be supported by the natural systems of the globe will no doubt be accompanied by failing health, conflict, ecological devastation, and gross inequalities. Uncontrolled collapse in the human footprint will come from rapid increases in mortality and rapid declines in consumption," [2] "growth does not necessarily lead to collapse. Collapse follows growth only if the growth has led to overshoot, to an expansion in demands on the planet's sources, and sinks above levels that can be sustained." [3] These perceptions triggered

---

① Donella Meadows, Jorgen Randers, Dennis Meadows: *Limits to Growth*, translated by Li Tao, China Machine Press, 2013.
② The same as above.
③ The same as above.

a wide range of discussions in the 1970s, and these discussions promoted some important international organizations including Economic and Social Council to pay attention to the environmental problems. In 1972, *Declaration of the United Nations Conference on the Human Environment (Stockholm Declaration)* was passed at the United Nations Conference on the Human Environment and Development in Stockholm, Sweden. This declaration proposed several important principles, such as protecting the natural resources, maintaining the earth's capability of producing the renewable energy, protecting the wild animals, sharing the non-renewable resources, and controlling pollution to the extent that the environment can clean itself up, among others.

Against that background, the UNESCO approved *The Convention Concerning the Protection of the World Cultural and Natural Heritage* in 1972 for the purpose of promoting the protection of the cultural and natural heritage "which are of Outstanding Universal Value" and "establishing an effective system of collective protection of the cultural and natural heritage of outstanding universal value, organized on a permanent basis and in accordance with modern scientific methods."[1] It's worth noting that the starting point of this stipulate is to protect the cultural and natural heritage which are of outstanding universal value. Although the discussions about the environmental problems had aroused widespread concern in this period, the "history" meaning and records were more emphasized at the level of the world heritage. This feature not only finds its way into the related criteria of the cultural heritage, but also into the criteria of the natural heritage. According to *The Operational Guidelines for the Implementation of The Convention Concerning the Protection of the World Cultural and Natural Heritage* passed by the World Heritage Committee in 1977, to evaluate whether the natural heritage has the universal value or not, there are four basic criteria:

1. be outstanding examples representing the major stages of the earth's evolutionary history;

2. be outstanding examples representing significant ongoing geological processes, biological evolution and man's interaction with his natural environment;

3. contain unique, rare or superlative natural phenomena, formations or features or areas of exceptional natural beauty, such as superlative examples of the most important ecosystems to man, natural features (for instance, rivers, mountains, waterfalls), spectacles presented by great concentrations of animals, sweeping vistas covered by natural vegetation and exceptional combinations of natural and cultural elements;

4. be habitats where populations of rare or endangered species of plants and animals still survive.

Cultural heritage and natural heritage alike showed the attention to the human history and the earth's evolutionary history in the initial period of *The Convention Concerning the Protection of the World Cultural and Natural Heritage*. They served as the evidence of human history and nature's evolutionary history, and strictly protecting them was the basic requirement in this period. The protection of the cultural heritage has to

---

[1] The United Nations Educational, Scientific and Cultural Organization: Convention Concerning the Protection of the World Cultural and Natural Heritage, 1972.

conform to the standards of authenticity while the protection of the natural heritage has to meet the standards of integrity. From the perspective of authenticity, the cultural heritage needs to focus on the legacy of the original physical form, including the design, techniques, materials and site, and the physical form is not the instantaneous form of the cultural heritage, but the form evolution that could reflect its outstanding universal value as the world heritage in its whole life process. As for the natural heritage, the declared heritage project adopting the criterion "be outstanding examples representing the major stages of the earth's evolutionary history" should include the landscape's all or most of the key elements of correlations and interdependence in the natural interrelationships. The declared area adopting the criterion of "be outstanding examples representing significant ongoing geological processes, biological evolution and man's interaction with his natural environment" needs to have enough scale, and include the elements necessary to demonstrate the continuity of the key aspects of the process. The declared heritage adopting the criterion of "contain unique, rare or superlative natural phenomena, formations or features or areas of exceptional natural beauty" should include the components of the ecosystem needed for species continuation and conservation. The integrity of the declared heritage adopting the criterion of "be habitats where populations of rare or endangered species of plants and animals still survive" lies in whether there are enough regions of sufficient scale for the survival and continuation of the populations of these species.

The protection of these legacies, which have outstanding worldwide value to humanity, is the fundamental objective of proposing *The Convention Concerning the Protection of the World Cultural and Natural Heritage*. And using protection to eliminate or mitigate the depletion of these cultural properties, the natural environment or resources in the course of human development and natural evolution has become what the Convention calls on Governments to participate in. To that end, the Convention suggested that Governments should also establish the corresponding protection systems in their own countries to protect cultural and natural heritage.

Integrating the Heritage Protection into the Dimension of Development

After the development in the 1970s and the 1980s, *The Convention Concerning the Protection of the World Cultural and Natural Heritage* became an "important tool for international cooperation"[1] and received wide attention from the international community. But during this period, there was widespread controversy over both the standards of world heritage and the basic standards of authenticity and integrity. These controversies focused on whether these standards could cover the heritage characteristics of different regions of the world? What were the concepts and practices on which authenticity and integrity standards are based? These discussions contributed to the reflection of heritage from different levels of perception and practice, as

---

[1] UNESCO, activity-564-2.pdf, Léon Pressouyre.

well as to changes in heritage standards and authenticity and integrity principles in the 1990s.

It is worth noting that in the 1980s, after the end of the Cold War, the world entered a new process of development, and the need for development once again placed enormous pressure on the protection of cultural and natural heritage. During this period, attention began to be paid to the differences between developed and developing countries in the protection of the world heritage. It differed markedly between developed and developing countries as to how to understand and express the value of heritage, and how to understand and implement the requirements for operational guidelines. And the differences were not eliminated but expanded to some extent with the expansion of the World Heritage List. This reflected the differences in perceptions in the sense of preservation of the heritage in countries at different stages of development or economic status, as well as the imbalance in protection capacity.

International Development Strategy for the Third United Nations Development Decade, passed at the Special Sessions of the UN General Assembly in 1980, put forward the goal of promoting the economic development of the Third World countries and providing assistance for the development of them, aiming at the imbalance of world economic and social development. The economic development of East and South-East Asia has also provided important experience that has received wide attention from the international community during this period. Privatization and market liberalization have unleashed new drivers of development. In that case, the UNESCO, as the founder of *The Convention Concerning the Protection of the World Cultural and Natural Heritage*, was also concerned about the relationship between the protection of cultural and natural heritage and the strong development requirements of the contracting parties to the Convention. UNESCO emphasized the cultural dimension of development at the United Nations-sponsored "World Decade for Cultural Development" activity from 1988 to 1997. "The experience of the last two decades has shown that culture cannot be dissociated from development in any society, whatever its level of economic growth or its political and economic orientation," [1] *Federico Mayor*, then Director-General, wrote in *The Courier*, a magazine of UNESCO. *Mayor* stressed that "Thus culture is bound make an imprint on economic activity and define the strengths and weaknesses of a society's productive processes."[2] "These conclusions emerge from the experience, both positive and negative, of all countries. Whenever a country has set itself the target of economic growth without reference to its cultural environment, grave economic and cultural imbalances have resulted and its creative potential has been seriously weakened. Genuine development must be based on the best possible use of the human resources and material wealth of the community. Thus in the final analysis the priorities, motivations and objectives of development must be found in culture. But in the past this has

---

[1] UNESCO, The Courier, 1988/11, 5.
[2] UNESCO, The Courier, 1988/11, 5.

been conspicuously ignored."[1] In particular, *Mayor* proposed that the aim of *World Decade for Cultural Development* was to promote awareness of the cultural imperative and to foster a new state of mind that will lead to the emergence of a variety of proposals devoted to "a diversity which unites, a creativity which brings together, and a solidarity which liberates." Behind this expression, it is not difficult to see the awakening of people's attention to cultural diversity under the influence of convergent economic development patterns in the 1980s and 1990s lay in that people were beginning to realize the importance of cultural diversity for the development of human society.

In its *Medium-Term Plan for 1984-1989*, the UNESCO also placed special emphasis on the issue of cultural diversity in its "culture and the Future" section, arguing that cultural diversity should be an open system and that recognition of cultural diversity implied respect for all cultural diversity. This concept has been the basis of UNESCO's practice on the protection of cultural diversity. The awakening of the concept of cultural diversity has a very high similarity to the awakening of environmental protection consciousness in the 1970s. Respect for and protection of cultural diversity has greatly influenced the development direction of the world heritage after the 1990s.

In its *Medium-Term Plan for 1984-1989*, the UNESCO highlighted the *Declaration of the World Conference on Cultural Policies in 1982* in its "strategy of action" on culture: "Every people has the right and the duty to develop its culture," "in their rich variety and diversity, and in the reciprocal influences they exert on one another, all cultures form part of the common heritage,"[2] and proposed to renew the goal of cultural development through this diversity of creativity in order to promote the development of society. This expression shows the UNESCO's view of cultural development during this period.

The 1980s and 1990s was not only a period for the countries of the world to seek rapid economic development, but also a period of local wars and conflicts. These conflicts shifted from the ideological antagonism of the two camps during the Cold War to a more characteristic of civilization or intercultural conflict. *The Clash of Civilizations and the Remaking of World Order*, written by *Samuel P. Huntington* and published in 1996, attributed the conflicts in the world after the Cold War to a clash of cultures. *Huntington's* point of view has aroused widespread concern and discussion in the world and, to some extent, influenced the UNESCO's judgment on world development. This was clearly demonstrated in *The Medium-Term Strategy For 1996-2001 of UNESCO*. With the emphasis on development in *The Medium-Term Plan For 1984-1989*, peace and security became central in the *Medium-Term Strategy for 1996-2001*. It re-emphasized that "it is in the minds of men that the defences of peace must be constructed", as proposed in *The Constitution of UNESCO*. Addressing the root causes of war through development was also the way in which *The Medium-Term*

---

①   UNESCO, The Courier, 1988/11, 5.
②   UNESCO, 054611eb-MTP-1984-89, 11037.

Strategy proposes to address the threat of conflicts facing the world: "it is war itself that must be destroyed by eradication the economic poverty, social injustice, political oppression, discrimination and exclusion, in all their forms, that are the root causes of conflict" [1]. It has become important means of promoting development and building peace for the world to enhance cultural heritage, promote living cultures and encourage creativity.

When it comes to the contents of *The Convention Concerning the Protection of the World Cultural and Natural Heritage*, the *Medium-term Strategy for 1996-2001* points out "the World Heritage List, which contains monuments and sites considered to be of 'outstanding universal value,' must continue to be made more representative. In that regard further consideration needs to be given to the actual concept of world heritage which, in addition to the traditional categories, should be expanded to include other important markers of the diversity of world culture."[2] Cultural landscape is regarded as iconic objects that reflect cultural diversity. And the "actual concept" more closely links the protection of heritage and the contemporary development and peace building together. Heritage protection is not just the government's work, "the protection of world heritage is a huge task, in the long run, only to take an active part in local community can succeed. Preservation of the world heritage is such a vast undertaking that, in the long run, it can only be successful if there is active participation by local communities. New approaches must be developed in the areas of conservation and site maintenance, drawing on local traditions, techniques and knowledge."[3] "We shall have to help ensure that the heritage is more fully integrated into the economic and social life of the community. UNESCO has already begun that process by providing assistance for urban rehabilitation projects designed to reintegrate historic sites into the daily life of the city. At a time when tourism represents a significant source of revenue for many countries, safeguarding policies need to give greater consideration to the legitimate concern of host populations to share in the economic benefits of tourism. UNESCO's strategy will therefore be to promote the growth of cultural tourism of a kind that respects cultural identities and encourages a strengthening of international understanding, while at the same time offering solutions to the needs of local communities over the long term." [4] In this description, heritage is no longer the static protected object, but becomes the active power that is deeply involved in the contemporary social and economic development.

Based on UNESCO's position, intercultural conflicts stem from a lack of intercultural dialogue and mutual respect, so the most important approach to the construction of peace is to encourage intercultural communication and dialogue, and the preservation and presentation of heritage projects that reflect this exchange and dialogue as historical experience becomes the important objective of heritage protection. In

---

[1] UNESCO, 102501e-MTS-96-01, Foreword.
[2] UNESCO, 102501e-MTS-96-01, 125.
[3] UNESCO, 102501e-MTS-96-01, 130.
[4] UNESCO, 102501e-MTS-96-01, 131.

the "strategy for peace-building" section of the *Medium-term Strategy for 1996-2001*,"encouraging cultural diversity and cultural dialogue" is an important part: "Since its foundation UNESCO has striven to develop dialogue between cultures as an essential element of any peace-building strategy. By encouraging exchanges between the world's principal cultural areas, in particular between the East and the West, and by helping newly independent countries to affirm their cultural identity. The UNESCO helped to promote broad awareness of the fruitful diversity of cultures referred to in the Constitution...The international co-operation that developed under the impetus of UNESCO has, among other things, "helped to bring out the concept of the 'common heritage' of humankind, to make many cultures better acquainted with one another," [1] "as we are confronted with worst-case scenarios focusing on the hermetic barriers and the unstable fault lines that may lead to an impending 'clash of civilizations', it behoves us to identify, in a spirit of dialogue and openness, a set of values that may be shared by all individuals - whatever cultural identity may constitute their prime reference - and thus to lay the foundations of a desire to live together.[2]

Through heritage, mobile or immobile, physical or nonphysical, natural or cultural, people can form a kind of spirit of openness and dialogue, establish common values of mutual respect and tolerance between cultures, avoid "a clash of civilizations", build peace and promote the development and creation of culture, which are the basic ideas put forward by the UNESCO in its Medium-term Strategy at this stage. This understanding of the actual value of heritage was not the same as that of the heritage value in 1972 when *The Convention Concerning the Protection of the World Cultural and Natural Heritage* was passed. It no longer just focused on the protection of heritage, but also began to pay close attention to how to exert the role of heritage in the peace-building and the social, economic and community development in the contemporary society. Heritage protection has been more explicitly incorporated into the dimension of development as a tool for building open cultural values and promoting peace-building and development.

The Heritage Protection in the 21ˢᵗ Century Based on the Sustainable Development

In the 54ᵗʰ United Nations General Assembly in 2000, the participating leaders passed the "United Nations Millennium Declaration" and pointed out "We believe that the central challenge we face today is to ensure that globalization becomes a positive force for all the world's people. For while globalization offers great opportunities, at present its benefits are very unevenly shared, while its costs are unevenly distributed. We recognize that developing countries and countries with economies in transition face special difficulties in responding to this central challenge. Thus, only through broad and sustained efforts to create a shared future, based upon our common humanity in all its diversity, can globalization be made fully inclusive and

---

① UNESCO, 102501e-MTS-96-01, 177.
② UNESCO, 102501e-MTS-96-01, 177.

equitable. These efforts must include policies and measures, at the global level, which correspond to the needs of developing countries and economies in transition and are formulated and implemented with their effective participation. "[1]

The United Nations and the world leaders believed that with the advent of the 21st century, the challenges facing the world are imbalance and injustice brought about by globalization, so it is necessary to achieve inclusive and equitable development of globalization on the basis of the diversity shared by mankind. They proposed fundamental values, including freedom, equality, solidarity, tolerance, respect for nature and shared responsibility, and also proposed basic goals of peace, security and disarmament, development and poverty eradication, environmental protection, human rights, democracy and good governance, protection of vulnerability, meeting the special needs of Africa and strengthening the role of the United Nations. And they especially identified the specific goals to alleviate poverty:

To halve, by the year 2015, the proportion of the world's people whose income is less than one dollar a day and the proportion of people who suffer from hunger and, by the same date, to halve the proportion of people who are unable to reach or to afford safe drinking water.

To ensure that, by the same date, children everywhere, boys and girls alike, will be able to complete a full course of primary schooling and that girls and boys will have equal access to all levels of education.

By the same date, to have reduced maternal mortality by three quarters, and under-five child mortality by two thirds, of their current rates.

To have, by then, halted, and begun to reverse, the spread of HIV/AIDS, the scourge of malaria and other major diseases that afflict humanity.

To provide special assistance to children orphaned by HIV/AIDS.

By 2020, to have achieved a significant improvement in the lives of at least 100 million slum dwellers as proposed in the "Cities Without Slums" initiative.[2]

In view of such global challenges, the protection of the world heritage has increasingly emphasized the contribution to these basic goals, and governments have also paid more and more attention to the contribution of heritage protection to and its impact on the social and economic development. This situation further boosts the appeal of countries to inscribe their heritage items on the World Heritage list, and to some extent has led to the controversial politicized tendency to review the world heritage.

Considering the "United Nations Millennium Declaration" as a consensus on the challenges ahead with the entry into the 21th century, the United Nations launched "The Millennium Development Goals (MDG) to meet these challenges, including eight basic goals: eradicate extreme poverty and hunger; achieve universal

---

[1]　https://documents-dds-ny.un.org/doc/UNDOC/GEN/N00/559/50/PDF/N0055950.pdf?OpenElement.

[2]　https://documents-dds-ny.un.org/doc/UNDOC/GEN/N00/559/50/PDF/N0055950.pdf?OpenElement.

primary education; promote gender equality and empower women; reduce child mortality; improve maternal health; combat HIV/AIDS, malaria and other diseases; ensure environmental sustainability; develop a global partnership for development. With regard to such an integrated objective of sustainable development involving economy, education, health, environment and global participation, how the world heritage should function as the UNESCO's flagship project was also an important question that should be faced and answered in the field of the world heritage protection.

In 2012, the UNESCO designated "World Heritage and Sustainable Development: the Role of Local Communities in the Management of UNESCO" as the theme of the celebrations marking the 40th anniversary of *The Convention Concerning the Protection of the World Cultural and Natural Heritage*. Promoting the sustainable development that centered on local communities became the important issue of the world heritage, and "This reflects individuals' profound awareness of the relationship between economic and social development and the growing status of the participation of local masses in the preservation of cultural and natural heritage."[1] During the celebrations, the UNESCO and the governments of the contracting parties organized a series of activities, all of which highlighted the relationship between the world heritage and sustainable development as well as the important role of the community. The meetings include "International Expert Meeting on 'World Heritage and Sustainable Development'" (in February 2012 in Brazil) , "'Living with World Heritage' Inter-regional Conference" (held in Norway in May 2012) ; "'Involving communities in the World Heritage Protection: Concepts and Action' International Conference (held in South Korea in September 2012) , "International Expert Workshop on the *The World Heritage Convention* and Indigenous Peoples" (held in Denmark in September 2012) ; "'Living with World Heritage in Africa' International Conference" (held in South Africa in September 2012) . The International Seminar "Heritage and Sustainability: from Principle to Practice" was co-sponsored by the World Heritage Center, Japanese Ministry of Culture and the Toyama Prefectural Government of at Toyama, Japan in November 2012. This meeting passed *Toyama Proposal on Heritage and Sustainable Development*, suggesting that when guided by the three overarching principles of sustainability, equality and human rights, the appropriate conservation and management of the natural and cultural heritage, as well as of the traditional/established knowledge and skills associated to its care, can make a powerful contribution to sustainable development across all of its core dimensions of environmental sustainability, inclusive social development, inclusive economic development, and peace and security[2]. The proposal also acknowledges that "it will be necessary to deepen an understanding of the relationship between heritage conservation and sustainable development and identify, as much as possible, quantitative and

---

[1] UNESCO, activity-664-10, 1.
[2] unesco/whc/event-930-1.

qualitative indicators that express the contribution of heritage to sustainable development";[1] The basic ways to achieve the contribution of heritage protection to sustainable development are "integrating its conservation within the policies and processes of the local governance and, accordingly, by building the related capacities of all those concerned, including local authorities, local people, tourism and other business sectors, and the wider civil society."[2]

Through the discussions on the relationship between the world heritage and sustainable development, more attention has been paid to the impact and promotion of the world heritage to the sustainable development, which has a more direct impact on the communities where the heritage site is located. Based on this understanding, the world heritage also shows a shift from the protection based on the value of the heritage to the people-centered protection that can promote the sustainable development. This shift reflects that with 40 years of development, the world heritage has become an important way to affect the development of human society. On the other hand, this development and shift also makes the protection of the world heritage more than a technical approach based solely on its heritage value, but gives the protection of the world heritage more appeal for social development, which inevitably adds a more political dimension to the world heritage. How to realize the new balance between the protection of heritage value and the need to promote the sustainable development of society on the basis of realistic needs is also a major challenge facing the world heritage today.

Kyoto Vision, an achievement of the celebration, acknowledges that "the relationship between World Heritage and local communities is indeed at the heart of the Convention and is fundamental to address the challenges currently facing all regions of the world, through increasing demographic and development pressures, global financial crises and climate change" [3]. According to *Kyoto Vision*, "one of the aims of the Convention is to 'give heritage a role in the life of the community' (Article 5), then the concerns and aspirations of communities must be centrally involved in conservation and management efforts. Only through strengthened relationships between people and heritage, based on respect for cultural and biological diversity as a whole, integrating both tangible and intangible aspects and geared towards sustainable development, will the 'future we want' become attainable."[4] "Unless such a sustainable development perspective is integrated in the management of a World Heritage property, it will be difficult in the long run to ensure the conservation of its Outstanding Universal Value."[5] Taking the community as the foundation of protecting the world heritage, promoting the sustainable development of human society through the community development brought about by the heritage protection is the basic orientation of the development of the world heritage in the early 21st

[1] The same as above.
[2] The same as above.
[3] UNESCO, activity-664-10, 11.
[4] The same as above.
[5] The same as above.

century.

As an important symbol of the contemporary global culture, the world heritage reflects the basic concepts of contemporary culture. The "'Culture: the Key to Sustainable Development' International conference" was held in Hangzhou by the UNESCO and the Chinese Government in 2013, *Hangzhou Declaration* passed at the conference states "culture should be considered to be a fundamental enabler of sustainability, being a source of meaning and energy, a wellspring of creativity and innovation, and a resource to address challenges and find appropriate solutions. The extraordinary power of culture to foster and enable truly sustainable development is especially evident when a people-centred and place-based approach is integrated into development programmes and peace-building initiatives," [1] "the potential of culture as a driver for sustainable development, through the specific contributions that it can make-as knowledge capital and a sector of activity-to inclusive social, cultural and economic development, harmony, environmental sustainability, peace and security. "[2]

Hangzhou Declaration put forward nine actions about further exerting the role of culture in sustainable development:

Integrate culture within all development policies and programmes;

Mobilize culture and mutual understanding to foster peace and reconciliation;

Ensure cultural rights for all to promote inclusive social development;

Leverage cultural for poverty education and inclusive economic development;

Build on culture to promote environmental sustainability;

Strengthen resilience to disasters and combat climate change through culture;

Value, safeguard and transmit culture to future generations;

Harness culture as a resource for achieving sustainable urban development and management;

Capitalize on culture to foster innovative and sustainable models of cooperation. [3]

Hangzhou Declaration expresses an important recognition that the influence of culture on the sustainable development is holistic, comprehensive and all-sided. The same is true of the world heritage for the sustainable development.

The UNESCO stated in its Medium-term Strategy for 2014-2021 "In the coming years, UNESCO will generate initiatives and mobilize energies, ideas and commitments to forge a new understanding of peace and sustainable development through culture. At the multilateral level, the Organization will capitalize on

---

[1]   UNESCO, CLT-2013/WS/14, 2.

[2]   The same as above.

[3]   UNESCO, CLT-2013/WS/14.

recent achievements in promoting culture as a driver and enabler of peace and sustainable development, as a human-centered approach to development, yielding sustainable, inclusive and equitable outcomes, can only be achieved with a strong culture component. Heritage, understood in its entirety - natural and cultural, tangible and intangible - constitutes assets inherited from the past that we wish to transmit to future generations because of their social value and the way in which they embody identity and belonging. These assets shall be used for promoting social stability peace-building, recovery from crisis situations, and development strategies."[1]

For the UNESCO, *The Convention Concerning the Protection of the World Cultural and Natural Heritage* is based on shared values and at the same time respects cultural diversity, and through the cooperation and dialogue in the field of the world heritage, it respects different cultural concepts, and eliminates the ideological foundation of conflicts in people's mind to achieve peace and create conditions for sustainable development. From this perspective, the world heritage's contribution to the sustainable development is not only to provide a possibility of economic development for heritage sites, but also makes more contribution to providing shared values on the ideological level and creating a platform for intercultural communication and dialogue. The role of the world heritage in and its influence on the sustainable development are multifaceted and holistic, and one-sided emphasis on the role of one aspect may affect its integral role.

In 2015, the 20th Congress of Contracting Parties to the World Heritage Convention adopted *Policy Document on Integrating a Sustainable Development Perspective into the Word Heritage Convention Process*, which suggested that "the Protection of the World Cultural and Natural Heritage is an integral part of UNESCO's overarching mandate to foster equitable sustainable development and to promote peace and security." [2] Based on the perspective of the sustainable development, the protection and management of the world heritage is not only to protect its outstanding universal value, but also to maintain a good condition for the contemporary and future generations; its protection and management strategy should be based on the related Charter of the United Nations and Agenda 2030, especially the concepts of human rights, equality and the sustainable development; the close correlation and interdependence between biodiversity and cultural diversity should be fully recognized; the sustainable development of all dimensions; achieving the sustainable development may be beyond the scale of the world heritage, so the plan of the sustainable development should be considered in a larger context; integrating the concept of the sustainable development into the protection and management of the world heritage needs capacity building. These basic principles describe the basic cognition of the relationships between the protection and management of the world heritage and the sustainable development. Under such a framework of principles, *Policy Document on Integrating a Sustainable Development Perspective into the Word Heritage Convention Process* put forward several basic dimensions of

---

[1]   UNESCO, 227860e-MTS-14-21, 66.
[2]   UNESCO, activity-834-5. 1.

the role of sustainable development in the protection and management of the world heritage:

Environment sustainability;

Protecting biological and cultural diversity and ecosystem services and benefits;

Strengthening resilience to natural hazards and climate change;

Inclusive social development;

Contributing to inclusion and equity;

Enhancing quality of life and well-being;

Respecting, protecting and promoting human rights;

Respecting, consulting and involving indigenous peoples and local communities;

Achieving gender equality. [1]

Conclusion

With nearly 50 years of development, the protection and management of the world heritage has developed from the protection based on the value of natural and cultural resources into an important part of the human sustainable development. The development reflects the extensive and tremendous influence of *The Convention Concerning the Protection of the World Cultural and Natural Heritage*, and also reflects the values that are represented by it and promotes its own development has become one of the basic values of human society.

The promotive effect of the World Heritage to the sustainable development is holistic, which is embodied not only in providing job opportunities and generating economic benefits, but also in promoting cultural exchanges and dialogue, building peace, creating the basic conditions for the sustainable development, improving the cognition of cultural consciousness and cultural identity, enhancing the community cohesion, strengthening capacity building, and providing education and training, and so forth.

The community where the heritage site is located is the basic unit of the heritage protection and management for the sustainable development. The role of the world heritage protection in the sustainable development of the community is also comprehensive and holistic. The community participation in the protection and management of heritage sites is an important way for the community development. Besides, through the participation in the heritage protection and management, the educational level in the community is enhanced, the cultural characteristics of the community are displayed, cultural diversity and heritage sites are integrated, the cultural development and innovation is promoted and the living standard of the community is improved, all of which are also the basic way for the World Heritage to promote the sustainable development.

---

① UNESCO, activity-834-5.

世界遗产支持计划

捷克共和国　文化部文化遗产保护司　伊里·瓦吉奇纳尔 [①]

摘要：

捷克文化部于 2008 年开始实施一项名为"支持联合国教科文组织世界遗产"的计划。该支持计划主要旨在履行捷克共和国作为《保护世界文化和自然遗产公约》缔约国的承诺。计划确定了由捷克文化部提供拨款的 3 个基本优先方向：一是制定或更新管理规划（即文化财产保护规划），二是支持符合该计划宗旨的、与遗产相关的科学研究项目，三是支持与遗产相关的展示、宣传和教育项目（如遗产的保护级别认定以及相关基本信息；有关遗产展示、保护或世界遗产申报的研讨会和研修班；针对不同类型的遗产参观者的出版项目和与遗产相关的教育项目，特别是专业论文出版项目）。

关键词：世界遗产，世界遗产预备名单，拨款支持计划

1991 年，捷克斯洛伐克签署了《保护世界文化和自然遗产公约》。根据该公约创建了《世界遗产名录》[②]，同时该公约规定了缔约国对列入名录的遗产（即世界上最为重要的古迹）所应履行的义务。

加入公约后，捷克共和国针对极为重要的国家古迹遗址列入名录的工作陆续制定了相关政策。目前，世界遗产委员会这一政府间组织已将捷克的 12 处古迹遗址 [③] 列入名录，包括：布拉格历史中心、克鲁姆洛夫历史中心、泰尔奇历史中心、库特纳霍拉历史中心及其圣·芭芭拉教堂和塞德莱茨的圣母

---

① 伊里·瓦吉奇纳尔（Jiří Vajčner）博士，自 1994 年起在捷克文化部工作，现任文化遗产保护司司长，捷克查理大学和公共管理研究所讲师，查理大学工业遗产研究中心顾问小组成员。先后就读于斯特拉尼日采工业中等学校（1987 至 1991 年）、布拉格商业学校（1992 至 1994 年）、查理大学（1995 至 2000 年）和捷克理工大学（2004 至 2007 年，建筑学专业，获得博士学位）。曾获献血者金质奖章。

1. Vajčner J.（2005 年），《布尔诺最高行政法庭关于文化古迹的先例判决》，发表于 Zprávypam-átkovépéče 65，2005 年第 1 期，第 74—77 页。

2. Vajčner J.（2006 年），《米洛维采的圣·凯瑟琳新哥特式教堂及其壁画》（米洛维采）。

3. Vajčner J. 和 Hlubuček P.，Tupý M.（2011 年），《2011 至 2016 年捷克共和国古迹保护理念》（布拉格）。

4. Vajčner J. 和 Zídek M.（2015 年），《遗产保护法案草案》，发表于 Zprávypamátkovépéče 75，2015 年第 1 期，第 75—79 页。

② 《联邦外交部通讯汇编》第 159/1991 号：关于《保护世界文化和自然遗产公约》的谈判。

③ 《世界遗产名录》，世界遗产委员会已将 153 个缔约国的 936 项遗产列入名录，其中包括 725 项文化遗产、183 项自然遗产和 28 项文化和自然混合遗产。此信息更新截至 2012 年 3 月。来源：联合国教科文组织网站：世界遗产／世界遗产名录。网址：whc.unesco.org.

玛利亚大教堂、泽雷纳荷拉的内波穆克圣·约翰朝圣教堂、雷德尼兹—瓦尔提兹的文化景观、克罗梅律什的花园和城堡、荷拉索维兹的历史村落保护区、利特米谢尔城堡、欧罗摩兹的圣三一纪念柱、布尔诺的图根达特别墅，崔比奇的犹太社区和圣·波罗寇帕斯教堂。从这个意义上来讲，毫无疑问，捷克共和国可以为其众多的国家瑰宝列入《世界遗产名录》而感到自豪。

（公众）对《世界遗产名录》是在联合国教科文组织批准的《保护世界文化和自然遗产公约》的基础上而创立的这一事实的认识程度是相对较高的。而另一方面，人们对于世界遗产的《预备名单》则了解甚少。众所周知，预备名单是缔约国想在未来列入名录的文化遗产的清单；这些文化遗产被认为是突出普遍价值的载体，因此适合列入名录的备选遗产。如果某项文化遗产未被列入预备名单，则其不具备被列入名录的资格。文化遗产在列入预备名单至少一年之后，缔约国方可向世界遗产中心提交世界遗产申报文本。预备名单不是穷尽和封闭的。预备名单宜在缔约国与国内各方（包括文化遗产的所有者和管理者、当地和地区自治机构、社会组织以及其它利益相关方和合作伙伴）广泛合作的基础上制定。捷克共和国于1991年制定了首个预备名单，并于2000年批准了更新的预备名单（几乎是全新的），因为几乎所有此前纳入预备名单的文化遗产均已列入《世界遗产名录》。最近一次预备名单更新于2017年。这一名单与其他缔约国的名单均可在世界遗产中心网站上查询[①]。捷克共和国的预备名单上目前有16处古迹遗址，包括1处自然遗产（波西米亚天堂的石头小镇）和15处文化遗产。2001年，以下遗产地被纳入预备名单：卡尔什特因城堡、库克斯附近的Betlém石雕群、米库勒茨采的大摩拉维亚山堡（2001年列入，是捷克和斯洛伐克联合申报的大摩拉维亚古迹的一部分，该申报项目包括米库勒茨采的斯拉夫山堡和考普采尼的圣·玛格丽特大教堂）、Velké Losiny的造纸坊、斯拉沃尼采的哥特时期晚期和文艺复兴时期的民居建筑群、特热邦的温泉遗产、泰雷津的要塞军镇、俄斯特拉发的工业遗产群、卢哈科维奇的温泉以及布拉格历史中心世界遗产地扩展项目（其中包括维诺拉第区的圣心教堂、斯特舍维兹的穆勒别墅、布雷诺夫修道院和星星夏宫）。2007年，预备名单又增添了几处遗产，包括：扎泰茨的啤酒花产区、克拉德鲁比的养马场文化景观和耶塞尼克的电视塔和山间酒店。2008年预备名单新增了西波西米亚温泉三角地区，包括3个温泉小镇：卡罗维发利、玛利亚斯基和弗朗齐歇克。最新纳入捷克预备名单的是厄尔士山脉（克鲁什内山脉）采矿文化景观。

长期以来，捷克文化部就已经认识到展示世界遗产地的必要性，这不仅仅是因为这些遗产地十分重要且日益受到大众欢迎，更重要的是缔约国对这些遗产地具有相应的义务（上述义务重要反映在《保护世界文化和自然遗产公约》的第4和5条）。《公约》规定，缔约国具有为子孙后代认定、保护、展示和传承文化和自然遗产的责任，为此应当采取必要措施同时对遗产资源尽可能地加以利用。认识到在相关领域保护世界遗产的这一责任，捷克文化部于2008年制定了名为"支持联合国教科文组织世界遗产"的计划[②]。该计划旨在支持已列入或通过国际上规定的渠道计划列入《世界遗产名录》的遗产地

---

① 《捷克共和国申报联合国教科文组织世界遗产名录的预备名单》（2011年，布拉格），第14—16页。
② 该计划于2008年根据2008年2月5日捷克文化部通过的《文化部预算非投资资金用于支持联合国教科文组织世界遗产计划的原则》而设立。用于管理计划拨款的原则根据《文化部长第25/2010号指示》（其中规定了从文化部政府预算中提供非投资和投资补贴的办法）以及《预算规定法案第218/2000号》和《若干相关法案修订案》中的条款而制定。该计划的文化部主管司局为文化遗产保护司。

的发展，以及对正在由国家遗产研究院编制申报文本的遗产项目提供支持。该计划拨款仅为已列入名录或正式考虑申请列入名录（以纳入预备名单的方式）的遗产的价值发展项目提供资助[①]。换句话说，目前该项目可用于向所有列入《世界遗产名录》和《预备名单》上的遗产项目（其世界遗产申报文本正在编制）提供资助。

支持计划确定了捷克文化部提供拨款的 3 项基本优先方向[②]。第一是制定或更新管理规划（即文化财产保护计划），这是保证对已经列入或正在申报世界遗产的遗产地进行有效保护的途径。确定保护规划目的的出发点是《世界遗产公约实施指南》[③]。关于保护规划的性质，指南指出："每一个计划列入《世界遗产名录》的遗产必须已有保护规划或其它管理体系文件，这些规划文件必须准确规定利用参与机制对突出普遍价值进行保护的方式。"[④] 第二是具有研究性质的，可用于支持符合该计划宗旨的，与遗产相关的科学研究项目。这些研究项目应能提升对遗产历史的认识以及对涉及保障高质量保护的价值的认识，如档案研究、更为具体和补充的历史研究、技术知识等等[⑤]。第三是支持与遗产相关的展示、宣传和教育项目（如古迹的保护级别认定以及相关基本信息；有关遗产展示、保护或世界遗产申报的会议、研讨会和研修班；针对古迹遗址不同类型参观者的出版项目和与古迹遗址相关的教育项目，特别是专业论文出版项目）[⑥]。

根据《预算规定》[⑦]符合条件的个人或法人实体均可申请支持计划拨款。拨款金额最多不超过项目总费用的 70%（在合理的情况下，个别项目的拨款额度可最多为总费用的 90%，但须得到文化部批准）[⑧]。拨款以决定的形式提供。决定文件规定了拨款受益人、拨款金额和拨款使用以及提取条件。拨款按每个日历年度向实施的项目或项目阶段提供。项目最终报告、拨款总额和项目成果须在下一年 1 月 15 日之前向文化部提交。支持计划的管理者审查项目拨款金额，支持计划的委员会评估项目是否符合基本优先方向。支持计划的所有必要信息，包括原则、计划申请表和拨款金额申请表、招标文件以及此前支持的项目，在文化部网站的"拨款和补助"一栏发布[⑨]。

支持计划年度拨款金额分别为：1800 万捷克克朗（2008 年），1100 万捷克克朗（2009 年），700 万捷克克朗（2010 年），620 万捷克克朗（2011 年），700 万捷克克朗（2012 年），500 万捷克克朗（2013 年），600 万捷克克朗（2014，2015，2016，2017 年），500 万捷克克朗（2018 年）。

---

① 《文化部预算非投资资金用于支持联合国教科文组织世界遗产计划的原则》，参考编号：总则 / 第一条 MK 1572/2010 OPP。

② 同上。总则 / 第二条。

③ 《世界遗产公约实施指南》。

④ 在与国家遗产研究院合作以及借鉴此前管理规划试点工作的基础上，文化部编制了规划基本大纲。鉴于文化遗产的多样性，这一文件只是一个框架文件，可针对列入名录的世界遗产地或希望列入名录的遗产地的具体情况加以调整。

⑤ 同上。总则 / 第二条。

⑥ 同上。总则 / 第二条。

⑦ 《预算规定法案第 218/2000 号》第 1 条第 4、5、6、7、8、9 款。

⑧ 同上。总则 / 第 2 条。

⑨ http://www.mkcr.cz/scripts/ detail.php?id=2433

　　"荷拉索维兹的历史村落保护区管理规划的编制"这一项目的首期实施体现了支持计划第一个优先方向（管理规划的制定或更新）。拨款受益者为扬科夫市。项目总费用为 43 万捷克克朗，其中 38.7 万捷克克朗由支持计划拨款。项目成果为一份全面的《世界遗产地管理规划》。

　　"对最具价值的国家遗产进行记录和展示的新途径：3D 扫描技术"这一项目体现了支持计划的第二个优先方向（科学研究项目）。项目总费用为 189.5 万捷克克朗，其中 132 万捷克克朗由支持计划拨款。项目成果为对便携式 3D 激光扫描技术的验证。这一成果确认了该技术适合用于记录古迹遗址（移动设备、实用程序操作软件、使用电脑线上监测扫描过程的途径等）。该项目以"使用高精 3D 扫描技术对若干世界遗产地进行记录和展示"的项目名称于 2009 年继续实施。新的项目费用为 112 万捷克克朗，其中 39.2 万捷克克朗由支持计划拨款。

　　"泽雷纳荷拉的内波穆克圣·约翰朝圣教堂建筑记录"是一项分两个阶段实施的项目，体现了支持计划的第二个优先方向（科学研究项目）。拨款受益者为国家遗产研究院地区特尔奇办事处。该项目 2008 年的总费用为 75.015 万捷克克朗，其中 37 万捷克克朗由支持计划拨款。该项目 2009 年的总费用为 54.4451 万捷克克朗，其中 38 万捷克克朗由支持计划拨款。项目成果为一份高质量的综合建筑记录文件，使用大地测量和摄影测量方法以及空间激光扫描技术编制。记录文件根据 S-JTSK 坐标系统和 BVP 垂直系统编制。记录文件可供遗产保护专家在修缮和修复该教堂建筑时使用。该文件所记录的新发现的粉饰和绘画也可用于遗产的宣传推广。支持计划在 2010 年的成果最为辉煌。这一年，实施了"泽雷纳荷拉的内波穆克圣·约翰朝圣教堂修复勘察"项目。国家遗产研究院地区特尔奇办事处以该项目获得支持计划的 30 万捷克克朗拨款（项目总费用为 69.1 万捷克克朗）。

　　布尔诺市立博物馆实施了一个名为"图根达特别墅藏品记录项目：档案和当代照片、影像和有声资料的收藏、评估和技术与艺术处理"的项目，该项目分为 3 个阶段。2009 年，该项目总费用为 68.5 万捷克克朗，其中 48 万捷克克朗由支持计划拨款。2010 年，该项目总费用为 42.9279 万捷克克朗，其中 30 万捷克克朗由支持计划拨款。2011 年，该项目总费用为 50 万捷克克朗，其中 35 万捷克克朗由支持计划拨款。

　　总而言之，2008 至 2018 年，捷克文化部的世界遗产支持计划为 300 多个项目总计拨款 8000 万捷克克朗（折合 350 万美元）。这些项目绝大多数都完成了目标，并为捷克的世界遗产地全面发展做出了贡献。这也证明了相对少量的资金可产生真正专业的成果。尽管设立时间不长，世界遗产支持计划已成为利用政府资金促进捷克文化遗产发展的良好典范。

Programme for the Support of World Heritage Sites

Jiří Vajčner[①]

Monument Preservation Department of the Ministry of Culture Czech Republic

Abstract:

The programme entitled "Support for UNESCO heritage properties" was set up by the Ministry of Culture in 2008. Its main aim is to fulfil the commitments the Czech Republic took on as a party to the Convention on the Protection of World Cultural and Natural Heritage. This programme specified three basic priorities for which grants can be provided through the Ministry of Culture. The first priority is the creation or updating of a Management Plan (Cultural Assets Care Plan) , the second priority is of a research nature, as it can be used to support scientific-research projects relating to the monuments for which the programme is intended and finally, the third priority can be used to support projects for presentation, promotion and education relating to the monuments for which the programme is intended (e.g. the designation of monuments and related basic information; conferences, seminars and workshops on topics associated with the presentation or care of monuments, or preparation for nomination; publishing projects aimed at different target groups of visitors to monument sites and educational projects related to these sites, especially professional monograph publications) .

Keywords: World Heritage, Tentative List, GrantSupportProgramme

In 1991 Czechoslovakia signed the Convention concerning the Protection of the World Cultural and

① Studied at the Industry Secondary School in Strážnice (1987-1991) , the Business School in Prague (1992-1994) , the Charles University (1995-2000) and the Czech Technical University in Prague - architecture, higher degree Ph.D. (2004-2007) . Since 1994, he has been working in the Ministry of Culture, now at the position of Director of the National Heritage Department. He is a lecturer on the Charles University in Prague and on the Institute for Public Administration in Prague. Member of Consultation Grouping of Research Centre for Industrial Heritage by Czech Technical University in Prague. Blood donor-a gold medal.

1. Vajčner J. (2005) , "Precedens verdicts of Supreme Administrative Court in Brno to the designations of objects as cultural monuments", in: Zprávypamátkovépéče 65, issue 1 - 2005, pp. 74 - 77.

2. Vajčner J. (2006) , Neo-Gothic church St. Catherine in Milovice and its mural painting, Milovice

3. Vajčner J., Hlubuček P., Tupý M. (2011) , Concept of Monument Care in the Czech Republic for 2011-2016, Praha

4. Vajčner J., Zídek M. (2015) , "Draft bill on the protection of the heritage sites", in: Zprávypamátkovépéče 75, issue 1 - 2015, pp. 75 - 79.

Natural Heritage, which led to the establishment of the World Heritage List[1] (UNESCO monuments) and defined countries' obligations towards the sites on the List, i.e. the most important monuments in the world.

Following the acceptance of this Convention, the Czech Republic gradually prepared proposals for exceptionally important national monuments to be included in the World Heritage List, twelve of which were accepted by the intergovernmental World Heritage Committee:[2] the historical core of Prague, the historical core of Český Krumlov, the historical core of Telč, the historical core of Kutná Hora with St. Barbara's Church and the Church of the Assumption of Our Lady in Sedlec near Kutná Hora, the Pilgrimage Church of Saint John of Nepomuk at Zelená Hora in Žďár nad Sázavou, the Lednice-Valtice Cultural Landscape, the gardens and chateau in Kroměříž, the village of Holašovice, the chateau in Litomyšl, the Holy Trinity Column in Olomouc, Villa Tugendhat in Brno and the Jewish Quarter and St. Procopius Basilica in Třebíč. In this regard it is essential to state that the Czech Republic can undoubtedly be proud of how many of its national treasures appear on the World Heritage List.

Awareness of the fact that the World Heritage List is compiled on the basis of the Convention concerning the Protection of the World Cultural and Natural Heritage, adopted in UNESCO, is relatively high. On the other hand, less is heard of the Tentative List in relation to world heritage. As it's known, it's an inventory of cultural asscts that countries would like to see included in the World Heritage List in the future, as they are assumed to be the bearers of outstanding universal value and are therefore suitable candidates for inclusion. If a cultural asset does not appear on the Tentative List, it cannot be entered in the World Heritage List. Cultural assets must be entered in the Tentative List at least one year before the actual nomination documentation is submitted to the World Heritage Centre, while the Tentative List is not considered exhaustive or closed. It is recommended that the Tentative List be drawn up at the national level in collaboration with a wide range of parties concerned, including the owners and administrators of the cultural assets, local and regional self-government bodies, civic associations and other stakeholders and partners. The Czech Republic defined its first Tentative List in 1991; the updated, almost entirely new Tentative List was approved in 2000, as in the meantime nearly all the sites on the previous list had been successfully nominated for inclusion on the World Heritage List. The Tentative List was last updated at the national level in 2017. It is available, together with other countries' proposals, on the World Heritage Centre website. [c] The Tentative List of the Czech Republic[d] includes a total of 16 sites, only

---

[1] Federal Ministry of Foreign Affairs Communication No. 159/1991 Coll., on negotiation of the Convention concerning the Protection of the World Cultural and Natural Heritage

[2] World Heritage List; The 936 properties which the World Heritage Committee has inscribed on the World Heritage List (725 cultural, 183 natural and 28 mixed properties in 153 States Parties) ; The List is current as of March 2012. Source: UNESCO website - World Heritage - World Heritage List (whc.unesco.org)

[3] Věra Kučová, *Indikativní seznam České republiky pro nominaci k zápisu na Seznam světového dědictví UNESCO* (*Indicative List of the Czech Republic for Nomination for Inclusion in the UNESCO World Heritage List*) , Prague 2011, pp. 14 - 16.

[4] Source: UNESCO website - World Heritage - Tentative Lists (whc.unesco.org) .

one of which, the Rock Towns of the Bohemian Paradise, represents natural heritage, meaning that there are 15 cultural heritage sites. In 2001 the following sites were included in this list: Karlštejn Castle, the complex of rock sculptures called Betlém in Nový les near Kuks, the Great Moravian hillfort in Mikulčice (2001) , which is part of the joint Czech - Slovak nomination referred to as the Monuments of Great Moravia - the Slavic hillfort in Mikulčice and the Church of St. Margaret of Antioch in Kopčany, the Paper Mill in Velké Losiny, the complex of burgher houses from the late Gothic period and the Renaissance in Slavonice, the Třeboň ponds heritage, the fortress town of Terezín, the industrial complexes in Ostrava, the spa in Luhačovice and the extension of the World Heritage site of the historical core of Prague, with candidates for expansion including particularly the Church of the Most Sacred Heart of Our Lord in Vinohrady, the Villa Müller in Střešovice, the Břevnov Monastery and the Letohrádek Hvězda ("Star Summer Palace") . In 2007 further sites were added: hop-growing in Žatec, the stud farm cultural landscape in Kladrubynad Labem and the TV tower and mountain hotel on Ještěd; these were followed in 2008 by the West Bohemian Spa Triangle, comprising three spa towns in West Bohemia - Karlovy Vary, Mariánské Lázně and Františkovy Lázně. The most recent cultural asset on the Tentative List of the Czech Republic is the Mining Cultural Landscape Erzgebirge/Krušnohoří.

The Ministry of Culture has long been very aware of the need to present World Heritage (UNESCO) sites, not only due to their importance and growing popularity, but particularly with a view to contracting states' obligations towards those sites, which are mainly reflected in Art. 4 and 5 of the Convention concerning the Protection of the World Cultural and Natural Heritage. These stipulate that contracting states primarily have the duty of ensuring the identification, protection, conservation, presentation and transmission to future generations of the cultural and natural heritage, and for this purpose should take the necessary measures while making the greatest possible use of their own resources. Aware of this duty in the respective areas of care for world heritage, in 2008 the Ministry of Culture set up a programme entitled Support for UNESCO Monuments ("programme") . [1] The aim of this programme is to support the development of monuments on the World Heritage List or monuments proposed for inclusion through the internationally prescribed channels, or those for which the nomination documentation is being prepared by the National Heritage Institute. Grants from the programme are only provided to fund projects designed to develop the values for which the monument was listed or is being officially considered (by inclusion on the Tentative List) for nomination for entry into the

[1] The programme was established in 2008 on the basis of the Principles for the Use of Non-investment Funds from the Ministry of Culture Budget Earmarked for the Support for UNESCO Monuments Programme, approved by the Ministry of Culture on 5 February 2008. The principles governing the provision of grants from the programme are based on Minister of Culture Instruction No. 25/2010, which defines the rules forthe provision of non-investment and investment subsidies from the state budget of the Ministry of Culture, and on the provisions of Act No. 218/2000 Coll., on Budgetary Rules and on the Amendment of Some Related Acts (Budgetary Rules) , as amended. The relevant Ministry of Culture department is the Department of Conservation

World Heritage List.[①] In other words, at present the programme can be used to fund all monuments on the World Heritage List and those on the tentative List for which detailed nomination documentation is actively being prepared.

This programme specified three basic priorities for which grants can be provided through the Ministry of Culture.[②] The first priority is the creation or updating of a so-called Management Plan (Cultural Assets Care Plan) , which is a means of assuring effective care for world heritage sites, or for sites nominated for inclusion in the World Heritage List. The starting points for defining the purpose of the Management Plan document are the Operational Guidelines for the Implementation of the World Heritage Convention.[③] In relation to the nature of the Management Plan, these Guidelines state: "Each property proposed for inclusion on the World Heritage List must have an existing care plan or other documented administrative system, which must precisely specify the manner in which the outstanding universal value is to be protected, applying the participation mechanism wherever possible".[④] The second priority is of a research nature, as it can be used to support scientific - research projects relating to the monuments for which the programme is intended and raising awareness of their history and the values involved in assuring quality heritage care (e.g. archival research, more detailed and additional historical research, technical expertise, etc.) .[⑤] Finally, the third priority can be used to support projects for presentation, promotion and education relating to the monuments for which the programme is intended (e.g. the designation of monuments and related basic information; conferences, seminars and workshops on topics associated with the presentation or care of monuments, or preparation for nomination; publishing projects aimed at different target groups of visitors to monument sites and educational projects related to these sites, especially professional monograph publications) .[⑥]

Grants may be applied for by individuals and legal entities eligible for a grant according Budgetary Rules.[⑦] Grants are provided up to a maximum of 70% of the total calculated costs of the project (in particularly justified cases, the proportion of the grant to the total costs of the project may be increased to 90%; such an

---

① Principles for the Use of Non-investment Funds from the Ministry of Culture Budget Earmarked for theSupport for UNESCO Monuments Programme, Ref. No.: MK 1572/2010 OPP, Article I. General Provisions
② Ibidem, Article II. General Rules
③ Operational Guidelines for the Implementation of the World Heritage Convention / Orientations devant guider la mise en oeuvre de la Convention du patrimoine mondial, as amended.
④ In cooperation with the National Heritage Institute and drawing on experience of previous results of work on pilot Management Plans, the Ministry of Culture prepared the basic outline of a plan which, owing to the diversity of the cultural heritage, must be seen as a framework which can be adapted to the specific conditions of those monuments or heritage conservation areas entered in the World Heritage List in accordance with the World Heritage Convention, or which aspire for entry in the List
⑤ Ibidem, Article II. General Rules
⑥ Ibidem, Article II. General Rules
⑦ § 7 Para. 1. d) , e) , f) , g) , j) and l) of Act No. 218/2000 Coll., on Budgetary Rules

increase requires the approval of the Ministry of Culture) .[1] Grants are provided by decision and this decision specifies the grant beneficiary, the amount of the grant and the conditions governing the use and drawing of the grant. Grants are always provided for projects (project phases) implemented in a single calendar year. The final report on the project, the grant accounts and the outcomes of the project must be submitted to the Ministry of Culture no later than by 15 January of the following year. The programme administrator checks the grant accounts and the Commission assesses whether the project meets the priorities of the programme. All the necessary information about the programme (principles, application and accounts form, the call to tender and projects supported in previous years) are published on the Ministry of Culture website, in the Grants and Subsidies section.[2]

In 2008 the sum of 18 million CZK was allocated for the programme; in 2009 - 11 million CZK; in 2010 it was 7 million CZK; in 2011 - 6,2 million CZK, in 2012 - 7 million CZK; in 2013 - 5 million CZK; in 2014, 2015, 2016 and 2017 it was 6 million CZK every year and finally, 2018, the sum allocated was 5 million CZK.

The first priority (Management Plan - Preparation or Updating of Existing Plan) saw the implementation of the first phase of the project, entitled "Preparation of the Holašovice Village Conservation Area Management Plan (UNESCO) ". The beneficiary of the grant was the Municipality of Jankov. The total costs of the project amounted to 430 000 CZK, of which 387 000 CZK (90%) comprised grant funds from the programme. The outcome of the project was a comprehensive UNESCO Site Management Plan.

As part of the second priority (scientific - research projects) , a project was prepared entitled "New Options for the Documentation and Presentation of the Most Valuable National Heritage Monuments Using 3D Scanning Technology". The total costs of the project amounted to 1,895,000 CZK, of which 1,320,000 CZK comprised grant funds from the programme. The result of the project was the verification of the Handy Scan 3D laser scanning technology. This confirmed that this technology is suitable for use in documenting monuments (mobile devices, utility operational software, the option to monitor the scanning process on-line on a computer, etc.) . The project also continued in 2009 under the name "Use of Precision 3D Scanning Technology for the Documentation and Presentation of Selected UNESCO Monuments". The costs of the project amounted to 1,120,000 CZK, of which 392,000 CZK comprised grant funds.

A two-step project entitled "Zelená hora - Pilgrimage Church of Saint John of Nepomuk - Construction Documentation" was implemented as part of the second priority (scientific - research projects) . The beneficiary of the grant was the Telč Regional Office of the National Heritage Institute. In 2008 the total costs of the project amounted to 750,150 CZK, of which 370,000 CZK were grant funds; in 2009 the project costs totalled 544,451 CZK, of which 380,000 CZK comprised grant funds. The outcome of the project was very high quality

[1] Ibidem, Article II. General Rules
[2] http://www.mkcr.cz/scripts/ detail.php?id=2433

comprehensive construction documentation, compiled using geodetic and photogrammetry methods and spatial laser scanning. The documentation was prepared in the S-JTSK coordinate system and BVP vertical system. The documentation can be used particularly by monument care experts when repairing and restoring the church. Part of the documentation which captured the newly discovered stucco and paintings may also be used for promotional purposes. This plan culminated in 2010 with a project entitled "Zelená hora - Pilgrimage Church of Saint John of Nepomuk - Restoration Survey", for which the Telč branch of the National Heritage Institute received a grant of 300,000 CZK (total project costs 691,000 CZK) .

Brno City Museum prepared a three-step project entitled "Villa Tugendhat - Collection Documentation Project - Collection, Evaluation, Technical and Artistic Treatment of Archival and Contemporary Photographic, Film and Phonetic Sources". In 2009 the total costs of this project amounted to 685,000 CZK, of which 480,000 CZK comprised grant funds; in 2010 the total costs of the project amounted to 429,279 CZK, of which 300,000 CZK comprised grant funds, and in 2011 the total costs were 500,000 CZK, 350,000 CZK of which were grant funds.

In conclusion, it may be stated that between 2008 and 2018 more than 80 million CZK (3.5 million USD) was drawn from the Ministry of Culture Support for UNESCO Monuments Programme and more than 300 projects were implemented. The great majority of these projects fulfilled their purpose and contributed to the all-round development of UNESCO monuments in the Czech Republic, proving that a relatively small amount of funds can generate truly professional results. Despite not having existed for long, the programme is also a good example of how the state-funded promotion of the cultural heritage of the Czech Republic may be implemented.

中国的世界文化遗产保护与监测

中国文化遗产研究院　赵　云①

摘要

我国基于《保护世界文化和自然遗产公约》框架，在世界文化遗产保护领域进行了大量探索和创新，取得了一系列既符合国际规则和要求，又适合我国国情的理论和实践成果，其中最突出的是议事协调制度（尤其针对超大规模系列遗产申报和保护）、世界文化遗产保护管理规划、世界文化遗产监测等方面的成果和经验。这些成果和经验在大运河申遗和保护中得到了充分应用和发展。

关键词：世界文化遗产保护，遗产监测，大运河

1972 年，联合国教科文组织通过了《保护世界文化和自然遗产公约》（以下简称《公约》），旨在保护对全人类具有突出普遍价值的文化和自然遗产。中国于 1985 年正式加入这一公约，并于 1987 年将长城、北京故宫、莫高窟、秦始皇陵及兵马俑、周口店北京人遗址、泰山等首批 6 处遗产申报列入《世界遗产名录》。至 2018 年底，我国拥有世界遗产 53 项，世界遗产总数位居世界第二位；其中文化遗产 36 项，自然遗产 13 项，文化和自然混合遗产 4 项。

我国的世界文化遗产是中华优秀传统文化的精髓，从时间跨度、空间分布、遗产类型等方面，对中华文明成果进行了全景呈现。从遗产类型上看，我国世界文化遗产类型齐全，包含文物、建筑群、遗址等传统类型，也包含文化景观、历史城镇和城镇中心、遗产运河、遗产线路等特殊类型。从价值内涵上看，我国世界文化遗产符合的标准覆盖全面，标准 III、标准 VI 的使用比例较全球水平明显偏高，见证了中华文明史上一系列重大历史事件和中华民族"多元一体"的文明格局，也反映了我国在

---

① 赵云，中国文化遗产研究院研究馆员，中国世界文化遗产中心主任。主要研究方向围绕世界文化遗产，包括遗产价值研究、保护利用研究、遗产监测研究。主持、参与了约 90 项文化遗产保护研究项目，获得国家级奖 1 项、省部级奖 6 项。个人获国家文物局嘉奖 1 次。中国文化遗产研究院第一批青年学术带头人。代表性成果包括：红河哈尼梯田文化景观申遗文本、中国大运河保护与管理总体规划、中国大运河申遗文本和管理规划、左江花山岩画文化景观申遗文本、海上丝绸之路·中国史迹申遗文本和管理规划、中国世界文化遗产监测预警信息系统国家总平台建设、中国世界文化遗产基础数据库建设、中国世界文化遗产地年度总报告编制、中国文化景观类文化遗产阐释与展示研究、《世界文化遗产地风险管理原则和指南》标准编制等项目。《文化遗产数字化展示研究》、《中国世界文化遗产监测》等专著；《真实性标准和不改变文物原状原则在大运河遗产保护中的应用》、《左江花山岩画文化景观突出普遍价值解读——杰出的岩画艺术与独特的文化景观》、《跨海和声——"海丝"与中国》等论文。

物质文化遗产和非物质文化遗产价值识别和保护方面的密切联系。

我国依据国内各层级文物保护法律法规实施世界文化遗产保护。以《中华人民共和国文物保护法》为上位法，制定了一系列专项法规、规范，探索积累《公约》及其《操作指南》与我国现行法律体系衔接的实践经验。基于法定保护，建立了政府为主、民间力量积极参与保护文化遗产的保护格局。

1 世界文化遗产保护领域的中国探索和创新

世界文化遗产保护理念的传播，直接推动了我国文物保护视野的拓展。在保护实践中，更加注重对文物本体、周边环境及其所承载的文化传统的整体保护，更加强调对利益相关者权益的尊重，更加提倡以监测为基础的科学管理和预防性保护机制。

同时，我国进行了大量探索和创新。从缔约国的角色而言，这些努力都旨在回答一个问题：作为"全人类的共同遗产"，基于《公约》框架、全人类共有的保护需求，如何得到国内层面、不同行业机构、相对小的团体、甚至个体的认同？多年来，我们取得了一系列既符合国际规则和要求，又适合我国国情的理论和实践成果，其中最突出的是基于大量实践的议事协调制度（尤其针对超大规模系列遗产申报和保护）、世界文化遗产保护管理规划、世界文化遗产监测等方面的成果和经验。

· 议事协调制度：44 个遗产地政府建立了议事协调制度，统筹协调遗产保护机构、当地政府、以及建设、宗教、旅游等相关部门。

· 世界文化遗产保护管理规划：遵循"规划先行"策略，把制定保护管理规划作为世界文化遗产地保护管理的首要步骤，尤其是针对文物保护单位区划（保护范围和建设控制地带）和世界遗产区划（遗产区和缓冲区）及其相应的管理规定，进行统筹安排和管理。

· 世界文化遗产监测：我国自 2012 年起系统性地全面推进世界文化遗产监测预警体系建设工作，目前已初步建成了中国世界文化遗产监测预警系统国家总平台和约 20 个地方平台，形成了以日常监测、年度报告、定期评估、基础数据库、交流共享为一体的世界文化遗产监测预警体系，在世界文化遗产工作中取得了显著成绩，初步实现了支持管理决策的目标。

2 中国的世界文化遗产监测

《公约》框架下，世界文化遗产监测指通过对衡量遗产保护状况指标的测定，确定遗产突出普遍价值以及完整性和 / 或真实性的保持状况及其变化趋势。反应性监测制度和定期报告制度是《操作指南》中确立的世界遗产监测规则的核心。

基于对历年来接受反应性监测和参与两轮定期报告的反思，我国于 2012 年从国家层面系统规划并启动了中国世界文化遗产监测预警体系建设。国家文物局在中国文化遗产研究院设立了中国世界文化遗产监测中心（现名中国世界文化遗产中心）。由该中心负责编制并推广全国世界文化遗产地监测工作制度规范和监测指标体系，牵头建设中国世界文化遗产监测预警系统，并在中国文化遗产研究院内建设国家总平台。总平台于2014年上线运行，其定位是与各地平台、各相关行业信息系统互联互通的"文化遗产保护监测大数据服务系统"。

目前，总平台能够支持开展世界文化遗产监测的各类主要工作，包括：

·年度报告：各世界文化遗产地于每年三月通过总平台向国家文物局提交《中国世界文化遗产地监测年度报告》，中国世界文化遗产中心负责编制全国总报告。

·定期评估：各世界文化遗产地以半年为周期开展在线评估，包含遗产地自评估和省级审阅两个层面。

·基础数据采集与更新：依据中国世界文化遗产地基础数据库数据规则，按照基础信息、保护管理、文献等3大类32项数据标准，持续搜集、核对、完善各遗产地基础数据，并补充新列入《世界遗产名录》的遗产地信息。

·监测预警系统对接：已建成监测预警信息系统的遗产地，通过接口服务对接到国家总平台，共享日常监测、预警处置、地图服务、每日舆情等监测数据。

·保护管理状况调研评估：通过总平台设立调研评估指标体系，辅助开展世界文化遗产地保护状况调研评估、监测预警体系建设评估等工作，建立在线档案、实现系统评分评级。

·交流共享：通过集成在总平台中的门户网站和资源共享平台，向社会公众普及和宣传世界遗产相关知识，提升公众世界遗产的保护意识，并为行业机构和公众分别提供符合其需求的世界遗产相关服务。

作为总平台的支撑，"监测云"移动应用系统、中国世界文化遗产监测年会制度、中国世界文化遗产中心遗产地项目专员制度从专业监测数据采集和移动端应用、行业内部交流培训、以及公众参与世界文化遗产事务等方面发挥着各自作用。其中，世界文化遗产监测年会自2013年至今已成功举办6届，会议内容包括全国世界文化遗产保护状况总体报告、重点问题讨论和经验分享、重要文件和规章制度解读，并对上年度工作进展予以回顾、对下阶段工作提出建议和指导。监测年会现已成为我国世界文化遗产地的重要交流平台。

可见，我国的世界文化遗产监测已远远超越了《指南》中有关监测的内容和成果，而是立足我国实际，形成了基于《公约》框架的中国遗产监测需求和创新。进一步说，中国世界文化遗产监测是对世界遗产5C战略的全面响应。

·增强《世界遗产名录》的可信度：通过信息系统进行数据统计、趋势分析、信息公开，将专业途径和管理手段结合确保保护管理状况的可信度。

·保证世界遗产的有效保护：通过设立国家层面的监测指标体系，引导遗产地系统地开展保护管理工作；监测和预警处置结合，预先发出警示信息，以便于保护管理机构及时采取相应的处置措施，有效防范风险。

·推进各缔约国有效的能力建设；监测融入日常管理工作，监测与培训深度结合，发挥世界文化遗产在国内不可移动文物保护领域的探索和示范作用。

·通过宣传增强大众对世界遗产保护的认识、参与和支持；总平台向公众展示准确、丰富的信息，是在公众与遗产之间建立强联系的基础。

·在实施《世界遗产公约》的过程中强化社区角色：监测云专业版和公众参与版实现社区参与功能。

综上所述，经过多年探索和努力，中国世界文化遗产监测已成为以总平台为核心，综合了数据、服务和交流功能，将专业、事物和人联系起来的世界文化遗产保护管理体系。

3　大运河保护和申遗实践所展现的中国世界文化遗产保护创新

大运河遗产规模巨大、构成要素丰富，包含 3000 余公里河道，涉及沿线 8 个省 / 直辖市的 35 个城市。作为一项复杂的巨型遗产，除部分为遗址状态外，多数遗产要素仍发挥着实用功能，与周边的人民、经济、社会发生着千丝万缕的联系。大运河处于我国中东部人口高度密集地区，在经济社会快速发展的新形势下，对其实施科学保护与合理利用是一项非常紧迫且高度繁难的事业，大运河申遗被认为是世界上最难的申遗项目。我国议事协调机制、保护管理规划体系、遗产监测方面的经验和成效在大运河申遗和保护中得到了充分应用和发展。

针对复杂的保护管理现状，国家层面由文化部、国家文物局牵头，会同发改委、财政部、国土资源部、环保部、交通运输部、水利部等 13 个相关部委和大运河沿线 8 省、直辖市人民政府组成大运河保护和申遗省部际会商小组。遗产地层面，也成立了相应的省、市、县级会商机构，协调处理保护和申遗中的重要问题、决定重大项目。此外，由大运河沿线 35 个城市成立大运河沿线城市联盟，促进了城市间的合作，协同做好大运河全线遗产的保护管理工作。

2008 年至 2012 年，由中国文化遗产研究院牵头，集 54 个机构部门、245 人合力，编制建立了大运河遗产保护管理规划体系，包括国家级保护规划、省级保护规划、地市级保护规划、重要点段保护规划和各类详细规划。各阶段、各级规划相互衔接、各有侧重，共同构建了对全国范围内大运河遗产实施全面保护的整体性政策。而且，大运河遗产保护管理规划体系至今仍在不断完善、动态更新。依据保护管理规划体系，国家文物局组织编制了大运河文化遗产及周边环境保护、展示、整治相关技术导则，指导运河沿线城市编制相关项目技术方案。中央财政和地方各级财政不断加大投入大量资金，在各级大运河保护、管理规划和相关技术导则的指导下，分类组织实施了一批运河遗产本体保护工程、环境整治工程、展示阐释工程，使大运河遗产的保护状况得到了显著改善。

2014 年，包含 31 个组成部分的大运河遗产成功列入《世界遗产名录》，其突出普遍价值得到国际社会的高度认可，推动中华优秀传统文化和中华文明成果"走出去"，使世界各国人民进一步加深了对古代中国和当代中国的认识、理解和欣赏。同时，这是"线性遗产"概念提出以来，中国单独申报的第一项超大型线性文化遗产，反映了国际文化遗产保护理念与中国文化遗产保护实践的成功结合，对我国文物保护理念和实践产生了深远的影响，也反映了我国世界文化遗产申报保护能力的较好水平。

申遗成功后，大运河沿线部分城市以运河文化为主题，以运河遗存保护为核心，对周边环境进行综合整治，重点加快基础设施和配套服务设施建设，建成一批运河休闲公园、运河文化博物馆和展示馆，为周边社区居民提供了公共文化空间；同时，改善了运河沿线的生活环境，提高了生活质量，提升了公共服务水平，使沿线居民切实感受到大运河遗产保护给日常生活带来的积极变化。大运河保护与利用有力推动了遗产地旅游经济的发展，成为推动当地经济社会可持续发展的重要力量。

大运河遗产监测系统在申遗、保护和管理中发挥了重要作用。申遗期间，国家文物局发布了《大运河遗产监测和档案系统建设要求》。依据要求，中国文化遗产研究院建立了大运河监测与档案国家中心和总平台，各遗产区都设有相应的遗产地平台，系统整体覆盖了 31 个遗产区。申遗成功后，大运河监测系统成为实现该遗产科学管理的重要抓手。2018 年世界遗产大会上，大运河作为世界遗产保护管理状况三个优秀案例之一获得高度赞赏。世界遗产中心和咨询机构的分析和总结中写到："显著的成果是遗产综合监测系统，通过对数据进行持续不断地收集、集中化管理、分析和评估，为支持决策奠定了数据基础。"近日，国家发布《大运河文化保护、传承、利用规划纲要》，通过大运河文化带整合起沿线的不可移动文物、博物馆、自然遗产和非物质文化遗产，再一次为实现大运河遗产的有效保护和可持续发展提供了新的契机。

参考文献：

[1] 国家文物局、中国古迹遗址保护协会 . 中国世界文化遗产 30 年，2017 年 1 月 .

[2] 赵云 . 中国世界文化遗产监测 . 中国建筑工业出版社，2017 年 7 月 .

[3] 中国世界文化遗产监测中心 . 中国世界文化遗产监测 2014 年度报告 . 中国文物科学研究，2015（3）.

[4] 罗颖、王芳、宋晓微 . 我国世界文化遗产保护管理状况及趋势分析——中国世界文化遗产 2017 年度总报告 . 中国文化遗产，2018（6）.

[5] 赵云 . 中国世界文化遗产监测预警总平台建设现状与发展思路——基于需求研究的思考 [J]. 中国文化遗产，2018（1）.

[6] UNESCO.（1972）. 保护世界文化和自然遗产公约 [EB/OL]. http：//whc.unesco.org/archive/convention-ch.pdf

[7] UNESCO.（2017）. 实施《世界遗产公约》操作指南 [EB/OL]. http：//whc.unesco.org/document/140239

Conservation and Monitoring of World Cultural Heritage in China

Zhao Yun[①]

Chinese Academy of Cultural Heritage

Abstract:

Under the framework of the UNESCO *Convention Concerning the Protection of the World Cultural and Natural Heritage*, China has made many explorations and innovations for the conservation of World Cultural Heritage properties across the country and achieved a number of theoretic and practical results meeting international rules and requirements while fitting national conditions. In particular, good results and experiences have been gained to develop a deliberation and coordination system (with particular focus on the nomination and conservation of extra-large serial properties) , formulate protection and management plans, and carry out monitoring activities. These results and experiences were fully used with further progress in nominating and protecting the Grand Canal as a World Cultural Heritage property.

Key words: World Cultural Heritage conservation, heritage monitoring, Grand Canal

In 1972, UNESCO adopted the *Convention Concerning the Protection of the World Cultural and Natural*

---

① Researcher, Director of World Cultural Heritage Center of China, Chinese Academy of Cultural Heritage. The main research direction of Zhao Yun is world cultural heritage, including researches on value, protection and use, and monitoring of world heritage sites. So far Zhao has led and participated in about 90 cultural heritage conservation researches and projects, among which 1 was honored with national award and 6 were honored with provincial and ministerial awards. Zhao herself was also praised and rewarded by China's National Cultural Heritage Administration. Zhao is among the first group of Young Academic Leaders of Chinese Academy of Cultural Heritage. Zhao's representative works include the compilation of nomination dossier for Cultural Landscape of Honghe Hani Rice Terraces, Grand Canal, ZuojiangHuashan Rock Art Cultural Landscape and Maritime Silk Road; the protection and management planning for Grand Canal and Maritime Silk Road; the construction of database for world cultural heritage sites in China; the establishment of National Platform for Monitoring & Early Warning System; annual reports of world cultural heritage sites in China; researches on interpretation and presentation of Chinese cultural landscape; and the formulation of principles and guidelines for risk management of world cultural heritage. Zhao has numerous monographs and theses, such as Digital Presentation of Cultural Heritage, China World Cultural Heritage Monitoring, Interpretation of Outstanding Universal Value of ZuojiangHuashan Rock Art Cultural Landscape - An Outstanding Rock Painting, A Unique Cultural Landscape, Harmony across the Ocean - Maritime Silk Road and China, etc.

Heritage (hereinafter referred to as the Convention), with the purpose of protecting the cultural and natural heritage that bear outstanding universal value for all mankind. China ratified the Convention in 1985 and its first group of six properties were inscribed on the World Heritage List in 1987, including the Great Wall, the Imperial Place of the Ming and Qing Dynasties in Beijing, the Mogao Caves, the Mausoleum of the First Qin Emperor, the Peking Man Site at Zhoukoudian, and Mount Taishan. As of the end of 2018, China had had 53 properties inscribed on the List, ranking second place in the world, among which there are 36 cultural, 13 natural and 4 mixed heritages.

World Cultural Heritage properties in China are the masterpieces representing the best of Chinese traditional culture. They exhibit a panorama of Chinese civilization from perspectives of chronological span, spatial distribution and heritage category. World Cultural Heritage properties in China contain all heritage categories inscribed on the List, ranging over not only conventional types such as monuments, sites and groups of buildings, but also special types including cultural landscapes, historic towns and centers, canal heritages and route heritages. All criteria for the selection of World Cultural Heritage properties have been used for these heritages, among which criteria (iii) and (vi) were applied for much more times than the average level worldwide. World Cultural Heritage properties in China bear a evidence to a number of significant events happening in the history of Chinese civilization and the civilizational development of Chinese people that features "unity in diversity", demonstrating close association between tangible and intangible cultural heritage regarding their value identification and conservation.

World Cultural Heritage properties in China are preserved and protected in accordance with laws and regulations at all levels. With the *Law of the People's Republic of China on the Protection of Cultural Relics* as the higher law, a number of laws, regulations and departmental norms have been developed and efforts made to keep the Convention and its Operational Guidelines in parallel with the country's existing legal system. A conservation structure has been developed that highlights the government as the principal player and the private sector as the active participant.

1. World Cultural Heritage Conservation: China's Explorations and Innovations

The promotion of theories on World Cultural Heritage conservation has directly widened visions for the conservation of cultural heritage properties in China. More emphasis has been placed on the integrated conservation of heritage properties, their settings and cultural traditions they bear, with particular respect for interests of stakeholders. More efforts have been made to encourage the establishment of mechanisms of scientific management and preventive conservation based on monitoring activities.

Meanwhile, many explorations and innovations have been made in this regard. All the efforts made by the State Party of China are aimed at answering the following question: How the "common heritage of all mankind" gains the recognition of various sectors and institutions at all domestic levels, in particular smaller groups or even individuals, under the framework of the Convention and based on common conservation needs of all mankind? For many years, China has achieved a number of theoretic and practical results that meet international rules and requirements while fitting its national conditions. In particular, good results and experiences have been gained to develop a deliberation and coordination system (with particular focus on the nomination and conservation of extra-large serial properties), formulate protection and management plans, and carry out monitoring activities.

· The deliberation and coordination system. Governments from 44 World Heritage sites across the country have established their own deliberation and coordination systems to coordinate conservation institutions, local governments, as well as construction, religious and tourism departments.

· The development of protection and management plans. The strategy of "planning first" has been formulated to require the development of protection and management plans as the first step, with particular focus on coordination between areas of priority protected sites (protected areas and construction control areas) and areas of World Heritage sites (Property Area and buffer zones) as well as between their management documents.

· World Cultural Heritage monitoring. From 2012, China began to speed up the building of the early-warning system for World Cultural Heritage properties in a systematic and all-round manner. So far, the national general platform of early-warning and 20 local platforms have been initially developed. They are combined to form an integrated early-warning system to provide daily monitoring, annual reporting, periodic assessment, basic database and information sharing. As a result, remarkable results have been scored and the objective to provide support for management decision-making initially achieved.

2. Monitoring of World Cultural Heritage Properties in China

Under the framework of the Convention, World Cultural Heritage monitoring is carried out to identify the state of OUV and integrity and/or authenticity as well as their changing trends through measuring State of Conservation (SOC) indicators. The reactive monitoring and periodic reporting systems are the core components of the monitoring rules specified in the *Operational Guidelines*.

Based on the reflection on past reactive monitoring missions and two cycles of periodic reporting, China started from 2012 to plan and launch the building of the early-warning system for World Cultural Heritage properties at the national level. The National Cultural Heritage Administration (NCHA) established China World Cultural Heritage Monitoring Center (currently named China World Cultural Heritage Center) within the Chinese Academy of Cultural Heritage (CACH). The center is responsible for developing and promoting working norms and monitoring indicators nationwide and for organizing the building of the early-warning system for World Cultural Heritage properties in China, with the national general platform set up within CACH. The general platform was put in use in 2014, functioning as the "big data service system for cultural heritage conservation and monitoring" that connects itself with all local platforms and information systems of related sectors.

Currently, the general platform is able to support all types of activities for World Cultural Heritage monitoring, including:

· Annual reporting. Via the general platform, management authorities of World Cultural Heritage properties across the country submit to NCHA the *Annual Report on the Monitoring of the World Cultural Heritage Property* in March each year, and China World Cultural Heritage Center prepares the national annual report.

· Periodic assessment. Each World Cultural Heritage property carries out online assessment over a half-year cycle, including self assessment and provincial-level review.

· Basic data collection and updating. In accordance with the rules governing the basic database of World Cultural Heritage properties in China, basic data are collected, verified and completed based on the 32 criteria governing three categories of basic information, protection and management, and documentation. Information on new heritages on the List will be added timely.

· Connecting with the national general platform. The early-warning and monitoring system for each World Cultural Heritage property is connected with the national general platform via interface service so as to share data on daily monitoring, early-warning disposal, mapping service, and daily opinion monitoring.

· Status of Convention (SOC) research and assessment. A system of research and assessment indicators is established at the general platform to support SOC research and assessment activities and assessment of monitoring and early-warning system building. Online archives are developed to score and grade monitoring and early warning systems.

· Information exchange and sharing. Portal websites and resources sharing platforms integrated in the general platform are used to publicize and promote knowledge on World Heritage properties, boost the general public's awareness of World Heritage conservation, and provide related services that meet needs of professional institutions and the general public.

· As the supporting facilities to the general platform, the "Monitoring Data Cloud" mobile application, the Annual Session on World Cultural Heritage Monitoring in China, and the Project Specialist System of China World Cultural Heritage Center function to facilitate professional monitoring data collection, mobile application, internal communication and training within the heritage sector, and public participation in World Cultural Heritage affairs. In particular, the Annual Session on World Cultural Heritage Monitoring in China has been successfully convened for six consecutive years since 2013, whose agenda includes overall SOC reporting on World Cultural Heritage sites in China, discussion of key issues and experience sharing, explanation of important documents and rules, review of the work in the previous year, and recommend actions and guidance on the next stage of work. The annual monitoring session has established itself as a key communication platform for World Cultural Heritage properties in China.

Monitoring of World Cultural Heritage properties in China has obviously gone far beyond the scope of contents and outcomes specified in the Operational Guidelines, with needs and innovations developed according to the country's actual conditions and under the framework of the Convention. Moreover, it represents a full-scale response to the 5Cs Strategic Objectives of the World Heritage Convention as follows:

· Strengthen the Credibility of the World Heritage List. To ensure the credibility of SOC through data statistics, trend analysis and access to information and by employing both professional approaches and management tools.

· Ensure the effective Conservation of World Heritage properties. To guide protection and management activities to be carried out systemically through the establishment of a monitoring indicators system at the national level. To combine monitoring with early-warning disposal and send warnings in advance so that protection and management institutions can timely take disposal measures and effectively prevent risks.

· Promote the development of Capacity Building measures. To integrate monitoring in daily management activities and combine monitoring with training closely so as to give play to the role of World Cultural Heritage properties as pioneering examples in the country's conservation of immoveable cultural properties.

· Increase public awareness, involvement and support for World Heritage through Communication. The national general platform provides accurate and rich information and serves as the bridge to build strong connection between the public and the heritage.

· Enhance the role of Communities in the implementation of the World Heritage Convention. The professional and public editions of the "Monitoring Data Cloud" App have enabled the involvement of communities.

In conclusion, with explorations and endeavors for many years, a protection and management system for the monitoring of World Cultural Heritage properties in China has been developed with the national general platform as the core component, integrating functions in data collection, service provision and communication and connecting the profession, heritage properties and people together.

3. Innovation in World Cultural Heritage Conservationin China: The Case of the Grand Canal

The Grand Canal is a huge heritage property with rich and sophisticated components, containing waterways totaling over 3,000 km that run through 35 cities under the jurisdiction of eight provinces or municipalities directly under the Central Government. In addition to some components protected as historical remains, most other components still function as water facilities today to serve people's life and their economic and social activities. The Grand Canal is located in the highly populous area in the mid-eastern region of China. It is an urgent and extremely difficult task to ensure scientific conservation and reasonable use of the heritage property. The nomination of the Grand Canal is considered the most difficult of its kind in the world. The experiences and results gained from the country's deliberation and coordination mechanisms, the protection and management planning system and heritage monitoring activities have been fully used with further progress in the nomination and conservation of the Grand Canal.

To address sophisticated protection and management realities, the Inter-provincial/ministerial Consultation Group on the Conservation and Nomination of the Grand Canal was established as a national-level body, led by the Ministry of Culture and NCHA with the participation of other 13 central ministries and commissions and 8 provincial governments along the canal. Provincial, city and county-level consultation bodies were also set up to coordinate and handle significant issues and decide significant projects regarding the conservation and nomination of the canal. Moreover, the Grand Canal Alliance of Cities was also founded, consisting of 35 member cities, with the aim of promoting inter-city cooperation and collaborating to protect and manage the whole heritage property.

From 2008 to 2012, CACH organized the preparation of the planning framework for the protection and management of the Grand Canal, with the participation of 245 professionals from 54 institutions and government departments across the country. The national-level conservation plan, provincial and city-level conservation plans, conservation plans for key sections and sites and all other types of detailed plans have been developed. Planning documents for various stages and at various levels supplement each other with different areas of focus and are combined to develop an overall policy for implementing full-scale conservation of the Grand Canal nationwide. Moreover, the planning framework is still being improved and updated. Under the planning framework, NCHA has developed documents of technical guidance on the conservation, presentation and enhancement of the Grand Canal and its settings to guide the preparation of related technical plans to be carried out by cities along the canal. Fiscal funds from the Central Government and local governments at various levels have continued to increase. In accordance with conservation plans, management plans and related technical guidance documents formulated at various levels, a number of works on heritage conservation, environmental enhancement and presentation and interpretation have been conducted, bringing about significant improvement in the state of conservation of the Grand Canal.

In 2014, the Grand Canal, comprising of 31 component sites and monuments, was successfully inscribed on the World Heritage List, with its OUV highly recognized by the international community. The property's inscription has helped promote the best of Chinese traditional culture and the accomplishments of Chinese civilization worldwide and enabled the people from the rest of the world to have deeper and better knowledge, understanding and appreciation of ancient China and contemporary China. Meanwhile, the Grand Canal was the first giant linear cultural heritage property nominated by the State Party of China on its own since the concept of "linear heritage" was proposed. Its nomination and inscription demonstrates the successful integration of international conservation theories with Chinese conservation practices, has far-reaching impact on the development of conservation theories and practices in China, and exhibits the country's good capacity for World Cultural Heritage nomination and conservation.

After the inscription on the World Heritage List, several cities along the Grand Canal have conducted comprehensive environmental enhancement, speeded up the construction of infrastructure and supporting service facilities, and built a number of leisure parks, museums and exhibition halls that feature the theme of canal culture and focus on the protection of canal remains, providing public cultural spaces for residents in surrounding communities. These facilities and public spaces have contributed to the improvement of living environments, quality of people's lives and public service capacity in areas along the Grand Canal. The people living along the Grand Canal have become highly aware of positive changes happening in their daily lives. The conservation and utilization of the Grand Canal has significantly facilitated the development of local tourism and economy and played an important role in promoting local sustainable development.

The Grand Canal Monitoring System played an important role in the property's nomination, conservation and management. When nominating the property for inscription on the World Heritage List, NCHA issued the document entitled "Requirements for the Building of the Monitoring and Archival System of the Grand Canal". According to the document, CACH established the National Center and General Platform on the Monitoring and Archiving of the Grand Canal. Local platforms were also set up in each of the component areas. The whole system covers all the 31 component areas. After the inscription, the Grand Canal Monitoring System has become an important instrument to conduct scientific management of the heritage property. At the World Heritage Committee's annual session in 2018, the Grand Canal was highly applauded as one of the three outstanding cases in the protection and management of World Heritage properties. It was written in the analysis and review report by the World Heritage Centre and the Advisory Bodies that "A significant result is the property's integrated monitoring system that has developed a data basis to support decision-making through continued collection, central management, analysis and assessment of data." Recently, the State Council has publicized the *Planning Outline on the Conservation, Continuation and Utilization of the Culture of the Grand Canal*, with the aim of integrating immoveable cultural properties, museums, natural heritage properties and intangible cultural heritage elements through the Cultural Belt of the Grand Canal so as to provide a new opportunity for its effective conservation and sustainable development.

Bibliography

1. NCHA, ICOMOS China. *30 Year of World Cultural Heritage in China*, January 2017.

2. Zhao Yun. *World Cultural Heritage Monitoring in China*. China Architecture & Building Press, July, 2017.

3. China World Cultural Heritage Center. *The Annual Report on World Cultural Heritage Monitoring in China 2014*. China Cultural Heritage Research Journal, Issue 3 of 2015.

4. Luo Ying, Wang Fang, Song Xiaowei. *State of Protection and Management of World Cultural Heritage Properties in China and Trend Analysis: The General Report on World Cultural Heritage Properties in China 2017*. Chinese Cultural Heritage Journal, Issue 6 of 2018.

5. Zhao Yun. *Current Construction and Development Strategy of the General Monitoring and Early-warning Platform for World Cultural Heritage Properties in China: Reflections Based on Need Research*. Chinese Cultural Heritage Journal, Issue 1 of 2018.

6. UNESCO, 1972. *The Convention Concerning the Protection of the World Cultural and Natural Heritage*. http://whc.unesco.org/archive/convention-ch.pdf

7. UNESCO, 2017. *The Operational Guidelines for the Implementation of the World Heritage Convention*. http://whc.unesco.org/document/140239

波兰世界文化遗产的保护、保存与管理

波兰共和国　国家遗产局　芭芭拉·弗玛尼克[①]

摘要：

必须指出，波兰是联合国教科文组织最早成立时的创始国之一。波兰于 1976 年批准通过联合国教科文组织《保护世界文化和自然遗产公约》。不久之后的 1978 年，第一批共 12 处遗址列入世界遗产名录，其中有两处来自波兰：克拉科夫历史中心和维利奇卡盐矿。1979 年又有两处列入：奥斯维辛德国纳粹集中营（1940—1945）和比亚沃维耶扎原始森林（自然遗产地，波兰—白俄罗斯跨境遗产）。1980 年有一处：华沙历史中心。

今天，在《世界遗产名录》存在 40 多年之后，波兰拥有 15 处被公认为具有突出普遍价值的世界遗产，以及数千处在国家古迹名录中受保护的历史遗迹。它们代表了波兰文化和历史的多样性和丰富性。

我们已形成了一个完善的抢救、保护和保存文化遗产的传统。波兰考古和古迹保护领域的专业人士以其知识、经验和奉献精神闻名于世。几十年来，他们不仅一直致力于保护波兰文化遗产，而且也保护世界各地的文化遗产。

波兰世界遗产中心的建立以及 2017 年在克拉科夫组织的世界遗产委员会第 41 届大会是多年来波兰专业遗产保护工作的顶峰。

关键字：世界遗产地，保存，保护，管理，监测

波兰的世界遗产

波兰是联合国教科文组织成立时的创始国之一。随后波兰于 1976 年批准通过了联合国教科文组织《保护世界文化和自然遗产公约》。不久，在 1978 年首批列入世界遗产名录的 12 处遗址中有两处来自波兰。今天，在《世界遗产名录》存在 40 多年之后，波兰有 15 处被公认为具有突出普遍价值的世界遗产——14 处文化遗产和 1 处自然遗产；其中有 3 处是跨境遗产。

[①]　芭芭拉·弗玛尼克（Barbara Furmanik），2000 年进入波兰国家文化遗产局。2013 年，开始在世界遗产分部工作，主要处理一系列与世界遗产相关的工作.曾参与多个历史公园和花园的保护指南和修复项目的执行.同时编写了世界遗产——穆斯考公园申遗文本。此外，曾在斯陀园工作为英国国家信托基金，且在旅游和娱乐系获得世界遗产旅游的本科学位。

四个历史城市

克拉科夫历史中心（1978 年列入世界遗产名录，列入标准 iv）

克拉科夫历史中心由 3 个城市建筑群构成：中世纪的克拉科夫城址、华威山综合建筑群和卡齐米日城（包括 Stradom 郊区）。它是欧洲城市规划的杰出典范，主要建筑特点在于集众多建筑风格于一身并和谐发展。这些建筑风格囊括了罗马早期到现代主义时期的所有建筑风格。

华沙历史中心（1980 年列入世界遗产名录，列入标准 ii 和 vi）

华沙老城在二战中受到严重破坏，波兰在原址采用历史建筑风格对华沙老城进行了重建，这体现了波兰拯救华沙老城这一最重要的国家文化代表的决心与努力。重建工作包括对城区规划的整体再造，重现了老城市场、市政厅、环绕四周的古城墙、皇家城堡以及一些重要的宗教建筑。

扎莫希奇古城（1992 年列入世界遗产名录，列入标准 iv）

扎莫希奇古城是 16 世纪晚期中欧城镇的典范，其设计和建筑风格充分体现了意大利文艺复兴时期的"理想城市"理论。它是这座古城开明的建立者扬·扎莫伊斯基（Jan Zamoyski）与意大利出色的建筑师贝尔南多·莫兰多（Bernardo Morando）密切配合的杰作。

图 1　扎莫希奇古城航拍图

摄于 2017 年，作者：彼得亚雷·奥斯托夫斯基（Piotr Ostrowski），© NID.

中世纪古镇托伦（1997 年列入世界遗产名录，列入标准 ii 和 iv）

中世纪古镇托伦是保存完好的中欧贸易中心和行政管理中心的范例。它向人们完整地展示了中世纪时期人们的生活方式。古城的空间布局为研究中欧城市的发展提供了珍贵的原始资料；另外，许多建筑都代表了中世纪的教会、军事以及民用砖房建筑的最高成就。

三处典型的木结构建筑遗产

扎沃尔和思维得尼加的和平教堂（2001 年列入世界遗产名录，列入标准 iii、iv 和 vi）

位于扎沃尔和思维得尼加的和平教堂是欧洲最大的巴洛克风格木结构宗教建筑。1648 年签署的《威斯特伐利亚和约》，结束了"欧洲三十年战争"，之后，也就是 17 世纪中叶和平教堂建成，其宏大的规模和建筑的复杂性在当时的欧洲木结构建筑史上前所未有。

南部小波兰木制教堂（2003 年列入世界遗产名录，列入标准 iii 和 iv）

6 座木结构教堂代表了罗马天主教文化中，中世纪教堂建造传统的不同方面。它们分布于布里兹列（Blizne）、比那洛瓦（Binarowa）、德布诺·圣米歇尔（Dę-bno Podhalańskie）、哈克佐夫（Haczów）、雷尼克·姆洛瓦纳（Lipnica Murowana）和赛库瓦（Sękowa）等城镇或乡村，从小波兰（Małopolska）历史区一直延伸到西喀尔巴阡山脉北面的丘陵地带。

图 2　比那洛瓦（Binarowa）教堂内景
摄于 2017 年，作者：彼得亚雷·奥斯托夫斯基，© NID.

波兰和乌克兰在喀尔巴阡山地区的木制教堂（跨境）（2013 年列入世界遗产名录，列入标准 iii 和 iv）

波兰和乌克兰境内的 16 座木结构教堂代表着曾广泛分布在斯拉夫国家的东正教木屋建筑传统，这种传统一直延续到今天。这些教堂有哈苏、哈利奇、博伊科和西莱姆科四种风格。

两处文化景观

卡瓦利泽布日多夫斯卡：风格独特的建筑和园林景观群与朝圣公园（1999 年列入世界遗产名录，列入标准 ii 和 iv）

卡瓦利泽布日多夫斯卡是一处具有伟大精神意义的文化景观。就其自然环境而言——这里有众多建成于 17 世纪的、与《耶稣的受难记》和《圣母玛利亚的一生》有关的具有象征意义的宗教活动场所——保护完好，几乎未变。时至今日，它仍是朝拜圣地。

斯科夫公园／马扎科夫斯基公园（波兰—德国跨境遗产）（2004 年列入世界遗产名录，列入标准 i 和 iv）

这座横跨尼斯河的园林公园，由赫尔曼·普克勒—穆斯考王子于 1815—1844 年间建造。公园将周围的农耕景观天衣无缝地融合在一起，开创了景观设计的新方法，并影响了欧洲和美洲景观建筑的发展。

图 3　波兰和德国部分的公园景色
摄于 2017，作者：彼得亚雷·奥斯托夫斯基，© NID.

两处建筑综合体

马尔堡的特多尼克奥尔多城堡（也称为条顿骑士团城堡）（1997 年列入世界遗产名录，列入标准 ii，iii 和 iv）

这座 13 世纪修建的日耳曼修道院属于条顿骑士团（Teutonic Order），1309 年骑士团大头领将总部从威尼斯迁到马尔堡后进行了大幅扩建和装饰。它是中世纪砖砌城堡的典范，后来逐渐衰败，但在 19 世纪和 20 世纪初得以精心修复。许多现在被公认为标准的保护技术就起源于这里。

弗罗茨瓦夫百年厅（2006 年列入世界遗产名录，列入标准 i，ii 和 iv）

弗罗茨瓦夫百年厅是钢筋混凝土建筑史上的一个里程碑，是由建筑师 Max Berg 于 1911—1913 年间建造的一座多功能娱乐休闲建筑，坐落于展览中心。从外形上看它是一个对称的四叶结构，巨大的圆形中心可容纳约 6,000 人。23 米高的圆顶顶部有一盏钢铁和玻璃制成的灯笼。

图 4　百年厅航拍照片
摄于 2017，作者：彼得亚雷·奥斯托夫斯基，© NID.

两处工业遗产

维利奇卡和博赫尼亚皇家盐矿（1978、2013 年列入世界遗产名录，列入标准 iv）

维利奇卡盐矿的岩盐矿床从 13 世纪开始开采。这个重要的工业企业具有皇家地位，是欧洲同类企业中最古老的一个。该遗址是由维利奇卡和博赫尼亚盐矿及维利奇卡盐厂城堡组成的系列遗产。

塔尔诺夫斯克山铅银锌矿及其地下水管理系统（2017 年列入世界遗产名录，列入标准 i，ii 和 iv）

作为中欧的主要矿区之一，该遗产包括整个地下矿山的坑道、竖井、走廊和其他水管理系统。大部分遗产位于地下，地上采矿地形以竖井和废堆遗迹以及 19 世纪蒸汽抽水站遗迹为特征。塔尔诺夫斯克山对全球铅和锌的生产做出了重大贡献。

一处纪念遗址

前纳粹德国奥斯维辛—比克瑙集中营（1940—1945）（1979 年列入世界遗产名录，列入标准 vi）

奥斯维辛—比克瑙是前纳粹德国政权蓄意灭绝犹太人的历史纪念碑，也是无数人的死亡之地，该遗址有无可辩驳的证据证明这是有史以来对人类犯下的最大罪行之一。它也是人类精神力量的纪念碑，在可怕的逆境中，人类抵抗了前纳粹德国政权压制自由和自由思想、消灭整个种族的企图。

图 5：前奥斯维辛—比克瑙集中营的碎片
摄于 2017，作者：彼得亚雷·奥斯托夫斯基 © NID.

一处自然遗产

比亚沃维耶扎原始森林（波兰—白俄罗斯跨境遗产）（1978、1992、2014 年列入世界遗产名录，列入标准 ix 和 x）

比亚沃维耶扎原始森林是位于波兰和白俄罗斯边境的一片巨大的广袤森林。这一遗产包括一系列具有中欧复合生态系统特征的低地森林。由于原始森林规模巨大，且包括大片未被干扰的、依自然规律正常发展的地区，所以对该地区实施保护具有特殊意义。

历史遗迹和文化遗产的保护

几十年来，波兰已经建立了完善的历史遗迹保护体系。《历史古迹保护和维护法》（2003 年 7 月 23 日法案，2017 年法律杂志，第 1257 项，已修订）是波兰的主要法律文件，其中明确规定了古迹的保护目标、保护范围和保护形式。该法案还制定了几项保护原则，包括制定古迹保护的国家规划原则、为古迹的保护、修复及相关工作筹措资金的原则，组织成立遗产保护机构的原则。

根据该法案的规定，"历史遗迹"（波兰语：*zabytek*）指一个遗产（不动产）或可移动文化遗产，其构成部分或全部，是人类的作品，或与人类的活动有关，它们是过去时代或事件的证明。由于历史古迹具有历史、艺术或科学价值，对其实施保护符合社会利益。

现有体系中已建立的关于遗产保护的法律形式有：

1. 列入古迹名册——地区古迹监督员负责按照职权或应任意一方（遗迹拥有者或使用者）的要求，启动古迹列入程序，将古迹登记入册。准备阶段的工作包括收集相关信息和文件资料，以确认相关古迹的价值符合国家遗产标准。

2. 认定为国家历史古迹——这是指任何列入名册的不可移动遗迹或具有特定文化价值的文化公园等。国家历史古迹是波兰共和国主席应文化和国家遗产部长的请求，通过颁布特别条例而设定，因此具有重要的地位。只有获得国家历史古迹称号的遗址，才有可能被提名列入联合国教科文组织世界遗产名录。

3. 成立文化公园——用来保护特定文化景观和具有不可移动性质特征的历史遗迹所在的区域，这些地区应具有当地建筑特色或传统聚落特色。文化公园的认定和除名，可经征求当地古迹监督员后，由公社委员会执行。跨市的文化公园可由多个市政机构或市政联盟设立。

4. 制定地方遗产保护协议，其内容与空间开发及一系列决策有关，决策涉及：地方公共投资、建筑环境、优先进行公路投资、铁路本地化、同意建造当地机场等。空间规划问题受《空间规划和地区发展法》（2003 年法律杂志，第 80 期，第 717 项，已修订）的管理和约束。各市政当局负责制定并实施本地的空间管理政策。

负责历史古迹保护的政府当局和机构有：

文化和国家遗产部长，在文化部担任国务秘书或副秘书，代表历史古迹保护总干事，负责行使与历史古迹保护相关的职责。

地区古迹监督员——作为省级联合管理机构的成员，是第一实体机构，而文化部长则是第二实体机构，负责处理法案和单行管理条例中所规定的事项。地区古迹监督员的工作，尤其包括下述内容：承担国家遗产保护和保存项目的相关工作职责；制定规划，为历史古迹的保护提供财政支持，使用获得的基金保护遗产；保存遗产登记册和地区遗产目录，整理核对相关文档；根据决定和决议，为法案和单行管理条例中的事项颁发许可证；监督所开展的保护研究、建筑研究、建筑工程的保护、修复及其他与遗迹相关的活动以及考古研究等，并进行质量控制；制定在发生武装冲突和危机情况下省级遗产保护规划；宣传关于历史古迹的知识。

对历史古迹的保护，尤其应包括各政府机构所采取的行动：提供法律的、组织的和财政相关信息，以便永久保护历史古迹及其发展；防止可能损害历史古迹价值的风险；防止对历史古迹的破坏和滥用；防止文物被盗、丢失或非法运往海外；控制历史古迹保护的状态和目标；重视空间规划和发展，重视营造环境以保护历史古迹。

另外，在历史古迹监督员的要求下，文化和国家遗产部长可将他或她职权范围内（颁发行政决定除外）的工作任务委托给专门负责古迹保护的文化机构负责人来执行，但部长必须是组织者。这些机构包括波兰国家遗产局（波兰语：Narodowy Instytut Dziedzictwa）。

波兰国家遗产局的主要目标是确认、研究和记录遗产资产，收集与历史环境、文化景观和文化古迹相关的信息，制定历史环境保护相关政策和策略，提升公众对历史环境、文化景观和遗产资产的认知。遗产局的总部位于华沙，在全国各地建有 16 个办事处。

在与世界遗产相关的事项方面，波兰国家遗产局局长有权代表古迹保护总干事行事。自 2007 年以来，该局一直负责管理世界遗产单位、管理与波兰世界遗产相关的规划及其他事项。另外，自 2014 年以来，波兰国家遗产局世界遗产中心一直努力致力于改善波兰世界遗产的保护和管理。该中心也被指定为波兰世界遗产协调中心。

尽管波兰在 1976 年批准通过了联合国教科文组织《实施保护世界文化与自然遗产公约操作指南》，但该指南通过 4 年后，波兰仍没有形成特定的、关于世界遗产认定和保护的法律规范。《历史古迹保护和维护法》仅提到了世界遗产的地位。根据《历史古迹》——获得这一地位是将古迹列入联合国教科文组织世界遗产名录的必要条件。

《波兰宪法》（1997 年）指出，所有国际条约均对国内法律有约束作用，即使未直接实施的国际条约也同样具有约束力。很遗憾，波兰并没有任何关于保护和维护波兰世界遗产的执行条例和文件。因此，从理论上来说，《世界遗产公约》（1972 年）和《实施保护世界文化与自然遗产公约操作指南》对波兰来说是适用的。但事实上，说服历史古迹／世界遗产的拥有者和相关管理机构来执行这些国际文件的要求，是非常困难的。

保护和管理

历史古迹的保护、保养、维护和安全保卫是古迹的拥有者或持有人的责任，尤其适用于：开展关于该历史古迹的科学研究和记录工作；确保对古迹进行专业保护、修复和重建；为历史古迹及其周边地区的保护和维护提供最好的条件；确保对历史古迹的利用必须能够永久保护其价值；创造条件宣传和推广历史古迹的知识及其历史和文化重要性。

所有上述原则都应无条件适用于世界遗产。世界遗产地的拥有者或管理人员可向波兰国家遗产局世界遗产中心寻求支持。根据操作指南第 172 条规定，如有意对世界遗产进行较大干预或开展大规模的工作，应向世界遗产中心汇报，因为这些行为可能会影响世界遗产的突出普遍价值。

世界遗产中心还应负责下述事项：加强世界遗产地拥有者或管理人员和保护机构的能力建设；制定遗产保护状况报告；监测世界遗产；定期报告；组织开展咨询任务或专家会议和影响评估。

监测

当地政府／中央政府／机构为古迹建立的档案记录和开展的各类实践，为有效监测世界遗产地的状况奠定了基础。尤其是，地方古迹监督员在广义上的开发和建筑保护方面，具有法律规定的自由裁量权。另外，2019 年 1 月，历史古迹总干事还对历史古迹和世界遗产展开了监测和控制活动，其目的是从国家层面改善对遗产的保护、提高个别遗产的管理效率。

参考文献

1. 联合国教科文组织保护世界文化和自然遗产公约（1972 年）.

2. 实施保护世界文化与自然遗产公约操作指南（2017 年）.

3.《历史古迹保护和维护法案》（2003 年 7 月 23 日法案，2017 年法律杂志，第 1257 项，已修订）.

4.《空间规划和地区发展法》（法律杂志 2003 年，第 80 期，第 717 项，已修订）.

5. 网址信息 https://whc.unesco.org/en/statesparties/pl.

World Cultural Heritage in Poland Protection, Conservation, Management

Barbara Furmanik[①]
National Heritage Board of Poland

Abstract:

It is important to state that Poland was among the founding states of the new established UNESCO. As the following action Poland ratified the UNESCO Convention Concerning the Protection of the World Cultural and Natural Heritage in 1976. Soon after, among the first 12 sites inscribed on the World Heritage List there were 2 sites from Poland inscribed in 1978: *Historic Centre of Kraków* and Salt Mines of Wieliczka, than 2 sites in 1979: Auschwitz Birkenau German Nazi Concentration and Extermination Camp (1940-1945) and Białowieża Forest (natural site, transboundary Poland/Belarus) , and 1 site in 1980: Historic Centre of Warsaw.

Today, after over 40 years of existence of World Heritage List, Poland has 15 properties that have been recognized as worthy of their Outstanding Universal Value, and thousands of historical monuments protected within the national register of monuments. They represent the vast diversity and richness of Polish culture and history.

Our experience in rescuing, protection, and conservation of cultural heritage has become a well-established tradition. Polish professionals from the fields of archaeology and monuments conservation are worldwide known for their knowledge, experience and devotion. They have been working for decades on only to protect Polish heritage but also all around the world.

The culmination of many years of such professional work was establishing the Centre for World Heritage in Poland and organizing the 41st session of the World Heritage Committee in Kraków in 2017.

Keywords: WH sites, conservation, protection, management, monitoring

---

① Barbara Furmanik, employee of the National Heritage Board of Poland in Warsaw since 2000. She prepared and worked for implementation of the conservation guidelines and restoration projects for many historic parks and gardens. She is also a co-author of nomination dossier for inscription the Muskauer Park on the UNESCO WH List. Since 2013 she has been working in World Heritage Unit, which deals with a wide range of work related to world heritage. Worked for the National Trust (UK) at Stowe Landscape Gardens. Additionally, received BA in the Faculty of Tourism and Recreation, with diploma concerning tourism in the WH properties.

WORLD HERITAGE IN POLAND

Poland was among the founding states of the new established UNESCO. As the following action Poland ratified the UNESCO Convention Concerning the Protection of the World Cultural and Natural Heritage in 1976, and soon after, among the first 12 sites inscribed on the World Heritage List there were 2 sites from Poland. Today, after over 40 years of existence of WH List, Poland has 15 properties that have been recognized as worthy of their Outstanding Universal Value - 14 cultural and 1 natural site; among them 3 transboundary sites:

4 historic cities

Historic Centre of Kraków (inscribed in 1978, criterion iv)

The Historic Centre of Kraków is formed by three urban ensembles: the medieval chartered City of Kraków, the Wawel Hill complex, and the town of Kazimierz (including the suburb of Stradom) . It is an outstanding examples of European urban planning, characterised by the harmonious development and accumulation of features representing all architectural styles from the early Romanesque to the Modernist periods.

Historic Centre of Warsaw (1980, ii and vi)

The reconstruction of the Old Town in Warsaw after the World War II destruction in its historic urban and architectural form was the manifestation of the care and attention taken to assure the survival of one of the most important testimonials of Polish culture. The reconstruction included the holistic recreation of the urban plan, together with the Old Town Market, townhouses, the circuit of the city walls, the Royal Castle, and important religious buildings.

Fig. 1　Aerial photo of the Old City of Zamość, 2017, author Piotr Ostrowski, © NID.

Old City of Zamość (1992, iv)

Old City of Zamość is an example of a late 16th century Central European town designed and built in accordance with Italian Renaissance theories on the creation of "ideal" cities. It is a result of a very close cooperation between the town's enlightened founder Jan Zamoyski, and the distinguished Italian architect Bernardo Morando.

Medieval Town Toruń (1997, ii and iv)

Toruń is a remarkably well preserved example of a medieval European trading and administrative centre. It provides an exceptionally complete picture of the medieval way of life. Its spatial layout is a valuable source material for research into the history of urban development in medieval Europe, and many of its buildings represent the highest achievements in medieval ecclesiastical, military, and civil brick-built architecture.

3 properties being examples of wooden architecture

Churches of Peace in Jawor and Świdnica (2001, iii, iv and vi)

The Churches of Peace located in the towns of Jawor and Świdnica are the largest timber-framed Baroque ecclesiastical buildings in Europe. They were built in the mid-17th century to a scale and complexity unknown in European wooden architecture before or since, following the provisions of the Peace of Westphalia, which concluded the Thirty Years' War in 1648.

Wooden Churches of Southern Małopolska (2003, iii and iv)

The six wooden churches represent different aspects of medieval church-building traditions in Roman

Fig. 2   Interior of the church in Binarowa, 2017, author Piotr Ostrowski, © NID.

Catholic culture. They are located in the towns and villages of Blizne, Binarowa, Dębno Podhalań skie, Haczów, Lipnica Murowana and Sękowa, which lie within the historic region of Małopolska, foothills of the northern part of the Western Carpathians.

Wooden Tserkvas of the Carpathian Region in Poland and Ukraine (transboundary) (2013, iii and iv)

The sixteen wooden tserkvas (churches) in Poland and Ukraine are examples of the once widespread Orthodox ecclesiastical timber-building tradition in the Slavic countries that survives to this day. They include Hutsul, Halych, Boyko and western Lemko types.

2 cultural landscapes

Kalwaria Zebrzydowska: the Mannerist Architectural and Park Landscape Complex and Pilgrimage Park (1999, ii and iv)

Kalwaria Zebrzydowska is a cultural landscape of great spiritual significance. Its natural setting - in which a series of symbolic places of worship relating to the Passion of Jesus Christ and the life of the Virgin Mary was laid out at the beginning of the 17ᵗʰ century - has remained virtually unchanged. It is still today a place of pilgrimage.

Muskauer Park / Park Mużakowski (transboundary with Germany) (2004, i and iv)

A landscaped park astride the Neisse River, it was created by Prince Hermann von Pückler-Muskau from 1815 to 1844. Blending seamlessly with the surrounding farmed landscape the park pioneered new approaches to landscape design and influenced the development of landscape architecture in Europe and America.

Fig. 3   View of the Polish and German parts of the park, 2017, author Piotr Ostrowski, © NID.

2 architectural ensembles

Castle of the Teutonic Order in Malbork (1997, ii, iii and iv)

This 13th century fortified monastery belonging to the Teutonic Order was substantially enlarged and embellished after 1309, when the seat of the Grand Master moved here from Venice. A particularly fine example of a medieval brick castle, it later fell into decay, but was meticulously restored in the 19th and early 20th centuries. Many of the conservation techniques now accepted as standard were evolved here.

Centennial Hall in Wrocław (2006, i, ii and iv)

The Centennial Hall, a landmark in the history of reinforced concrete architecture, was erected in 1911-1913 by the architect Max Berg as a multi-purpose recreational building, situated in the Exhibition Grounds. In form it is a symmetrical quatrefoil with a vast circular central space that can seat some 6,000 persons. The 23m-high dome is topped with a lantern in steel and glass.

Fig. 4   Aerial photo of the Centennial Hall complex, 2017, author Piotr Ostrowski, © NID.

2 industrial properties

Wieliczka and Bochnia Royal Salt Mines (1978, 2013, iv)

The deposit of rock salt in Wieliczka and Bochnia has been mined since the 13th century. This major industrial undertaking has royal status and is the oldest of its type in Europe. The site is a serial property consisting of Wieliczka and Bochnia salt mines and Wieliczka Saltworks Castle.

Tarnowskie Góry Lead-Silver-Zinc Mine and its Underground Water Management System (2017, i, ii and iv)

One of the main mining areas of central Europe, the property includes the entire underground mine with adits, shafts, galleries and other features of the water management system. Most of the property is situated underground while the surface mining topography features relics of shafts and waste heaps, as well as the remains of the 19th century steam water pumping station. Tarnowskie Góry represents a significant contribution to the global production of lead and zinc.

1 memory site

Auschwitz Birkenau, German Nazi Concentration and Extermination Camp (1940-1945) (1979, vi)

Auschwitz Birkenau, monument to the deliberate genocide of the Jews by the German Nazi regime and to the deaths of countless others, bears irrefutable evidence to one of the greatest crimes ever perpetrated against humanity. It is also a monument to the strength of the human spirit which in appalling conditions of adversity resisted the efforts of the German Nazi regime to suppress freedom and free thought and to wipe out whole races.

Fig. 5   Fragment of the former camp Auschwitz II-Birkenau, 2017, author Piotr Ostrowski, © NID.

1 natural property

Białowieża Forest (transboundary with Belarus) (1978, 1992, 2014, ix and x)

Białowieża Forest is a large forest complex located on the border between Poland and Belarus. This property includes a complex of lowland forests that are characteristics of the Central European mixed forests terrestrial ecoregion. The area has exceptionally conservation significance due to the scale of its old growth forests, which include extensive undisturbed areas where natural processes are on-going.

PROTECTION OF MONUMENTS AND CULTURAL HERITAGE

Poland for decades has well organised system of monuments protection. The main legal document in Poland that specifies the purpose, scope and forms of protection of monuments and the care for them is the *Act on protection and care of historical monuments* (Act of 23 July 2003, Journal of Laws of 2017, item 1257, as amended) . It also indicates the principles of establishment of a national programme for the protection of monuments and care of monuments and the financing of conservation, restoration and other works at the monuments, as well as the organisation of monument protection authorities.

According to the Act, a *monument* (Polish: *zabytek*) is a property (real estate) or a movable cultural item, their parts or ensemble being the work of humans, or connected with their activity, and constituting a testimony of the past epoch or event, the preservation of which is in the social interest because of historical, artistic, or scientific value.

The legal forms of protection established by the current system are:

1. Entries in the Register of Monuments - administrative actions in the field of the monuments' entry in the Register of Monuments are carried out by the Regional Monuments Inspector who, ex officio or at the request of a party (the monument's owner or user) , launches the entry procedure. The preparatory stage consists in collection of information and documentary materials meant to confirm the value of the monument for the national heritage.

2. Recognition as a national Monument of History - this status can mean any immovable monument listed in the register or a cultural park of special cultural value. The importance of national Monument of History is highlighted by the fact that it is instituted by the President of the Republic of Poland by special regulation issued at the request of the Minister of Culture and National Heritage. Obtaining this status is a necessary condition required for a monument to be nominated for the UNESCO World Heritage List.

3. Establishment of a cultural park - it protects a specific area of the cultural landscape and landscape areas with immovable monuments that are characteristic for the local tradition of building and settlement. The cultural park may be appointed and dismissed by the commune council after consulting the Regional Monuments Inspector. Parks that go beyond the area of one municipality can be established jointly by municipalities or a union of municipalities.

4. Local preservation agreement in the matter of spatial development, or in the decisions concerning localisation of public investments, building conditions, privilege to deliver road investment, localisation of railways, or consent to build a local public airport. The issues of spatial planning are regulated by the *Act on spatial planning and area development* (Journal of Laws 2003, No. 80, item 717, as amended) . Formulation and conduct of spatial policy in the municipality is its own responsibility.

Authorities and bodies responsible for monuments protection are:

The Minister of Culture and National Heritage, on behalf of whom the tasks and purview related to protection of historic monuments are exercised by the *General Conservator of Monuments*, who holds the position of Secretary or Undersecretary of State in the Ministry of Culture.

The Regional Monuments Inspector-a member of the joint provincial administration, is the first instance body, whilst the Minister of Culture is the second instance body in the matters specified in the Act and in separate regulations. The tasks of the Regional Monuments Inspector include, in particular: carrying out duties arising from the National Heritage Preservation and Protection Programme; preparing plans for financing monument preservation and protection from granted funds; maintaining the Heritage Register and Regional Heritage Inventory, and collating relevant documentation; issuing, in keeping with decisions and resolutions, licences concerning the issues specified in the Act and separate regulations; supervising and carrying out quality control of conducted conservation studies, architectural research, conservation, restoration and construction works and other activities related to monuments, as well as archaeological research; preparing provincial heritage protection plans in the event of armed conflict and crisis; promoting knowledge about monuments.

Protection of monuments, in particular, consists in taking action by the government bodies to: provide legal, organisational and financial information in order to allow permanent conservation of monuments, their development and maintenance; prevent risks that could cause damage to the monuments' value; prevent destruction and misuse of the monuments; prevent theft, loss or illicit export of monuments abroad; control the state of preservation and purpose of monuments; take into account the protection tasks in spatial planning and development and in shaping the environment.

Moreover, at the request of the General Conservator of Monuments, the Minister of Culture and National Heritage can entrust the execution of some tasks which fall within his or her remit (except for the issuing of administrative decisions) to managers of cultural institutions specialising in monument protection, for which the Minister is the organiser. The said institutions include the *National Heritage Board of Poland* (Polish: Narodowy Instytut Dziedzictwa) .

The primary objectives of the National Heritage Board of Poland are to identify, study and document heritage assets, gather information related to the historic environment, cultural landscape and cultural monuments, develop policies and strategies on historic environment conservation and raise public awareness of the historic environment, cultural landscapes and heritage assets. The Board has its headquarters in Warsaw and 16 regional offices around the country.

In the case of World Heritage properties, the Director of the National Heritage Board of Poland has a mandate to act on behalf of the General Conservator of Monuments. Within the Board, since 2007, has operated the World Heritage Unit, responsible for management plans and other matters related to World Heritage properties in Poland. Additionally, since 2014, the Centre for World Heritage in the National Heritage Board of Poland has been working, to improve conservation and management of World Heritage properties in Poland. The Centre also is designated the Polish Focal Point for World Heritage.

Although Poland ratified the UNESCO Convention Concerning the Protection of the World Cultural and Natural Heritage in 1976, only four years after its issue, in Polish legislation still there is no dedicated designation to World Heritage properties and their protection. In the *Act on protection and care of historical monuments* World Heritage status is only mentioned, in accordance to Monuments of History - obtaining this status is a necessary condition required for a monument to be nominated for the UNESCO World Heritage List.

The *Constitution of Poland* (1997) indicates, that all international agreements are binding for the national law even they are not directly implemented. Unfortunately any executive regulations and documents on protecting and maintenance of World Heritage in Poland does not exist. Therefore, in theory, the World Heritage Convention (1972) and the Operational Guidelines for the implementation of the WH Convention are applicable. In practise, however, it is much more difficult to put it in force, and convince the authorities and owners of the monument/WH site to implement in accordance to these documents.

CONSERVATION AND MANAGEMENT

Conservation, care, maintenance and safeguarding of monuments are responsibility of the owner or holder. In particular, this applies to: conducting scientific research and documentation of the monument; assuring professional conservation, restoration and construction works at the monument; providing protection and maintenance of the monument and its surroundings in the best possible condition; ensuring use of a monument in a way that ensures permanent preservation of its value; providing promotion and dissemination of knowledge on the monument and its significance for the history and culture.

In case of World Heritage all the above-mentioned principals are obligatory. The owners or managers of the WH sites can look for support of the Centre for World Heritage in the National Heritage Board of Poland. Also in accordance of para. 172 of the Operational Guidelines, any intention to undertake major interventions or work in the WH property should be reported to the Centre, as it may affect its Outstanding Universal Value.

The Centre for World Heritage is also responsible for: capacity building among the owners or managers of WH sites, and conservation authorities; preparing SOC reports; monitoring of WH properties; Periodic Reporting; organizing advisory missions or experts meetings and impact assessments.

MONITORING

The basis for most of the effective monitoring of WH sites is already in place through the established records and practices of the local and central authorities and agencies. In particular Regional Monuments Inspectors have statutory and discretionary powers in respect of any development and building conservation in its widest sense. In addition General Conservator of Monuments launch monitoring and control of Monuments of History and WH properties in January 2019. It is designed to serve the improvement of heritage protection at the national level as well as management effectiveness of individual properties.

BIBLIOGRAPHY

1. UNESCO Convention Concerning the Protection of the World Cultural and Natural Heritage (1972) .

2. Operational Guidelines for the implementation of the World Heritage Convention (2017) .

3. *Act on protection and care of historical monuments* (Act of 23 July 2003, Journal of Laws of 2017, item 1257, as amended) .

4. *Act on spatial planning and area development* (Journal of Laws 2003, No. 80, item 717, as amended) .

5. Information on the website https://whc.unesco.org/en/statesparties/pl.

龙门石窟的预防性保护

中国　龙门石窟研究院　余江宁 [①]

摘要

石窟的预防性保护，是指在石窟尚未发生大的病变之前，在风险监测、评估的基础上，有计划、主动性开展的科学保护工作。本文主要从龙门石窟的环境特征、价值特点、保护工作历程回顾、预防性保护的主要工作以及面临的困难和挑战、预防性保护工作的深化拓展和工作展望等方面对世界文化遗产龙门石窟的预防性保护工作进行探讨分析。

关键词：龙门石窟，价值特点，预防性保护，展望

龙门石窟位于洛阳市区南五公里的伊河两岸，1961 年被国务院公布为全国重点文物保护单位；1982 年，被国务院公布为首批国家级风景名胜区；2000 年 11 月被联合国教科文组织列入《世界遗产名录》。

一、龙门石窟的环境特征

1. 地理环境

龙门山系秦岭余脉熊耳山的分支，走向近东西，该山体被伊水横切，分为东西两山，形成深切峡谷，形如"门阙"。石窟区地貌上属低山、丘陵地貌，龙门山和伊河河谷是区内的主要地貌单元，峡谷两岸立壁岩体为石窟开凿和雕刻提供了优良的地理条件；西山为石窟主要洞窟所在地，西山的南段陡壁高大，崖壁的高差最大达 50m，集中雕凿了奉先寺、古阳洞等大型洞窟；北段陡壁高差约 20m，分布了摩崖三佛、宾阳三洞、潜溪寺等大型洞窟；东山石窟分布于万佛沟内，大型洞窟有擂鼓台三洞、高平郡王洞、看经寺等。

2. 地质环境

龙门石窟区岩石属于寒武纪、奥陶纪和石炭纪地层，地层层厚大；岩性为石灰岩、白云岩，主体

---

① 余江宁，男，1973 年生，安徽省潜山市人，历史学博士，时任龙门石窟研究院院长。

图 1　龙门石窟优美的环境风貌

矿物系方解石和白云石。

3.气象环境

龙门石窟区属暖温带大陆性季风气候，冬季寒冷，少雨雪，春季干旱风大，夏季炎热多雨，秋季多晴。年平均降雨量约 580mm，年平均气温 14.7℃，年平均蒸发量 1829.7mm，年平均相对湿度 64.5%。

二、龙门石窟的价值和特点

龙门石窟具有无与伦比的价值和极其崇高的遗产地位，她的价值特点集中体现在如下五个方面：

一是典型的皇家艺术风范。作为北魏晚期和盛唐时期皇室贵族发愿造像最为集中的区域，龙门石窟的造像风格、审美风尚、美学理念和雕刻技艺引领着当时社会的雕刻艺术潮流，特别是"中原风格"和"大唐风范"两种划时代的造像艺术，在龙门臻于成熟后逐渐辐射影响至全国乃至东亚其他地区。

二是史诗般的文化内涵。龙门石窟现存 2345 座窟龛、10 万余尊造像、2800 余块碑刻题记，保存有反映古代建筑、雕刻、音乐、舞蹈、服饰、书法、医药、地名、职官、中西交通和文化交流等方面的珍贵资料，是研究北魏晚期至盛唐时期历史、政治、经济、宗教、文化的极好佐证。

三是集众多佛教宗派之大成。龙门石窟造像内容广涉佛教众多宗派，如净土宗、华严宗、三阶教、禅宗以及密宗等等；除佛教外，道教、景教等在龙门也有体现。

四是代表中国石刻艺术的最高峰。龙门石窟规模宏大、雕刻精美、蕴涵丰富，展现了人类杰出的艺术创造力，是世界上最伟大的古典艺术宝库之一。

五是天然形胜、风光秀美。龙门石窟东西两山对峙，中间伊水北流，远望形如天然门阙，历史上是拱卫京城的重要关隘之一，也是文人骚客留恋吟咏之地，有"伊阙""龙门"之称。

世界遗产委员会对龙门石窟的评价为："龙门地区的石窟和佛龛展现了中国北魏晚期至唐代四百余年间，最具规模和最为优秀的造型艺术。这些详实描述佛教中宗教题材的艺术作品，代表了中国石刻

图 2　美轮美奂的龙门石窟石刻艺术

艺术的最高峰"。这高度说明了龙门石窟的重要价值，应该受到全人类的重视和保护。

三、龙门石窟的保护工作历程回顾

1. 成立保护管理机构（上世纪五十年代到七十年代初）

20 世纪 50 年代，龙门石窟的保护工作开始引起国内专家和管理部门的重视。1951 年成立"龙门森林古迹保护委员会"，1953 年成立"龙门文物保管所"，1961 年国家科委将龙门石窟的"围岩崩塌、洞窟漏水、雕刻品风化"三大病害列入十年科研规划。1965 年龙门文物保管所成立保护组，进行气象、洞窟观察，筹建保护技术实验室。

2. 石窟抢险加固（从七十年代初至八十年代中期）

从 1971 年开始，龙门石窟连续进行了一系列的抢险加固工程。1971 至 1974 年实施奉先寺加固工

图 3　奉先寺卢舍那大佛修复前　　图 4　奉先寺卢舍那大佛修复后

程，将岩土工程中的锚杆加固、化学灌浆技术首次应用到大型石窟寺的维修保护工程中。经过这一阶段的加固维修，有效地防止了石窟围岩的倒塌崩落。

3. 石窟综合治理工程（从八十年代中期至九十年代）

1986年，制定了"龙门石窟保护维修规划"，实施东西两山的全面整治工程。1987年正式开始实施，前后历时5年，加固了大部分洞窟、岩体，基本解决了龙门石窟的稳定性问题，洞窟渗漏在一定时期内得到改善；修建了保护围墙、游览栈道，奠定了龙门石窟作为文物保护区和文物游览区的基本框架，基本完成了以解决石窟安全稳定为主的大规模的抢救性保护工作。

图5　龙门石窟综合治理工程施工现场

4. 申报世界文化遗产至今

2000年成功申报世界文化遗产后，龙门石窟研究院连续开展了"联合国教科文组织龙门石窟保护修复工程""中意合作双窟修复工程"等国际合作项目，取得了重要的科研成果，特别是一些先进的保护理念和完善的保护修复计划，为不可移动石质文物修复积累了宝贵经验。

图6　龙门石窟保护修复工程三方专家会议

近十余年来，龙门石窟持续开展了包括洞窟修复、渗漏水综合治理、遗产监测体系建设、石窟保存状况调查、保护材料研究、保护管理规划和管理条例修订等石窟保护方面的主要工作。

四、石窟预防性保护的主要工作

主要包括如下六个方面的工作：

1. 龙门石窟的监测

对石窟文物本体状况、本体病害以及石窟保存环境的监测是石窟保护最基础的工作，它可以使我们了解石窟的保存状况和变化情况，以及与这些变化相关的环境因素；同时，监测也作为一种研究手段，针对石窟特种病害采取的研究性监测，可以探究石窟文物之所以发生病害变化的原因，了解病害发生发展的趋势，进而提出相应的保护方案和修复措施。

图 7　双窑修复工程现场

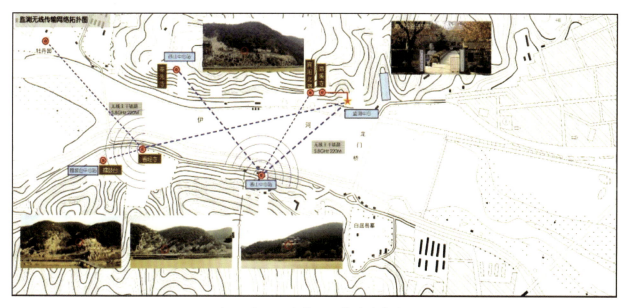

图 8　龙门石窟监测预警体系布局图

龙门石窟的监测始于 20 世纪 60 年代，2000 年以后，龙门石窟研究院逐步升级和完善了监测系统。购置了大气质量连续自动监测仪器，对大气中二氧化硫、氮氧化物的含量进行自动监测；建立了两个自动气象环境监测站,监测大气温湿度、降雨量、蒸发量、风向风速等;建立了水环境监测系统监测地下水位变化和泉水、河水变化。目前正在运行的监测预警体系始于 2013 年,分四期实施,2017年完工。基本构建起石窟文物与石窟环境监测的框架,并最终实现与省、国家监测平台的对接。其中监测的核心内容是对龙门石窟区域环境、洞窟微环境、文物本体病害、大气环境质量等进行连续自动监测,通过无线传输汇入监测平台。

图 9　龙门石窟气象观测场　　　　　　　　图 10　雕像风化监测

　　龙门石窟重点区域环境和重点洞窟文物本体病害是体系监测的重点,区域环境监测内容包含:石窟区域环境温湿度、风向、风速、大气降水、光强、土壤含水率、震动、河水、泉水等;文物本体病害监测包括:洞窟环境温湿度、洞窟渗漏水、凝结水、风化、岩体稳定性等(见表一)。根据龙门石窟自身特点和需求,设计了风化、渗水等方面的研究性监测内容。例如,利用红外成像技术对洞窟渗漏水进行监测,突破了传统照相等手段的局限性,不仅能够全天候不间断监测记录,而且可以近似模拟渗漏水量,满足了定量监测的需求;利用高精度工业摄像机对典型风化雕刻进行连续监测,长期观察风化状况,进行风化的定量研究。

表一　龙门石窟监测体系各期实施情况汇总

时间	监测位置	监测内容	监测指标	传感器数量	指标数
一期 2013 年 11 月开始	万佛洞和奉先寺两个监测点位	分为环境(综合气象、土壤含水、微环境、噪声)、稳定性、渗漏水、风化等 4 个监测类型	温度、湿度、风速、风向、气压、雨量、总辐射、壁面温度、土壤水分、噪声、裂隙、倾角、渗漏水、紫外线、风化	29	35
二期 2014 年 4 月开始	潜溪寺、宾阳北洞、万佛洞、极南洞、牡丹园、擂鼓台、看经寺、白园等 8 个监测点位	分为环境(综合气象、土壤含水、酸雨、空气质量)、微环境、稳定性、渗漏水、风化、凝结水、振动等 7 个监测类型	温度、湿度、风速、风向、气压、雨量、总辐射、壁面温度、土壤水分、CO_2、SO_2、NO_2、PM2.5、负氧离子、裂隙、倾斜、渗漏水、风化、凝结水、PH	50	76

时间	监测位置	监测内容	监测指标	传感器数量	指标数
三期 2015 年 11 月开始	西山入口、监测中心、潜溪寺、宾阳洞、敬善寺、奉先寺、皇甫公窟、西山路洞、极南洞、西山顶部、西山码头、伊河水、东山入口、西方净土龛、千手千眼观音龛、看经寺等 16 个监测点位	分为环境（地下水位、水质）、微环境、稳定性、渗漏水、风化、游客量等 6 个监测类型	温度、湿度、壁面温度、地下水位、PH、电导率、溶解氧	54	56
四期 2016 年 11 月开始	潜溪寺、宾阳中洞、万佛洞、奉先寺、西山南北侧、牡丹园、伊河水、擂鼓台、看经寺、白园、东山南北侧等 11 个监测点位	分为环境（蒸发量、水位、CO_2 等）、渗漏水、振动、凝结水等 4 个监测类型	温度、湿度、CO_2、蒸发量、水位、渗漏水、凝结水、震动	25	27

在众多监测项目和指标中，洞窟的渗漏水、危岩体（裂隙）与石窟的安全性、稳定性关系最为密切，直接关系到石窟保护计划的制定和保护工程的设计安排，是石窟寺预防性保护的前提要素。

图 11 潜溪寺裂缝计安装现场

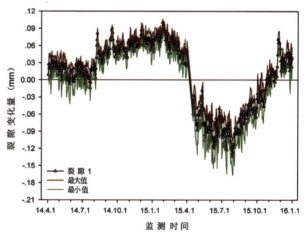

图 12 潜溪寺裂隙 1 日平均变化量与波动范围

以潜溪寺为例：龙门石窟潜溪寺位于龙门西山，自北端开始的第一个大型洞窟，同时也是龙门石窟大型洞窟中病害最为严重的洞窟之一。针对石窟病害的主要原因，即石窟岩体的变形和长期渗漏水作用，重点监测了洞窟岩体的变形和渗流状态及其变化，内容包括石窟岩体内部水平位移、石窟岩体裂隙开度、石窟岩体内部渗透水压力、渗水流量等。

针对岩体裂隙，在潜溪寺内外安置裂缝计 3 个，标注为裂隙 1、裂隙 2、裂隙 3，分别位于潜溪寺洞顶东侧、潜溪寺洞顶东北角和潜溪寺洞口北侧。通过对潜溪寺的裂隙和渗漏水监测，可以评估洞窟病害的变化、验证保护工程的效果，为潜溪寺的长期保护提供依据。

2. 龙门石窟保存状况调查

龙门石窟区岩石属于寒武纪、奥陶纪和石炭纪地层；岩性为石灰岩、白云岩，主体矿物系方解石和白云石，其力学强度适中，具有较强抗风化能力，同时宜于开凿。但是层面裂隙、构造裂隙、卸荷裂隙发育，主导着石窟渗漏水病害的发展；石灰岩的可溶蚀性，又决定了石窟溶蚀病害的发生。

龙门石窟从开凿之初就与各种地质病害相伴相生，地质病害的发生发展和石窟的保存状况息息相关。2013 年以后，为全面认识龙门石窟的保存现状，完善洞窟的保存状况档案，启动了龙门石窟保存现状调查工作，主要从地质病害的角度，对每个洞窟的保存状况进行记录、评价，以期为龙门石窟的保护规划服务，为以后的洞窟地质病害治理提供依据。调查将龙门石窟东西两山近 2 公里长范围内的洞窟按照不同地层结构分成 7 个区段进行，内容包括洞窟裂隙、渗水、岩溶、危岩体、生物病害、风化病害等，调查各洞窟主要病害类型、病害发育程度及形成的初步机理，对病害的趋势进行预测，对洞窟保存状况等级进行划分，并提出应对措施。

图 13　龙门石窟病害现状调查现场

在洞窟完整性调查方面：洞窟本体完整性主要指洞窟内造像、题刻等的完整性，是衡量石窟保存状态的重要指标；洞窟形制完整性与本体完整性具有一定相关性，前者是后者的基础，但部分洞窟形制完整的洞窟，却存在比较严重的本体完整性问题（见表二、三）。

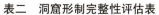

表二　洞窟形制完整性评估表

编号	命名	定义	典型洞窟
A	完整	洞窟整体形态完好，极易辨别洞窟组成与形制，一般窟檐、窟门、窟顶等关键受力部位基本完好。	潜溪寺、宾阳三洞、奉先寺等
B	局部破损	洞窟局部破坏，但整体形态可辨，极易恢复洞窟原始形制，主要破坏为窟檐、窟门、窟顶等部位。	大部分洞窟
C	缺失	洞窟一侧及以上坍塌破坏，洞窟原始形制毁坏，洞窟进深等关键参数难以取得等。	擂鼓台南洞、西方净土变龛等
D	残存	洞窟位置可辨，但基本不存在文物本体。	

表三　本体完整性评估表

编号	命名	定义	典型洞窟
A	保存完好	洞窟形制 A 或 B 类，洞窟内造像与雕刻较完整。主体造像的头、手大部分完好，造像人物身份容易辨认。	潜溪寺、宾阳三洞、奉先寺等
B	基本完好	洞窟形制 A 或 B 类，造像分布位置清晰，主要破坏部位为头、手，身体大部完好。主佛身体完好，其余造像整体盗凿或者整体缺失数量少于 1/3。	
C	损毁中等	洞窟形制 C 类，均属于此类。洞窟形制好于 C 类的，主要根据造像完整性进行评估，主佛头、身破损，其余造像整体缺失数量大于 1/3。	千手观音
D	严重损毁	洞窟形制属于 D 类的，均属于此类。好于 D 类的，根据造像完整评估。主佛严重破损，或者风化后弥漫不清，大部分造像破坏严重。	擂鼓台北洞
E	遗迹	已经不存在文物本体，但在考古资料帮助下，可以大致辨认出原为洞窟。	

　　洞窟的保存状况在不同的地质条件中的差异明显，石窟的状况固然受后期人为作用干预影响（盗凿、破坏、保护工程等），但地质条件仍然是控制龙门石窟保存状态的关键因素，主要控制因素为地层岩性和地质构造条件（见表四）。

表四　不同地层岩性本体保护评估表

单位：%

类型	保存完好	基本完好	损毁中等	严重损毁	遗迹
凤山组	7.21	22.95	25.57	7.87	36.39
崮山组	0.00	10.53	0.00	0.00	89.47
张夏组	13.14	43.20	22.25	5.80	15.62
徐庄组	2.60	18.20	29.20	24.40	25.60

3. 龙门石窟地质灾害调查研究

龙门石窟目前正在进行区域地质灾害调查的研究工作。在龙门石窟区域，地质灾害造成的洞窟渗水病害、风化、岩体稳定性、山体滑落、溶蚀等病害严重威胁着文物的安全；另一方面，龙门石窟每年的游客量居于全国石窟之首，地质灾害造成的岩体开裂、脱落时有发生，对密集游人的安全形成了严重的安全隐患。通过全面调查和评估龙门石窟地质灾害的状况，可以为编制龙门石窟地质灾害防治工程方案，做好地质灾害的预防提供有力支持。主要研究内容概括如下：

1）危岩体调查评估

在已有研究工作基础上，对龙门石窟区域进行更为详细的地质灾害调查，绘制高精度岩石地层剖面图，绘制工程地质立面图；对地质灾害相关的危岩体进行调查，绘制危岩体剖面图，并对危岩体进行稳定性分析；对松动块石进行调查，并绘制相关图件，总结该区域的地质灾害状况。

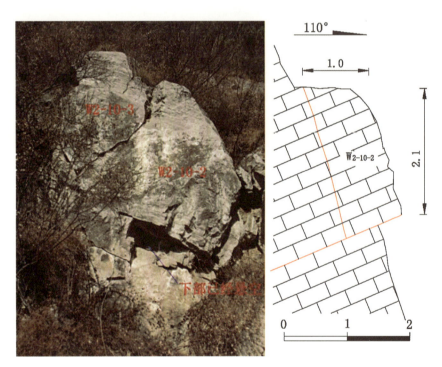

图 14　龙门石窟危岩体调查

2）建立地灾数据库

对龙门石窟的地质灾害相关因素岩体裂隙、岩溶、山体滑塌、水文地质、风化、渗漏水等进行详细调查，按照不同岩性进行岩石的矿物成分、化学成分、物理性质测定，结合不同岩性分布区域的裂隙发育同岩溶状况和发育程度的控制关系，建立岩石地层数据资料数据库，评估地质灾害发生规律和破坏性。

3）编制防灾预案

根据前期调查成果，可以科学高效的圈定龙门石窟地质灾害发生的危险区域及其诱发因素，了解地质灾害在龙门石窟的发展演化；掌握龙门石窟地质灾害的分布和发生规律，为龙门石窟地质灾害的综合治理提供科学有效的支持，最大限度减小地质灾害的影响。

4. 龙门石窟的保养维护

《中国文物古迹保护准则》第 29 条明确说明：日常保养是及时化解外力侵害可能造成损伤的预防性措施，适用于任何对象。石窟寺也像其他文物一样，保护要从预防做起，保养维护是预防性保护理念的根本体现。

龙门石窟的保养维护工作主要内容包括：

1）危石积尘清理

坚持制度化的杂草危石清除、积尘清扫工作。及时的杂草清理，消除杂草灌木对洞窟雕刻品以及围岩的自然破坏作用；对窟内体量较大的佛像表面进行积尘清扫，避免其带来的吸湿、板结、吸附有害气体以及视觉改变等问题。

图 15 龙门石窟奉先寺保养维护现场

2）保护设施的维护

对已有窟檐、雨篷平台进行保养维护，排水沟清理与修补等，确保其发挥作用。近年来主要对宾阳洞、摩崖三佛的雨篷、石牛溪保护窟檐平台实施了清理、裂隙灌浆加固封堵、重新铺设防渗层等保障措施；对潜溪寺、奉先寺顶部等排水沟采取了定期清理碎石、砌补加固边坡、修补挡水墙等措施。

3）露天雕刻品及其围岩的保养维护

龙门石窟仅西山南北长 1 公里，洞窟分布在几米到数十米的岩壁上，有计划地、分区段搭设脚手架对石窟进行细致检查，对发现的问题或隐患利用成熟的技术手段因地制宜地进行及时的处理，主要包括：(1)表层裂隙封堵、灌浆加固；(2)小体量危岩体粘接归位；(3)露天雕刻品的修复；(4)坍塌窟龛的顶、底部的必要部分进行试验性修补，保护窟内雕刻品。已经维护处理过的区段如西山的摩崖三佛区域、莲花洞区域、奉先寺区域、极南洞区域，东山的二莲花洞区域等效果良好。

图 16　露天雕刻品的保养维护前　　　　　　　　图 17　露天雕刻品的保养维护后

图 18　露天碑刻加装保护性窟檐前后对比

通过这些工作，积累了一定的经验，也遇到了一些疑惑和问题，例如如何建立保养维护的标准化操作规范、保养维护工作内容的取舍、保养维护如何与其他保护工程有机结合起来等，有待于在今后工作过程中去解决。

5. 编制洞窟考古报告

编写系统、客观、科学的石窟寺考古报告，全面、详实的记录和保留文化遗产信息，既是石窟寺首要的学术工作，又是传承和弘扬好中华历史文化的迫切需要。正如著名考古学家宿白先生指出的：编写洞窟考古报告，是当前石窟研究的首要工作。

石窟档案和以此为基础的石窟寺考古报告的编写是全面记录石窟信息的重要方式，也是石窟长久保护的基础工作。编写龙门石窟这样遗存洞窟数量大、遗迹现象复杂的石窟寺考古报告，是一项长期和艰巨的工作，为便于工作并保证各期工作的延续性，将东、西两山划分为若干区段，按照东山从南至北、西山从北至南的顺序分期逐步实施。

图19 著名考古学家宿白先生亲临龙门石窟指导考古报告编写工作

在著名考古学家、北京大学资深教授宿白先生的高度关注、亲自指导下，历经十三载的艰辛和接续努力，《龙门石窟考古报告——东山擂鼓台区》于2018年4月由科学出版社正式出版发行。这是进入二十一世纪以来，中国人自己对大型石窟寺编写科学系统考古报告的一次重要探索和生动实践，考古报告编写过程中，在团队组织、记录方式类型、使用的科技手段、报告编排体例及其不同的记录形成的成果在报告中的学术作用等方面的探索，丰富了石窟寺考古的理论和方法，为各地区石窟群运用考古学的方法，结合本地区石窟寺的具体实际，全面、客观、系统、科学地记录相关遗迹、编写考古报告提供了有益的参考和借鉴。同时，也是龙门石窟研究史上首次在科学考古发掘基础上形成的窟前遗址和洞窟遗存有机统一、系统完整的石窟考古报告，为国内国际学界研究龙门乃至中国石窟寺构筑了资料平台，推动了龙门石窟研究的深化和升华。

图 20 《龙门石窟考古报告——东山擂鼓台区》出版

6. "数字龙门"建设

龙门石窟研究院自 2005 年开始开展"龙门石窟三维数字化工程",经过十多年的现场扫描,至今已完成 80% 窟龛的数据采集工作,具备了建立龙门石窟数字档案的基础条件,并对部分洞窟进行了三维建模和应用展示,通过数字记录的方法在文物的研究、保护、展示以及文化衍生品等方面提供依据,加快了龙门石窟利用新科技进行文物保护和宣传展示的进程。

特别是在文物保护方面,利用三维建模,可以方便快捷的在模型上标示出地质病害,对了解各洞窟主要病害类型和病害发育程度及趋势进行预测,为保护工作提供了更为简便的方法和应对措施。

此外,在三维数字应用推广方面,龙门石窟研究院进行了有益的探索和尝试:

1)虚拟复原

2005 年流失海外回归我国的古阳洞高树龛佛首,通过数字化技术将其身首虚拟复原。在虚拟修复

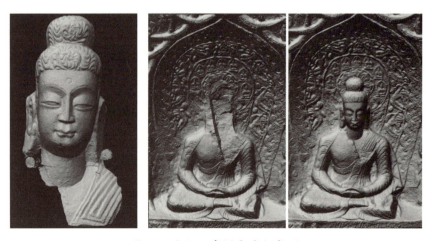

图 21 古阳洞高树龛虚拟复原

过程中，综合现存部分的几何信息以及其包含的对象属性信息，结合文物专家意见和文献的记载，最后生成虚拟复原图像，完美再现了高树龛的艺术价值。

2）互动体验

万佛洞 VR 是龙门石窟第一个虚拟现实项目，不仅实现了在洞窟内自由行走，还具备了一些操作体验功能。龙门石窟大部分洞窟属于半开放状态，通过这种方式，可以近距离观察洞窟内每一处细节。

图 22 万佛洞 VR 体验

3）文化创意

根据三维数据，可以研发出很多创意产品，促进龙门石窟的文化传播，提高龙门石窟的影响力。龙门石窟研究院与浙江大学文化遗产研究院合作进行陈抟十字卷碑和古阳洞北壁四龛数据采集和 3D

图 23 "数字龙门"研讨会

打印，以满足当前新形势下龙门石窟展示工作的需求；同时与洛阳龙章文化传播有限公司合作进行龙门二十品数字化互动展示项目，不仅展示了中国的北魏时期高超的书法技艺，而且寓教于乐，让观众在互动参与中更好的了解龙门二十品。

五、龙门石窟预防性保护面临的困难和挑战

龙门石窟的预防性保护工作虽然在实践中逐步丰富和不断提高，但依然存在诸多的困难和挑战：

1. 石窟寺监测体系有待完善

监测体系已经初步建立，开展了文物本体保护状况、文物环境的连续的系统性的监测，监测的技术和方法上也有所创新，并在此基础上开展了一些病害机理、工程效果等与监测相关的研究，但是整体监测体系的运行远不成熟，甚至有些问题才刚刚显现。比如监测项目的目的性、有效性问题，表现在有些项目的针对性不强；监测结果的解读、使用问题，震动监测的数据量大，专业性强，解读困难。风化监测的周期长，表征有难度；监测标准的制定滞后，预警值界定有待进一步的研究；监测设备的更新维护是长期的问题，存在人员、资金上的局限等。

2. 石窟寺的防护设施有待提升

石窟寺的附属设施作为物理防护手段，相比较化学保护方法，安全性上具有优势，例如龙门石窟修建的窟檐、导排水沟等，修建时间有些可以追溯到开窟的年代，沿用至今仍可发挥保护石窟的作用。但是往往因为一些设计上的不足，使得对窟檐等附属设施的合理性存在一些质疑，表现在影响洞窟微环境、影响岩体稳定、影响文物景观环境等，这些完全可以通过更加合理、完善的设计，来消除或减弱。在龙门石窟风化较严重区段修建窟檐等防护附属设施，防止、减缓区域内文物的劣化，是最直接有效的方式，比如在莲花洞至唐字洞段、千手千眼龛至西方净土变龛、擂鼓台三洞区域段、看经寺区域等，只需在修建设计时全面考虑其对石窟文物本体、微环境以及石窟景观等的影响，趋利避害，就可以更好地发挥其保护作用。

3. 石窟寺管理层面的保护与控制乏力

石窟寺和环境是紧密结合体，不只是自然环境，人文社会环境对石窟寺的影响也日趋深刻而全面。作为优质的人文资源，石窟寺大多地处风光优美的自然环境当中，越来越成为旅游市场的热点，从荒郊野外的历史遗迹逐渐成为游客众多的旅游胜地，甚至会逐渐变成城市盆景。龙门石窟与城市中心的距离，在教科书中的离城 13.5 公里，已经缩短至 5 公里，与城市的界限正变得模糊。社会需求既是文物保护的初衷和动力，也与文物保护的客观要求存在矛盾，因此从石窟寺的预防性保护角度考量，社会管理层面的提升不容忽视。

4. 保护技术遭遇瓶颈

石窟病害的治理遇到了科研技术瓶颈，亟需进行科研攻关，如保护加固材料及施工工艺研究、防风化治理等，特别是后者，已经到了刻不容缓的地步。

5. 保护机构和专业人才力量亟待加强补充

目前，无论是为应对石窟病害治理，还是为加强预防性保护工作，最终达到长期保护的目的，都亟需加强保护机构和专业人才队伍的建设。

图 24　游客如织的龙门石窟

六、龙门石窟预防性保护工作的深化和拓展

对龙门石窟而言，预防性保护理念并不是突然之间产生的，是在抢救性保护工作的经验和积累上发展而来，且抢救性保护与预防性保护是长期并存的一种状态，只不过不同时期会有所侧重；再者，预防性保护应当包含技术性保护和管理性保护两个层面，技术性保护是核心，管理性保护是保障；其次，预防性保护的各项工作需平衡推动发展，缺一不可。仅从石窟预防性保护理念出发，其所涵盖的工作内容应当包括：

1. 石窟保存状况调查与评估

主要内容包括，对石窟本体以及石窟赋存的自然山体的现状、病害发育状况等，进行科学调查和等级评估。

2. 石窟与环境的监测

进一步完善石窟寺监测体系，特别是石窟与环境的常规性监测、风化等病害的长期监测，以及岩体稳定等病害的预警监测、病害机理的研究性监测和保护工程的有效性监测等。

3. 附属保护设施的建设和有效性保障

适当的窟檐、防水雨棚、排水沟、挡水墙、栈道等保护性附属设施建设，以及定期的维护，保证其有效发挥作用。

图 25　地质雷达监测　　　　　　　　　　图 26　洞窟渗水监测

4. 石窟的日常巡视和保养维护

制度化的巡查和规范化的保养维护，及时发现并处理石窟病变，防止进一步的劣化发生。

图 27　窟檐及窟顶排水设施　　　　　　图 28　奉先寺保养维护

5. 石窟重大病害的及时保护和修复

有计划地开展洞窟、岩体加固的保护工程，残损文物必要的修复工程，以解决石窟稳定和展示的根本问题。

6. 石窟数字化档案的建立

建立石窟数字化的完整档案，记录和保存石窟保护的现状。

图 29 潜溪寺渗漏水治理工程

图 30 擂鼓台综合治理工程

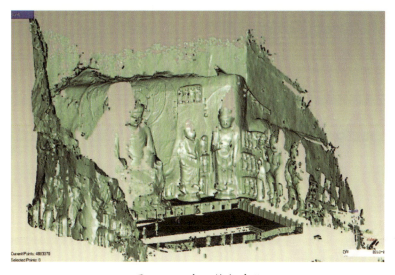

图 31 石窟三维数字化

7. 自然灾害的保护预案

针对突发地质灾害、极端天气、洪水等非常规事件，要有有效的预警机制和应对方案。

图 32 洪水灾害

8. 安全保卫

杜绝人为因素破坏的发生。

9. 规划、管理条例等社会环境的控制

保证保护管理规划、条例的适用性、有效性，协调文物管理与社会民生、旅游、经济建设的互动关系。

石窟预防性保护理念是为了使我们对石窟保护面临的目标和任务更加明确，在此基础上建立健全预防性保护工作的框架，其后深入了解石窟文物病害的发生、发展及变化规律，制定评价标准，研究石窟文物风险防范与控制技术，减缓或降低各类风险带来的危害，进而科学构建石窟文物风险监测与评估体系，实现对石窟保护管理的综合评估、全程管控。

七、龙门石窟预防性保护工作展望

展望未来，龙门石窟的预防性保护工作依然任重道远，防风化材料的科研攻关和龙门石窟大卢舍那像龛保护性建筑设施的修建是重中之重。

1. 防风化材料的科研攻关

在文物保护技术中，保护材料及其工艺是最为重要的技术之一，制约着我国石质文物保护工作的发展。龙门石窟研究院和中国地质大学（武汉）经过多年合作攻关，取得了相关科研成果，针对龙门石窟

图 33　露天碑刻风化

特殊的灌浆要求，研究出以偏高领土为主料的新型环保无机灌浆材料 PC20-10，目前已在大足石刻等重要石窟推广应用，效果良好，但是露天石刻的防风化材料研究进展缓慢。龙门石窟一千五百多年来受风吹、雨淋、日晒等自然原因和人为破坏等影响，造像表面风化剥落、缺失、裂隙、粉化等病害普遍存在，尤其以奉先寺以南至极南洞区段风化最为严重，亟待修复加固和保护。加强国际合作，深入研究风化机理，开展表层加固与修复技术试验研究，积极探索改善露天石刻保存状态的新方法新思路。

2. 奉先寺保护性窟檐建设

1963 年第七期《文物》刊载的《闲话文物建筑的重修与维护》中，著名建筑大师梁思成先生专门谈到龙门奉先寺修建保护性建筑设施的问题："奉先寺卢舍那佛一组大像原来是有木构楼阁保护的，但不知从什么时候起（推测甚至可能从会昌灭法时），就已经被毁……但今天，我们不能让这组中国雕刻史中最重要的杰作之一继续被大自然损蚀下去，必须设法保护，不使再受日晒雨淋。给它做一些掩盖是必要的。"如今，时间已经过去了将近 60 年，梁思成先生的愿望还没有实现，这项工作仍然面临着很多困难，这是我们的责任和重点要解决好的问题之一。

图 34 龙门石窟奉先寺

八、结语

石窟寺的抢救性保护和预防性保护两个概念都具积极的现实意义，在经历过抢救性保护阶段之后，石窟寺预防性保护无疑是更积极的认识和态度。"科学保护、预防为主、改善环境、最小介入"，通过创造一个适宜的最佳保存环境，最终达到长期保护的目的。

"保护固态、传承活态、发展业态"。龙门石窟研究院作为龙门石窟的守门人，肩负着龙门石窟保护的重任，我们愿意和全世界共同努力，携手做好龙门石窟这一珍贵文化遗产的预防性保护工作。同时，龙门石窟研究院将以拥抱世界的胸怀，着力建成世界一流石窟科研机构、奋力争当文化遗产保护典范，为洛阳国际历史文化旅游名城建设、河南省打造全国文化高地，乃至为文化强国建设，做出龙门石窟应有的担当和贡献！

Preventive Conservation of Longmen Grottoes

Yu Jiangning[①]

China Institute of Longmen Grottoes

Abstract:

The preventive conservation of grottoes refers to the scientific conservation carried out systematically and proactively on the basis of risk monitoring and assessment in order to prevent grottoes from developing major diseases. This paper chiefly discussed and analyzed the preventive conservation of the world heritage site Longmen Grottoes in terms of environmental characteristics, value features, review of conservation efforts, the chief content of preventive conservation of Longmen Grottoes, as well as difficulties and challenges, the deepening of preventive conservation and outlook.

Keywords: Longmen Grottoes, value characteristics, preventive conservation, outlook

Longmen Grottoes, situated on the banks of the Yi River, five kilometers south of Luoyang City, was designated by the State Council as an important heritage site under state protection in 1961. In 1982, it was designated as one of the first national tourist attractions by the State Council. In November 2000, it was inscribed by UNESCO on the List of World Heritage Sites.

I. Environmental Characteristics of Longmen Grottoes

1. Geographical environment

Longmen Mountains is a branch of Xiong'er Mountain which is part of Qinling Mountains, running in an east and west direction. The mountains are divided by the Yi River into the East Mountain and West Mountain, forming a deep canyon like a "tower". The grotto area is characterized by a low mountain and hilly landform. The Longmen Mountains and Yi River Valley are the principal geomorphic units in the area. The cliff rock on both sides of the valley provides excellent geographical conditions for grotto digging and carving; the caverns

---

[①] Yu Jiangning, male, born in 1973, native of Qianshan, Anhui province, Ph.D. in history. He was the director of the Institute of Longmen Grottoes.

are chiefly concentrated in West Mountain, which has sheer cliffs in the south, with a height difference of up to 50m. Large caverns dug include Fengxian Temple and Guyang Cave; the steep cliff in the north has a height difference of some 20m, and has large caverns including Three Buddhists Carved on Cliff, Binyang Cave, and Qianxi Temple. East Mountain Grottoes are distributed in Wanfo Valley, which has such large caverns as Drum Beating Cave, Gaoping County Prince Cave, and Kanjing Temple.

Fig.1   Beautiful landscape of Longmen Grottoes

2. Geological environment

The rocks in Longmen Grottoes belong to the Cambrian, Ordovician and Carboniferous strata, with their thick stratum; the rocks are limestone and dolomite, and the main minerals are calcite and dolomite.

3. Meteorological environment

The Longmen Grottoes area has a warm temperate continental monsoon climate with little rain and snow in cold winter, high wind in dry spring, hot and rainy summer, and mostly a fine autumn. The annual average precipitation is roughly 580mm, the annual average temperature is 14.7°C, the annual average evaporation capacity is 1829.7mm, and the annual average relative humidity is 64.5%.

II. Value and Characteristics of Longmen Grottoes

Longmen Grottoes are blessed with unrivalled value and a noble status as a heritage site, with its value and characteristics manifested the following five aspects:

One is the typical royal art style. As the best embodiment of statues of royal aristocrats expressing wishes in the late Northern Wei Dynasty and the Tang Dynasty, Longmen Grottoes led the way in carving art at the time in terms of statue style, aesthetics trend and ideas and sculpting skills. In particular, "Central Plain Style" and "Tang Style" epoch-making art gradually exerted an influence in the whole country and even other areas of East Asia following its maturity.

The second is the epic cultural connotations. Longmen Grottoes contain 2,345 shrines, over 100,000 statues, and over 2,800 pieces of inscriptions. These rare artefacts reflect the ancient architecture, sculpture, music, dance, costume, calligraphy, medicine, place names, officials, Chinese and Western transport and cultural exchanges, which bear witness to the history, politics, economy, religion and culture from the late Northern Wei Dynasty to the Tang Dynasty.

The third is the collection of many Buddhist schools. Longmen Grottoes statues involve many schools of Buddhism, such as Pure Land school, Hua-yen school, three stages school, Zen Buddhism and Esoteric Buddhism. In addition to Buddhism, Taoism and Nestorianism are also reflected in Longmen Grottoes.

Fourth, it stands for the acme of Chinese stone carving art. Large-scale Longmen Grottoes with its exquisite statues and rich connotations showcase the outstanding artistic creativity of mankind. It is one of the world's greatest treasure troves of classical art.

The fifth is the grand and beautiful landscape. The east and west mountains of Longmen Grottoes sit opposite to each other, with the Yi River running northward in the middle. Viewed from far away, it is a natural watchtower. It is historically one of the important passes for defending the capital. With inscriptions and poems written by the literati, it is known as the "gate of the Yi River" and "Longmen".

Fig.2　Gorgeous Longmen Grottoes' stone carving art

The World Heritage Committee comments on Longmen Grottoes as follows: "The grottoes and niches of Longmen contain the largest and most impressive collection of Chinese art of the late Northern Wei and Tang Dynasties (316-907) . These works, entirely devoted to the Buddhist religion, represent the high point of Chinese stone carving." This amply demonstrates the important value of Longmen Grottoes which should be valued and conserved by mankind.

III. Review of Longmen Grottoes' conservation work

1. Establish a conservation management organization (from the 1950s to the early 1970s)

In the 1950s, the conservation of Longmen Grottoes began to attract the attention of Chinese experts and authorities. The "Longmen Forest Historical Site Protection Committee" was established in 1951. The "Longmen Cultural Relics Protection and Management Office" was established in 1953. In 1961, the State Scientific and Technological Commission included Longmen Grottoes' three major diseases "wall rock collapse, cavern leakage, and weathering of carved works" in the ten-year scientific research plan. In 1965, the Longmen Cultural Relics Protection and Management Office founded the conservation group to perform meteorological and cavern observations and established the conservation technology lab.

2. Rescue and reinforcement of grottoes (from the 1970s to the mid-1980s)

Since 1971, a whole slew of rescue and reinforcement projects have been carried out for Longmen Grottoes. From 1971 to 1974, the reinforcement project of Fengxian Temple was implemented, and anchor rod reinforcement and chemical grouting technology in geotechnical engineering were applied to the maintenance and conservation of large grotto temple for the first time. After this stage of reinforcement, the collapse of surrounding rock of grottoes has been effectively prevented.

Fig.3 Vairocana Buddha at Fengxian Temple before restoration **Fig.4 Vairocana Buddha at Fengxian Temple after restoration**

3. Comprehensive governance of grottoes (from the mid-1980s to the 1990s)

In 1986, the "Plan of Conservation and Maintenance of Longmen Grottoes" was formulated for a comprehensive renovation of the east and west mountains. For 5 years since 1987, most of caverns and rock mass were reinforced; the stability problem of Longmen Grottoes was basically solved, and cave leakage was improved in a certain time; protective fence and plank roads for tourists were built. It serves as the basic framework of Longmen Grottoes as the heritage protected zone and cultural relic tourist area. Large-scale rescue protection that chiefly solved the safety and stability of grottoes was basically completed.

Fig.5　On-site renovation of Longmen Grottoes

4. From nomination until today

After the successful inscription as a World Cultural Heritage Site in 2000, the Longmen Grottoes Institute has carried out international cooperation projects such as "UNESCO Longmen Grottoes Conservation and Restoration Project" and "China-Italy Cooperative Restoration Project for Double Caves" and achieved remarkable scientific research results. In particular, some advanced conservation concepts and sound conservation and restoration programs have amassed valuable experience for the restoration of immovable stone cultural relics.

Fig.6　Tripartite Expert Meeting for Conservation and Restoration of Longmen Grottoes

In the past ten years, the conservation project of Longmen Grottoes carried out includes cavern restoration, comprehensive governance of water leakage, construction of heritage monitoring system, survey of conservation status of grottoes, research on conservation materials, conservation and management planning and management regulations.

IV. Main work of preventive conservation of Longmen Grottoes

It mainly includes the work in the following six aspects:

1. Monitoring of Longmen Grottoes

The monitoring of the status of cultural relics in grottoes, diseases of grottoes and grotto conservation environment is most fundamental to grotto conservation. It helps us understand the conservation state and changes to grottoes, as well as the environmental factors related to these changes. Monitoring also serves as a means of research. Research monitoring for special diseases of grottoes can identify the causes of diseases to grottoes, and help us understand the trend of disease development, so that corresponding conservation programs and restoration measures are proposed.

Fig.7　Restoration Project Site of Double Caves

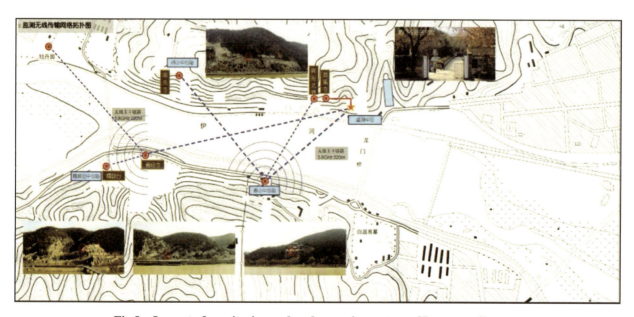

Fig.8　Layout of monitoring and early warning system of Longmen Grottoes

The monitoring of Longmen Grottoes was initiated in the 1960s. After 2000, the Longmen Grottoes

Institute gradually upgraded the monitoring system by purchasing continuous automatic monitoring instrument for atmospheric quality for automatic monitoring of the content of sulfur dioxide and nitrogen oxides in the atmosphere; establishing two automatic meteorological environmental monitoring stations to monitor the atmospheric temperature and humidity, precipitation, evaporation capacity, wind direction and speed; establishing water environment monitoring system to monitor changes in groundwater level and changes in spring water and river water. The monitoring and early warning system currently in effect was initiated in 2013 and was completed in 2017 over four phases. A framework for grotto cultural relics and grotto environmental monitoring is basically put in place, and is finally connected to the provincial and national monitoring platforms. The monitoring is geared to continuous automatic monitoring of the environment Longmen Grottoes area, cavern micro-environment, diseases of cultural relics, and the quality of atmospheric environment, and is connected to the monitoring platform through wireless transmission.

| Fig.9   Meteorological observation field for Longmen Grottoes | Fig.10   Monitoring of statue weathering |

The environment of the key area of Longmen Grottoes and the diseases of key cultural relics in grottoes are the focus of the system monitoring. Regional environmental monitoring includes: ambient temperature and humidity, wind direction, wind speed, atmospheric precipitation, light intensity, soil moisture content, vibration, river water, spring water, etc. at the grotto area. The monitoring of diseases of cultural relics cover: ambient temperature and humidity of caverns, water leakage, condensate, weathering, rock mass stability, among others (see Table 1). According to the characteristics and needs of Longmen Grottoes, the research monitoring of weathering and water seepage and leakage was designed. For instance, the use of infrared thermography technology to monitor water leakage in caverns removes the limitations of traditional photography, in that it has continuous monitoring and recording throughout the day, and also simulates the amount of leakage to meet the needs of quantitative monitoring. High-precision industrial cameras are used to continuously monitor

Table 1   Summary of the implementation of Longmen Grotto monitoring system in stages

Time	Monitoring position	Monitoring description	Monitoring indicators	Number of sensors	Number of indicators
The first phase began in November 2013	Two monitoring points at Wanfo Cave and Fengxian Temple	Include four monitoring types of environment (comprehensive meteorology, soil water content, microenvironment, noise) , stability, water leakage and weathering	Temperature, humidity, wind speed, wind direction, atmospheric pressure, rainfall, total radiation, wall temperature, soil moisture, noise, cracks, angle of inclination, leakage, UV, weathering	29	35
The second phase began in April 2014	8 monitoring locations including Qianxi Temple, Binyang North Cave, Wanfo Cave, Ji'nan Cave, Peony Garden, Drum Beating Cave, Kanjing Temple, and White Garden	Include 7 monitoring types of environment (comprehensive meteorology, soil water content, acid rain, air quality) , microenvironment, stability, water leakage, weathering, condensate, and vibration	Temperature, humidity, wind speed, wind direction, atmospheric pressure, rainfall, total radiation, wall temperature, soil moisture, CO_2,SO_2,NO_2, PM2.5, negative oxygen ions, cracks, angle of inclination, water leakage, weathering, condensate, PH	50	76
The third phase began in November 2015	16 monitoring locations including Entrance to West Mountain, Monitoring Center, Qianxi Temple, Binyang Cave, Jingshan Temple, Fengxian Temple, Duke Huangfu Cave, Xishan Road Cave, Ji'nan Cave, West Mountain Top, West Mountain Wharf, Yi River, entrance to East Mountain, Heavenly Paradise Shrine, Guanyin Shrine, and Kanjing Temple	Include 6 monitoring types of environment (groundwater level, water quality) , microenvironment, stability, water leakage, weathering, and tourist capacity	Temperature, humidity, wall temperature, groundwater level, pH, conductivity, dissolved oxygen, water temperature, UV light, weathering, cracks, angle of inclination, water leakage, tourists	54	56
The fourth phase began in November 2016	11 monitoring locations including Qianxi Temple, Binyang Middle Cave, Wanfo Cave, Fengxian Temple, West Mountain south and north sides, Peony Garden, Yi River, Drum Beating Cave, Kanjing Temple, White Garden, East Mountain south and north sides	Include 4 monitoring types of environment (evaporation, water level, CO_2, etc.) , water leakage, vibration, condensate	Temperature, humidity, CO_2, evaporation, water level, water leakage, condensate, vibration	25	27

typical weathered engravings to observe weathering conditions in the long run, and conduct quantitative research on weathering.

Of the many monitoring items and indicators, cavern's water leakage and dangerous rock (cracks fracture) are most closely related to the safety and stability of grottoes. It has a direct bearing on the formulation of grotto conservation plan and the design of conservation engineering. It is a prerequisite for preventive conservation of grotto temples.

| Fig.11 Installation of crack meters at Qianxi Temple | Fig.12 Average daily crack variation and fluctuation range at Qianxi Temple |

In the case of Qianxi Temple: Qianxi Temple is situated on the west mountain of Longmen, and is first large cavern from the north end. It is one of the caverns with the severest diseases at Longmen Grottoes. As the deformation of grottoes and the long-term water leakage are the main causes of grotto diseases, the monitoring focuses on the deformation of cave rocks and water seepage and its changes, including the horizontal displacement of grotto rock, cracks in rocks, and seepage pressure, seepage flow, etc. inside grotto rocks.

For the cracks in rock mass, three crack meters are placed inside and outside Qianxi Temple, and are marked as crack 1, crack 2, and crack 3, which are located in the east side of the top of Qianxi Temple, the northeast corner of the top of Qianxi Temple and the north side of the entrance to Qianxi Temple. By means of the monitoring of the cracks and water seepage in Qianxi Temple, the changes in cavern disease can be assessed and the effect of the conservation project can be verified, providing a basis for the long-term conservation of Qianxi Temple.

2. Survey of conservation state of Longmen Grottoes

The rocks at Longmen Grottoes belong to the Cambrian, Ordovician and Carboniferous strata. The nature of rocks is limestone and dolomite, and the main minerals are calcite and dolomite. With a moderate mechanical strength, it has strong weathering resistance ability, and is suitable for digging. However, the development of surface cracks, tectonic cracks and unloading cracks dominates the water leakage of grottoes. Limestone prone to corrosion determines the occurrence of corrosion diseases of grottoes.

Longmen Grottoes has been plagued by different geological diseases since its digging. The occurrence and development of geological diseases are intimately linked to the conservation of grottoes. To fully understand the conservation state of Longmen Grottoes and improve the conservation archives of caverns, the survey of conservation state of Longmen Grottoes was launched in 2013 to record and evaluate the conservation of each cavern from the perspective of geological diseases, with a view to serving the conservation plan of Longmen Grottoes and providing a basis for future geological disease treatment of caverns. The survey divided the caverns in the east and mountains of Longmen Grottoes in a length of nearly 2 km into 7 sections according to stratigraphic structures, including cavern cracks, water seepage, karst, dangerous rock body, biological diseases, weathering disease, etc. The survey investigated the main diseases of each cavern, disease development and initial mechanism of formation, predicted the trend of disease development, classified the conservation state of caverns, and proposed countermeasures.

Fig.13　On-site survey of diseases caused to Longmen Grottoes

In the case of integrity survey of caverns: The integrity of cavern mainly refers to the integrity of the statues, inscriptions, etc. in the caverns, and is an important indicator to gauge the conservation state of grottoes. Cavern integrity has certain relevance with the integrity of the body, as the former is the basis of the latter. However, some caverns with a complete structure have serious integrity problems of the body (see Tables 2 and 3) .

Table 2   Evaluation of Cavern Structure Integrity

Number	Naming	Definition	Typical caverns
A	Complete	Cavern has a sound overall structure, and it is easy to identify the composition and shape of the cavern. Key stress-bearing parts such as cave eaves, cave door and the top of the cave are basically intact.	Qianxi Temple, Binyang Caves, Fengxian Temple, etc.
B	Partial damage	The cavern is damaged in parts, but the overall shape is discernible, and it is very easy to restore the original structure of the cavern. The damaged parts include eaves, cave door, and the cave top.	Most caverns
C	Missing parts	Cavern collapsed or is damaged on one or more sides. The original shape of the cavern is damaged, and key parameters such as depth of cavern are difficult to obtain.	Drum Beating South Cave, Heavenly Paradise Shrine, etc.
D	Ruins	Cavern position is discernible, but the body of cultural relics is basically nonexistent.	

Table 3   Evaluation of the Integrity of Grotto Body

Number	Naming	Definition	Typical caverns
A	In good condition	Cavern shape belongs to class A or B. The statues and carvings inside the cavern are complete. The head and hands of the main statues are mostly intact, and the identity of statue is easily recognizable.	Qianxi Temple, Binyang Caves, Fengxian Temple, etc.
B	Basically in good condition	Cavern shape belongs to class A or B. The statues are clearly distributed. The damaged parts are mainly the head and hands, while the torso is mostly intact. The torso of main Buddha is in good condition, and the other statues were stolen or the total number of loss is less than 1/3.	
C	Moderate damage	Caverns in class C belong to this category. The cavern structure is better than class C, and it is mainly evaluated according to the integrity of the statues. The head and torso of the main Buddha are damaged, and the total number of loss of other statues exceeds 1/3.	Thousand Hands Guanyin
D	Serious damage	Caverns in class D belong to this category. Those above Class D are evaluated according to the integrity of statues. The main Buddha is severely damaged, or becomes unclear due to weathering, and most of statues are seriously damaged.	Drum Beating North Cave
E	Ruins	The cultural relics are nonexistent, but cavern can be roughly identified with the aid of archaeological data.	

The conservation state of caverns varies markedly according to different geological conditions. The condition of grottoes is affected by human activities (cavern robbing, destruction, conservation work, etc.) , but the geological conditions are the key factors in the conservation of Longmen Grottoes. The controlling factors are formation lithology and geological structure conditions (see Table 4) .

Table 4 Evaluation table of conservation of bodies under different formation lithology

%

Type	In good condition	Basically in good condition	Moderate damage	Serious damage	Ruins
Fengshan Group	7.21	22.95	25.57	7.87	36.39
Gushan Group	0.00	10.53	0.00	0.00	89.47
Zhangxia Group	13.14	43.20	22.25	5.80	15.62
Xuzhuang Group	2.60	18.20	29.20	24.40	25.60

3. Geological disaster investigation and research of Longmen Grottoes

Research on regional geological hazards to Longmen Grottoes is ongoing. In Longmen Grottoes area, diseases caused by geological disasters such as water seepage in caverns, weathering, rock mass instability, landslide, and erosion pose a grave threat to the safety of cultural relics. On the other hand, Longmen Grottoes ranks top among other grottoes in terms of tourist capacity. The rock cracking and falling off trigger by geological disasters occur from time to time, posing a serious threat to the safety of tourists. The comprehensive survey and evaluation of geological disasters facing Longmen Grottoes provides strong support for the formulation of geological disaster prevention and control programs for Longmen Grottoes. The main research content is summed up as follows:

1) Survey and evaluation of dangerous rock body

On the basis of existing research, a more detailed survey of geological hazard is carried out on Longmen Grottoes area, and high-precision litho-stratigraphic profile and the engineering geological elevation diagrams are drawn up; dangerous rock body related to geological disasters is investigated, dangerous rock profile is drawn up, and the stability of dangerous rock body is analyzed; loose stones are investigated, and relevant drawings are made to sum up the geological disasters in this area.

2) Establish a disaster database

Geological hazard factors of Longmen Grottoes, such as rock cracks, karst, landslide, hydrogeology, weathering, and water seepage are investigated in detail, and the mineral composition, chemical composition and physical property of rocks are measured according to different lithology. Based on the relationship between the crack development in different lithological distribution areas and the karst status and development, the database on rock stratum is set up to evaluate the law of occurrence and destructiveness of geological disasters.

Fig.14　Survey of dangerous rock body at Longmen Grottoes

3) Prepare disaster prevention programs

According to the results of preliminary investigations, it is possible to scientifically and efficiently identify the dangerous areas of Longmen Grottoes prone to geological disasters and its triggering factors, and understand the evolution of geological disasters at Longmen Grottoes; the distribution and occurrence law of geological disasters at Longmen Grottoes are mastered to provide scientific and effective support for the integrated treatment of geological disasters at Longmen Grottoes and to minimize the impact of geological disasters.

4. Maintenance of Longmen Grottoes

Article 29 of the "Principles for the Conservation of Heritage Sites in China" states that: Routine maintenance is a preventive measure to prevent in a timely manner the damage possibly caused by external forces, and applies to any object. Like other cultural relics, the conservation of grottoes and temples shall begin with prevention. Maintenance is the fundamental embodiment of the preventive conservation concept.

The main contents of the maintenance of Longmen Grottoes include:

1) Cleaning of dangerous stone and dust: week and dangerous stones and dust shall be cleaned in an institutional manner. Weed shall be cleaned in a timely manner, and the destruction of weeds and shrubs on cavern carved works and surrounding rocks shall be eliminated; the surface of large Buddha statues in the caverns shall be cleaned to prevent moisture absorption, compaction, and adsorption of noxious gases, visual changes, among others.

Fig.15   Maintenance Site of Fengxian Temple of Longmen Grottoes

2) Maintenance of protective facilities: Existing cavern eaves and awning platforms are repaired and drainage ditch, etc., are cleared and repaired to ensure their normal functions. In recent years, safeguard measures have been adopted for the awnings of Binyang Caves and Three Buddhists Carved on Cliff, and the protection platform of Shiniu River, such as cleaning, crack grouting and reinforcement, and re-laying of anti-seepage layer. For the drainage ditches for the top of Qianxi Temple and Fengxian Temple, etc., the measures such as regular cleaning of gravel, repair and reinforcement of slopes, and repair of retaining wall have been taken.

3) Maintenance of open-air carved works and surrounding rocks: In the 1km-long west mountain of Longmen Grottoes from the south to the north, caverns are distributed on the rock wall several meters to several tens of meters high. Scaffolding is carefully erected in sections to check the grottoes in detail. Problems or hidden dangers discovered are treated in a timely manner by virtue of mature technologies, including: (1) surface crack plugging and grouting reinforcement; (2) bonding of small-size hazardous rock body; (3) repair of open-air carved works; (4) test repair of necessary parts of the top and bottom of collapsed shrines to protect the carved works in the cave. The treated sections such as Three Buddhists Carved on Cliff, Lotus Cave, Fengxian Temple, Jinan Cave in the West Mountain and Second Lotus Cave in the East Mountain have sound conservation effect.

Fig.16   Open-air carved works before maintenance   Fig.17   Open-air carved works after maintenance

Fig.18   Comparison of open-air inscriptions before and after the installation of protective eaves

Through these measures, there is both experience, and some doubts and problems, such as how to prepare standardized operation specifications for maintenance, how to choose maintenance work, and how to combine maintenance with other conservation projects. These remain to be answered in the future work.

5. Compile the archaeological report on caverns

The systematic, objective and scientific archaeological report on the Grottoes Temple is compiled to record and preserve cultural heritage information comprehensively and exhaustively. It is the chief academic work of grotto temples, and also a crying need to pass on and promote the Chinese history and culture. As the well-known archaeologist Mr. Su Bai pointed out: The preparation of archaeological report on caverns is the paramount task of the current research on grottoes.

The preparation of archives on grottoes and the subsequent archaeological reports is an important way to record information on grottoes and is also the basis for long-term conservation of grottoes. It is a long-term and herculean task to prepare archaeological report on the grotto temples like Longmen Grottoes, which have a wealth of caverns and complicated ruins. In order to facilitate the work and ensure the continuity of work in each period, the east and west mountains are divided into several sections. Implementation is carried out gradually in stages from south to north in the east mountain and from north to south in the west mountain.

Fig.19   Famous archaeologist Mr. Su Bai visited Longmen Grottoes to guide the preparation of archaeological report

With the guidance of the famous archaeologist and Peking University senior professor Mr. Su Bai, "Archaeological Report on Longmen Grottoes - Drum Beating cave Area in East Mountain" was published in April 2018 by the Science Press after 13 years of sustained hard work. This is a major exploration and vivid practice of the Chinese people in preparing scientific and systematic archaeological reports on large grottoes in the 21st century. In preparing archaeological reports, exploration was made in the organization of team, recording methods, the use of technological means, the report layout, as well as the academic role of the results of different records in the report. Richer archaeological theory and methods of grottoes have been accumulated, providing useful reference for use of archaeological methods for the grotto cluster, the specific reality of grottoes, comprehensive, objective, systematic and scientific recording of relevant relics, and the preparation of archaeological reports. At the same time, it is also the first systematic grotto archaeological report on the organic integration of heritage site in front of caves and cavern remains on the basis of archaeological excavation in the research history of Longmen Grottoes. It built a data platform for domestic and international academic circles to study Longmen Grottoes and even other grotto temples in China, and promote the in-depth study of Longmen Grottoes.

Fig.20   Publication of "Archaeological Report on Longmen Grottoes – Drum Beating cave Area in East Mountain"

6. Construction of "Digital Longmen"

The Longmen Grottoes Institute carried out "3D Digital Engineering of Longmen Grottoes" since 2005. After more than a decade of on-site scanning, it has completed data collection of 80% of shrines, and the basic conditions for establishing digital file of Longmen Grottoes are satisfied. Three-dimensional modeling and application demonstration are performed on some caverns. A basis for the research, conservation, display of cultural relics as well as cultural derivatives is provided through digital recording, which facilitates the use of new technology for cultural relic protection and publicity of Longmen Grottoes.

In terms of conservation of cultural relics, geological diseases can be marked on the three-dimensional models conveniently and quickly, so as to learn about main disease types and disease development in each cavern and predict the trends, and provide more convenient methods and countermeasures for conservation work.

Moreover, the Longmen Grottoes Institute has made useful exploration and attempts in the promotion of 3D digital use:

1) Virtual restoration

The Buddha head of Gaoshu Shrine at Guyang Cave was returned to China in 2005. Its torso and head were restored using digital technology. In the virtual restoration process, the virtual restoration image was generated based on the geometric information of the existing part and the object attribute information contained it contained, coupled with the cultural relic expert opinions and documents. It eminently reproduces the artistic value of Gaoshu Shrine.

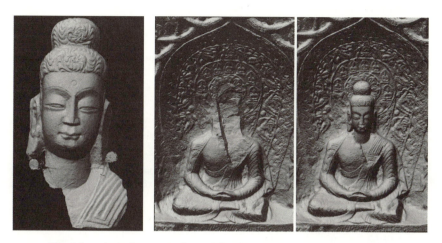

Fig.21   virtual restoration of Gaoshu Shrine at Guyang Cave

2) Interactive experience

Wanfo Cave VR is the first virtual reality project of Longmen Grottoes. It makes possible free walking in the cavern, and also offers some operational experience. Longmen Grottoes is mostly semi-open. Users can view every detail in the cavern at close range through this way.

Fig.22   VR Experience of Wanfo Cave

3) Cultural creativity

A wealth of creative products can be developed using 3D data to promote the cultural communication of Longmen Grottoes and raise its influence. The Longmen Grottoes Institute cooperated with Zhejiang University Cultural Heritage Research Institute in carrying the data collection and 3D printing of Chen Tuan ten-word monument and four shines on the north wall of Guyang Cave, in order to meet the display needs of Longmen Grottoes under new circumstances. It cooperates with Luoyang Longzhang Cultural Communication Co., Ltd. in the digital interactive display of 20 Longmen products, which showcase the superior calligraphy in the Northern Wei Dynasty, and enable the audience to better understand the 20 Longmen products through edutainment.

Fig.23   "Digital Longmen" Seminar

5. Difficulties and Challenges Facing Preventive Conservation of Longmen Grottoes

Although the preventive conservation work of Longmen Grottoes has gradually improved in practice, many difficulties and challenges remain:

1) Monitoring system of grotto temples needs to be improved

The monitoring system has been initially put in place, and the continuous systematic monitoring of conservation of cultural relics and the environment cultural relics have been carried out. Innovative monitoring techniques and methods are used, and on this basis, monitoring-related research such as disease mechanisms and engineering effects has been performed. Nevertheless, the overall monitoring system is far from mature in operation, and some problems have just cropped up. The problems include lack of targeted purpose in some monitoring projects; problems in interpretation and use of monitoring results, huge data of vibration monitoring, and the difficulty of interpretation due to high level of professionalism; difficulty characterization due to a long period of weathering monitoring; the delayed predation of monitoring standards, and further study of definition of early warning values; maintenance and upgrading of monitoring equipment, and limitations on personnel and funds.

2) The protective facilities of grotto temples remain to be improved

The ancillary facilities of the grotto temples used as physical conservation methods have advantages in safety vis-à-vis chemical conservation methods. For example, the eaves and drainage channels at Longmen Grottoes date back to the time of cave digging. These still protect grottoes today. However, due to inadequate design, there are some doubts over the auxiliary facilities such as eaves, which affect the cavern micro-environment, the stability of rock body, and the cultural landscape. These can be removed or weakened through more reasonable design. It is the most direct and effective way to prevent and mitigate the degradation of cultural relics in Longmen Grottoes by building ancillary facilities such as cave eaves in the severely weathered sections. For instance, in the section from Lotus Cave to Tangzi Cave, the section from Guanyin Shrine to Heavenly Paradise Shrine and Drum Beating Caves, and Kanjing Temple, it is only necessary to take full account of its influence on the cultural relics, micro-environment and grotto landscape at the time of design and construction. This makes use of advantages and avoids harm, thus playing a better role of conservation.

3) Grotto temple management shows anemic protection and control efforts

The grotto temples and the environment are closely intertwined. Apart from the natural environment, the cultural and social environment has an increasing and comprehensive impact on grotto temples. As stellar cultural resources, grotto temples are mostly located in the beautiful natural environment, and increasingly become hot tourist attractions. What were wild historical sites have gradually become popular tourist attractions, and even urban bonsai. The distance between Longmen Grottoes and the city center has shrunk to 5 kilometers, and the boundaries of the city are becoming blurred. Social demand is the intention and incentive of cultural relic conservation, and is also in conflict with the objective requirements of cultural relic conservation. Therefore, the improvement of social management cannot be overlooked from the perspective of preventive conservation of grotto temples.

4) Bottlenecks in conservation technology

The treatment of grotto diseases hits bottlenecks in scientific research and technology, which need to be solved, such as study of conservation and reinforcement materials and construction technology, anti-weathering treatment, etc., especially the latter, which require urgent solution.

5) Conservation agencies and highly-skilled professionals are in demand

Whether it is the treatment of grotto

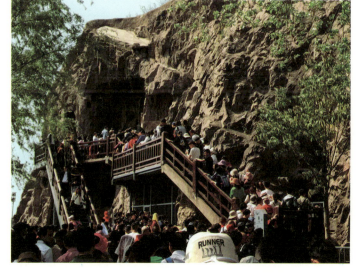

Fig.24　Longmen Grottoes thronged with tourists

disease, or better preventive conservation work, the conservation agencies and highly-skilled professionals are urgently required to achieve the long-term conservation objective.

6. Deepen preventive conservation work of Longmen Grottoes

For Longmen Grottoes, the concept of preventive conservation does not come overnight, but is based on the experience in rescue conservation work. The rescue conservation and preventive conservation coexist for a long time, on that there is different focus in different periods; further, preventive conservation should include technical conservation and management conservation. Technical conservation is the keystone while management conservation offers the guarantee. Second, preventive conservation needs to be balanced in all respects. The concept of preventive conservation of grottoes shall include:

1) Investigation and evaluation of grotto conservation status

The main work include the scientific investigation and level evaluation of the grottoes, status of the natural mountain body where grottoes are located, and the disease development.

2) Monitoring of grottoes and the environment

Improve the monitoring system of grotto temples, especially the routine monitoring of grottoes and the environment, long-term monitoring of diseases such as weathering, as well as early warning monitoring of diseases such as rock instability, research monitoring of disease mechanisms, and the effectiveness monitoring of conservation projects.

| **Fig.25　Geological radar monitoring** | **Fig.26　Water seepage monitoring in caverns** |

3) Construction of ancillary conservation facilities and effectiveness guarantee

Appropriate protective ancillary facilities such as eaves, canopies, drainage ditches, water retaining walls, and plank roads, as well as regular maintenance ensure their effective role.

4) Daily inspection and maintenance of grottoes

Institutional inspections and standardized maintenance can detect and treat diseases to grottoes in a timely manner to prevent further degradation.

Fig.27   Drainage facilities at cave eaves and cave top

Fig.28   Maintenance of Fengxian Temple

5) Timely repair of major diseases to grottoes

Conservation projects for cavern and rock mass reinforcement, and necessary restoration works for damaged cultural relics are carried out according to plan to solve the fundamental problems in terms of grotto stability and display.

Fig.29   Seepage control project

Fig.30   Comprehensive treatment project at Drum Beating Cave at Qianxi Temple

6) Establishment of digital files of grottoes

Complete files of grottoes are established to record the current state of grotto conservation.

Fig.31   Three-dimensional records of grottoes

7) Protection plan to guard against natural disasters

Effective early warning mechanisms and response plans are put in place for unexpected events such as sudden geological disasters, extreme weather, and floods.

Fig.32   Flood disaster

8) Security

Guard against destruction due to human activities.

9) Control of social environment such as planning and management regulations

Ensure the enforcement and effectiveness of conservation and management plans and regulations, and coordinate the interaction among cultural relic management, people's livelihood, tourism, and economic development.

Preventive conservation concept of grottoes makes clear the goals and tasks of grotto protection we face. On this basis, a sound framework for preventive conservation work is established. After an in-depth understanding of occurrence, development and change of diseases of cultural relics in the grottoes, evaluation standards are formulated, risk prevention and control technology of cultural relics in grottoes are studied to slow down or mitigate the hazards caused by various risks, and the risk monitoring and evaluation system for cultural relic in the grottoes is built for comprehensive evaluation and control of grotto conservation and management.

7. Outlook of preventive conservation work of Longmen Grottoes

Preventive conservation work of Longmen Grottoes still has a long way to go. Breakthroughs in anti-weathering materials and the restoration of preventive facilities of Vairocana Buddha Shrine at Longmen Grottoes are the overriding priority.

1) Breakthroughs in anti-weathering materials

In the protection technology of cultural relics, protective materials and their processes are the most important technologies, as it hampers the conservation of stone cultural relics in China. Longmen Grottoes Institute and China University of Geosciences (Wuhan) have made related scientific research after years of cooperation. Given the special grouting requirements of Longmen Grottoes, new environmentally friendly inorganic grouting material PC20-10 featuring metakaolin has been developed. At present, it has been applied to key grottoes such as Dazu Rock Carvings, with good results. However, the research on anti-weathering materials for open stone inscriptions is advancing slowly. Due to natural factors such as the elements and human activities for over 1,500 years, Longmen Grottoes suffer surface weathering, loss, cracks, and powdering

Fig.33　Weathered open-air inscriptions

generally, especially in the section from the south of Fengxian Temple to Jinan Cave. Reinforcement and conservation are urgently required. Efforts are made to foster international cooperation, conduct in-depth study of weathering mechanism, perform experimental research on surface reinforcement and repair technology, and explore new methods and ideas for improving the preservation of open stone inscriptions.

2) Protective eaves for Fengxian Temple

In the article "Talk on Restoration and Maintenance of Cultural Relics" published in the seventh issue of *Cultural Relics* in 1963, the well-known architect Liang Sicheng talked about the construction of protective architectural facilities for Fengxian Temple at Longmen: "Vairocana Buddha statues at Fengxian Temple were originally protected by wooden structures, but it is unclear when these were destroyed (presumably since the Huichang Buddhism destruction) ... But today, we can't see these works, one of the masterpieces in the Chinese carving history, being eroded by nature. These must be prevented from the elements. It is necessary to cover it up." Today, after a period of nearly 60 years, Mr. Liang Sicheng's wish is still not fulfilled. This task still faces a host of difficulties. It is our responsibilities and a priority issue for us.

Fig.34   Fengxian Temple of Longmen Grottoes

8. Conclusion

The two concepts of rescue conservation and preventive conservation of grotto temples have positive and practical significance. Following the rescue conservation, the preventive conservation of grottoes is without a doubt more positive understanding and attitude. Through "scientific conservation, focus on prevention, environmental improvement, and minimal intervention", a suitable optimal conservation environment is created for the goal of long-term conservation.

"Conserve the solid state, pass on the living state, and develop the heritage." Longmen Grottoes

Institute, as the guardian of Longmen Grottoes, shoulders the responsibility of protecting Longmen Grottoes. We stand ready to work with the international community in the preventive conservation of Longmen Grottoes, the precious cultural heritage. At the same time, Longmen Grottoes Institute with its global perspective strives to become a world-class grotto research institute, and try its best to become a role model in protecting the cultural heritage, and contribute to making Luoyang a world-renowned historical and cultural tourist city, making Henan Province the culturally advanced region in China, and making China a strong country through culture!

斯特茨中世纪墓地管理规划

波斯尼亚和黑塞哥维那　文化历史与自然遗产保护研究所　米里亚娜·奥克伊里奇[①]

摘要

斯特茨中世纪墓地是根据标准（Ⅲ）和（Ⅳ）于 2016 年列入联合国教科文组织《世界遗产名录》的系列遗产。该系列遗产由 28 处墓地组成，分布于波黑、塞尔维亚、黑山和克罗地亚等 4 国，是具有地域特色的中世纪墓碑的代表（斯特茨）。这些墓地建造于 12 至 16 世纪期间，以行列的方式排列，这是自中世纪以来欧洲常见的习俗。墓碑大多以石灰岩雕刻而成，在某些方面受到早期、史前和中古传统的影响。通过与负责墓地日常维护的机构和组织以及与对墓地享有特殊利益的当地社区和其他团体的密切合作，制定了遗产地管理规划。管理规划的主要目的包括：为墓地及其周边环境制定管理目标以确保其突出普遍价值得到保护和提升；为今后的管理设计可持续发展模式，兼顾墓地管理与周边环境管理之间的平衡以及旅游的可持续发展；确定研究所需的必要水平以对未来的管理工作提供信息；提升公众意识等。除总体管理规划外，也为每一处墓地制定了具体管理规划。其中一个关键问题是，如何确定斯特茨墓碑永久和系统保护的解决方案。

关键词：斯特茨，墓地，中世纪，管理，保护

斯特茨中世纪墓地是根据标准（Ⅲ）和（Ⅳ）于 2016 年列入联合国教科文组织《世界遗产名录》的系列遗产（世界遗产委员会第 40 COM 8B.24 号决定）。该系列遗产由 28 处墓地构成，包括 4000 座墓碑（斯特茨）。这些墓地分布于 4 个国家，其中波黑 20 处，克罗地亚 2 处，黑山 3 处，塞尔维亚 3 处。

这些墓地建造于 12 至 16 世纪期间，以行列的方式排列，这是自中世纪以来欧洲常见的习俗。墓碑大多以石灰岩雕刻而成，在某些方面受到早期、史前和中古传统的影响。这些墓碑当时建在道路两旁，史前墓地内，要塞聚居地旁，教堂周边，或水井旁边。最近一次系统普查的结果显示，上述 4 国境内约 3300 处墓地共计有 70000 座左右的已登记墓碑（集体作者，2015，123）。

墓碑的艺术设计体现在其形式和装饰中。装饰图案以浅浮雕和凹浮雕两种技艺雕刻而成，代表了

---

① 米里亚娜·奥克伊里奇（Milijana Okilj）拥有建筑学和文化遗产保护学的博士学位。1995 年开始从事建筑保护工作，并于 1999 年担任波黑文化历史与自然遗产保护研究所文化处处长。波黑巴尼亚卢卡大学建筑、土木工程及测地系和科学系的客座教授。著有多部专著，并曾在专业杂志上发表过数篇文章。此外，她也是世界遗产协调人之一。

斯特茨墓碑的主要艺术品质。墓碑装饰图案的主题强调中世纪艺术的典型象征，可分为以下几种类型：社会和宗教象征（不同类型的十字架、工具、武器、新月和星星、拟人化百合花、太阳图案等）；人物造型（男女形象、骑士比武场景、竞技比赛、狩猎、队列游行、葬礼上的车轮舞蹈以及动物形象等）；众多植物和几何装饰图案（M. Wenzel，1965）。

对斯特茨墓碑所在地区出现的不同文化现象的大量研究表明，这些地区存在大量与死亡有关的非物质遗产以及为逝者修建的墓地和其它场所。除了其作为墓地（建有斯特茨墓碑的墓地以及其它墓地）的主要功能之外，这些墓地也是祭祀传统的构成部分，是该地区社会、艺术、宗教以及人们精神生活其它方面在一个特定历史时期发展的重要体现。

图 1　波黑斯特茨中世纪墓地分布图（来源：https://www.stecciwh.org/）

通过与负责墓地日常维护的机构和组织以及与对墓地享有特殊利益的当地社区和其他团体的密切合作，制定了遗产地管理规划。管理规划的主要目的包括：为墓地及其周边环境制定管理目标以确保其突出普遍价值得到保护和提升；为今后的管理设计可持续发展模式，兼顾墓地管理与周边环境管理之间的平衡以及旅游的可持续发展；确定研究所需的必要水平以对未来的管理工作提供信息；提升公众意识等。

该遗产地列入《世界遗产名录》后，在 4 国层面并在各个国家分别建立了遗产地管理体系。

除总体管理规划之外，也为每一处墓地制定了具体管理规划。多个领域的专家参与了具体管理规划的制定，包括建筑学家、考古学家、生物学家、律师、人类学家等。

表 1：国际层面的管理组织架构（来源：https://www.stecciwh.org/）

跨国协调委员会

秘书处

波黑	塞尔维亚	黑山	克罗地亚
国家协调架构	国家协调架构	国家协调架构	国家协调架构
遗产地管理	遗产地管理	遗产地管理	遗产地管理

以下国际文件直接适用于制定遗产地各处墓地具体管理规划的需要：

1. 联合国教科文组织《世界遗产公约实施指南》（联合国教科文组织世界遗产委员会，巴黎，2011）；

2.《巴拉宪章：国际古迹遗址理事会澳大利亚国家委员会保护具有文化重要性的场所宪章》（1999）；

3. 联合国教科文组织《保护世界文化和自然遗产公约》（联合国教科文组织大会第 17 届会议 1972 年 11 月 16 日于巴黎通过，WHC-2001/WS/2）（来源：http://whc.unesco.org/en/conventiontext）；

4. 世界遗产委员会《世界遗产文件、信息和教育活动战略计划》（巴黎，1998，WHC-98/CONF.203/15）。

每处墓地的管理规划包括愿景、目标、价值的介绍，当前状况描述，保护，场所精神，旅游，保护措施，风险，行动计划等内容。对斯特茨墓碑类型数量，具有装饰图案的墓碑准确数量和装饰图案类型，以及每一座斯特茨墓碑的状况进行了总体概述。管理规划还包括墓碑尺寸和类别的具体数据。

文化遗产保护的目的是为了当代利用和启迪后世而保护历史文化资源的重要价值。所有保护决定都是基于文化遗产基本价值的重要性而做出的。价值要素的类型各有不同，包括历史、建筑、审美、精神和社会价值。价值是根据遗存特点、口头传统、档案研究而确定的，并通过所在场所体现的。保护遗产意味着对具有社区重要性的有价值的构成部分进行保护和展示。

《巴拉宪章》提供了通过管理流程进行保护的系统而具有逻辑性的方法。宪章开篇对重要性进行了阐述，之后对遗产潜力进行了SWOT分析（优势、劣势、机会和威胁）。对重要性的申明和SWOT分析是制定保护政策的基础。保护政策是支撑管理规划制定的理念基础。

图2　位于内韦西涅市克雷克维的卡鲁菲墓地（波黑塞族共和国文化、历史和自然遗产保护研究所文件）

一个关键问题是，如何确定斯特茨墓碑的永久和系统保护解决方案。大多数斯特茨墓碑是由石灰岩所造，这是该地区最常见的岩石，非常适于雕刻。在不产石灰岩的地区，斯特茨墓碑由蛇纹石、板岩、砾岩、凝灰岩或其它岩石雕刻而成。

这些斯特茨墓碑在漫长的历史时期经历了不同程度的物理退化。这一方面是由于岩石本身的矿物学和岩相学特点所造成的，另一方面也是由于墓碑所处的宏观和微观环境发生变化而导致的。

岩石退化的最常见原因和过程包括（Hadžić A.，Fočo M.，Okilj M.，2014）：

No:	the name of the necropolis and location
009	**Gvozno polje, Municipality Kalinovik**
type	sljemenjak-gabled roof stećak
dimension	160x75x77 cm
material	limestone
orientation	NW-SI
condition	damaged edges, partially covered with lichen, sunken
inscriptions and decorations	a woman with horses, a scene of hunting
note	-
photos	
	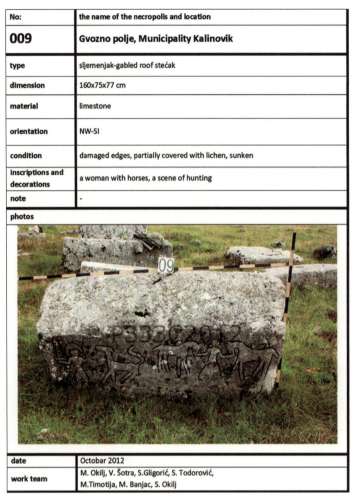
date	Octobar 2012
work team	M. Okilj, V. Šotra, S.Gligorić, S. Todorović, M.Timotija, M. Banjac, S. Okilj

图 3 墓碑记录卡示例（波黑塞族共和国文化、历史和自然遗产保护研究所文件）

生物腐蚀

了解垂直稀释和相互依赖的生物群落的功能作用，对发现斯特茨墓碑石存在的生物威胁从而采取足够的清理工作具有十分重要的意义。这里主要是指：藻类（以粉状形式存在），生存在菌类和地衣生物群落，对岩石表面起破坏作用。菌类（附着在岩石表面），与藻类共同作用，是地衣生长的基础，其齿列对岩石产生最重要作用。地衣（多成分植物）是对岩石危害最大的大型物种，在新陈代谢过程中产生二氧化碳和分泌物，腐蚀岩石表面。苔藓，主要是对其附着的多孔岩石表面造成威胁。藤蔓，其强壮根茎能够穿透进岩石结构中的缝隙。

化学腐蚀

化学腐蚀由二氧化硫和二氧化碳与水分的融合作用而造成，这会导致石灰岩墓碑的变形。岩石荧光、结晶或开裂会造成斯特茨墓碑瓦片的残缺或装饰构件的不完整,这主要发生在斯特茨墓碑制作的最初阶段。

物理腐蚀

逆温现象与这一地区特有的日晒和风锈以及石灰岩墓碑的透水性(透水率 2.8%)共同作用,造成对墓碑的物理腐蚀。

磨损和磨蚀

风对岩石产生持续的轻微破坏作用,如果不加以足够保护,这会导致墓碑石表面装饰构件渐进的缺失。

水的作用(水的负面影响)

与水的负面作用作斗争是一个艰巨的过程,这主要是指对路面和墓穴的修复和斯特茨墓碑石表面的保护。

为制定斯特茨墓碑永久和系统保护解决方案并进行项目记录,有必要开展多个阶段的工作,以做出正确的诊断和治理,即消除威胁和损害的保护程序。

为制定项目文件,有必要:

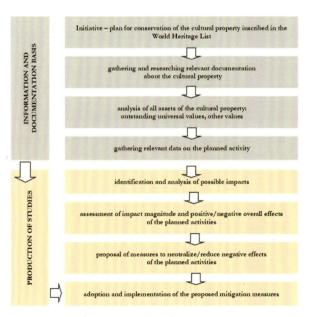

表2 行动计划实施流程图

·深入研究这一领域，确定遗产地内斯特茨墓碑数量、形式和装饰构件，并形成配套的文字和影像文件；

·确定生物、物理和化学损害的类型、成因和程度；

·如有可能（且必要的话），采用非破坏性方法（热图像测量分析和超声波诊断）对墓碑石结构进行分析。

为制定合适的解决方案，2017年于黑山共和国的扎布利亚克举办了斯特茨中世纪墓碑保护研讨会，Simon Warrack 作为石质文物保护领域的国际专家受邀参加。研讨会的主要目的是分享不同领域专业人士的知识，为所有的斯特茨墓地制定共同的保护策略（Warrack S.，2017）。

参考书目

1. 集体作者，2015，《斯特茨中世纪墓碑列入世界遗产名录申报文本》，波黑、克罗地亚、黑山、塞尔维亚。

2. M. Wenzel，1965，《波斯尼亚及周边地区中世纪墓碑的装饰主题》（第1和2卷），萨拉热窝。

3. A. Hadžić，M. Fočo 和 M. Okilj，2014，《斯特茨墓碑永久和系统保护的方法》（管理规划摘录），萨拉热窝、巴尼亚卢卡。

4. S. Warrack，2017，《斯特茨中世纪墓碑保护研讨会》，黑山，扎布利亚克。

使用的文献

1. Бандић, Д. (1990.) Царство земаљскоицарствонебеско, *Библиотека XX век 69*, Београд

2. Бандић, Д. (2004.) *Народна религијаСрбау 100 појмова*, Београд

3. Бешлагић, Ш. *Стећци*, Каталошко-топографски преглед, Сарајево, 1971

4. Ћоровић, В. (1989.) *ИсторијаСрба 1*, БИГЗ, Београд

5. Ђорђевић, Т. *Наш народни живот I–IV*, Просвета, Београд, 1984

6. Зечевић, С. (1982). , *Култ мртвих код Срба*, Вук Караџић, Београд

7. Ringbeck, B., 2008，《世界遗产地管理规划实用指南》，ICOMOS 德国国家委员会，波恩

8. Stovel, H., 1998，《风险预防：世界文化遗产管理手册》，ICCROM，罗马

9. Feilden, B. M 和 Jokilehto, J., 1998，《世界文化遗产管理指南》（第二版），ICCROM，罗马

Individual Management Plans for Stećci - Medieval Tombstone Graveyards

Milijana Okilj[①]

Institute for the Protection of Cultural-Historical and Natural Heritage of Republic of Srpska

Bosnia and Herzegovina

Abstract

Stećci Medieval Tombstone Graveyards, serial nominations, were inscribed on the UNESCO World Heritage List, based on criteria (iii) and (iv) , in 2016. This serial property combines 28 sites, located in Bosnia and Herzegovina, Serbia, Montenegro and Croatia, representing these cemeteries and regionally distinctive medieval tombstones, or stećci. The cemeteries, which date from the 12th to 16th centuries CE, are laid out in rows, as was the common custom in Europe from the Middle Ages. The stećci are mostly carved from limestone. In addition, stećci were, in some respects, influenced by earlier, prehistoric and ancient, traditions.The Management plan has been developed in close cooperation with the institutions and organizations responsible for the day to day care of the Medieval Tombstone Graveyards, together with the local communities and others witha special interest in it. The main aims of the MP are: to provide objectives for the management of the necropolis, their settings and environment, so that the universal outstanding value is conserved and improved, to outline a sustainable approach to future management which balances conservation of the necropolis and management of the environment, and sustainable development of tourism; to identify the necessary level of research whose result will inform future management; to increase public awareness etc. In addition to the general management plan, management plans have been made for each individual necropolis. One of the key questions is how to find solution for permanent systematic conservation of stećci.

Keywords: stećci, necropolis, Middle Ages, management, conservation

---

① Milijana Okilj has a PhD in History of Architecture and Protection of Cultural Heritage. Since 1995 she has worked as an architect-conservator, from 1999 she is a Head of Department for Cultural-Historical Heritage, for the Institute for Protection of Cultural-Historical and Natural Heritage of Republic of Srpska. She also has the experience in working for Faculty of Architecture, Civil Engineering and Geodesy and Faculty of Sciences, University of Banja Luka, B&H as a Visiting Professor. She has published several monographs and articles in professional journals. She is also the Focal Point for World Heritage.

Stećci Medieval Tombstone Graveyards, serial nominations, were inscribed on the UNESCO World Heritage List, based on criteria (iii) and (iv) , in 2016 (Decision: 40 COM 8B.24 of WHC) .The serial property of 28 component sites includes a selection of 4,000 medieval tombstones (stećci) on the territory of four states: Bosnia and Herzegovina (20) , the Republic of Croatia (2) , Montenegro (3) and the Republic of Serbia (3) .

The cemeteries, which date from the 12ᵗʰ to 16ᵗʰ centuries CE, are laid out in rows, as was the common custom in Europe from the Middle Ages. In addition, stećci were, in some respects, influenced by earlier, prehistoric and ancient traditions. At the time when they were made, they were arranged next to roads, on prehistoric tumuli, so-called gomile, at prehistoric fortified settlements, so-called gradine, around churches, next to wells, etc. The last systematic inventory of these monuments resulted in the figure of around 70,000 registered tombstones at about 3,300 sites on the territory of the mentioned states (Group of authors, Stećci-Medieval Tombstones, 2015, 123) .

The artistic design of stećci is reflected in their form and decoration. Decorations were done in two carving techniques,bas-relief and sunk relief, represent the main artistic quality of stećci. Decorative motifs on stećci have an accentuated symbolic typical for medieval art and may be divided into several groups: social and religious symbols (different types of crosses, tools, weapons, crescent moon and stars,anthropomorphic lilies, solar motifs, etc.) , figural compositions (images of men and women, jousting scenes, tournaments, hunting,

Fig. 1 Map of Bosnia and Herzegovina, with marked necropolises (https://www.stecciwh.org/)

parades of people, so-called funeral wheel-dances - kolo, and images of animals) and numerous vegetal and geometric ornaments (Wenzel, M. 1965) .

Numerous studies of different cultural phenomena in the areas where stećci appear indicate a large number of intangible heritage refering to death and everything related to it, which includes cemeteries and other places intended for the deceased. In addition to its primary function - burial sites, necropolis with stećak tombstones, and other cemeteries, they are part of cult traditions and a significant indicator of social, artistic, religious and other aspects of the development of the spiritual life of the people of that region for a certain period of time.

The Management plan has been developed in close cooperation with the institutions and organizations responsible for the day to day care of the Medieval Tombstone Graveyards, together with the local communities and others with a special interests in it.The main aims of the MP are:to provide objectives for the management of the necropolis, their settings and environment, so that the universal outstanding value is conserved and improved, to outline a sustainable approach to future management which balances conservation of the necropolis and management of the enviroment, and sustainable development of tourism; to identify the necessary level of research whose result will inform future management; to increase public awareness etc.

After inscription on the World Heritage List, a system of managament was established at the level of the four states and in each state separately.

In addition to the general management plan, management plans have been made for each individual necropolis.Experts from several professions participated in the development of individual management plans; architects, archaeologists, biologists, lawyers, ethnologists, etc.

Table 1　Organisational management structure at international level(https://www.stecciwh.org/)

The following international documents have been directly applied for the needs of the development of individual management plans:

1. *UNESCO Operational Guidelines for the implementation of the World Heritage Convention*, UNESCO WHC, Paris, 2011.

2. *The Burra Charter*: The Australia ICOMOS Charter for Places of Cultural Significance, 1999

3.UNESCO, *Convention concerning the protection of the world cultural and natural heritage*, adopted by the General Conference at its seventeenth session, Paris, 16 November 1972, WHC-2001/WS/2 (http://whc.unesco.org/en/conventiontext)

4.World Heritage Committee, *A Strategic Plan for World Heritage Documentation, Information and Education Activities*, Paris 1998 (WHC-98/CONF.203/15) .

Each individual management plan contains information about the visions, goals, values of the necropolis, a description of the current situation, conservation, the spirit of the place (genius loci) , tourism, protection measures, risks, action plans etc.There is an overview of the number of stećci by types (chest, slab, sljemenjak-gabled roof stećak, monumental cross or only fragments are preserved) , the exact number of decorated ones and types of decoration, as well as the state of each individual stećak. It also contains data on dimensions and orientation.

Conservation of cultural heritage is undertaken in order to preserve the value and importance of cultural resources from the past, to use the present and to inspire future generations. All conservation decisions are

Fig. 2　Necropolis Kalufi in Krekovi, Municipality Nevesinje（Documentation of Republic Institute for Protection of Cultural-Historical and Natural Heritage of Republic of Srpska）

based on the significance of the basic values of cultural heritage. There are different kinds of values, such as historical, architectural, aesthetic, spiritual or social. Values are determined based on physical characteristics, oral traditions, archival research and studies, and embodied in the place itself. Preserving the heritage implies protection and presentation as valuable components of a community's significance.

The Bura Charter provides a systematic and logical approach to conservation through the management process. It starts with a statement of significance, followed by a SWOT analysis (strength, weakness, opportunity and threat) of the heritage potential. Declaration of importance and SWOT analysis are the basis for conservation policy. Conservation policy is the philosophy behind the management plan.

No:	the name of the necropolis and location
009	**Gvozno polje, Municipality Kalinovik**
type	sljemenjak-gabled roof stećak
dimension	160x75x77 cm
material	limestone
orientation	NW-SI
condition	damaged edges, partially covered with lichen, sunken
inscriptions and decorations	a woman with horses, a scene of hunting
note	-
photos	

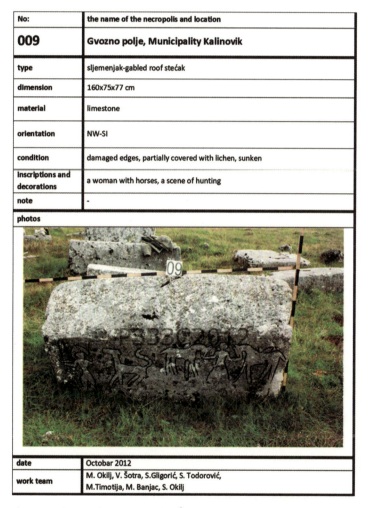

date	Octobar 2012
work team	M. Okilj, V. Šotra, S.Gligorić, S. Todorović, M.Timotija, M. Banjac, S. Okilj

Fig. 3   An example of a record card for each stećak (Documentation of Republic Institute for Protection of Cultural-Historical and Natural Heritage of Republic of Srpska)

One of the key questions is how to find a solution for permanent systematic conservation of stećci. Stećci were mostly made of limestone - a most common type of stone in this region very suitable for carving. In the areas where there was no limestone, stećci were carved from serpentine, slate, conglomerate, tuff and other types of stone.

During their long-lived existence there has been a certain degree of physical degradation. Inpart, the cause of these phenomena lies in the mineralogical-petrographic characteristics of the stones from which the stećci were made, and on the other hand, in the changed macro and micro-ambient conditions in which these monuments were found.

The most common causes and processes of stone degradation are (Hadžić A. Fočo M. Okilj, M. 2014) :

-Biological corrosion

Knowing the functioning of vertically diluted and mutually dependent bio-communities is of great importance for the detection of the biological threat of stone slabs of stećci, in order to apply an adequate cleaning treatment. Here, it primarily means: algae (in powder form) , which in the community with fungi and lichens have a detrimental effect on the stone surface; fungi (seal on stone surfaces) with algae form the basis for the development of lichens, whose dentition is the most important for stone; lichen (multicomponent plants) - the most damaging of the colossal species that are characteristic of the stone; endangerment is manifested by the presence of carbon dioxide and secretion as a result of the metabolic process (organic and inorganic acid) , which corrode the surface of the stone and cause its corrosion; mosses (mostly endangering porous stone surfaces where moisture is retained) ; ivy (with its strong root penetrates the cracks in the structure of the stone.)

-Chemical corrosion

Chemical corrosion caused by the interaction of sulfur and carbon dioxide with moisture, leads to the deformation of stone limestone. Some of the damage in the form of florescence, or crystallization or blossoming of stone, can be manifested in the form of missing parts of stećak tiles, or the unfinishedness of decorative compositions, which occurred during the production of stećci in the original time of their making.

-Physical corrosion

Temperature inversions, combined with the insolation and rust of winds characteristic of this area and the permeability of stone limestone (2.8%) .

-Abrasion and erosion

Wind effect has the effect of constant light blasting, which leads to a gradual loss of decorative compositions on stone surfaces, if they are not adequately protected.

-Operation of water (negative impact of water)

Combating the negative effects of water is a demanding process, mostly referring to the rehabilitation of the pavement, the caverns and the protection of the stone surface of the stećci.

In order to find an adequate solution for the permanent systematic conservation of stećci and to do the project documentation, it is necessary to perform several stages of work in order to establish the correct diagnostics and curative segment, i. e. the conservation procedure for elimination of threats and damage.

For the purposes of designing project documentation, it is necessary to:

· Perform an insight into the field with the finding of the number of stećci at the site, forms and decorative compositions with the production of accompanying narrative and photo documentation;

· Determining the types, causes and degrees of damage of biological, physical and chemical origin;

· If it is possible (and necessary) to analyze stone structures using non-destructive methods (thermographic stone analysis and ultrasound diagnostics) .

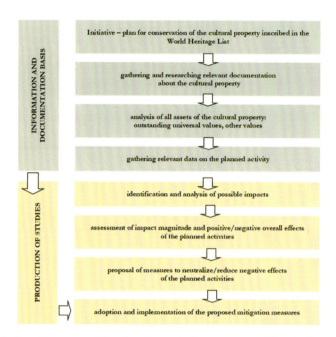

Table 2   Diagram of the implementation process of the Action plan

In order to find an adequate solution, the Conservation Workshop on Stećci - Medieval Tombstones was organized, which was held in Žabljak, Montenegro, 2017. An international expert in the field of stone preservation Simon Warrack was engaged. The main goal of the workshop was to share the knowledge from professionals from different fields of work, and to develop common conservation strategies for all stećci necropolis (Warrack S. 2017) .

BIBLIOGRAPHICAL REFERENCES

1. Group of authors, (2015) *Stećci-Medieval Tombstones*, Nomination Document for the Inscriptionon the UNESCO World Heritage List, Bosnia and Herzegovina,

Republic of Croatia, Montenegro, Republic of Serbia

2. Wenzel, M (1965) *Ukrasni motivi na stećcima I i II, Ormanental motifs on tomb-stones from medieval Bosna and surroundding regions I and II*, Sarajevo

3. A. Hadžić, M. Fočo and M. Okilj *Methodological approach to permanent systematic conservation of*

stećci (An extract from the MP) , Sarajevo-Banja Luka, 2014

4. Warrack S. (2017) *Conservation Workshop on Stećci - Medieval Tombstones*, Žabljak, Montenegro

USED LITERATURE

1. Бандић, Д. (1990.) Царство земаљскоицарствонебеско, *Библиотека XX век 69*, Београд,

2. Бандић, Д. (2004.) *Народна религијаСрбау 100 појмова*, Београд,

3. Бешлагић, Ш. *Стећци*, Каталошко-топографски преглед, Сарајево, 1971.

4. Ћоровић, В. (1989.) *ИсторијаСрба 1*, БИГЗ, Београд

5. Ђорђевић, Т. *Наш народни живот I-IV*, Просвета, Београд, 1984.

6. Зечевић, С. (1982) ., *Култ мртвих код Срба*, Вук Караџић, Београд,

7. Ringbeck, B. (2008) *Management Plans for World Heritage Sites, A practical guide*, German Commission for UNESCO, Bonn,

8. Stovel, H. (1998) , *Risk Preparedness: a Management Manual for World Cultural Heritage*, ICCROM, Rome,

9. Feilden, B. M, and Jokilehto, J. (1998) , *Management Guidelines for World Cultural Heritage Sites*, ICCROM, Rome, Second Edition

浅谈《澳门历史城区保护及管理计划》的编制

中国　澳门特别行政区政府　文化局文化遗产厅　关俊雄[①]

摘要：

　　"澳门历史城区"于 2005 年正式列入《世界遗产名录》，是我国第 31 处世界遗产。作为澳门重要的遗产和资源，"澳门历史城区"在社会文化和经济发展等方面均具有突出的地位，它是澳门城市可持续发展的宝贵财富，而为使这一宝贵的财富在未来后世得以永续传承，澳门特区政府积极有序持续推进《澳门历史城区保护及管理计划》的编制及相关的立法工作，本文指出《澳门历史城区保护及管理计划》的编制依据，并尝试浅析《澳门历史城区保护及管理计划》咨询文本相关内容。

　　关键词："澳门历史城区"，《澳门历史城区保护及管理计划》，《文化遗产保护法》，咨询文本

一、"澳门历史城区"概述

　　"澳门历史城区"由 22 座被评定的不动产，即澳门本地的法定文物保护单位，及 8 个广场空间、连接各广场空间及历史建筑的街道组合而成，其保存了澳门 400 多年中西文化交流的历史精髓，是我国境内现存年代最远、规模最大、保存最完整和最集中，以西式建筑为主、中西式建筑互相辉映的历史城区；是西方宗教文化在中国和远东地区传播历史重要的见证；更是 400 多年来中西文化交流互补、多元共存的结晶。在四百多年的历史里，中国人与葡萄牙人在澳门历史城区内，合力营造了不同的生活社区。这些生活社区，除了展示澳门的中、西式建筑艺术特色外，更展现了中葡两国人民不同宗教、文化以至生活习惯的交融与尊重。这种中葡人民共同蕴酿出来的温情、淳朴、包容的社区气息，是澳门最具特色、最有价值的地方。所以，"澳门历史城区"见证了西方文化与中国文化的碰撞与对话，证明了中国文化永不衰败的生命力及其开放性和包容性，以及中西两种相异文化和平共存的可能性。[②]2005 年 7 月 15 日，联合国教科文组织第 29 届世界遗产委员会会议上，"澳门历史城区"以符合世界

---

　　① 关俊雄，现职澳门特别行政区政府文化局文化遗产厅研究及计划处首席高级技术员，为澳门青年学者，先后于南京大学历史学系取得学士、硕士学位，从事澳门历史、文化遗产、考古学、街道地名等范畴的文化研究，至今在《长江文化论丛》、《澳门研究》、《文化杂志》、《城市经纬》等国内及澳门学术刊物发表相关论文超过二十篇。

　　② 澳门特别行政区政府. 澳门世界遗产 [M]. 澳门：澳门特别行政区政府，2005：127、131—132.

遗产遴选标准（Ⅱ）、（Ⅲ）、（Ⅳ）、（Ⅵ），[①] 正式被列入《世界遗产名录》，成为中国第 31 处世界遗产。

作为澳门重要的遗产和资源，"澳门历史城区"在社会文化和经济发展等方面均具有突出的地位，它是澳门城市可持续发展的宝贵财富，而为使这一宝贵的财富在未来后世得以永续传承，有必要以法律手段规范其保护及管理工作。

二、《澳门历史城区保护及管理计划》的编制依据

澳门回归祖国后，依照"一国两制，高度自治"的方针，按《中华人民共和国澳门特别行政区基本法》（下文简称《基本法》），全国性法律除了规定的《关于中华人民共和国国都、纪年、国歌、国旗的决议》《关于中华人民共和国国庆节的决议》《中华人民共和国国籍法》等 11 项外，其余均不在澳门特别行政区实施，而澳门现行的文化遗产保护制度由本地的第 11/2013 号法律《文化遗产保护法》（下文简称《文遗法》）订定。

《文遗法》于 2013 年 8 月通过及公布，并自 2014 年 3 月 1 日正式生效，其立法初衷是为进一步加强澳门的文化遗产保护工作，让文化遗产得到更全面、深入的法律保障，因此，澳门特区政府广泛吸纳社会各界意见拟订的《文遗法》，是本澳文化遗产保护事业的里程碑。较之以往澳葡政府时期的文化遗产保护相关法例，《文遗法》不仅具有更高的法律地位，而且其涵盖范围更广，保护对象包括被评定的不动产、被评定的动产、非物质文化遗产、考古遗产、古树名木等类别，其中，《文遗法》第 50—57 条独立成章规范"澳门历史城区"的保护。

《文遗法》关于保护"澳门历史城区"的法律条文，围绕《澳门历史城区保护及管理计划》（下文简称《保护及管理计划》）而展开，《保护及管理计划》的编制，正是旨在透过特定措施及方法，对"澳门历史城区"作出合适的管理，确保其突出普遍价值得到严格的保护，永续传承。另外，《文遗法》规定《保护及管理计划》须符合该法律的规定和联合国教育、科学及文化组织的指引，并应载明特定措施，以确保"澳门历史城区"所处空间在城市生活、文化、环境方面可持续地发挥作用，[②] 由于"澳门历史城区"已列入《世界遗产名录》，故《保护及管理计划》的编制除须遵守《文遗法》外，亦须遵守相关的国际公约，以及须符合联合国教科文组织世界遗产委员会的决议要求。

三、《澳门历史城区保护及管理计划》咨询文本主要内容浅析

2018 年，文化局公布的《保护及管理计划》咨询文本，具体提出了"澳门历史城区"保护的对象

[①] "澳门历史城区"所符合的世界遗产遴选标准为：（Ⅱ）能在一定时期内或世界某一文化区域内，对建筑艺术、纪念物艺术、城镇规划或景观设计方面的发展产生过大影响；（Ⅲ）能为一种已消逝的文明或文化传统提供一种独特的至少是特殊的见证；（Ⅳ）人类历史发展中某一建筑风格的杰出范例；（Ⅵ）与具特殊普遍意义的事件或现行传统或思想或信仰或文学艺术作品有直接或实质的联系。

[②] 澳门特别行政区第 11/2013 号法律《文化遗产保护法》，第 51 条。

和措施，以咨询公众意见，首先，咨询文本提出"澳门历史城区"的核心区及缓冲区应被视为文化价值相互关联的统一整体，其价值须得到真实、完整的保护，表示保护范围涵盖核心区及缓冲区，符合《文遗法》规定"缓冲区应确保保存其特色，以配合澳门特别行政区城区特色生活的方式，尤其是保存其地貌及形态、自然物与环境景观的结合、往昔港口城市的城市布局，以及保存被评定的不动产在建筑艺术上的完整性"[①]的精神。另外，咨询文本提出《保护及管理计划》的目标及愿景是对"澳门历史城区"作出合适的管理，确保其突出普遍价值得到严格的保护，永续传承，并通过对世界遗产的公众参与、优化管理和合理利用，以促进本澳社会及城市整体的可持续发展，以及为本澳建设成世界旅游休闲中心的发展定位提供基础。

建筑及城市空间是"澳门历史城区"的重要载体，其价值与特色的维护和弘扬，关系到其普世价值与历史文化的延续，而根据《文遗法》，为有效保护"澳门历史城区"，《保护及管理计划》应包括四个方面内容：（1）景观管理监督，尤其是街道风貌、景观视廊等方面的规定；（2）建筑限制条件，尤其是建筑的高度、体量、样式等方面的规定；（3）城市肌理的维护措施及改造限制；（4）建筑修复准则。[②] 因此，咨询文本的主体内容便是按上述内容展开。

1. 景观管理监督

对于"澳门历史城区"，尤其是当中的历史建筑景观、自然景观、特色街道景观与城市整体景观，均是"澳门历史城区"文化特色及历史意义内涵的载体，是其突出普遍价值的反映。因此，上述景观的保存状况与完整性体现的程度，是"澳门历史城区"保存与延续的关键要素。因此，咨询文本按《文遗法》规定提出循景观视廊、街道风貌两方面实施景观管理监督。

（1）景观视廊

咨询文本提出重点考虑以下类别景观视廊的维护：城区制高点与海洋的景观联系、重要历史建筑物之间的景观联系、重要历史建筑物与重要开敞空间的景观联系，并明确提出 11 条须作特别保护的重要景观视廊，同时，明确提出每条景观视廊的景观价值及管理措施，例如塔石广场是澳门半岛城市中心以及"澳门历史城区"东西两个缓冲区之间最主要的公共开敞空间，而东望洋炮台及灯塔作为城区内海拔最高的主要公共观景处及制高点，故该两处地点均属城市的重要观景地点，且其均相互作为对方的景观视觉焦点，它们间相互方向的景观体现了"澳门历史城区"重要建筑物与周边主要公共空间节点间的重要视觉联系，提出之管理措施为该景观范围须由相关职权部门以城市规划手段，共同对其发展制定合适的建筑高度，并在日后的城市规划中体现。另外，注重邻近东望洋山的建筑设计与山体环境的协调性，各职权部门相互合作，逐步制定相应的屋顶设计指南。

---

① 澳门特别行政区第 11/2013 号法律《文化遗产保护法》，第 50 条。
② 澳门特别行政区第 11/2013 号法律《文化遗产保护法》，第 52 条。

（2）街道风貌

街道风貌是指街道或公共开敞空间主要通过沿街建筑外观及空间格局，以至铺地、历史遗迹、公共设施、街道功能、人文元素、自然环境及社会关系等所综合形成的整体氛围。街道及开敞空间的风貌是"澳门历史城区"特色的视觉体现，能让人们最直观地感受城区的空间特色与历史氛围。街道的走向、街道及开敞空间的尺度、铺地、设施、两旁的建筑等，共同展现了"澳门历史城区"的城市特色，是"澳门历史城区"突出普遍价值的载体之一。咨询文本明确提出能反映"澳门历史城区"突出普遍价值的 19 组"风貌街道"，指出应在宣传物品、外立面设计、特色铺地、街道设施四方面要素上作适当管理，同时，就每组风貌街道明确提出其风貌特征及价值、管理措施，例如关前后街特色建筑集中，建筑风格统一且界面具较好连续性，是体现该类建筑形式及风格在"澳门历史城区"内延续至今的典型代表，其主要管理措施包括建筑物外立面的设计，尤其立面材质、色彩及墙身的虚实比例，须与该"风貌街道"西侧，由果栏街至炉巷，及由炉巷至短巷间的两组历史建筑物群组之外观相协调；应适当限制广告招牌等宣传物品及相关结构物的安装、张贴或放置位置、大小、数量及色彩；维持现有或恢复原有特色铺地。

2.建筑限制条件

为使城区发展方向、方式、规模及强度等处于可控与可接受的程度，"澳门历史城区"的建筑限制条件除了须考虑城区的"景观视廊"、"城市肌理"及"街道风貌"外，亦应遵从相关建筑限制条件，以制定较全面及综合的管理要求。

"澳门历史城区"内被评定或待评定的不动产，是城区文化价值或特色的重要物质载体，必须确保其得到妥善的保护。对涉及被评定或待评定的不动产地段之建筑限制条件之制定，整体上应采取保护为主，适度活化利用的原则，除严格遵守《文遗法》的要求外，尚须按其文物类别遵守以下其他要求：

（1）纪念物

须完整保留不动产；对有利于保护、恢复或彰显该纪念物的价值之情况下，经文化局评估及发出意见后，可进行局部的建筑复原或优化工程与工作；须保留范围内之《古树名木保护名录》中的树木，且职权部门须在取得文化局的意见后，尽可能保留范围内倘有之古树、大树。

（2）具建筑艺术价值的楼宇

须完整保留不动产；对有利于保护、恢复、彰显或不贬损该建筑物的价值之情况下，经文化局评估及发出意见后，可对其内部进行局部的更改；须保留范围内之《古树名木保护名录》中的树木，且职权部门须在取得文化局的意见后，尽可能保留范围内倘有之古树、大树。

（3）建筑群

原则上楼宇均须保留全部的沿街立面，但在不降低建筑群价值的情况下，经文化局评估及发出意

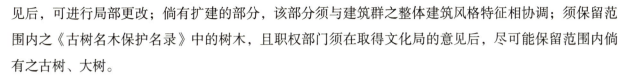

见后，可进行局部更改；倘有扩建的部分，该部分须与建筑群之整体建筑风格特征相协调；须保留范围内之《古树名木保护名录》中的树木，且职权部门须在取得文化局的意见后，尽可能保留范围内倘有之古树、大树。

（4）场所

须维持或彰显场所的环境特征，如地形地貌、绿化空间、整体绿地率、土地覆盖率、土地利用现状等特征；涉及山体的场所，建筑物的高度应与场所的形态特征相协调，且山体主要受观赏面的轮廓线不得被干扰；须保留范围内之《古树名木保护名录》中的树木，且职权部门须在取得文化局的意见后，尽可能保留范围内倘有之古树、大树；保留范围内倘有的与场所有密切关联的历史或特色建构筑物。

另外，为延续被评定的不动产与其周边背景环境的文脉关系，或避免受与之相邻的建筑环境的妨碍或干扰，或是对被评定的不动产的管理维护及结构安全性的考虑，或期望促使其周边具有良好的景观质量以营造良好文化场景及景观视线的体验等考虑，一般情况下，须在建筑高度、体量、色彩以及立面设计上，与相邻的被评定的不动产相协调，同时，避免在空间上对被评定的不动产构成压迫感或影响其景观质量，此外，需注意不干扰及遮挡从主要街道节点或开敞空间观视被评定的不动产的视线，以确保其良好展现。此外，为维护城区的整体性及空间氛围，缓冲区内楼宇高度限制在20.5米或以下。

3. 城市肌理的维护措施及改造限制

城市肌理是体现城区突出普遍价值的重要元素，同时也是城区内的社会组织模式、邻里关系、情感记忆、宗教仪式及风俗习惯等人文活动的载体，体现了城市发展的特征、逻辑、痕迹以及城市的规划理念。"澳门历史城区"的街道是城市中重要的公共空间，也是城区城市肌理主要的构成部分，其作为城市空间特征与人文活动的载体，是人们认识、理解和体会"澳门历史城区"空间特征及多元文化融合的人文特色的重要渠道，是观察、感受和体验"澳门历史城区"城市特色风貌的最主要途径，对在城区内的步行经验的建立积累和心理感受方面具有重要作用。咨询文本提出24组"具重要城市肌理特征的区域及街道线路"，并就各组指出其肌理价值，提出其相应的主要管理措施。例如，苦力围是"澳门历史城区"内反映出传统华人生活聚居特色的居住组团空间，当中仍保留有完整的门楼及土地公，反映了传统围、里的街道肌理，体现了"澳门历史城区"多元文化共存及延续的突出普遍价值，管理措施包括维持具围合性且只有一个街道出入口的空间形态特征，避免因道路拓宽或收窄而改变其空间尺度感；避免改变围内街道与其他街巷的连接关系等。

4. 建筑修复准则

为了"澳门历史城区"的良好保存，对于城区内具重要文化价值的不动产之修复，其工作须有具体及严谨的要求，包括修复具重要文化价值的不动产时，须事前确认其价值特色，保留其具价值特色的部位或构件，同时须保留能反映该不动产的历史时期及建筑风格等信息的内容；修复工作应确保具重要文化价值的不动产的原位置、形式、材质、工艺、功能，以及环境氛围的真实，避免臆测性修复或制造"假古董";同时,修复工作应考虑对不动产各部分所组成的整体连同周边环境的完整保护,延续其文脉背景的完整性。修复过程需依赖考证,多方面透过历史及文物史料作为辩证不动产原貌的依据,同时,考究其他旁证,在掌握确切可靠的资料时,方可考虑恢复缺失的部分;修复时对于一些不可避免的新增或后加物,必须与原建筑物的建筑构件有所区别。要使建筑物本身的时间痕迹,以及有意义的添加、缺失和改变都清晰地显示出来,避免影响对建筑物历史信息的解读;对具重要文化价值的不动产的修复,应视其为停止、延缓建筑破损趋势,或恢复、保持其强度的措施,修复过程中须以最小干预为原则,即尽可能采用最少、最低程度及必要的修复处理工作,以保留原不动产最多的、最大程度的历史信息;为修复具重要文化价值的不动产而必须设置的附加物应具可逆性,在其移除时不会对原不动产造成破坏;为确保具重要文化价值的不动产之修复工作的科学性与严谨性,其工作流程应符合以价值保护为导向及合理性的原则,当对具重要文化价值的不动产的价值未有充份理解与认识,或对其位置、形式、材质、工艺、功能,以及环境氛围等的情况及信息未能确认或完全掌握时,应咨询相关专业人士、部门或机构之专业意见,以确保该等不动产能得到正确及适当的修复;为使修复工作在一定的长时间内具有延续性,并为每次的修复工作提供可供依循的、科学性的参考,文化局及其他主管的公共部门可按实际情况,制定相应的、具针对性或普遍性的技术指南。

除了上述按《文遗法》所规定《保护及管理计划》应包括的四个方面内容,咨询文本还提出其他保护管理工作,包括提出城区内向公众开放的被评定的不动产应制定日常使用管理计划,其内容尤其包括管理人员及工作人员的管理、场地使用管理,如使用功能、防火措施、结构安全、节庆活动特别措施、游客管理、景点承载力管理。此外,为防止或减少灾害事故对城区内被评定的不动产的保存状况造成负面影响,科学有效地保存城区内被评定的不动产,对风险情况进行事前预防工作,并提前制定相应的应急预案,咨询文本提出不动产权利人及占有人必须对各种可能影响不动产的风险有充分了解,做好预防工作,根据实际情况制定应急预案和通报机制,同时,定期进行检查,加强人员培训,提高事故应变能力,并在事故后作出检讨。此外,应对消防、虫害、结构安全等各类风险具管理措施。

此外,为动态了解"澳门历史城区"的保护状况,掌握及预警其变化趋势,咨询文本提出监测"澳门历史城区"的突出普遍价值的组成部分,尤其是指核心区内的 8 个广场空间、22 处被评定的不动产。针对核心区内的 8 个广场空间,其监测重点内容为设计、环境及内涵意义的变化;针对核心区内 22 处被评定的不动产,其监测重点内容为设计、材料、工艺、环境方面的真实性,以及建筑结构、外观、室内外环境的保存状况。有关工作旨在按监测结果进行决策,从而有效、及时地避免"澳门历史城区"突出普遍价值受到破坏或损害。

"澳门历史城区"是一个"活的文化遗产",与单纯的考古遗迹或历史建筑不同,其作为一个每日仍然有大量居民于其中开展生活及生产活动的、复杂的城市系统,其突出普遍价值的全面及有效保护,除了以遗产本体及其景观特征的保存延续为基础外,必然亦涉及其他方面、不同层次的工作范畴。为此,咨询文本亦针对财政资源、特色生活方式的延续、旅游、交通、市政设施、城区绿化、宣传与教育,以及研究工作共八个方面的范畴,提出相应的管理方向。例如,在宣传与教育,文化局与相关职

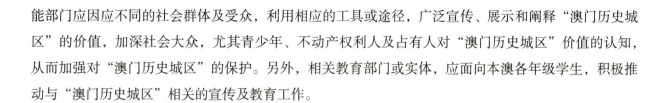

能部门应因应不同的社会群体及受众，利用相应的工具或途径，广泛宣传、展示和阐释"澳门历史城区"的价值，加深社会大众，尤其青少年、不动产权利人及占有人对"澳门历史城区"价值的认知，从而加强对"澳门历史城区"的保护。另外，相关教育部门或实体，应面向本澳各年级学生，积极推动与"澳门历史城区"相关的宣传及教育工作。

结语

落实"澳门历史城区"的保护及管理工作是一项极大的挑战，需要全澳市民共同参与，发挥身为世界遗产地主人翁的精神，为"澳门历史城区"的保护出谋献策，齐心合力，相互配合和支持，因此，2018 年 1 月 20 日至 3 月 20 日期间，文化局就上述《保护及管理计划》咨询文本具体提出的保护对象和措施公开咨询，广泛听取公众的意见，集思广益，咨询期间共收到 1790 份，合共 2050 条意见，① 为制定《保护及管理计划》行政法规，打下坚实的基础，目前，特区政府正继续完善和推进《保护及管理计划》的行政法规草案编制及相关的立法工作，期望凝聚社会共识而编制的《保护及管理计划》能为"澳门历史城区"带来更全面的保护，使其突出普遍价值得以永续传承。

---

① 澳门特别行政区政府.澳门历史城区保护及管理计划公开咨询意见总结报告 [M]. 澳门：澳门特别行政区政府，2018：1.

A Tentative Discussion on the Preparation of the Conservation and Management Plan for the Historic Centre of Macao

Kuan Chon Hong[1]

Department of Cultural Heritage of Cultural Affairs Bureau

Macao SAR Government of China

Abstract:

The Historic Centre of Macao was officially inscribed on the World Heritage List in 2005, becoming the 31st World Heritage property in China. As an important heritage property in Macao, the Historic Centre of Macao occupies an outstanding position in the city's social, cultural and economic development and establishes itself as the city's valuable asset for sustainable development. In order to hand down the valuable property to future generations, the Macao SAR Government has actively worked to prepare the *Convention and Management Plan for the Historic Centre of Macao* and formulate related legislations. The essay intends to explain the basis for the preparation of the plan and analyze the content of its advisory text.

Key words: Historic Centre of Macao, Convention and Management Plan for the Historic Centre of Macao, Cultural Heritage Convention Law, advisory text

I. An Overview of the Historic Centre of Macao

The Historic Centre of Macao comprises of 22 immoveable properties designated as monuments under legal convention of Macao, 8 squares as well as streets linking squares and historic buildings. It bears a testimony to the history of cultural encounters between China and West that occurred in Macao for more than 400 years. It is the oldest, largest and best preserved historic urban center in China that has the highest

---

① Kuan Chon Hong is chief senior technician in the Division of Research and Planning, Department of Cultural Heritage, Cultural Affairs Bureau of Macao SAR Government. As a young Macao-based scholar, he obtained BA and MA degrees from the History Department of Nanjing University and is engaged in research of Macao's history, cultural heritage, archaeology, and street names. He has published over 20 treatises and essays in journals of Mainland China and Macao, such as Symposium on Yangtze River Culture, Review of Culture, Atlas of Cities and Journal of Macau Studies.

concentration of Western-style buildings supplemented by those mixing Chinese and Western elements. It is also the important evidence to testify to the dissemination of Western religion and culture in China and other parts of Far East, crystalizing China-West cultural encounters and co-existence of diverse cultures. Over a period of some 400 years, Chinese and Portuguese developed distinct living communities within the Historic Centre of Macao. In addition to Chinese and Western architectural styles, these living communities also demonstrate fusion and mutual respect between different religions, cultures and living habits of Chinese and Portuguese people. The community spirit of warmth, honesty and inclusion jointly developed by Chinese and Portuguese is the most characteristic and valuable element of Macao. That is why the Historic Centre of Macao bears a testimony to the meeting and dialogue of Western and Chinese cultures, the everlasting vitality, openness and inclusion of Chinese culture, and the possibility of peaceful coexistence of the two different cultures of China and West[①]. On 15 July 2005, the World Heritage Committee at its 29th session inscribed the Historic Centre of Macao on the World Heritage List on the basis of criteria (ii) , (iii) , (iv) and (vi) [②], which became the 31st World Heritage property in China.

As an important heritage property in Macao, the Historic Centre of Macao occupies an outstanding position in the city's social, cultural and economic development and establishes itself as the city's valuable asset for sustainable development. It is therefore necessary to regulate its convention and management through legal means in order to hand it down to future generations.

II. The Basis for the Preparation of *Convention and Management Plan for the Historic Centre of Macao*

In accordance with the principle of "one country, two systems with a high degree of autonomy" and the *Basic Law of the Macao Special Administrative Region of the People's Republic of China* (hereinafter referred to as the Basic Law) , no other national laws shall be applicable to Macao SAR, except the 11 national laws, including the *Resolution on the Capital, Calendar, National Anthem and National Flag of the People's Republic of China*, the *Resolution on the National Day of the People's Republic of China*, and the *Nationality Law of the People's Republic of China*. The existing system for the convention of cultural heritage in Macao was established in accordance with the *Cultural Heritage Convention Law No.11/2013* (hereinafter referred to as the Law) which is a local law of Macao.

---

① Macao SAR Government. The World Heritage Property of Macao (M) . Macao, Macao SAR Government, 2015, p.127, pp.131-132.

② The Historic Centre of Macao meets the following criteria for the selection of World Heritage sites: (ii) to exhibit an important interchange of human values, over a span of time or within a cultural area of the world, on developments in architecture or technology, monumental arts, town-planning or landscape design; (iii) to bear a unique or at least exceptional testimony to a cultural tradition or to a civilization which is living or which has disappeared; and (vi) to be directly or tangibly associated with events or living traditions, with ideas, or with beliefs, with artistic and literary works of outstanding universal significance.

The *Cultural Heritage Convention Law* was adopted and promulgated in August 2013 and officially came into effect on 1 March 2014. The purpose of the Law is to strengthen legislation on cultural heritage convention and provide more comprehensive and stronger guarantees for cultural heritage protection. The Law, which was developed by drawing from extensive comments from all walks of life in Macao, is a milestone legal instrument for the cause of cultural heritage convention in Macao. Comparing to previous laws and regulations on cultural heritage convention during the period of the Portuguese administration, the Law enjoys a higher legal status and governs a wider range of protected properties, including designated immoveable properties, designated moveable properties, intangible cultural heritage, archaeological properties, and ancient and famous trees. Among others, the convention of the Historic Centre of Macao is specified in a separate chapter (articles 50-57) in the Cultural Heritage Convention Law.

Legal clauses on the convention of the Historic Center of Macao specified in the Law focuses on the *Convention and Management Plan for the Historic Centre of Macao* (hereinafter referred to as the Convention and Management Plan) . The preparation of the *Convention and Management Plan* aims to exercise appropriate management of the Historic Center of Macao and ensure strict convention of its Outstanding Universal Value through the development of specific measures and methods. In addition, pursuant to the Law, the *Convention and Management Plan* shall meet provisions of the Law and guidelines of UNESCO and contain specific measures in order to secure the role of the Historic Centre of Macao in urban life, culture and environment[①]. Due to the inscription of the property on the World Heritage List, the preparation of the *Convention and Management Plan* shall also come up with relevant international conventions and decisions of the UNESCO World Heritage Committee.

III. A Tentative Analysis of the Advisory Text of the *Convention and Management Plan*

In 2018, the Cultural Affairs Bureau of Macao publicized the advisory text of the *Convention and Management Plan* to invite public comments and advice, in which protected properties and protective measures are proposed. First, the advisory text states that the core area and buffer zone of the Historic Centre of Macao should be deemed as an integrated whole whose cultural values are inter-related and shall be protected in an authentic and integral manner. The protected area shall cover both the core area and the buffer zone, which reflects the the spirit as stated in the Law that "The buffer zone should preserve its characteristics in order to respond to the characteristic lifestyle of Macao, with particular preservation focusing on the combination of its landforms with natural objects and environmental landscapes, the urban layout of the past port city, and

---

① Macao SAR Cultural Heritage Convention Law No. 11/2013, Article 51.

integrity of designated immoveable properties in terms of architecture and the arts." In addition, the advisory text also proposes the objectives and visions of the *Convention and Management Plan* which should be to exercise appropriate management of the Historic Centre of Macao, ensure strict convention and continuation of its OUV, promote overall social and urban sustainable development of Macao through public participation, optimized management and reasonable utilization of the World Cultural Heritage site, and lay a foundation for the development of Macao as a global travel & leisure center.

Buildings and urban spaces are important physical carriers of the Historic Centre of Macao. Safeguarding and promoting their values and characteristics are crucial to the continuation of the property's OUV and its history and culture. Pursuant to the Law, in order to effectively protect the Historic Centre of Macao, the *Convention and Management Law* should contain regulations on the following four aspects: 1) landscape management and supervision, with particular focus on street scenarios and landscape corridors; 2) building restrictions, with particular restrictions on height, size and form of buildings; 3) safeguarding measures and innovation restrictions on urban fabrics; and 4) building restoration principles[①]. The advisory text was prepared with focus on the above-mentioned four areas.

1.Landscape management and supervision

Historic building landscapes, natural landscapes, characteristic street landscapes and overall urban landscapes are all physical carriers of cultural features and historical meanings of the Historic Centre of Macao. Their state of preservation and degrees of integrity are key factors for the preservation and continuation of the property. Pursuant to the Law, the advisory text proposes regulations on management and supervision of landscape corridors and street scenarios.

(1) Landscape corridors

In the advisory text, safeguarding of the following categories of landscape corridors are given priority consideration: association of urban commanding heights with the ocean, landscape association between important historic buildings, and landscape association of important historic buildings with important open spaces. It is also clearly specified that 11 important landscape corridors shall be given special protection. Landscape values and management measures have been proposed for each of the landscape corridors. For example, Tap Seac Square is the urban center of Macao Peninsula and the most principal public open space between the eastern and western buffer zones of the property, while Guia Fortress and Lighthouse is the highest public view point and commanding height in the urban area. The two sites are therefore important urban view points. They are visual focuses of each other and landscapes viewed from each other demonstrate important visual association between key buildings of the property and nodes of its surrounding public spaces. Therefore,

---

① Macao SAR Cultural Heritage Convention Law No. 11/2013, Article 52.

competent authorities should develop appropriate restrictions on height of buildings within the range of the landscapes and incorporate them in the future urban plan. In addition, attention should be paid to harmony between buildings on the neighboring Guia Hill and in its mountain setting. Competent authorities should collaborate with each other to work out corresponding guidelines for roof designing.

(2) Street scenarios

Street scenarios refers to an overall environment of streets and public open spaces presented by street-front buildings and their spatial layouts, pavements, historic remains, public facilities, street functions, cultural elements, natural environment and social relationships. Scenarios of streets and public open spaces are visual embodiments of characteristics of the Historic Centre of Macao, enabling people to experience spatial features and historical scenarios of urban areas. Directions of streets and sizes, pavements, facilities of streets and open spaces as well as buildings along them are combined to demonstrate urban features of the Historic Centre of Macao and serve as physical barriers of its OUV. The advisory text proposes 19 groups of "characteristic streets" that can exhibit the OUV of the Historic Centre of Macao, noting that appropriate management should be exercised regarding publicity materials, façade designing, characteristic pavements, and street facilities. Features and values of each group of characteristic streets and management measures are also defined in the advisory text. For example, Rua dos Ervanarios has a high concentration of characteristic buildings which have a unified style and a good continuity in their architectural interfaces. They are typical surviving examples to demonstrate the style and forms of this type of buildings. Therefore, management measures have been developed to ensure that their facades, in particular their materials, colors and wall proportions of facades, shall keep harmony with the two groups of historic buildings on the west side of the street that extend from Rua Da Tercena to Travessa do Fogão and from Travessa do Fogão to Travessa Curta. Regulations shall be applied to the installation, location, size, number and color of publicity materials and their related structures such as advertising signboards, and existing characteristic pavements shall be maintained or original ones restored.

2.Building restrictions

In order to keep the direction, pattern, scale and intensity of urban development to a controllable or acceptable degree, building restrictions should be also developed as part of comprehensive management requirements, in addition to landscape corridors, urban fabrics and street scenarios.

Immoveable properties designated or to be designated within the Historic Centre of Macao are important physical carriers of cultural values and characteristics of the urban area and must be properly protected. In formulating building restrictions on urban sections that are involved with immoveable properties designated or to be designated, the principle of "emphasis on convention with appropriate activation and utilization" should

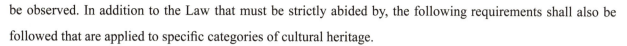

be observed. In addition to the Law that must be strictly abided by, the following requirements shall also be followed that are applied to specific categories of cultural heritage.

(1) Monuments

Immoveable properties shall be integrally preserved. Partial restoration or optimization works that shall be beneficial to protecting, restoring or highlighting monument values can be carried out with assessment and approval of the Cultural Affairs Bureau. Trees included on the List of Ancient and Famous Trees under Convention shall be preserved. Competent authorities shall use best possible efforts to preserve ancient and large trees in line with suggestions of the Cultural Affairs Bureau.

(2) Buildings with architectural and artistic values

Immoveable properties shall be integrally preserved. Partial modifications to building interiors that shall be beneficial to protecting, restoring, highlighting or not degrading building values can be carried out. Trees included on the List of Ancient and Famous Trees under Convention shall be preserved. Competent authorities shall use best possible efforts to preserve ancient and large trees in line with suggestions of the Cultural Affairs Bureau.

(3) Building complexes

All street-front facades of historic buildings shall be preserved in principle. Partial modifications that shall not reduce values of building complexes can be carried out with the assessment and approval of the Cultural Affairs Bureau. In case of extensions, extended parts shall keep harmony with overall style and features of the building complex. Trees included on the List of Ancient and Famous Trees under Convention shall be preserved. Competent authorities shall use best possible efforts to preserve ancient and large trees in line with suggestions of the Cultural Affairs Bureau.

(4) Places

Environmental features of places shall be maintained or highlighted, such as landform, green space, overall greening rate, state of land use, etc. As regards places that are involved with mountains, building height should keep harmony with form of places and mountain outlines in sightseeing parts shall not be intervened. Trees on the List of Ancient and Famous Trees under Convention shall be preserved. Competent authorities shall preserve surviving ancient or large trees to the extent possible upon receipt of decisions of the Cultural Affairs Bureau. Historic or characteristic buildings that have close association with places shall be preserved.

In addition, in order to continue the cultural context of designated immoveable properties in relation to their settings, or to prevent them from intervention of neighboring building environments, or to ensure the management, safeguarding and structural safety of designated immoveable properties, or to enable a good landscape setting so as to create a good cultural place and a landscape view, height, size, color and facade of buildings should keep harmony with neighboring designated immoveable properties and should not have impact of oppression on designated immoveable properties or affect their landscape quality. Moreover, visual lines of designated immoveable properties viewed from major street nodes or open spaces should not be intervened or blocked. Height of buildings within the buffer zone shall be restricted to 20.5m or below in order to maintain the integrity and spatial context of the urban area.

3. Safeguarding measures and innovation restrictions on urban fabrics

Urban fabrics are important elements to exhibit the property's OUV and physical carriers of social organization, neighborhood relationship, memories of feeling and emotion, religious rituals, customs and habits, demonstrating features, logics and traces of urban development and urban planning ideas. Streets in the Historic Centre of Macao are important public spaces in the city and major components of urban fabrics. As carriers of the city's spatial features and cultural activities, they are important means for people to know, understand and perceive spatial features and multicultural fusion of the Historic Centre of Macao and the most principal channel to observe, conceive and experience urban characteristics and scenarios of the Historic Centre of Macao. They play an important role in developing pedestrian and mental experiences within the urban area. The advisory text proposes the 24 groups of quarters and street routes with important urban fabric features and management measures in response to their specific urban fabric values. For example, Pátio dos Culcs is a residential community that reflects the traditional lifestyle of Chinese residents in the Historic Centre of Macao, with the integrally preserved entrance gate tower and statue of Land Deity that demonstrate street fabrics of traditional neighborhoods and the property's OUV as represented by multicultural coexistence. Management measures include maintaining spatial form and characteristics of the enclosed community with only one entrance so as to prevent changes in its size due to road expansion or narrowing or changes in connections between streets inside and outside the community.

4. Building restoration principles

In order to better preserve the Historic Centre of Macao, specific and strict requirements shall be formulated to regulate restoration activities for immoveable properties with important cultural values in the urban area. Values and characteristics of immoveable properties with important cultural values shall be identified and characteristic parts or components retained when a restoration works is to be carried out. Information that exhibits historical periods and architectural styles of immoveable properties to be restored shall also be retained. Restoration works should ensure the preservation of original locations, forms, materials processes and functions of the immoveable properties as well as the authenticity of their settings so as to avoid speculation-based restoration or creation of "bogus monuments". Meanwhile, restoration works should also take into account integrated convention of comprising components of the immoveable property as a whole and its setting so as to continue the integrity of its cultural context. Restoration works should be conducted based on research results, in particular historical and heritage evidence that justifies original state of the immoveable property. Restoration of missing parts can be considered only on the basis of concrete and reliable evidence. New additions that are necessary for restoration must distinguish themselves from original parts so as to clearly show chronological traces of buildings and meaningful additions, missing parts and modifications and not affect interpretation of historical information about buildings. Restoration of immoveable properties with important cultural values should be deemed as a measure to stop or slow down the process of degradation and destruction and to restore or maintain building intensity. The principle of minimal intervention shall be observed to exercise minimal, least intensive and necessary restoration measures so as to retain the historical information of the original immoveable property to the extent possible. Additions that are necessary to be added to immoveable properties with important cultural values should be reversible; its removal should not cause damage to the original property. The restoration work process should abide by the principle focusing on value convention and restoration reasonability and ensure full understanding and recognition of the property's values so as to guarantee restoration works are carried out in a scientific and standard manner. When there is no full recognition and understanding of location, form, materials, process, functions and setting of the immoveable property. The restoration team should consult experts or professional departments or institutions so as to ensure correct and appropriate restoration of the immoveable property. In order to guarantee its durability and continuity, scientific references should be provided for restoration works and the Cultural Affairs Bureau and other competent authorities can formulate specific or common technical guidelines.

In addition to the four focus areas that should be included in the *Convention and Management Plan* pursuant to the Law, the advisory text also proposes other requirements. For example, daily management plans should be formulated for designated immoveable properties in the urban area that are open to public, including regulations on management of staff members and places, special regulations on facility functions, fire control, structural safety and festivals and events, and management of tourists and accommodation capacity. In order to prevent or reduce adverse impact on the state of conservation of designated properties in the urban area and preserve them in a scientific and effective manner, risk preparedness should be conducted and emergency plan formulated. It is proposed in the advisory text that stakeholders and owners of immoveable properties must have a full understanding of all possible risks that may affect the immoveable properties, conduct risk preparedness and develop emergency plans and reporting mechanisms based on actual situations. Meanwhile, inspections should be conducted on a regular basis and personnel training strengthened so as to enhance capacity for accident response and after-accident review. Specific measures should also be formulated to address risks of fire, insect hazards and structural safety.

In order to keep informed of the state of conservation of the property and its changes and trends and to conduct early warnings, monitoring of components of the property's OUV is also proposed in the advisory text, with particular focus on the 8 squares and 22 designated immoveable properties in the core area. Key areas of monitoring for the 8 squares include changes in theirs designs, environments and meanings. Key areas of monitoring for the 22 designated immoveable properties include authenticity of designs, materials, processes and environments, as well as the state of preservation in architectural structures, facades, interior and exterior environments. Decisions shall be made based on monitoring results so as to effectively and timely prevent damage or destruction to the OUV of the Historic Centre of Macao.

The Historic Centre of Macao is a living cultural heritage property. Different from archaeological sites or historic monuments, it is a huge, sophisticated urban system where an enormous number of residents are living and engaging in production activities everyday. The comprehensive and effective convention of its OUV, based on the preservation and continuation of its heritage components and landscape features, must be involved with work on various fronts and at various levels. For that reason, the advisory text also proposes management guidelines in eight areas, including continuation of characteristic lifestyle, tourism, transport, municipal infrastructure, urban greening, publicity and education, and research. For example, as regard publicity and education, the Cultural Affairs Bureau and other competent departments should use appropriate tools and approaches to promote, present and interpret values of the property so as to deepen understanding of the property's values, in particular among young people and stakeholders and owners of immoveable properties so as to improve the conservation of the property. In addition, relevant education departments or entities should work actively to promote the publicity and education related to the property among students at all grades.

IV. Conclusion

The convention and management of the Historic Centre of Macao is a huge challenge that requires participation of all Macao citizens who should take the initiative as the stakeholders of the World Heritage site to provide advice and support. That is why the Cultural Affairs Bureau publicized the advisory text of the *Convention and Management Plan* to invite public comments and advices from 20 January to 20 March 2018. A total of 1,790 feedback questionnaires were received that contain 2,050 comments and advices[①], laying a solid foundation for the convention of the *Convention and Management Plan*. Currently, the Macao SAR Government is working to improve and finalize the preparation of the *Convention and Management Plan* and related legislations, hoping that the *Convention and Management Plan* that crystalizes social consensus can enable more comprehensive conservation of the Historic Centre of Macao and everlasting continuation of its OUV.

---

① Macao SAR Government. The Summary Report on Public Comments and Advices on the Convention and Management Plan for the Historic Centre of Macao (M) . Macao, Macao SAR Government, January 2018.

斯图德尼察修道院（12世纪）从文物古迹的保护到景观管理

塞尔维亚　文化遗产保护研究所　内维娜·德布约维奇·里斯蒂奇 [①]

摘要：

文化遗产的保护和管理，是一条确保遗产永久性之路，同时也是一个不断识别遗产新价值的过程。除了具有历史、建筑和艺术价值之外，还涉及独特的精神和宗教价值，以及组成遗产的地点和环境的价值。这些价值和环境彼此关联，不能分割，对文化遗产的保护和管理至关重要。

本文以 1986 年列入世界文化和自然遗产名录的斯图德尼察修道院（12世纪）为例，介绍了识别遗产价值的方法和步骤，从而有利于改进保护实践。作为中世纪最高级别的修道院，当引入国家法规或制度时，斯图德尼察修道院的价值集中体现在其文化、历史、建筑、艺术和保护措施等方面。将斯图德尼察修道院列入世界遗产名录并扩大其国际名声，需要更深入研究修道院的环境，保留修道院的文化和宗教传统，在这过程中，发现修道院独特的宗教地形环境。用地理术语来讲，如今它属于 "Golija-Studenica" 生物圈保护区，或更准确地说，属于联合国教科文组织世界生物圈保护区网络（MAB）。

在为斯图德尼察修道院编制《特殊用途区域的空间规划》（Special Purpose Area Spatial Plan）和《管理规划》时，文化景观作为一个整体价值体系出现了：有形价值、无形价值、文化价值、自然价值和精神价值。为了保护这些价值，需要当地社区群众和其他利益相关方的积极参与，以便使遗产整体保护和可持续发展的主要需求，能够在更广泛的范围内展开。

关键词：斯图德尼察修道院，古迹，保护，景观管理

[①] 内维娜·德布约维奇·里斯蒂奇（Nevena Debljovic Ristic），建筑保护专家，目前在塞尔维亚文化遗产保护研究所担任文化遗产顾问，索普察尼修道院（Sopocani）和斯图德尼察修道院（Studenica）项目和现场负责人，也是塞尔维亚世界遗产团队的成员。毕业于贝尔格莱德大学建筑系，获得中世纪建筑历史、理论和美学博士学位。Ristic 女士经常在国际和塞尔维亚科学杂志上发表文章，特别是在中世纪宗教建筑和历史建筑的复兴领域，撰写了大量保护和修复方面的文章。此外，她还积极参加了众多国际和地区会议。

斯图德尼察修道院建筑（12 世纪）

在漫长的历史岁月中，斯图德尼察修道院一直备受尊崇，主要因为修道院是塞尔维亚共和国的创立者，斯特凡·纳曼亚大公（1171—1196）创建的，他统治了接下来的两个世纪。斯图德尼察修道院建筑群是所有塞尔维亚 12—13 世纪修道院的典范，代表了纳曼亚王朝时期的建筑风格（Popovic-Mojsilovic，1994）。

斯图德尼察修道院建在斯图德尼察河上的开阔地带，群山环抱，四周城墙围成一圈，呈理想的几何圆形，中心是一座教堂。圆拱形空间的起源和象征，代表天国耶路撒冷是基督教徒对地球上天国的一种想象（Markovic，1920）。

图 1　从北面俯瞰斯图德尼察修道院（12 世纪）

修道院建筑群的中心有一座专门用来供奉圣母的教堂，修建于 1183 年至 1198 年。教堂是忠于 *Rascia School* 建筑风格的杰出典范，这是由于中世纪塞尔维亚国的特殊地位和政治形势所致。圣母大教堂综合两种建筑风格 —— 拜占庭风格和来自西方（仿罗马式的厚重外墙和建筑雕塑）的风格。教堂内部最突出的特征反映在 1208—1209 年完成的精致壁画上，这些壁画的艺术造诣使得斯图德尼察修道院成为 13 世纪最重要的拜占庭艺术作品之一。圣母大教堂还有 1569 年完成的壁画，代表那个年代的精湛艺术水平和特色。

约 1230 年，王朝奠基人纳曼亚之孙 Radoslav，在圣母大教堂加建了宽敞的外前廊和两座 parekklesions（小教堂）。14 世纪初，纳曼亚的曾孙 Milutin，修建了另一座重要教堂，即"国王大教堂"，来供奉圣母的父母——乔西姆和安娜。国王大教堂内有保存完好的壁画，色彩和谐，技法精湛，代表了 14 世纪上半叶塞尔维亚最有价值的绘画艺术，都是价值连城的珍品（Kasanin，Korac，1986）。

进入遗产地，大小教堂等其他宗教建筑，见证了斯图德尼察修道院的复杂发展。在主教堂的南部，有两座独立的教堂，一座建于13世纪上半叶，是供奉圣尼古拉斯的教堂，另一座是供奉圣约翰的教堂，建于13世纪晚期或14世纪初。在18世纪中期竖立的斯图德尼察修道院铜版蚀刻，刻有在修道院内及附近共14座教堂的名字（Pejic，2010）。

从修道院内的建筑遗迹来看，教堂坐落在建筑群中显要位置，说明修道院直至20世纪下半叶都是该地区的中心。修道院僧侣生活最重要的地方是食堂，建于12世纪晚期，坐落在圣母大教堂入口西面，曾被拆毁重建多次（Nenadovic，1957）。相对于教堂，食堂的位置和半圆后殿的空间外形，指向修道院内其他建筑。僧侣宿舍一般在楼上，沿着修道院的城墙兴建，地下是储物室和工作间。修道院的北面是一座名为"The Great Cells"的大型住宅楼。宿舍和住宅楼的东面是修道院东北建筑群的一部分，沿着围墙有一座供奉圣德梅特尔的小教堂。修道院遗址还有建于16世纪的住宅宿舍，以及后期兴建的新住宅楼及其他建筑（Popovic，2015）。

今天的斯图德尼察修道院是一座宝库，收藏了精美的雕像，供各种礼拜仪式之用的物件，和大理石装饰品，还有图书馆、档案资料室。在斯图德尼察修道院内的大片空地，发现有僧侣住所、小教堂、中世纪聚落和道路、一套中世水系和一个古老的矿井。所有这些遗迹，说明一直有人在这里生存、活动，与修道院的文化、历史和功能息息相连。

斯图德尼察修道院的保护、保存和展示

根据已确认的价值，斯图德尼察修道院于1979年被列入国家重点文物保护单位，具有突出价值，继而在1986年，列入世界文化和自然遗产名录。所以，当评价修道院的价值时，我们需要通盘考虑在

图 2　建筑图纸和雕塑详图（1880 年）

过去的几年里所有在保护、保存和展示方面已实施的方法和过程，还要考虑斯图德尼察修道院的现状和将来的目标。

修道院在漫长的历史长河中受过多次摧毁。其中最严重的一次，发生在 1805—1806 年，圣母大教堂遭到严重损毁。1833 年塞尔维亚脱离奥斯曼土耳其的统治，塞尔维亚第一次有条件修复修道院。1839 年又进行了大范围的整修，包括新建 36 扇窗户，竖起大理石柱，修复地板、屋顶和门楣（Medic，Boskovic，1986）。这些修复非常重要，把圣母大教堂的主要建筑和雕塑的特征作了还原。

19 世纪下半叶，第一次对修道院进行了基于学术的调查，主要是收集资料：教堂的历史，艺术和建筑特征。这次调查，追溯研究塞尔维亚中世纪历史、艺术和建筑的首个科学术语和方法论过程，并建立了斯图德尼察修道院的参考文库，为 20 世纪晚期进行的大量广泛调查奠定了基础。

1877 年对斯图德尼察修道院内的建筑进行结构勘测，国王大教堂的勘测延续至 1880 年。当年对圣母大教堂进行了仔细勘测，而后编制了 30 张图纸和水彩画。除了结构和极其精确的建筑图纸，还有一组引人注目的关于教堂正门和窗户的雕刻。透视图描绘了整个檐口石材细节、拱廊、翅托、柱顶、双形柱（立柱）（Valtrovic，Milutinovic，2006）。

1947 年第二次世界大战结束后，基于已确认的保护价值，斯图德尼察修道院被列为国宝，随后几十年，塞尔维亚政府对修道院进行了研究，调查，修复和保护。1949 年曾对圣母大教堂进行小规模整修。20 世纪 90 年代初，对整个修道院进行了大翻修，范围覆盖教堂、住宅楼、食堂，并重建了部分 18 世纪门廊。1970 年代—1980 年代初，修复了圣母大教堂的穹顶，拆掉 Radoslav（9 世纪塞尔维亚国王）的偏厅、门楣中心的拱形装饰，拆除了食堂老旧门廊等等。在诠释修道院的建筑和艺术时，古迹的突出特征对如何评价其历史和艺术价值有重大影响，一般是从学术和历史的角度评价，由此构建出文化遗产的发展前景（Debljovic-Ristic，2015）。

随着时间流逝，跨学科的互动交流会产生不同观点与视野。回顾历史和政治形势，从中我们可以了解中世纪君王的角色和责任、建造修道院的原则和王位继承法，了解斯图德尼察修道院作为宗教和精神中心对一个王朝的崇拜，以及对圣人世袭门第的崇拜。同样重要的是，从考古调查中我们还能了解到以下几个方面的内容：修道院聚落的空间布局、所有新建活动和拆毁活动的日期、修道院内的教堂和建筑是按种类和大小划分的、圣人崇拜仪式和"风格"特征、建筑雕刻的艺术风格和图像特征等等。

这一独特的中世纪斯图德尼察修道院建筑群，作为拜占庭精神和艺术世界的一部分，具有众多无可争议的价值，根据既定列入文化遗产标准（Ⅰ，Ⅱ，Ⅳ，Ⅵ），修道院于 1986 年被列入联合国世界文化和自然遗产名录。当初提名文件没有包括标准（Ⅰ），后来根据国王大教堂内壁画的独特性特征将其纳入。标准（Ⅱ）是由于圣母大教堂对 13 世纪塞尔维亚和拜占庭建筑和艺术产生了重大影响。至于标准（Ⅳ），ICOMOS 评估后，认为斯图德尼察修道院以及僧侣住所、教堂和采石场，其突出价值体现在它们是"塞尔维亚东正教会修道院的独特典范"，完好保存了"13 世纪到 18 世纪"的建筑结构，同时也是"一种建筑综合体或景观"的杰出范例。标准（Ⅵ）强调了塞尔维亚中世纪最重要的历史人物与斯图德尼察修道院之间的关系。列入世界遗产名录和列入标准的肯定，提醒我们要关注修道院的周边环境。为此，两年后重新确定了遗产地周边环境边界和修道院自然区域，并在 1991 年成立了斯图德尼察修道院管理委员会。但自 1992 年，所有与世界遗产委员会的正式沟通全部停止，原因是国际制裁塞尔维亚。到 2001 年全体大会正式通过塞尔维亚为成员国之后，塞尔维亚才恢复与世界遗产委员会的关系（KesicRistic，2016）。

20 世纪 90 年代，塞尔维亚国家和社会经历了一个"去世俗化"过程，加上南斯拉夫解体，社会和经济的动荡导致政府在保护文化遗产方面的经费大大缩减。与此同时，塞尔维亚东正教会（SOC，Serbian Othodox Church）在政府事务上逐渐取得话语权。随着国家经济力量削弱，修道院附近的公共和旅游设施日渐荒废，最后关门，当地居民也纷纷搬离。另一方面，2010 年代，斯图德尼察修道院越来越受欢迎，经济实力也越来越强，有些国有建筑落入修道院手中，随后几年，修道院有经济能力买下所有修道院附近的建筑物。

20 世纪 90 年代末，由国家文化遗产保护研究所负责，对圣母大教堂的大理石外墙进行大规模保护和修复。经过深入调查研究，获得了大量大理石化学成分的重要数据，并按照原始材料选择混合砂浆的中型性能。确认损毁范围和原因后，制定出大理石外墙的修复方法。这项特别为大理石外墙进行保护和修复的工程，涉及不同学科，用了差不多二十年时间才完成，颇有成效（Barisic，2012）。唯独圣母大教堂主外墙北面的双形柱两个世纪以来没有修复。1956 年的修复工程，发现两块大理石残片，刻有以鸟类为特征的浮雕。

在过去数十年的考古调查中发现的文物资料信息，帮助我们确定了这个重要雕塑单位的整体外观，还原了其本来面目（Popovic，2016）。修复北面的双形柱是一个非常复杂的过程。所有缺失

图 3　从教堂东北方眺望斯图德尼察修道院（12 世纪）外墙修复后的圣母大教堂

的装饰都用原来的材料修复，修复象征三位一体的圆圈，也使用了和修复圣母大教堂外墙一样的材料。经过这次大修复，直到近些年双形柱才恢复旧日完整的建筑外形，浮雕装饰也恢复了神圣意义。（DebljovicRistic，2017）。此外，翻修后的圣母大教堂最大程度地还原了它本来的面目，显示了工匠的高超手艺和技巧。

其中一项修复，为了证明圣母大教堂等同于文化遗产，拆卸了 19 世纪的圣像保护装置，取而代之是使用剩下来的大理石重新建造的祭坛屏风（Barisic，2012）。专家对此做法有不同意见，但壁画和屏风修复后，教堂内部焕然一新，胜过所有礼拜仪式的价值。

修道院的生活方式直至今日基本没变，因此被确认为真实的非物质文化遗产形式，从斯图德尼察修道院建成及典籍编写完成时起保存到现在。直到今天所有塞尔维亚修道院都遵从典籍的指示（Markovic，1920）。从更广泛的角度解释和评估宗教礼仪时，其互相交织彼此关联的非物质过程，通过祷告仪式，隐居方式，拓展的礼拜仪式、劳动和祈祷等来表达活生生的特征，呈现宗教的生命力。这些礼仪，让人类在宗教的启示下，体会生命的存在。

图 4　重建斯图德尼察修道院圣母大教堂祭坛后殿的祭坛屏风和壁画，1208/1209

由此，评估和保护遗产的重心从专注于建筑有形遗产转向更广泛的方面，需要重新界定"古迹"的含义，以便更好地了解历史、艺术、宗教的文化价值和构成生命的精神价值，以及千百年来与人类生活起居息息相关的自然环境，这些都是普世的文化价值观（DebljovicRistic，2011）。

所以，文化遗产保护重点逐渐转向修道院僧侣的日常修行生活及其可持续性方面，在规划和管理方面则集中为僧侣的生活提供宽阔的场所，而斯图德尼察修道院就是僧侣生活的中心。保护和保存的重点仍然集中在与保护有关的具体问题和特征上，还有提升所有已确认的价值。管理方面则包括一套规划和行政制度，以便使上述价值在现在和将来得以持续保存（Jokilehto，2018）。

近几年，修道院与附近的社区、建筑师、文物保护人员合作开展保护活动，帮助人们提升对修道院的认识，促进遗产地的可持续发展。基于此，对建于18世纪用作储物的住宅楼底楼做了大规模修复，以还原其真实面貌。住宅楼以前有一个酒窖，在那里举办品酒活动，供宾客品尝产自Aleksandrovac地区斯图德尼察葡萄园的葡萄酒。住宅楼的用途广泛，除了酒窖，重要会议或宣传斯图德尼察地区的活动也在那举行。

在修道院内的食堂内，启动了一个"数字斯图德尼察"项目。项目借助新技术、新媒体设立一个教育和信息平台，展示修道院的所有地标性文物建筑和文化历史遗产。这个设计理念是让游客在St Sava食堂的餐桌边就可以欣赏到"虚拟的精神食粮"，这其实是介绍斯图德尼察修道院历史和艺术的短片。项目还包含全景虚拟实景体验，戴上HTC虚拟眼镜，就可以欣赏修道院里所有无法接近的建筑和壁画。除此之外，游客教育中心摆放平板电脑播放各种虚拟实景短片，游客也可以在全世界任何一个地方，直接从手机应用商店或Google Play（实时视图应用商店）下载安装 *Holograd* 来欣赏。

作为全新展示斯图德尼察宝库的一部分，展览运用现代化手段，分年代、分类型展示上千年的僧侣生活遗留下来的宗教圣物、遗物盒、福音等。

斯图德尼察修道院还提供一年一度的教堂和活动日历。教堂日历上分别列出七个最重要的圣徒节日，而文化活动日历包括几十年前的活动：艺术殖民地，唱诗班节日，以及其他文化艺术活动。

为了强调修道院周围环境的文化和自然价值，让更多人看到这些价值，一条文化旅游线路（包含本地区三处颇有潜力的景点Rudno，Savovo和Pridvorica）被添加到斯图德尼察地区的旅游图上。当地居民的作用也被肯定，在Rudno地区的Sekler家庭住宿——由当地妇女创业发起的乡村旅游酒店式房间，成功推广当地农家自制产品之余，也让游客感受到了塞尔维亚人民的殷勤好客。众多个人活动，以及重视历史环境和社区（具有成熟自然环境），这些都需要我们编制一个斯图德尼察修道院管理规划，并在《特殊用途区域空间规划》里，把修道院及其周边环境纳入为文化景观。

斯图德尼察修道院神圣的景观

在斯图德尼察修道院附近，多处宗教场所已被确认并得到保护。考古发掘也发现了大量宗教建筑的遗存，都已记录在案，还发现几个堡垒和不少当地建筑。

通过对修道院周边区域进行符号学方面的研究和理解，一种突出的宗教性质的文化历史意义出现了，即在更广阔的空间区域内呈现出一种圣地的地形特征。这种现象，当然归功于修道院一直以来传播宗教意识所发挥的强大作用，所以设立了多个礼拜场地，一般沿墓地服务于当地小社区。景观特征显示，虽然出现了一些小而分散的聚落，但同时也有可能追溯到中世纪至今连续不断的建筑活动（Pešic, Pejic, 1990–1991）。

为了认识和保护整个区域的众多价值，斯图德尼察修道院遗产地的边界已在《特殊用途区域空间规划》里划定，遗产地被确认为特殊的文化景观，以众多圣地为特色。

《特殊用途区域空间规划》的设想，从全面保护和保存出发，加强文化、精神和自然遗产之间的相互作用。这种设想需要对修道院周围更广阔空间区域有整体理解和认识，从而使之成为一种文化景观。这样，属于过去各民族社区的文化物质遗存得以保护和保存，包括具有宗教和传统文化特色的建筑，以及在特定的地理、自然、社会、文化及年代背景下的价值。该规划所涵盖的区域是"人类与环境相互作用"的地方，强调人类历史，文化和宗教传统的持续性、社会价值和一个国家在历史长河中的和愿景。

另外，修道院附近的土地，有一部分属于"Golija–Studenica"生物圈保护区，更准确地说，属于联合国世界生物圈保护区网络（WNBR），人与生物圈计划（Man and the Biosphere Programme（MAB）的一部分，同时也是"Golija 国家公园"的一部分，是具有突出价值的自然综合体。

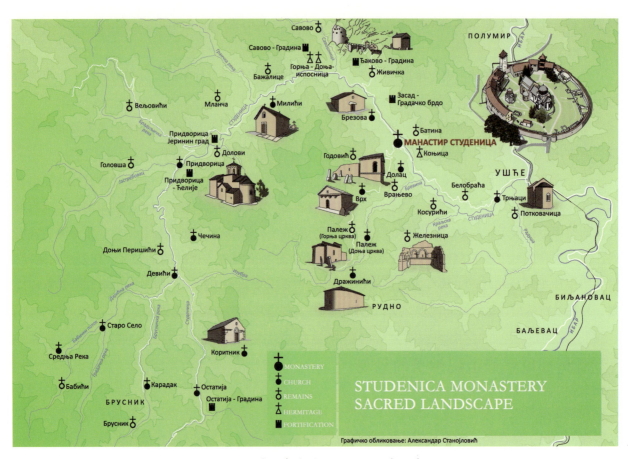

图 5　斯图德尼察修道院的文化 / 神圣景观

介绍斯图德尼察修道院周边特殊用途区域的文化景观概念，作为有形和无形、自然和文化的整体价值体系，从文化遗产保护和整体保护的角度来看，是一个必要条件，因为这一地区的特征和普遍突出价值已被国际法确认。由此，保护修道院的突出普遍价值、真实性和完整性的主要目标，也成为可持续发展的全球目标中的一部分。以景观作为规划的出发点，把公共空间系统界定为文化遗产，同时又是自然遗产。这样界定，可以帮助我们更好地理解复杂的过程，如何化解文化遗产和自然遗产的冲突以及所有其他影响保护的因素，从文化、社会、经济、环境及其他方面，为这地区的经济和社区可持续发展提供有力的支持。

另一方面，斯图德尼察修道院管理规划着眼于保护、使用和管理文化景观的战略方向，主要是从更广阔的视角解读修道院层层叠叠的文化和自然特征。管理规划的一个重点是文化景观的风险识别，所以规划里也要包括一个《风险管理规划》。

斯图德尼察修道院《特殊用途区域空间规划》和《管理规划》属于操作性文件，目的是保护和保存修道院，同时也考虑如何在整个文化景观中，善用文化景观的圣神的，文化的和自然性特征。两份规划都是更广泛开发过程的一部分，重点是从开发和控制环境动态变化方面的应用。

文化景观作为有力推动文化遗产保护的独特概念，将自然、文化和精神融为一体，呈现不同价值，整个修道院遗产地变成实实在在的"统一地"，"过去所用的，今天继续用，将来接着用"（Fairclough，2009）。

参考文献

Barišić S.，（2012），斯图德尼察圣母大教堂原来祭坛屏风的重建，《通讯》，XLIV，第33—42页。

Barišić，S.，（2012），"斯图德尼察修道院圣母大教堂大理石外墙和雕塑装饰的保护和修复"，2012年4月19日在斯图德尼察举行的研讨会上发表的其中一篇论文，ed. BrankaŠekarić，ICOMOS 2012. 第1—6页。

DebljovićRistić，N.（2017），"斯图德尼察圣母大教堂西墙上竖框窗 —— 分析形状和雕塑装饰"，《通讯》，XLIX，第25—42页。

DebljovićRistić，N.（2015），"中世纪神圣遗产 —— 考古保护的原则和程序"，SCS 39，第290 —301页。

DebljovićRistić，N.（2013），"探讨塞尔维亚中世纪修道院建筑的保护方法"，《现代文物保护》，1，第87—96页。

Fairclough，G.（2009），欧洲理事会《遗产及其之外的新遗产领域》，2009，第29—42页。

Jokilehto，J.（2016），"什么是地区管理"，《现代文物保护》，4，第22—31页。

Kašanin M.，Korać V. et al.（1986），斯图德尼察，贝尔格莱德，第102，134页。

KesićRistić，S.（2016）"世界遗产 —— 斯图德尼察修道院"，《现代文物保护》，4，pp128—130.

KesićRistić，S.，Pejic S. et al.（2010），世界遗产，塞尔维亚，贝尔格莱德，第 63 页。

Marković L.（1920），"中世纪塞尔维亚东正教修行及修道院"，SremskiKarlovci，第 2—5 页。

Millet G.（1930），《研究 塞尔维亚王国 *Rascie* 教堂，斯拉夫民族的拜占庭艺术》，巴黎。

Popović-Mojsilović，S.（1994），"圆圈内的十字架：中世纪塞尔维亚的修道院建筑"，贝尔格莱德，第 67—78 页。

Popović M.（2015），斯图德尼察修道院：考古发现，贝尔格莱德，第 134—137 页。

ešic B.，PejićS.（1990-1991）"斯图德尼察教堂古迹"，《通讯》，XXII-XXIII，第 182—225 页。

Nenadović，S.，（1957），"斯图德尼察的问题"，贝尔格莱德。

Valtrović，M.，MilutinovićD.（2006-2008），文件 I —— 实地调查资料 1871-1884；Ed. Tanja Damljanović. 贝尔格莱德。

Čanak-Medić M.，BoškovićĐ.（1986），《纳曼亚时期 I 的建筑》，贝尔格莱德，第 77—117 页。

图一，三，四（Live View studio）

图二（塞尔维亚历史博物馆）

图五（作者：A. Stanojlovic）

Studenica Monastery (12th Century) from Cultural Monument Conservation to Landscape Management

Nevena Debljovic Ristic[①]

Institute for the Protection of Cultural Monuments of Serbia

Abstract:

Cultural heritage resources protection and management is a road to ensure its permanence, but at the same time, it is a process that involves constant recognition of numerous new values. Besides historical, architectural and artistic values, there is a distinct group of spiritual and religious values, as well as those that constitute the heritage place or the environment. Their inseparable interconnection in making strategic decisions on the cultural heritage care is crucial for its management and preservation.

The paper presents a recognition process of a group of values that led to improving the conservation practice, taking an example of the Studenica Monastery (12th century), inscribed in the World Cultural and Natural Heritage List in 1986. When introducing institutional activities in protecting the cultural heritage within the national framework, valorisation of the Studenica Monastery, as one of the highest ranking mediaeval monasteries, was focused on its cultural, historical, architectural and artistic properties and the protection thereof. Inscription in the WH List as well as broadening the notion of heritage itself on an international level, spurred some more intensive investigations of the environment, continuity of the cultural and religious tradition, which led to a discovery of an unusual religious topography in the monastery surroundings. In geographical terms, today it belongs to a "Golija-Studenica" biosphere reserve, or more precisely, the UNESCO World Network of Biosphere Reserves (MAB).

While drawing up a Special Purpose Area Spatial Plan, and then a Management Plan for the Studenica

---

① Architect conservator, graduated from Faculty of Architecture, University of Belgrade, where she defended her PhD in Department of History, Theory, and Aesthetics of Architecture in the Middle Ages. She is employed at the Institute for the Protection of Cultural Monuments in Serbia as Cultural Heritage Advisor. She is a Project and Site Manager for the monasteries Sopocani and Studenica, and is a team member responsible for the World Heritage Serbia. Mrs Ristic is an author of numerous conservation and restoration projects in the fields of medieval sacred architecture and revitalization of historic buildings. She regularly publishes articles in numerous international and national scientific journals. She is an active participant in many international and regional conferences.

Monastery, a cultural landscape emerged as an integral system of values: tangible, intangible, cultural, natural and spiritual. In order to preserve those values, it would be necessary to provide active involvement of the local community and other stakeholders, so that the integrated conservation and sustainable development primary requirements could be produced on a much broader level.

Key words: Studenica Monastery, monument, conservation, landscape management

STUDENICA MONASTERY ARCHITECTURE (12ᵗʰ CENTURY)

From the very beginning and throughout its long history, the Studenica Monastery has been highly venerated mostly due to Stefan Nemanja, the Great Prince (1171-1196) , the founder of the independent Serbian state and the entire dynasty that would rule for the next two centuries. This monasterial complex is the prototype of the Serbian monasteries built in the 12ᵗʰ and the 13ᵗʰ centuries and represents the architecture of the Nemanjic Dynasty (Popovic-Mojsilovic, 1994).

It was built on a spacious flat area above the Studenica River, surrounded by mountains, with the walls in a shape of an ideal geometrical circle and a church in its centre. The origin and symbolism of a circular spatial concept can be found in a symbolic representation of the celestial Jerusalem as a Christian vision of a celestial state on Earth (Markovic, 1920).

Fig.1   Studenica Monastery (12ᵗʰ century) , aerial view from the northern side

In the centre of the monasterial complex there is a church dedicated to the Virgin Evergetide, built between 1183 and 1198. It is the most outstanding example of an authentic architectural style called the *Rascia School*, resulting from a specific position and political orientation of the mediaeval Serbian state. The Church of the Virgin came about as a synthesis of two architectural practices - one coming from the Byzantium and the other coming from the West (the Romanesque mode of façade shaping and the architectural sculpture) . The most prominent feature of its interior are the fresco paintings dating from 1208-9. Their artistic scope keep the Studenica Monastery among the most significant 13th century Byzantine works of art. The Virgin Church paintings also feature the frescoes dating from 1569, honouring the period they were made in.

In about 1230, a dynasty founder's grandson, Radoslav, added a spacious exonarthex and two parekklesions (small chapels) to the church, and in the early 14th century, a great-grandson, Milutin, erected another important church dedicated to the Virgin's parents, Joachim and Anna, the so-called "King's Church". That church features well-preserved fresco paintings that are ranked among the most valuable examples of the Serbian painting in the first half of the 14th century, due to their colouristic harmony and sophisticated artistic strokes (Kasanin, Korac, 1986).

Other religious structures inside the site testify to a rather complex development of the Studenica Monastery. To the south of the main church there are two other free-standing churches, one dedicated to St Nicholas, dating from the first half of the 13th century and the remains of another dedicated to St John, dating from the late 13th or early 14th century. There is a copper plate etching of the Studenica Monastery from the mid-18th century, showing even 14 churches within the monasterial compound or immediately beside it (Pejic, 2010).

An organised search for the monasterial complex architectural remains, where the church and its dominant position indicated that it was a regional centre, did not start until the second half of the 20th century. Particularly important in the monks' life was the monasterial refectory, built in the late 12th century, situated to west from the entrance to the Virgin's Church that was demolished and restored several times (Nenadovic, 1957). Its position in relation to the church and the spatial shape with an apse pointed to the arrangement of other built structures on the site. Residential quarters used to be on the upper floors, along the monasterial border wall, and on the ground floor there were storage rooms and workshops. On the north side there was a large residential building, called "The Great Cells". On the east side of the settlement, as part of the north-east structures, along the fence wall, a smaller parekklesion was found, dedicated to St Demetrios. There is also a 16th century residential quarter and some new residential and other buildings erected on a later date (Popovic, 2015).

Today, the monastery houses a rich treasury of icons and various divine service liturgical objects, a collection of stone ornaments, a library and an archive. In the Studenica Monastery wider area, there are material traces and numerous structures that tells us about continuous life activities and strong cultural, historical and functional clinks with the monastery, and those are hermitages, chapels, remains of mediaeval settlements and roads, a mediaeval water system and an old mine.

STUDENICA MONASTERY PROTECTION, CONSERVATION AND PRESENTATION

According to its recognised values, the Studenica Monastery was listed in 1979 as a national monument of outstanding value, and in 1986 was inscribed in the World Natural and Cultural Heritage List. Therefore, when considering the monastery, we need to take into account all the methods and processes already implemented in its preservation, conservation and presentation in the past years, the condition of the complex today, as well as the goals for its future.

Throughout its history, the monastery has undergone a lot of destruction. In one of the most severe torches and devastations in 1805 and 1806, the Church of the Virgin was extremely damaged. When in 1833 Serbia was liberated from the Ottoman rule, it was the first time that the conditions for its restoration were provided. In 1839 some extensive works were conducted that included building 36 windows, erecting marble columns, floor, roof and cornice repairs (Medic, Boskovic, 1986). Those works were crucial for bringing back the primary architectural and sculptural characteristics to the Church of the Virgin.

Fig.2　Drawings of architectural plans and sculpturing details (1880)

However, the first scholarly based investigations conducted in the second half of the 19th century, referred mostly to gathering all the material information on church historical, artistic and architectural characteristics. Tracing the first scientific terms and methodological processes in researching the Serbian mediaeval history, art and architecture started with establishing the reference material of the Studenica Monastery, which created a basis for numerous and extensive investigations conducted later on in the 20th century.

The structural survey of the Studenica Monastery structures started in 1877 when the King's Church architecture was examined to be continued in 1880. The Church of the Virgin was surveyed in detail and 30 drawings and watercolours were made of the extant situation at that time. Besides structural and extremely precise architectural plans, an outstanding set of architectural sculpturing details was created of the portal and window openings, perspective drawings of the full cornice stone details, arcades, corbels, capitals and bifora columns (mullions) (Valtrovic, Milutinovic, 2006).

For its recognised preserved values, Studenica listed as a national treasure after the Second World War, in 1947. Then the institutionalised work on its study, investigations, restoration and conservation lasted for decades. In 1949 there were some minor scope works on the Church of the Virgin. In the early 1960s, extensive investigations coupled with conservation and restoration works started on the entire complex. The works were conducted on the church, the residential quarters and the refectory and a section of the 18th century porch were partially reconstructed. Then in the 1970s and early 1980s the works ensued on the Virgin's Church dome, the Radoslav's narthex tympanum when the arcade decorations were removed, a porch dating from one stage of the refectory history dismantled, etc. When interpreting its architecture and art, an outstanding character of the monument had an impact on how the historical and artistic values are to be viewed, often based on scholarly, critical and historical evaluation that creates an outlook of the cultural property (Debljovic-Ristic, 2015).

However, with time, an interdisciplinary interaction of knowledge eventually produced numerous results. Observing historical and political circumstances, we learned about the role and duties of a mediaeval ruler were, about the principles of founding a monastery and the hereditary law, about Studenica as a monasterial and spiritual centre that gave rise to a dynastic cult and its saint generating lineage. Equally significant knowledge came from the archaeological investigations of the monasterial settlement spatial organisation; dates were determined for all the construction and demolition activities; the structures classified according to types and proportions; iconographic programmes and "stylistic" features defined, as well as artistic and iconographic features of the architectural sculpture, etc.

The numerous indisputable values of this unique mediaeval Serbian monasterial complex, as part of both the spiritual and artistic world of Byzantium, were acknowledged when Studenica was inscribed in the UNESCO World Cultural and Natural Heritage List in 1986, based on the set criteria (i, ii, iv, vi) . The first criterion had not been included in the nomination dossier, but subsequently, the ICOMOS Mission included it, having in mind the unique nature of the King's Church paintings. The second criterion was accepted, owing to a crucial impact the Church of the Virgin had on the 13th century Serbian, as well as Byzantine architecture and art. Also, owing to the ICOMOS evaluation of the fourth criterion, the outstanding value of Studenica was recognised as a unique "example of the Serbian Orthodox Church monastery", which was developing and preserving its "13th to 18th centuries" structures, as well as its "outstanding example of a type of ensemble or landscape" with its hermitages, churches and quarries. The sixth criterion highlighted a link between the most significant figures of the Serbian mediaeval history and the Studenica Monastery. Inscription in the List and the criteria acknowledgment raised awareness of the monastery surroundings, so two years later the boundaries of the immediate surroundings and the monastery natural area were defined, so in 1991 a Studenica Managing Board was formed. Then in 1992, all official communications with the World Heritage Committee ceased due to the international sanctions imposed on Serbia. In 2001 relations with the Committee were re-established after Serbia was reinstated as a member, which was confirmed at the General Assembly (KesicRistic, 2016).

In the 1990s, Serbia saw a process of desecularisation in both the state and its society. Very unfavourable social and economic circumstances that came about after the disintegration of Yugoslavia resulted in serious cuts in government funding the cultural heritage, whilst, the SOC was gradually gaining on its authority. With the weakening of the economic power of the state, numerous structures in the immediate vicinity of the monastery, meant for public use and tourism, were being deteriorating, which led to shutting down the vital functions of the place, causing the local population to move away. On the other hand, in the 2010s, the role of the Studenica Monastery was gaining on its popularity and economic strength, so that some of the state owned structures went to the hands of the monastery and in the years to follow, the monastery was able to buy out all the structures in its vicinity.

In the late 1990s, an extensive conservation and restoration project was started on the Virgin's Church marble façades. The Project was being conducted under the auspices of the Republic Institute for the Protection of Cultural Monuments. Some particular investigations yielded a host of important data on the chemical composition of the marble and a choice of neutral properties of the mortar mixed according to the original material. When the scope and cause of the damages had been identified, the restoration of the marble façade methodology was selected. Undertaking of such a unique, multidisciplinary conservation and restoration project on the marble elements took almost two decades, giving some significant results (Barisic, 2012). Only the north bifora on the main façade of the Virgin's Church was left unrestored for almost two centuries. Two stone fragments with an ornamental relief featuring birds were found during the conservation works in 1956.

The information obtained from the finds discovered in archaeological investigations conducted in the previous decades helped us to identify the entire appearance of such an important sculptural unit (Popovic, 2016). The north bifora restoration entailed a highly complex process. All the missing elements were carved in the original material, whilst restoration of the symbolic trinity circular form was done with the same material used for restoration of the church façade. Only recently the has obtained its full architectural shape and the ornamental reliefs their profound theological sense (DebljovicRistic, 2017). In addition, the works on the Virgin's Church largely presented its original outlook, as well as high skill and artisanship.

One of the activities where the church proved its equal status with the cultural heritage preservation

Fig.3   The Church of the Holy Virgin, Studenica Monastery, 12th century, view from the northeastern side, after restoration of the church façade.

services was a removal of a 19th century iconostasis and making an altar screen as it used to be, reconstructed based on the available original marble remains (Barisic, 2012). The views of the experts differed about this issue, but after the work on the frescoes and the templon, the church interior gained a new, above all liturgical value.

In its primary form, the monastic way of life has remained unchanged to the present day, so it was recognised as an authentic form of intangible cultural heritage that survived from the period the monastery was built and when the *Studenica Typicon* was written, whose instructions are still in use today at all the Serbian monasteries (Markovic, 1920). Interlaced and mutually connected intangible processes in interpreting and evaluating the broader religious field point to a living character of symbolic expression through liturgy, divine service, hermitage and extended liturgy, labour and prayer. Religious functions are manifested in those interactions that suppose human beings, their existence and their presence.

For that reason, a shift in the evaluation focus and heritage preservation from the architectural and tangible to broader aspects has led to a necessary action of redefining the notion of a "monument", aiming at better understanding the cultural values of the historical, artistic, religious and spiritual values that constitute the life itself, as well as the natural environment that is linked to the centuries old human activities, as general universal cultural values (DebljovicRistic, 2011).

Therefore, the conservation activities are increasingly directed to the monasterial life, its sustainability and

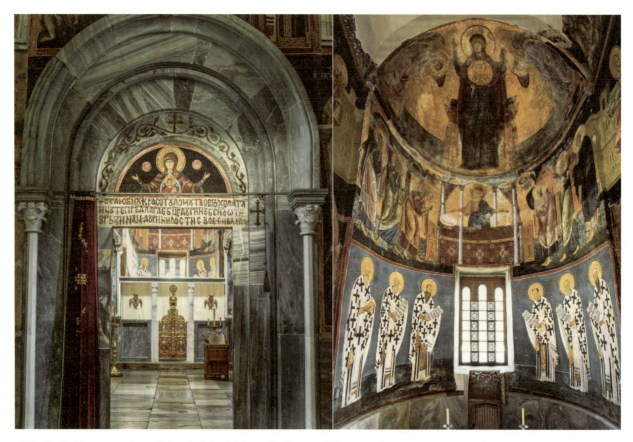

Fig.4   Reconstruction of the Original Altar Screen and Frescoes in the altar apse of the Church of the Holy Virgin, Studenica Monastery, 1208/1209

particularly to planning and managing its broader area where the Studenica Monastery is actually its centre. Protection and conservation are still focused on specific issues and characteristics related to preservation and enhancement of all identifying values, whilst management comprises a system of planning and administration that enables preservation of the said values and their upkeep in the future (Jokilehto, 2018).

A series of activities conducted in collaboration with the monastic brotherhood and the architects conservators in the last few years helped to enhance the monasterial content and its sustainability. For that reason, some extensive conservation works have been done on the 18th century ground floor residential quarters that were used as a storage, now regaining their authentic outlook. A wine cellar is envisioned inside the structure, where wine tasting events are organised, presenting the wines produced from the Studenica vineyards from the Aleksandrovac region. The quarters are envisioned as multifunctional, so other important meetings can be held there, as well as various promotion activities for the Studenica region.

In the monasterial refectory, a project "Digital Studenica" has been launched. With a help of the new technology and media, an educational and informational platform has been set up, presenting all the monasterial landmarks and cultural and historical heritage. The idea is for the visitors to sit at the St Sava refectory tables and help themselves with the virtual, spiritual food which is actually visual narratives of the Studenica Monastery history and art. There is also a Vertical VR 360, using the HTC Vive glasses for virtual reality to allow the visitors to experience all the physically inaccessible sections of architecture and fresco paintings. Furthermore, some various VR material is available with a use of tablets at the educational visitors' centre or through a *Holograd* application that can be installed from any place in the world at an App Store and Google Play (Live View Studio) .

As part of the new Studenica Treasury exhibition display, using a modern style presentation and a chronological and typological concept, religious objects, numerous reliquaries and gospels mirroring various epochs from the centuries of the monasterial life have been presented.

There is also an annual church and events calendar. The church calendar cites celebrations of seven most important patron saints' days. The cultural events calendar includes decades old events: art colonies, choir festivals and other cultural and artistic programmes.

In order to strengthen the numerous cultural and natural values of the wider monastery surrounding and to render them more visible, a network of cultural routes have been established towards Rudno, Savovo and Pridvorica, which are gradually being integrated into a tourist map of the Studenica region as places of high potential. The role of the local population have also been recognised and in the place of Rudno there is the Sekler household - apartments, who are initiators of women's entrepreneurship and rural tourism, successfully promoting homemade produce and at the same time, offering a well-known Serbian hospitality. Numerous individual activities, as well as valuing the historical environment and its communities with a developed natural context, finally required a Studenica Monastery Management Plan to be drafted. The Special Purpose Area Spatial Plan has identified the monastery and its wider area as cultural landscape.

STUDENICA MONASTERY SACRED LANDSCAPE

In the Studenica Monastery surroundings, a large number of religious sites have been identified and valorised. Also, a great number of archaeological remains of religious structures have been recorded, as well as a few forts and a number of vernacular structures.

Studying and understanding the semiotic aspect of the area around the monastery, an outstanding cultural and historical significance of religious character emerged, i.e. a character of sacred sites topography in a broader spatial area. The phenomenon certainly owes much to a strong role of the monastery that had been spreading religious awareness, so numerous places of worship were erected, often along the cemeteries to service small communities. The landscape characteristics indicate emergence of some small and scattered settlements, but at the same time it is possible to trace continuous and live building activities from the Middle Ages up to the present day (Pešic, Pejic, 1990-1991).

In recognising and trying to preserve numerous values of the entire area, the Studenica Monastery Special Purpose Area Spatial Plan boundaries have been defined. The place has been valorised as a special cultural landscape featuring numerous sacred sites.

The Plan envisages the heritage integrated protection and conservation approach based on enhancing the interaction between the cultural, spiritual and natural heritage. Such an approach implies a holistic understanding of the broader spatial area around the monastery, thus making it a cultural landscape. In this way, the past ethnic communities' cultural tangible remains are preserved and protected, building on the characteristics of live religious and traditional culture, as well as on the values within a particular geographical, natural, social, cultural and time context. The area covered by the Plan comprises "human interaction with the environment", where the emphasis is on human history, cultural and religious tradition continuity, social values and aspirations of a nation through history.

Furthermore, a part of the land around the monastery belongs to the "Golija-Studenica" biosphere reserve, or better still, the UNESCO World Network of Biosphere Reserves (WNBR) as part of the Man and the Biosphere Programme (MAB) , and also to the "Golija Nature Park", a nature complex of outstanding value.

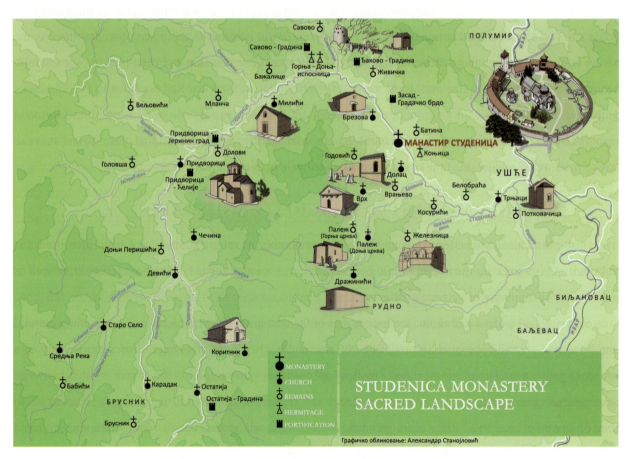

Fig.5　Studenica Monastery Cultural /Sacred Landscape

Introduction of the cultural landscape concept for the special purpose area around the Studenica Monastery, as an integral value system - tangible and intangible, natural and cultural - from the aspect of the cultural property protection and integrated conservation, was a condition sine qua non, considering the character and the outstanding universal values of the area, confirmed in the international legislation. In this way, the primary goals in preserving the outstanding universal values, authenticity and integrity of the property become part of the global goals of sustainable development. An approach to planning from the aspect of a landscape, provides for the common spatial systems to be identified as both cultural and natural heritage. It also helps to understand the complex processes, how to overcome conflicts, and all other influences that combined may contribute to the area protection and preservation, provide a common support to an economic development and the development of the community, which is sustainable from the cultural, social, economic, environmental and other aspects.

On the other hand, the Studenica Monastery Management Plan envisions some strategic directions of cultural landscape preservation, use and management, deriving from layers of cultural and natural characteristics viewed in a broader context. A special significance in this area was given to the cultural landscape risk identification, so Plan is to include a Risk Management Plan, as well.

The Studenica Monastery Special Purpose Area Spatial Plan and the Management Plan are now operational instruments aiming at preservation and protection, but also at an optimal use of the potentials of the sacred, cultural and natural features of the area within the entire cultural landscape. Both plans are part of a broader development process focused on the ways of use from the development aspect and control of the dynamic changes in the environment.

Establishing a cultural landscape as a unique concept of heritage active preservation, where the nature, culture and spirituality are placed in one context featuring multitude of values, is now made into an existentially experienced "unified site", where the use of the past is in the present and its renewal into the future" (Fairclough, 2009).

BIBLIOGRAPHICAL REFERENCES

Barišić S., (2012) ,A Reconstruction of the Original Altar Screen in the Church of the Virgin at Studenica, in *The Communications*, XLIV, pp. 33-42.

Barišić, S., (2012) , "Conservation and Restoration Works on the Marble Façade and Sculptural Decoration on the Virgin's Church in the Monastery of Studenica", in the Collection of Papers from a workshop held on 19 April 2012 in Studenica, ed. BrankaŠekarić, ICOMOS 2012. pp. 1-6.

DebljovićRistić, N. (2017) , "Mullioned Windows in the West Façade of the Church of the Virgin at Studenica - An Analysis of the Shapes and Sculptural Decoration", in *The Communications*, XLIX, 25-42.

DebljovićRistić, N. (2015) , "Medieval Sacred Heritage - Principles and Procedures in Architectural Conservation", in the SCS 39, pp. 290 - 301.

DebljovićRistić, N. (2013) , "Reviews of the Conservation Approaches in Interpretation of the Medieval Monasteries Architecture in Serbia", *Modern Conservation*, 1, pp. 87-96.

Fairclough, G. (2009) , *New Heritage Frontiers* in *Heritage and Beyond*, Council of Europe, 2009, pp. 29-42.

Jokilehto, J. (2016) , "What is Territorial management?" *Modern Conservation*, 4, pp. 22-31.

Kašanin M., Korać V. et al. (1986) , *Studenica*, Belgrade, pp. 102,134.

KesićRistić, S. (2016) "World Heritage - the Studenica Monastery", in *Modern Conservation*, 4, pp128-130.

KesićRistić, S., Pejic S. et al. (2010) , *World Heritage, Serbia*, Belgrade, pp. 63.

Marković L. (1920) , "Orthodox Monasticism and Monasteries of Mediaeval Serbia", SremskiKarlovci, pp. 2-5.

Millet G. (1930) , *Etude sur les eglises de Rascie, dans L'artbyzantin chez les Slaves I*, Paris.

Popović-Mojsilović, S. (1994) , "*A Cross in a Circle: Monasterial Architecture of Mediaeval Serbia*", Belgrade, pp. 67-78.

Popović M. (2015) , *The Monastery of Studenica: Archeological Discoveries*, Belgrade, pp.134-137

Pešic B., PejićS. (1990-1991) "Les Monument du bassin de la Studenica" in *Communication*, XXII-XXIII, pp.182-225.

Nenadović, S., (1957) , "*The Studenica Issues*", Belrgade.

Valtrović, M.,MilutinovićD. (2006-2008) , *Documents* I - *field material 1871-1884*; Ed. Tanja Damljanović. Belgrade.

Čanak-Medić M., BoškovićĐ. (1986) , *Architecture of the Nemanja Period I*, Belgrade, pp. 77-117.

Fig 1,3,4 (Live View Studio)

Fig 2 (Historical Museum of Serbia)

Fig 5 (author: A. Stanojlovic)

斯皮思城堡缓冲区土地使用保护和规划的新问题

斯洛伐克共和国　科希策文化遗产局　罗伯特·基拉尔 [①]

摘要

自 2017 年起，联合国教科文组织世界遗产地，斯皮思（SPIŠ）城堡缓冲区内泽赫拉（Žehra）村的新土地使用规划一直在准备中。本文深入研究了受保护区域面临的具体问题，并提出了具体的解决方案，制定了相关管理规定，以保护遗产景观的突出文化价值。通过与科希策文化遗产局和编制规划的主要作者（建筑师）合作，确定了列入保护遗迹名单的特色景观的土地使用要求，并根据附近罗姆人聚居地区人口不断增长的情况，规划了新的住宅区。其中一个已经解决的问题是，目前已完成对城堡下方区域高级路网的追踪。

关键词：斯皮思城堡—联合国教科文组织遗产地，泽赫拉村—联合国教科文组织遗产地，土地使用规划，文化景观

图 1　斯皮思城堡概貌（左侧）及泽赫拉村缓冲区

土地使用（城市）规划是保护和发展受保护地区重要而有效的工具。泽赫拉村决定采纳 2017 年第一个土地利用规划。由于村庄包括两处重要的列入遗产名录的联合国教科文组织遗产地，且整个城堡区都位于遗产缓冲区内，为此有必要进一步细化该规划。除两处已列入名录的中世纪遗迹（城堡和教堂）外，该联合国教科文组织世界遗产的突出价值还反映在真实的景观结构方面，它们仍然保留了遗产的历史特征。

---

① 罗伯特·基拉尔（Róbert Királ），斯洛伐克科希策文化遗产局保护专家，主要负责遗产地和保护区的保护工作。2008 年毕业于位于布拉迪斯发的斯洛伐克技术大学建筑系。

简要介绍联合国教科文组织世界遗产地

斯皮思城堡及其邻近区域相关遗迹是斯洛伐克一处独特的、风景如画的联合国教科文组织遗产地，包括多个完整的历史遗迹、遗产和广阔的缓冲区。该遗产于1993年列入世界遗产名录，2009年进行了扩展，将邻近有城墙的中世纪小镇勒沃卡（距城堡以西13公里处）囊括进来，小镇珍藏了16世纪雕刻大师保罗的精美木制品。1993年列入世界遗产名录时，该地区是一处令人瞩目的建筑群，是由多个不同的中世纪建筑组成的真实景观。主要包括城堡（SpišskýHrad/斯皮思城堡）、Suburbium（SpišskéPodhradie镇）、牧师礼堂（SpišskáKapitula教会遗址，内有大教堂和教会人员房屋）、和教堂（教区圣灵教堂，内有Žehra村中世纪壁画）。城堡像一座纪念碑一样矗立在独特的岩石层上，从四面八方勾勒出一幅令人惊叹的轮廓。总的来说，它是欧洲最大的城堡遗址之一，由一个位于顶部城堡的中心主楼（公元12/13世纪）和三个低矮院落组成（公元13—15世纪）。如今该城堡已对外开放，设有博物馆文物展厅。每年有超过250,000名游客前来参观，成为斯洛伐克最受欢迎的历史遗迹之一。游客主要被它的雄伟和适合拍摄的优美视觉景观所吸引，附近的高速公路（2010年开通）是前来遗址地参观的主要通道。对艺术历史学家来说，最有价值的地方是建于13世纪早期的罗马式宫殿。

从广义历史观点来说，该遗址位于斯皮思地区的中心。这个小镇建于12世纪，是匈牙利王国北部边境地区，历史上紧邻波兰王国。地区中心位于霍尔纳德河河谷，周围是林地和山脉。河谷正中央出现了一组四座独特的石灰华（一种白色的沉积灰岩）山丘。12世纪中叶，匈牙利国王在其中一座山丘上修建了斯皮思城堡，并将其作为新成立的斯皮思行政区的管理中心，同时也是连通南北贸易路线的重要交通要塞。这是史前时期的一个分支，被称为东方琥珀之路，它将巴尔干半岛国家与波罗的海相连——从更近的范围来说，将克拉科夫—科希策—贝尔格莱德等城镇连接起来。城堡下方，逐渐发展成为一个城镇（即今天的斯皮思凯波德赫拉杰小镇，见图5），并在地理上成为城堡的郊区。另外国王还在城堡西郊建造了牧师礼堂——教会的行政管理机构。这是一个有围墙的罗马式大教堂和教会人员住所，在18世纪中叶成为基督大主教和神学院所在地。城堡是国王的财产，一直由其指派的管理人员管理，直至1528年。之后，由贵族家族拥有，直至第二次世界大战。1780年城堡遭遇火灾，后来被遗弃，现今成为一处引人注目的城堡废墟。

泽赫拉（Žehra）村

现在，城堡区的联合国教科文组织遗产地被分为两个自治郡（见图4）。普雷绍夫（Prešov）郡，包括Suburbium、牧师礼堂、以及位于缓冲区西部和北部的多个村庄。科希策（Košice）郡，遗产地相对较小，主要有泽赫拉村的宗地、城堡和教堂等。泽赫拉现有2,250名村民，高出了斯洛伐克的平均人口水平。这是一个很小的村庄，仅包括三个不同的独立建成区。其中一个是历史村本身（见图2），包括建在一座小山上的列入世界遗产名录的教堂。人口为300人。第二个是一处围绕巴洛克贵族家族企业宅邸建造的小型赫德科夫（Hodkovce）聚落，这里有一个比较有价值的历史公园——也是构成遗产地的相关历史遗迹。赫德科夫人口约为 150 人——其中超过百人是在这座贵族府邸为智障人士设立的福利机构的客户。总的来说，在这个村庄里，人们可在一层或两层家庭住房里享受平静的乡村生活。当地的两家木制窗户生产商和两个主要饲养牛羊等牲畜的农场是提供就业的主要机构。在赫德科夫，当地居民还经营了四个小型游客住宿设施。

图 2 从南面看泽赫拉村，右侧为拟议的旁道

第三个也是最复杂的建成区是位于西南边缘的聚落，称为 Drevenik/Dobra Vola（见图 3）。这是一座罗姆人（吉普赛）社区，现在有 1850 人定居。其中一部分人住在政府 20 世纪 90 年代建造的标准平房内，但还有小部分人则生活在缺乏自来水和下水道的条件简陋的村舍中。这个社区通常都是被排斥和不受欢迎的，居民大多没有工作，依靠社会救助体系生存，住房附近产生大量垃圾。较低的受教育水平、较低的卫生标准（相当缺乏）、非法采伐木柴、90% 的失业率以及高利贷是 Drevenik 聚落日常生活中面临的最紧迫的问题。幸运的是，该聚落与列入名录的历史遗迹（位于缓冲区边界，被一处石灰华山丘所遮盖）之间不存在直接的视觉联系。但是它仍是通往联合国教科文组织世界遗产地南部道路上一个具有较强干扰的因素，是当地社会保障机构和遗迹保护机构都需面对的一个问题。

值得指出的是，现在 Drevenik 社区已自然延伸到了邻近的多布拉沃拉（Dobra Vola）聚落（见下图 4），该聚落位于 SpisskeVlachy 小镇（Košice 郡）宗地。多布拉沃拉是石瓦匠聚居地（19/20 世纪之交，在当地采石场工作的石瓦匠），现在计算下来，这里约有 20 个小型的石屋和一座粮仓。过去几十年来，来自 Drevenik 的移民已经占领了这些早就被其主人所遗弃的房屋。多布拉沃拉早就不在联合国教科文组织世界遗产地缓冲区之内。

图3　罗姆人聚落（Drevenik）一览，位于同一名称石灰华山丘下——从毗邻的多布拉·沃拉聚落视角欣赏

问题和挑战

泽赫拉村的城市规划面临两大挑战。由于大部分领地都具有文化和自然景观价值，这大大限制了新建成区扩展的可能性。城堡、教堂和Hodkovce宅邸的视觉外观必须作为文化历史景观价值加以保护。由于它是联合国教科文组织世界遗产地和缓冲区，为此，根据斯洛伐克历史遗迹法律，设置了一个所谓的保护特色景观（远景）的网络体系，用来监测和保护列入名录的遗迹所处环境的真实性特征。已界定的最重要的景点包括：

1. 从南面看泽赫拉村及其教堂景观（见图2）；

2. 从东部公路入口处看城堡景观；

3. 连接教堂与城堡的 Hodkovce 宅邸。

除此之外，该地区西部被认定为自然保护区。这里有三处较为瞩目的石灰华山丘（Drevenik，Sobotisko，城堡山），构成了一个喀斯特地貌——洞穴、当地特有的盐碱植物、岩石峭壁、以及从旧石器时代到罗马时期的大量考古发现等。不允许在该保护区内建造任何住宅群。

第二个主要的挑战是 Drevenik/ Dobra Vola 聚落人口增长带来的问题。罗姆人最早于 20 世纪早期来到这里。据记载，在 20 世纪 50 年代大约仅有 10 处罗姆人村舍。后来，罗姆人口数量快速增长，且呈持续增长态势。2007 年 Drevenik 有 1400 名居民，到了 2017 年则增长到 1850 名，其中包括 1200 名儿童。约五分之一的居民生活在未按规定建造的简陋村舍中。这里的幼儿园、小教堂、市民住宅和商店可提供的公共服务也很少。通过对土地利用规划的分析，估计到 2030 年人口数量还会增加 1300 人。预计的人口增长和恶劣的居住环境意味着需要新的地方来满足住房和公共建设需求。

现在很多有冒险精神和技能的罗姆人携家带口搬到了英国或比利时，这进一步强化了上述居民需求。因为他们在外边赚了钱之后，又重回泽赫拉村，其中大部分人都希望在这里按最新的标准建造又大又新的房子，或者直接重建或扩建位于村庄历史区内的老房（教堂下方）。这自然导致了世代居住在本村的居民和过去几十年入侵的罗姆人之间的独特仇恨。随着英国脱欧临近，估计不久的将来会有更多的罗姆人从英国回归。

　　既要保护珍稀的景观，又要应对不断增长的边境居民对居住地的需求，新制定的土地利用规划必须平衡这两种矛盾。

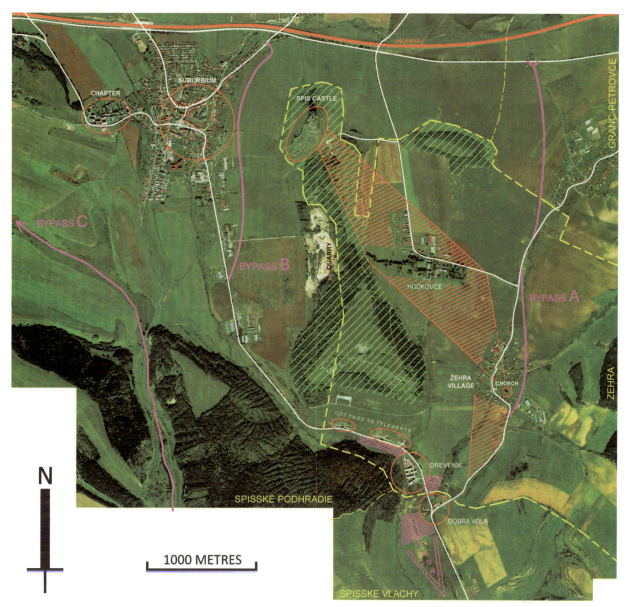

图4　当地地图：黄线——宗地边界，白线——主要道路，红线——公路，桔色舱口形状——受保护景观区，绿色舱口形状——自然保护区，洋红色舱口形状——拟议建成区，洋红线——3个拟建的旁道旁道

解决方案和管理规定

　　最早制定土地使用规划时，科希策文化遗产局——作为一级古迹保护机构对当前的文化景观所具有的价值进行了初步分析。作为斯皮思城堡下真实的建成区的一个基本特征，孤立（分离的）的外观

得到了认可——历史上的聚落，有着清晰可辨的边界，分别矗立在各自的国度里。考虑到这个特征，将三个现存的聚落融合（连接起来）（Drevenik –Zehra– Hodkovce）起来并不符合这一特征。这种孤立的外观也与泽赫拉村南入口道路的真实轮廓相关联（在南面受保护的视野看，见图 2）。教堂区最后一排具有本地特色的历史建筑物构成了真实而典型的斯皮思村庄，代表了文化景观价值的真实本质。为此，科希策文化遗产局做出了强烈的保护决定，避免在距教堂约 700 米的南部视野范围内建造任何建筑物。另一方面，该视野区域内平坦的南部田地也可被规划出来，用于扩大 Drevenik 聚落居住地，没有任何领地限制。Drevenik 聚落位于狭窄的谷地，这里只有一小部分土地可用来建造新的房屋（见图 4），但未来 20 年却需要新建 200—300 个公寓。土地利用规划的主要作者——建筑师 JánPastiran 从一开始就有强烈的保护家乡遗产价值的意识。为此，制定规划时，在不允许在南部土地上建造新房屋这一问题上没有出现任何激烈讨论。另外，这些南部土地 20 世纪早期之前是个池塘，因此，如果允许这里新建房屋，将有可能妨碍池塘的重建。

处理了保护界限的问题后，Drevenik 城市发展的问题也应该已经解决了。人们将关注点转向了邻近的 Dobra Vola 聚落，它位于附近 SpisskeVlachy 镇。两个市政当局和首席建筑师进行了艰苦的谈判，最终决定在 Dobra Vola 聚落实施《土地利用变更》（2018 年通过），其中划定了可容纳约 20 座房屋的新居民区，还选择了一个地点建设新的污水处理厂，处理 Drevenik 聚落产生的污水。Dobra Vola 南部一片狭长的平地本来有可能为 Drevenik 提供更多的土地供给，但是 SpisskeVlachy 镇的居民可能不会同意在他们的选区增加大量的罗姆人。为此，未来可能的解决方案是在上述两个市镇之间交换土地，这也是一项艰难的行政任务——过去几十年来从未有过先例。未来发展到底会提出什么样的土地需求，我们将拭目以待。到时，也许 Dobra Vola 的土地交换将不可避免。

下面是其他一些复杂性不太高的、已通过的解决方案、管理规定和要求：

1. 制定了重新养护公路两侧历史古树的要求。

2. 规定泽赫拉和 Hodkovce 的家庭住房不能超过两层。

3. 建议新建的当地传统马鞍式屋顶的坡度应设为 30°—42°，颜色为红色、棕色或灰色（缓冲区建筑限制成平屋顶是令人满意的）。

4. 建议设置透明（半透明）篱笆（面向街道），材质为木制或金属。篱笆墙不得高于 1.8 米。

5. 在村庄中部（距教堂约 200 米）的边道适度设置旅游巴士停车位置——不在教堂视野范围内。

6. 教堂南部场地，仅允许建造简单的运动／足球场地，不得建造任何更衣室、卫生间、看台或自助餐厅等服务设施。

15 年前，圣灵教会曾出现过轻微的视觉损害——这是土地使用规划要解决的次要问题。现在整个村庄所有村民共享一处公共墓地（大部分斯洛伐克人和罗姆人都是罗马天主教徒），就在教堂遗址石墙的后边。2002 年罗姆酋长的葬礼之后，泽赫拉村出现了一种新的风俗，富裕的罗姆人开始建造大型墓碑。为了纪念逝去的亲人，罗姆人在新墓地建造了垂直的黑色石制墓碑，并在上边雕刻了与逝者真人大小的画像。这种真人大小的墓碑在斯洛伐克墓地很少见。泽赫拉村真实的历史墓碑通常更为简陋，不会如此显眼突出，因此泽赫拉村民对这种"新"风尚很反感。这些超大墓碑被竖立在教堂前边（未获得任何批准），对遗产的视觉价值也造成了负面影响。为避免这些行为——科希策文化遗产局、卫生部门和泽赫拉村市政当局通过谈判协商，在村子通过了一项新的、详细的墓地使用法令。考虑到有些村民可能会尝试不遵守法令的规定，新的土地利用规划还划定了一处新的墓地区，位于 Drevenik 聚落。希望未来所有超大墓碑都只出现在新划定的墓地范围内，永远停止前述对教堂所造成的视觉损害。

简要介绍的泽赫拉村土地利用规划应在未来几个月通过。希望这能成为一个长期有效的工具，保护和鼓励斯皮思城堡景观的视觉完整性和真实性特征。

关于旁道的问题

过去十年，斯皮思城堡的旁道成为城市化讨论中的一个严肃议题，因为它与整个联合国教科文组织遗产地相关。之前所提议的旁道路线可能会对文化景观的突出价值带来威胁。

2010 年从城堡往北开通了一条高速公路后，将高速公路与霍尔纳德河河谷公路和 Krompachy 的工业区（城堡东南部 12 公里处）连接起来的需求开始凸显。泽赫拉村和 SpisskePodhradie 镇的主要公路对卡车通行来说都比较狭窄。较大的交通噪音给这两个城区的居民带来了困扰。两个镇的相关机构都提议在地区土地使用规划中采用直接穿过联合国教科文组织遗产地的旁道（见图 4 - 红线）。科希策镇提议修建泽赫拉村旁道（A），沿教堂往东仅 100 米（见图 2）。这条旁道对教堂周边环境会造成较大损害，对从南面看村庄轮廓也有视觉上的影响。在另一边，普雷绍夫（Prešov）镇提议修建旁道（B），穿过城堡和 Suburbium 之间区域（见图 5）。这条旁道将切断这两个遗产点，对历史上一直将城堡及 Suburbium 相连的地方形成一道屏障。

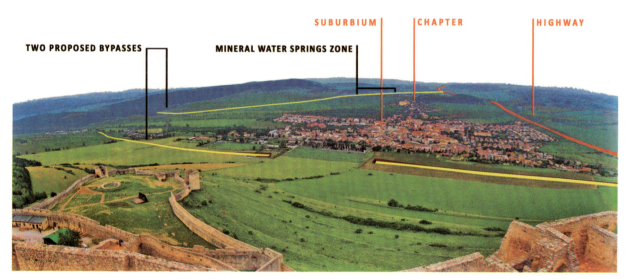

图 5　从城堡向西看 SpisskePodhradie（Suburbium）和 SpisskaKapitula（牧师礼堂），黄线为拟建的旁道 B（下）和旁道 C（上）

古迹保护部门对两个旁道提案提出了异议。尽管如此，2008 年 SpisskePohradie 的旁道还是被纳入该镇土地利用规划。关于泽赫拉村的旁道，人们提议在泽赫拉教堂附近山下修建一条隧道，作为折中方案——但是人们认为该方案花费较大。古迹管理机构和一些当地建筑师提议在联合国教科文组织遗产地西侧修建旁道 C（见图 5）。该旁道主要修建于市区外，不会干扰最有价值的文化景观，但是缺点是太长（造价高）。在公路尽头（高速公路附近）这条旁道将穿过一处矿泉保护区。自然保护机构不同意，但直至今日尚未对在矿泉区修建公路的可能性进行全面分析。

在过去几年，县、镇的代表和古迹管理机构、斯洛伐克国际古迹遗址理事会经过多轮协商后，最终决定重新评估关于修建旁道的决定。其中一个常被引用的论据是，2009 年德国德累斯顿境内的联合国教科文组织遗产地从世界遗产名录中被移除，原因就是新修建了一座桥梁，该桥梁横穿了该遗产地中心位置的易北河。

结果，科希策镇将在教堂附近修建旁道的提案从土地使用规划中撤回了。同样，SpisskePohradie 镇也从当地土地使用规划中撤回了他们的旁道修建提议。事实上，前述公路上的卡车通行已经停滞。Krompachy 工业区的生产也停滞不前。一些生产厂家甚至搬离了工业区。尽管目前在遗产保护方面取得了暂时性进展，但是随着未来经济发展，当地的旁道问题仍会重新提上日程。因此，科希策文化遗产局必须做好准备，再次保护联合国教科文组织遗产斯皮思城堡及其相关遗迹。

参考文献

网址

https://www.spisskepodhradie.sk/mesto/dokumenty–listiny/dokumenty–unesco/

https://whc.unesco.org/en/list/620

Recent Questions of Land-use Protection and Planning in Buffer Zone One of Spiš Castle

Róbert Királ[①]

Regional Monument Board of Slovak Republic

Abstract:

Since 2017 new land-use plan of village Žehra in buffer zone of Spiš Castle UNESCO site is being prepared. Paper provides closer look on specific problems in protected area, and also presents concrete solutions and regulations which were set to preserve outstanding cultural values of the landscape. In cooperation of Regional Monument Board and main author of plan (architect) were defined land-use requirements on protection of characteristic views of listed monuments and new areas for residential buildings were defined due to growing population of adjacent Romani people settlement. One of solved questions was tracing of superior road network in the area under the Castle.

Keywords: Spiš Castle - Unesco site, Zehra - Unesco site, Land-use planning, Cultural landscape

Fig. 1   General view of Spiš Castle (on the left) and area of buffer zone with village Zehra.

Land-use (urban) plan is a crucial and effective tool to preserve and develop protected sites. Village Žehra has decided to prepare and adopt its very first Land-use plan in 2017. The need to elaborate the plan was strengthened by the fact that the territory of village includes two important properties of listed UNESCO site

---

① Heritage supervisor of Regional Monument Board in Košice (Slovakia) dealing mainly with protection of heritage sites and protected zones. Graduated in 2008 at Faculty of architecture of Slovak University of Technology in Bratislava.

and its whole cadastral territory lies in its buffer zone. Beside two of listed medieval monuments (castle and church) the outstanding value of this UNESCO site is composed also by the structure of authentic landscape, which still preserves its historic features.

BRIEF DESCRIPTION OF UNESCO SITE

Spiš Castle and associated monuments in its vicinity is an extraordinary and picturesque UNESCO site of Slovakia, consisting of several intact monument properties and sites and of a wide buffer zone. It was listed in 1993. In 2009 locality was extended to include neighboring medieval walled town of Levoča (13 km west of castle) with an exquisite wood-work of the sculptor Master Paul from the 16ᵗʰ century. The area, listed in 1993, is a remarkable ensemble of different medieval structures in its authentic landscape. It consists primarily of the Castle (SpišskýHrad / Spiš Castle) , Suburbium (town of SpišskéPodhradie) , Chapter (ecclesiastical site of SpišskáKapitula with the Cathedral and the Canonist-Houses) , and the Church (parish church of the Holy Spirit with medieval frescoes in the village Žehra). The Castle stands monumentally on a distinctive rocky mount, creating an astonishing silhouette from all sides. Generally, it is one of largest castle ruins in Europe, compounding of the core on top (12/13ᵗʰ century) and of 3 lower walled courtyards (13ᵗʰ-15ᵗʰ century) . Today it is an opened-to-public castle ruin with a museum exhibition. Over 250 000 visitors a year make it the most visited monument in Slovakia. Visitors are mainly attracted by its monumentality and photogenic visual appearance, mainly from a near going highway (opened in year 2010) . For art-historians most valuable part of the castle is the Romanesque palace on its very top from the early 13ᵗʰ century.

From a broader historical point of view, the locality lies in the very center of Spiš Region. This county was constituted in the 12ᵗʰ century as a north-border region of the Kingdom of Hungary. Region was historically neighboring with Kingdom of Poland. The center of region takes place in the Valley of Hornad River surrounded by woodland mountains. From the very center of the valley a group of four distinctive travertine (white sort of sedimentary limestone) hills emerges. On one of them the Hungarian king founded the Spiš Castle in mid 12ᵗʰ century as an administrative center of newly constituted Spiš administrative region and as a stronghold on important trade route connecting north to the south. This was a branch of even prehistoric, so called *EastAmber road*, linking Balkan countries to Baltic Sea - in closer scale connecting towns of Krakow-Košice-Beograd. Right with foundation of castle a town under it originated (todays Spišské Podhradie - see Fig. 5) as its suburbium and on its west outskirts the king also founded the Chapter - seat of clerical administration of the Church. It is a walled settlement of a Romanesque Cathedral, Canonist-Houses, which in mid 18ᵗʰ century became a seat of bishop and seminary. Castle was a property of the king and was managed by his governor until 1528 - afterwards it

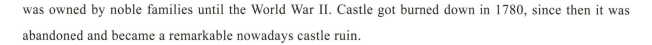

was owned by noble families until the World War II. Castle got burned down in 1780, since then it was abandoned and became a remarkable nowadays castle ruin.

VILLAGE ŽEHRA

UNESCO locality under the Castle is today split in two self-governing counties (see Fig. 4) . In the Prešov County is lies the Suburbium and the Chapter together with several villages in west and north part of the buffer zone. Smaller part, belonging to the Košice County includes only the cadastral area of the village Zehra with the Castle and the Church. Zehra is a rather small village, though its population of 2250 inhabitants is over Slovak average. The village consists of three different solitery built-up areas. One is the historical village itself (see Fig. 2) with a listed Church on a small hill. It has 300 inhabitants. The second is small settlement of Hodkovce built around a Baroque noble family mansion with a valuable historic park - which is an associated monument of the Site. Hodkovce has 150 inhabitants - hundred of them are clients of social-care facility for people with mental disabilities, that is run in the mansion. Generally, village provides calm rural living in one and two-storey family houses. Employment is provided by two producers of wooden windows and two agricultural farms breeding mostly cattle and horses. In Hodkovce four small tourist-accommodation facilities are run by local people.

Fig. 2   View of village Zehra from the south with depiction of proposed road bypass variant on the very right.

The third and most complicated built-up area is the settlement on southwest margin, called Drevenik / Dobra Vola (see Fig. 3) . It is a settlement of Romani (Gypsy) community having today 1850 inhabitants. Part of them lives in standard flat houses built by government in 1990s but a smaller part of community still lives in poor cottages without running water and sewerage. This community is generally excluded and unappealing, its people are mostly unemployed, living from social-care system and producing a lot of garbage around their houses. Low level of education, low (rather absent) hygienic standards, illegal harvesting of firewood, 90% of unemployment and usury among the settlers are the most pressing questions of everyday life in Drevenik settlement. Fortunately, this settlement is not in a direct visual connection with the listed monuments (it is on the margin of the buffer zone, covered by a travertine mound) , but still is a strong disturbing point on the south-entry road to the UNESCO site, that not only social-care authorities but also monument-protection authorities have to deal with.

Important remark to be mentioned with Drevenik community is that today it is spontaneuosly reaching over to the neighboring settlement Dobra Vola (see down on Fig. 4) , which is located in the cadastral territory of a small town Spišské Vlachy (Košice County as well) . Dobra Vola was founded as a stone-masons settlement (turn of the 19/20th centuries, stone-masons for the local quarry) , counting today apx. 20 small stone houses and a granary. In past few decades settlers from Drevenik have overtaken all these houses, abandoned by their owners before. Dobra Vola is already out of the buffer zone of the UNESCO site.

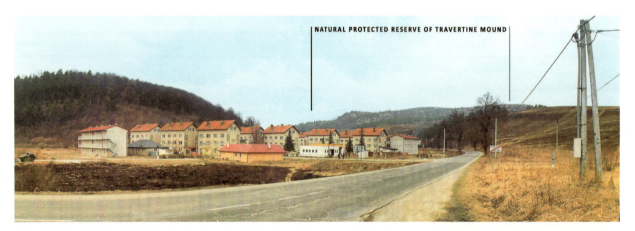

Fig. 3   View of Romani settlement called Drevenik under a same named travertine hill - a view from Dobra Vola.

PROBLEMS AND CHALLENGES

In terms of urban planning in Zehra there are two major challenges. Landscape values of cultural and natural character are present on most of its territory what should strongly limit possibilities of extension of any new built-up areas. Visual appearance of the Castle, Church and Hodkovce mansion has to be preserved as a value of cultural-historic landscape. Since it is a UNESCO site and a buffer zone in terms of Slovak Monument Law - a net of so called protected characteristic views (vistas) was set to monitor and protect authenticity of the listed monument´s environment. The most important defined views are:

1. View of Zehra village and its Church from the south (see Fig. 2) ;

2. View of Castle from the east-entry road;

3. View linking Church and Castle over the Hodkovce mansion.

Beside that, west part of the territory was declared Natural Protected Reserve. It is a group of three remarkable travertine mounds (Drevenik, Sobotisko, Castle Hill) forming a karst area with caves, endemit saline flora, rocky cliffs and plenty of archeological findings from Paleolithic era to Roman era. Any residential built-up is excluded from this natural reserve.

Second major challenge is population growth in the settlement Drevenik / Dobra Vola. First Romani settlers came to this locality at the beginning of the 20th century. In 1950s only apx. 10 Romani cottages were recorded. Later on, the number of Romani people grew rapidly and this trend continues. In 2007 Drevenik

Fig. 4   Map of locality: yellow line - cadastral border, white line - main roads, red line - highway, orange hatch - area of protected views, green hatch - natural protected reserve, magenta hatch - proposed built-up area, magenta line - 3 proposed variants of road bypasses.

had 1400 inhabitants, in 2017 it had 1850 inhabitants of which 1200 are children. Probably 1/5 of them lives in poor unauthorized cottages. And there is only a very few civic services in the settlement - kindergarten, small chapel, civic house and one store. Analysis of Land-use plan estimates increase of population by 1300 people till 2030. Expected population grow and poor living conditions mean a strong demand on new areas for housing and civic buildings.

These demands are strengthened also by fact that many daring and skilled Romani citizens moved with families for work to United Kingdom or Belgium. After making enough money they come back to village Zehra mostly with a will to build a big new house in recent standards, or to reconstruct and enlarge older house directly in the historic part of the village (under the Church) . Naturally, this causes distinctive animosities between rural inhabitants, living in Zehra for generations, and the Romani settlers - intruding in the last decades. With oncoming Brexit a big return from UK is expected in close future.

Protection of valuable landscape and territorial needs of a growing border settlement were two main contradictory moments, which newly prepared Land-use plan had to harmonize.

SOLUTIONS AND REGULATIONS

At the very beginning of the preparation of the Land-use plan Regional Monuments Board of Košice - as 1st instance monument-protection authority - did an elementary analysis of present cultural-landscape values. As a basic feature of authentic built-up areas under Spiš Castle solitary-like (detached) appearance was recognized historical settlements have clearly recognizable margins, they stand in the country separately. Regarding this feature, no merging (joining) together of the three existing settlements (Drevenik - Zehra - Hodkovce) is eligible. With this solitary appearance is related also the authentic silhouette of the village Zehra from south-entry road (on the south protected view, see Fig. 2) . Here, the last rowof the historic vernacular buildings under the Church form an authentic and typical picture of a Spiš village, which represents a real essence of cultural-landscape value. Therefore a strong, conservative decision on Regional Monuments Board was taken to avoid any buildings within this south view - in a distance of 700 meters from the Church. On the other hand, flat south fields in the area of this view could have been a zone for a straight enlargement of the growing Drevenik settlement - without territorial limitations. Drevenik settlement stands in a narrow valley, where only a few land for new buildings is left (see Fig. 4) , while new 200-300 flats will be needed in next 20 years there. However, chief author of the Land-use plan - architect Ján Pastiran - had from the beginning a strong sense for preservation of values of his native village Zehra. It was therefore, no serious discussion during planning took place on the matter of no-built-up zone on the south field. What more, these south fields used to be a pond until early 20ᵗʰ century, so the possibility of pond´s regeneration mustn´t be avoided by permitting new buildings.

Despite this achieved preservation restriction, the problem of urban growth of Drevenik should have been solved. Attention was turned to the close Dobra Vola settlement, which is however in a neighboring cadaster of the town Spišské Vlachy. Difficult negotiations of two municipalities and chief architects led to a Land-use Change (adopted in 2018) in settlement of Dobra Vola, where new residential area for apx. 20 houses was defined and also a place for the new wastewater treatment plant to treat water from Drevenik settlement was chosen. A long flat area to the south of Dobra Vola has a potential to provide the land for growth of Drevenik, but citizens of town Spišské Vlachy may not agree on massive increase of Romani people in their cadaster, in their electoral ward. Therefore, a possible future solution is an exchange of lands between two mentioned municipalities, which is a difficult administrative task - with no precedence in past decades. We will see what exact land demands will the future development bring, and then the matter of land exchange on Dobra Vola might become inevitable.

Some less complex adopted solutions, regulations and requirements should be mentioned, either:

1. Requirement on regeneration of historical tree allees along road was set.

2. Family houses in village Zehra and Hodkovce was limited to 2-storeys.

3. Recommendation on saddle roofs of new buildings with locally traditional slope of 30°-42° was set, together with red, brown or grey colour of roofing. (It is desirable to have a restriction for flat roofs in the buffer zone ...)

4. Recommendation on transparent (semi-transparent) fences made of wood or metal rods (oriented to street) was set. Maximum height of fences was limited to 1,8 metres.

5. Modest parking place for tourist-buses in the center of the village (200 m from Church) was defined in a side street - out of any views on Church.

6. On the fields south of the Church only a simple sport / football playground was permitted, without possibility of any service-buildings, such as dressing room, toilets, tribune or buffets.

Minor visual nuisance of the presentation of the Church of Holy Spirit has rose up 15 years ago - which was a secondary question also for Land-use plan. Today there is only one common cemetery in the village for the whole population (both Slovak and Romani are mostly Roman-Catholics) right behind the stone wall of the listed Church. With a burial of deceased Romani chief in 2002 a fashion of erecting large tombstones among wealthier Romani people of Zehra started. To honour deceased relatives Romani people built vertical black stone tombstones on the new grave-places with life-size depiction of the deceased person. Life-size tombstones are unusual in Slovakian cemeteries. The authentic historic tombstones in Zehra have been usually more humble, not so magnificent, so the citizens of Zehra feel annoyed with this "new" fashion. Oversized tombstones, placed in front of the Church wall (without any permission), are also negatively interfering the visual values of the Site. To avoid such activities - negotiations between the Regional Monument Board, Hygiene authorities, and the local municipality of Zehra led the village to adopt a new and very detailed cemetery order. To prevent those who try not to respect the order, new Land-use plan defines an area for a new second cemetery, right over Drevenik settlement. All future oversized tombstones will be hopefully erected only on new grave-yard and described visual nuisance beside church will stop for good.

Briefly described Land-use plan of village Zehra should be adopted in a next few months. Hopefully, it will be an effective and long-term tool to preserve and encourage visual integrity and authenticity of landscape under the Spiš Castle.

QUESTION OF ROAD BYPASS

In the past decade a great question of the road bypass under the Spiš Castle came to serious urbanistic discussions, involving the whole UNESCO site. The earlier proposed routes of the bypass could have endanger the outstanding values of its cultural landscape.

After opening a highway in 2010 north from the Castle, the need to connect the highway with the roads in the Hornad river valley and the industrial zone in town Krompachy (12km south-east of the Castle) emerged. The main roads in the village Zehra and in the town SpisskePodhradie are quite narrow for truck traffic and heavy traffic noise annoys citizens in these two urban areas. Both concerned county authorities have proposed and adopted to Regional Land-use plan a variant of a road bypass right through the UNESCO site (see Fig. 4 - magenta lines) . Košice County proposed the bypass (A) of village Zehra, tracing a road only 100 meters eastward from the listed Church (see Fig. 2). This bypass would spoil very drastically the surrounding of the Church, and the silhouette of the village from south as well. On the other side, the bypass (B) , proposed by the Prešov County, would cross the area right between the Castle and its Suburbium (see Fig. 5) . This bypass route would cut off these two listed properties, making a barrier in a land that was historically always interconnecting the Castle with its Suburbium.

Fig. 5 **West view from Castle on town SpisskePodhradie (Suburbium) with SpisskaKapitula (Chapter) , depicting in yellow lines the proposed bypass B (down) and bypass C (up) .**

Monument-protection authorities expressed disagreements with both bypass proposals. Despite that, the bypass beside the town SpisskePohradie was adopted even into the Land-use plan of the town in 2008. For the bypass in Zehra a tunnel under the hill beside the Church in Zehra was discussed as a compromise solution-which was however considered expensive. Monument-protection authorities and some local architects proposed the bypass C variant on the west margin of the UNESCO site (see Fig. 5) . This variant goes outside of urban areas, doesn't interfere most valuable cultural landscape, but is too long (expensive) and at the end (near the highway) it crosses a protected area of mineral-water springs. Nature-protection authorities disagree on this matter, though till today possibilities of building a road in mentioned water-spring zone wasn´t thoroughly analyzed.

In the past few years, after series of negotiations of Counties and Town representatives with Monument-protection authorities, involving also Slovak ICOMOS committee, decisions on a bypass were finally reassessed. One of the used arguments was a case of delisting UNESCO site in Dresden, Germany (in 2009) , due to the new bridge crossing over Elbe River in the very center of the listed site.

As a result, Košice County withdrew a proposal of the bypass near the Church from the Regional Land-use plan. Also town of SpisskePohradie withdrew a bypass from its local Land-use plan. The fact also is, that truck traffic on mentioned roads stagnates today. The production in industrial zone of the town Krompachy stagnates as well, and some of the producers even left the zone. Despite this temporary preservation success, future development can reopen the question of a bypass in the locality. Therefore, Regional Monuments Board must be prepared to protect the area of UNESCO listed Spiš Castle and associated monuments once again.

BIBLIOGRAPHICAL REFERENCES

SITES

https://www.spisskepodhradie.sk/mesto/dokumenty-listiny/dokumenty-unesco/

https://whc.unesco.org/en/list/620

保加利亚内塞伯尔古城保护和管理

保加利亚共和国　文化部文化遗产、博物馆与艺术司　伊凡·科列夫 [①]

摘要

1983 年，保加利亚内塞伯尔古城基于标准Ⅲ和Ⅳ列入联合国教科文组织世界遗产名录，成为保加利亚第七处列入名录的世界文化遗产地，也是其中唯一一处包含城市区域的遗产地。因此，对该古城的保护有别于保加利亚其他遗产，有一定的独特性。

自列入名录以来，古城的管理和保护随不同时期发生了不同变化。20 世纪 80 年代，国家开展了大量工作对古城进行保护和修复。到了 90 年代，国家对于世界遗产地内的新建项目失去了管控，结果，曾经以其真实性著称于世的世界遗产地差点列入濒危世界遗产名录。

2010 年，经过二十多年奋争保护遗产的努力，在国际社会的反应和世界遗产委员会的监督下，内塞伯尔当局和当地居民对该世界遗产地的保护有了新方向。世界遗产委员会决议指出："深切关注该遗产的总体保护状况，尤其是，因不可接受的城市结构开发带来的严重改变可能会威胁遗产突出普遍价值、完整性和真实性。"

另外，生活在内塞伯尔旧城的居民对该遗产地所具有的世界遗产地位持怀疑态度，也对遗产所带来的大规模旅游是否能给他们带来更好的生活表示怀疑。

显然，"保加利亚内塞伯尔古城"迫切需要来自内部和外部专家的帮助。

如今将近十年过去了，我们可以坚定地说，内塞伯尔正在重获新生。地方当局和中央政府，与民间社会团体一起，正在为加强该世界遗产地的保护和管理做出新的努力。

关键词：内塞伯尔，古代，中世纪，乡土

国内立法和保护

1956 年，保加利亚内阁会议首次将内塞伯尔古城作为文化遗产加以保护，认为古城是"一个具有

---

① 伊凡·科列夫（Ivan Kolev），建筑师，保加利亚文化部文化遗产、博物馆与艺术司不可移动文化遗产处处长，保加利亚古遗址协会执行委员会成员，并参加了一些致力于遗产保护的保加利亚民间组织。曾在保加利亚不可移动文化遗产国立研究所工作 6 年，并在文化遗产保护领域参与过建筑实践。研究领域为文化遗产研究和遗产地民间社会与管理。

国内外重要意义的集博物馆、旅游观光和度假胜地为一体的综合体",同时也是一处建筑、城市和考古保护区。在当时该文件足以保护遗产,因为它首次确定了遗产作为一个整体的价值存在——既是一系列独立的文化遗迹,也反映了多层次的城市结构。

1981年,文化部通过了"关于索佐波尔和内塞伯尔作为建筑、历史保护区和旅游胜地的法令"。在七八十年代,发布一个文件来保护具有共同建筑和城市结构的历史遗迹群是非常普遍的做法。该法令界定了遗产的边界——整个半岛及其与陆地相连的地峡。一般而言,这些文件是为了控制与保护相关的建筑而制定的,并未明确说明保护区域的历史及文化重要性。这也是为什么有必要为每一个独立的城市保护区制定相应文件的原因,该文件应明确指出每一遗产地的重要性及其独特特征。

1986年,国家文化遗产研究所提出了内塞伯尔总体规划的概念。这一国家管理规划是实施总体规划这一新的国家政策的一部分内容。

总体规划明确指出,之前所有文件都有助于提升内塞伯尔文化遗产的利益,但是却并未形成相应的关于老城区旅游管理活动的规范。这些旅游活动与当地特定的历史环境不相符,且对遗产环境造成了一定影响。

1991年,在总体规划的基础上批准通过了考古、建筑和城市保护区"内塞伯尔"的边界。

2009年,随着文化遗产法案的通过,保加利亚内塞伯尔古城得到了"考古保护区"法令的保护,但该法令并未明确回应古城文化价值所具有的全部含义。

2015年,根据现行立法,通过了新的保加利亚内塞伯尔古城保护体制,其中包括保护指南和可接受的干预等。该体制覆盖了世界遗产及其缓冲区——包括陆地和海洋部分。根据法律要求,该遗产地重新命名为:不可移动文化遗产群"内塞伯尔古城"——"'国家意义'类别下的考古保护区、建筑—结构和城市不可移动文化遗产'历史聚居地'"。

图1　保加利亚内塞伯尔古城,景观特色,1926年(https://pou-nesebar.org)

不可移动遗产地

考古遗址。内塞伯尔不可移动文化遗产由多个关键要素构成，其中每个独立要素根据其功能和建造时期而界定。大部分可追溯至远古的构成要素都被统一划为考古类别，包括古城墙遗址、早期拜占庭温泉浴场、默森布里亚史前坟墓等。

宗教建筑。内塞伯尔古城受到了来自保加利亚陆地和拜占庭文化区域的宗教影响。内塞伯尔的教堂建筑建于多个历史时期，这些历史时期具有同等重要性，且跨越了整个东正教建筑和文化发展的1500年历史。

本地建筑。内塞伯尔房屋建筑向保加利亚东南方延伸，同时保留了与当地居民捕鱼及其他日常生活活动相关的独特元素。由这些建筑所造就的城市结构也成为其突出普遍价值的重要特征。

图 2　保加利亚内塞伯尔古城，古老的圣索菲亚大教堂遗址，作者：Ivan Kolev

图 3　保加利亚内塞伯尔古城，街道特色，作者：Ivan Kolev

保护和管理问题

内塞伯尔列入世界遗产名录之时，其岩石山坡就已经出现了问题。持续不断的潮汐侵蚀把陆地的一部分冲进了黑海，该城市大部分历史时期都有这个问题。保加利亚政府看到了问题所在，并采取了一些被证明较为有效的措施，但这同时也改变了这些山坡的自然形状和用途，随后——人们日常生活中对遗产地的使用方式也被改变了。这些来自海里的新地层包围了整个半岛，并由此建造了新的渔港码头，且面积得到了扩大。

由于缺少相关法律来限制涌入古城的旅游流量，旅游人数呈现逐步上升的趋势。对食宿设施和贸易商店的需求改变了内塞伯尔居民对自己城市的使用方式。功能上的改变促进了一些建筑和城市特色的改变。在 90 年代，这一具有较高旅游价值的遗产地与保加利亚的政治和社会变迁息息相关。旅游文化给内塞伯尔带来了非常大的变化，以致于古城差点被列入濒危世界遗产名录。

对遗产地的改变持续了将近二十年之久，直至 2010 年，政府表现出新的从政治和专业层面治理的决心，通过限制负面做法、引入保护和管理规划来加强对遗产地的保护和管理，该规划是 2009 年文化遗产法案框架内的新工具。

保护和管理规划的影响

参与制定保护和管理规划的人员包括保加利亚遗产保护领域理论和实践领域的领军人物，以及来自国家不可移动遗产学院的专家学者。该规划历时两年完成，包括了大量关于城市历史、文化、现行政策、目前的保护状况、新的保护指南和几个试点保护项目等信息。其目标是成为未来最佳实践的案例。

保护和管理规划有两个方面值得注意。第一，最早制定该规划时，规划中的财务部分并未得到批准，理由是在当时，融资工具从法律上来讲并不可行。这推迟了最终规划方案的形成，直至 2019 年，还未形成终稿。

第二，该规划对本地居民和当局带来了一定影响，当时并未得到政府官方批准。随着这些行动方案的各个阶段连续得到实施，这才得到地方当局、当地居民和国际专家的认可。

在国际古迹遗址理事会保加利亚国家委员会的大力支持下，地方当局开始实施规划所提议的试点项目。2010—2018 年间，内塞伯尔成功完成了多个大型保护项目。这些项目主要针对公共空间，通过适当的保护措施来保护几个最重要的遗产。

仅列举下述几个项目为例：

"圣斯蒂芬"教堂、"圣帕拉斯凯维"教堂、"施洗者圣约翰"教堂、"内塞伯尔"文化线路的保护和修复项目，反映出宗教在内塞伯尔历史发展过程中的重要意义和作用。

最近，保加利亚国际古迹遗址理事会和内塞伯尔市政府获得了保加利亚美国大使基金资助，这有助于对"圣约翰阿利特格托斯"教堂实施保护。修复工程于 2018 年完成。

除这些项目外，保加利亚还采取了其他措施：

1. 2015 年重新更新了不可移动文化遗产的状况并明确了保护机制。

2. 记录和拍摄未发掘的考古遗址、街景和中世纪教堂等。制作建筑、考古和文化遗产监控卡。

3. 分阶段拆除非法建筑。自 2010 年以来，未得到授权的人为干预大幅减少，这是文化部"文化遗产保护督察组"总司和东部海港布尔加斯"国家建筑控制"指挥部共同管控的结果。

4. 每年都会开展关于水下文化遗产的研究，相关报告显示，这将有可能增强该遗产地的突出普遍价值。

另外，2011 年，内塞伯尔市政府对新建筑开发进行了限制。该举措在数年内都将有效，事实证明，这给当地居民也带来了全新的感受。自此以后，世界遗产地范围内很少出现新建项目，大部分项目都是对现有建筑的保护、修复和改造。

保护和管理规划及实施带来了巨大影响，事实证明，这对公共空间的开发也具有重要作用。规划所开展的项目对当地居民及其在遗产保护中所起的作用有正面促进，更为重要的是，人们看到有希望通过当地社区和专家的坚强意志和共同努力重现内塞伯尔的生机和活力。

内塞伯尔市政府对这些重焕公共空间、并为游客创造了解遗产地突出普遍价值全貌的行动表示认可。通过重新铺砌道路，使其尽可能恢复真实状态，不少重要街巷逐渐得到复原。

为更好地移除不真实的柏油马路，限制私有车辆在古城内通行，在古城北部，即缓冲区内划出了用于车辆通行的管制区域。这样，内塞伯尔居民和游客得以享受更为真实、更为缓慢的生活节奏，这与城市的结构和建筑也非常契合。

另一个重要的改变是关于商铺店面的指南，这对遗产地的整体艺术性产生了持续影响。这些指南规定使得城市很多地区的贸易功能更为均衡，街道整体重新展现出本地建筑特色。

图 4 保加利亚内塞伯尔古城，圣斯蒂芬教堂，作者：Ivan Kolev

图 5　保加利亚内塞伯尔古城，圣帕拉斯凯维教堂，作者：Ivan Kolev

内塞伯尔咨询及监测任务的影响

2017 年内塞伯尔咨询任务：

"咨询小组认为世界遗产保加利亚内塞伯尔古城保留了支撑其突出普遍价值的关键属性特征。最近，在保护遗产突出普遍价值、改变过去所造成的负面影响方面取得了重要进展，但是……"

尽管保加利亚内塞伯尔古城取得了有目共睹的成功，但我们前面仍有许多工作需要开展。2017 年咨询任务提出来许多建议，其中较为重要的有：

管理规划的通过和实施（正在最终定稿中）；

实施全面的遗产影响评估（HIA）框架（正在保加利亚文化遗产法框架内通过）；

建议小幅调整遗产边界，将水下文化遗产纳入遗产范围（国家水下考古中心每年都开展水下遗产研究）；

支持拆除非法增加的建筑物，改善城市环境（鉴于法律程序较长，仍在进行中）；

鼓励当地社区居民仍居住在半岛内；

与联合国教科文组织及其合作伙伴合作，开展能力建设项目，改善水下文化遗产的鉴定、评估、研究和保护。

备注：

1. 保加利亚内塞伯尔古城于 1983 年基于标准 III 和 IV 列入联合国教科文组织世界遗产名录。

标准（Ⅲ）：保加利亚内塞伯尔古城是多层次文化和历史遗产的杰出见证。许多文明都在此留下了实实在在的痕迹：公元前两千年的考古结构、希腊黑海殖民地与保存完好的防御工事、古老的希腊风格别墅和宗教建筑、保存完好的中世纪教堂建筑（其中一些教堂仅保存了部分考古结构）。内塞伯尔在许多方面展现出其作为一个边境城市所具有的历史重要性。这个古城数千年来都是重要的基督教信仰中心，现在是一个不断发展、充满活力的城市机体。

标准（Ⅳ）：保加利亚内塞伯尔古城是独特的建筑群，保存了保加利亚文艺复兴时期 * 的建筑，并与岩石半岛突出的自然特色形成和谐统一的共生，古城通过一段狭长的人工地峡与大陆相连。长期以来人类的活动共同造就了该城市的特质，使其得以存在至今，它见证了不同的历史时期——城市中既有公元前两千年的结构，还有古典时期和中世纪时期的遗物；中世纪时期的宗教建筑外立面有丰富的塑胶制品和多彩的陶瓷装饰饰品，是当时代表性的风格；古城还见证了特色民居建筑不同的发展阶段，证明了巴尔干半岛和东地中海地区高超的建筑技艺。以中世纪教堂和考古为主的极具本地特色的城市建筑群，与独特的沿海浮雕一起，呈现出高质量的城市肌理特征。

* （该术语并不准确，因为大部分房屋并不具有保加利亚文艺复兴时期的特点，使用本地一词更为准确）

2. 保加利亚立法中，《文化遗产法》将管理规划列为法案的一部分，并将遗产地关于保护、修复和适应的指南文件，管理工具和责任悉数纳入。

参考书目

保加利亚共和国档案馆国家不可移动文化遗产研究所档案馆

保加利亚共和国文化部档案馆

IvanchevI.（1957），内塞伯尔及其房屋，索菲亚

ChambulevaZ.，SaselovD.（1993），保加利亚内塞伯尔古城，索菲亚

内塞伯尔咨询任务报告 2017

保护状况报告 2018

保护状况报告 2017

内塞伯尔咨询任务报告 2015

保加利亚内塞伯尔古城反应性监测任务 2012。国际古迹遗址理事会

存在风险的遗产。世界濒危遗迹和遗产报告 2011—2013。国际古迹遗址理事会

网址

https://whc.unesco.org/en/list/217

http://nessebarinfo.com/

http://ancient-nessebar.com/

The Ancient City of Nessebar Conservation and Management

Ivan Kolev[①]

Department "Immovable Cultural Heritage" in Ministry of Culture of Republic of Bulgaria

Abstract:

The Ancient City of Nessebar was inscribed in the UNESCO World Heritage List in 1983 based on criteria iii and iv. It is one of the seven Bulgarian heritage sites with that statute, while it is the only one that consists of urban area. As such, its protection within the Bulgarian heritage preservation practice is unique.

Since its inscription the city has had challenging times concerning its management and conservation. The 80's were a decade of a huge state effort dedicated to conservation and restoration; the 90's and were infamous for the decline in state control on new building development within the world heritage site. As a result, the property, once acclaimed for its authenticity, was on a brink of being enlisted in the List of World heritage in Danger.

In 2010, following more than two decades of struggle in conservation efforts, for both the authorities and the local people of Nessebar, the world heritage site preservation took new direction, with international reaction and the Decision of the World Heritage Committee which stated: *"deep concern regarding the overall state of conservation of the property, and in particular, serious changes due to unacceptable development of the urban fabric that are a threat to the Outstanding Universal Value, integrity and authenticity of the property."*

Moreover, the people living in the old city of Nessebar were having doubts on the World Heritage status of the site, and whether the mass tourism it brought, changed their livelihood for benefit.

It was clear that "The Ancient City of Nessebar" was in a great need for internal and external expert help. Almost ten years had passed since then and we can strongly say that Nessebar is regaining its spirit.

Local and central authorities, together with civil society are enhancing fresh efforts in conservation and

---

[①] Ivan Kolev is an architect, head of Department "Immovable cultural heritage" in the Ministry of Culture of the Republic of Bulgaria. Before that, he has been working for six years in the National Institute for Immovable cultural Heritage in Bulgaria and has had architectural practice in the field of cultural heritage preservation. His interests are in cultural heritage research, civil society and management of heritage sites. He is a member of the Executive Committee of the ICOMOS - Bulgaria and takes part in few other civil organizations dedicated to heritage preservation in Bulgaria.

management on the world heritage property.

Keywords: Nessebar, Ancient, Medieval, Vernacular

NATIONAL LEGISLATION AND PROTECTION

The Ancient City of Nessebar was first protected as a cultural heritage site in 1956 by the Council of Ministers of Bulgaria as a "Museum, tourist and resort complex of national and international importance", and at the same time as an Architectural, urban, and archeological preservation area. This document was adequate to the age as it was the first to establish the value of the site as a whole - both as series of individual monuments of culture, and as a layered urban structure.

In 1981 the Ministry of Culture approved an "Ordinance for Architectural and Historical Reserves and tourism sites Sozopol and Nessebar". During the 70s and the 80s it was common for historic group monuments of common architectural and urban structure to be preserved by shared documents. The Ordinance defined the borders of the site - the whole peninsula with the isthmus, connecting it with the land. These documents, as a general rule, were made for building control relevant to the conservation and did not state the specific historical and cultural importance of the preservation areas. That is why a new document was needed for each urban preservation area that would clearly state the importance and unique characteristics of each site.

In 1986 the National institute for Monuments of Culture proposed the General plan-Concept for Nessebar. It was part of a new state policy for the implementation of General plans, who were a national formulae of Management plans.

The General plan confirmed that all previous documents give a push for the development of the interest toward the cultural heritage of Nessebar, though they did not give the regulations for releasing of the Old city of activities connected with tourism, which were not conforming to the specific historical context and were affecting its atmosphere.

In 1991, on the basis of the General plan, the boundaries of the Archaeological, architectural and Urban reserve "Nessebar" were approved.

In 2009 with the adoption of the Culture Heritage Act the Ancient City of Nessebar was given the statute of *"Archaeological Reserve", which clearly did not respond to the full meaning of its cultural value.*

In 2015, under the current legislation, the new Conservation regimes of the Ancient City of Nessebar were adopted and they included the guidelines for conservation and acceptable interventions. The Regimes cover the area of the world heritage property and its buffer zone - on land and sea. Following the requirements of the law the new name of the site is: Group immovable cultural property "Ancient city of Nessebar" - "archaeological reserve and an architectural-structural and urban immovable cultural properly "historical settlement" with a category "national significance".

Fig. 1   The Ancient City of Nessebar, Characteristics of The Landscape, 1926 (https://pou-nesebar.org)

IMMOVABLE HERITAGE SITES

Archaeological Sites. The immovable cultural heritage of Nessebar consists of several key elements, amongst which, the single ones are defined by their functions and period of construction. Most of the elements dated back to antiquity are generalized as archaeological, including the remains of the city walls, Early Byzantine thermae, the Necropolis od Messembria etc.

Religious Architecture. The city of Nessebar has had an influence of a religious center not only on the Bulgarian lands, but also in the Byzantine cultural sphere. The churches of Nessebar date back to several

Fig. 2   The Ancient City of Nessebar, Ruins of the Old Metropolitan church St. Sophia, Author Ivan Kolev

equally important periods and span throughout 15 centuries of development of the Orthodox Christian architecture and culture.

Vernacular Architecture. The houses of Nessebar present a type of housing spread onto the South-East part of Bulgaria, while retaining some unique elements connected with the fishing and other everyday activities of the local people. The urban structure that they define is also a key feature of the OUV.

Fig. 3   The Ancient City of Nessebar, Street Characteristics, Author Ivan Kolev

CONSERVATION AND MANAGEMENT PROBLEMS

When Nessebar was enlisted in the World Heritage List it already had problems with its rocky slopes. The tidal erosion was taking away parts from the land into the Black sea as it has been for the good part of the town's history. This problem was faced by the Bulgarian state with measures that proved sufficient, while in the process changing the natural shape and use of the slopes, and subsequently - the way people used the site within their everyday life. This new layer of land, taken back from the sea, surrounds the whole peninsula and created new and expands the fisherman port area.

Due to lack of legal instruments to narrow down the tourist flow in the Old town, the crowds were reaching escalating levels. The need for accommodation, places to eat and drink and trade shops led to changes in the way people of Nessebar use their own city. These changes in function led to changes in some architectural and urban characteristics. This moment of high touristic interest for the site was combined with the political and social changes in the Bulgarian society in the 90's. The strength of the tourism culture led to a sufficient change of Nessebar and to the point where the Ancient city was on threatened to be enlisted in the List of World heritage in danger.

This process of change within nearly twenty years was stopped in 2010 when the state showed new political and expert will to restrict the negative practices and enforce conservation and management tools with the introduction of the Conservation and Management plan - A new instrument within the Cultural Heritage Act of 2009.

THE IMPACT OF THE CONSERVATION AND MANAGEMENT PLAN

The team that took upon themselves to create the Conservation and management plan comprised of the leading figures in the Bulgarian theory and practice in the field of heritage conservation, along with experts from the National Institute for Immovable Heritage. The development of the plan took two years and included vast information about the city, its history, cultural layers, existing policies, current state of conservation, along with the new conservation guidelines and several pilot projects, which were aimed as an example for good practices that should multiply in the future.

The Conservation and Management plan development has two aspects. First, when it was introduced it was not approved in its financial part - it suggested finance tools that were not legally possible by the time. This led to several years of delaying the final preparation of the plan and until 2019, it is not ready as a final document.

The second aspect of the plan however is the impact it had on local people and authorities, without even being an official document, approved by the government. One by one, the different stages of the action plan were being carried out and they were followed by the approval of authorities, local people and international experts.

The local authorities, with the huge help of the Bulgarian National Committee of ICOMOS started to implement the pilot projects suggested by the Plan. In the years 2010-2018 several huge conservation projects were successfully completed in Nessebar. They were all dedicated to public space and brought several of the most important monuments in the light, with appropriate conservation measures.

Just to name a few of the projects:

Conservation and restoration of churches "St. Stephan", "St. Paraskeva", "St. John the Baptist", the "Faith in Nessebar" cultural route, showing the significance of religion for the historical development of Nessebar.

Most recently, ICOMOS Bulgaria and Municipality of Nessebar won a grant from the USA Ambassador's Fund in Bulgaria, which helped the conservation of "St. John Aliturgetos". The restoration was completed in 2018.

Besides these projects, other steps were taken by the state:

1. In 2015 the immovable cultural property status was updated and Conservation regimes were determined.

2. The uncovered archaeological sites, street silhouettes, medieval churches were documented and

photographed; monitoring cards were prepared for architectural, archaeological, and artistic cultural heritage properties;

3. The illegal constructions are being removed in a phased manner, and since 2010 a sharp reduction of the unauthorized interventions was noticed. Their removal is under the control of General Directorate "Cultural Heritage Conservation Inspectorate" of the Ministry of Culture and the Regional Directorate "National Construction Control" - Burgas.

4. Each year, the research on underwater cultural heritage is carried out and the reports show great promise on addition to the outstanding universal value of the site.

Furthermore, the Municipality of Nessebar introduced a restriction on new building development in 2011. This measure was active for several years and the process proved refreshing for the local community. Since then, the new building proposals are rarity, while most of the projects within the world heritage site are conservation, restoration and adaptation of existing buildings.

The impact of the Conservation and Management Plan and its implementation proved to be of great importance for the development of public spaces, the example it carried out to local people and their role in the preservation of the site, but most importantly - the hope that Nessebar could revive through the will and common work of the local community and experts.

The Municipality of Nessebar acknowledged its mission to revive the public space, creating the opportunity for the visitors to grasp whole spectrum of the key elements of the OUV. One by one, important street ensambles are being restored through restoration of the authentic paving of the streets.

The removal of unauthentic asphalt street is enhanced by access limitations of personal vehicles within the Old town. A controlled access for all vehicles is set on the north part of the old town, in the area of the buffer

Fig. 4　The Ancient City of Nessebar, The church St. Stephen, Author Ivan Kolev

zone. This way people of Nessebar and visitors can enjoy more authentic and slow kind of life, suitable to the urban structure and architecture of the city.

An important change was the guidelines on shop fronts, which instantly affected the overall aesthetics of the site. Through the guidelines, a more balanced approach was achieved in most of the trade functions in the city, and the street ensambles regained the views on the vernacular architecture.

Fig. 5   The Ancient City of Nessebar, The church St. Paraskeva, Author Ivan Kolev

THE IMPACT OF THE ADVISORY AND MONITORING MISSIONS IN NESSEBAR

The 2017 Advisory mission to Nessebar:

"The mission team concluded that the World Heritage property The Ancient City of Nessebar retains the key attributes that underpin its Outstanding Universal Value (OUV). There has been significant recent progress to protect the OUV of the property and to reverse negative impacts that took place in the past. However..."

Despite the unarguable success stories within the Ancient City of Nessebar, a lot of work stands ahead of us. Among many of the 2017 Advisory Mission recommendations, some key ones are:

1. Adoption and implementation of Management plan (in final editing);

2. Implementation of thorough and comprehensive Heritage Impact Assessment (HIA) framework (in process of adoption in the Culture Heritage Act of Bulgaria);

3. Proposing a minor boundary modification to include the underwater cultural heritage (each year underwater research is carried out by the state Center for Underwater Archaeology);

4. Support the removal of illegal additions to buildings and to improving the urban environment (still in process, due to the long legislation procedures);

5. Encouraging the local community to remain resident within the peninsula;

6. Establishing a capacity - building programme in cooperation with UNESCO and its partners to improve the identification, evaluation, research and protection of underwater cultural heritage.

Notes:

1. The Ancient City of Nessebar was inscribed in the UNESCO World Heritage List in 1983 based on criteria iii and iv.

Criterion (iii) : The Ancient City of Nessebar is an outstanding testimony of multilayered cultural and historical heritage. It is a place where many civilizations left their tangible traces: archaeological structures from the Second millennium BC, a Greek Black Sea colony with surviving remains of fortifications, a Hellenistic villa and religious buildings from the Antiquity, preserved churches (in some of them preserved only parts of archaeological structures) from the Middle Ages. Nessebar has demonstrated its historical importance as a frontier city on numerous occasions. Having been a remarkable spiritual centre of Christianity for a thousand years, today it is a developing and vibrant urban organism.

Criterion (iv) : The Ancient City of Nessebar is a unique example of an architectural ensemble with preserved Bulgarian Renaissance* structure, and forms a harmonious homogenous entity with the outstanding natural configuration of the rocky peninsular, linked with the continent by a long narrow stretch of land. Its nature and existence is a result of synthesis of long-term human activity, which has witnessed significant historic periods - an urban structure with elements from 2nd millennium BC, classical antiquity, and the Middle Ages; the development of medieval religious architecture with rich plastic and polychrome decoration on its facades in the form of ceramic ornamentation typical for the period; the different stages in the development of the characteristic residential vernacular architecture, which testify to the supreme mastery of the architecture of the Balkans as well as the East Mediterranean region. The vernacular architecture of the urban ensemble, dominated by medieval churches and archaeology, together with the unique coastal relief, combine to produce an urban fabric of the high quality.

* (the term was not appropriate since most of the houses were not examples ofthe Bulgarian Renaissance, while vernacular is more adequate)

2. In Bulgarian Legislation the Management plan was introduced in the Culture Heritage Act as a *Conservation and Management plan*, thus incorporating both the guidelines for conservation, restoration and adaptation of the heritage sites, and the management tools and responsibilities.

BIBLIOGRAPHY

National Institute of Immovable Cultural Heritage of the Republic of Bulgaria Archive

Ministry of Culture of the Republic of Bulgaria Archive

Ivanchev I. (1957) , *Nessebar and Its Houses*, Sofia

Chambuleva Z., Saselov D. (1993) , *The Ancient City of Nessebar*, Sofia

Advisory Misson Report Nessebar 2017

State of Conservation Report 2018

State of Conservation Report 2017

Advisory Misson Report Nessebar 2015

Reactive Monitoring Mission to the Ancient City of Nessebar, 2012. ICOMOS

Heritage at Risk. World Report on Monuments and Sites in Danger2011-2013. ICOMOS

SITES

https://pou-nesebar.org/en/

https://whc.unesco.org/en/list/217

http://nessebarinfo.com/

http://ancient-nessebar.com/

恢复当地社区与文化遗产间的联系：
考纳斯现代主义建筑案例

立陶宛共和国　文化部文化纪念与遗产政策司　卢卡斯·斯特拉瑟维切斯 [①]

摘要

1919 年，由于政治原因，立陶宛失去了历史都城维尔纽斯，国家第二大城市考纳斯成为临时首都。急剧增长的人口、政府机构和外国使馆的办公住房需求使考纳斯城市发生了迅速变化。快速扩张和现代主义建筑赋予了这座城市独特的面貌——这些变化不仅体现在城市化和建筑风格中，同时也使这个新成立的首都和它的居民形成了一种积极乐观的特质。1940 年考纳斯丧失独立，尽管多年来它们与当地社区的宝贵联系已渐渐削弱，但其现代主义建筑依然成为过去辉煌遗产的代表，屹立于世。

如今，随着重要项目"2022 年考纳斯欧洲文化之都"的开展以及考纳斯现代主义建筑正筹备申请列入联合国教科文组织世界遗产名录，这些遗产正逐渐恢复生机。这些行动为该市的文化运动奠定了良好的基础。市政府与当地社区正在利用文化遗产来恢复当地社区与文化遗产之间的联系。本文将回顾、展现当地社区参与考纳斯的行动以及所取得的积极成果，并尝试说明社区参与保护和利用文化遗产中的重要作用。因此，通过回顾为恢复与考纳斯现代主义建筑间的联系所采取的各种行动，本文试图证明，重点关注社区及遗产的可持续利用，或许可为文化遗产保护利用中出现的诸多问题提供答案。

关键词：考纳斯，立陶宛，现代主义，社区，联合国教科文组织

简介

世界遗产公约第 30 周年庆之后，《布达佩斯宣言》强调了 4 个战略性目标，也称为"4C"目标。2007 年增加的"第 5 个 C"目标明确提出，要努力确保当地社区在各个层面参与到世界遗产地的确认、保护和管理过程中。《2012—2022 年实施世界遗产公约战略行动计划》指出，非常有必要加强社区在

[①]　卢卡斯·斯特拉瑟维切斯（Lukas Straševičius）先生，立陶宛共和国文化部文化纪念和遗产政策司副司长，参与了国家文化遗产保护政策的制定过程，同时也是欧盟颁发的特别荣誉——"欧洲遗产标识"的国家协调员。曾在立陶宛维尔纽斯大学获得历史学硕士学位，专攻遗产保护领域。

世界遗产公约实施过程中的作用。

最近几年，在立陶宛越来越能感受到强大社区所带来的益处。文化遗产可作为催化剂解决许多社会问题，带来正面改变。立陶宛有深厚的历史渊源，立陶宛人对自己的历史和文化深感自豪，并致力于保护这一历史及文化。鉴于立陶宛这一社会特质，通过向市民传递资讯，并提供咨询，使其了解参与文化遗产保护及可持续利用的方法途径，极有可能提高公众在参与性管理和遗产保护方面的参与程度。这将进一步鼓励社区凝聚起来，努力改善自身的环境。

考纳斯现代主义建筑

考纳斯现代主义建筑是 1918—1940 年间立陶宛政治环境的产物。1919 年，由于政治原因，立陶宛失去了历史都城维尔纽斯，国家第二大城市考纳斯成为临时首都。这些年间，急剧增长的人口、政府机构和外国使馆的办公住房需求使考纳斯城市发生了迅速变化。快速扩张和现代主义建筑赋予这座城市独特的面貌。考纳斯边界扩张了 7 倍，人口从 90000 增长到 155000（Drėmaitė M.，2018）。这些变化不仅体现在城市化和建筑风格中，同时也使这个新成立的首都和它的居民形成了一种积极乐观的特质。这成为快速城市化和现代化的例子，反映出乐观的、直面独立未来的信仰所激发出的独特价值观——这是当时许多中东欧城市都存在的态度（Drėmaitė M.，2018）。1940 年考纳斯丧失独立，尽管多年来与当地社区的宝贵联系已渐渐削弱，但其现代主义建筑依然成为过去辉煌遗产的代表，屹立于世。

图 1　考纳斯化学学院屋顶（图片来源：考纳斯 2022 项目 "Ekskursas" 图片来源：M.Plepys）

当前的行动

如今，随着重要项目"2022 年考纳斯欧洲文化之都"的开展以及考纳斯现代主义建筑正筹备申请列入联合国教科文组织世界遗产名录，这些遗产正逐渐恢复生机。这些行动为该市的文化运动奠定了良好的基础。市政府与当地社区正利用文化遗产来恢复当地社区与文化遗产间的联系。本文将回顾、展现当地社区参与文化遗产保护和利用的行动、以及所取得的积极成果，并尝试说明社区参与在保护和利用文化遗产中的重要作用。因此，通过回顾为恢复与考纳斯现代主义建筑间的联系所采取的行动，本文尝试证明，重点关注社区及遗产的可持续利用，或许可为文化遗产保护利用中出现的诸多问题提供答案。

艺术与文化遗产间的协同效应：国际考纳斯双年展

"国际考纳斯双年展"是一个当代艺术节，自 1997 年以来，由非政府组织举办。艺术节的举办地往往融合了文物或历史遗迹。2015 年，在考纳斯原纺织厂和中央邮政局两处文化遗产建筑均举办了展览。中央邮政局建于 1932 年，是考纳斯现代主义建筑最具代表性的建筑之一。过去十年中仅有部分建筑得到了利用，大部分房间均处于空置状态。这一展览吸引了众多参观者，远超出主办方的预期。其中大部分参观者期望探究中央邮政局大楼这一现代主义建筑的内部构造，参观这一曾被关闭且空置十余年的标志性建筑。在这个实例中，文化遗产向公众开放，使展示区域具有临时功能。这种艺术与遗产之间的协同效应是重新焕发闲置遗产建筑活力和价值的良好范例。

2017 年，"国际考纳斯双年展"致力于展现历史遗迹及其与人、社区和城市间的关系。纪念活动反对那些保守派做法，例如，简单移除 / 竖立历史纪念碑、或模拟新的当代方式等。日本艺术家 Tatzu Nishi 使用立陶宛独立后的标志性象征物——立陶宛著名艺术家 Juozas Zikaras 于 1921 年设计的自由纪念碑，创办了一场展览。1921 年，著名的立陶宛艺术家 Juozas Zikaras 设计出自由纪念碑，但该纪念碑在前苏联占领时被拆除，其中的青铜天使则保存在博物馆中。当时，人们只能在餐桌旁私下谈论自由（bienale.lt，2017）。为此，这个艺术家制作了一个典型的厨房，原来的青铜天使放在房间中央。整个装置被精心放置在约 12 米高的纪念碑上。用 T.Nishi 的话来说，在纪念碑建成后，社区和纪念碑之间的联系正迅速消失。这位艺术家试图重新建立这种联系，并为他所创作的纪念碑赋予新的意义（bienale.lt，2017）。

面向未来的现代主义

"面向未来的现代主义"（*Modernizmas ateičiai*）是"2022 年考纳斯欧洲文化之都"项目下开展的活动之一，这是一个专门的平台和开放空间，可用于人们开展活动、召开会议、也欢迎遗产社区和文化行动代表前来讨论和参加研讨会，为现代主义遗产的保护、阐释和传播制定策略。其目标是使人们认识并赞同，在考纳斯这座城市中，他们对围绕他们的周边环境应承担责任，激发他们与城市景观和文化之间的情感联系（modernizmasateiciai.lt，2018）。该行动鼓励当地居民分享他们与居住建筑之间发生的故事，从而构建遗产的重要组成部分——与社区间的联系。遗产社区已开始提交关于当时的现代主义建筑故事，并依托文化遗产创建了可讲述不同故事的旅游路线。

"Ekskursas"是"面向未来的现代主义"的一个子项目，它提供了一个平台，供不同专家学者组织公共参观和旅游活动。截至目前，已有多名建筑师、艺术历史学家、城市规划专家、社会学家和其他学者分享了他们关于考纳斯现代主义建筑的知识和观点，且活动已持续3年之久。这一子项目旨在将著名的建筑物面向公众开放，并通过故事和现代建筑独特的内部构造将其对外推广。通过这些游览活动，现代主义建筑以及广义上的文化遗产价值得以传递给普通公众，从而加深人们的理解。

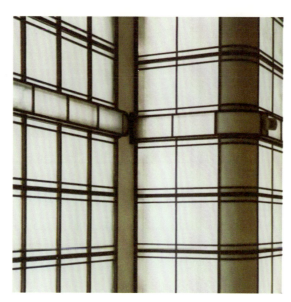

图2　国家储蓄银行（图片来自：考纳斯2022项目"Ekskursas"摄影：M.Plepys）

考纳斯开放档案

"Atminties vietos"或"考纳斯开放档案"是一项针对考纳斯集体记忆的项目。这是一个开放平台，当地社区可在其中发布各种关于这个城市的故事。人们可以通过网站发布不同时间轴上发生的故事，并标示在交互式地图上。网站目前汇集了各类科学的、通俗的和文学的文字，以及研究成果、艺术类相关研究项目、照片、视频和音频记录等，并持续更新记忆场所的虚拟地图。但是，该数据库最大的价值是城市居民所讲述的个人记忆和故事（atmintiesvietos.lt，2018）。其中还有对生活在考纳斯的少数民族代表进行的视频采访，这些视频资料记录了他们的生活经历、捕捉了过去的点滴细节、创建了一幅更为多样、具有丰富情感的考纳斯记忆画卷。不仅如此，许多年轻人也得到邀请，来分享他们的故事，表达他们所在的环境对自身生活所产生的影响。这些更为深入地反映出城市景观与文化遗产对人们日常生活的影响，以及这些影响是如何不断变化的。该项目鼓励与遗产有联系的社区行动起来，探索和研究他们自身的文化遗产，从而创造出更大的价值。

图 3　体育大学屋顶（图片来自：考纳斯 2022 项目 "Ekskursas" 摄影：M.Plepys）

让我们建设更美丽的考纳斯

"让我们建设更美丽的考纳斯"（"Gražinkime Kauną"）是一家位于考纳斯的非政府组织，主要关注文化遗产的保护和历史的传承，并致力于打造更美丽的遗产环境。该组织举办了不少旅游活动，重点推介两战之间的装饰艺术的设计。其中一个主题线路是"两战期间的考纳斯—设计之城"短途旅行，建议人们参观位于考纳斯 Žaliakalnis 区的公共机构、私人别墅、住所及其他名胜。这些活动的联合组织方包括立陶宛农业商会、考纳斯国家图书馆古稀新闻部、考纳斯艺术体育馆、个人艺术家和收藏家等（grazinkimekauna.Wordpress.com，2018），其目的是将收藏文化遗产的私密空间向公众开放，使公众有机会感受原先无法接触到的文化遗产。非政府组织 "Gražinkime Kauną" 还与应用科技大学合作，为老人和年轻人共同学习提供帮助。其中的一个项目——"Medžio talka"，旨在教授当地居民制作木工、纪念品等 DIY 课程，目的是激发非经济活动人口提升其在就业市场中的地位（grazinkimekauna.wordpress.com，2018）。除此之外，"让我们建设更美丽的考纳斯"项目还通过组织多种多样的主题游览活动参与了"欧洲遗产日"活动。其组织设计的线路"考纳斯最漂亮的大门"将考纳斯现代主义建筑最珍贵、最真实的大门展现给公众。"Gražinkime Kauną" 的主要目的之一是开放考纳斯现代主义博物馆。

其他与考纳斯现代主义无关的活动

2018 年是欧洲遗产年。虽然一些活动将考纳斯看作是俄罗斯帝国某个省的中心城市，但在遗产年框架下，重点则放在了考纳斯的现代主义建筑上。1879 年，沙皇亚历山大二世认为考纳斯具有战略重要意义，遂命令在该城建造一座堡垒。到了 1911 年，大部分一级堡垒和军事要塞已建成。其中大部分建筑仍是考纳斯景观的重要组成部分，且形成了 Šančiai 或 Panemunė 等小地区的全貌。这些军事设施在一战中发挥了作用，后来则作为监狱、仓库和军事学校使用。1993 年俄罗斯军离开立陶宛后，大部分军事建筑要么被遗弃，要么无人维护。这些会令人感觉不愉快的遗产地后来被用于实际需要——收集砖块、开辟出蔬菜园或建造庇护所等。

卷心菜地

这个名称来源于一处 19 世纪军用地窖，用来储藏腌制的卷心菜。与其他堡垒建筑一样，这个地方也是最近才向公众开放。卷心菜地与其他军用堡垒建筑一同建造，是 19 世纪至 20 世纪军事基地的一部分。1993 年军事学校被当地人遗弃，并被视为占领的遗产。2004 年，有投资者购买了主干道沿线的老旧营房并计划对其重建，这是重焕 Šančiai 地区生机的第一步。

卷心菜地是当地社区开展的一项自下而上的行动。这个社区位于低阶层的 Šančiai 地区。行动在 2013 年由 Ed Carroll 和 Vita Gėlūnienė 发起。尽管 Šančiai 地区对大多数考纳斯民众来说不是很有吸引力，但他们依然看到了该地区具有的潜力。他们发现了一个不同寻常的、被遗弃的地块，其中有不少存放公共包裹和垃圾的地窖。第二年，他们组织对这些地窖进行清理——"尽管该活动规模很小，但却反映出当地社区对物理恢复概念的不断演进、以及社区民众不断提升的积极认知"（Carroll，2017）。现在这些地窖被用来开展各式各样的展览和研讨会。当地社区还利用这些空间举办社区活动——卷心菜地已成为社区生活的中心。Šančiai 社区也是 2022 年考纳斯欧洲文化之都的合作伙伴。该社区的活动向所有人开放，也是 2022 年考纳斯欧洲文化之都项目的一部分。卷心菜地是 Faro 公约网络组织的成员之一，该组织致力于将欧洲的遗产社区联合起来。这个地方能反映出 Šančiai 地区所有的特

图 4 圣诞节期间的卷心菜地（摄影：Darius Petrulis）

质——红色的石砌军营在考纳斯非常显眼，被 Šančiai 视为自己独特的地标。

过去几年，Šančiai 社区组织了各种各样的活动，将社区成员聚集在一起。圣诞期间他们会用香脂白杨（一种立陶宛较为稀有的树种）来代替圣诞树做装饰，并创作了社区歌剧 "Kopūstų laukas"（"卷心菜地"）。每年他们都会发行日历，2019 年日历主题为 Šančiai 地区的当地建筑。2018 年，他们组织成立了社区艺术培训学校。一年多的活动让他们找到了更多的合作伙伴和其他想要进行合作的活动。卷心菜地成功地改善了他们的环境，并按照他们的需求，将其所尊敬的遗产也融入进来。结果就是，社区变得更为强大，不同社会群体建立了社会联系，而且，文化遗产重新焕发了活力，并服务于社区需要。

Parakas

Parakas 是一个社区活动，旨在利用其生活社区的遗产，努力使沙皇时期防御要塞的文物重新焕发活力，并服务于社区。例如，一个建于 19 世纪晚期的老旧火药地窖曾是防御工程的一部分，已用于军事目的长达 100 多年。与许多其他建筑一样，它也没有任何用途。当地人知道了之后，将它开发成为无家可归者和地下组织的庇护所。最近当地人开始清理该地窖，仔细处理那些存在危险的洞穴和其他障碍。不久之后，人们逐渐发现了这个有趣地窖的潜力。当地社区在此举办了各种各样的聚会活动、周日宴会、研讨会、装置艺术、巡演以及音乐盛会等。去年，这个火药地窖成为 "Baterija" 遗产节的主要场景之一。

Baterija

Baterija 是一个跨领域的文化遗产节日，旨在为已遗忘的文物"充电"，使它们重焕新生，并服务于社区和艺术专业人员，并作为聚会或开展艺术演出的场所。该艺术盛会由考纳斯城堡公园（负责城

图 5 Baterija 庆祝活动中升起了标志性白旗（图片来源：Baterija 脸书页面）

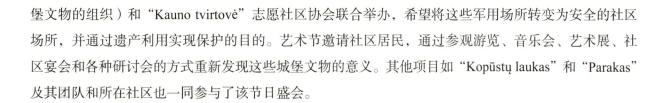

堡文物的组织）和 "Kauno tvirtovė" 志愿社区协会联合举办，希望将这些军用场所转变为安全的社区场所，并通过遗产利用实现保护的目的。艺术节邀请社区居民，通过参观游览、音乐会、艺术展、社区宴会和各种研讨会的方式重新发现这些城堡文物的意义。其他项目如 "Kopūstų laukas" 和 "Parakas" 及其团队和所在社区也一同参与了该节日盛会。

结论

通过考察考纳斯现代主义建筑发现，整个社会已准备好参与到遗产保护和可持续利用的活动中，以提升生活品质。另一个值得一提的事情是，政府机构或专业人士的帮助可以促进这种自下而上的运动发展壮大，并积极参与到文化遗产保护体系中来。文中这些例子反映出文化遗产如何使人们聚集和团结起来，并鼓励他们加入到社区活动中来。合作是双向的，已确定各自遗产的社区有决心保护自身遗产，而遗产文物可以成为社区团结融合的一个重要因素。文化遗产和社区间的协同效应刺激人们学习遗产的历史，并采取措施保护他们的遗产，因此遗产与社区之间的联系加强了。代表非政府组织的社区与市政当局的对话有助于确保参与式治理，这也是可持续发展的关键要素之一。

参考书目

a）书集

Drėmaitė M.，Akmenytė–Ruzgienė V. et.al.eds（2018），乐观主义建筑：考纳斯现象，维尔纽斯。

b）网址

https://grazinkimekauna.wordpress.com/

https://modernizmasateiciai.lt/en/apie/

http://www.atmintiesvietos.lt/en/informacija/about–the–project/

https://ec.europa.eu/eurostat/tgm/refreshTableAction.do?tab=table&plugin=1&pcode=tps00177&language=en

http://www.bienale.lt/

Reviving Connection between Local Communities and Cultural Heritage: Kaunas Modernism Architecture Case

Lukas Straševičius[①]

Ministry of Culture of the Republic of Lithuania

Abstract

In 1919, due to political aspects Lithuania lost its historical capital Vilnius and Kaunas, the second biggest city in the country, became the temporary capital. Rapid transformation of Kaunas was dictated by vastly growing population and demand for new estates to house governmental institutions and foreign embassies. Fast expansion and modernism architecture formed unique appearance of the city - these changes were seen not only in urbanization and architecture, but it also formed a new optimistic identity of re-established state and its residents. After the loss of independence in 1940, Kaunas modernism architecture stood as a legacy of the glorious past, though through long years of negligence valuable connection with local community faded.

Today that legacy is being gradually revived in connection with development of the highly important project "Kaunas European Capital of Culture 2022" and with the preparation process of inscription of Kaunas Modernism Architecture on the UNESCO World Heritage List. These initiatives gave a great base for cultural motion in the city. Municipal and local community initiatives are using cultural heritage to revive connection between local community and its cultural heritage. This paper will review and present initiatives and positive outcomes of local community involvement in Kaunas and try to demonstrate the importance of community involvement in preserving and utilization of cultural heritage. Therefore this review of initiatives connected to Kaunas modernism architecture tries to prove that the focus on communities and sustainable use of heritage is an answer to many problems concerning conservation and utilization of cultural heritage.

---

① Mr. Lukas Straševičius has a Master's Degree in History from Vilnius University, Lithuania; specializing in Heritage Preservation. Currently Mr. Straševičius has been working as a Chief Officer at the Department of Cultural Memory and Heritage Policy at the Ministry of Culture of the Republic of Lithuania. He is involved in the development process of the national policies in the field of cultural heritage protection. Lukas Straševičius is also a National Coordinator of the European Heritage Label, which is a special award by the European Union.

Keywords: Kaunas, Lithuania, modernism, community, UNESCO

Introduction

Following the 30th anniversary of World Heritage Convention, Budapest Declaration emphasizes 4 strategic objectives, also known as "Four Cs". The "Fifth C", added later in 2007, clearly states to seek to ensure the active involvement of our local communities at all levels in the identification, protection and management of our World Heritage Sites. The Strategic Action Plan for the Implementation of the World Heritage Convention 2012-2022 points out that it is essential to enhance the role of communities in the implementation of the World Heritage Convention.

The benefits of strong communities are becoming more and more visible in the recent years in Lithuania. Many social challenges can be solved using cultural heritage as catalyst for positive changes. As a country that has strong historical background, Lithuanians are proud of their history and culture and have commitment to preserve it. Keeping in mind this quality of Lithuanian society and reaching out by informing and consulting how citizens can participate in protection and sustainable use of cultural heritage, it is possible to achieve higher public involvement in assuring participatory governance and heritage conservation. This further encourages communities to gather and seek to improve their environment.

Kaunas modernism architecture

A phenomenon of Kaunas modernism architecture was a consequence of political situation in Lithuania during 1918-1940. In 1919, due to political aspects, Lithuania lost historical capital Vilnius and Kaunas, the

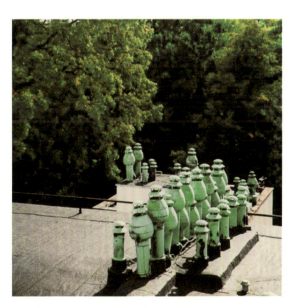

Fig. 1   Roof of Kaunas faculty of chemistry (Photo from Kaunas 2022 project "Ekskursas" by M. Plepys)

second biggest city in the country, became the temporary capital. During those years, rapid transformation of Kaunas was caused by vastly growing population and demand for new estates to house governmental institutions and foreign embassies. Fast expansion and modernism architecture formed unique appearance of the city. Kaunas boundaries expanded 7 times and population grew from 90,000 to 155,000 (Drėmaitė M., 2018) . These changes were not only seen in urbanization and architecture, but it also formed a new optimistic identity of re-established state and its residents. It became an example of rapid urbanization and modernization and an expression of the values inspired by optimistic belief in an independent future - an attitude shared by many cities in Central Eastern Europe at that time (Drėmaitė M., 2018). After the loss of Lithuania independence in 1940, Kaunas modernism architecture stood as a legacy of the glorious past, although through long years of negligence, valuable connection with local community faded.

Current initiatives

Today that legacy is being gradually revived in connection with development of the highly important project "Kaunas European Capital of Culture 2022" and with the preparation process of inscription of Kaunas Modernism Architecture on the UNESCO World Heritage List. These initiatives gave a great base for cultural motion in the city. Municipal and local community initiatives use cultural heritage to revive connection between local community and its cultural heritage. This paper will review and present initiatives and positive outcomes of local community involvement in conservation and utilization of cultural heritage and try to demonstrate the importance of it in preserving and utilization of cultural heritage. Therefore, this review of initiatives connected to Kaunas modernism architecture tries to prove that the focus on communities and sustainable use of heritage is an answer to many challenges concerning conservation and utilization of cultural heritage.

Synergies between art and cultural heritage: the International Kaunas Biennal

The International Kaunas Biennial is a contemporary art festival, which has been organized by the non-governmental organization "Kaunas Biennial" since 1997. Festival space often integrates heritage objects or even monuments. In 2015 exhibitions were held in the cultural heritage buildings - in the former factory of textile and in the Central Post Office in Kaunas. The Central Post Office building was built in 1932 and it is one of the most iconic buildings of Kaunas modernism architecture. For the past 10 years it was used only partially, and most of its rooms were empty. This event attracted more visitors than organizers would have expected; most of them were interested in exploring modernism interiors of the Central Post Office building and visiting this iconic building which used to be closed and empty for more than 10 years. In this case, cultural heritage was made accessible to general public and enabled temporary function of exhibition area. This synergy between art and heritage is a good example of revitalization of unused heritage buildings.

In 2017, the International Kaunas Biennial was dedicated to reflect the notion of monument and its relation to person, community and city. Festival opposed for conservative practice of removing/erecting monuments and simulated new contemporary approach to monuments. The Japanese artist Tatzu Nishi created an exhibition using an iconic symbol of independent Lithuania, the Freedom Monument designed by the famous Lithuanian artist Juozas Zikaras in 1921. During the Soviet occupation of Lithuania, this monument was demolished and the bronze angel of the monument was stored in the museum. At that time, the freedom was only talked about in private, around the kitchen table (bienale.lt, 2017). Therefore, the artist created a typical kitchen room with the original bronze angel in the middle. The whole installation was carefully put around standing monument in about 12 meter height. In T. Nishi words, the connection between community and the monument is fading fast after the erection of the monument. The artist tried to renew that connection and gave new meanings for the monument he has been worked with (bienale.lt, 2017) .

Modernism for the future

"Modernism for the future" (*Modernizmas ateičiai*) is one of the initiatives created under the project "Kaunas European Capital of Culture 2022". This initiative is a special platform and an open space for initiatives and meetings, welcoming heritage community and representatives of cultural initiatives for discussions and workshops to create strategy for preservation, interpretation and dissemination of modernism heritage. Its goal is to endorse the people's responsibility for the environment that surrounds them in Kaunas

Fig. 2   National Savings Bank (Photo from Kaunas 2022 project "Ekskursas" by M. Plepys)

and to stimulate their emotional connection with the urban landscape and culture (modernizmasateiciai.lt, 2018). Initiative encourages locals to share stories about buildings they live in, thus creating important part of heritage - connection with community. Heritage community has already started to submit stories about modernism buildings of the time, also create themed touristic routes that tell different stories with the help of cultural heritage.

One of the sub-project of the initiative "Modernism for the future" is called "Ekskursas", which is a platform for different specialists to hold public routes and tours. So far, architects, art historians, urbanists, sociologists and others have been sharing their knowledge and insights about the modernism architecture in Kaunas already for 3 years. This sub-project aims to open the doors of well-known buildings for the public and introduce them with stories and unique interiors of modern architecture. Throughout these tours, the value of modernism architecture and cultural heritage in general is being revealed to the public, thus creating deeper understanding of it.

Open archives of Kaunas

"Atminties vietos" or an "Open archive of Kaunas" is a project dedicated for collective memory of Kaunas. It's an open platform for community to post various stories about the city. Website publishes stories on the timeline and represents them on the interactive map. The website stores scientific, popular, literary texts and research studies, artistic and research projects, photos, audio and video recordings and the continuously updates the virtual map of memory places. However, the greatest value of this database is related to the personal memories and stories told by the city residents (atmintiesvietos.lt, 2018). Part of the project is video interviews with the representatives of the national minorities, which live in Kaunas, documenting their experience and

Fig. 3　Roof of University of Sports (Photo from Kaunas 2022 project "Ekskursas" by M. Plepys)

capturing details from the past, creating even more diverse and emotional picture of Kaunas. Nevertheless, project invites young people to share their stories and show what impact in their life had the environment they grew up in. This creates a deeper perspective of perception how urban landscape and cultural heritage influenced lives of the people and how that impact has been changing. This project encourages community that has a connection with heritage to explore and research their cultural heritage, thus creating even greater value of it.

Let's Make Kaunas More Beautiful

"Let's Make Kaunas More Beautiful" ("Grąžinkime Kauną") is a non-governmental organization based in Kaunas concentrating on cultural heritage preservation, history and simply making their environment more beautiful. Organization runs tours that mostly focus on interwar art-deco designs. One of the thematic routes for excursion "Interwar Kaunas - a City of Design" suggests visiting public institutions, private villas, residencies and other places of interest in Kaunas Žaliakalnis district. The tours are organized in cooperation with the Lithuanian Chamber of Agriculture, the Rare and Old Press Department of the Kaunas State Library, the Kaunas Art Gymnasium, private artists and collectors (grazinkimekauna.wordpress.com, 2018) . Initiative tries to open private spaces where hardly accessible cultural heritage objects are shown to the public. The NGO "Gražinkime Kauną" presented projects for Kaunas eldership and youth together with University of Applied Sciences. One of them - "Medžio talka" intends to educate local residents in DIY tasks such as woodwork and souvenir making, thus motivating economically inactive people to improve their status in the employment market (grazinkimekauna.wordpress.com, 2018) . Apart from those initiatives, "Let's Make Kaunas More Beautiful" participated in the European Heritage Days initiative by organizing various thematic tours. Organization created route of "Most beautiful door of Kaunas" that presents rare authentic doors of Kaunas modernism buildings. One of the great aims of "Gražinkime Kauną" is to open Kaunas modernism museum.

Other initiatives not connected to Kaunas modernism

2018 was declared the heritage year of Europe, in Kaunas context spotlight was put on modernism architecture, though some initiatives choose to explore Kaunas as a center of governorate in Russian empire. In 1879, Tsar Alexander II ordered to construct a fortress in Kaunas as a strategically important place. Until 1911, most of the I class fortress batteries and forts were finished. Most of these buildings are still seen in the landscape of Kaunas and shaping the look of the entire micro-districts like Šančiai or Panemunė. These military constructions served in the Great War and then were used as prisons and warehouses and military campus. After soviet army left Lithuania in 1993, most of the fortress buildings were left abandoned or without care. This uncomfortable heritage was used for practical needs - collected bricks, created vegetable gardens or built shelters.

Cabbage field

A name derived from an old 19th century army cellars that were used to store pickled cabbages. This place, like many other fortress buildings, was newly open for public - it was constructed together with army barracks and was part of military base through 19th and 20th century. After the 1993 military campus was abandoned and rejected by locals as a heritage of occupation. Only in 2004 investors bought old barracks along the main street and prepared reconstruction project. This was the first step in reviving Šančiai micro-district.

Cabbage field is a bottom-up initiative from local community of lower Šančiai micro-district. It was started in 2013 by Ed Carroll and Vita Gėl ū nienė. They saw potential in Šančiai district, which was not very appealing for most residents of Kaunas. An unusual abandoned public parcel with cellars full of rubbish was spotted. Next year they organized cleaning of the cellars - "While small scale, it reflected the evolving physical recuperation and increased positive perception by the community" (Carroll, 2017) . The cellar is now being used for various exhibitions and workshops. Local community uses this space for hosting community events - cabbage field became a center of community life. Šančiai community is a partner of Kaunas European Culture Capital 2022. Events of the community, which are open for everyone, are a part of Kaunas - European Capital of Culture 2022 programme. Cabbage field is a member of Faro Convention Network which unites heritage communities in Europe. This place reflects the whole character of Šančiai district - red masonry barracks are easily recognized by Kaunas residents while residents of Šančiai consider this their unique landmark.

In the past year, Šančiai community organized various events gathering community members. At

Fig. 4   Cabbage field during Christmas (Photo by Darius Petrulis)

Christmas time they decorated balsam poplar (an unusual tree in Lithuania) as Christmas tree and created community opera "Kop ū stų laukas" ("*Cabbage field*") . They are also issuing calendars every year - 2019 calendar is dedicated for local architecture of Šančiai district. In 2018 they organized Community Art Training School. Over a year of activity they found many partners and other initiatives that want to cooperate. Cabbage field managed to transform their environment and transform it for their need incorporating heritage they respect. By doing that, community has grown stronger, social links were created between various social groups and cultural heritage was revitalized and used for community needs.

Parakas

Parakas is a community initiative seeking to utilize heritage in their living space and tries to revive tsarist fortress objects and use them for community needs. An old gun powder cellar built as a part of fortress project in the late 19th century was used by military for more than 100 years. Like many other buildings, this object stood without purpose, yet it was known for locals and served as a shelter for homeless and underground parties. Recently local community started to clean it up and took care of dangerous holes and other obstacles. Soon after that, they saw a potential in this interesting place and started to organize various gatherings for community, Sunday dinners, workshops, art installations, tours and musical events. Last year it was one of the main scenes for heritage festival "Baterija".

Baterija

Baterija is an interdisciplinary cultural heritage festival trying to "charge up" forbidden objects for new

Fig. 5   A symbolic white flag was hoisted during Baterija festival (Photo from Baterija Facebook page)

life ant present them as potential places for communities and art professionals to be used for their needs as places of gathering or art performances. This festival was organized by Kaunas fortress park (Organization responsible for fortress objects) and voluntary community association "Kauno tvirtovė". Their aim was to transform these places from military objects to safe community spaces and adapt a concept of preservation through utilization. Festival invited residents to explore fortress objects through tours, concerts, art exhibitions, community dinners and various workshops. Other initiatives like "Kop ū stų laukas" and "Parakas" participated in the festival together with their teams and communities surrounding them.

Conclusion

This overview of initiatives related to Kaunas modernism architecture reveals that society is ready to participate in the field of heritage preservation and sustainable use in order to improve quality of living. Another thing worth mentioning is that a help from governmental institutions or professionals can help bottom-up initiatives to grow stronger and get involved into cultural heritage conservation system. These examples illustrate how cultural heritage can unite and encourage people to gather into communities. Cooperation works both ways - communities that have identified their heritage are very committed to preserving it while objects can be a uniting factor for the communities. This synergy of cultural heritage and community stimulates to learn about their history and preserve their heritage, therefore connection between heritage and community strengthens. The dialog between community representing NGO's and municipality contributes to assuring participatory governance that is one of the keys for sustainable development.

Bibliographical references

a) Collective book

Drėmaitė M., Akmenytė-Ruzgienė V.et. al. eds (2018) , *Architecture of optimism: The Kaunas Phenomenon*, Vilnius.

b) Sites

https://grazinkimekauna.wordpress.com/

https://moderniamnoentoioini.lt/en/npio/

http://www.atmintiesvietos.lt/en/informacija/about-the-project/

https://ec.europa.eu/eurostat/tgm/refreshTableAction.do?tab=table&plugin=1&pcode=tps00177&language=en

http://www.bienale.lt/

阿尔巴尼亚培拉特与吉洛卡斯特拉世界遗产地历史建筑的保护

意大利　米兰理工大学　格里戈尔·安基柳 [①]
阿尔巴尼亚共和国　文化部　柯泽塔·安基柳
阿尔巴尼亚共和国　文化部　奥罗拉·坎贝里

摘要

作为联合国教科文组织世界遗产名录的一部分，培拉特与吉洛卡斯特拉历史中心在历史建筑的保护和管理方面面临巨大的挑战。在可持续发展的背景下，应将传统技艺等综合知识体系与现代结构分析方法的应用结合起来，推动保护实践的开展，这具有非常重要的意义。因此，为确保历史建筑的完整性特征不受破坏，在实施任何保护性干预之前，必须开展详细的跨学科研究。本文重点讨论下述内容：

– 分析培拉特与吉洛卡斯特拉历史中心历史建筑的类型、传统建筑材料和建造工艺；

– 运用有限元素法分析建筑结构体系在应对地震等自然灾害时的有效性；

– 保护传统建筑体系及组成部分对于研究建筑结构安全性方面的独特意义。

关键词：培拉特与吉洛卡斯特拉，世界遗产地，历史建筑，真实性，结构评估

简介

吉洛卡斯特拉历史中心于 2005 年成为世界遗产地，并于 2008 年进行了扩展，将培拉特历史中心纳入进来，形成了系列遗产——培拉特与吉洛卡斯特拉历史中心，这是具有奥斯曼帝国时期典型建筑特征的罕见范例。从古自今，这两处有防御保护功能的历史中心一直有人居住。这两处遗址地位于阿尔巴尼亚南部，且彼此相连，它们见证了所在城市和建筑遗产的丰富和多样。培拉特与吉洛卡斯特拉

[①]　格里戈尔·安基柳（Grigor Angjeliu），米兰理工大学土木和环境工程学院博士、研究员、讲师。曾在宾夕法尼亚大学担任访问学者。专业领域是历史建筑的结构修复，包括复杂数字模型的开发，安全评估和缓解历史砖石建筑地震易损性的，并在该领域撰写了多篇研究论文。

是一种生活方式的见证，这种生活方式在奥斯曼帝国时期，长期受伊斯兰传统影响且融入了更多古代风格。这种生活方式尊重东正教的传统，使得东正教的思想和文化得以继续发扬光大，尤其在培拉特地区（联合国教科文组织世界遗产名录 2008）。

　　培拉特位于阿尔巴尼亚中部，见证了多个世纪以来不同宗教和文化社区和谐并存的状况。它的特点是一处大型防御工事，当地人称之为"kala"，其中大部分建于公元 13 世纪，但最早可追溯至公元前 4 世纪（图 1a）。城堡区有许多拜占庭式教堂建筑，大部分建于公元 13 世纪，另有几座建于 1417 年奥斯曼帝国时期的清真寺。培拉特是一座坚固开放的小城，长期以来是手工艺人和商人的居住地。培拉特城市中心反映了巴尔干半岛的乡土住宅传统，其中一些可追溯至 18 世纪晚期至 19 世纪时期（联合国教科文组织世界遗产名录 2008）。

　　吉洛卡斯特拉位于阿尔巴尼亚南部 Drinos 河谷地带，由拥有土地权的大地主建造而成。小城随处可见 17 世纪建造的，引人注目的传统房屋建筑，还有建于 19 世纪早期的更为精致的房屋建筑（图 1b）。小城还保留了一处集市、一座建于 18 世纪的清真寺、和两座教堂（联合国教科文组织世界遗产名录 2008）。

图 1　历史中心一览
a）培拉特，b）吉洛卡斯特拉（阿尔巴尼亚文化部提供）

吉洛卡斯特拉历史中心的建筑类型

　　不同类型历史建筑的发展会受很多因素影响，例如，社会和经济发展状况、地形特征、环境条件、当地建筑材料、地方建造技术和社区生活方式等。下文根据 Riza 教授的研究对吉洛卡斯特拉房屋建筑进行了类型划分。

在国内类型划分的框架内，吉洛卡斯特拉的住宅建筑被归类为用于城市防御住宅范畴（Riza 2009）。建筑的总体朝向和平面情况遵循当地独特的地形。在阿尔巴尼亚其他地区（如培拉特、克鲁亚、斯库台等地）也发现了过去建造的用于防御目的的住宅，如"kulle"，但在吉洛卡斯特拉发现的房屋是最具代表性的（Baçe, Meksi et al. 1980）。

随着时间推移，吉洛卡斯特拉住宅在平面设计和体积构成等方面发生了很多变化。在吉洛卡斯特拉，16世纪建造的历史房屋比较简单，而17世纪早期建造的房屋则较为高级。根据Riza教授的研究（2009），用一个基本的标准来衡量吉洛卡斯特拉房屋的平面和体积构成，可划分出三种不同的类型（图2）：

垂直类型：是其中最简单的类型，也是吉洛卡斯特拉房屋发展进程中最基本的构成方式（图2a）。它形成了一种柱状的楼体，一般建在两层或三层楼高的矩形房基上。前两层通过外部的楼梯相连。

单翼类型：是吉洛卡斯特拉最为流行的房屋类型，所以当地泥瓦匠对这种房屋的建造技巧非常精通（图2b）。Kikino房屋是其中最突出的代表。

双翼类型：是最复杂的吉洛卡斯特拉房屋类型（图2c）。据可查的资料显示，这种房屋类型最早出现在18世纪早期或更早时候。Zekate（1812年）或Skendulate（1823年）房屋是其中的典型代表。

图2　吉洛卡斯特拉传统房屋的代表
a）垂直类型，b）单翼类型，c）双翼类型（Riza 2009）

传统建筑技术

墙壁是阿尔巴尼亚传统房屋主要的结构元素，通常使用简单石块、土坯砌体或内有填充物的木结构石墙。大部分情况下都会使用黏土或石灰粘合剂，偶尔也看到使用干砌墙方法（没有任何粘合剂）建造的房屋。

基于对历史建筑的调查，建议对房屋的建筑施工技术进行如下分类：

砖石墙：60—120厘米厚，使用枕木（不同层面）进行加固，用于改善在土壤沉降或地震情况下的结构性能。对于60—70厘米厚的墙壁，需要使用两个纵向枕木；更厚的墙壁则需要使用3个或更多枕木来覆盖整个墙体。有些情况下用于加固的木料会隐藏于墙壁内部，以便更好地应对环境状况，保护墙壁的稳定。

木结构砖墙：通常作为房屋内部的隔墙，有时也用于建筑物的外立面，减少窗户的嵌入。橡木和松木是最常用的木材种类。后来木材框架逐渐使用石块、砖坯或窄小的木板（çatma）来填充。19 世纪早期开始运用 çatma 技术，为不同建筑造型提供了可能性（图 3）。1851 年发生大地震后，很多培拉特历史中心房屋的上层遭到了严重破坏，Çatma 技术得到了广泛应用。这一技术中，木材框架的重量比沉重的石砌体建筑轻得多，为此房屋有很强的抗震性。

土坯砖墙：在培拉特与吉洛卡斯特拉历史中心较少见到这种建筑类型。土坯砖墙是阿尔巴尼亚中部和北部地区常用的类型。有各种规模大小的风干砖坯。建造过程中还常常使用枕木。

除墙壁外，传统房屋的建造过程中还大量使用石柱（由石墩或木材制成）、石拱或筒形拱顶。

木桩常用于建筑物前部，hajat 和 çardak。有时为了支撑石拱或筒形拱顶也会在建造楼体时使用石墩。石拱或筒形拱顶是培拉特与吉洛卡斯特拉传统房屋的典型构造。门窗或拱廊也会出现拱门的造型。石筒拱顶常被用来覆盖水箱、地窖或用于楼梯建造。

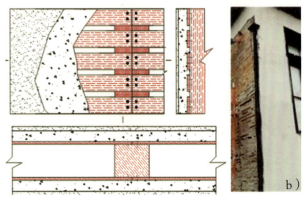

图 3　使用 catma 技术可创建不同的建筑造型
a）Angonate 房屋、Gjrokastra，b）木板条和石膏的详细使用方法（çatma）

建筑体系的结构评估

在实际进行人工干预时，使用钢筋或混凝土等现代建筑材料来代替传统建筑材料的某些特殊部件（木栓、屋顶或地板等）一直有很大的争议。对这一现象进行研究很有意义，因为材料的转变不仅仅会影响历史建筑的完整性特征，在某些情况下还会使建筑物更难抵御地震等自然灾害（Langenbach 2007）。

根据"奈良真实性"（国际古迹遗址理事会 1994）的建议，历史建筑的真实性特征应从不同维度评估：结构、材料、施工技术、建造环境等。所选择的干预方法必须尊重原始功能，且应确保可与现有的材料、结构和建筑价值相兼容。因此，开展任何保护工程之前，必须对传统建筑进行详细研究，以便全面了解其建筑结构、施工技术和材料。同时还应用现代结构分析方法，以便更好地了解现有结构体系的有效性或实施改进措施的必要性。

随着时间的推移，在培拉特与吉洛卡斯特拉历史中心记录了大量因自然和或人类行为造成的威胁：

地震、水灾、山崩滑坡、土壤下沉、火灾等（Milutinovic，Spirollari et al. 2003）。运用基于有限元素法的结构分析等科学方法可充分理解并预测历史建筑在这些情况下的结构化反应及安全性。通过模拟不同的应急情况、评估建筑物的安全性以及设计更好的技术干预方案等，为人们更好地理解和预测结构化反应提供了解决方法。下文是两个应用有限元素法对地震作用下的历史建筑进行分析的案例。

了解现有结构化体系的有效性

第一个用于结构化分析的案例是一处典型的砖石填充的木结构建筑物。该建筑位于爱尔巴桑镇，城堡的围墙内（图4a），建于19世纪晚期。本次研究的目的是，使用有限元素法研究在地震时，如果最高地面加速度达到 ag，475=0.269g、且假定逆程周期为475年（50年内超过10%的概率）时（Aliaj，Muço et al. 2010）现有的木结构的性能。

图4　a）Elbasan 地区的传统房屋；b）外立面填充砖石的木框架测量

该结构有较为规则的形状，尺寸约为8.6米×12米。外石砖体（含石灰砂浆）厚度约为51厘米，使用枕木进行加固（图6a）。一层结构为石砌体并使用枕木进行加固，上层则是砖石填充的框架结构（图6b）。所填充的砖块大小为22×15×5厘米。

运用有限元素法分析的结果表明，现有结构体系也能抵抗中等强度地震（Angjeliu et al. 2013）。反应频谱分析表明，尽管整个建筑都会受到地震的破坏，但建筑上层是最脆弱的部位（图5a）。填充了砖石的木框架结构减轻了来自建筑物上层的重量，有利于减小地震能量的破坏。对角支撑通过维持不同角落中的拉力，改善了砖体间的连接（图5a）。分析预测，地震荷载可能会导致力的高度集中，因此，如今后进行修复，应重点加强结构节点和连接处。

为强调原始木结构的重要性，对没有上层枕木和角落支柱的情况（第二个案例）也进行了结构分

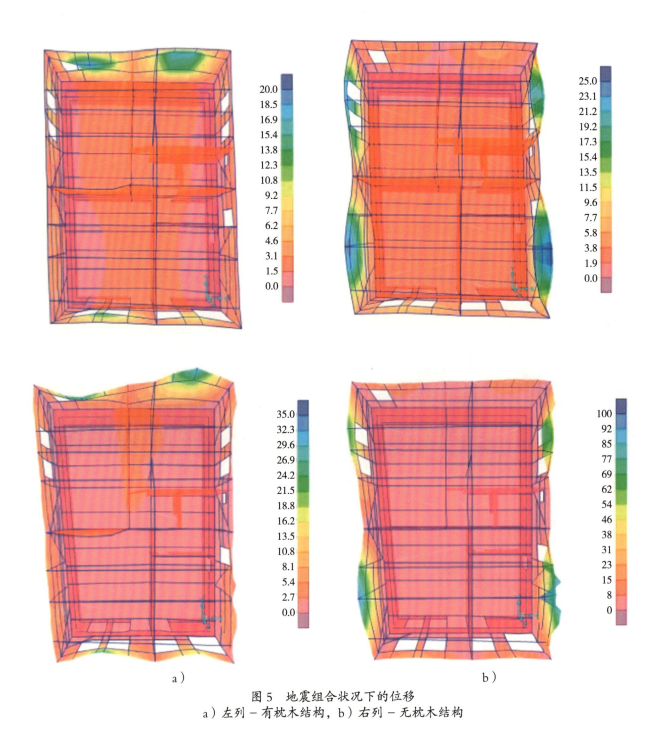

a）   b）

图 5　地震组合状况下的位移
a）左列 – 有枕木结构，b）右列 – 无枕木结构

析。对比结果显示，第二个案例中，由于出现了地震组合状况，X 和 Y 方向的位移大了 2—5 倍（图 5a，b）。水平方向的枕木有助于减轻砖砌体的变形程度，改善了石砌墙的平面外特性。

识别现有结构体系的脆弱性

第二个案例的研究目的是运用有限元素结构分析方法来了解地震过程中的结构化反应，凸显现有的脆弱点。

选取意大利驻阿尔巴尼亚地拉那前大使馆（图6）作为案例研究的对象（Angjeliu and Baballeku 2013）。该建筑位于阿尔巴尼亚首都地拉那中部，始建于20世纪20年代，因具有独特的建筑价值被列为阿尔巴尼亚的建筑遗产，受到国家级保护。

 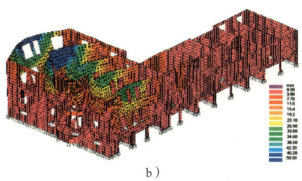

a）   b）

图6　确认结构脆弱点
a）前意大利大使馆；b）墙壁平面外问题

非线性时程分析显示，由于建筑物中央出现平面外问题，形成一个脆弱点。究其原因，一是原有的结构形态，二是多年来开展的各种人工干预改变了建筑物的原有内部空间结构。仅通过设计师的经验很难识别历史建筑中此类脆弱点。支持该说法的一个证据是，尽管近期已经对该建筑进行了修复，但从未发现这种问题。

总结及讨论

本文对培拉特与吉洛卡斯特拉历史中心传统建筑的类型、技术和建筑材料以及保护历史建筑的现代结构评估方法进行了综述。

在开展实际保护项目前，必须对文化遗产进行跨学科研究，以清晰了解该建筑的价值，了解其受保护的原因。保护工程的目的在于保护与这些建筑、材料和建筑技术等真实性特征相关的价值，因为这些价值很脆弱，可能会因为遗弃或者错误的人为干预而受到损害。

本文描述的现代结构分析方法有助于评估建筑物原有结构体系，理解建筑物应对自然灾害及安全性。数值分析结果验证了传统的木框架结构体系在各构成元素完好无损时，具有良好的抗震性能。另外，由于力的高度集中，建议对节点处和建筑上层进行调查。如果在勘查中发现相关破坏，有必要改善这些接合处的状况，重新恢复其结构上的完整性。无论何种情况都应使用与现有材料兼容的建筑材料。在第二个案例中，数值方法被证明是识别建筑结构中薄弱环节行之有效的方法，同时还得出了建筑结构体系需要改进的结论。

最后，结构分析方法的运用，对优化与最小干预原则下的人类干预措施有重要意义。运用这种方法得出的结果，有助于设计师更好地把控建筑遗产技术干预的安全性。

参考书目

Aliaj，S.，B. Muço 和 E. Sulstarova（2010）. "Sizmiciteti, sizmotektonika dhe vleresimi i rrezikut sizmik ne Shqipëri / 阿尔巴尼亚地震活动、地震构造和地震灾害评估"，阿尔巴尼亚科学院，地拉那，阿尔巴尼亚.

Angjeliu，G.，K. Angjeliu 和 L. Çapeli（2013）. 阿尔巴尼亚历史悠久的木结构砖石建筑. 地中海地区历史抗震木结构国际会议.

Angjeliu，G. 和 M. Baballeku（2013）. 历史砖石结构的抗震性评估：原意大利大使馆。第二届巴尔干国际土木工程问题会议.

Baçe，A.，A. Meksi，E. Riza，G. Karaiskaj 和 P. Thomo（1980）. Historia e Arkitekturës shqiptare / 阿尔巴尼亚建筑史. 地拉那.

国际古迹遗址理事会（1994）. 奈良真实性文件. 奈良.

Langenbach，R.（2007）. "从 'Opus Craticium' 到 "芝加哥框架"：传统建筑方法的抗震性 ". 国际建筑遗产杂志 1（1）：29-59.

Milutinovic，Z.，M. Spirollari 和 A. Galperin（2003）. Vlerësimi i rreziqeve nga fatkeqesitë në Shqipëri / 阿尔巴尼亚自然灾害风险评估.

Riza，E.（2009）. Qyteti dhe banesa qytetare shqiptare e shek. XV-XIX，Botimet "Dita 2000".

联合国教科文组织世界遗产名录（2008）. "培拉特与吉洛卡斯特拉历史中心 ." 检索自 2019 年 2 月 24 日，https：//whc.unesco.org/en/list/569.

Conservation of Historic Buildings in the World Heritage Site of Berat and Gjirokastra, in Albania

Grigor Angjeliu, Italy Politecnico di Milano[①]

Kozeta Angjeliu, Ministry of Culture of Albania

Aurora Kamberi, Ministry of Culture of Albania

Abstract

The management of the Historic Centres of Berat and Gjirokastra, part of the World Heritage List of UNESCO, presents great challenges in relation to the conservation and safeguarding of historical buildings. Within a context of sustainable development, it is important to promote a conservations practice through an integrated knowledge of traditional techniques and application of modern methods of structural analysis. Hence, to guarantee the integrity of historical buildings, any conservation intervention must be preceded by a detailed multidisciplinary study. This article will focus on:

- the analysis of the typologies of historical buildings in the Historical Centre of Berat and Gjirokastra, the traditional materials and techniques used for their construction;

- the application the finite element method in assessing the effectiveness of building's structural system to natural disasters e.g. earthquake;

- the particular importance of the conservation of traditional constructive systems and components for the structural safety of buildings object of study.

Keywords: Berat and Gjirokastra, World Heritage Site, Historical buildings, Authenticity, Structural assessment

---

① Grigor Angjeliu is a Researcher and a Lecturer at the Department of Civil and Environmental Engineering at Politecnico di Milano, where he also completed his PhD studies. He has also been a visiting scholar at the Pennsylvania State University. His field of expertise in the structural restoration of historical buildings includes: the development of complex digital models, safety assessment, and mitigation of seismic vulnerability in historical masonry buildings, where he is author of several research papers.

INTRODUCTION

Historic Centre of Gjirokastra was listed as World Heritage Site in 2005 and extended in 2008 to include the Historic Centre of Berat as series properties. Historic Centres of Berat and Gjirokastra are rare examples of an architectural character typical of the Ottoman period. These two fortified historic centres have been continuously inhabited from ancient times to the present day. Situated in Southern Albania and close to each other, they bear witness to the wealth and diversity of the urban and architectural heritage of this region. Berat and Gjirokastra are testimony to a way of life which has been influenced over a long period by the traditions of Islam during the Ottoman period, while at the same time incorporating more ancient influences. This way of life has respected Orthodox Christian traditions which have thus been able to continue their spiritual and cultural development, particularly at Berat (UNESCO World Heritage List 2008) .

Located in central Albania,Berat,bears witness to the coexistence of various religious and cultural communities down the centuries. It features a large fortification, locally known as the "Kala", most of which was built in the 13th century, although its origins dates back to the 4th century BC (Fig. 1a) . The citadel area numbers many Byzantine churches, mainly from the 13th century, as well as several mosques built under the Ottoman era which began in 1417. Berat is testimony of a town which was fortified but open and was over a long period inhabited by craftsmen and merchants. Its urban centre reflects a vernacular housing tradition of the Balkans, examples of which date mainly from the late 18th and the 19th centuries (UNESCO World Heritage List 2008) .

Gjirokastra is located in the Drinos river valley in Southern Albania. It was built by major landowners. Gjirokastra contains several remarkable examples of traditional houses which date from the 17th century, while more elaborate examples date to the early 19th century (Fig. 1b) . The town also retains a bazaar, an 18thcentury mosque and two churches of the same period (UNESCO World Heritage List 2008) .

BUILDING TYPOLOGIES IN THE HISTORICAL CENTRE OF GJIROKASTRA

The development of different typologies of historic buildings depends on factors such as social and economic development, terrain features, environmental conditions, local building materials, local building techniques and the way of life of the community. In the following a typological classification of Gjirokastra house is presented following studies of Prof. Riza.

Within a typological classification on a national scale, the dwelling house of Gjirokastra is included in the category of urban fortified house with a closed character, appropriate for defensive purpose (Riza 2009) . The general orientation and planimetric development of the buildings follow the peculiarity of the terrain. Other examples of fortified houses, known also as "*kulle*" were previously developed also in other regions of Albania (e.g. Berat, Krujë, Shkodër, etc.) , but the best examples are found in Gjirokastra (Baçe, Meksi et al. 1980) .

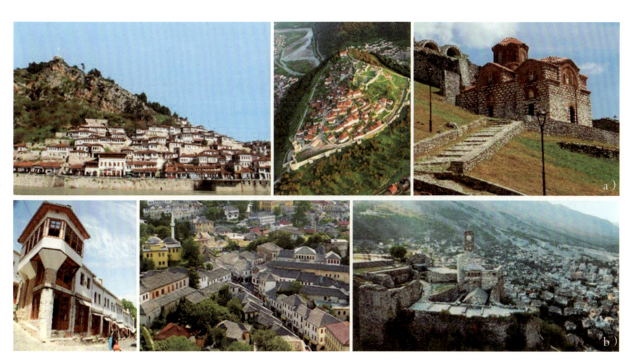

Fig. 1　View of the historic centre
a) Berat, b) Gjirokastra (Courtesy of Ministry of Culture, Albania)

The dwelling house of Gjirokastra has undergone important development in time, in its planimetric and volumetric composition. The simple examples of historic houses in Gjirokastra are of the 16th century while the most advanced examples at the beginning of the 17th century. According to the studies by Prof. Riza (2009) , using as a basic criterion the planimetric and volumetric composition of the Gjirokastra houses, they classified in three variants (Fig. 2) :

- *The perpendicular variant* is the simplest one, and at the same time is the basic compositional unit for the development of the Gjirokastra house (Fig. 2a) . The unit represents a prismatic block with a rectangular

Fig. 2　Example of traditional buildings of Gjirokastra
a) The perpendicular variant; b) One-wing variant; c) Two-wing variant (Riza 2009)

basis of two or three storeys. The first two storeys are connected by stairs in the exterior.

- *The one-wing variant* constitutes the most diffused kind of the Gjirokastra house, hence well mastered by the masons (Fig. 2b) . The most outstanding example of this typology is the Kikino House.

- *The two-wing variant*, is the most elaborate example of the Gjirokastra house (Fig. 2c) . Available data has shown that the development of this typology dates back to the beginning of the 18th century or even earlier. The Zekate (1812) or Skendulate (1823) House are the most outstanding examples of this typology.

TRADITIONAL BUILDING TECHNIQUE

Walls are the main structural element of the Albanian traditional houses. They are built as plain stone or adobe masonry or as timber frame walls with material infill. In most cases, clay or lime binder is used, while other cases are found examples of application of the dry-wall technique (with no binder) .

Based on the surveys of the historical buildings is proposed the following classification of the building construction technique:

- Masonry walls vary from 60 to 120 cm in thickness and are reinforced with timber ties (at different levels) to improve the structural behaviour under soil-settlements or earthquakes. The timber ties consist of two longitudinal elements for wall thickness varying from 60 to 70 cm, while for wider walls can be used 3 longitudinal elements or even more to cover all the complete section of the wall. In some cases, the timber reinforcements are hidden inside the wall to better protect them from environmental conditions.

- Timber framed masonry walls are typically used as partition walls in the interior, or in some cases are used in the building's facades, easing the insertion of many windows. The most commonly used woods are oak and pine. The timber frame is later filled with stone, adobe or narrow planks of wood (*çatma*) . The *çatma* technique which was adopted at the beginning of the 19th century, offers vast possibilities for architectural

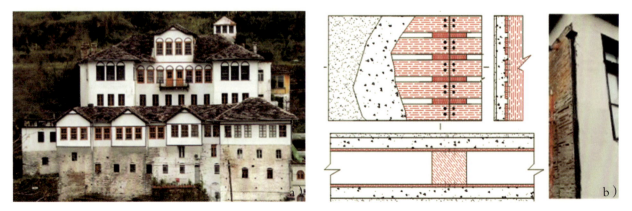

Fig. 3   Use of *catma* technique allowed to create vast architectural shapes
a) Angonate House, Gjirokastra, b) Detail of the lath and plaster technique (*çatma*)

shapes (Fig.3) . It was largely used in the historic centre of Berat after the earthquake of 1851, which caused significant damage to the upper floors. It has a good response during seismic events, because of its reduced weight compared to heavy stone masonry buildings.

- Adobe masonry walls are rarely encountered in the Historic Centre of Berat and Gjirokastra, while are more common in central and norther parts of the country. Adobe bricks are made of different dimensions and timber ties are frequently used during the construction.

Beside walls, also piers (made of stone piers or timber) , stone arches or barrel vaults are largely used in the construction of the traditional house.

Timber piers are usually found in the building's front, *hajat* and *çardak*, while stone piers are used in the construction of stairs, to support a system of stone arches and barrel vaults. Arches and barrel vaults are typically used in traditional houses of Berat and Gjirokastra. Arches are also found in doors and windows, or in the creation of arcades. Stone barrel vaults are used to cover water cisterns, basements, or in the construction of stairs.

STRUCTURAL ASSESSMENT OF THE CONSTRUCTIVE SYSTEM

During practical interventions, the replacement of some peculiar components of traditional buildings as timber ties, roofs or floors with modern materials as steel or concrete is highly questionable. Study of these phenomena is of interests as these transformations not only affect historical buildings integrity, but in some cases make them also more vulnerable to natural disasters e.g. earthquakes (Langenbach 2007) .

Following the recommendations, the "Nara Document on Authenticity" (ICOMOS 1994) , the authenticity of historical buildings should be evaluated at different levels: architecture, materials, construction technique, context, etc. The chosen intervention must respect the original function and ensure compatibility with existing materials, structural and architectural values. Hence, conservation projects must be preceded by a detailed study of traditional buildings for a comprehensive understanding of its architecture, constructing technique and materials. This shall include also application of modern structural analysis methods in order to understand the effectiveness of the existing structural systems or the need to provide necessary improvements.

In time, in the historic centres of Berat and Gjirokastra are documented a number of natural and human induced threats: earthquake, flood, landslide, soil - settlements, fire, etc. (Milutinovic, Spirollari et al. 2003). The structural response and the safety of historical buildings under these conditions can be understood and predicted through the application of scientific methods such as the structural analysis based on the finite element method. It offers solutions to understand and predict the structural response by simulating different emergency scenarios, evaluating the buildings safety, and designing better technical interventions. In the following are shown two examples of the application of the finite element method for the analysis of historical buildings in the case of a seismic event.

Understand the effectiveness of the existing structural systems

The first case study for the structural analysis is representative of the typology of timber-frame buildings with masonry infill. The building is located in the town of Elbasan, within the walls of the castle and was built in the late 19th century (Fig. 4a) . The objective of the study is to use the finite element method to study the performance of the existing timber frame structure in the case of an earthquake with peak ground acceleration is ag, 475=0.269g assuming a return period of 475 years (probability of exceedance of 10% in 50 years) (Aliaj, Muço et al. 2010) .

The structure has a regular shape with approximate dimensions 8.6 m x 12 m. The external stone masonry walls (with lime mortar) have a thickness of 51 cm and are reinforced by timber ties (Fig.6a) . The structure of the ground floor is made of stone masonry reinforced with timber ties, while the upper floor of the system is a timber frame with masonry infill (Fig.6b) . The infill bricks dimensions are $22 \times 15 \times 5$cm.

The finite element analysis results shows the effectivness of the existing structural system to withstand also moderate earthquakes (Angjeliu et al. 2013) . The response spectrum analysis concludes that the upper storey of thebuilding is the most vulnerable to seismic actions even though damage is distributed through all the building (Fig.5a) . The timber frame with masonry infill system reduces the weight of the upper storey and helps in the dissipation of the seismic energy.The diagonal bracing elements improve the masonry walls connections by sustaining the tensile forces in the corners (Fig.5a) . In case of a future restoration care should be provided in

Fig. 4 a) Traditional house in the region of Elbasan ; b) Survey of the timber frame with masonry infill in the façade

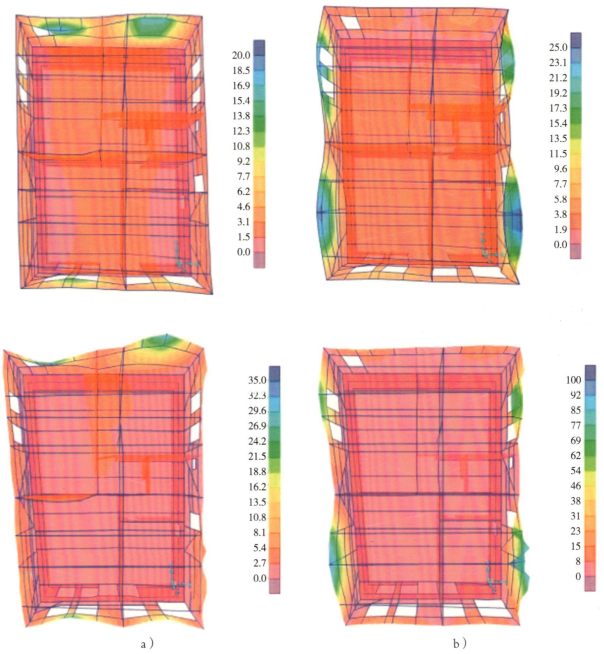

Fig. 5   Displacement from seismic combinations.
a) Left column-structure with timber ties, b) Right column-structure without timber ties.

the structure joints, because the analysis predicts high concentration of forces due to the seismic loading.

To highlight the importance of original timber elements the structure analysis was carried out even without the upper level timber ties and the bracing elements in the corners. The comparison shows that the displacement in the X and Y direction due to the seismic combinations are 2-5 times larger in the second case (Fig. 5a, b) . The horizontal timber ties reduces the deformations and improves the out-of-plane behavior of the masonry wall.

Identification of weaknesses of the existing structural systems

The objective of this second example is to use the finite element structural analysis method to understand the structural response during an earthquake and to highlight existing weak points. The former Italian embassy (ex-Legazione d'Italia) in Tirana, Albania (Fig. 6) was chosen as a case study (Angjeliu and Baballeku 2013) The building was built in the 1920s. It is located in central Tirana, Albania, and is part of the Albanian built Heritage because of its architectural values and thus set under the protection of the state.

a)   b)

Fig. 6   Identification of structural weaknesses
a) the former Italian Embassy ;   b) Out-of-plane failure of walls

The results of a nonlinear pushover analysis show a weakness due to out of plane failure of the central block of the building. The reasons are found in its structural configuration, but also in several interventions in different years that transformed the original buildings internal spaces. The prediction of such vulnerabilities in historical buildings would be difficult to be identified only though the experience of the designer. In support this statement is the evidence that although this building has been subject to recent restoration works, such problem has never been spotted.

CONCLUSION AND DISCUSSION

This article presented a summary on the traditional building typologies, techniques and construction materials in the Historic Centre of Berat and Gjirokastra as well as modern methods of structural assessment for safeguarding historical buildings.

Practical conservation projects must be preceded by a multidisciplinary study of the cultural property to clearly understand the values for which it is being protected. The conservation project should aim to preserve these values in relation with the authenticity of its architecture, materials, construction technique, etc., as they could be equally damaged from abandonment as well as from wrong interventions.

Modern methods of structural analysis, presented in this paper, help in the evaluation of the original structural system and in understanding the buildings response or safety to natural disasters. The numerical analysis results confirmed that the traditional timber frame structural system is suitable to resist the seismic action if each member is undamaged. Furthermore, a survey of the nodal zones and the upper ties is recommended due to high concentration of stresses. It is necessary to improve these connections and restore their structural integrity, in case damage is observed during the survey. In all cases the new materials shall be compatible with the existing ones. In the second example, the application of the numerical method was proved to be a suitable diagnostic tool for identifying weak points of the structural system and to concluded on the need for improvements of building structural system.

Finally, the application of structural analysis methdos bring invaluable benefits for optimization of interventions in relation with the principle of minimal interventions. Its results crucial to help the designer on the safety of technical innervations in the built heritage.

BIBLIOGRAPHICAL REFERENCES

Aliaj, S., B. Muço and E. Sulstarova (2010) . "Sizmiciteti, sizmotektonika dhe vleresimi i rrezikut sizmik ne Shqipëri / Seismicity, seismotectonics and seismic hazard assessment in Albania." Academy of Sciences of Albania, Tirana, Albania.

Angjeliu, G., K. Angjeliu and L. Çapeli (2013) . Historic timber framed masonry buildings in Albania. International Conference of Historical Earthquake-Resistant Timber Frames in the Mediterranean Area.

Angjeliu, G. and M. Baballeku (2013) . Seismic assessment of historical masonry structures: The former Italian Embassy. 2nd International Balkans Conference on Challenges of Civil Engineering.

Baçe, A., A. Meksi, E. Riza, G. Karaiskaj and P. Thomo (1980) . Historia e Arkitekturës shqiptare / History of Albanian Architecture. Tiranë.

ICOMOS (1994) . The Nara Document on Authenticity. Nara.

Langenbach, R. (2007) . "From 'Opus Craticium' to the 'Chicago Frame' : Earthquake-Resistant Traditional Construction." International Journal of Architectural Heritage 1 (1) : 29-59.

Milutinovic, Z., M. Spirollari and A. Galperin (2003) . Vlerësimi i rreziqeve nga fatkeqesitë në Shqipëri / Risk evaluation of natural disasters in Albania.

Riza, E. (2009) . Qyteti dhe banesa qytetare shqiptare e shek. XV-XIX, Botimet "Dita 2000".

UNESCO World Heritage List. (2008) . "Historic Centres of Berat and Gjirokastra." Retrieved 24 February 2019, from https://whc.unesco.org/en/list/

第二届中国—中东欧国家文化遗产论坛文集

考古研究与实践

中国文化遗产研究院文物保护与考古国际合作交流实践

中国　中国文化遗产研究院　柴晓明[①]

近年来，中国文化遗产研究院与国际古迹遗址理事会、国际文化财产保护与修复研究中心、联合国教科文组织亚太世界遗产培训与研究中心、全球文化遗产基金会、德国考古研究院、意大利国家研究委员会、法国文化遗产学院、法国远东学院、日本国立东京文化财研究所以及塞尔维亚伏伊伏丁那文化遗产研究院等多个专业机构开展了多种形式的合作与交流。同时，中国文化遗产研究院积极实践文化遗产保护与考古国际合作项目，相继在柬埔寨、肯尼亚、蒙古、乌兹别克斯坦、尼泊尔等国家开展工作。经过二十余年的工作实践，中国文化遗产研究院取得了丰硕的成果，积累了大量的工作经验，逐渐成为中国文物保护与考古国际合作交流的重要平台。

一、实践案例

吴哥古迹保护工作是一项成功范例。26 年前，中国参与了由柬埔寨政府和联合国教科文组织发起的"拯救吴哥古迹国际行动"，明确表示将为吴哥保护做出自己的努力。1996 年，国家文物局派出第一个专家组赴柬，翌年选择了周萨神庙作为中国参与吴哥保护的项目。1997 年，中国文物研究所（中国文化遗产研究院前身）正式组建"中国吴哥古迹保护工作队"。自此，拉开了中国吴哥古迹保护和考古的序幕。周萨神庙由 11 座单体建筑组成，建筑损毁严重，部分建筑仅基座尚存，其他建筑也出现不同程度的倾斜、歪闪。工作队对坍塌情况严重的 8 座建筑进行了整体维修。经过了十年努力，中国文化遗产研究院于 2008 年完成了周萨神庙保护项目。经维修后的建筑不仅全部排除了险情，而且将大部分塌落的构件复位。周萨神庙单体建筑的结构、形式得以展现，整座建筑的真实性和完整性得以提升，周萨神庙再现了昔日的风采。

[①] 柴晓明，男，生于 1961 年。中国文化遗产研究院研究馆员。现任中国文化遗产研究院院长，兼任中国考古学会理事及中国古迹遗址保护协会第四届理事会副理事长等。历任中国社会科学院考古研究所副研究员（兼学术秘书）、国家文物局文物保护司副司长、国家文物局水下文化遗产保护中心主任。主要研究方向包括文物保护与考古，文物保护法规、政策研究，文物保护管理和世界遗产管理。曾作为首席科学家主持国家社科基金重大项目《大遗址保护行动跟踪研究》（2012 年—2014 年），质检公益性行业科研专项《文化遗产保护与利用技术标准分类研究》，《北京琉璃河西周遗址的田野发掘》，《山西襄汾陶寺考古发掘研究》及国家文物局《长城资源调查项目》、《明长城资源调查报告》项目等。曾出版包括《大遗址保护行动跟踪研究》在内的多部学术著作。

2006 年，在援助柬埔寨吴哥古迹一期周萨神庙保护工程进入尾声之际，中柬两国政府正式确认茶胶寺为中国援助柬埔寨二期吴哥古迹保护项目。2010 年，为期八年的茶胶寺保护修复项目正式开工。茶胶寺保护修复项目内容包括建筑本体保护修复、排水与环境整治、须弥台石刻保护、考古研究及辅助设施建设工程。项目按期完成了计划内南内塔门、东外塔门、二层台东北角及角楼等 24 项全部修复内容，并增加了庙山五塔整体维修以及东内塔门、西内塔门、北内塔门排险加固工程。修复后的整体效果良好，达到了保护修复项目要求，改善了茶胶寺整体的安全状况，排除了文物险情，展现了原有的历史风貌。

为加强吴哥古迹保护与考古国际合作，中国文化遗产研究院还对柬埔寨吴哥古迹王宫遗址、柏威夏寺和崩密列寺开展前期研究和考古工作。中国文化遗产研究院对王宫遗址、柏威夏寺开展了初步勘察测绘工作，收集相关基础资料，梳理历史沿革，获得了建筑测绘数据，对建筑结构、基础和残损现状进行初步调查及评估，为后续保护工作提供数据支持。中国文化遗产研究院与柬埔寨吴哥古迹保护与发展管理局签署关于崩密列研究与保护的谅解备忘录。中柬双方成立了联合考古工作组，共同开展崩密列的考古与研究工作。

乌兹别克斯坦花剌子模州历史文化遗迹修复项目是中国在中亚地区实施的第一个文物保护工程援助项目。2013 年 9 月，习近平主席访问乌兹别克斯坦，期间与卡里莫夫总统签署两国关于进一步发展和深化战略伙伴关系的联合宣言和友好合作条约。为落实此次访问成果，2014 年 4 月，中乌双方决定在希瓦古城选择两处历史古迹进行保护修复。经调研与磋商，双方商定项目内容包括阿米尔·图拉经学院与哈桑·穆拉德库什别吉清真寺的建筑本体修缮及环境整治工程。项目由中国文化遗产研究院承担。目前，项目正在有序进行，已经完成了建筑主体修复及地基基础加固。

2015 年，尼泊尔发生 8.1 级地震，中国政府立即派出中国文化遗产研究院专家赴现场参与尼泊尔震后文物损毁调研评估工作。在前期工作的基础上，中国文化遗产研究院承担了尼泊尔加德满都杜巴广场九层神庙修复项目，为受到地震灾害严重影响的尼泊尔文物古迹伸出援助之手。尼泊尔加德满都杜巴广场九层神庙修复项目包括文物建筑本体保护修缮工程、文物安全防范工程、文物展示利用工程等。项目于 2017 年 8 月正式启动，计划工期为 58 个月。目前，项目正在有序实施中。2017 年 8 月，中国文化遗产研究院还开展了尼泊尔另外一处受地震影响的古迹——努瓦科特杜巴广场王宫及周边附属文物建筑的初步调查。

二、理念与方法

中国文化遗产研究院开展的文物保护与考古国际合作始终遵循最小干预原则、不改变文物原状原则、真实性原则、完整性原则，坚持尊重当地的传统做法和工艺，最大限度的保留历史信息。这些既是国际社会公认的保护理念，也是中国特色的文物修复原则。基于不同文化遗产案例的建筑特点和残损现状，采用不同的保护策略和修复方法。针对柬埔寨周萨神庙周边散落 4000 余块砂石构件的情况，保护修复以"遗址保护、抢险加固、重点修复"。面对茶胶寺建筑巨大体量和现状险情，中方基于全面勘察和重点局部检测，因地制宜地使用钢结构支护、锚杆、拉杆等保护措施，即对断裂的石构件使用锚杆进行修复，对未断裂的石构件通过拉杆或钢结构支护的方式进行保护，在措施的安全性、持续性和尊重遗产的真实性、完整性之间达到平衡，既保证了建筑结构的安全，又尊重了原有建造技术特征以及材料特性。对于在国际上长期存在修复理念、方法争议的柬埔寨崩密列遗址，中国文化遗产研究院设立研究课题，试图通过开展崩密列建筑考古和修复实验，为崩密列的后续保护和研究奠定基础。在尼泊尔九层神庙保护修复过程中，坚持"原材料、原形制、原工艺、原做法"原则，尊重当地的传统做法和工艺，最大限度的保留历史信息，以现状整修为主，对局部结构薄弱部位采取适当方法进行加固补强。

中国文化遗产研究院将国内最新的保护技术手段和在大量实践中积累的保护经验应用于文物保护与考古国际合作项目。中国文化遗产研究院结合中国文物保护的经验和成果，将国际社会公认的保护理念与具有中国特色的文物保护修复原则相结合，摸索出一套行之有效的项目管理方法和技术路线，逐渐在文物古迹保护国际舞台中形成了独特的"中国模式"。在茶胶寺保护项目实施过程中，根据施工现场的实际情况，使用传统施工工具、吊装机械，这种传统施工机械替代了一些现代大型起吊机械设施，极大提高了保护修复效率。在对王宫遗址的现场初步勘察测绘中，中国文化遗产研究院应用最新的三维激光扫描、无人机倾斜摄影技术手段快速、准确的采集基础数据，使用无损雷达探测设备以不对遗址扰动为前提开展地基与基础勘察及评估。

中国文化遗产研究院始终坚持研究与修复并重，围绕文物保护工程，开展了大量前期勘察测绘与相关研究。研究涉及建筑学、历史学、考古学、地质学、材料学、结构科学、岩土科学和保护科学等多学科，为文物价值评估和价值特征的确定、病害机理研究、保护工程的设计、保护技术和材料的选择奠定了基础。在周萨神庙通过考古探方的合理布设，揭露了建造、使用和废弃的遗存，促进我们对基础建造程序的认识，了解了寺院的宗教属性从印度教转向佛教再改为印度教的复杂过程。茶胶寺是一座特殊的建筑，它在历史上是一座未完成的寺庙。通过对碑铭的解读，我们了解了因遭到雷击而停工的历史信息。根据这一特殊性，我们将排险加固作为修复工程的定位，有效保证文物的真实性和完整性，最大限度地保留历史信息。在实施周萨神庙、茶胶寺保护项目前进行了建筑测绘、工程地质勘测、考古调查、石材修复研究等，为制定保护工程的设计方案提供了科学依据。中柬双方共同开展了崩密列的资料收集、整体格局初探，重点开展了崩密列东神道的考古调查、测绘、考古勘探和考古发掘，揭露了神道不同区域的建筑结构、形制和建造程序，发掘出土了近500件丰富的遗物，包括建筑陶器、本地陶器、中国瓷器、铁器等。相关成果以《茶胶寺庙山建筑研究》、《茶胶寺修复工程研究报告》、《柬埔寨吴哥古迹茶胶寺考古报告》等形式出版。

三、国际交流与合作

在文物保护与考古工作中，中国文化遗产研究院积极与外方技术人员进行交流，聘用当地工人实施技术工作，不仅向当地工人学习地方传统工艺和技术方法，促进了当地传统工艺的传承和发展，也向他们传授了文物保护理念和技术，进行施工管理培训，对当地工人进行了有效的能力建设和人才培养。在尼泊尔九层神庙保护项目中，中国文化遗产研究院聘用当地工人施工，通过与尼方技术人员进行沟通和交流，中方技术人员从当地工匠身上学到了尼泊尔传统木建筑建造和雕刻方面高超、精湛的技术工艺，使尼泊尔传统工艺得以进一步传承与发展。在周萨神庙保护项目中，中国文化遗产研究院还对当地技术工人进行培训，在现场将石材加工与雕刻、构件安装等技术传授给当地工人，为当地建立一支技术队伍。在茶胶寺保护项目实施中，工作队与柬埔寨金边皇家艺术大学考古系师生联合开展了考古工作，共同研究探讨茶胶寺及相关古迹的保护与研究。在这个过程中，培训了一批柬埔寨本地大学毕业后从事文物保护的专业人员。

中国文化遗产研究院还与当地专家及联合国教科文组织国际专家等开展技术研讨，分享文物保护技术理念、方法和经验。2012 年，中国文化遗产研究院与法国远东学院在北京共同举办"柬埔寨吴哥古迹保护与研究论坛"及"考古与柬埔寨吴哥古迹——法国远东学院历史照片特展"。在每年召开的联合国教科文组织吴哥古迹保护国际协调委员会大会和柏威夏寺保护国际协调委员会大会上，中国文化遗产研究院技术人员与来自法国、日本、美国、德国、意大利等国专家在柬埔寨暹粒齐聚一堂，共同研讨文物保护的理念、方法和经验。2016 年，中国文化遗产研究院承办的第二届"加德满都文化论坛"在尼泊尔加德满都举办。2018 年，中国文化遗产研究院和乌方举办了"'一带一路'文物保护技术国际研讨会——希瓦古城保护与利用国际交流"，来自中国、乌兹别克斯坦、塔吉克斯坦、哈萨克斯坦与土耳其的文化遗产专家齐聚乌兹别克斯坦首都塔什干，共同分享文化遗产保护与研究的经验。

中国文化遗产研究院的文物保护理念、技术和方法以及实践获得地方政府和国际社会的认可与肯定。柬埔寨吴哥古迹保护与发展管理局出具的《吴哥古迹茶胶寺保护修复项目对外验收证明函》指出，"柬方认可中国政府援助柬埔寨吴哥古迹保护工作队在吴哥古迹修复项目中取得的整体成就。"联合国教科文组织吴哥古迹保护国际协调委员会专家组曾高度评价中国队一直坚持的做法，认为中国队的理念是"保护"而不是"修复"，意味着最大限度的保护文物历史信息，尽可能采取可逆措施，最小扰动文物。联合国教科文组织吴哥古迹保护国际协调委员会常务科学秘书阿泽迪纳·贝肖克教授评价说："中国队在塔门入口处设置钢结构支撑措施，专家组一致认为有效保证了游客安全与建筑安全，没有伤及文物，为日后更先进的技术应用留有余地。这种使用新材料加固而不伤及文物的做法，完全符合《吴哥宪章》，不仅有效地保护了文物，也是对吴哥古迹保护理念方法的完善。"柬埔寨文化艺术大臣彭萨格娜曾对新华社记者说："非常感谢中国帮助柬埔寨保护吴哥古迹。我认为中国专家修复文物的水平非常高，得到了国际认可。柬埔寨的文物修复人员通过和中国专家的合作也增加了学习和交流的机会。"

在文物保护与考古工作开展的同时，中国文化遗产研究院还举办了专题展览，开展对外宣传和展示，介绍项目相关成果，阐释项目的意义，积极推动了考古与文物保护的国际合作与交流。2014 年，中国文化遗产研究院在柬埔寨暹粒设立中国吴哥古迹保护研究中心，该中心是开展吴哥古迹保护和研究工作的国际学术平台。2017 年，中国文化遗产研究院建造的吴哥古迹保护中国中心在柬埔寨暹粒落成，该中心介绍了中国政府援助柬埔寨吴哥古迹保护的工作历程和成果，是中国对外宣传和展示援柬文物保护与研究的窗口。

四、思考与展望

过去的二十余年，从柬埔寨周萨神庙的小试牛刀，茶胶寺的庞大壮丽，到柏威夏寺保护修复中国主席国的地位提升，从乌兹别克斯坦花剌子模州希瓦古城的古迹保护，再到尼泊尔九层神庙王宫建筑的修复，中国文化遗产研究院在文化遗产保护与考古国际合作领域经历了从小到大、由点到面、由浅入深的发展历程。第一阶段以周萨神庙为代表，是探索前行，寻找如何完成吴哥古迹保护之路的过程；第二阶段以茶胶寺为代表，开展综合保护项目，强调保护修复与研究并重；目前，即第三阶段，正向着以研究先行，加强国际交流合作，建设综合整体保护队伍，提升中国文物保护和综合研究水平的方向迈进。

从东南亚灿烂辉煌的吴哥文明走到中亚古老悠久的伊斯兰文化，再到尼泊尔加德满都谷地建筑独特的艺术风格，中国文化遗产研究院文物保护工作者面临更多的机遇和挑战。基于文物保护与考古国际合作项目，中国文化遗产研究院正在开展一系列相关的历史、建筑、考古、文化、艺术等研究，将外国文物古迹蕴藏的文化历史内涵介绍到中国，并逐步探索中外古代文明之间的交流与互鉴。

我们很荣幸能借此机会和国际同行分享和探讨文物保护领域的经验、技术和方法，碰撞出智慧的火花。中国文化遗产研究院将继续做好文物保护与考古国际合作项目，进一步加强文化遗产领域的国际合作与交流，为保护世界文化遗产贡献一份力量！

International Exchanges and Cooperation in Heritage Conservation and Archaeology: A Case Study of CACH

Chai Xiaoming[1]

China Chinese Academy of Cultural Heritage

Over the recent years, the Chinese Academy of Cultural Heritage (CACH) has worked in multilateral forms of cooperation and exchanges with different specialized institutions, including the International Council on Monuments and Sites (ICOMOS) , International Centre for the Study of the Preservation and Restoration of Cultural Property (ICCROM) , World Heritage Institute of Training and Research for the Asia and the Pacific Region under the auspices of UNESCO (WHITRAP) ,World Monuments Fund (WMF) , the German Archaeological Institute,the National Research Council of Italy (CNR), the Institut National du Patrimoine (INP), the French School of Asian Studies (EFEO) , the Tokyo National Research Institute for Cultural Properties, the Vojvodinan Academy of Culture Heritage in Serbia and so on. At the same time, CACH has also actively participated in international collaborative programs on the field of heritage conservation and archaeology. CACH has carried out conservation works and archaeological projects in Cambodia, Kenya, Mongolia, Uzbekistan and Nepal, with fruitful achievements scored and much experience gained, establishing itself as a Chinese important platform in the field.

---

① Chai Xiaoming, male, born in 1961. He is a research fellow of Chinese Academy of Cultural Heritage (CACH) and currently CACH's director. He is also a council member of the Society for Chinese Archaeology and vice chairman of ICOMOS China. His previous positions include associate research fellow of CASS Institute of Archaeology (concurrently the institute's secretary for academic affairs) , vice director of the Department of Heritage Conservation of the National Cultural Heritage Administration, and director of the National Center of Underwater Cultural Heritage. His major research areas are cultural heritage conservation and archaeology, conservation laws, regulations and policies, management of cultural heritage with particular focus on World Heritage sites. He was a chief scientist for such diverse research projects as Longitudinal Study on Conservation Actions for Large-scale Archaeological Sites 2012-2014 (a major project financed by the National Social Sciences Fund) , Research of Categories of Technical Standards for the Conservation and Utilization of Cultural Heritage (a not-for-profit research project for quality inspection and control) , Excavations of the Western Zhou Site in Liulihe, Beijing, Research of Archaeological Excavations in Taosi, Xiangfen, Shanxi Province, as well as NACH-sponsored projects including Surveys of Resources of the Great Wall and A Report on Surveys of Resources of the Great Wall. Chai has published several academic works, including Longitudinal Study of Conservation Actions for Large-scale Archaeological Sites.

I. Practices

The conservation of Angkor monuments is a successful example that demonstrates CACH's engagement in international endeavors to protect cultural heritage. 26 years ago, China officially joined the international campaign to rescue the historic site of Angkor co-launched by the government of Cambodian and UNESCO, and explicitly committed to work for the conservation of Angkor. In 1996, the China's National Cultural Heritage Administration (NCHA) dispatched the first experts group to visit Cambodia and eventually chose Chau Say Tevoda as the site where the conservation works shall be carried out in the following year. In 1997, China Institute of Cultural Property (the predecessor of CACH) established the Chinese Working Team for the Conservation of Angkor Monuments, kicking off China's international assistance endeavors for the conservation and archaeology of Angkor monuments. Chau Say Tevoda comprises of 11 individual buildings that were badly damaged. Some of the buildings have only surviving foundations, while inclination and skewing existed in the rest of the buildings to various degrees. The working team conducted overall repair and maintenance for the 8 badly damaged and collapsed buildings. With efforts for ten years, CACH completed the conservation works of Chau Say Tevoda in 2008. Not only risks have been eliminated from all the repaired buildings but also most collapsed building components have been restored to their original positions. Structures and forms of individual buildings have been restored and the authenticity and integrity of Chau Say Tevoda as a whole complex have been enhanced to exhibit its original beauty and style.

In 2006 when the first-phase conservation works came to an end, the Chinese and Cambodian governments officially designated Ta Keo Temple as the site where the second-phase conservation works shall be carried out. In 2010, the restoration works of Ta Keo Temple was officially launched, that lasted for eight years. The restoration works include restoration of architecture, enhancement of the drainage system and the environment, protection of the inscription stone on the Pyramid Platform, archaeological study, and construction of supporting facilities. All the 24 monuments have been restored as scheduled, including the south inner tower gate, the east outer tower gate, the northeast corner at the second floor of the platform, and corner towers. In addition, the overall conservation of the Five Tower of the Temple Mountain and risk elimination and reinforcement for the east inner tower gate, the west inner tower gate and the north inner tower gate have been conducted. The restoration works is a quite successful project that has delivered good overall results, come up with requirements for conservation and restoration, improved the overall safety of the temple, eliminated potential risks, and recovered original historical features.

CACH has also carried out preliminary research and archaeological work at the site of the Royal Palace of Angkor, Preah Vihear Temple and Beng Mealea Temple. CACH conducted preliminary surveying and mapping activities at the site of the Royal Place of Angkor and Preah Vihear Temple to collect basic information, clarify history and developments, obtain data of architectural surveys, and achieve initial survey findings and assessment results as regards architectural structures, foundations and damaged situation, so as to provide data support for follow-up conservation work. CACH and APSARA National Authority signed an MOU on the research and conservation of Beng Mealea Temple. The two institutions set up a joint archaeological group to carry out archaeological research of the temple.

The restoration of historic and cultural monuments in Khwarezm Region of Uzbekistan was the first heritage conservation assistance project that China launched in Central Asia. In September 2013, Chinese President Xi Jinping signed with Uzbekistani President Karimov a joint declaration and a treaty of friendship and cooperation to further develop and deepen the bilateral strategic partnership during his state visit to Uzbekistan. In order to implement the outcomes achieved through the historic visit, China and Uzbekistan decided in April 2014 to choose two historic monuments in the ancient city of Khiva for conservation and restoration. Amir Tura Madrasah and Khasahmurad Mosque were the two properties eventually chosen for heritage conservation and environmental enhancement, which were conducted by CACH. The project is proceeding as scheduled, with their main architecture restored and their foundations consolidated.

Immediately after an 8.1-magnitude devastating earthquake hit Nepal in 2015, Chinese government dispatched CACH's experts to participate in post-quake investigations and assessments of damaged cultural heritage properties in Kathmandu. Based on preliminary work results, CACH launched the project for the restoration of the nine-storeyed tower on the Kathmandn Durbar Square. The restoration works include restoring of heritage architecture, security and protection engineering, and heritage display and utilization. Officially launched in August 2017, this 58-month project is currently proceeding well as scheduled. In August 2017, CACH also kicked off another conservation project in Nepal to conduct preliminary surveys of Nuwakot Durbar and its surrounding monuments which were also badly damaged in the devastating earthquake.

II. Concepts and Methodologies

In conducting international cooperation in heritage conservation and archaeology, CACH has always abided by the principles of minimal intervention, no alteration to original state, authenticity and integrity, respected local traditional practices and processes, and retained historical information to the extent possible. These are not only internationally recognized concepts but also principles with Chinese characteristics. Different conservation strategies and restoration methods have been adopted based on architectural features and damages of different heritage cases to be protected or restored. For example, a principle of "protecting the site, rescuing and consolidating damaged components, and giving priority to the restoration of key parts" has been followed to restore Chau Say Tevoda based on the fact that there were some 4,000 sandstone components scattered around the monument. In response to the huge size of Ta Keo Temple and risks existing in the monument, the Chinese team, based on comprehensive surveys as well as examinations of key parts, adopted protective measures as appropriate, such as steel frame support and application of anchor rods and drawbars. Anchor rods were applied to broken stone components, while drawbars and steel structures were installed to protect unbroken stone components. By doing so, the team enabled a balance between ensuring the safety and continuity of protection measures and respecting the authenticity and integrity of the property, which has guaranteed the safety of architectural structures and respected original technical and material characteristics. As regards the site of Beng Mealea where there existed long disputes over its restoration concepts and methodologies internationally, CACH set up a research team to conduct groundwork for its follow-up conservation and research through experiments in architectural archaeology and restoration. By following "the principles of the original materials, the original shapes, the original process, the original practice", respect for local traditional practices and processes, and preservation of historical information to the extent possible, the restoration works of nine-storeyed tower on the Kathmandu Durbar Square focused on restoration of the property on the basis of its existing state, using appropriate methods to conserve and reinforce fragile and vulnerable parts.

CACH has applied the latest technologies and numerous experiences developed in domestic conservation practices to international cooperation projects. Based on Chinese experiences and results in heritage conservation, CACH has combined internationally recognized concepts with conservation and restoration principles with Chinese characteristics, developing a set of effective project management rules and technical guidelines that is known as the "China Pattern" among the international conservation community. Traditional tools and hoisting devices were employed in implementing the conservation works of Ta Keo Temple, based on actual conditions of the site. Modern large hoisting machines were replaced by traditional devices, which significantly enhanced work efficiency. CACH also applied the leading 3D laser scanning and UAV oblique photographing technologies to collect basic data fast and precisely and used non-destructive radar detection equipment so as not to disturb the site to conduct foundation and base surveys and assessments when carrying out preliminary surveys and investigations of the site of the Royal Palace in Angkor.

CACH has always put equal emphasis on research work and restoration practices and carried out numerous surveys and related research activities for heritage conservation works. Its research activities rang over various disciplines, such as architecture, history, archaeology, geology, materials science, structural mechanics, rock and soil science, and conservation, laying the groundwork for value assessment and identification, research of hazard causes, designing of conservation works, and selection of conservation technologies and materials. Trial trenches were reasonably arranged in Chau Say Tevoda so as to discover traces of construction, use and abandonment and enable us to gain a better understanding of foundation construction procedures and the sophisticated process of transformation from a Hindu temple to a Buddhist temple and then back to a Hindu temple. Ta Keo Temple is a unique but uncompleted architectural complex. Study of inscriptions preserved in the temple has enabled us to learn that construction was stopped due to lightning strike. The restoration works focused on eliminating risks and consolidating vulnerable parts, which ensure the authenticity and integrity of the monuments and retain their historical information to the extent possible. Architectural, geological and archaeological surveys as well as research of stone material restoration had been conducted prior to the implementation of the conservation works of the conservation project of Chau Say Tevoda and Ta Keo Temple, which provide scientific evidence to the conservation design scheme. As regards Beng Mealea, the Chinese and Cambodian teams worked together to collect archaeological evidence and documentation and conduct preliminary investigations of its overall layout, with particular focus on archaeological surveys and excavations of its causeway. As a result, architectural structures, forms and construction processes of various components of the eastern causeway have been clarified, with nearly 500 objects unearthed, including ceramic architectural decorations, local potteries, Chinese porcelain wares, and iron wares. The research outcomes have been published in such works as the Architecture Research on Ta Keo Temple-Mountain of Angkor site, the Research on Conservation and Restoration of Ta Keo Temple, and the Report on Archaeological Investig action and Excavation at Ta Keo Mountain-Temple Site of the Angkor Monument in Cambodia.

III. International Exchanges and Cooperation

In implementing international projects for heritage conservation and archaeology, CACH has actively conducted communication with foreign technicians, employed local workers, and drawn from local traditional processes and methods, which promoted the dissemination and development of traditional local craft. In addition to that, CACH also introduced conservation concepts and technologies, whilst construction management training and talent training for local workers providing effective capacity building. For example, CACH employed local workers for the implementation of the conservation works of nine-storeyed Basantapur Tower, while learning from Nepalese artisans superb and outstanding traditional skills and processes in wooden architecture and sculpture which facilitated the inheritage and development further. As regards the conservation works of Chau Say Tevoda, CACH conducted training for local technicians and workers and introduced to the technologies in stone processing and carving and component installation and assembling, thus developing a group of technicians and artisans for the local area. In implementing the conservation works of Ta Keo Temple, the Chinese team conducted archaeological work together with teachers and students from the Archaeology Department of the Royal University of Fine Arts, Phnom Penh, and trained a group of local university graduates who later engaged in heritage conservation.

CACH has also conducted technical communication with local experts and international experts from UNESCO to share with each other concepts, methods and experiences as regards conservation science and technology. In 2012, CACH and EFEO co-organized in Beijing the "Forum on Conservation and Research of Angkor Monuments" and "Archaeology and Angkor Monuments: A Special Photo Exhibition on the History of EFEO". At the ICC-Angkor International Coordinating Committee for the safeguarding and development of the historical site of Angkor Plenary Session and the ICC-Preah Vihear Plenary Session held every year, technical professionals from CACH and Cambodia together with experts from France, Japan, USA, Germany and Italy have assembled in Siem Reap, to share conservation concepts, methods and experiences. In 2016, CACH organized the Second Kathmandu Culture Forum in Nepal. In 2018, CACH co-organized with Uzbekistani partners the Belt and Road International Symposium on Cultural Heritage Conservation Technology: International Exchanges in the Conservation and Utilization of the Ancient City of Khiva. Cultural heritage experts from China, Uzbekistan, Tajikistan, Kazakhstan and Turkey gathered in Tashkent, capital of Uzbekistan, to share their experiences in the conservation and research of cultural heritage.

CACH's conservation concepts, technologies, methods and practices have won recognition of both local governments and international community. The Acceptance Certificate on the Conservation and Restoration of Ta Keo Temple in Angkor, issued by the APSARA National Authority of Cambodia, stated that "APSARA Authority, representative authority of the Royal Government of the Kingdom of Cambodia. recognized and accepted the overall achievement of the restoration work of the Chinese Government for safeguarding Angkor Team at Ta Keo Temple in Angkor." The UNESCO ICC-Angkor's experts group highly commended the practices conducted by the Chinese working team, considering that the team emphasizes conservation rather than restoration, which means the preservation of historical information to the extent possible and minimal intervention to the monument. Professor Azedine Beschaouch, the scientific secretary of ICC-Angkor, said that "The experts group unanimously considered that the supportive steel frames that the Chinese team has installed at tower gate entrances have effectively ensured the safety of both tourists and heritage buildings, causing no damage to heritage properties and sparing space for the application of more leading technologies in the future. The practice, using new materials to reinforce heritage properties while causing no damage to them, completely conforms with the Angkor Charter, which has effectively protected the heritage while contributing to the improvement of concepts and methods for the conservation of Angkor monuments." Phoeurng Sackona, Cambodian Minister of the Culture and Art Department, said in an interview with Xinhua News Agency, "I would like to thank China very much for its assistance to the conservation of Angkor monuments. Chinese experts have great capacity for cultural heritage conservation, which has been recognized worldwide. Cambodian conservation professionals have also learned a lot through their collaboration with Chinese experts."

CACH has also organized thematic exhibitions in order to publicize and promote achievements in conservation and archaeological projects, increase international exchanges and cooperation. In 2014, CACH established the Research Center of Chinese Government Team Safeguarding Angkor in Siem Reap, Cambodia, whose mission is to provide an international academic platform for the conservation and research of Angkor monuments. In 2017, Chinese Center for Safeguarding Angkor was constructed and completed by CACH in Siem Reap. The research center is a window to publicize and present Chinese government assistance project for safeguarding Angkor monuments, with particular focus on China's practices and achievements in the conservation of Angkor monuments.

IV. Reflections and Prospects

CACH's engagement in international cooperation in heritage conservation and archaeology has seen a gradual process of development over the past two decades, from the initial trial at Chau Say Tevoda, to the sophisticated project at Ta Keo Temple, to one of the presidency for ICC-Preah Vihear, to the heritage conservation of the ancient city of Khiva in Uzbekistan, to the restoration of nine-storeyed tower in Kathmandu in Durbar Square in Nepal. In the first stage as represented by the conservation of Chau Say Tevoda, CACH made tentative explorations in how to better protect Angkor monuments. In the second stage as represented by the conservation of Ta Keo Temple, CACH conducted a comprehensive conservation project to emphasize on both restoration and research. In the ongoing third stage, CACH follows the principle of "research first" and aims to develop a comprehensive professional team for integrated conservation through increased international cooperation so as to improve China's capacity for cultural heritage conservation and comprehensive research.

From the glorious Angkor civilization in Southeast Asia to the time-honored Islamic culture in Central Asia to the unique art expression exhibited by historic buildings in the Kathmandu Valley in Nepal, conservators from CACH are faced with more opportunities and challenges today. On the basis of previous international conservation and archaeological projects, CACH is carrying out a series of research in terms of relevant histories, architecture, archaeology, cultures, arts, with the aim of introducing the cultures and history of foreign heritage properties, to China and increasing communications and mutual learning between ancient civilizations of China and other nations across the world.

It is our honor to share and exchange our experiences, techniques and approaches within the field of heritage conservation with all the professionals and experts today, hoping more fruitful outcomes can be produced through this opportunity. And CACH will continue its efforts to increase international cooperation and exchanges in heritage conservation and archaeology and make its due contribution to the safeguarding and development of cultural heritage across the world.

城市与考古：世界遗产地里加历史中心的保护

拉脱维亚　国家遗产局局长　丘瑞思·达米比斯 [①]

拉脱维亚　国家遗产局里加地区司司长　亚尼斯·阿萨瑞斯 [②]

摘要：

里加历史中心于 1997 年列入联合国教科文组织《世界遗产名录》。为减少开发项目对遗产价值造成的损失，2003 年通过了《里加历史中心保护法》。该法律对里加历史中心及其缓冲区进行了界定，明确了需要加以保护的真实文化和历史价值要素，包括其考古文化层。

2004 年通过的《部长内阁规定》制定了针对里加历史中心及其缓冲区更为具体的保护条款和开发项目的实施程序。该规定指出，文化层和考古证据均为受保护的价值要素。考虑到遗产区和缓冲区规模较大（共 2102.5 公顷），其古迹遗址分布在不同历史时期，在文化和历史环境价值方面存在差异，因此这一遗产地被划分为 11 个区域，由不同的保护部门进行管理。在其中 5 个区域，当建设项目需要对文化层或考古证据进行暴露时，将对其开展考古研究（即考古发掘和考古监督）。

遗产地最古老的部分，即里加老城，面积相对较小（约 50 公顷），是被认定为国家级重要古迹的考古遗址群。对这一区域的保护（发掘）措施最为严格。对建筑结构（包括地下室）已经在 20 世纪消失的区域，仅需要进行考古监督就足够了。对需要进行考古发掘的其他区域，如存在文字资料或初步研究成果，则其可作为考古证据。

关键词： 保护，开发，文化和历史环境价值，考古研究

里加历史中心于 1997 年 12 月 6 日列入联合国教科文组织《世界遗产名录》。作为一项独特的杰作，该遗产地由中世纪及之后时期的城市结构所组成，集中了众多高品质的新艺术运动建筑和 19 世纪木构建筑。

遗产区面积 438 公顷，占城市总面积的 1.4%，包括 4500 多座建筑。缓冲区面积 1574 公顷，占城

---

①　丘瑞思·达米比斯（Juris Dambis），从 1988 年开始担任拉脱维亚国家遗产局局长。1979 年，在里加综合技术研究所建筑与建筑设计系接受高等教育。2010 年，获得建筑学博士学位。在获得建筑师资格后，开始在文化遗产领域工作，同时从事私人执业，且从中积累了丰富的建筑技术经验。1993 年参与欧洲文化遗产委员会的工作，并从 1999 年到 2001 年担任委员会主席。1992 年加入古遗址保护协会。2014—2017 年担任拉脱维亚国家文化理事会主席。

②　亚尼斯·阿萨瑞斯（Jānis Asaris），生于 1960 年，考古学家，拉脱维亚国家遗产局里加地区司司长，从 2013 年起担任拉脱维亚考古学家协会委员会主席。在文化遗产领域工作三十余载，多次在西拉脱维亚和里加地区主持古遗址考古挖掘工作。出版了 120 多部关于考古遗址和文化遗产保护问题的科学和大众出版物。

市总面积的 6.5%。

里加历史中心的价值包括：

1. 城市规划结构，建造原则体系，城市与自然环境的关系；

2. 里加老城的全景和轮廓；

3. 历史建筑：中世纪建筑、新艺术运动建筑、19 世纪木构建筑；

4. 开放公共空间：绿地、公园、广场、花园、历史水系等；

图 1　里加历史中心景观
摄影：J. Dambis

在里加历史中心申报世界遗产期间，制定了一套具体的措施规定。然而，在保护管理规划完成之前，因受到巨大的经济压力，里加市政府在 2000 年和 2001 年批准了多个与遗产保护原则相冲突的开发项目。

经济压力造成的主要问题包括：

1. 交通设施的配置导致在市区中心不计后果地建造了一批建筑；

2. 为建造停车场腾出空地而拆除了一批建筑，而不是在拆除之后新建建筑；

3. 拆除了一批历史建筑，其动机是因为新建建筑比改造历史建筑更加容易，成本更低；

4. 大型超市的建设危及了历史建筑中小店铺的生存，从而切断了保护这些历史建筑的基本收入来源；

5. 新建建筑由于其体量规模，并未与里加历史中心的特点保持一致；

6. 建造开放空间和绿地，以及将历史上并未存在建筑的区域改造成为公众认可的开放空间；

7. 针对历史建筑的事故和蓄意处置；

8. 使用不适当的现代材料和构件对历史建筑进行改造，采用现代技术进行品质低劣的更换；

9. 对历史建筑中的斜坡屋顶和阁楼进行改建，改变了原有建筑的体量；

10. 建筑外立面上过于突出的广告牌匾干扰了对历史环境的感受；

11. 为了尽快获得利润，建设活动变得过度、低廉和快速，这通常会导致所建建筑超出了所在位置的特征所能支撑的程度，或是建在了一个不合适的位置。这些建筑物和构筑物会在未来造成一系列问题，因为对一个退化的地点进行审美提升需要大量的资源，远远超过一个廉价和未经深思熟虑的建造项目（而不是一个平衡的、规划良好的、甚至是成本昂贵的项目）所能获取的利润。这意味着，我们今天的存在是基于对未来的投资；我们从环境中透支的成本将不得不在未来由我们的后代所偿还。

12. 由于缺乏意识和尊重而拆除工业历史建筑；

13. 用现代元素替换建筑的原始要素（如塑料门窗等），从而失去了建筑的真实性；

14. 在里加历史中心价值最为突出的位置建造从建筑学角度上被视为低劣的新建筑。

图 2 新艺术运动风格的建筑细部
摄影：J. Dambris

国家遗产保护检查署发起了一项大众媒体运动，要求里加市政府加快制定该遗产地的保护和发展规划，并要求议会和政府通过一项保护这一世界遗产地的特别法律。检察署制定了一份文件，对该遗产地的遗产价值、"2020 年愿景"这一发展概念及其修订版"2002—2020 年愿景"进行了概述。

尽管出台了上述一系列法律法规，里加市政府在未经检查署同意和未考虑现行规划指导文件的情况下，仍然批准在缓冲区内的 Kīpsala 地区建造一栋高层建筑。

鉴此，2003 年 6 月 26 日通过了《里加历史中心保护法》，明确指出，文化遗产对社会具有价值，对这一世界遗产地的保护和发展是一项优先任务。

里加市政府对此表示抗议并向拉脱维亚共和国宪法法院提出诉讼，要求废除一系列基本规范。作为拉脱维亚现行制度中的最高法院，宪法法院裁定该法律符合拉脱维亚的宪法并认可了文化遗产的保护要求。

2003 年 10 月，里加历史中心保护和发展理事会成立。该理事会是一个由 10 位成员组成的公共咨询机构，包括国家遗产保护检查署、市议会、联合国教科文组织拉脱维亚全国委员会和其他政府部门的负责人和专家，以及建筑师代表。理事会每月召开两次会议，审议涉及里加历史中心保护与发展的问题。

图 3　国家遗产局——理事会会议召开地点
摄影：J. Dambis

经过了几个月的讨论，里加市议会最终于 2006 年通过了《里加历史中心及其缓冲区保护发展规划》。

上述法律文件以及发展规划确保了在里加历史中心及其缓冲区内所有建设开发项目均须审议；所有新建建筑均须尊重该遗产地的视觉统一性。随后，制定了一套有效的变化管控体系并在机构之间开展了对话交流。

对里加历史中心列入《世界遗产名录》这一事件，当地社会存在着两种不同的情绪：一派人对遗产地价值得到认可而表示高兴；而另一派人则对限制开发表示担心。城市不是一个停滞不前的地方，如果人们在这里生活和工作，它就需要发展；然而，发展的质量则是一个很重要的考量方面。文化遗产是多个世纪积淀的产物，对其任何一个构成部分的降级或破坏都会使得社会变得贫瘠。在管理历史城市的过程中，仅考虑单个古迹遗址是不够的，必须将一个地区作为一个整体对待。

文化遗产是可以通过理智的方式开发的经济资产，而不是通过破坏的方式攫取经济利益。破坏文化遗产不仅是指拆除文化古迹，而且是指对在某个地方建造超出其所需体量的建筑，在有价值的地方建造廉价的建筑，或是在不需要的地方建造建筑的行为不加以阻止。这是贪婪的行为，是赚取快钱的企图。

没有变化，是不可能发展的；同时，时间也会留下它的足迹。对城市环境的变更应作为当代的行为，为未来的品质做出贡献。为了实现这一点，在各个层面上遵守道德准则是极其重要的。在别国经营的投资者必须遵守总体的道德准则，即从文化遗产保护的角度而言，不得从事其本国都不允许的行为，即使别国当地法规允许这么做。

只有原始要素才构成最高价值。如果原始要素损失，遗产的某一构成部分则会缺失并将不可能再复原。因此，研究受保护的价值要素和有问题的方面，然后找到解决方案，确保高质量的人居空间，这是非常重要的。

城市是一个集体系统，民主不是消极的代名词。社会应当始终将共同利益置于单个团体利益之上。土地规划是创建平衡的居住环境最有效的手段之一。规划是所有利益相关方之间就地区发展达成的民主共识；每个单个团体均能够参与谈判，实现价值的增值，即历史城镇中心保护与发展的清晰规则。因此，厘清社会的利益有哪些，这是重要的：

1. 我们希望保护的价值是什么？

2. 哪些是不必要的，阻碍性的，应当被祛除的利益？

3. 哪些是我们所缺乏的新的和必要的利益？

世界上的良好范例证明，品质优良的当代建筑并未使文化遗产降级，而良好的文化遗产政策也未阻碍现代建筑的发展。优秀的当代建筑和设计构成了人类未来的文化遗产——它们体现某个具体环境的主流品质水平，遵循建筑体量原则和特点，尊重传统材料和建筑营造的氛围。品质优良的当代建筑和设计为环境增添了附加值。

建筑师和城市规划师决不能为金钱所驱使，而应是一个从长远角度为营造有品质的居住环境肩负责任的艺术家。我们当然不用把所有要素都保留下来；但是对情况进行预测和把控，以避免损失最具价值的细节、特点和文化遗产所唤起的情感，这是极其重要的。只有实现新的和更好的品质，损失才能是被允许的。

开放的公共空间对城市功能运转是具有重要价值的。这一人造环境同时也构成了人的本身。一个有品质的、民主的环境会促进社会的学术、民主和人文价值的形成。

我们首先需要好的想法，然后才需要考虑用于开发的钱；否则，如果有了钱，我们就会把文化遗产毁掉。

就里加历史中心而言，立法已经制定。应当在未来继续讨论敏感的当代开发和文化遗产保护的问题：因为，一方面，我们需要保护文化遗产的真实性；另一方面，需要支持高品质的当代建筑，从而在过去和未来之间建立一条纽带。高品质的当代建筑同样将在未来成为文化和历史古迹。

考古层面的里加历史中心保护

《里加历史中心保护法》第 5 章对里加历史中心及其保护区进行了界定，规定了要求加以保护的真实文化和历史价值要素，包括其考古文化层。

2004 年 3 月通过的《部长内阁规定》制定了针对里加历史中心及其缓冲区更为具体的保护条款和开发项目的实施程序。该规定指出，考古文化层和考古要素均为受保护的价值要素。考虑到遗产区和缓冲区规模较大（共 2102 公顷），其古迹遗址为不同历史时期所建造，在文化和历史环境价值方面存在差异，因此这一遗产地被划分为 11 个区域，适用不同的建设限制规定。在其中 5 个区域，当建设过程需要对文化层或考古证据进行暴露时，将开展考古研究工程，包括考古发掘和考古监督。根据《欧盟考古遗产保护公约》第 6 章 "考古研究和保护资金筹措" 以及拉脱维亚的立法，与土地开发相关的考古工程所需费用由开发承包单位承担。

里加历史中心最古老的部分，即里加老城，面积相对较小（约 50 公顷），是被认定为国家级重要古迹的考古遗址群。与总体上的考古研究历史相比，针对拉脱维亚境内城镇的考古历史较短——这一领域的考古活动从 1939 年才开始，当时里加历史博物馆组织了考古发掘，但是城镇考古发掘从 1957 年才开始定期进行。Andris Caune 博士编写了关于里加老城考古研究历史和趋势的更多具体著作（Caune，2007 年）。同时，他还从 1970 年起对里加老城 40 多处遗址的考古发掘进行了监督。里加老城的文化层从 12 世纪开始形成，经过几个世纪的积累达到 3 至 5 米，利泽内河的淤积河床里的文化层更厚。文化层的厚度在老城不同地区各有不同，这是由于决定历史层积增长强度、结构和保护的不同条件所造成的：例如，最初地形的特征，该区域在城市生活中的功能和作用，建筑类型等等。最初的构筑物仅仅包括木构建筑，经常会被大火损毁。在之前的位置上重建建筑，在家庭垃圾和稳定粪肥的作用下，促进了文化层的密集形成。为防止破坏性火灾的发生，里加市议会于 1293 年通过了首个建筑标准，禁止在城市区域建造木构建筑。随着石构建筑比例的增加，文化层的积淀速度降低了。不过，里加老城主要部分的地面层自 18 世纪以来几乎保持未变（Celmiņš，1998 年）。

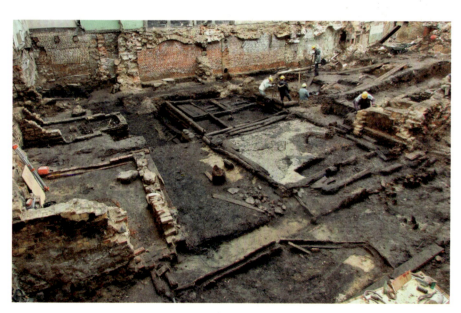

图 4　里加老城 Audēju 大街 13 号发掘区域全景（2011 年）
摄影：U. Kalējs

对文化层的破坏始于石构建筑的建造。在房屋底部建造地下室，促进了对建设用地更为合理的利用。几个世纪以来在里加一直建造的几乎均为 2 至 3 层石构建筑，地基相对较浅，未深达下层土，这意味着浅层考古表面得到保护，未被触及。这一状况随着多层建筑的引入而发生改变，基坑的建造完全将文化层移除了。

里加老城的考古要求（考古发掘）最为严格，这并不包括其建筑结构因各种破坏活动已经在 20 世纪或更晚时期消失的区域——在这些区域，仅对地下室地面之上进行考古监督即可。个别考古学家（Caune，2007 年）仍然认为，在建设工程施工过程中，对里加老城文化层中至下层土之上部分均应进行检查，以获取从科学角度而言更为重要的、年代更久远的文化层信息。我们认为，这些要求并不适用所有情况，这应视新建建筑的地基建设解决方案而定。比如，当钢筋混凝土铺装装置用作建筑地基并覆盖了文化层未经检查的表面，同时根据《瓦莱塔公约》为后代的研究者将其完好无损保护起来时，则不需要进行上述检查。问题更大的情况是，用打桩的方式建造地基。穿过未经检查的文化层钻孔打桩是完全不可接受的，至少地基桩的数量要减到最少并集中在此前已经研究过或价值更低的位置，不能够对具有历史价值的构筑物造成损害。

在里加历史中心进行的其它考古发掘，应根据关于该遗址历史重要性的文字资料或初步研究成果展开发掘。比如，在本世纪，对 15 世纪建造的老格特鲁德教堂墓地遗址进行了大量的考古研究（发现了 700 多座墓葬）。对 17 世纪的要塞建筑 Cobronskans 也进行了考古研究。

图 5　里加，老格特鲁德教堂。发掘现场工作场景（2007 年）
摄影：U. Kalējs

我们生活的这片土地以及自然、历史和文化的珍宝不仅属于我们，而且属于我们的子孙后代。我们享有理解、评价和享受这些价值的机会，同时也被赋予创造我们这个时代新的价值的责任。

参考书目：

Caune A.（2007 年），*PētījumiRīgasarheoloģijā: Rakstuizlase*，里加，第 10 — 22 页。

Celmiņš A.（1998 年），《地下之城》，里加，第 10 页。

Dambis J.（2018 年），《拉脱维亚的文化遗产保护》，里加。

Pickard R.（2001 年），《遗产保护政策和法规》，伦敦。

Preservation of Riga Historical Centre as the UNESCO World Cultural and Natural Heritage Site-Urban and Archaeological Aspects

Juris Dambis[①] and Jānis Asaris[②]

National Heritage Board of Latvia

Abstract:

In 1997, Riga historical centre (RHC) was included in the UNESCO World Heritage List. To reduce loss of heritage values due to development projects Law on Preservation and Protection of the Historic Centre of Riga was approved in 2003. Law defines RHC and its buffer zones (RHC BZ) - authentic cultural and historical values that require preservation and protection, including the archaeological cultural layer.

More detailed preservation provisions of the RHC and RHC BZ and development project implementation procedure is determined by the Regulations of the Cabinet of Ministers adopted in 2004. Regulations state that not only cultural layer, but also archaeological evidence are value that shall be preserved. Considering the vast territory of RHC and RHC BZ (2012.5 ha) and its development in different periods, as well as differences of the cultural and historic environment values, this territory is divided into 11 zones with different preservation regimes. In five zones if the construction requires exposure of cultural layer or archaeological evidence, archaeological research shall be performed (archaeological excavations and archaeological supervision) .

Oldest part of RHC-Old Riga - is comparatively small (~ 50 ha) and as archaeological complex protected as monument of national importance. In this area requirements are the strictest (excavations) . In places where

---

a   Juris Dambis. In 1979 obtained higher education at the Faculty of Construction and Architecture of Riga Polytechnical Institute. After acquiring the qualification of an architect, started working in the field of cultural heritage. At the same time, worked in private practice, acquired skills in construction craft. In 2010 obtained Dr. Sc. degree in Architecture. Since 1988 Head of the National Heritage Board of Latvia. From 1993 involved in the work of the Cultural Heritage Committee of the Council of Europe. Committee Chairman from 1999 to 2001. Since 1992 member of ICOMOS. From 2014 to 2017 Chairman of National Culture Council of Latvia.

b   Jānis Asaris (1960) , Archaeologist, Head of Riga Regional Office of National Heritage Board, has worked in the cultural heritage industry for more than 30 years, has led several archaeological excavations at ancient sites in Western Latvia and Riga, author of over 120 scientific and general publications on archaeological monuments and problems of preserving cultural heritage, chairman of the Board of Latvian Society of Archaeologists (since 2013) .

the buildings were lost during 20th century until the basement floor level it is enough with archaeological supervision. In other zones archaeological excavations are required, if there are written sources or preliminary research, that indicates archaeological evidence.

Keywords: conservation, development, cultural and historic environment values, archaeological research

The Historic Centre of Riga was inscribed in the UNESCO World Heritage list on 6 of December 1997 as a unique masterpiece, formed by medieval and later urban structure, density and quality of Art Nouveau and 19th century wooden architecture.

The site territory covers 438 hectares and it is 1.4% of the city area containing more than 4500 buildings. The buffer zone territory forms 6.5% of total city area and its 1574 hectares.

The values of the Historic Centre of Riga are:

1. town planning structure, system of building principles, city's relation with natural environment;

2. panorama and silhouette of the Old Riga;

3. historical buildings: medieval architecture, art-nouveau architecture, 19th century wooden architecture;

4. open public space - green area, parks, squares, gardens, historical watercourses.

Fig. 1   View of the Historic Centre of Riga. Photo: J. Dambis

During the inscription process for the Historic Centre of Riga a programme of specific measures was developed. However in 2000 and 2001, before the planning was completed and under significant economic pressure, the municipality accepted several projects that conflicted with the principles of heritage protection.

The main problems caused mainly by economic pressure are:

1. collocation of the transport attracted buildings in the city centre disregarding the eventual consequences;

2. demolishing of buildings with the purpose to obtain empty spaces for construction of parking places instead of new buildings;

3. demolishing historical buildings, motivating that it is easier and cheaper to build up a new one than to renovate the historical buildings;

4. construction of big supermarkets that endangers the existence of small shops in the historical buildings thus ruining essential income resource for preservation of these buildings;

5. new built constructions that due to their spectrum do not correspond to the character of the Historic Center of Riga;

6. attempts to build up public open space, green zones as well as places where historically there has been constructions, but which have transformed into public acknowledged qualitative open space;

7. accidents or deliberate disposal from historic buildings;

8. renovation of historic buildings by using inappropriate contemporary materials and wares, low-grade complements of buildings with help of contemporary technologies;

9. alteration of mansards and attics in the historical buildings changing their volume;

10. too active promotional signs on the facades that disturbs the perception of the historical environment;

11. in order to gain immediate profits, construction activities become excessive, cheap and fast, usually resulting in buildings bigger than the specific site characteristics would normally support or structures located in unsuitable places. Such buildings and structures represent a number of future problems, as aesthetic improvements to a degraded site require significant resources, which are much bigger than the margin gained through cheap and poorly considered construction effort instead of balanced, well-planned and even expensive

Fig. 2   Detail of the building of the Art Noveau style. Photo: J. Dambis

activities. It means that our existence today is based on investments to be made tomorrow - we take out a loan from our environment that will have to be repaid by the coming generations.

12. demolishing of historical industrial buildings due to lack of awareness and respect;

13. changing the original elements of the buildings to the modern ones (plastic windows, doors etc.) and losing the authenticity;

14. construction of architectonically inferior and cheap new buildings in the most outstanding places of the Historic Centre of Riga.

The State Inspection for Heritage Protection launched a mass media campaign, asked the municipality to hasten the production of the preservation and development plan for the site and then asked the parliament and government to adopt a special law for the protection of the World Heritage site. The Inspection produced a document outlining the heritage values of the site and the development concept "Vision 2020" and its revised version "Vision 2002-2020".

In spite of this, the municipality of Riga gave permission for construction of a tall building in Ķīpsala, in the buffer zone of site, without agreement from the Inspection and without consideration of existing planning guidance.

As a result a law "On Preservation and Protection of the Historic Centre of Riga" was adopted in June 26, 2003 which was a clear signal that cultural heritage has value for society and that the development and preservation of the World Heritage Site is a priority.

The Riga municipality protested and brought an action to the Constitutional Court of the Republic of Latvia to annul a number of essential norms. The Constitutional Court, the highest court institutional in the Republic of Latvia, ruled that the law is in accord with the Constitution of the Republic of Latvia and approved the demand for cultural heritage preservation.

In October 2003 the Council for the Preservation and Development of the Historic Centre of Riga was created as a public, consultative institution consisting of ten members, including the Head and experts from the Inspection, the City Council, and National Commission for UNESCO, other authorities and architects' representatives. The Council meets twice a month and reviews topical issues concerning the preservation and development of the Historic Centre of Riga.

After several years of discussions, the Riga City Council finally adopted the Preservation and Development Plan of the Historic Centre of Riga and its Buffer zone in 2006.

The creation of these legal instruments and the development plan ensure that all projects in the Historic Centre of Riga and its buffer zone can be reviewed and that all new buildings respect the visual unity of the site. Consequently an effective control system of changes and a dialog between institutions have been achieved.

When the historical centre of town is inscribed in the list of World Heritage Sites, there are mixed feelings

Fig. 3   National Heritage Board–Place of the Council meetings. Photo: J. Dambis

in the society - one group of people is usually pleased with the acknowledgment of its value, while the other is concerned about restrictions of development. No town is a stagnating place, if people want to live and work there, and it needs development, however, the quality of development is an important aspect. Cultural heritage is accumulated over many centuries and degrading or destroying any part of it makes the society poorer. In the management of the historic town it is not enough to view a separate monument; a place must be regarded as a whole.

Cultural heritage is an economic asset to be exploited sensibly rather than destroyed to gain economic benefits. Destroying cultural heritage does not mean only tearing down cultural monument, but also not to prevent from building something bigger than the particular site demands, from building cheap constructions in worthy place or from building in a place where it is not necessary. It is greediness - willingness to gain quick profits.

Development is impossible without modifications, and time also leaves its footprints. Modifications to the urban environment should serve as the contemporary contribution to the future quality. In order to achieve that, it is important to obey ethical principles in different levels. Investors dealing in other countries have to obey overall ethical principle - not to perform such activities in other countries that, from the point of view of cultural heritage preservation, are not allowed in their own countries, even if the local regulations allow it.

Only the original elements comprise the highest value. By losing the original elements we lose a part of heritage that is impossible to recover. Therefore it is very important to study the values to be preserved, problematic issues and then find a solution for ensuring high quality human living space.

A town is a collective system - democracy is not permissiveness. The society should always place its common interests higher than those of individual groups. Territorial planning is one of the most efficient instruments in developing a balanced living environment. Planning is a democratic agreement on territorial development concluded by and between all groups of stakeholders, where each individual group is open to negotiations and yielding that result in increased value - clear rules of preservation and development of historical town centers. Therefore it is important to clarify the interests of the society:

1. What is the value we want to preserve;

2. What is unnecessary, impeding and should be removed;

3. What we lack as new and necessary.

Good examples in the world prove that high quality contemporary architecture does not degrade cultural heritage, and good cultural heritage policy does not hinder the development of modern architecture. Good contemporary architecture and design constitute future cultural heritage - it corresponds to the dominating quality level in the particular environment, observes building scale, characteristics, respect traditional materials and atmosphere created by architecture. High-quality contemporary architecture and design is added value to the environment.

An architect or urban-planer must not be a money-minded person, but rather an artistic individual responsible for creating a quality living environment in a long-term perspective. Not all elements may be preserved, however, it is highly important to forecast and control the situation, avoid losing the most valuable details, the special character and feelings evoked by cultural heritage. A loss is permitted only through gaining new and better quality.

Open public space is of important value in the functioning of a city. This man-made environment also forms the person himself/herself. A quality and democratic environment foster the intellectual, democratic and human values in the society.

First we need good ideas and only then the money for development, otherwise with money we spoil cultural heritage.

In case of the Historic Centre of Riga effective legislation has been created. Discussion about sensitive contemporary development and the preservation of cultural heritage should continue in the future as on the one hand we need to preserve the authenticity of the cultural heritage; and on the other, there is the need to support good contemporary architecture to build a bridge from the past to the future. Good contemporary architecture will become a cultural and historic monument of the future.

PRESERVATION OF RIGA HISTORICAL CENTRE - ARCHAEOLOGICAL ASPECTS

Section 5 of the law "On Preservation and Protection of the Historic Centre of Riga" defines Riga historical centre and its protection zones as authentic cultural and historical values that require preservation and protection, including also the archaeological cultural layer.

More detailed elaboration of the Riga historical centre and its protection zones preservation provisions, as well as development project implementation procedure is determined by the Regulations of the Cabinet of Ministers adopted on March 2004. Regulations state that not only archaeological cultural layer but also archaeological elements are value that shall be preserved. In considering the vast territory of Riga historical centre and its protection zone (in total 2012 ha) and its construction development chronologically in different periods, as well as differences of the culturally historical environment value, this territory is conditionally divided into 11 zones with different construction restrictions. Five of the zones establish that in case of construction requires exposure of archaeological cultural layer or archaeological evidence, then archaeological research works shall be performed - both archaeological excavations and archaeological supervision. According to the Section 6 of the European Convention on the Protection of the Archaeological Heritage "Financing of archaeological research and conservation" and Latvian legislation, costs of archaeological works related to territory development are covered from the funds of the contracting entity.

Oldest part of Riga historical centre - Old Riga - is comparatively small (~ 50 ha) and as "archaeological complex" protected as the national importance archaeological monument. In comparison to the history of archaeological research in general, the history of archaeology of cities and towns in Latvia is of quite recent origin - it begun in 1939 with the archaeological excavations organised by the Museum of History of Riga but only since 1957 these excavations were organised on regularly basis. Dr. Andris Caune has provided more detailed writings about the history and trends of the archaeological research of Old Riga (Caune 2007) , also since 1970 he has supervised archaeological excavations in more than 40 objects in Old Riga. Cultural layer

Fig. 4   Riga. Old Town. Audēju street 13. Overview of the excavation area (2011) . Photo: U. Kalējs

started to form in the territory of Old Riga in 12th century and over time increased up to 3-5 m, but it was even thicker in the riverbed of the Ridzene River that was filled up. Stratigraphy of cultural layer varies in different areas of the old town due to different conditions determining the growth intensity of the historical layering of the land, as well as structure and preservation, for example, peculiarities of the original land relief, functional role of the territory in the city life, type of construction. Initially construction consisted of only wooden buildings that were frequently destroyed by fire. Buildings were rebuilt in the previous places promoting intensive formation of cultural layer with the help of household waste and stable manure.

To prevent destructive fires, Riga Town Council in 1293 adopted first construction standards prohibiting construction of wooden buildings within the town territory. As the proportion of stone buildings increased, the growth of cultural layer declined but since 18th century ground level has almost remained intact in the majority part of Old Riga (Celmiņš 1998) .

First destructions of cultural layer started with the beginning of the construction of stone buildings. Basements were made under the houses to facilitate more rational use of the construction area. Still for several centuries mostly two or three storied buildings were constructed in Riga with comparatively low foundations that did not reach the subsoil, which meant that the lower archaeological horizons were preserved untouched. This situation changed with the introduction of multi-storey buildings, when foundation trenches removed the cultural layer entirely.

Archaeological requirements (excavations) are the strictest in Old Riga, excluding places where the construction was lost on 20th century and later due to various destructions, archaeological supervision is acceptable until the basement floor level. Separate archaeologists (Caune 2007) still consider that during any construction works the cultural layer of Old Riga should be examined until the subsoil to gain information about chronologically older layers with more significance from the scientific point of view. We consider that these requirements are not justified in all cases - it depends on the constructive solutions of foundations of newly constructed buildings as, for example, in cases when the reinforced concrete paving units are used as foundations of the buildings and they form a cover that seals the unexamined horizons of cultural layer, and in light of the Valletta Convention preserves them intact for the next generations of researchers. More problematic are situations when piles are used as foundation solution for newly constructed buildings and drilling of these piles through unexamined cultural layer is not acceptable at all or at least number of piles should be minimised, concentrating them in previously researched or less valuable places without causing harm to historically valuable constructions.

Other excavations within the RHC territory are required in cases that are based on the statements of written sources or preliminary research about the historical significance of the site. Thus in 21st century, for example, extensive research of the Old St. Gertrude's Church cemetery created in the 15th century in Riga was performed

Fig.5   Riga. The cemetery of the Old St. Gertrude Church. Work scene in the excavation area (2007). Photo: M. Lūsēns

(revealing more than 700 burials) , as well as fortification construction that dates back to 17ᵗʰ century-Cobronskans.

The land where we live, treasures of the nature, history and the culture do not belong to us but to our children. We are given the chance to understand, evaluate and enjoy the values, and to create new values of our own time.

BIBLIOGRAPHY

Caune A. (2007) , *PētījumiRīgasarheoloģijā: Rakstuizlase*, Riga, pp. 10-22.

Celmiņš A. (1998) , *Zemēapslēptāpilsēta. A City under the Ground,* Riga, p. 10.

Dambis J. (2018) , *Protection of cultural heritage Latvia,* Riga

Pickard R. (2001) , *Policy and Law in Heritage Conservation,* London

河南古代大遗址保护利用基础与模式的探讨

中国　河南省文物局　田　凯[①]

河南地处中原腹地，是中华民族和华夏文明的重要发祥地，是全国重要的文物资源大省。全省现有不可移动文物 65519 处，其中世界文化遗产 5 处；全国重点文物保护单位 420 处，省级文物保护单位 1231 处；国家级历史文化名城、名镇、名村 20 个。中国八大古都河南占 4 座（郑州、开封、洛阳、安阳）。

作为全国重要的文物资源大省，河南境内的古代聚落、都城遗址、帝王陵寝等大遗址分布密度令世人瞩目。十三五时期国家确定的 152 处大遗址河南涉及 22 处，数量居全国首位。这些大遗址主要有以下特征：

一是相对集中整体连片。洛阳、郑州两大片区，长城、大运河、丝绸之路 3 条线性大遗址包含了河南大遗址的主体部分。

二是时代连续。囊括了我国重要历史时期最主要的考古学文化遗存，是中华五千年灿烂文明史的主要组成部分，对于传承创新中华优秀传统文化具有十分重要的意义。

三是内涵丰富形态多样。有新石器时代聚落遗址、古城址；有从夏代至北宋的都城遗址；有邙山陵墓群、巩义宋陵等墓葬群；还有宝丰清凉寺等瓷窑遗址。

四是这些遗址特别是都城遗址在发展上连续不断形成今天的中原主要城市框架，所以郑州商城、郑韩故城、隋唐洛阳城、北宋开封城等古代城市与现代城市形成叠压关系。

五是这些遗址更多的是深埋于地下的土遗址，地上遗存较少。

根据这五大特征，河南省大遗址保护围绕强化基础工作，彰显遗址价值，探讨保护模式，着力发挥作用等方面展开工作。

一、强化基础工作彰显遗址价值

（一）加强考古发掘研究，深挖大遗址文化内涵，讲好大遗址故事

河南省考古发掘研究力量雄厚，几乎每一处重要的大遗址，都有专门的考古发掘研究机构常年持

[①] 田凯，1985 年北京大学考古系毕业，现任河南省文物局局长、国际博协安全专业委员会执行委员、国务院特殊津贴专家、文化部优秀专家、文博二级研究员，郑州大学、河南大学、中央民族大学、中国科技大学研究生导师。曾任河南博物院院长、中国博物馆协会副理事长。主要从事文物、博物馆管理与研究，发表近百篇论文，出版多部学术论著。

续开展考古发掘研究工作。二里头遗址、偃师商城、殷墟、汉魏洛阳故城、隋唐洛阳城遗址等 5 处大遗址，社科院考古所的 5 支队伍常年在这里开展工作，其相关考古发掘研究成果，对于这几处大遗址的保护展示、规划编制、遗址公园建设等工作，起到了至关重要的支撑作用。另外，河南省文物考古研究院、郑州市、洛阳市文物考古研究院也分别有各自负责发掘研究的大遗址。

自 2005 年以来，二里头遗址、三杨庄遗址、北阳平遗址群·西坡遗址、邙山陵墓群、郑韩故城、安阳高陵、隋唐洛阳城、汉魏洛阳故城等大遗址范围内的考古发掘研究频频获得重大新发现，多个考古发掘项目入选"全国十大考古新发现"。《二里头》、《偃师商城》、《隋唐洛阳城》、《邙山陵墓群考古调查报告》、《安阳高陵考古发掘报告》、《贾湖遗址考古发掘报告》等一批考古发掘报告相继出版，考古发掘研究整体水平获得长足进步。近期，经过我们的努力，河南、陕西、山西、河北四省文物考古研究机构联合启动了"中原地区文明化进程研究项目"，主要目的就是要针对那些在华夏文明起源过程中起关键作用的重点、核心大遗址做持续性的、科学的考古发掘研究工作，深挖大遗址文化内涵，讲好大遗址故事。

（二）逐步完善大遗址保护政策法规体系，高标准推动大遗址保护规划编制工作

针对各主要大遗址，河南各地相继完成了《安阳殷墟保护管理条例》（2001 年）、《洛阳市汉魏故城保护条例》（2006 年）、《洛阳市隋唐洛阳城遗址保护条例》（2008 年）、《洛阳市偃师二里头遗址和尸乡沟商城遗址保护条例》（2009 年）、《洛阳市邙山陵墓群保护条例》（2011 年），《郑韩故城遗址保护管理条例》（2014 年）等 7 处大遗址的专项立法工作。到目前为止，河南省有关大遗址保护的专项法规、规章、规范性文件等已近 20 部，涉及全省 40 余处大遗址。以上地方性文物保护专项法规的出台，为相关大遗址的保护提供了长期的、制度性的法律保障，对于加强全省大遗址保护工作具有特殊重要的历史意义。

另一方面，我省持续高标准推动大遗址保护规划编制、审批和公布工作。自 2005 年国家启动大遗址保护工作以来，河南省列入国家大遗址保护规划的 18 处大遗址中，已有 17 处完成或部分完成保护规划的编制，其中 15 部已经获国家文物局批准，14 部已经由省人民政府公布实施。这些保护规划的编制、批准和公布，整体上保证了河南大遗址保护工作的规范化和科学化。

（三）积极争取经费支持，实施了一批具有带头和示范作用的大遗址保护展示工程

保护展示工程是大遗址保护的重要抓手，也是考古遗址公园建设中展示遗址价值的核心内容。据统计，自 2005 年以来，河南省已完成建设的大遗址保护展示工程超过 30 项，已使用国家大遗址保护专项经费约 15 亿元人民币，地方财政用于环境整治、居民拆迁、基础设施建设方面的配套投入将近 200 亿元。

这其中取得较好效果的工程包括：隋唐洛阳城定鼎门遗址保护展示工程、明堂、天堂遗址保护展示工程、九州池遗址保护展示工程、含嘉仓遗址保护展示工程、回洛仓遗址保护展示工程；汉魏洛阳

城间阖门遗址保护展示工程、宫城二号门、三号门址保护展示工程、永宁寺塔基保护展示工程、西阳门内大街保护展示工程、铜驼大街保护展示工程；郑州商城内城城垣遗址保护展示工程，郑韩故城郑国贵族墓地保护展示工程、郑韩故城东南城墙遗址保护展示工程，内黄二杨庄二号庭院遗址保护展示工程，贾湖遗址前七次考古发现重要遗迹保护展示工程，宝丰清凉寺汝官窑遗址核心烧造区保护展示工程，城阳城七号墓保护展示工程等等。

一大批重要大遗址保护展示工程的实施，不仅使这些大遗址中的重要节点得到了保护，使大遗址本身的价值得到了阐释，而且还推动了与大遗址保护展示工程相关的考古发掘研究、环境整治、配套基础设施建设等工作，使大遗址保护总体工作取得全面进步。

（四）满足公众文化需求，加快遗址博物馆建设和考古遗址公园建设

遗址博物馆是国家考古遗址公园建设中的点睛之笔，同时也是大遗址保护服务社会公众的重要文化设施。国家文物局《"十三五"大遗址保护专项规划》明确要求，"十三五"期间，全国要建成20—30个遗址博物馆。截止目前，河南省已经建成并对公众开放的遗址博物馆有：殷墟遗址博物馆、仰韶村遗址博物馆、郑韩故城郑国贵族大墓车马坑遗址博物馆、大河村遗址博物馆、城阳城遗址博物馆、定鼎门遗址博物馆、宝丰清凉寺汝官窑遗址博物馆等7处。另有二里头遗址博物馆、郑州商代都城遗址博物馆、贾湖遗址博物馆、庙底沟遗址博物馆、安阳高陵遗址博物馆、北宋东京城新郑门遗址博物馆等6处正在建设或筹建过程中。

另一方面，作为大遗址研究保护的成果，考古遗址公园依托大遗址保护展示工程，通过配套相关的基础服务设施，对周边环境进行绿化美化、并面向社会大众开放，成为一种集教育、科研、游览、休闲等多项功能于一体的大遗址保护成果形式。截止目前，河南省已经建成或部分建成4处国家考古遗址公园，另有9处考古遗址公园入围国家考古遗址公园立项名单。通过建设考古遗址公园，不仅保护了大遗址，维护了文化遗产的尊严，而且改善了人居环境、带动了相关产业发展，在城镇化建设中还发挥了提升城市文化品位，凸显城市特色等作用。因此，最近几年，各大遗址所在地人民政府纷纷仿效这一大遗址保护利用新模式，依托那些位于城市建成区或城市近郊的大遗址，建设各类考古遗址公园，极大促进了文化遗产保护与经济社会的和谐发展。

二、探讨保护模式，着力发挥作用

（一）郑州片区的"生态保遗"模式

2017年初，郑州开始全面实施"生态保遗"工程。主要内容包括：在未来3至5年内，针对分布在郑州市中心城区、城市毗邻区、城郊地区的75处遗址类文物保护单位（含全国重点文物保护单位、省级文物保护单位和市级文物保护单位），采用生态绿化、美化的方式，将其建设成为供市民开展休闲

活动的生态文化主题公园。这一工程初步计划建设遗址生态文化公园 75 处，完成生态绿化面积 5 万亩，财政投资总额近百亿。为确保生态保遗工作中的文物安全和公益属性，遗址生态文化公园建设坚持以政府为主导，鼓励引导社会力量参与，确保便民利民、服务社会的公益属性。遗址生态文化公园设计方案编制必须以文物勘探报告和考古工作资料为依据。

和传统的大遗址保护工程主要围绕考古遗址中的重要节点，开展考古发掘研究、揭示其文化内涵、进而开展保护展示工程不同，"生态保遗"的工作重点，并不在考古遗址的发掘、研究和展示方面，而是把重心放在了"保护"上。以目前正在建设的苑陵故城遗址公园为例，其建设过程，首先是在整个遗址上进行覆土，将文化层彻底封存在地下，然后在覆土之上，设计建设游园道路、服务设施、进行绿化美化，最终建成生态文化公园。整个公园建设过程不会对地下古遗址造成任何破坏。

郑州市的"生态保遗"工程，是在国家大力推进生态文明建设的大背景下，结合城市生态绿地建设需要，对古遗址类文物保护单位进行保护利用的一次大胆尝试。这种保护模式的最大优点，是保证了遗址文化内涵的完整性，同时盘活了遗址上土地资源的有效利用。虽然在短期内不能有效揭露展示遗址的文化内涵，但从长远看，是有利于遗址保护的，我们可以在未来时机成熟的时候，再来做考古工作，揭露研究展示遗址的文化内涵。我们认为，对于那些遗址类文物资源分布比较密集的城市，如果目前尚没有财力对所有的遗址都进行展示性保护，都可以借鉴郑州市"生态保遗"的模式，开展大遗址保护工作。

（二）远离老城建新城的"洛阳模式"

为了完整保护隋唐洛阳城洛南里坊区遗址，早在 20 世纪 90 年代第三期城市规划时，洛阳市就提出了跨越洛河和隋唐洛阳城里坊区遗址向南建设新区的城市发展思路，将 22 平方公里的隋唐城里坊区遗址划为非建设用地。这一"远离老城建新城"的大遗址保护模式，被称为"洛阳模式"。在第四期城市总体规划修编中，为避开城市周边的大遗址和重要历史遗迹，洛阳市又提出了跨越伊河、在城市东南方向寻求城市发展空间的思路，再一次用实际行动践行了"洛阳模式"。我们认为，"洛阳模式"是解决大遗址保护与城市发展关系的最终出路，对于中国大遗址的保护工作具有广泛而深刻的示范与启示意义。

（三）安阳优势互补、利益共享的"殷墟模式"

中国社会科学院考古研究所安阳工作站作为殷墟的主要发掘单位，收藏有大量出土自殷墟的珍贵文物，但是没有必要的文物展示；安阳市政府在殷墟大遗址保护和申遗的过程中，想要建设殷墟博物馆，但是缺少文物藏品的支持；而人民群众在游览殷墟大遗址时，看不到殷墟出土文物的展示，体会不到殷墟价值的珍贵，对殷墟保护缺乏基本认知和自觉保护意识。为了改变这一现状，经多方协调，安阳市人民政府和中国社会科学院考古研究所合作，共同建设殷墟遗址博物馆。2005 年底，殷墟博物馆建成并对外开放，它由安阳市财政投资建造，武警部队负责安全保卫，中国社会科学院考古研究所安阳工作站和当地文物部门共同管理，共同受益，从而创造了一个国家科研机构和地方部门优势互补、

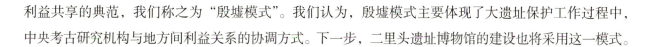

利益共享的典范，我们称之为"殷墟模式"。我们认为，殷墟模式主要体现了大遗址保护工作过程中，中央考古研究机构与地方间利益关系的协调方式。下一步，二里头遗址博物馆的建设也将采用这一模式。

（四）信阳城阳城址管委会模式

为加强对城阳城址大遗址保护，2004 年 12 月，信阳市人民政府、信阳市平桥区人民政府将城阳城址涉及区域的四个行政村，从原先的长台关乡分离出来，组建成立城阳城址保护区管委会，管委会为财政全供科级事业单位，其职能主要为文物保护和利用，同时兼负乡镇行政管理职能，下设财政所、民政所、社保所、武装部、综治办、计生服务中心、文化事业服务中心、农业发展服务中心等行政职能部门。保护区党委对所辖各部门及四个行政村村支两委成员均有任免权。保护区总面积 25 平方公里，其中文物保护面积 12 平方公里，总人口 11000 人。

城阳城址管委会除了依靠国家大遗址保护专项补助经费，开展城阳城址保护展示利用工程外，还带动了上级政府各部门对城阳城址的整合集中式投放，并有效撬动社会资金力量参与城阳城址的文物保护与经济社会发展。比如吸纳财政、交通、扶贫部门资金，修建了约 45 公里的遗址内、外和村组间道路；整合电力项目，将涉及遗址区的线路迁移到城址之外，将有碍遗址风貌的高压线进行迁埋；整合美丽乡村项目，对遗址区内部分村庄进行环境美化和房屋改造等等。社会资金吸纳方面，通过招商引资吸引社会资本在遗址周边区域建设城阳新城文化创新区，引导遗址区内群众逐步迁出；通过招商引资开展农业观光旅游项目，同时对旧的村舍进行改造，发展民宿旅游，既丰富了城阳城考古遗址公园的内涵，又缓解了财政投入的压力，解决了绿化和服务设施的投资问题。考古遗址公园的建设，还带动了周边土地的增值，城阳新城文化创新区的价值逐步提升，间接增加了当地群众的经济收入。

信阳城阳城址的管委会模式，既有效保护了大遗址，又统筹考虑了区域内城乡建设发展，因此，是一种非常值得借鉴的大遗址保护模式。我们认为，河南境内的汉魏洛阳故城、内黄三杨庄遗址、新密古城寨城址、北阳平遗址群、仰韶村遗址等这些分布在广大田野中或城乡结合部的大遗址，都适合采用这样的保护管理模式。

三、几点体会

通过近年来的工作，我们感觉到，在当前形势下，要做好大遗址保护工作，必须做好以下几个方面的工作：

1.地方政府的重视是保护好大遗址的内动力。必须充分调动地方政府保护大遗址的积极性。要使地方政府看到大遗址保护对于改善城市环境、提升城市品位、促进地方文化旅游业发展等方面的积极意义，对大遗址保护工作有兴趣、有积极性，并进而将大遗址保护工作纳入政府重点工作计划，力促大遗址保护与地方经济社会在和谐发展中获得共赢。

2.政策引导是保护好大遗址的外引力。国家文物局等有关部委是我国大遗址保护工程的发起者，同时也是大遗址保护工作最有力的倡导者。中央政府和有关部委在政策、项目、经费方面的大力支持，会极大鼓舞广大文物工作者保护大遗址的热情，同时也会极大地激发地方政府保护大遗址的积极性。

3. 规划先行是保护好大遗址的约束力。大遗址保护范围广大，保护对象众多，牵涉利益方方面面，保护工作要求长期开展，因此，必须制定严谨科学的总体保护利用规划。大遗址的保护展示利用项目要根据相关研究工作开展的深度分步骤实施，对目前尚没有展示利用条件的项目不宜仓促上马；大遗址周边环境的改善不仅要配合重大项目进行集中整治，更应该在一个较长的时期内依照规划严格控制，实行有机更新；文物保护与周边各种利益团体的关系要通过法律的形式规定下来，且不能朝令夕改。这些方面都需要规划来统一约束。

4. 造福社会是保护好大遗址的生命力。必须将大遗址保护和改善人民群众生活结合起来。如将城市区域内的大遗址建设成为城市遗址公园、公共绿地、文物旅游展示景点等，使人民群众切实感受到大遗址保护工作给其生活质量改善带来的好处，吸引他们更自觉地加入到对大遗址的保护中来，这也是大遗址保护应对城市化进程加快的根本对策。

总之，近年来河南大遗址保护探索的经验表明，大遗址保护只有坚持"以人为本"，面向社会、服务社会，引导社会力量共同参与保护实践，让大遗址的文化内涵"活"起来，才能为文物工作全局营造积极、良好的发展氛围，并最终推动大遗址保护向更深入的方向发展。

Explore the Foundation and Model for the Conservation and Utilization of Large Ancient Sites in Henan

Tian Kai[①]

China Henan Provincial Administration of Cultural Heritage

Located at the heart of China, Henan is an important birthplace for Chinese nation and civilization, as well as a large province where most of the China's cultural heritage reside. Today, Henan is home to 65,519 immovable heritage sites, out of which, 5 World Cultural Heritage properties, 420 State Priority Protected Sites, 1,231 Provincial Priority Protected Sites and 20 State Priority Historical Famous Cultural Cites/Towns/Villages. Among 8 ancient capitals in China, 4 are in Henan (Zhengzhou, Kaifeng, Luoyang, Anyang) .

Henan is a province with rich heritage resource. The world is amazed at the grand scale of ancient settlement, sites of national capitals and ancient royal tombs densely distributed over a large area in the province. Among the 152 large heritage sites designated by the State during the "13th Five-Year" period, Henan is on the top of the list with 22 sites in the province. These large sites have the following main features:

1. Cluster around a wide area. In Luoyang and Zhengzhou, the three serial heritage - Great Wall, Grand Canal and Silk Roads make up most of the large ancient sites in Henan.

2. Carry over different periods. Henan encompasses all the important archaeological relics in main periods of history in ancient China.They are the major components of China's five thousand years of history and glorious civilization. In terms of significance, they are important to inheritance and innovation of Chinese

---

① Tian Kai was graduated in 1985 with a degree in Archaeology from Peking University. He is now the Director of the Henan Provincial Administration of Cultural Heritage and an Executive Member of the International Committee for Museum Security in the International Council of Museum (ICOM) . Tian Kai is an expert under the special allowance of State Council, also a distinguished expert for the Ministry of Culture. As a Class II Researcher in Museology, Tian Kai is a Postgraduate Mentor in Zhengzhou University, Henan University, Minzu University of China and University of Science and Technology of China. Previously he was the Director of Henan Museum and Vice Chairman of Chinese Museums Association. With profound expertise in the management and research of cultural heritage and museology, Tian Kai has published nearly a hundred papers as well as numerous books on these subjects.

splendid tradition and culture.

3. Rich connotation and diverse forms. There are settlement sites dating back to New Stone Age, sites of ancient cities, sites of capitals from Xia to Northern Song Dynasty, Mangshan Mausoleum Complex and the Imperial Tombs of the Northern Song Dynasty in Gongyi City, also the Qingliangsi state-owned kiln site in Baofeng County.

4. The characteristics of these sites, especially the continuous development of capital sites, shape the framework of main cities today. The Zhengzhou Shang City, Capital of Kingdoms Zheng and Han during the Spring and Autumn/Warrior States Period, Sui-Tang Luoyang City, Northern Song Kaifeng City, these ancient cities criss-cross and overlap with Henan's modern cities.

5. These grand sites are usually buried deeply under the ground, few of them lying exposed on the surface.

In view of the above 5 features, conservation for these large ancient sites in Henan Province focuses on the fundamental works to exhibit their values, explore how to protect them and let them play a role.

I. Fundamental measures for presentation of heritage values

(1) More archaeological excavation/research in an effort to find out their cultural context with a narrative for each

Henan has a strong team in archaeology. Nearly every large site has a dedicated institute to conduct archaeological excavation and research.

Five teams from Institute of Archaeology, Chinese Academy of Social Sciences work at the five large sites (Erlitou, Yanshi Shang City, Yin Ruins, Han-Wei Luoyang City and Sui-Tang Luoyang City) all year round. The outcomes of their archaeological work play a major role in supporting the conservation and presentation, as well as planning and building ruins parks for these sites. There are also archaeological teams from Henan Provincial Institute of Cultural Heritage and Archaeology, Zhengzhou/Luoyang Municipal Institute of Cultural Heritage and Archaeology working at these sites.

Since 2005, archaeological teams discovered numerous artefacts during field works at these large sites of Erlitou, Sanyangzhuang, Beiyangping · Xipo, Mangshan Mausoleum Complex, Capital of Kingdoms Zheng and Han, Anyang Gaoling Mausoleum or Caocao Mausoleum, Sui-Tang Luoyang City and Han-Wei Luoyang City. Some of them are listed in the "Top 10 Archaeological Discoveries" followed by publications such as: *Erlitou, Yanshi Shang City, Sui-Tang Luoyang City, Archaeological Survey on Mangshan Mausoleum Complex, Archaeological Excavation at Anyang Gaoling Mausoleum, Archaeological Excavation at Jiahu Ruins*. All these outcomes and publications show the great archaeological progress of Henan. Recently, through our efforts, the four provincial institutes of cultural heritage and archaeology from Henan, Shaanxi, Shanxi and Hebei joined together to initiate a "Project on the Study of Civilized Central Plain Region". The project aims to conduct continuous, scientific archaeological works at large critical sites which are crucial to the origin of Chinese civilization, in an effort to find out their cultural context with a narrative for each other.

(2) Enhanced regulatory framework for protection of these large sites at the highest standard

Legislative measures and regulatory systems have been prepared for 7 large sites. These include: *Regulations on the Conservation and Management of Anyang Yin Ruins (2001)* , *Regulations for the Conservation of Han-Wei Luoyang City (2006)* , *Regulations for the Conservation of Sui-Tang Luoyang City (2008)* , *Regulations for the Conservation of Site of Yanshi,Erlitou in Luoyang and Site of Shixianggou Shang City (2009)* , *Regulations for the Conservation of Mangshan Mausoleum Complex in Luoyang (2011)* and *Regulations on the Conservation and Management of Capital of Kingdoms Zheng and Han (2014)* . As of today, a total of nearly 20 volumes of laws, regulations and normative documents have been in place for the conservation of over 40 large heritage sites in Henan province. The above local laws and regulations not only provide long-term institutional protection for the conservation of concerned sites, but also bear historical significance in preserving these grand historical sites of Henan.

On the other side, Henan actively involves in the preparation, approval and promulgation of conservation plans for these sites. The government started the conservation programme for large ancient sites in 2005. Since then, conservation plans have been completed or partially completed for 17 large sites out of the 18 in Henan listed under national protection.Among them, 15 plans have been approved by National Administration of Cultural Heritage, 14 plans have been announced by the People's Government of Henan Province for implementation. These plans, after going through the stages of preparation, approval and promulgation, ensure that the conservation of large heritage sites in Henan are met in a standard and scientific manner.

(3) Secure funding on conservation and presentation of large ancient sites

Conservation and presentationare crucial to protect large ancient sites, as well as a key item in building ruins parks for the presentation of their values. According to statistics, beginning from 2005 there are over 30 protection and presentation projects completed. An approximate of RMB 1.5 billion from government funding has been spent on these projects, while nearly RMB 20 billion of local fiscal spent on environmental treatment, relocation of residents and infrastructure.

The protection and presentation projects of the archaeological sites in Henan Province that have achieved good results include the following heritage: Dingding Gate at the Site of Sui-Tang Luoyang City, Bright Hall and Heavenly Hall at the Site of Imperial Palace of Tang Dynasty, Jiuzhouchi or royal garden at the Site of Imperial Palace of Tang Dynasty, Hanjia granary site, Huiluo granary site, Changhe Gate at the Site of Han-Wei Luoyang City, Secong Palace Gate and, Third Palace Gate at the Site of Han-Wei Luoyang City, earthen foundation of Yongning Pagoda/ Temple, Xiyang Gate at the Site of Han-Wei Luoyang City, Processional Way inside Xiyang Gate at the Site of Han-Wei Luoyang City, Tongtuo Drive at the Site of the Han-Wei Luoyang City, outer wall at the Zhengzhou Shang City, nobility tombs of Kingdom Zheng at the Site of Capital of Kingdoms Zheng and Han, southeast city wall at the Site of Capital of Kingdoms Zheng and Han, No.2 Courtyard at the Site of Sanyangzhuang Han settlement near the Yellow

River, ruins discovered during the previous seven archaeological excavations at Jiahu Site, porcelain-making zone at the BaofengQingliangsi Ru Kiln Site and No.7 ancient tomb in the ruins of Chengyang city.

The implementation of numerous such projects preserves the main context of these large ancient sites in order to interpret their values. It also drives the archaeological works, environmental treatment and infrastructure construction that are essential to the conservation of these sites.

(4) Site museums, heritage parks take public through the culture of archaeological ruins

Site museums not only add a garden folly to national archaeological site parks, but also serve as cultural facilities for the public besides conserving the ruins. As stipulated by the "13th *Five-Year" Conservation Plans for Large Heritage Sites*, 20-30 site museums have been built during the "13th Five-Year" period. As of today, 7 new site museums in Henan province are now open for public. They are: The Garden Museum of Yin Ruins, Yangshao Culture Museum,Museum of Capital of Kingdoms Zheng and Han - Chariot Pits at a Nobility Tomb of the Kingdom Zheng, Dahe Village Ruins and Museum, Museum of Chengyang City Ruins. Dingding Gate Museum and Museum of BaofengQingliangsi Ru Kiln Site. Further, 6 museums are under construction or in preparation for the following sites - Erlitou, Museum, Zhengzhou Shang City, Jihua Ruin,Miaodigou Ruin, Anyang Gaoling Mausoleum, Xinzheng Gate in Eastern Capital of Northern Song Dynasty.

Archaeological site parks are the outcome to conserve the ruins of large ancient sites. In order to protect and exhibit the ruins, these parks with all the facilities, infrastructure and greenery surrounding are open to public, providing a beautiful corner for education, research, tourism and leisure. As of today, Henan province has 4 archaeological sites parks (some still under construction) , 9 in the national project list. Archaeological site parks protect these large sites and pay full respect to cultural heritage. Further, they improve our living environment and drive other developments to promote a beautiful city with unique charm, culture and character. As a result, local people's governments follow this new model of conservation and reuse of large ancient sites. And for those large ancient sites located in the downtown or suburb, archaeological site parks play a role in harmonious development between heritage preservation and economic society.

II. New models to fulfill conservation

(1) "Ecological Heritage Conservation" in Zhengzhou

"Ecological Heritage Conservation" is a project started in Zhengzhou in early 2017. The main activities involved in the project: within the next 3 to 5 years, 75 heritage sites (national/provincial/municipal heritage) located in Zhengzhou's downtown, suburbs or outskirts will be converted to ecological theme parks which are beautiful grand green spaces for public leisure. According to the initial plan, 75 eco parks will be built to provide 50,000 acres of greenery area with a fiscal investment of nearly RMB 1 million. To ensure that these ancient sites are safe and open to public, government will take the leadership and encourage all concerned parties to participate. These beautiful parks are for everyone, for the society. Their designs strictly follow heritage survey reports and archaeological findings.

Different from former practice focusing on archaeological excavation to study the cultural context and present the sites, the main concern of "Ecological Heritage Conservation" is "conservation" rather than excavation, research and presentation. An example is the Yuanling Ancient City Ruins Park under construction now. The construction of the park starts from covering the site with soil to conceal the entire cultural layer under the ground. Above the ground is a new eco-cultural park with a tour route, service facilities and green space. During the construction, the underground ancient site remains intact.

China government has made great efforts to promote ecological progress. Against this backdrop, the "Ecological Heritage Conservation" project in Zhengzhou is a bold attempt to protect ancient ruins by combining greenery with dynamic heritage uses. To conserve ancient ruins in this way has the biggest advantage, since the integrity of their cultural context is preserved while at the same time making full use of the land above the ruins. Though the cultural context of the site may not be effectively presented for the time being, yet this is good for the conservation in the long-term. In the future when the right opportunity comes, we can always continue archaeological works and exhibit the cultural context of the site. In our opinion, cities packed with ancient ruins can learn from "Ecological Heritage Conservation" to protect large ancient sites, if there is not enough funding to protect all.

(2) "Luoyang Model" - new city away from old city

In the 1990s during the third phase of urban planning, in order to preserve the residential ruins south of Luoyang at the Site of the Sui-Tang Luoyang City, local government proposed to build a new district to the south of the residential ruins crossing Luo River and Site of the Sui-Tang Luoyang City, the 22 square kilometers of residential ruins are demarcated as non-construction land. This "new city away from old city" for conservation of large ancient sitesis called "Luoyang Model". Again, during the four phase of urban planning, local government proposedto look for new land across the Yi River to the southeast of Luoyang, so as to avoid the large ancient sites and key historical ruins within the periphery of Luoyang. "Luoyang Model" was put into practice once again. In our opinion, "Luoyang Model" is the final solution to address the relation between conservation of large ancient sites and urban development. It also offers a profound insight about the conservation of large ancient sites in China.

(3) "Yinxu Model" - mutual benefit, shared interest in Anyang

Anyang Working Station of the Archaeological Institute of the Chinese Academy of Social Sciences, the main team responsible for the archaeological excavation at Yinxu (Ruins of Yin) , has collected numerous treasure and artefacts unearthed from the site but without any necessary presentation or exhibition. During the conservation of the site for World Heritage nomination, Anyang Municipal Government was thinking to build a site museum for Yinxu. Yet there was nothing to display. Visitors coming to the site cannot see the splendid and brilliant artefacts unearthed and their priceless value. As a result, there is a lack of understanding in how to conserve these treasures. In order to change the situation, after discussion Anyang Municipal People's Government and Archaeological Institute of the Chinese Academy of Social Sciences agreed to build a new site museum together. By end of 2005, the Garden-Museum of Yin Ruins was open to public. The new museum was funded by Anyang local government, guarded by armed police and jointlymanaged by Anyang Working Station of the Archaeological Institute of the Chinese Academy of Social Sciences and local cultural heritage departments. This is a typical example of "mutual benefit, shared interest" between a national science and technology institute and local government departments, or "Yinxu Model" as we called it. In our opinion, Yinxu Model mainly demonstrated the coordination between a national archaeological institute and local government for the conservation of large ancient sites. In the next step, the Erlitou Museum will be built based on this model.

(4) Model of Xinyang Chengyang Site Management Committee

In December 2004, with an aim to conserve the ruins of Chengyang City, The People's Government of Xinyang Municipality and People's Government of Xinyang Pingqiao District separated the related 4 administrative villages from the former Changtaiguan Village. A new Protected Zone of Chengyang Site Management Committee was formed. The committee was a research division funded by local governments. Its main responsibility is heritage preservation and reuse on top of village-town administration. Under this division has offices for finance, civil affairs, social security, armed police, public order, as well as family planning center, cultural service center, agricultural service center. The CPC party committee of the protected zone has the authority to appoint/dismiss the staff of all offices and members of 2 CPC party committees in 4 administrative villages. The protected zone, with a population of 11,000, covers an area of 250,000 square kilometers, where 12 square kilometers reserved for heritage conservation.

The Chengyang Site Management Committee, besides funded by central government for conservation of large ancient sites to exhibit and reuse of the site, also receives funding from various departments of governments at higher level. The committee has successfully solicited funds from the society to conserve the ruins and stimulate social and economic development in the area. For example, funds from government fiscal, transport/poverty alleviation departments have been used for reconstruction of 45 kilometers of roads inside/ outside the site and between the villages. Electricity wires within the site were moved out. All high-voltage wires that obstructed the site landscape were relocated or buried. After "Beautiful Village" project, the ancient fabric and houses in some of the villages were purged, repaired and beautified. To strengthen fund attraction, efforts have been made to attract investors to build a Chengyang Cultural Innovation Zone next to the ruins. Residents were asked to relocate. New investment was used for agricultural tourism project and makeovers of old houses and villages for bed-and-breakfast inns. Besides alleviating the tight fiscal pressure, with all these investments in greenery and amenities, the ruins park now has become more attractive than ever. Moreover, the ruin park creates higher value to the land around the site. The increasing value of Chengyang Cultural Innovation Zone indirectly brings more income to the local residents.

The Xinyang Chengyang Site Management Committee is a new model to conserve a large ancient site effectively, while full consideration is given to the development of rural villages. This model to conserve large ancient sites affords us lessons that merit attention. In our opinion, the Han-Wei Luoyang City, Sanyangzhuang Site in Neihuang County, Site of Ancient Xinmi Stockade, Beiyangping Site, Yangshao Village Site, these numerous large ancient sites scattered over a wide area or urban-rural areas in Henan can be protected and managed using this model.

III. Afterthoughts

From our efforts in recent years, in view of the present situation, our opinion on the conservation of large ancient sites should include the following:

1. Internal driving force comes from the concerns of local governments. In other words, local governments must be involved. By protecting these large ancient ruins, they can see the benefits such as improving urban environment, enhancing urban charm and promoting local cultural tourism. Beginning with a strong interest, local governments should actively participate and put conservation of large ancient sites into government plans, and to achieve win-win during the harmonious development between conservation and local economy.

2. External driving force comes from policies. National Administration of Cultural Heritage and other concerned state departments are the initiators and strongest advocate in the conservation of large ancient sites in China. The full support Central Government, ministries and commissions in terms of policies, projects and funding is an impetus to encourage all heritage professional as well as local government to protect these sites.

3. Planning binds conservation. Large ancient sites spanning over a wide area involve numerous countermeasures, interests of different parties and long-term planning. Hence, there must be strict, scientific overall plans for the conservation and reuse of these sites. The protection and presentation projects are based on in-depth research and implemented in phases. For sites with no condition for display and reuse at the moment, planning should not be in a hurry. The improvement to the immediate setting of these sites should coincide with the works of large projects. Within a longer period, strict control should be exercised according to plan in order to organically revitalize their surroundings. Laws should be enforced to lay down the rules and relation between heritage conservation and stakeholders. These laws cannot be issued in the morning and rescinded in the evening. All of these should be considered first before planning.

4. Benefits to society gives life to conserve large ancient sites. Conservation and improvement of people's livelihood should be combined under one goal. For instance, large sites located in urban districts are converted

into ruin parks, public green spaces or cultural attractions for all to enjoy, to feel the living improvement and benefits brought by the conservation. In this way, more people are attracted to protect the sites. Conserving large ancient sites is also a fundamental measure to counter the rapid progress of urbanization.

To conclude, from the experience of looking for new ways to protect large ancient sites in Henan, the principle is "care for people", for the society, serve the society, people from all walks of life are encouraged to protect these sites, to "rejuvenate" their cultural context. Only this can heritage conservation be continued in good momentum and ultimately moved forward.

水下考古与海上丝绸之路

中国　国家文物局水下文化遗产保护中心　姜　波[①]

　　沉船、港口与贸易品，是考古学家解读古代海上丝绸之路的金钥匙。二十世纪后半叶以来，沉船考古成果尤其令人瞩目，出人意料的水下考古发现层见叠出，著名者如广东川岛海域的"南海一号"（南宋时期）、韩国新安沉船（元代）和印尼的"黑石号"沉船（晚唐）等，这些水下考古新成果，揭开了海上丝绸之路研究的新篇章。

　　中国海域发现的海上丝绸之路沉船以泉州后渚沉船、"南海一号"和"华光礁一号"最有代表性，三者均属我国古代海洋贸易的高峰时期——宋元时期，发现地点恰在起航港、"放洋之地"（古人对出海通道的称呼）和远洋航线上。从航向来看，"南海一号"与"华光礁一号"是从中国港口满载出海的商船，后渚沉船则是从东南亚归航泉州的海舶，他们的发现，非常生动地展示了宋元时期海上丝绸之路的历史风貌。

图 1　清理出来的"南海一号"船体轮廓

　　① 姜波，男，博士，研究员，时任国家文物局水下文化遗产保护中心水下考古所所长。1992 年毕业于武汉大学历史系考古专业，获学士学位；2001 年毕业于中国社会科学院研究生院，获博士学位。2016 年获评国务院特殊津贴专家，2017 年获评国家"万人计划"领军人才。兼任国际古迹遗址理事会（ICOMOS）执行委员、中国古迹遗址理事会（ICOMOS-CHINA）副理事长。主要研究领域为水下考古、海上丝绸之路研究与汉唐都城考古。主要代表作有《汉唐都城礼制建筑研究》（专著）、《中国古代都城考古学研究》（专著、合作）、《从泉州到锡兰山》（论文）等。曾先后就职于中国社会科学院考古研究所、中国文化遗产研究院；并曾以访问学者身份赴美国哈佛大学、美国国家美术馆研修。

图 2 "南海一号"船舱码放货物的情形

"南海一号"是迄今为止海上丝绸之路水下考古最为重要的成果，该沉船 1987 年在广东川岛海域被发现，2007 年整体打捞出水并移入"水晶宫"（广东海上丝绸之路博物馆）。这是世界上首次采用沉箱整体打捞沉船，堪称世界水下考古史上的创举。目前，"南海一号"的室内发掘工作还在有条不紊地进行中。考古发掘显示，这是一艘满载出航且保存完好的南宋海船，船体残长约 22 米，最大船宽近 10 米，总计有 14 个隔舱（含艉尖舱）（图 1）。船舱里各色货物码放有序，品类繁多，琳琅满目！此外，船内还发掘出大量的个人物品，如戒指、手镯、臂钏、项链等金制饰品，以及金叶、玉器、银铤、漆器等。尤其令人称奇的是，船体左舷外发现的一个小木盒，是一个"珠宝箱"，里面盛放了 70 余件金器！截止至 2016 年 1 月 5 日，总共出土文物 14392 件（套），其中瓷器 13497 件套、金器 151 件套、银器 124 件套、铜钱约 17000 枚，等等。另据最新的样品检测数据，"南海一号"上已经发现丝绸遗留的化学成分，"海上丝绸之路"名不虚传！

1974 年发掘的泉州湾后渚古船，出土有香料、胡椒、瓷器、铜钱乃至记录货物的签牌等，为我们提供了研究海洋贸易的珍贵实物资料。船壳上采集的海洋贝壳遗骸，经鉴定为南洋物种，表明这条海船曾经远航至东南亚海域。尤其值得注意的是，船上发现的一把"量天尺"，表明宋代海船不但使用了中国人传统的罗盘导航技术，也开始借鉴阿拉伯商人"牵星过洋"的天文导航技术，生动揭示了古代东西方航海技术方面的交流。

与泉州古船和"南海一号"不同，西沙群岛海域发现的"华光礁一号"沉船，则是发现于远洋航线上的海上丝绸之路商船（图 4）。"华光礁一号"发现于西沙海域的华光礁礁盘内侧，年代属南宋时期，这也是中国水下考古学界第一次在远海海域完成的水下考古发掘项目。"华光礁一号"出水遗物近万件，有瓷器、铁器、铜镜、铜钱等，瓷器产地除江西景德镇以外，主要为福建窑口的产品，包括德化窑、磁灶窑、闽清窑、南安窑、松溪窑等。"华光礁一号"的发现，证明至迟在宋元时期（依据水下考古的发现，有可能早至五代时期），我国先民就已经开辟了取道西沙群岛直航东南亚地区的航线（以前受限于航海技术水平，远航东南亚多贴岸航行），标志着我国古代航海技术和导航技术已经达到一个新的高度。

中、日、韩三国一衣带水，自古以来就有密切的海上交流，留下了徐福入海求仙、鉴真东渡扶桑、圆仁入唐求法等诸多佳话。水下考古成果非常生动地展示了东北亚地区的海上交流活动，其中最重要的发现是 1975 年在韩国群山列岛海域发现的新安沉船。经过连续多年的水下考古发掘，考古队员从沉船里发掘出了两万多件青瓷（图 5）和白瓷，两千多件金属制品、石制品和紫檀木，以及 800 万枚重达 28 吨的中国铜钱，这一水下考古成果震惊了全世界。考古学家据新安沉船出水的刻"庆元"铭文铜

图 3　考古发掘出来的泉州后渚古船   图 4　"华光礁一号"沉船遗迹

权和"使司帅府公用"青瓷盘推断，新安沉船的始发港应为庆元港，即今天的浙江宁波。目前学术界普遍的看法是，新安沉船是元代至治三年（1323 年）前后，从中国的庆元港（宁波）启航，驶向日本博多港地区的海洋贸易商船，途中不幸沉没在朝鲜半岛新安海域。

图 5　新安沉船出水龙泉窑荷叶盖罐在杭州展出情形

爪哇（印度尼西亚）是联接印度洋与太平洋的十字路口，这里发现的水下沉船广受关注，如印旦沉船、井里汶沉船和"黑石号"沉船等。1998 年，德国打捞公司在印尼勿里洞岛海域一块黑色大礁岩附近发现了一艘唐代沉船，即著名的"黑石号"。2005 年，新加坡"圣淘沙"集团（SentosaLeisure）筹资 3000 万美元购得"黑石号"沉船文物，使得这批重要文物最终落户狮城。据水下考古队员仔细观察，"黑石号"船体保存完整，船底发现破损的大洞，推测"黑石号"为触礁沉没。"黑石号"之所以保存完好，主要是因为海床上沉积有厚厚的淤泥，满载船货的船体因为负荷较重，很快就被海底淤泥

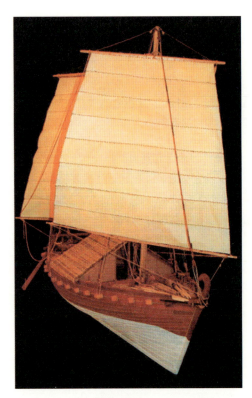

图 6　复原的"黑石号"沉船

图 7　黑石号上出水的长沙窑瓷盘

掩埋覆盖，避免了海潮的冲刷和船蛆的吞噬，从而使得船体和货物得到了很好的保护。从结构和工艺上看，"黑石号"应该是一艘阿拉伯式的单桅缝合帆船，制作船体时不使用铁钉而用棕榈绳缝合船板（图6）。关于"黑石号"的年代，因为出水长沙窑瓷碗上带有唐代"宝历二年"（826年）铭文，故沉船的年代被确认为9世纪上半叶。

"黑石号"出水文物十分精彩。船上共出金器10件，其精美程度可媲美1970年西安何家村唐代窖藏出土金银器。其中的一件八棱胡人伎乐金杯高10厘米，比何家村窖藏出土品体量还大。另有银器24件、银铤18枚和铜镜30枚，银铤单件重达2公斤。其他还发现了一些船上乘员的个人物品，其中包括2件玻璃瓶、一件漆盘（残）、象牙制游戏器具（似为游艺用的双陆）和砚、墨（残）等文房用具。"黑石号"打捞文物陶瓷制品多达67000多件，其中98%是中国陶瓷。长沙窑瓷约56500件，器型以碗为主，其次为执壶。这是长沙窑大规模生产外销瓷的一个生动写照（图7）。"黑石号"出水的3件完好无损的唐代青花瓷盘尤为引人注目，它们应该是在洛阳地区的巩县窑烧制，经隋唐大运河运抵扬州港，再从扬州转运出海，最终抵达印尼海域的。唐·贾耽"广州通海夷道"曾非常详细地描述了从广州出发，经越南、马六甲抵达印度洋海域的航线。另据《全唐文》记载，唐德宗贞元年间，曾有波斯船抵达中国东南沿海。有鉴于此，印尼海域发现满载中国船货的阿拉伯帆船，应属意料之中的事情。

15—16世纪，欧洲迎来了"地理大发现"的时代，以此为背景，以欧洲为中心，欧洲航海家开辟了向东、向西两条抵达东方的航线：向东的航线，自葡萄牙里斯本启航，经开普敦—果阿—马六甲—澳门，最终抵达日本九州的长崎港，活跃在这条航线上的，先后有葡萄牙人、荷兰人和英国人等；向西的航线，包括横跨大西洋的里斯本—里约航线和横跨太平洋的马尼拉—阿卡普尔科航线，主导这条航线的，最主要的是西班牙人。水下考古发现的瑞典"哥德堡号"沉船和西班牙"圣迭戈号"沉船，堪称东、西两条航线上颇具代表性的沉船。限于篇幅，这里就不一一介绍了。

Underwater Archaeology and the Maritime Silk Road

Jiang Bo[①]

China National Center of Underwater Cultural Heritage

Shipwrecks, ports and traded products are the golden keys for archaeologists to discover the ancient Maritime Silk Road. Remarkable achievements in shipwreck archaeology have been scored since the second half of the 20th century. Surprising underwater archaeological finds have been made one after another, such as the South China Sea No.1 Shipwreck (the Southern Song Dynasty) in the waters of Chuandao of China's Guangdong Province, the Sinan Shipwreck (the Yuan Dynasty) in the Republic of Korea, and the Batu Hitam Shipwreck (the late Tang Dynasty) in Indonesia. These achievements in underwater archaeology have ushered in a new era for the study of the Maritime Silk Road.

The Houzhu Shipwreck in Quanzhou, the South China Sea No.1 Shipwreck and the Huaguang Reef No.1 Shipwreck are the most representative discovered on the Maritime Silk Road within China's territorial waters. All the three shipwrecks were built during the Song and Yuan dynasties, the heydays of maritime trade in ancient China, and discovered at a departure port, a gateway to the sea or a maritime route respectively. In terms of heading, South China Sea No.1 and Huaguang Reef No. 1 were fully-laden merchant boats departing from a Chinese seaport, while the Houzhu Shipwreck was a marine boat on its return voyage from Southeast Asia to Quanzhou. These archaeological finds are the vivid evidence demonstrative of the historical scenario of the Maritime Silk Road during the Song and Yuan dynasties.

The South China Sea No.1 Shipwreck marks the most important achievement of underwater archaeology

---

① Jiang Bo, male, Ph.D., research fellow, director of China National Center of Underwater Cultural Heritage. In 1992, he graduated from the History Department of Wuhan University, with a B.A. degree in archaeology. In 2001, he graduated from the Graduate School of the Chinese Academy of Social Sciences (CASS), with a doctoral degree. In 2016, he was honored as an expert to receive the State Council Special Allowance. In 2017, he was chosen as a leading talent for the National Ten Thousand Talents Program. Jiang is also a member of the ICOMOS Board and vice chairman of ICOMOS China. His major research areas include underwater archaeology, study of the Maritime Silk Road, and archaeology in capital sites of the Han and Tang dynasties. His major publications include Research of Ritual Buildings in Capitals of the Han and Tang Dynasties (monograph), Archaeological Research of Capitals of Ancient China (monograph co-authored with others), and From Quanzhou to Ceylon Hill (treatise). Jiang worked in CASS Institute of Archaeology and Chinese Academy of Cultural Heritage (CACH) successively and conducted research as visiting scholar at Harvard University and the National Gallery of Art in USA.

that has ever been scored along the Maritime Silk Road. The shipwreck was discovered in the waters of Chuandong of Guangdong Province in 1987. The whole shipwreck was salvaged in 2007 and later housed in the Crystal Palace (another name of the Maritime Silk Road Museum of Guangdong) . It was the world's first shipwreck integrally salvaged by using caissons, setting a pioneering example in the world history of underwater archaeology. Currently, excavations are being carried out in the shipwreck's interior. Archaeological excavations show that it is fully-laden, well-preserved Southern Song marine boat on its departure voyage. The remnant length is approximately 22m and the maximum width is nearly 10m, with a total of 14 bulkhead compartments (including the after peak compartment) (see the Fig.1 below) . There is a dazzling array of products orderly stacked up in the boat's compartments. An enormous number of personal items were also excavated, such as gold rings, bracelets, armlets and necklaces, as well as gold leafs, jade wares, silver ingots and lacquer wares. More surprisingly, a wooden jewelry box was found beyond the port side, containing up to 70 gold wares. As of 5 January 2016, a total of 14,392 objects (in items or sets) had been excavated, including 13, 497 porcelain wares, 151 gold wares, 124 silver wares, and 17,000 copper coins. According to the latest sample testing data, chemical components from silk fabrics have been found in the shipwreck, which is a true testimony to the existence of the Maritime Silk Road.

Fig.1　The excavated shipwreck body of South China Sea No. 1

Spice herbs, pepper, porcelain, copper coins and even product-recording chips were excavated from the Houzhou Shipwreck found in Quanzhou Bay in 1974, which provide the valuable physical evidence for the study of maritime trade. Shell remnants collected from boat hulls were identified to be species from the South China Sea, the evidence to testify to the marine boat's voyages to Southeast Asia. The "Celestial Measuring Ruler" found in the shipwreck indicates that not only the Chinese traditional navigation technology using the compass but also the Islamic navigation knowledge known as "Fettering Stars" were applied to Song Dynasty marine boats, which is the vivid evidence to testify to East-West exchanges of navigational technology in ancient times.

Different from the Houzhou Shipwreck and South China Sea No. 1 found in a port area or coastal waters, the Huaguang Reef No. 1 Shipwreck was a merchant boat found on a seafaring route of the ancient Maritime Silk Road on the inner side of Huaguang Reef in the Xisha Islands. The Southern Song shipwreck was the first underwater excavation project carried out by Chinese archaeologists in offshore waters. Nearly 10,000 objects were excavated from the shipwreck, including porcelain, iron wares, bronze mirrors and copper coins. In addition to a small number of porcelain wares produced in Jingdezhen of Jiangxi Province, most of the excavated porcelain wares were produced in Fujian's kilns, including Dehua, Cizao, Minqing, Nan'an and Songxi kilns. The shipwreck is the evidence that Chinese ancestors had pioneered a maritime route to Southeast Asia via the Xishan Islands no later than the Song and

Fig.2   Products stacked up in compartments of the South China Sea No.1 Shipwreck

Yuan dynasties (probably as early as in the Five Dynasties period according to underwater archaeological finds) (due to restraints in navigation technology, most boats sailing to Southeast Asia had followed coastal routes). The discovery of the shipwreck indicates that maritime and navigation technologies in this period of ancient China developed into a new height.

Fig.3   The Houzhou Shipwreck excavated in Quanzhou

Fig.4   The remains on the Huaguang Reef No. 1 Shipwreck

China, Japan and Korea are close neighbors facing each other across a strip of water. Intensive maritime exchanges among them over the sweep of history have left behind many unforgettable figures and stories such as Xu Fu who was sent to cross the sea to find the secret of immortality, Chinese Monk Jian Zhen's six attempts to cross the sea to Japan for the promotion of Buddhism, and Japanese monk Ennin's heroic adventure to China's Tang Empire for the study of Buddhism. Achievements of underwater archaeology vividly exhibit maritime encounters occurring in Northeast Asia. The most important of its kind is Sinan Shipwreck found in the waters of the Republic of Korea in 1975. More than 20,000 celadon wares (see the Fig. 5 below) and white porcelain wares, over 2,000 metal, stone and sandalwood wares, as well as 8 million Chinese copper coins weighing 28 tons have been unearthed as a result of archaeological excavations for many years. The underwater archaeological discovery stunned the whole world. Based on the bronze weight inscribed with characters "Qing Yuan" and the celadon plate inscribed with a line of characters meaning "for the use of the High Pacification Commissioner's Office only", archaeologists have inferred that the Sinan Shipwreck should depart from Qingyuan Port (present-day Ningbo of China's Zhejiang Province) . The academic community generally considers that the Sinan Shipwreck was a merchant boat sunk in Sinan waters of the Korean Peninsual during its voyage from China's Qingyuan Port (present-day Ningbo) to Japan's Hakata Port around 1323 (the 3rd year of the Zhizhi reign of the Yuan Dynasty) .

**Fig. 5   The Longquan Kiln celadon pot with lotus-shaped cover unearthed
from the Sinan Shipwreck, on display in Hangzhou City of China**

Java Island in Indonesia is a crossroad linking the Indian Ocean and the Pacific Ocean. The shipwrecks discovered in the waters here have drawn extensive attention, such as the Intan Shipwreck, the Cirebon Shipwreck and the Batu Hitam Shipwreck. In 1998, a German salvage company found a Tang Dynasty shipwreck near a black reef in the waters of Belitung Island of Indonesia, known as "Batu Hitam Shipwreck". In 2005, the cargo on the shipwreck was purchased for around 30 million USD by the Singapore-based corporation Sentosa Leisure Group and was later housed in Singapore. Archaeologists found that the shipwreck was well-preserved and the big hole at the shipwreck bottom indicates that it was sunk probably because of hitting a huge reef. The shipwreck was well preserved as the fully-laden boat was covered by thick silt on the seabed so as to avoid washing of tides and biting of shipworms. In terms of structure and technical process, the shipwreck should be an Arabic-style sloop vessel whose shipboards were sewn by palm ropes, instead of being fixed by iron nails (see the Fig. 6 below). Based on the inscription on the excavated Changsha Kiln porcelain bowl that reads "the second year of the Baoli Reign" (826 AD, Tang Dynasty), it is confirmed that the shipwreck should date back to the first half of the 9th century.

Fig.6   The restored Batu Hitam Shipwreck

There are marvelous objects excavated from the Batu Hitam Shipwreck. For example, the 10 gold wares excavated are as exquisite as gold and silver wares unearthed from a Tang Dynasty cellar in Hejiacun Village of Xi'an in 1970. In particular, the 10cm-high octagonal gold cup with design of barbarian musicians is even larger than those excavated from Hejiacun. Other objects excavated from the shipwreck include 24 silver wares, 18 silver ingots (each weighing 2kg) and 30 bronze mirrors, as well as personal items of passengers and sailors, including 2 glass bottles, 1 lacquer plate (fragmented), ivory games and stationery items such as ink slab and ink bar (fragmented). 67,000 porcelain wares have been excavated from the shipwreck, 98% of which are Chinese products. Most of the excavated porcelain wares are Changsha Kiln products, totaling 56,500 items, with bowls

Fig.7   The Changsha Kiln porcelain plate excavated from the Batu Hitam Shipwreck

as the largest portion, followed by ewers. These porcelain wares are the vivid evidence to testify to the large-scale production of export-oriented porcelain in Changsha Kiln sites at that time (see the Fig.7 below). The most attractive excavated objects from the shipwreck are the three completely-preserved Tang Dynasty blue-and-white porcelain plates. They should be produced in a kiln from Gongxian County in Luoyang and then transported to Yangzhou Port via the Grand Canal of the Sui and Tang Dynasties and eventually shipped to

Indonesia. The *Maritime Routes Starting from Guangzhou*, a documentation written by Jia Dan of the Tang Dynasty, contains a detailed inscription of the maritime route departing from Guangzhou and arriving at the Indian Ocean via Vietnam and Malacca. According to *Quan Tang Wen* (a complete collection of literatures in the Tang period) , Persian boats reached coasts of southeast China during the Zhenyuan reign of the Tang Dynasty. It is therefore not surprising to find an Arabic-style boat loaded with Chinese cargo in the waters of Indonesia.

Europe embraced the Era of Great Geographic Discovery in the 15th-16th centuries. Starting from Europe, navigators pioneered two maritime routes destined to the East. The eastward route started from Lisbon of Portugal, passed through Cape Town, Goa, Malacca and Macao, and eventually reached Nagasaki Port in Kyushu of Japan. Portuguese, Dutch, and British navigators were active along the route. There were two westward routes: one crossing the Atlantic Ocean from Lisbon to Rio and the other crossing the Pacific Ocean from Manila to Acapulco. The latter was long dominated by Spanish. The Goteborg Shipwreck of Sweden and the San Diego Shipwreck of Spain are the two most typical examples representing the eastward and westward maritime routes. I will not elaborate on them due to time restraints.

骨头海湾（Plocha Michov Grad）——奥赫里德湖的帕拉菲特遗址

北马其顿共和国　考古博物馆　亚历山德拉·帕帕佐夫斯卡[①]

简介

不得不说，骨头海湾的故事与马其顿整个领土范围内的湖边桩屋和湿地[②]是分不开的。马其顿湖泊和湿地是史前巴尔干半岛中部重要的区域。

湖泊景观位于马其顿南部和西南部，主要分布在奥赫里德湖（Ohrid）、布里斯帕湖（Prespa）和多依兰湖（Dojran）周边区域。奥赫里德湖、布里斯帕湖和马利希（位于阿尔巴尼亚）是位于亚得里亚海盆地的新第三纪大 Dasaretia 湖的遗存，而多依兰湖和希腊北部其他 13 个湖泊（如 Keletron、Koroneia Limne、Prasias Limne、Kirkinitis、Bolbe Limne、Limne Loudiake、Begorritis Limne 等）则是位于爱琴海盆地的新第三纪大爱琴湖的遗存（图 1）[③]。

关于这些地区湖边桩屋的数据和描述最早可见于公元前 5 世纪中叶希腊历史学家希罗多德的记载。他在著作《历史》中描述了发生在色雷斯的波斯战争，并指出"波斯指挥官 Megabas 打败了奥尼亚人部落，将其驱赶至亚洲地区，但没能打败居住在 Praise 湖边的部落。"[④]他描述到，"这些部落的族人生活在湖边平台的木屋中，而平台是搭建在湖底木桩上的。"希罗多德详细介绍了这些湖泊聚居部落的生活状况（或当时所称的桩屋聚落）、他们如何养活自己、以及如何在这片宁静的湖泊和酷刑区存活下来。[⑤]我们从希罗多德的文字和那些帮助我们重建帕拉菲特湖聚落的人们那里找到这些数据资料。

---

① 亚历山德拉·帕帕佐夫斯卡（Aleksandra Papazovska），现供职于北马其顿共和国考古博物馆。2002 年，担任该博物馆铁器时代展览策展顾问。从 1995 年至今，在马其顿及其他国家多次参与考古挖掘。曾是佩林切、库马诺沃、内戈蒂诺、杰夫格里雅、瓦兰多沃和史高比耶要塞等地考古发掘的协调人。2009 年，在圣基里尔麦托迪大学艺术史和考古系获得史前考古专业硕士学位。毕业论文题目为"瓦尔达尔河谷铁器时代陶器的分类"，并于 2015 年以"马其顿铁器时代的开端"为题获得博士学位。曾在圣基里尔麦托迪大学和巴尔干大学参加了不同科目的多项课程。目前与 Mario Gavranovic 博士、奥地利科学学院和东方巴尔干考古研究所（OREA）共同参与"马其顿的金属——技术，贸易与分销"项目。
② Van de Noort R., & O'Sullivan A., 2006, 34–35.
③ Papazoglou F., 1957,281.
④ 希罗多德 V, 16.
⑤ Porozanov K., 1997, 162.

根据在紧邻湖泊或河流地带开展的考古发掘情况、以及过去十年间进行的水下考古发掘活动（以及 20 世纪调查所获得的第一手资料），我们对远古时期生活在这些遗产地的人们有了一个完整的了解。在奥赫里德湖（8 个遗址）发现的帕拉菲特遗址最多，而在布里斯帕湖和多依兰湖，各发现了一个遗址。在 Šum 河进入 Drim 河的入口处也只记载了一个聚落（图 1）。史前时期，在马其顿湖泊上、或湖泊附近、或湿地水域分布着较为密集的此类聚落，偶尔在中世纪时期的古代遗迹中也会发现其中的踪迹。20 世纪在斯科普里地区一个名为 Taor 的村庄里也发现了这类聚落（图 1）。[①]

图 1

考古发掘历史及建筑特征

在文化部的财政支持下，从 1997 年到 2006 年，每年都在 Gradishte 半岛南海岸奥赫里德湖水域骨头海湾遗址地 "Plocha Michov Grad" 开展一次水下考古发掘活动。这是在马其顿北部最早开展的水下考古调查活动之一，也标志着正式开始对这些水下文化遗存进行考古研究、保护和保存。在面积为 8500 平方米的骨头海湾遗址地，发现了青铜器时代晚期至铁器时代早期的史前帕拉菲特聚居遗址（湖上桩屋）（图 2）。[②]

从开始进行调查研究直至今日，在湖底约 3—5 米的地方共发现了约 6000 个木桩遗存，它们很有可能建造在一座公共平台上，也就是说，这个平台共支撑了约 20 个用木材建造的史前住宅建筑。聚落

---

① Kuzman P., 2013, 308.
② Kuzman P., 2013, 330.

与当地环境（湖滨）之间通过一座木桥相连（可能是可移动的）。最外边的木桩距湖滨南部约71米，而最近的木桩则距湖泊12米，这个距离是搭建木桥的长度。考古发掘和调查确定了该聚落的情况，放置了一个方形水下考古网，并在多勘测点进行了挖掘（图3）。[1]

由于这一遗产地的湖底建有密集的木桩，并保存了大量关于该聚落居住形态的各类实物文化遗存，我们可得出聚落布局的相关结论。所有这些遗迹和不可计数的各尺寸木材建筑遗存，反映出在所考察的空间内，这些聚落应是一个统一的整体，也就是说，该聚落建于一个独立的木制平台上，而且该平台根据居民建造新房屋的需求不断扩大。调查表明，在湖中或湖岸出现的此类湖泊聚落有一个独特的特征。给人的初始印象是，木桩附着在湖泊底部，这在当时（三千年前）很可能是3米左右的低水位。

只有高超的史前建造技术才能解开这些居民

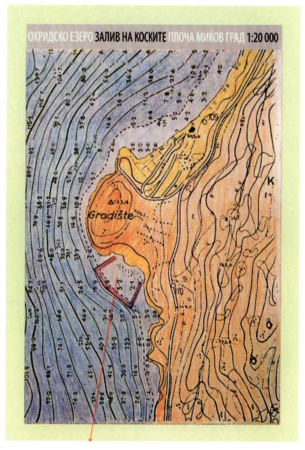

图 2

如何将木桩坚固地安放于水下这一谜题。通过系统的调查以及对聚落特定地段的分析表明，在距离南部50米左右的平整湖面上，第一行木桩所插入的湖面深度为2.1×3.2×4.8米。之后湖泊底部突然下降至15.9米，当地称为"眉"。这一段在岸边的区域被夷平并很干燥。[2]如果假设这些大直径的木桩有根，那么结论就是，这些房屋立于平台之上，而且该平台与沼泽地带或临湖的干燥地带相连。这种安置聚落的方式，一边靠近湖泊，另一边则靠近森林地带，这样可以保护聚落远离洪水侵蚀也从一定程度上远离来自陆地的威胁。另外居民也可以通过捕鱼享用湖泊带来的益处，同时还能通过农业培植和狩猎在陆地获得生存资源。

现在，对这一遗址地的湖泊底部也开展了地形学分析，尽管只发现了一块可追溯至新石器时代早期的陶器碎片，并未发现多层地形。这块陶器碎片仅是偶然发现的，所以我们无法得出关于它的更多信息。从已发现的文化遗迹（烧焦的树木残骸、煤碳和细烟灰）来看，这些房屋曾经遭遇过多次火灾，且多次重建。

研究者还对湖底发现的木桩的配置情况进行了数学（几何）分析。分析显示建筑物地基呈长方形、正方形或圆形，在桩基上建造平台，然后又在平台上建造了房屋。起初平台仅能用于建造几个独立房

① Kuzman P., 2013, 335-337.
② Kuzman P., 2013, 343.

图 3

屋，但后来随着房屋数量的不断增加，这些平台逐渐合并成为一个大平台，其最大容量约能支撑 20 个房屋。支撑房屋的木桩约 2—3 米高，尺寸约 3×3 米、4×4 米或 3×6 米。房屋的墙壁由两个或多个榛子树枝编织成的"木板"构成，通过大麻类植物或一条条的动物皮毛相连。潮湿的表面使用泥土和稻草加以覆盖。屋顶倾斜，为圆形或倾斜状，使用木材和树枝制成的一整块盖子搭建，上边还用湖泊中茂密丛生的稻草或芦苇进行覆盖。[①]根据对聚落不同年代范围的分析，这些房屋内部布局肯定进行了规划，这意味着一些规模较大的民居在重建时用了同样的材料作为底层墙。由于木材作为主要建筑材料使用，房屋往往在频繁火灾后进行重建，方法是在湖底用新木桩将旧木桩逐渐压实。这些修复的迹象解释了为何现在湖底有如此密集的木桩。

湖底发现的房屋遗存有助于我们重现房屋的内部结构：大口陶瓷坛这样的大型器皿被放于靠近房屋入口的地方，其他较大的坛子则置于距离壁炉近的地方，常常是房屋的中部。其他可移动的器物，如陶器、工具和个人物品等，则安放在房屋的各个角落或沿房屋旁边排放。房屋内部拐角处分割出来的空间或其他独立隔开的空间很可能是睡觉的地方。

考古发现

考古发掘发现了大量青铜器时代和铁器时代的文物（主要是破碎的陶器、石器和打火石、小部分

---

① Kuzman P., 2013, 345–348.

青铜器以及大量动物骨骼碎片等。其中，部分动物骨骼碎片作为工具使用）（图4）。

图 4

陶器主要是手工制品，包括各种各样的单手柄小杯子、壶、罐、双耳容器、深碗、puranois 和 pitoi 等。总的来说，这些文物中没有发现任何装饰的痕迹，仅有少数物品带有塑料带子和手柄，但它们很可能更多地有实用性价值而非装饰。

单手柄的半球状杯子[①]是红铜时期至青铜器时期常见的物品。在 Varos Prilep[②] 发现的铁器时代早期的陶瓷杯子与此类似。在 Kritsana、Hagios Mamas、Vardarophtsa、Saratse、Sedes、Armenochori 等遗址地也发现了这一类型物品。[③] 带有半球主体和伞状手柄的 Kantharoi[④] 是巴塔哥尼亚地区铁器时代早期非常典型的器物。在 Saraj – Brod、Martha Zovik、Visoi – Petilep 等考古遗址地发现了一些类似物品。[⑤] 瓦兰多沃镇附近的 Glos 以及 Chaushitsa、Saratse 和 Olinthos 等希腊北部遗址地[⑥]也发现了同时期的类似物品。其中一个最具当地特色的陶器是手柄上有尖头的 kantharos[⑦]，可追溯至公元前13世纪下半叶和公元前12世纪，即青铜器时代晚期。在 Vardar（Axios）河谷（Dimov Grob–Ulanci）[⑧]地区、希腊北部 Vardarophtsa 和 Pateli 地区[⑨]也发现了大量此类陶器遗存。

带有单手柄、主体形状为球形或半球形，底部突出[⑩]的罐子通常是不规则的、没有任何装饰，而

---

① Kuzman P., 2013, 378, T.XIV 1–6, 8.

② Kitanoski B., 1983, 21–22, 31. 图 2.3.

③ Heurtly W.A., 1939, 168（171），172（183,184, Pl. XI/183/184），178（221, 222, 223, Pl.XIV/221–223），183（254, 256），187（279–281），188（283,284），190（304–306），192（319），217（411, 412, Pl. XXI/411/412），Pl.XXIII（s–u）.

④ Kuzman P., 2013, 375, 图 51, T. XIX 7,9,11.

⑤ Simoska D., Sanev V., 1976, 53, 图 258; 54, 图 271.

⑥ Heurtly W.A., 1939, 236（486），239（499,500）.

⑦ Kuzman P., 2013, 379, T.XVII 1–5, T.XVIII 1–3, T. XIX 10,12.

⑧ Mitrevski D., 2013, 185, 206, 图 61.

⑨ Mitrevski D., 2010, 139, T.II 3,4.

⑩ Kuzman P., 2013, 379, T.XV 1–6, T.XVI 8,9,11.

且使用了较长时间。这种类型的罐子在青铜器时期早期和整个铁器时期的希腊北部地区、沿亚得里亚海海岸（从东部伊斯特里亚到北达尔马提亚的利比利亚人群）[1]非常普遍（Hagios Mamas，Saratse 等）[2]。罐腹有出水口且只有一个手柄的容器[3]较为罕见。它们起源于 Pelagonia 的 Toumbas 地区（如：Kanino 村庄的 Tumba）发现的青铜器时代中期的类似文物。[4]

有四个垂直侧把手的两耳细颈酒罐[5]很可能受到了巴尔干半岛东部或小亚细亚地区的影响。[6]有两个垂直把手和两个塑胶的球型酒罐[7]出现在青铜器时代向铁器时代过渡时期。这些文物发现于希腊北部的 Kritsana 和 Saratse[8]遗址地、Donja Brnica（Kosovo）和 Togočevac 遗址地。[9]

无把手的圆底椭圆形瓦罐[10]也起源于小亚细亚，在那里有较长的使用历史（Tara II-V）[11]。在这一遗产地发现的用于火上使用的容器（puranoi）[12]都已破碎，从重新仿制的一个样品来看，这种容器通常由两部分构成，主要放在火上使用。此类文物主要发现在希腊北部的 Varos Prilep、Veles 附近的 Manastir、Vardino 和 Tumba Asiros，可追溯至青铜器时代晚期和青铜器时代向铁器早期的过渡时期（公元前 12—10 世纪）。[13]

除陶器外，还发现了大量黏土制造的重物。大部分文物为圆形——呈盘状，带两个孔眼，主要用于捕鱼；带双锥形珠子的瘦长型器皿则主要用于纺纱和编织。[14]

石器和燧石文物数量不多，发现了一些石斧和石制的挖掘工具。这些文物的制造技术及其形状反映出新石器时代的传统特征。除石斧外，还发现了一些石砖、石块制成的护身符和谷物手磨机。[15]

当时的金属物品极为罕见。仅保存了一把青铜鱼叉和一把铜斧、一根铁针、一个三角形针头的双铜针。[16]铜斧很有年代感，可视为聚落开始定居的象征。这些斧子主要发现于约公元前 1800—1300 年间的特洛伊六世地层。三角形针头的铜针则主要发现于公元前 7 世纪末至 6 世纪铁器时代的遗产地——瓦达—摩拉维亚河谷。它们也反映出聚落存在的年代。

---

① Čović B., 1987,237,240, T.XXIV（9,19）, 261 T.XXIX（20）.

② Heurtly W.A., 1939, 172（195）и 247, Т. XII（195）, 174（197）, 179（228）and 248, T.XIV（228, 183（255）), 187（277, 278）, 189（293–295）, 235（477）, 237（488）.

③ Kuzman P., 2013, 380, T.XIV 9–12, 图 54,55.

④ Simoska D., Sanev V., 1976, 51–52, 图 251.

⑤ Kuzman P., 2013, 380, T.XXII 1.

⑥ Troia, 1992, 56（88）.

⑦ Kuzman P., 2013, 377, 图 52.

⑧ Heurtly W.A., 1939, 171（176, TXIII/176）, 189（299）, 222, 172（195）и 247, Т. XII（440, Pl. XV/440）.

⑨ Garašanin M., 1983d,733, T.CI, 6.

⑩ Kuzman P., 2013, 380–381, T.XX 3, T.XXX 2, T.XXI 1,2.

⑪ Troia, 1992, 68（155）.

⑫ Kuzman P., 2013, 377, T.XXVI 10–12, 14, 16, T.XXV 1.

⑬ Kitanovski, 1986, 26, 图 7; Jovčevska T., 2008, 92, T. XXIII; Heurtly W.A., 1939, 234（474）, 252, Pl. XXII（474）; Wardle K.A., Wardle D., 2007, 467, 470（pl.5）.

⑭ Kuzman P., 2013, T.XXVII 1–18; T.XXVII 19–26.

⑮ Kuzman P., 2013, T.XXVII 27–41.

⑯ Kuzman P., 2013, T.XXVIII 1–4.

结论

在骨头海湾（Plocha Michov Grad）遗产地开展的水下考古研究是巴尔干半岛开展的最全面的调查研究之一。为此，2008 年至 2009 年，对存在于青铜器时代晚期至铁器时代早期的湖居进行了重建（图 5）。

图 5

骨头海湾聚落（民居）主要建于一个木制平台之上，而位于湖对岸的 Vrbnik 遗址，它的每间房屋都建于一个单独的平台之上，两者存在不同之处。欧洲已经发现了多个这种类型的聚落，如苏黎世湖 Mailen 的湖边桩屋。[①] Ferdinand Keller 证实，这些渔民的房屋并不是独立存在的，而是形成了一片湖边民居。在意大利北部特伦蒂诺区原卡雷拉湖地区发现的青铜器时代的 Fiave 民居也属于这种类型，将木制房屋建造在湖中的木桩之上。[②] 根据这些研究，我们认为这些湖居可能是：位于湖泊附近木桩上的离岸建筑或湖上民居，立在木桩和平台之上的民居，立于木桩和河流或河岸（曾经也立于木桩上）上的酷刑民居。在奥赫里德湖地区的民居中，只有位于骨头海湾（Bay of the Bones）、海湾地区（Gulf of the Bay）及 Trpejca 地区的属于湖居，位于 Peshtani 的炸弹海湾（Gulf of Bombs）和位于 Sv.Naum 的 Bučila 等地的是离岸民居，位于奥赫里德的 Penelopa 和位于 Struga 的 Vrbnik 则是离岸—酷刑民居。只有位于 Vranishta 的 Crkveni Livadi 遗址地和 Ustie of Drim 是河岸民居。[③]

为此我们可以得出结论，湖泊聚落这一现象应始于公元前 5000 年左右，直至公元前 1000 年，即公元前 7 世纪。

奥赫里德湖地区如此密集的民居为未来开展年代学研究、进行新的水下考古发掘提供了可能。

---

① Rouff U., 2004, 9.
② Rouff U., 2004, 19–21.
③ Kuzman P., 2013, 350.

参考书目：

Garašanin M.，（1983）　　　　　Paraćinska grupa，Praistorija Jugoslovenskih Zemalja IV，Bronzano doba，Sarajevo

Jovčevska T.，（2008）　　　　　Manastir - 从青铜时代向铁器时代过渡期的史前墓地，Veles

Kitanoski B.，（1983）　　　　　Prilep 史前陶器仓库，马其顿科学院考古学报 6，斯科普里，21—36.

Kuzman P.，（2013）　　　　　马其顿史前湖居，斯科普里，297—430.

Mitrevski D.，（2010）　　　　　Gloska Chuka 的考古发掘情况，马其顿科学院考古学报 19，斯科普里，127—146.

Mitrevski D.，（2013）　　　　　史前时期的马其顿共和国，83—266.

Van de Noort R.，& O'Sullivan A.，　重新思索湿地考古学，伦敦
（2006）

Papazoglou F.，（1957）　　　　罗马时期的马其顿城镇，斯科普里

Porozanov K.，（1997）　　　　Подводната археология-разговор със „света на мълчанието"，Човекът зед находките-Археологията днес и утре（Иван Гацов），Интела，София，155-165.

Rouff U.，（2004）　　　　　自'1854 年 Meilen 湖'以来瑞士的湖居研究，生活在史前欧洲的湖上（Menotti），伦敦—纽约.

Simoska D.，Sanev V.，
Kitanoski B.，Sarzoski S.，（1976）　马其顿史前时期（目录），斯科普里

Troia（1992）　　　　　目　录 - Ausstellungskataloge der Prahistorischen Staatssammlung Herausgegeben von Hermann Dannheimer，Band 21

希罗多德 V　　　　　历史，Subitica 1966

Heurtly W.A.，（1939）　　　　史前时期的马其顿，剑桥

ČovićB.，（1987）　　　　Grupa Donja Dolina-Sanski most，Prahistorija Jugoslovenskih Zemalja IV，Željeszno doba，Sarajevo.

Wardle K.A.，Wardle D.，（2007）

Bay of Bones (Plocha Michov Grad) -Palafite site on Lake Ohrid

Aleksandra Papazovska[1]

Archaeological Museum of North Macedonia

Introduction

The story of the Gulf of the Bones cannot but be linked in general with the pile dwellings and with the wetland[2] on the territory of Macedonia generally. Macedonian lakes and wetlands were an important region in the prehistory of the Central Balkans.The lake landscapes are geographically located in the south and southwestern part of the country, mainly in the region around Ohrid, Prespa and Lake Dojran. Lake Ohrid, Lake Prespa and Lake Malich (in Albania) are the remains of the great Neogene Dasaretia Lake which belongs to the Adriatic Basin, while Lake Dojran and the remaining of 13 lakes in Northern Greece (such as Keletron, Koroneia Limne, Prasias Limne, Kirkinitis, Bolbe Limne, Limne Loudiake, Begorritis Limne, etc.) are the remains of the great Neogene Aegean Lake which belongs to the Aegean Basin (Fig. 1) .[3]

The first historical data and descriptions of the lake dwellings in these regions date back to the middle of the 5th century BC to Herodotus, who in his work "History" describes the Persian Wars in Thrace and speaks about "the Persian commander Megabas who defeated the Paionian tribes and moved them to Asia, but did

① Dr. Aleksandra Papazovska, Archaeological Museum of Republic of North Macedonia. In 2009 I get the Master degree in the Prehistoric archaeology at St. Cyril and Methodius University in Skopje, at Faculty of Philosophy, Department of Art history and Archaeology on a subject "Typology of the Iron age pottery in Vardar Valley" and a PhD degree in 2015 with a title "The beginning of the Iron Age in Macedonia". I am employed at the Archaeological Museum in Skopje from 2002, on a position of curator adviser for Iron Age. Coordinate and participate in numerous archaeological excavations in the country and abroad, started from 1995 till now. I was a coordinator of the excavations at Pelince, Kumanovo, Mali Dol - Negotino, Vardarski Rid -Gevgelija, Lisicin Dol-Valandovo, Skopsko Kale etc. I also participated at lots of congresses and symposiums in a field of archaeology. I take a lot of classes at the different subjects at the University of St. Cyril and Methodius in Skopje and at the Balkan University in Skopje. Now I am working on a project with the Austrian Academy of science, the Institute for Oriental and Balkan Archaeology - orea on a project "Macedonian metals - technology, trade and distribution" together with Dr Mario Gavranovic

② Van de Noort R., & O'Sullivan A., 2006, 34-35.

③ Papazoglou F., 1957,281.

Fig. 1

not defeat those tribes who lived around the Lake of Praise." [1] He describes that they lived in wooden houses built on platforms, placed on wooden piles at the bottom of the lake. "Herodotus gives a detailed description of the life in the Lake settlements (or dwelling settlements at that time), how they fed themselves and how they existed in the so-called quiet lakes and torture regions.[2] We find these data from Herodotus and from those who helped us reconstruct the lake palafitte settlements.

Based on the archaeological excavations in the immediate vicinity of lakes or rivers, as well as the underwater archaeological excavations in the past ten years (together with the first data from the research in the last century), we almost have a complete picture of the population at these sites in the prehistory. The largest number of palafite sites have been found around Lake Ohrid (8 sites), while in Lake Prespa and Lake Dojran, only one site has been recorded by each lake, and also only one site has been recorded at the location of the River Šum's inlet into in the River Drim (Fig. 1). The dwellings above the lakes or near them or in the marshy waters in Macedonia existed very intensively in the period of prehistory, and occasionally appeared in the Antiquity and in the Medieval period. Examples of this type of settlements were found in the 20ᵗʰ century in Taor, a village in the Skopje region (Fig. 1).[3]

---

① Herodotus V, 16.
② Porozanov K., 1997, 162.
③ Kuzman P., 2013, 308.

History of excavation and architectural features

The underwater archaeological excavations at the site "Plocha Michov Grad" at the Bay of Bones, in the waters of Lake Ohrid, by the south coast of the peninsula Gradishte, were performed in the champagnes each year from 1997 until 2006, with financial support from the Ministry of Culture. These were among the first investigation activities in the underwater archaeology in North Macedonia, and it became an official branch of archaeology dealing with the remains, protection and presentation of the underwater cultural heritage. At the site of the Bay of Bones at an area of cca 8500m², a prehistoric palafitte settlement (pile dwelling) from Late Bronze and Early Iron Age has been discovered (Fig.2) .[1]

In the course of the investigations performed until this period, 6000 remains of wooden piles

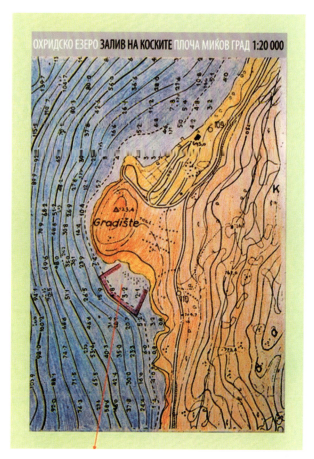

Fig. 2

were registered at the bottom of the lake at the depth of 3 to 5m, which were most probably the support of a common platform on which about twenty prehistoric dwelling buildings, built also out of wood, functioned. The connection between the settlement and the environment (shore) was made with a wooden bridge (probably movable) . The outermost piles are at 71m from the coast to the south, and the nearest piles at cca 12m in the lake, indicating that this is the distance at which the bridge was laid. The archaeological excavations and survey had given the surface of the settlement, a square underwater archaeological net was placed and excavations at several investigation fields were performed (Fig.3) .[2]

Taking into consideration that the bottom of the lake at the place of the site is densely covered with wooden piles and enormous concentration with remains of the material culture of the inhabitancy of the settlement, we can draw relevant conclusions for the layout of the settlement. Namely, all these remains together with the numerous remains of wooden construction material with different diameters, point to the fact that the settlement at the available space was monolithic, i.e. it was built on a single wooden platform that

---

①   Kuzman P., 2013, 330.

②   Kuzman P., 2013, 335-337.

Fig. 3

was extended according to the needs of the inhabitants for building new houses. The investigations had shown one exceptional feature when we speak of a lake settlement of this type in the water or at the lake shore. The initial impression is that the wooden piles were attached to the bottom of the lake, which in that period (three millennia ago) was probably with lower level for cca. 3m.

The technology achievement of the prehistoric constructions was the only way in which the inhabitants could manipulate with squatting of the wooden piles at the bottom. The systematic investigation and the analysis of certain spots in the settlement indicate that on the flattened surface on the lake shore to the south cca.50m, i.e. to the first line ending with water depth of 2.1 × 3.2 × 4.8 m, after which the bottom of the lake suddenly descends to a depth of 15.9 m, here so-called "eyebrow", this area by the shore was flattened and dry.[①] If we add to this information that the wooden piles with large diameter had roots, we can conclude that the dwelling was raised on a platform that for sure was attached in a marshy terrain or on a dry land near the water. This way of setting the settlement near the water from one side and near the forest from the other side shows how the settlement was protected from the waives and also from the land in a particular way. On the other hand, in this way the inhabitants could use the benefits offered by the lake, such as fishing, and at the same time, they could operate on the mainland by agriculture and hunting.

Today, the stratigraphy of this site at the lake bottom does not show any multiple layers even though only one fragment of pottery has been found that could be dated earlier in the Eneolithic period. We cannot talk more about the presence of that fragment, which in this context can be found by chance. Among the cultural layer of mould, remains of burnt trees, coal and fine soot have been found, which indicates that the houses had

---

① Kuzman P., 2013, 343.

suffered in fires and had been renewed several times.

The researchers at the site had done the mathematical, i.e. geometrical analysis of the disposition of the piles found today at the bottom of the lake, and they show rectangular, square and circular bases of buildings, above them the platform was built and above it the houses. In the first time the platform was built for several individual houses, but later, with the increase of the numbering of the houses, the platforms were merged into one single platform of maximum capacity of around 20 houses. The houses were built on wooden supports up to a height between 2 and 3 m, with dimensions of 3 × 3 m, 4 × 4m, or 3 × 6m. The walls were comprised of two or more "boards" prepared by knitting of hazel branches, interconnected with hemp or stripes of animal's leather. Then, the waived surfaces were coated with mud and straw. The roofs were pitched, circular or askew with a monolithic cover built of timber and branches, and covered with straw or reed found abundantly in the lake.[1] According to the chronological phase of this settlement, there must have been internal planned disposition of the houses, which means that some of the dwellings with larger dimensions were rebuilt with the same material as the base wall canvases. The houses were often rebuilt after frequent fires, according to the use of the wood as a main material, by compaction of new piles on the lake bottom. All these repairs explain the present bottom of the lake with a huge frequency of the piles.

The remains of the house inventory found at the bottom of the lake can help us with the reconstruction of the inner look of the houses: the large vessels as pithoi were placed near the entrance of the houses, while the other larger vessels were placed near the fireplaces, always set in the central part of a room. The rest of the movable finds, such as pottery, tools and personal items, were located in different positions in the house, or laterally alongside it. The partitioned spaces or other separated spaces, cornering the interior, were probably used for sleeping.

Archaeological finds

The excavations provided huge concentration of Bronze Age and Iron Age artefacts (mainly fragmented pottery, stone and flint objects, less bronze, and many fragments of animal bones, but some of them were used as tools) (Fig.4) .

Pottery production is handmade, represented by a variety of small cups with one handle, jugs, pots, amphora shaped vessels, deep bowls, puranois and pitoi. Generally in this production we found absence of decorations, excluding several samples decorated with plastic bands and handles, which have more practical uses than decorative.

The one handled cups with a hemispherical body,[2] are very common from the Eneolithic Period until

①   Kuzman P., 2013, 345-348.
②   Kuzman P., 2013, 378, T.XIV 1-6, 8.

Fig.4

the Bronze Age. We found analogies with cups from the ceramic depot from Varos Prilep,[1] where this type is dated in the Early Iron Age. The same type was found at the sites of Kritsana, Hagios Mamas, Vardarophtsa, Saratse, Sedes, Armenochori etc.[2] Kantharoi with hemispherical body and mushroom applications on the handles[3] are typical for the Early Iron Age in Pelagonia. Such samples were found at the archaeological sites at Saraj - Brod, Martha Zovik, Visoi - Petilep,[4] Glos near Valandovo, as well as on some sites in northern Greece as Chaushitsa, Saratse and Olinthos[5] dated in the same time. One of the most common local pottery type is kantharos with a pointed tip of the handles[6] dated in the Late Bronze Age in the second half of the 13th and 12th centuries BC. Massive production of this type was found at the sites in the region of Vardar (Axios) Valley (Dimov Grob-Ulanci) ,[7] Vardarophtsa and Pateli in northern Greece. [8]

One handled jugs with a spherical or hemispherical body and an emphasized bottom[9] are generally atypical without any decoration and had been used for a long period. This form is most prevalent in the Early Bronze Age and throughout the Iron Age in Northern Greece (Hagios Mamas, Saratse, etc.) [10] and along the Adriatic Coast (the Liberian group from Eastern Istria to North Dalmatia) [11]. The vessels with a drain on a

① Kitanoski B., 1983, 21-22, 31. Fig.2.3.

② Heurtly W.A., 1939, 168 (171) , 172 (183,184, Pl. XI/183/184) , 178 (221, 222, 223, Pl.XIV/221-223) , 183 (254, 256) , 187 (279-281) , 188 (283,284) , 190 (304-306) , 192 (319) , 217 (411, 412, Pl. XXI/411/412) , Pl.XXIII (s-u) .

③ Kuzman P., 2013, 375, fig.51, T. XIX 7,9,11.

④ Simoska D., Sanev V., 1976, 53, fig.258; 54, fig.271

⑤ Heurtly W.A., 1939, 236 (486) , 239 (499,500) .

⑥ Kuzman P., 2013, 379, T.XVII 1-5, T.XVIII 1-3, T. XIX 10,12.

⑦ Mitrevski D., 2013, 185, 206, fig. 61;

⑧ Mitrevski D., 2010, 139, T.II 3,4.

⑨ Kuzman P., 2013, 379, T.XV1-6, T.XVI 8,9,11.

⑩ Heurtly W.A., 1939, 172 (195) и 247, Т. XII (195) , 174 (197) , 179 (228) and 248, T.XIV (228, 183 (255)) , 187 (277, 278) , 189 (293-295) , 235 (477) , 237 (488) .

⑪ Čović B., 1987,237,240, T.XXIV (9,19) , 261 T.XXIX (20) .

stomach[1] and one handle appeared very rarely. They originate from similar samples found on the Toumbas in Pelagonia (e. g. Tumba in village Kanino) from the Middle Bronze Age.[2]

The amphorae with four profiled handles,[3] vertically placed, probably had influences by the eastern Balkan or Asia Minor regions.[4] The amphorae with a spherical body,[5] two vertical handles and two plastic applications appeared in the Transitional period from Bronze to Iron Age. Such samples were found at the sites of Kritsana and Saratse in northern Greece[6] and at the sites of Donja Brnica (Kosovo) and Togočevac.[7]

The pots without handles,[8] with an elliptical shape and a rounded bottom, also originate from Asia Minor, where they had a long period of use (Tara II-V)[9]. Fire containers (puranoi)[10] found at this site are fragmented, except one reconstructed sample, usually composed of two parts and placed on the fire. Such samples were found in Varos - Prilep, Manastir near Veles, Vardino and Tumba Asiros in northern Greece, dating back to the Late Bronze Age and in the Transitional period from Bronze to the Early Iron Age (12th - 10th century BC).[11]

Besides pottery, a large quantity of weights made of clay has been found. Most often they had a circular shape - discoid with two perforations, used for fishing and biconical beads with an elongated shape used for spinning and weaving.[12]

Stone and flint artifacts are not numerous. Several stone axes and a stone digger were discovered. The technology and shape of these objects had a Neolithic tradition. Besides stone axes, several stone bricks, one amulet made of stone and a grain hand mill were discovered.[13]

The metal objects were very rare, so one bronze harpoon and one copper ax, an iron stitch and a fragment of a double bronze needle with a triangular head were preserved.[14] The bronze ax is a chronologically sensitive object and can be treated as *terminus a quo* for settlement date. Such axes were found in the layer of Troy VI, dated between 1800 and 1300 BC. The needles with a triangular head were found very often at the Iron Age sites in the Vardar - Moravian valley at the end of the 7th and in the 6th centuries BC, and they represent *terminus ad quem* for the existence of the settlement.

---

[1]   Kuzman P., 2013, 380, T.XIV 9-12, Fig.54,55.
[2]   Simoska D., Sanev V., 1976, 51-52, fig.251.
[3]   Kuzman P., 2013, 380, T.XXII 1.
[4]   Troia, 1992, 56 (88).
[5]   Kuzman P., 2013, 377, Fig.52.
[6]   Heurtly W.A., 1939, 171 (176, TXIII/176), 189 (299), 222, 172 (195) и 247, T. XII (440, Pl. XV/440).
[7]   Garašanin M., 1983d,733, T.CI, 6.
[8]   Kuzman P., 2013, 380-381, T.XX 3, T.XXX 2, T.XXI 1,2.
[9]   Troia, 1992, 68 (155).
[10]   Kuzman P., 2013, 377, T.XXVI 10-12, 14, 16, T.XXV 1.
[11]   Kitanovski, 1986, 26, fig. 7; Jovčevska T., 2008, 92, T. XXIII; Heurtly W.A., 1939, 234 (474), 252, Pl. XXII (474); Wardle K.A., Wardle D., 2007, 467, 470 (pl.5).
[12]   Kuzman P., 2013, T.XXVII 1-18; T.XXVII 19-26.
[13]   Kuzman P., 2013, T.XXVII 27-41.
[14]   Kuzman P., 2013, T.XXVIII 1-4.

Conclusion

The underwater archaeological researches at the site Plocha Michov Grad in the Bay of Bones are one of the most comprehensive surveys done in the Balkans. Therefore, in the period from 2008 to 2009, a reconstruction of the lake settlement, which existed in the period of the Late Bronze Age and the Early Iron Age, was made (Fig.5) .

Fig.5

The way the settlement (dwellings) in the Bay of Bones was set on a wooden platform is different from the settlement of the site Vrbnik on the other side of the lake, where the houses were placed on each platform. Several settlements of this type have been noticed in Europe, such as lake dwellings in Mailen on the Zurich Lake,[1] where Ferdinand Keller proved that fishermen's houses were not isolated but organized like lake settlements. These types of settlements can also be found in the Bronze Age settlement in Fiave, discovered in the region of the former Lake Carrera in the Trentino district of northern Italy, where the wooden buildings were placed on piles in the lake.[2] According to these researches, we can conclude that the settlements can be: offshore lifted on piles near the lakes or lake settlements, raised on piles and platforms, torture settlements raised on piles and rivers or river coastal ones also raised on piles. On the territory of Lake Ohrid only the settlement in the Bay of the Bones and the Gulf of the Bay, Trpejca are lake settlements, the others, such as the Gulf of Bombs in Peshtani and Bučila in Sv.Naum are offshore settlements, whereas Penelopa in Ohrid and Vrbnik in Struga are offshore - torture settlements. Only the settlements located at the sites of Crkveni Livadi in Vranishta and Ustie of Drim are river coastal settlements.[3]

At this phase we can conclude that the phenomenon of the lake settlements began in the 5ᵗʰ millennium BC and ended in the 1st millennium BC, i.e. 7ᵗʰ century BC.

This concentration of settlements in the region of Lake Ohrid is certainly a potential for further

---

① Rouff U., 2004, 9.
② Rouff U., 2004, 19-21.
③ Kuzman P., 2013, 350.

dendrochronological analyses, as well as new underwater explorations.

Bibliography:

Garašanin M., (1983)   Paraćinska grupa, Praistorija Jugoslovenskih Zemalja IV, Bronzano doba, Sarajevo

Jovčevska T., (2008)   Manastir –necropolis from the Transitional period from Bronze to the Iron Age, Veles

Kitanoski B., (1983)   Prehistoric pottery depot in Prilep, Macedoniae Acta Archaeologica 6, Skopje, 21-36.

Kuzman P., (2013)   Praehistorian palafitte settlements in Macedonia, Skopje, 297-430.

Mitrevski D., (2010)   Archaeological excavations in Gloska Chuka, Macedonia Acta Archaeologica 19, Skopje, 127-146.

Mitrevski D., (2013)   Prehistory in the Republic of Macedonia, 83-266.

Van de Noort R., & O' Sullivan A., (2006)   Rethinking Wetland Archaeology, London

Papazoglou F., (1957)   Macedonian towns in Roman time, Skopje

Porozanov K., (1997)   Подводната археология-разговор със „света на мълчанието", Човекът зед находките-Археологията днес и утре (Иван Гацов) , Интела, София, 155-165.

Rouff U., (2004)   Lake-Dwelling studies in Switzerland since 'Meilen 1854', Living on the lake in prehistoric Europe (Menotti) , London-New York.

Simoska D., Sanev V., Kitanoski B., Sarzoski S., (1976)   Prehistory in Macedonia (Catalogue) ,

Troia (1992)   Catalog – Ausstellungskataloge der Prahistorischen Staatssammlung Herausgegeben von Hermann Dannheimer, Band 21

Herodotus V   History, Subitica 1966

Heurtly W.A., (1939)   Prehistoric Macedonia, Cambridge

ČovićB., (1987)   Grupa Donja Dolina-Sanski most, Prahistorija Jugoslovenskih Zemalja IV, Željeszno doba, Sarajevo.

Wardle K.A., Wardle D., (2007)

从考古遗址到世界文化遗产：良渚古城的价值认定与保护利用 ①

中国　浙江省文物考古研究所　刘　斌 ②　王宁远　陈明辉

摘要

　　良渚古城遗址八十多年来的考古发掘工作充分揭示了遗址的重要价值，证明它是良渚文明的都邑性遗址，是实证五千多年文明史的圣地，是规模庞大的世界级城址，遗址的价值得到国内外学界的高度关注和广泛认可。在各方面的配合和努力下，良渚古城遗址的文物保护也随着考古工作的开展而不断推进，并取得了举世瞩目的成就。2012 年以来良渚古城遗址申遗工作的正式启动，良渚博物院展陈完成更新换代，良渚国家考古公园建设也已大体成型，良渚古城遗址已进入全面展示和利用的新时代。

　　关键词：良渚古城　考古　良渚考古　考古遗址　价值认定　保护利用　展示　申遗　世界文化遗产

　　良渚古城遗址是我国已公布的 500 余处大遗址中重要的史前时期大遗址。近年来，有关大遗址考古与大遗址保护越来越受到国家文物局和考古界的重视。2005 年财政局、国家文物局联合发布的《大遗址保护专项经费管理办法》中指出"大遗址"定义为"价值突出、规模体量较大、影响深远的遗址，主要包括反映中国古代历史上涉及政治、宗教、军事、科技、工业、农业、建筑、交通、水利等方面重要历史文化信息的大型聚落、城址、宫室、陵寝、墓葬等遗址、遗址群及文化景观"。大遗址的产生除了历史上著名的古城址（如汉唐长安城）、古墓葬（如历代帝王陵）外，史前时期大遗址的发现与确立主要依赖于考古工作的积累，是一个从无到有、从小到大的积累过程。良渚古城遗址便是如此。

　　良渚遗址通过八十余年的考古发掘与研究，大致可分为三大阶段：单一遗址的发现，遗址群聚落的确认，良渚古城及水利系统的发现及总体格局的认识。在研究方法、技术手段和研究内容上，良

　　①　本文正式发表于《东南文化》2019 年 1 期。

　　②　刘斌　1985 年毕业于吉林大学历史系考古专业。1985 年至今一直在浙江省文物考古研究所从事考古工作，现任浙江省文物考古研究所所长、良渚遗址考古与保护中心主任。曾参加过浙江余杭反山、瑶山遗址，湖北宜昌中堡岛等著名遗址的考古发掘工作，主持发掘过浙江海宁荷叶地、海宁余墩庙、余杭汇观山，嘉兴南河浜等许多重要的新石器时代遗址。2006 年至 2007 年主持良渚遗址的钻探调查，发现了良渚古城。自 2008 年至今一直主持良渚古城的考古发掘工作。主要著述有：《南河浜——崧泽文化遗址发掘报告》，文物出版社，2005 年；《中国出土玉器全集——浙江卷》，科学出版社，2005 年；《神巫的世界——良渚文化纵论》，浙江摄影出版社，2007 年。

渚遗址的考古也从以研究器物和遗迹为主，而走向多学科合作、关注动植物和气候等自然环境、遗址兴废过程与原因、材料分类与来源等全方位的全息式的考古模式。从 2007 年发现良渚古城开始逐渐揭示出了一座距今 5000 年的超大规模的古工国都城，实证中华五千多年的文明史。数十年来的考古实践证明，长期而扎实的考古工作是认识文化遗产、认定文化遗产价值的基础。而考古发现、研究与保护的互动，才能最终实现遗产价值，让古代遗产成为当今文化的一部分。

一、良渚考古与良渚古城遗址的价值认定

（一）良渚考古八十年历程

1936 年浙江西湖博物馆的施昕更先生（以下省略敬称）在余杭良渚镇一带进行调查，发现了十余处以黑陶为特征的新石器时代遗址，对其中 6 处遗址进行了小规模发掘，并出版了《良渚（杭县第二区黑陶文化遗址初步报告)》[①] 一书，成为良渚文化和浙江史前考古的发端。在传播论与黄河中心论旧史观的影响下，良渚一带的发现被认为是龙山文化向东南传播的一支。

20 世纪 50 年代，随着基本建设的蓬勃发展，中国的考古事业进入了黄金时代。长江下游地区发掘了十余处新石器时代的遗址。学界逐步建立起长江下游地区新石器时代的文化序列，并认识到与山东龙山文化等的差异性，1959 年夏鼐正式提出了 "良渚文化" 的命名 [②]。作为良渚文化命名地，良渚遗址于 1961 年被公布为浙江省重点文物保护单位。

浙江省文物考古研究所于 1979 年正式成立，于 1981 年发掘余杭瓶窑吴家埠遗址 [③]，发现了马家浜、崧泽和良渚文化的堆积与墓葬；并在当地建立工作站，从此良渚一带开始有了长期稳定的考古工作。随后组织了两次调查，新发现不少遗址，1986 年在 "良渚发现 50 周年会议" 上，王明达提出 "良渚遗址群" 的概念，并公布了 "已知的地点多达四五十处" [④]。

1973 年，南京博物院在江苏吴县草鞋山遗址第一次发现随葬玉琮、玉璧等大型玉礼器的良渚文化墓葬 [⑤]，良渚文化的玉器从此被认识。到 20 世纪 80 年代初期，学界先后在江苏吴县张陵山 [⑥]、武进寺墩 [⑦]、上海青浦福泉山 [⑧] 等地陆续发掘随葬玉器的良渚文化大墓。良渚文化的社会发展水平逐渐被认识。

浙江作为良渚文化的命名地，直到 1986 年才第一次在余杭反山遗址发掘到良渚文化的高等级墓地，出土了数以千计的精美玉器，尤其在反山 M12 的玉琮王和玉钺王上发现了完整的神徽形象，这对

---

① 施昕更：《良渚（杭县第二区黑陶文化遗址初步报告)》，浙江省教育厅 1938 年版。
② 夏鼐：《长江流域考古问题——1959 年 12 月 26 日在长办文物考古队队长会议上的发言》，《考古》1960 年第 2 期。
③ 浙江省文物考古研究所编：《余杭吴家埠新石器时代遗址》，《浙江省文物考古研究所学刊》，科学出版社 1993 年。
④ 王明达：《良渚遗址群田野考古概述》，余杭县政协文史资料委员会编《文明的曙光——良渚文化》，浙江人民出版社 1987 年。
⑤ 南京博物院：《江苏吴县草鞋山遗址》，《文物资料丛刊（第 3 辑）》，文物出版社 1980 年；南京博物院：《苏州草鞋山良渚文化墓葬》，《东方文明之光——良渚文化发现 60 周年纪念文集》，海南国际新闻出版中心 1996 年。
⑥ 南京博物院：《江苏吴县张陵山遗址发掘简报》，《文物资料丛刊（第 6 辑）》，文物出版社 1982 年。
⑦ 南京博物院：《1982 年江苏常州武进寺墩遗址的发掘》，《考古》1984 年第 2 期。
⑧ 上海市文物保管委员会：《福泉山——新石器时代遗址发掘报告》，文物出版社 2000 年。

于解读良渚玉器的纹饰内涵和器物造型具有划时代的意义[①]。

1987年，浙江省文物考古研究所在瑶山又发现了12座良渚文化的高等级墓葬，并且首次发现良渚文化的祭坛遗址[②]。1991年，在余杭瓶窑汇观山上又发现了与瑶山十分相似的良渚祭坛和墓地，从而使良渚祭坛的功能和性质得到进一步认识[③]。

图1　反山玉琮王上的神徽

图2　瑶山祭坛及墓地

1987年及1992—1993年，通过对莫角山遗址的发掘，学界认识到这个面积约30多万平方米、相对高度约10米的大型土台是良渚文化人工堆筑营建的大型宫殿基址[④]。如此规模宏大的建筑遗址以及与反山、瑶山、汇观山等出土的大量精美玉器，反映此地区应是良渚文化的中心所在。

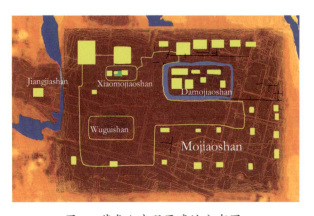

图3　莫角山宫殿区遗迹分布图

① 浙江省文物考古研究所反山考古队：《浙江余杭反山良渚墓地发掘简报》,《文物》1988年第1期。浙江省文物考古研究所：《反山》，文物出版社2005年。

② 浙江省文物考古研究所：《瑶山》，文物出版社2003年。

③ 浙江省文物考古研究所、余杭市文物管理委员会：《浙江余杭汇观山良渚文化祭坛与墓地发掘简报》,《文物》1997年第7期。

④ 杨楠、赵晔：《余杭莫角山清理大型建筑基址》,《中国文物报》1993年10月10日第版。浙江省文物考古研究所：《余杭莫角山遗址1992—1993年的发掘》,《文物》2001年12期。

从 20 世纪 80 年代末到 90 年代，良渚一带的考古工作几乎没有中断。1998—2002 年浙江省文物考古研究所对良渚一带约 50 平方公里的范围进行了拉网式的详细调查，共确认遗址 130 多处。

2006 年，葡萄畈遗址发现了一段良渚时期的古河道。对河岸进行解剖发现 3 米多高的河岸下面铺垫有一层石头，笔者推测葡萄畈村所在的南北向高地可能是良渚时期的苕溪大堤，也可能是围绕着莫角山的城墙。2007 年 3 月—11 月，经过发掘最终发现确认了四面城墙。2007 年 11 月 29 日由浙江省文物局和杭州市政府共同举行了新闻发布会，宣布发现了面积达 300 万平方米良渚古城。

自 2007 年之后，在国家文物局和浙江省文物局的大力支持下，良渚遗址的考古开始进入了长期的、有计划的考古阶段。随着良渚古城的发现，以往的以了解各个遗址的年代与性状的散点式的考古计划已无法适应新发现的要求，以古城为核心、厘清古城内外功能布局与发展过程，成为良渚古城发现以后的工作目标。因此，浙江省文物考古研究所于 2008 年在张忠培的指导下，按照"百年谋略"、"十年目标"、"三年计划"的方针，制定了良渚古城遗址的考古工作规划。十年来，浙江省文物考古研究所按照这一计划，总体勘探，重点发掘，先城外、后城内，逐渐厘清了以古城为核心的约 100 平方公里范围的遗址分布格局，以及古地貌、古环境等情况。

2010 年以来，通过对城内外 10.8 平方公里的勘探，摸清了良渚古城遗址的城墙、台地、河道的边界和演变过程；通过勘探和数字高程模型分析，发现了外郭城的城墙以及美人地等外郭城范围的遗址分布情况。经过对美人地、扁担山、里山等长条状台地的解剖发掘，确认了外郭城的堆筑形式、使用年代等情况。由于良渚古城西部紧邻瓶窑镇，目前仅确认围绕着良渚古城的北、东、南三面的 6.3 平方公里的外城。

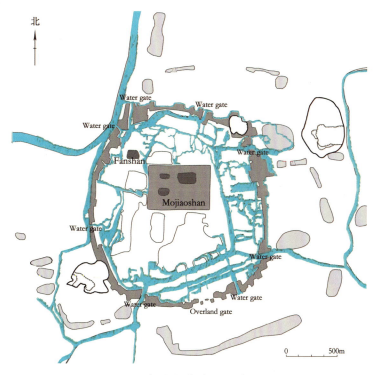

图 4　良渚古城城址区布局

2009 年，余杭彭公一带取土发现了岗公岭水坝，随后通过组织开展对其周边区域的调查，在岗公岭以西又发现了老虎岭、周家畈、石坞、秋坞等水坝遗址。2010 年初，发现岗公岭水坝堆筑的青泥是以草包裹的形式垒筑而成，经北京大学碳十四实验室测年确定为良渚文化时期。2013 年通过遥感分析和钻探，又发现鲤鱼山等另一组较低的水坝遗址，将这些连接两山的水坝与 1999 年确认的 5 公里长的塘山水坝相连接，最终我们厘清了由 11 条水坝构成的庞大的水利工程。2015 年浙江省文物考古研究所分别对鲤鱼山和老虎岭进行考古发掘，并在老虎岭发现了打破坝体堆积的良渚文化晚期的灰沟。11 条水坝的碳十四测年数据为距今 5100—4700 年。至此我们于 2016 年召开了新闻发布会，宣布发现了中国最早的水利系统。这一发现也使良渚遗址的范围扩大到了约 100 平方公里。

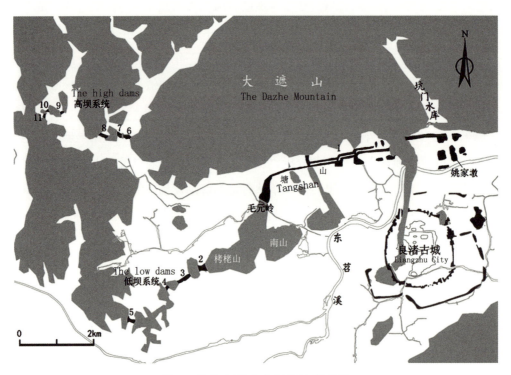

图 5　良渚古城及水利系统布局图

无论从其宏大的规模，还是从城市体系的复杂性及其建筑的工程量等而言，良渚古城都不亚于同时期的古埃及、苏美尔和哈拉帕文明；高等级的墓葬与玉礼器的发现也证实良渚时期甚至已经出现了统一的神灵信仰和森严的社会等级分化；如今学术界已普遍公认良渚文化已进入了早期国家社会[①]。

（二）多学科全息考古全方位揭示了良渚古城遗址的价值

良渚考古工作在大遗址考古理念的指导下，科技考古和多学科合作成为极重要的研究手段，取得

---

① 赵辉：《良渚的国家形态》，《中国文化遗产》2017 年第 3 期；Colin Renfrew，Bin Liu：The emergence of complex society in China：the case of Liangzhu，Antiquity 2018，92：975–990. 中文版见〔英〕科林·伦福儒、刘斌著，陈明辉、朱叶菲、宋姝、姬翔、连蕙茹译：《中国复杂社会的出现：以良渚为例》，《南方文物》2018 年第 1 期。

了显著的效果。

1. 考古测量控制网提高了测绘效率

随着良渚古城的确认，我们对良渚遗址的认识完成了遗址点→遗址群→都邑考古的跨越，考古工作的基本着眼点也相应的从对 130 多个遗址点的分散认识，发展到将整个遗址群作为一个特大型都邑遗址来认识。因此，其内部所有的发掘记录和研究必须建立在一个统一的考古测量控制系统之上。为此，我们与北京大学考古文博学院合作，建立了一个目前全国最大规模的田野考古测量控制系统，其实际应用范围为几百平方公里，并可根据需要无限扩大。

这套测量控制系统以良渚古城为中心，涵盖遗址区及周边范围。控制网分"区"、"块"、"方"三级。其中每个"区"为边长 2500 米的正方形，每"区"下分 25 个边长 500 米的"块"，"块"下又设 2500 个边长 10 米的"方"。"区"依坐标法编号，具有扩展性。控制网内的各项发掘的探方，都能各自对应唯一的探方编号。随着测量手段的发展，我们又对该系统的测控方式进行了改良。最初的控制网设计时，每区都需设置较高密度的固定测控点作测量控制，这种方式需要投入大量的人力和物力。后来我们使用 RTK（动态 GPS）设备，采用最新的 CORS 测量方式，实时引用测绘主管部门设置的测量基点的差分数据，不再埋设实体的加密控制点，从而在保证测量精度的前提下，极大地减少了投入，提高了测绘效率。

目前良渚遗址群内的所有考古发掘项目都是基于这套坐标系统进行记录的。

2. 地形图和地面影像为遗址分析及遗址规划保护提供了基础

遗址区矢量地图是建立地理信息系统（Geographic Information System，GIS）的基本要求。我们对遗址区进行测绘和航拍，并对原有的地图资料进行矢量化处理。目前我们已获得非常完备的各类地图资料，包括全余杭区 1：10000 比例、瓶窑和良渚两镇 380 平方公里的 1：2000 比例以及古城重点区 20 余平方公里的 1：500 比例的矢量地图。同时，我们也很关注对历史时期地图资料的收集，因为早期的地图可能保留原有的信息更丰富、破坏更少。我们收集了清代末期余杭地区的水系图、20 世纪 30 年的杭州地区都图地图、20 世纪 40 年代侵华日军 1：50000 比例的军用地图等资料，这些资料对现代实测地图具有很好的补充作用，对很多已被破坏消失的水道等信息都有记录。

数字正射影像是基础地理信息的另一种重要载体。我们除获得遗址群范围 GOOGLE 公司 60 厘米分辨率的地面影像外，陕西西安大地测绘及十月科技有限公司对古城及周边 120 平方公里范围进行了无人机航拍航测，获得了分辨率高达 8 厘米的高清数字正射影像图。

在全国各类大型遗址中，良渚地区可能是地图资料最为齐备的地区。这些基础地形信息的获取是 GIS 工作的前提，为遗址分析及遗址规划保护提供了基础。

3. 田野考古数据库系统满足了田野发掘和研究的实际需求

田野考古数据库是考古记录系统改进的一项重要工作。我们在 2003 年即开始以 ACCESS 方式自行设置田野考古的前端记录系统，随着十多年的改良和实践，我们的记录系统基本上已经可以满足田野工作的需要。与其他的一些类似软件比，田野考古数据库的系统因其基于田野发掘和研究的实际需求，由考古领队自己设计，所以在系统的易用程度、与实际考古工作流程的契合度、与考古工作各类表单的对应关系等诸多关键要素上，更符合实际考古工作的需要。在后期整理中，此系统在查询统计和纠错等环节的操作和界面简洁明了，通过与WORD软件的整合，各类考古表单的填写和考古报告的编写，均能做到一键完成，极大地提高了工作效率。目前经过若干个大型遗址发掘和整理过程的实践，此系统在维护和开放性等方面要优于专业开发的专用软件，是考古领队真正易于掌握且有效的工具。我们始终认为，一个考古软件系统的成功与否，关键在于考古领队和发掘人员是否愿意使用。而要领队和发掘人员愿意使用的前提是此软件可使考古记录工作量减少、在易用性和开放性具有优势，且符合考古工作的一般流程。

4. GIS技术成功寻找到良渚古城的外围结构

GIS在良渚遗址的考古工作中获得广泛应用，在良渚古城外围结构的寻找、水利系统的分析、溢洪道等结构的寻找中发挥了巨大作用。

2009年底，我们利用良渚古城区域1：500比例的线划图制作了数字高程模型（Digital Elevation Model，DEM），结果有惊人的发现。在这张图中，莫角山标准的长方形轮廓，以及其上的大小莫角山和乌龟山这三个高台显示得非常规清晰。更为重要的是，在这张范围相当局促的图里，我们可以明确地发现良渚古城东南部外侧存在着一个长方形的结构体，它由美人地、里山—郑村、卞家山分别构成北、东、南三面墙体，并和良渚古城的东墙和南墙相接续。经过对美人地等地点的发掘，证实这就是良渚古城外郭的一部分。

所谓"数字高程模型"，就是把地图上不同高程的范围依照某种色系的变化涂上不同的颜色。这样，即使一道城墙被破坏后呈若干分散的小段，若其基本高程一致，在DEM平面图上就显示为相同的颜色，这样就很容易把它们联系起来观察。DEM反应的是单纯的地表高程变化，所以能从复杂的地表植被和建筑的视觉干扰中，将纯粹的高程信息直观反应出来。因此，DEM是在本地区寻找城墙结构的最有效的方法。

发现水利系统之后，我们又利用DEM手段分别在高坝东区和西区发现了溢洪道的重要线索。根据水利工程的原理，良渚这种大规模的坝区一定会有溢洪道。水利专家认为，溢洪道无法设置在人工土坝之上，因为过水容易冲垮，推测可能会利用库区内低于坝高1—2米左右的石质山口用作溢洪。但是自然的石质山口通过一般的考古勘探等手段无法判断，因此，我们根据复原的坝顶高，将各个库区的数字地图制作DEM。通过设定，将低于坝高0.5、1、1.5、2、2.5的高程点，分别标注为特别的颜色，结果在高坝的东区和西区都发现了符合溢洪要求的山口。其中东区的溢洪道位于坝东侧的一处小山口，高程为28.9米，低于东组30米坝高1.1米。经过实地勘察，此山口为石质基础，后经水利测算，其宽度满足百年一遇的降水的泄洪要求，因此起到了溢洪道的作用，这是良渚人有意选择的结果。水库最高水位是由溢洪道高度决定的，因此，在明确了溢洪道高度之后，水利专家利用GIS软件计算出良渚水利系统的库区总面积为13.29平方公里、总库容4635万立方米。

5. 运用遥感（Remote Sensing，RS）手段完整揭示出良渚水利系统结构

遥感（Remote Sensing，RS）是良渚考古中应用的另一项重要手段。

在发现高坝系统后，我们利用解密美国 1960 年代的 coroana 间谍卫星影像进行观察。2011 年初，发现在高坝南面的约 3 公里的鲤鱼山存在一个明显具有人工痕迹的大型坝体。经钻探证实这个近 300 米长的坝体确是人工堆筑。同时发现在鲤鱼山的东西两侧共有 3 段人工坝体。这些坝体连接平原上的孤丘，坝高约 10 米，形成低坝系统。它不仅增加了坝体的数量，关键在于低坝通过其东面的小山体连接到塘山，又通过西侧绵延的低丘向北连接到高坝，从而揭示出塘山、高坝和低坝共同构成的良渚水利系统的完整结构，意义重大。

同时，RS 技术还被应用于良渚古城及塘山长堤的结构研究和功能分析。我们利用 corona 影像的立体像对古城和塘山进行高程复原，进而找到了良渚古城西水门位置，并经过勘探证实，并同时对塘山机结构和功能机理进行了分析。RS 技术成本低廉、影像直观，成为良渚大遗址考古中结构性研究中的最重要手段之一。

6. 动植物考古和良渚稻作农业调查全面再现良渚时期植物种类及古气候

通过对良渚遗址群内发掘出土的植物标本的鉴定及地层的孢粉分析，我们对良渚时期的植物种类及古气候有了全面的了解；并且获得了良渚时期的除水稻之外大量的其他可食用植物标本，如菱角、芡实、桃子、李子、甜瓜等。通过对遗址中出土的动物标本的研究，我们已经鉴定出 50 多种动物，其中猪骨占绝大多数。对动植物标本的研究为我们提供了良渚时期人们的食谱，同时也显示出良渚时期生动的生态景象。

通过对外郭城以内大面积的钻探调查，显示古城外郭之内区域现有高地基本为居住地，居住地之间为大面积水域，并无水稻种植。而钟家港等古河道发掘出土的大量陶片以及玉器、石器、漆木器、骨器等的加工废料和胚料，也反映了良渚城中当年的居住者除统治者外主要是工匠阶层。

另外，在城中宫殿区莫角山两侧及莫角山南面的池中寺遗址发现了总量达 20 多万公斤的碳化米废弃堆积，推测为宫殿区粮仓失火后的废弃堆积，说明良渚古城内有大量的粮食储备。我们与日本东京大学合作，对这些碳化稻米进行同位素分析，结果显示这些稻米来源于不同的产地。

7. 多学科合作的综合研究丰富了对良渚古城遗址的认识

近十年来，多学科合作研究是良渚考古的重要方面。我们和国际、国内很多科研单位和高校合作，从"资源与环境"、"技术与信仰"、"水利与工程"等方面，进行社会考古学角度的全面观察，使我们对良渚遗址的认识日益丰富和生动起来。

在古环境方面，我们对良渚古城出现之前的环境、气候、水文等进行研究，确定良渚文明出现的环境背景。在本地区良渚堆积之上普遍分布一层纯净的黄粉土，学界一般认为是洪水堆积层。通过分析，我们获知这层黄粉土的成分主要来自长江口的泥沙，是海相的咸水沉积物，且从濒临杭州湾的临平到西侧的良渚一带颗粒逐步变细，说明其成因应与钱塘潮有关。这为良渚后期的衰亡提供了一种可信的环境解释。

在地质考古方面，我们拓展了仅对石玉器出土物进行岩性鉴定的传统方法，对良渚整个区域的自然岩石分布进行了全面的勘察，从而在资源与环境的角度获得了很多的新信息。我们计划分三步完成石玉器的研究：第一步，研究作为建筑材料的良渚城墙垫石。岩石学家首先对古城四面城墙解剖点所有暴露的垫石（共 10524 块）进行岩性、磨圆度、块度的鉴定和统计，发现绝大部分垫石都是散石，很少为人工开采；地质学家对古城周边分水岭以内 200 平方公里的所有山地进行调查，形成区域岩性分布图，进而与垫石的质地磨圆度等对比，获知取石地点基本都是山脚和冲沟位置，并利用 RS 和地质及考古勘探资料恢复良渚时期的河道水系。考古学家根据垫石质地和形态对垫石进行分垄计算，推定良渚垫石的运载方式为竹筏运输；并根据河道及采石点位置，还原其可能的运输路径。通过实地的采集搬运和铺装等实验考古，进而计算整个垫石工程的用工量为 8.4 万工。

第二步是对整个 1000 平方公里 C 形盆地内的良渚文化石器进行全面鉴定，同时将野外岩性调查的范围扩大到整个区域的山地。目前研究尚在进行中，发现良渚时期人们对于石器石料的采集有非常明确的选择，并且若干种重要的石料经由跨流域的远距离运输而来。在石器石料的调查过程中，我们在天目山系还发现了玉矿的重要线索，为未来的第三步玉器来源研究奠定了重要基础。

在良渚水利系统研究过程中，我们还与河海大学共同成立"古代水利系统与工程技术"研究中心。在校地两处都设立联合实验室，将专业机构有机引入到良渚水利系统的研究中来，使我们对良渚水利系统的功能、结构、性质等的认识获得质的提高，并引起国家水利部门的高度关注。

二、良渚考古与良渚古城遗址的保护

距今约 4200 年，良渚古城所在的杭州余杭盆地遭遇了持续性的大洪水，良渚从此销声匿迹。直到战国时期，这一地区才开始重新有人类生活痕迹。汉代人口渐多，莫角山宫殿的高地上留下了许多汉六朝墓葬，这虽对良渚的史前遗址造成了一定程度的破坏，但并未伤及遗址的总体格局。南宋时期这一带成为临安城的郊区，我们在遗址边缘也发现了少量此期的房址和墓葬。因此良渚古城的核心区总体保存完好。

良渚古城保护的历程可以分为四个阶段。

第一阶段，从 1936 年到 20 世纪 80 年代，遗址区内的村镇仍然处于缓慢发展的状态，遗址与城镇化的矛盾并不突出，同时文物市场不发达，盗掘现象罕见。1958 年，杭州市民政局组建大观山果园，并兴建了社会福利院和儿童福利院。现知的良渚古城核心莫角山、皇坟山、姜家山等高地区域被划归果园，直到 2016 年均保持果园状态，客观上使这几处重要遗址避开了城镇化的侵蚀。1961 年良渚遗址被公布为浙江省重点文物保护单位。

第二阶段，20 世纪 80 年代到 90 年代中期，反山、瑶山遗址的发掘推动了遗址的保护力度。此阶段当地经济快速发展，城镇化的速率加快，城镇基本建设增加，村民富裕起来，兴起建房热潮，导致村镇建设规模不断扩大，人口密度不断增加，遗址保护及其与当地村民生产生活和经济发展的矛盾日益突出，遗址的保护问题成为考古和文物迫切需要解决的大问题。

这一时期的考古基本都是配合基本建设项目，主动性的考古发掘工作极少，但在此过程中，浙江省文物考古研究所始终有着较强的课题意识与保护意识。在反山、瑶山、汇观山、莫角山等发掘过程中，我们便决定采用保护性发掘；在发掘完重要遗迹后，即采用回填保护，并积极呼吁当地政府进行保护。余杭区政府对于保护遗址向来也高度重视，反山、瑶山发掘之后随即进行了征地保护，并在1987年成立了专门的保护机构——余杭县良渚文化遗址管理所，负责良渚遗址的日常巡查和保护工作，这一机构的设置对遗址保护起到了关键作用。

在1987年配合老104国道拓窗的考古发掘中，发现莫角山遗址，第一次认识到大观山所在的高地为良渚时期人工堆筑而成。在浙江省文物局和余杭政府的努力下，为了保护遗址，公路部门最后决定将104国道向南改道。1992—1993年为配合长命印刷厂扩建，在大观山果园台地的中心部位进行大面积揭露，发现了用一层沙一层泥夯筑的建筑基址，使我们进一步认识到莫角山遗址的重要性。在各方努力下，当地政府决定将长命印刷厂进行搬迁。

第三阶段，20世纪90年代中期至今，进入主动性保护为主的新阶段。

从20世纪90年代中期开始，学界对良渚遗址的研讨日益深入，其历史价值和地位也愈发彰显。1994年良渚遗址因其在中华文明起源阶段无与伦比的重要价值和保存的完整性，被国家文物局列入中国申报《世界遗产名录》预备名单。1996年国务院批准良渚遗址群为第四批全国重点文物保护单位。1996年在"纪念良渚文化发现六十周年国际学术研讨会"上，学界普遍认为良渚是中华五千年文明的曙光，甚至已进入文明时代[①]。

随着改革开放的深入，各地的建设热潮一浪高过一浪，地处杭州市郊的良渚、安溪、长命、瓶窑一带的城市化与工业化迅猛发展，乡镇企业迅猛发展，集镇与乡村急速翻新与膨胀。到20世纪90年代末，遗址群北侧的大遮山共出现大小石矿有30多家，使良渚每日笼罩在隆隆的炮声和弥漫的粉尘之中。2000—2002年，浙江省政府痛下决心，历经两年时间关停良渚遗址周边的31家石矿，彻底消除了采石经济对遗址环境风貌的破坏。

杭州市与余杭区政府为遗址保护制定了许多政策法规，同时建立和完善了有效的管理机制。1995年浙江省人民政府公布《良渚遗址群保护规划》，划定了33.8平方公里的保护区，并对遗址群内的建设规模进行了严格限制，从此良渚遗址进入了规划管理阶段。浙江省文物考古研究所专门成立了良渚工作站，负责良渚遗址的考古，并配合审批实地踏查、勘探出具考古意见。2001年9月，浙江省人民政府批准设立了杭州良渚遗址管理区，面积242平方公里，组建正区（副厅）级杭州良渚遗址管理区管理委员会，原良渚文化遗址管理所划归至良管委，更名杭州良渚遗址管理所，杭州良渚遗址管理区的设立是良渚遗址保护史上的里程碑，在管理区统一协调遗址保护与社会经济发展，为促进良渚古城遗址的长远保护提供了组织保证。2002年9月，成立杭州市公安局余杭分局瑶山派出所，专门负责打击针对良渚遗址的违法犯罪活动。2002年，杭州市颁布了《杭州市良渚遗址保护管理条例》，使良渚遗址保护有了专门的针对性法规，该条例于2013年进行了修订。2002年，浙江省政府成立良渚遗址

---

① 浙江省文物考古研究所编：《良渚文化研究——纪念良渚文化发现六十周年国际学术研讨会论文集》，科学出版社1999年。

保护专家咨询委员会，委托制定《良渚遗址保护总体规划》（该规划最终于 2013 年获得通过）。为配合保护规划的制定，浙江省文物考古研究所对良渚遗址群进行了进一步调查，制定了《良渚遗址 5 年考古工作规划》，提出了近期规划与远期目标，从而使良渚遗址的考古工作开始走向了有计划、有目标、有序的发展阶段。首创了文物保护补偿等新举措，2004 年以来，良管委颁布了《良渚遗址保护区文物保护补偿办法》，对保护范围内村社区的集体经济进行补偿奖励[①]。

第四阶段，21 世纪近十年，研究与保护走向国际。2006—2007 年良渚古城以及 2009—2015 年良渚古城外围水利系统的确认，使良渚古城遗址的规模位于同时期世界前列。2007 年之后，良渚古城考古开始进行系统的、持续的考古工作，每年的考古工作持续 300 天以上，考古工作人员也从原先的几人发展到如今的二十余人，包括 10 余名研究人员和 10 余名专业技工。良渚古城的研究方向除传统考古外，还包括了数字考古、动物考古、植物考古、地质考古、环境考古、文物保护等。同时还招聘勘探队伍，不间断地对遗址范围进行全覆盖式勘探和系统调查。

2009 年 6 月国家文物局在良渚召开"2009 大遗址保护良渚论坛暨良渚国家遗址公园启动仪式"。同时，国家文物局和浙江省文物局授牌成立了良渚遗址考古与保护中心。中心实行双重管理，由浙江省文物考古研究所和良管委共同管理。如今我们已经初步建成一个符合世界遗产地要求、具有国际标准的考古与保护的研究基地，开启了良渚遗址考古与保护的新篇章。良渚考古的实践证明，考古工作站的工作模式是一个地区的考古工作得以长期深入开展的有力保障，是百年大计的大遗址考古工作的内在要求。

三、良渚考古与良渚古城遗址的展示与利用

从 20 世纪 90 年代中期良渚文化博物馆建立开始，展示和利用便伴随着考古成果和遗址价值的深化而不断推进。1994 年，位于荀山南侧的良渚文化博物馆建成开放。随着考古发现与研究的进展，原博物馆已经无法容纳新的内涵。因此 2008 年又在异地兴建了新的场馆，并更名为良渚博物院。展陈设计与考古人员紧密合作，保证了学术性，吸收了良渚古城的最新成果，建成后的博物院每年吸引四五十万游客前来参观，成为宣传展示良渚文化的重要窗口。

2008—2017 年是良渚古城考古成果进展最迅速的十年。2008 年的展陈内容已经远远落后于良渚古城的最新认识，为配合良渚古城遗址申遗，2017 年 8 月，良渚博物院闭馆改陈，2018 年 6 月底最终完成重新开放。复旦大学的策展团队与良渚考古人员通力合作完成了改陈设计。使展陈尽量科学、完整地展示了良渚考古研究的新进展和新认知[②]。

良渚古城遗址展示的另一个重要组成部分是遗址公园内的现场展示，包括生态环境展示、遗址本

---

① 黄莉:《建立补偿机制有效保护遗址——良渚遗址文物保护补偿机制的实践与思考》,《浙江文物》2016 年第 1 期。
② 高蒙河、宋雨晗:《从"良渚全考古"到"良博全展示"——以良渚博物院 2018 年改陈策展为例》,《东南文化》2018 年第 6 期。

体、遗迹现场模拟展示、数字动画展示等。在遗址公园建设过程中，考古人员以张忠培提出的"遗址定性公园、公园衣饭遗址、切忌公园化遗址"的方针为原则，积极参与遗址公园的展示设计。

目前，良渚古城的环境整治已经初步完成，城内外可通视，站在古城的宫殿区，可清楚地看到古城正处于三山环抱之中，向东为开阔的平原，周边地形地貌一览无余，视野相当开阔。遗址本体展示已经基本完成，其中莫角山（包括大莫角山、小莫角山、乌龟山）、城墙、瑶山、反山、姜家山、池中寺、水坝遗址等均以绿植标识，遗址本体大部分明显可辨，遗产区的总体框架结构初显。

南城墙解剖点、反山剖面、老虎岭水坝剖面采取原真展示。反山王陵的墓葬采取复原展示，在墓地原地面覆土加高数十厘米，在原位置放置铜制墓坑，墓坑内以仿制的玉器、石器、陶器等随葬品按原有位置

图6　反山M12复原展示

摆放。每座墓均配以图文解读，基本复原了墓葬出土时的场景。

瑶山祭坛、大莫角山F2及小莫角山F17则采取地表模拟展示手段，同样在覆土加高的基础上，通过GRC手段原址在原位置展示出祭坛、墓坑或基槽、柱坑的形状，大致可模拟发掘出土时的土质、土色。

图7　瑶山祭坛及墓地地表模拟展示

莫角山宫殿区内的其余房屋台基和沙土广场、池中寺碳化稻谷堆积及房屋台基、姜家山和文家山墓地则均在原位置作了标识物展示，如房屋台基以树皮铺装展示、沙土广场以粗砂铺装展示、池中寺

的碳化稻谷堆积及房屋台基则以绿植标识、姜家山和文家山墓葬以卵石铺装展示等。

图 8 莫角山宫殿区标识物展示

四、结语

　　良渚遗址的考古、发掘、科学研究与保护、展示经历了八十多年的艰苦奋斗和不断探索,取得了丰硕的成果。尤其是 2013—2017 年,我们完成了《良渚古城综合研究报告》一书(将于近期出版)的撰写,为良渚古城遗址申遗文本的编撰提供了丰富详实的资料。根据最新考古成果,划定了 14.3 平方公里的包括城址、水利系统和瑶山在内的申遗区,基于城址、外围水利系统、分等级墓地、玉器这四个基本价值要素,认为良渚符合标准Ⅲ(能为延续至今或业已消逝的文明或文化传统提供独特的或至少是特殊的见证)和标准Ⅳ(是一种建筑、建筑或技术整体、或景观的杰出范例,展现人类历史上一个(或几个)重要阶段)这两条世界文化遗产价值标准。良渚古城遗址的申遗文本已于 2018 年 1 月 26 日正式上报联合国教科文组织,申遗工作进入最后的冲刺阶段。

　　良渚古城遗址的考古、保护、展示和申遗工作能取得今天的成绩,其中凝结了数代考古人的汗水和心血。历次重要的考古发现均都得到国家文物局、浙江省文物局以及浙江省杭州市、余杭区各级政府的大力支持,也得到了当地老百姓的理解、帮助与牺牲奉献。正是这一步步的发现和保护,从点到面,最终才有了今天这样一个保存基本完整的良渚古代王国。当我们站在这高高的五千年的良渚王国的宫殿基址上,我们的内心充满了敬畏和感恩!

From Archaeological Site to World Cultural Heritage: Value Identification of Liangzhu City and its Conservation and Utilization[①]

Liu Bin[②], Wang Ningyuan, Chen Minghui

China Zhejiang Provincial Institute of Cultural Relics and Archaeology

Abstract

The archaeological excavation of the Archaeological Ruins of Liangzhu City over the past 80 years fully demonstrates the important value of the site, since it proves that it is the capital site of Liangzhu culture, a sacred place that bears witnesses to the 5,000-year-old civilization, and a huge world-class urban site. The value of the site has been highly and widely recognized by scholars at home and abroad. Thanks to the cooperation and efforts of all parties concerned, the protection of cultural relics of Archaeological Ruins of Liangzhu City is advancing in lockstep with the archaeological work, and has scored remarkable achievements. The nomination for the Archaeological Ruins of Liangzhu City as a world heritage site was officially launched in 2012. The Liangzhu Museum has completed the updating of exhibition. The construction of Liangzhu National Archaeological Park has been basically completed. The Archaeological Ruins of Liangzhu City has entered a new era of comprehensive display and utilization.

Keywords: Liangzhu City, archaeology, Liangzhu archeology, archaeological site, value identification, conservation and utilization, presentation, nomination for inscription as world heritage site, world cultural heritage

---

① Officially published on the 1st issue of *Southeast Culture* in 2019

② Liu Bin. The author was graduated from Department of History and Archaeology from Jilin University in 1985. Since 1985, he has been engaged in archaeological works in Zhejiang Provincial Institute of Cultural Relics and Archaeology. He is now the head of this Institute, and also the Director of the Conservation Center for Liangzhu Archaeological Site. He has participated in several archaeological excavations at Fanshan and Yaoshan sites in Yuhang, Zhejiang province, Zhongbao Island site in Yichang, Hubei province and other famous sites. He presided over excavation of many important Neolithic heritage sites such as Heye Land and Shedun Temple in Haining, Huiguan Mountain in Yuhang and Nanhebang in Jiaxing, Zhejiang province. From 2006 to 2007, he led the drilling survey of Liangzhu site and found the ancient city of Liangzhu. He has led the archaeological excavation in ancient Liangzhu city since 2008. His major works are: Nanhebang - Report on Excavation of Songze Cultural Heritage, published by the Cultural Relics Press, 2005; Complete Collection of Chinese Unearthed Jade Artefacts - Zhejiang Volume, published by Science Press, 2005; Liangzhu Culture: World of Sorcerer, published by Zhejiang Photography Press, 2007.

Archaeological Ruins of Liangzhu City is an important prehistoric site among 500+ large sites in China. In recent years, the archaeology and conservation of major ruins have captured increasing attention from the China's National Cultural Heritage Administration and the archaeology community. The *Measures on the Administration of Special Funds for the Conservation of Major Ruins* jointly issued by the Ministry of Finance and State Administration of Cultural Heritage in 2005 state that "major ruins" are defined as "ruins with outstanding value, a large volume and far-reaching influence, mainly including ruins and ensemble of ruins such as large settlements, city sites, palaces, mausoleums, and tombs, as well as cultural landscapes that contain important historical and cultural information in politics, religion, military, science and technology, industry, agriculture, architecture, transportation, and water conservancy in the ancient Chinese history". Except the historically famous ancient city sites (such as imperial city of Chang'an during the Han and Tang dynasties) and ancient tombs (such as emperors' mausoleums), the discovery and establishment of major prehistoric ruins rely chiefly on the accumulation of archaeological work. It is a growth process from scratch. This is the case with Archaeological Ruins of Liangzhu City.

After over 80 years of archaeological excavation and research, the Archaeological Ruins of Liangzhu can be roughly divided into three stages: discovery of a single site, confirmation of the ruins ensemble cluster, and discovery of Liangzhu City and water conservancy system and the understanding of the overall pattern. In terms of research methodology, technical means and research content, the archaeology of the Archaeological Ruins of Liangzhu focuses on the study of implements and relics, and adopts the holographic archaeological model covering the multidisciplinary cooperation, focus on natural environments such as fauna and flora and climate, the rise and fall of ruins and its causes, and classification and sources of materials. Since the discovery of Liangzhu City in 2007, it gradually revealed a super-large capital of an ancient kingdom 5,000 years ago, demonstrating the history of Chinese civilization of more than 5,000 years. Archaeological practices over the decades prove that long-term meticulous archaeological work is fundamental to understanding cultural heritage and recognizing its value. The value of heritage is ultimately realized through the interaction between archaeological discovery, research and conservation, so that ancient heritage becomes part of contemporary culture.

I. Liangzhu archaeology and value identification of Archaeological Ruins of Liangzhu City

(1) Over 80 years of Liangzhu archaeology

In 1936, Mr. Shi Xingeng, of West Lake Museum in Zhejiang Province conducted a survey near Liangzhu Town in Yuhang. He discovered over ten Neolithic ruins characterized by black pottery, and carried out small-scale excavation of six sites. The book *Preliminary Report on the Black Pottery Culture Ruins in Liangzhu -*

Second District of Hangzhou[1] inaugurated the archaeology of Liangzhu culture and prehistoric period of Zhejiang. Under the influence of the communication theory and the Yellow River Center theory, the discovery of Liangzhu region is regarded as part of the southeastern spread of Longshan culture.

In the 1950s, China's archaeological work entered a golden age alongside the flourishing development of infrastructure construction. Over ten Neolithic sites were discovered in the lower reaches of the Yangtze River. The academic community gradually established the sequence of cultures in the Neolithic Age in the lower reaches of the Yangtze River, and recognized its difference with Longshan culture, among others. In 1959, Xia Nai officially put forward the name "Liangzhu Culture".[2]

As the place after which the Liangzhu culture is named, Archaeological Ruins of Liangzhu was designated as an important provincial heritage under the protection of Zhejiang Province in 1961.

Zhejiang Institute of Cultural Relics and Archaeology, formally established in 1979, discovered Wujiabu ruins in Pingyao Town, Yuhang in 1981,[3] and also discovered cultural accumulation and tombs of Majiabang, Songze and Liangzhu cultures. Long-term stable archaeological work began in Liangzhu area with the establishment of a local workstation. Many new ruins were discovered in the subsequent two investigations. At the "50th Anniversary of Discovery of Liangzhu" in 1986, Wang Mingda proposed the concept of "ensemble of archaeological ruins of Liangzhu" and announced that "there are over forty to fifty known sites".[4]

In 1973, Nanjing Museum discovered the Liangzhu culture tombs containing large sacrificial jade vessels such as long hollow piece of jades with rectangular sides and round flat piece of jades with a hole in its center[5] at Caoxie Mountain ruins in Wu County, Jiangsu Province. The jade articles of the Liangzhu culture gained public recognition since then. In the early 1980s, the academic community successively discovered the Liangzhu Culture tombs with burial jades in Zhangling Mountain,[6] Wujin Shidun in Jiangsu[7] and Fuquan

[1] Shi Xingeng: "Preliminary Report on the Black Pottery Culture Ruins in Liangzhu - Second District of Hangzhou", Zhejiang Provincial Department of Education, 1938 Edition.

[2] Xia Nai: "Issues on Archaeology of the Yangtze River Basin - Speech at the Meeting of Leaders of Cultural Relics and Archaeology Teams of the Yangtze River Office on December 26, 1959", Archeology, 1960, No. 2.

[3] Zhejiang Institute of Cultural Relics and Archaeology: "Neolithic Wujiabu Ruins in Yuhang", Journal of Zhejiang Institute of Cultural Relics and Archaeology, Science Press, 1993.

[4] Wang Mingda, Overview of Field Archaeology of Archaeological Ruins of Liangzhu, "The Dawn of Civilization - Liangzhu Culture" complied by Yuhang County CPPCC Literature and History Information Committee, Zhejiang People's Publishing House, 1987.

[5] Nanjing Museum: "Caoxie Mountain Site in Wu County, Jiangsu Province", "Books on Cultural Relics (volume 3) ", Cultural Relics Press, 1980; Nanjing Museum: "Tombs of Liangzhu Culture on Suzhou Caoxie Mountain", "The Light of Oriental Civilization - Collected Works on 60th Anniversary of the Discovery of Liangzhu Culture, Hainan International Press and Publication Center, 1996.

[6] Nanjing Museum: "Briefing on Excavation of Zhangling Mountain Site in Wu County, Jiangsu Province", "Books on Cultural Relics (volume 6) ", Cultural Relics Press, 1982.

[7] Nanjing Museum: "Excavation of Wujin Shidun Site in Changzhou, Jiangsu Province in 1982", "Archeology", 1984, No. 2.

Mountain in Qingpu District, Shanghai.[①]The social development of Liangzhu culture has gradually been recognized.

It was not until 1986 that Zhejiang, where Liangzhu culture is located, discovered the high-grade tombs of Liangzhu culture for the first time in Fanshan Ruins in Yuhang, and unearthed thousands of exquisite jade articles, especially the complete images of insignia on the chief long hollow piece of jade with rectangular sides and jade battle-axe at Fanshan M12. This is of epoch-making significance for interpreting the connotations of ornamentation on Liangzhu jade and shape of implements.[②]

In 1987, Zhejiang Institute of Cultural Relics and Archaeology discovered 12 high-grade tombs of Liangzhu culture at Yaoshan and discovered the altar ruins of Liangzhu culture for the first time.[③] In 1991, Liangzhu sacrificial altar and cemetery, highly similar to those at Yaoshan, were discovered on Huiguan Mountain in Pingyao, Yuhang, which assisted the recognition of function and nature of Liangzhu altar.[④]

Fig.1　Insignia on long hollow piece of jade
with rectangular sides unearthed in Fanshan

Fig.2　Yaoshan altar and cemetery

In 1987 and 1992-1993, the academic community realized that the large soil platform covering an area of over 300,000 square meters with a relative height of some 10 meters was the base of a large palace built during

---

① Shanghai Cultural Heritage Preservation Commission: "Fuquan Mountain - Briefing on Excavation of Neolithic Site", Cultural Relics Press, 2000.

② Fanshan Archaeological Team of Zhejiang Institute of Cultural Relics and Archaeology: "Briefing on Fanshan Liangzhu Cemetery in Yuhang, Zhejiang Province", "Cultural Relics", 1988, No. 1. Zhejiang Institute of Cultural Relics and Archeology: "Fanshan", Cultural Relics Press, 2005.

③ Zhejiang Institute of Cultural Relics and Archeology: Yaoshan, Cultural Relics Press, 2003.

④ Zhejiang Institute of Cultural Relics and Archaeology, Yuhang Cultural Heritage Management Committee: "Brief on Excavation of Huiguan Mountain Liangzhu Culture Altar and Cemetery in Yuhang, Zhejiang", "Cultural Relics" 1997, No. 7.

the Liangzhu culture through the excavation of Mojiao Mountain site.[1] This large-scale architectural site as well as a cornucopia of exquisite jade articles unearthed in Fanshan, Yaoshan and Huiguan Mountain show that this area should be the heart of Liangzhu culture.

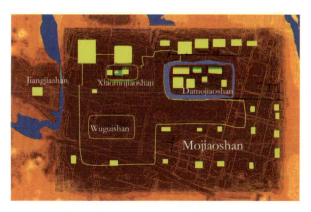

Fig. 3   Distribution of ruins of Mojiao Mountain Palace

From the late 1980s to the 1990s, the archaeological work in Liangzhu area was carried out almost nonstop. From 1998 to 2002, Zhejiang Institute of Cultural Relics and Archaeology conducted a detailed blanket survey of an area of about 50 square kilometers in Liangzhu area, and confirmed the existence of over 130 sites.

In 2006, the ancient river course during the Liangzhu Culture period was discovered at Putaofan Ruins. The anatomy of the river bank showed that there is a layer of stone under the 3-meter-high banks. The authors reckon that the north-south highland where Putaofan Village is located may be Tiaoxi enbankment during the Liangzhu period or may be the city wall surrounding Mojiao Mountain. After excavation, four city walls were confirmed from March to November 2007. On November 29, 2007, the press conference held by the Zhejiang Cultural Heritage Bureau and the Hangzhou Municipal Government announced the discovery of the Liangzhu City with an area of 3 million square meters.

Since 2007, the archaeology of Archaeological Ruins of Liangzhu has entered a long-term, planned stage with the support of the China's National Cultural Heritage Administration and Zhejiang Cultural Heritage Bureau. In the wake of the discovery of Liangzhu City, the previous scattered archaeological plans for understanding the ages and traits of various sites are inadequate to meet the requirements of new discoveries. An understanding of the functional layout and development process inside and outside the ancient city, with the ancient city as the center, becomes the work objectives following the discovery of Liangzhu City. Therefore, in 2008, Zhejiang Institute of Cultural Relics and Archaeology, under the guidance of Zhang

---

[1]   Yang Nan, Zhao Ye: "Large Building Site on Mojiao Mountain, Yuhang", "China Paper of Cultural Relics", October 10, 1993. Zhejiang Institute of Cultural Relics and Archeology: Excavation of Mojiao Mountain Site in Yuhang, 1992-1993, Cultural Relics, 2001, No. 12.

Zhongpei, formulated the archaeological work plan for the Archaeological Ruins of Liangzhu City pursuant to the "centennial strategy", "ten-year goals" and "three-year plan". In the past ten years, Zhejiang Institute of Cultural Relics and Archaeology has performed an overall exploration and focused excavation outside the city first and then inside the city according to this plan, and has gradually made clear the distribution of the site of some 100 square kilometers with the ancient city as the center, as well as the ancient landform, ancient environment, among others.

Since 2010, the exploration of an area of 10.8 square kilometers inside and outside the city shows the boundary and evolution process of walls, terraces and rivers at the Archaeological Ruins of Liangzhu City; through the exploration and digital elevation model analysis, the distribution of outer city walls as well as Meirendi ruins was presented. The anatomical excavation of long tablelands such as Meirendi, Biandan Mountain, and Lishan Mountain confirms the construction forms of the outer city wall and period, among others. As the western Liangzhu City abuts on Pingyao Town, only the outer city of 6.3 square kilometers on the north, east and south sides of Liangzhu City is confirmed.

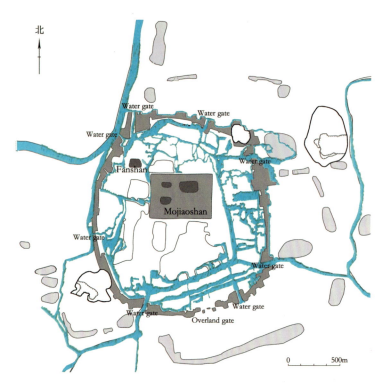

Fig.4　Layout of the Liangzhu City Ruins

In 2009, Ganggongling dam was discovered in Penggong, Yugong. The survey of its surrounding areas revealed the dam sites such as Laohuling, Zhoujiafan, Shiwu and Qiu wu to the west of Ganggongling. In early 2010, it was found that blue mud stacked at Ganggongling dam was in the form of grass bags. It was determined by the Carbon-14 Dating Lab of Peking University, belonging to the Liangzhu Period. In 2013, remote sensing analysis and drilling showed that another group of lower dam sites, such as Liyushan were discovered. These dams connecting the two mountains were connected with the 5 km long Tangshan dam confirmed in 1999. Finally, we ascertained the huge water conservancy project composed of 11 dams. In 2015, Zhejiang Institute of Cultural Relics and Archaeology carried out archaeological excavations on Liyushan and Laohuling respectively, and discovered the late Liangzhu culture ash ditch that broke the dam accumulation in Laohuling. The 11 dams can be traced back 5100-4700 years ago according to the Carbon-14 dating data. We held a press conference in 2016 to announce the discovery of China's earliest water conservancy system. This discovery expanded the size of the Archaeological Ruins of Liangzhu to some 100 square kilometers.

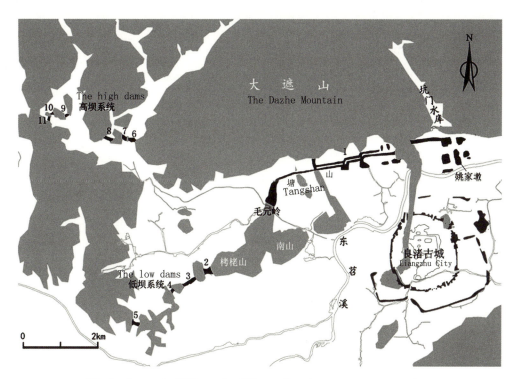

Fig.5　Layout of Liangzhu City and water conservancy system

Whether it be the grand scale, the complexity of the urban system and the amount of buildings, Liangzhu City is not inferior to the ancient Egyptian, Sumer and Harappan civilizations during the same period; high-grade tombs and jade sacrificial vessels discovered also confirmed that a unified divinity belief and a strict social hierarchy existed in the Liangzhu period. It is universally accepted in the academic community that the Liangzhu culture was an early state society.[1]

---

[1]　Zhao Hui: "State Form of Liangzhu", "China Cultural Heritage", No. 3, 2017; Colin Renfrew, Bin Liu: The emergence of complex society in China: the case of Liangzhu, Antiquity 2018, 92: 975-990., "Cultural Relics in Southern China" No. 1, 2018.

(II) Multi-disciplinary holographic archaeology demonstrates the value of Archaeological Ruins of Liangzhu City

Under the guidance of archaeological concept of the major sites, scientific archaeology and multidisciplinary cooperation become crucially important research methodology and yielded remarkable results.

1. Archaeological survey control network improves survey efficiency

After Liangzhu City was confirmed, our recognition of the Archaeological Ruins of Liangzhu spanned site location → site complex → archaeology of capital. The focus of the archaeological work also shifts from the scattered understanding of over 130 sites to the recognition of the entire site complex as the site of a huge capital. Therefore, all internal excavation records and research must be based on a harmonized archaeological survey control system. To this end, we cooperated with Peking University's School of Archaeology and Museology in setting up China's largest field archaeological survey control system, which can cover several hundred square kilometers in practice and can be scaled up infinitely as needed.

This survey control system, centering on Liangzhu City, covers the area of the ruins and its surroundings. The control network is divided into "zone", "block" and "square". Each "zone" is a square with a side length of 2,500 meters. Each "zone" is divided into 25 "blocks" with a side length of 500 meters. Each "block" has 2,500 squares with a side length of 10 meters. The "zone" is numbered according to the coordinate method and is scalable. The square for each excavation in the control network corresponds to a unique square number. With the improvement of measurement methods, we improved the measurement and control methods of this system. In the initial control network, each zone has a high-density fixed measurement and control point for measurement control, which requires immense manpower and material resources. Later, we used RTK (dynamic GPS) equipment, and adopted the latest CORS measurement method. The differential data on measurement base points set by the surveying and mapping departments are referenced in real time, without embedded physical dense control points. This greatly curtails input and improves mapping efficiency under the condition of ensuring measurement accuracy.

All archaeological excavations for the Archaeological Ruins of Liangzhu are recorded based on this coordinate system.

2. Topographic maps and ground images provide the basis for site analysis and site planning and conservation

The vector map of the ruins is the basic requirement for building the Geographic Information System (GIS). We surveyed and made aerial photography of the site area and performed vectorization on the original map data. At present, we have obtained a full variety of maps, including the vector maps of whole Yuhang District at a scale of 1:10000 , 380 square kilometers of Pingyao and Liangzhu towns at a scale of 1:2000 , and over 20 square kilometers of the key area of the ancient city at a scale of 1:500 . At the same time, we collected the map data in the historical periods, in that these early maps may contain more original information. We collected data such as the water system map in the Yuhang area at the end of the Qing Dynasty, the map of Hangzhou in the 1930s, and the military map at a scale of 1:50000 by the Japanese invaders in the 1940s. The information is a good complement to the modern measured maps, as it contains information on many waterways that were destroyed and disappeared.

Digital orthoimages are another key source of basic geographic information. We obtained the 60 cm resolution ground images of the ruins cluster from GOOGLE. Also, Xi'an Dadi Surveying and Mapping Co., Ltd. and Octcoo Company carried out aerial photography and survey of the ancient city and the surrounding area of 120 square kilometers, and obtained HD digital orthoimage map with a resolution of 8cm.

Of the large-scale sites nationwide, the Liangzhu area may have the most comprehensive map data. The acquisition of basic topographic information is a precondition for GIS work, providing the basis for site analysis and site planning and conservation.

3. Field archaeological database system satisfies the actual needs of field excavation and research

The field archaeological database is a key part in the improvement of archaeological record system. In 2003, we began to set up the frontend record system for field archaeology through ACCESS. After more than a decade of improvement and practice, our record system can basically suit the needs of field work. Compared to other similar software, the field archaeological database system was designed by archaeological team based on the actual needs of field excavation and research. Therefore, it better meets the needs of actual archaeological work in terms of the ease of use, the compliance with actual archaeological workflow, and correspondence to the various forms and sheets for archaeological work. In the subsequent arrangement, this system has simple and clear operations and interface in such links as query statistics and error correction. Through the integration with WORD documents, the filling of archaeological sheets and forms and preparation of archaeological reports can be completed easily, greatly boosting the work efficiency. At present, after its application to the excavation of several large-scale sites and data organization, this system is proved to be superior than professional software in terms of maintenance and openness, and is a truly easy-to-use effective tool for archaeological teams. We consistently believe that the key to the success of archaeological software lies in the willingness of archaeological leaders and excavation personnel to use it. Team leaders and excavation personnel use software on the condition that the software can cut down the archaeological record workload, has advantages in ease of use and openness, and follows the general process of archaeological work.

4. Peripheral structure of Liangzhu City is discovered with GIS technology

GIS has been widely applied to archaeological work of Archaeological Ruins of Liangzhu, and has played a vital role in the search for peripheral structure of Liangzhu City, the analysis of water conservancy system, and the search for spillway structures.

At the end of 2009, we harnessed the 1:500 scale line map of Liangzhu City to produce the Digital Elevation Model (DEM) , with staggering results. In this map, the standard rectangular profile of Mojiao Mountain, as well as the three elevations of large and small Mojiao Mountains and Turtle Mountain is clearly shown. More importantly, in this small-scale map, we can clearly see a rectangular structure on the outer side of the southeastern Liangzhu City. Meirendi, Lishan-Zhengcun and Bianjiashan constitute north, east and south walls and are connected to the east and south walls of Liangzhu City. The excavation of places such as Meirendi verifies that this is part of Liangzhu City.

The so-called "Digital Elevation Model" applies different colors to the range of different elevations on the map according to the changes in a certain color scheme. Even if a broken wall is shown in many scattered segments, it will be displayed in the same color on the DEM if the basic elevations are consistent. It is easy to link them up for observation. The DEM reflects simple changes in surface elevation. It can intuitively reflect the pure elevation information from among complex surface vegetation and architectural disturbances. Therefore, DEM is the most effective way to discover the wall structure in this region.

After the water conservancy system was discovered, we found key clues to the spillway in the eastern and western areas of the high dam using DEM. According to the principle of water conservancy project, there must be a spillway in the large dam area in Liangzhu. Water conservancy experts hold that the spillway cannot build on the artificial earth dam, because it can be easily washed away by water. it is presumed that the stone mountain pass lower than the dam by 1-2 meters in the reservoir area may be used as spillway. However, natural stone mountain pass cannot be judged using general archaeological exploration means. Therefore, we made DEM for the digital maps of each reservoir area based on the restored dam height. The elevation points lower than the dam height by 0.5, 1, 1.5, 2, and 2.5 are marked with special colors. Finally, the mountain pass as the spillway was found in the eastern and western areas of the high dam. The spillway in the eastern area is located at a small mountain pass to the east of the dam, with an elevation of 28.9 meters, which is lower than the east 30-meter high dam by 1.1 meters. After field investigation, this mountain pass has a stone foundation. Through water conservancy calculation, its width meets the flood discharge requirements for once-in-a-century rainfall. Therefore, it serves as a spillway. This was especially chosen by Liangzhu people. The maximum water level of the reservoir depends on the height of the spillway. Therefore, after the height of the spillway is determined, water conservancy experts calculated the total reservoir area of the Liangzhu water system at 13.29 square

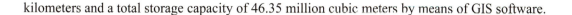
kilometers and a total storage capacity of 46.35 million cubic meters by means of GIS software.

5. Remote sensing (RS) means reveal the structure of Liangzhu water system

Remote Sensing (RS) is another key means in Liangzhu archaeology.

After the high dam system was found, we used the images from American Corona spy satellite for observation. In early 2011, it was found that there was a large dam with obvious man-made elements in Luyushan about 3 km south of the high dam. Drilling confirmed that the dam body of nearly 300 meters long was a man-made structure. At the same time, there were three man-made dams on east and west sides of Liyu Mountain. These dams, connected to the kop on the plain, are about 10 meters high, resulting in a low dam system. Not only was the number of dams increased. Importantly, the low dam is connected to Tangshan through the hills on the east side, and is connected to the high dam in the north through the low hills on the west side. This is of great significance as it reveals the complete structure of the Liangzhu water system composed of Tangshan, high dam and low dam.

At the same time, RS technology was used for the structural research and functional analysis of Liangzhu City and Tangshan embankment. We used the Corona images to restore the elevation of the ancient city and Tangshan, and found the location of the west water gate of Liangzhu City, which was confirmed through exploration. The structure and function mechanism of Tangshan were analyzed. The low-cost RS technology producing intuitive images is one of the most important means in the structural research of archeology of Liangzhu ruins.

6. Flora and fauna archaeology and survey of Liangzhu rice cultivation reproduce the plant species and geologic climate in Liangzhu period

We gain a comprehensive understanding of the plant species and geologic climate in the Liangzhu period through the identification of unearthed plant specimens from the Archaeological Ruins of Liangzhu and the sporopollen analysis of the strata; and obtained a wealth of edible plant specimens in addition to rice in the Liangzhu period, such as water chestnuts, fox nuts, peaches, plums, and melons. By studying animal specimens unearthed from the ruins, we have identified over 50 species of animals, mostly pig bones. The study of animal and plant specimens shows recipes for people in the Liangzhu period, and presents a vivid scene during the Liangzhu period.

A large-scale drilling survey within the outer city wall shows that the existing highland within the outer city wall is basically residential areas, with vast water body between the residential areas but no rice planting. A cornucopia of pottery shards as well as the processed wastes and raw materials of jade, stoneware, lacquers and wood artifacts, and bone implements unearthed from ancient rivers such as Zhongjiagang show that the inhabitants of Liangzhu City were mainly artisans apart from the rulers.

Moreover, a total of over 200,000 kilograms of carbonized rice waste were found on both sides of Mojiao Mountain in the palace area and the Chizhong Temple site in southern Mojiao Mountain. It is presumed to be the waste pile after a fire at the palace granary, indicating a wealth of grain reserves in Liangzhu City. We performed isotope analysis of these carbonized rice in cooperation with the University of Tokyo. The results show the rice from different origins.

7. Comprehensive multidisciplinary study enriches our understanding of Archaeological Ruins of Liangzhu City

In the past decade, collaborative multidisciplinary research has been a key part of Liangzhu archaeology. We perform a comprehensive observation from the perspective of social archaeology in terms of "resources and environment", "technology and belief", "water conservancy and engineering", and so on in cooperation with many international and domestic research institutes and universities. This makes our understanding of the Archaeological Ruins of Liangzhu richer and vivid.

In terms of ancient environment, we studied the environment, climate, hydrology, among others before the emergence of Liangzhu City, and determined the environmental background to the emergence of Liangzhu culture. A layer of pure yellow silt is generally distributed on the Liangzhu accumulation in this region, which is generally regarded by the academic community as the flood deposit layer. After analysis, we know that the composition of this layer of yellow silt is mainly the sediment from the Yangtze River estuary, the saline sediment. The particles gradually thin from Linping adjacent to the Hangzhou Bay to the west side of Liangzhu, indicating that its formation is related to Qiantang River tidal bore. This provides a convincing environmental explanation for the demise of the late period of Liangzhu.

In terms of geological archaeology, we expanded the traditional method of lithology identification for unearthed stone and jade articles, and carried out a comprehensive survey of the natural rock distribution in the entire Liangzhu area, thereby obtaining much new information from the perspectives of resources and the environment. We plan to complete the study of stone and jade articles in three steps: The first step is to study the underlying stones of Liangzhu walls as building materials. Petrologists identified and counted the lithology, roundness and lumpiness of all exposed slabs (totaling 10,524 pieces) on the anatomical points of the four walls of the ancient city. It was found that a vast majority of underlying stones are loose stones, with rare artificially mined stones; geologists surveyed all the mountains in an area of 200 square kilometers within the watershed around the ancient city to generate a regional lithology map. It is then compared to texture, roundness and others of underlying stones. It was found that stones were basically obtained from the foot of the mountain and gullies. The RS and geological and archaeological exploration data were used to restore the river course system during the Liangzhu period. Archaeologists calculated the underlying stones by the ridge according to texture and shape of underlying stones. It is presumed that the underlying stones of Liangzhu were carried by bamboo rafts. The transportation routes can possibly be restored according to the river course and location of quarrying locations. Through the experimental archeology such as field transport and paving, it can be calculated that the entire amount of labor used for underlying stone project is 84,000 workers.

The second step is to comprehensively identify Liangzhu Culture stoneware in the 1000 square kilometer C-shaped basin, and extend the scope of the field lithology survey to the entire region. The research is still ongoing. It is found that during the Liangzhu period, people had express purpose in gathering stone materials, and important stones were transported over long distances across the basins. During the investigation of stoneware, we discovered important clues to jade mines in the Tianmu Mountain System, which laid a key groundwork for the future research on the source of jade in the third step.

During the research of Liangzhu water system, we also set up the "Ancient water conservancy system and engineering technology" research center with Hohai University. A joint lab was set up in the university and locally. Professional organization was organically introduced into the research of the Liangzhu water system to greatly help us understand the function, structure and nature of the Liangzhu water system. It also attracted the attention of the national water conservancy authorities.

II. Liangzhu archaeology and conservation of Archaeological Ruins of Liangzhu City

The Yuhang Basin in Hangzhou, where Liangzhu City is located, was hit by a sustained great flood some 4200 years ago, and Liangzhu vanished without a trace thereafter. It was not until the Warring States period that this region saw human settlement again. As the population in the Han Dynasty grew, many Han and Six Dynasties tombs were preserved on the high grounds at Mojiao Mountain Palace. Much as this caused damage to the prehistoric ruins of Liangzhu, it did not compromise the overall pattern of the site. During the Southern Song Dynasty, this region was a suburb of Lin'an City. We also found some house sites and tombs at the edge of the ruins. Therefore, the central area of Liangzhu City remains generally intact.

The history of conservation of Liangzhu City can be divided into four stages.

In the first stage, from 1936 to the 1980s, the villages and towns in the site area were developing slowly, and there was no prominent conflict between the site and urbanization. At the same time, the cultural relic market was underdeveloped, with rare theft excavation. In 1958, the Hangzhou Municipal Civil Affairs Bureau built Daguanshan Orchard and the social welfare institution and children's welfare institution. The existing high ground area in the center of Liangzhu City such as Mojiao Mountain, Huangfen Mountain, and Jiangjia Mountain were placed under the jurisdiction of the orchard and the state of the orchard was maintained until

2016. As a result, these important sites are not affected by urbanization. Archaeological Ruins of Liangzhu was designated as an important provincial heritage site under the protection of Zhejiang Province in 1961.

In the second stage, from the 1980s to the mid-1990s, the excavation of Fanshan and Yaoshan sites promoted the conservation of the ruins. At this stage, the local economy developed apace, urbanization deepened, and the construction of urban infrastructure increased. As the villagers became rich, there was a wave of housing boom, resulting in the expansion of villages and towns and higher population density. There was a more prominent conflict between site conservation and the work and life local villagers and economic development. The conservation of the site is an urgent issue for archaeology and cultural relics.

Archaeology at this stage basically supports the infrastructure construction projects, with little initiative for archaeological excavation. In this process, however, Zhejiang Institute of Cultural Relics and Archaeology has a strong awareness of the subject and conservation. In the excavation of Fanshan, Yaoshan, Huiguan Mountain and Mojiao Mountain, we decided to adopt protective excavation; after important relics were discovered, we adopted backfill protection and appealed to the local government for protection. The Yuhang District Government also set great store by the protection of the site. After the excavation of Fanshan and Yaoshan, land acquisition was carried out immediately for conservation purposes. Liangzhu Cultural Relic Management Office of Yuhang County, a special conservation institution established in 1987, is responsible for routine inspection and protection of the Archaeological Ruins of Liangzhu. The establishment of this institution plays a key role in conservation.

In 1987, Mojiao Mountain site was discovered during the archaeological excavation for the widening project of the old National Highway 104. For the first time, it was found that the highland where Daguan Mountain is located was artificially structured during the Liangzhu period. Thanks to the efforts of Zhejiang Institute of Cultural Relics and Archaeology and the Yuhang Government, the highway department decided to divert the National Road 104 southwards to protect the site. For the sake of the expansion of Changming Printing Factory in 1992-1993, a large area in the center of Daguanshan Orchard was exposed. It was found that there was a building base with layers of sand and soil, making us aware of the importance of Mojiao Mountain site. Under the efforts of all parties, the local government decided to relocate Changming Printing Factory.

The third stage, from the mid-1990s to the present, is a new stage of proactive conservation.

Since the mid-1990s, the academic community has been carrying out in-depth study of Archaeological Ruins of Liangzhu, and the historical value and status are increasingly exhibited. In 1994, Archaeological Ruins of Liangzhu was included by China's National Cultural Heritage Administration in the tentative list of China's nomination for the World Heritage Site due to its unparalleled value and integrity at the beginning of the Chinese civilization. In 1996, the State Council designated the Archaeological Ruins of Liangzhu Group one of the fourth batch of important heritage site under state protection. At the International Symposium on Commemorating the 60ᵗʰ Anniversary of the Discovery of Liangzhu Culture in 1996, the academic community generally held that Liangzhu was the dawn of the 5000-year-old Chinese civilization and even entered the age of civilization.[①]

As reform and opening up deepens, the construction boom sweeps the whole country. Liangzhu, Anxi, Changming and Pingyao in the suburbs of Hangzhou see robust urbanization and industrialization. Township enterprises are developing at a fast clip, and towns and villages see rapid transformation and expansion. By the end of the 1990s, there were over 30 large and small stone mines on Dazhe Mountain on the north side of the site, bombarding Liangzhu with rumbling sound and immense dust every day. From 2000 to 2002, the Zhejiang Provincial Government decided to shut down 31 stone mines near the Archaeological Ruins of Liangzhu in two years, removing the destruction of the quarrying economy on the environment of the ruins.

Hangzhou and Yuhang District governments have formulated a host of policies and regulations for the conservation of ruins, and established sound effective management mechanisms. In 1995, the Zhejiang Provincial People's Government promulgated the *Conservation Plan for Archaeological Ruins of Liangzhu*, which designated a protected area of 33.8 square kilometers and imposed strict restrictions on the construction inside the site cluster. The planning and management stage of Archaeological Ruins of Liangzhu began since then. Zhejiang Institute of Cultural Relics and Archaeology set up Liangzhu Workstation which is responsible for the archaeology of the Archaeological Ruins of Liangzhu, and issues archaeological opinions on the field survey and exploration. In September 2001, the Zhejiang Provincial People's Government approved the establishment of the Archaeological Ruins of Liangzhu Management Area in Hangzhou, covering an area of 242 square kilometers. The district-level (deputy department-level) Management Committee of Archaeological Ruins of Liangzhu Management Area was set up. The former Liangzhu Cultural Site Management Office was incorporated into the Management Committee and renamed Hangzhou Liangzhu Archaeological Ruins Management Office. Archaeological Ruins of Liangzhu Management Area is a milestone in the protection history of Archaeological Ruins of Liangzhu, and coordinates site protection and socio-economic development in the management area, in order to guarantee the long-term conservation of the Archaeological Ruins of Liangzhu City. In September 2002, the Yaoshan Police Station of the Yuhang Branch of Hangzhou Municipal Public Security Bureau was set up to combat crimes against Archaeological Ruins of Liangzhu. In 2002, Hangzhou government promulgated the *Regulations on the Administration of the Conservation of Archaeological Ruins of Liangzhu Hangzhou*, which serve as targeted regulations for the protection of Archaeological Ruins of Liangzhu. The regulations were revised in 2013. In 2002, the Zhejiang Provincial Government established the Expert Advisory Committee on Archaeological Ruins of Liangzhu Protection and commissioned the formulation of the *Master Planon the Conservation ofArchaeological Ruins of Liangzhu*

---

① Zhejiang Institute of Cultural Relics and Archaeology: "Study of Liangzhu Culture - Collected Theses of the International Symposium on the 60th Anniversary of the Discovery of Liangzhu Culture", Science Press, 1999.

(finally adopted in 2013) . In cooperation with the formulation of the conservation plan, Zhejiang Institute of Cultural Relics and Archaeology conducted investigation of the Archaeological Ruins of Liangzhu, and formulated the *Five-yearArchaeological Work Plan for Archaeological Ruins of Liangzhu*, which proposes short-term planning and long-term goals. This marks the planned, targeted, and orderly development stage for the archaeological work of the Archaeological Ruins of Liangzhu. It pioneered new measures such as compensation for protection of cultural relics. In 2004, the Liangzhu Management Committee promulgated the *Compensation MeasuresforCultural Relics Protection at the Protected Archaeological Ruins of Liangzhu* to compensate the collective economy of village communities inside the scope of protection.[①]

The fourth stage, in the past decade of the 21st century, marks the international research and protection. The confirmation of Liangzhu City in 2006-2007 and the surrounding water conservancy system of Liangzhu City in 2009-2015 put the Archaeological Ruins of Liangzhu City at the forefront of the world in terms of scale during the same period. After 2007, systematic and continuous archaeological work was initiated for Liangzhu City. The annual archaeological work lasted over 300 days, and archaeological staff increased from few persons to over 20 people today, including over 10 researchers and more than 10 professional technicians. Apart from traditional archaeology, Liangzhu City's research covers digital archaeology, animal archaeology, plant archaeology, geological archaeology, environmental archaeology, and protection of cultural relics. At the same time, exploration team was recruited to conduct full exploration and systematic survey of the ruins nonstop.

In June 2009, the China's National Cultural Heritage Administration held the "2009 Liangzhu Forum on Protection of Major Ruins and Launching Ceremony of Liangzhu National Heritage Park" in Liangzhu. At the same time, the China's National Cultural Heritage Administration and Zhejiang Cultural Heritage Bureau founded the Archaeology and Protection Center of Archaeological Ruins of Liangzhu. The center is jointly managed by Zhejiang Institute of Cultural Relics and Archaeology and the Liangzhu Management Committee. We have established a research base for archaeology and conservation in line with the requirements of a world heritage site and international standards, inaugurating a new chapter in archaeology and protection of Archaeological Ruins of Liangzhu. The practice of archaeology in Liangzhu proves that the work mode of archaeological workstation guarantees the long-term in-depth archaeological work in a region. It is required for the archaeological work of major ruins.

III. Liangzhu archaeology, presentation and Utilization of Archaeological Ruins of Liangzhu City

Since the establishment of Liangzhu Cultural Museum in the mid-1990s, the presentation and application

---

① Huang Li: "Establish Compensation Mechanism to Protect Site - The Practice and Thoughts on Compensation Mechanism for Cultural Relics Protection of Archaeological Ruins of Liangzhu", "Zhejiang Cultural Relics", No. 1, 2016.

advance in lockstep with the growth of archaeological achievements and the value of the ruins. In 1994, the Liangzhu Cultural Museum on the south side of Xunshan Mountain was open to the public. As archaeological discoveries and research develop, the original museum is unable to accommodate new exhibits. Therefore, a new museum renamed Liangzhu Museum was built in 2008. The exhibition design and archaeological staff work together to introduce the latest achievements of Liangzhu City. The museum attracts 400,000 to 50,000 tourists every year and becomes a key window for showcasing the Liangzhu culture.

The decade of 2008-2017 saw the fastest growth in archaeological achievements of Liangzhu City. The exhibition in 2008 lagged far behind the new understanding of Liangzhu City. To assist the nomination for Archaeological Ruins of Liangzhu City as a world heritage site, the Liangzhu Museum was closed in August 2017 and reopened at the end of June 2018. The curatorial team of Fudan University and Liangzhu archaeological staff cooperated in completing the design of exhibition change, so that presentation and display showcase the latest progress and knowledge of Liangzhu archaeological research as scientifically and completely as possible.[1]

Another key component for the presentation of Archaeological Ruins of Liangzhu City is the on-site display inside the site park, including the ecological environment display, the ruins, on-site simulation of the ruins, and digital animation display. During the construction of the site park, archaeological staff were actively involved in the exhibition design of the site park based on the principle of "the nature of the ruins as the park, park expressed as the ruins, and avoidance of the park-type ruins" as proposed by Zhang Zhongpei.

At present, the environmental renovation of Liangzhu City has been initially completed, with an unobstructed view inside and outside the city. From the palace area of the ancient city, we can clearly see that the ancient city is surrounded by three mountains, with the open plain in the east. Unobstructed view of the surrounding landform is provided. The display of the site has been basically completed. Mojiao Mountain (including big Mojiao Mountain, small Mojiao Mountain, Turtle Mountain) , city wall, Yaoshan, Fanshan, Jiangjia Mountain, Chizhong

Fig.6   Fanshan M12 after restoration

① Gao Menghe and Song Yuhan: "From "Full Archaeology of Liangzhu" to "Full Exhibition of Liangzhu Museum" - Case of change of exhibition of Liangzhu Museum in 2018, "Southeast Culture", No. 6, 2018.

Temple, dam site, etc. are marked by vegetation. The ruins are mostly discernible. The overall frame structure of the heritage area begins to take shape.

The anatomy point of south City Wall, the section of Fanshan, and the section of dam at Laohuling are exhibited as they are. Restoration exhibition is adopted for tombs of Fanshan mausoleums. The original ground of the cemetery is covered by several tens of centimeters of soil. A copper tomb was placed in the original position. The burial objects such as imitated jade, stoneware and pottery in the tomb are placed in the original positions. Each tomb with graphic and text interpretation basically restores the scene when the tomb was unearthed.

Surface simulation display method is adopted for Yaoshan altar, big Mojiao Mountain F2 and small Mojiao Mountain F17. On the basis of soil cover, the shape of altar, tomb or foundation ditch and posthole are displayed in the original position through GRC. Soil texture and color at the time of being unearthed can be roughly simulated.

Fig.7　Surface simulation display of Yaoshan altar and cemetery

Fig.8　Display of marks for Mojiao Mountain Palace Area

The remaining house foundations and the sand-soil square at Mojiao Mountain Palace area, carbonized rice and the housing platform at Chizhong Temple, and cemetery at Jiangjia Mountain and Wenjia Mountain are marked out in the original locations. For example, the house foundation is displayed through barks, sand-sand square through coarse sand pavement, carbonized rice and house foundation at Chizhong Temple through green plants, and the tombs at Jiangjia Mountain and Wenjia Mountain through cobblestones.

IV. Conclusion

After more than 80 years of hard work and exploration, fruitful results have been achieved in the archaeology, excavation, scientific research and protection of Archaeological Ruins of Liangzhu. Especially in 2013-2017, we completed the compilation of the "Comprehensive Research Report on Liangzhu City" (to be published soon) , which provides a wealth of detailed information on the compilation of documents for nomination of Archaeological Ruins of Liangzhu City as a world heritage site. According to the latest archaeological achievements, an area of 14.3 square kilometers is designated for the applicant world heritage site, including the city site, water conservancy system and Yaoshan. Based on the four basic value elements of city site, peripheral water conservancy system, graded cemeteries and jade articles, it is considered that Liangzhu meets two criteria : iii (to bear a unique or at least exceptional testimony to a cultural tradition or to a civilization which is living or which has disappeared;) and iv (to be an outstanding example of a type of building, architectural or technological ensemble or landscape which illustrates (a) significant stage (s) in human history) . The nomination dossier for Archaeological Ruins of Liangzhu City as a world heritage site was officially submitted to UNESCO on January 26, 2018, and the nomination is now on the home stretch.

Archaeology, conservation, presentation and nomination as a world heritage site for Archaeological Ruins of Liangzhu City are the results of the hard work of several generations of archaeologists. All important archaeological discoveries were strongly supported by the China's National Cultural Heritage Administration, the Zhejiang Provincial Cultural Heritage Bureau, and the governments of Hangzhou and Yuhang District. It is also indispensable from the understanding, help and dedication of the local people. It is through the step-by-step discovery and protection that the basically intact ancient kingdom of Liangzhu is preserved. Standing on the ruins of the palace of 5,000-year-old Liangzhu Kingdom, we are overwhelmed with awe and gratitude!

波兰的预防性考古研究

波兰　国家遗产局　阿格尼尔斯卡·昂尼斯佐克[①]

摘要

本文首先简述了考古文化遗产管理及其法律框架。接着介绍了波兰以发展为导向的考古研究体系。作者通过从 20 世纪 90 年代兴起的高速公路考古，强调考古过程中从规划阶段到普查、大规模考古挖掘、对结果进行科学分析，再到考古结果的发布，应用系统性方法是具有相当优势的。特别是考古结果的发布和宣传，其方式应更具多样性，例如使用多种交流方式，将科学社群及更广大的公众群体纳入其中。为了使抢救性考古能够真正做到在防止遗迹的信息流失，并具有预防性，长期保护必须适用于所有考古文献类型，包括文物、纸质文档和电子化

关键词：预防性考古，开发引导考古，高速公路考古，波兰考古遗产管理

引言

无论小村庄还是大城市的考古遗产，都反映了这个地方的独特性特征。几乎在世界的每一个角落，人类历史的层层痕迹都是那些没被载入史册的人留下的。所以，考古遗址的真正价值在于它们的原有物质，但颇有讽刺意味的是，这些物质却在考古发掘过程中受到了破坏。考古是真正可以起到预防作用的，因为它采用非入侵式的方式研究遗址并确保它们在多年之后仍完好保存。"预防性"这个词常用于以开发为导向的研究中，然而在本文，当人们都一致认为原有物质受到破坏时，预防性考古是为了防止信息的丢失。在这样的背景下，当人们面临前所未有的发展压力时，需要制定一个全面完善的体系来管理考古遗产，并尽最大努力为子孙后代保护好这些遗产。

法律背景

波兰管理和保护考古遗产框架是在 2003 年 7 月 23 日颁布的《文化遗产保护法》（波兰，2003 年）

---

① 阿格尼尔斯卡·昂尼斯佐克（Agnieszka Oniszczuk），波兰国家遗产局考古遗迹研究及分析小组首席考古专家。同时担任欧洲考古理事会成员及该理事会欧洲考古档案工作组主席。业务领域涉及中世纪后期考古和城市考古，考古遗产管理、政策和相关法规标准，以及国际合作。

的基础上建立的。该法案解释了什么是历史遗迹、什么是考古文物；并区分了文物保护的管理行为与文物拥有者的监护行为。此外，法案还对法律保护形式、考古研究、资金来源和国家遗址保护机构（具体说明各自角色分工）等事项进行了约束。

值得注意的是，该法案的个别条款与波兰政府1996年批准认可的《欧洲保护考古遗产公约》的相关内容基本一致。该公约得到认可后成为波兰法律体系的一部分。对空间规划、高速公路建设中涉及到的考古遗产保护问题，也制定了相关法案或法律法规进行解决。对了《瓦莱塔公约》在波兰的执行情况，作者已在先前的文章中作过具体分析（奥尼茨祖克，2014年）。

关于考古遗产，由《文化遗产保护法》衍生出的最重要的几个法规包括：《国家遗产保护机构法》（波兰，2004年）、《考古研究法》（波兰，2018年）、《开展考古研究的国家捐赠法》（波兰，2014年）以及《文物的登记及清册法》（波兰，2011年）。

考古遗产的相关法律条款

考古遗址，法律解释为"不可移动遗迹，包含人类生存或活动留下来的地面、地下和水下遗存三部分，由文化层和其中的人类作品或人类痕迹构成；或包含上述内容的可移动遗迹"。然而，为进一步界定"考古遗址"，其概念必须首先符合遗址的一般意义，也就是说，考古遗址应具有历史、艺术和科学价值，值得保护（波兰，2003年，第三条）。无论保存状态如何，考古遗址都应受到保护（波兰，2003年，第六条）。

图1　奥斯托夫·莱德尼基，一座莱德尼基湖上的小岛，岛上有一处中世纪早期波兰第一个统治者的居住地遗址。该岛是第一批登记在册受保护文物之一，拍摄者：W·斯得皮恩。

考古研究指以发现、辨别、记录、并保护考古文物为目的的活动（波兰，2003年，第三条）。

考古发现的文物属于国家所有（波兰，2003年，第三十五条）。它们将被永久收藏在博物馆或其他文物保护单位里，或公有或私有的，以确保对它们进行永久保管、分类、保护，以及为科学研究提供帮助（波兰，2003，第三十五条）。

考古遗产管理体系

波兰是一个统一的国家，共有16个省，每个省设有省级文物保护局（办公室），并下设地方性分支机构（见图2）。它们是国家行政管理部门的地方单位，各省省长决定该省文物保护局（办公室）的财政预算和机构设置。从国家层面上说，省级遗产保护活动由文化与国家遗产部副部长进行协调和监督，其职能相当于古迹保护总干事。这种省级遗产保护的双重从属关系是波兰遗产管理的主要决定因素。

考古方面，国家遗产保护部门对登记在册的约7750个考古遗迹（如：有较高价值的受保护点）和超过45万处考古遗址进行管理和保护。这些遗迹或遗址多是通过野外实地勘探或先前探索发现的，并已列入《波兰考古记录大全》（奥尼茨祖克，2018年）。

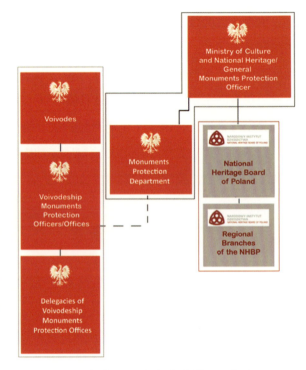

图2　负责波兰考古遗产管理的机构。

波兰国家遗产局不属于国家行政管理机构。它是文化和国家遗产部设立的一个机构，负责执行国家保护文化遗产的相关政策，并行使监督权，确保为文化遗产的保护提供最好最全面的条件。它的主要任务包括：收集并传播遗产信息、制定保护和保存标准、提高公民对波兰文化遗产的保护意识，按照可持续发展战略通过以上活动为后代保留文化遗产。

波兰考古研究的管理

按照《瓦莱塔公约》提出的"谁污染谁买单"原则，考古研究通常由投资者（开发商、土地所有人等）资助，并受到有明确规定的管理程序制约。

任何人想要开展任何可能对考古遗迹造成改变、甚至破坏的工程（建设、改变土地用途等），都必须依法承担必要的预防性考古研究费用。研究的范围由省级文物保护局（办公室）确定（波兰，2003年，第三十一条）。

开展考古实地研究之前需要得到省级遗产保护单位的许可。任何申请人，无论是个人还是机构（研究人员、土地所有者、开发商）都必须证明其研究合法，提供确切的研究地点及起止时间。实地研究结束后，申请人还必须按顺序依次提交如下材料：土地使用权证明或与土地所有者同意书、研究规划书、博物馆或其他组织单位的书面同意书（接受未来的研究发现成果）、以及研究区域的说明书（波兰，2018年，第几条）。

后续许可证件包括：申请人的姓名和住址、研究地点、研究范围及方式、许可证有效期、以及许可证内容。尤其注意以下内容：实地考察开始前14天必须将研究负责人的姓名与住址告知省级文物保护局（办公室）负责人，负责人应及时通知申请人任何有可能影响研究范围和持续时间的新情况，确保实地工作期间研究区域的安全，并在研究结束后恢复原状。此外，许可证中还应详细说明研究成果的永久存放地，并向省级文物保护局（办公室）说明移交各个考古档案资料的截止日期。这些材料的截止日期应从实地考察结束时算起，通常这样计算：准备初步发掘报告需要3个星期，移交研究成果清单及实地考察文件需要6个月，对研究结果进行全面科学论证并妥善保存需要3年。以上资料最后将移交到指定的博物馆或其他存放单位（波兰，2018年，第十八条）。

波兰开展以开发为导向的考古状况

概述

1992年《瓦莱塔公约》颁布后，包括大型基础设施建设在内的项目投资暴增，对于波兰考古遗产而言，这是一件幸运的事情。公约旨在抵消西欧曾经因疯狂实施大规模基础设施建设对考古遗址造成的严重破坏（威廉姆斯，2014年，第152页）。然而不管怎样，它推动了波兰形成了现行考古体系，将重点放在以开发为导向的救援发掘工作中。根据波兰国家遗产局提供的数据，大约有98%的考古实地考察工作（侵入式的或非侵入式的）都是以开发为导向的。

图3　波兰南部克拉科夫附近高速公路施工前的考古挖掘工作，摄影者：M·布加杰。

到目前为止，亚马尔—欧洲天然气管道建设项目大型基础设施建设开展前已组织了前期系统的考古研究。其中，1993 年—1998 年进行了考古研究（亚当奇克和吉尔拉赫，1998 年，第 18 期），从 1996 年开始进行考古实地考察，为高速公路建设项目做准备。数字能够说明高速公路建设项目实地调查工作的规模：截止 2012 年，实地调查面积超过 1000 公顷。共发掘出 2500 处考古遗址，包括：2250 处村落遗址、200 处墓地和 50 处其他遗址，包括生产遗址、矿山、军事遗址等（卡德罗，2012 年）。

高速公路考古采用的系统性方法

天然气管道挖掘工作取得的惊人成果（详见：克劳德尼基，柯瑞兹尼尔克，1998 年）表明了工业领域和遗产领域系统合作的优势。所以，高速公路建设项目立项之初就明确提出，要建立一个全面完善的预防性考古研究体系以应对这项在波兰预防性考古研究史上规模最大的项目。1995 年，一个专门的国家机构——考古救援研究中心（波兰国家遗产局的法定前身之一）成立了。它的主要任务是同国家道路与高速公路管理局（GDNRM）合作，并建立高速公路考古研究的框架结构（马西泽夫斯基，2005 年，第 36 页）。这一制度建立于 20 世纪 90 年代，现在仍在继续发挥作用，并不断被修正，及时反映法律制度变化及合作机构的重组状况。

考古勘探研究的整个过程利用了各种方式（野外徒步、物理勘探、ALS 数据分析、航空探测）对成果进行勘测研究、挖掘、保护，并对发掘结果进行科学研究。一般规则是，勘测研究过程中发现的所有遗迹都要进行挖掘。有些建筑工程因此受到考古监测的影响，比如：考古学家要在建筑工地现场向考古遗产保护部门？汇报某个先前未知的考古文物发现。之后，由于需要对该发现进行救援挖掘，此项工程被迫中止。

考古承包商通过公开招标确定。考古研究按照精确的指导方案（所有承包商必须同意）进行。研究结果以纸质版和电子版两种形式移交 GDNRM。其中，为方便后期在网上公开，电子版应为标准版本。

各阶段必要的考古研究范围和类型由相应省级文物保护局（办公室）（VMPO）决定。国家遗产保护部门依法负责实地调查的质量控制、文件归档，并参与到将研究成果移交给最终存放单位的过程中。

GDNRM 为整个考古研究提供资金支持。勘测研究经费按照固定费率或基于勘测路线和沟槽长度估算出来成本；至于余下两个阶段所需的费用，用相对成本估算法结合一系列指示符？计算。

计算方法根据劳动消耗，即标准公亩，而指示符用来描述特定遗址的状态，包括：功能（指示符 A）、居住期的数量（指示符 B）、位于 1 公亩内的特征数量（指示符 C）、这些特征的平均深度（指示符 D）、人类活动层的厚度（指示符 E）、以及土壤类型（指示符 F）。指示符 A—F 的值是基于波兰史前考古遗址的特征确定。在这个计算方法中，"1 标准公亩"的意思是赋值为 1 的指示符，也就是说在一个居住期有一个村落遗址或一个火葬墓地。1 公亩内的特征数量为 0.2—3.9 个，这些特征的平均厚度为 0.8 米，没有人类活动层，土壤类型是沙地。初步假设挖掘具备以上特点的一个区域需要 146 个工时。指示符的值按挖掘特定遗址的劳动力的变化而变化，如：特征的平均深度超过 2 米时，指示符

D 的值将由 1 提高到 1.6。

实际操作中，可根据正在进行的勘测研究，计算挖掘每个遗址 1 公亩所需的劳动消耗，具体计算方法如下：按照遗址状态调整的指示符值乘以 146，再乘以考古场地的面积（公亩）。得到的结果为遗址标准单位数。投标期间，考古承包商竞投挖掘 1 标准单位遗址的价格。如果遗址的实际情况与预期不一致，计算指示符的值，经 GDNRM 同意后，根据新情况对数值作相应调整。

另外一组指示符是用来计算科学研究的劳动消耗，涉及以下数据：不同年代特征占比、发掘数量、研究数量（可接受范围在 GDNRM 操作手册中加以界定）。

以上方法，待研究结束后用来计算最终费用。由于高速公路考古研究项目规模较大，已开始验收部分实地考古工作，并进行部分拨款。

经 GDNRM 同意，波兰国家遗产局（NHBoP）对勘测报告进行评估，并参与验收部分正在进行中的实地考古勘测，最后对勘测科学研究结果进行质量控制。质量控制由两名考古学家——高级学者进行同行评议，所以 NHBoP 的工作人员应保证这些报告的内部连贯性和科学性。

这些研究结果的发布，将由各研究机构负责出版，非公开发表的研究结果可在省级文物保护局（办公室）和 NHBoP 查阅。目前，GDNRM 已与多方合作完成了多次展览（例如：克拉科夫展，2005年）、出版了插图丰富的科普读物（如：维斯纽斯基，科特洛夫斯基，2013 年），并积极寻找更多的传播渠道。另外，目前正在研究在 NHBoP 网站上公开发布高速公路考古研究完整的科研报告事宜。

结论

综上所述，GDNRM 20 多年前启用的研究体系看似复杂，但多年实践却证明了它的实用性。该研究体系的众多特征对系统性考古遗址管理具有重要作用：

1. 它是基于波兰考古活动的实际经验编写的。

2. 它具备灵活性，能够根据法律条款的变化适时调整。

3. 它是众多利益相关者（投资人、国家遗产保护机构、考古承包商和 NHBoP）之间的合作的结果，现在仍需要各方继续合作。

4. 它涵盖整个考古过程。

5. 它有明确定义的工作流程和清晰的操作指南。

6. 最后，它通过展览和出版物来解决公众需要。

波兰开展的大规模以开发为导向的研究符合《瓦莱塔公约》和《洛桑宪章》（欧洲委员会，1992，国际古迹遗址理事会，1990）的规定，其优势不可否认。遗址管理者获得的数据来源空间范围广，遗址覆盖面广。工程的规模和重复性可以验证现行的研究方法（野外徒步和测试挖掘效果）和标准。考古研究一直在改变我们对历史的看法。最后，由于考古研究无处不在，人们与考古之间的距离不断拉近。从这个角度考虑，考古研究的潜力仍有待开发和充分利用。

参考文献

亚当奇克·K，吉尔拉赫·M.（1998），天然气运输管道的考古研究：方法、概念、实践，源源不断的考古宝藏，M·克劳德尼基，L·柯瑞兹尼尔克，波兹南编辑：15—20。

克劳德尼基·M，柯瑞兹尼尔克·L 等 .（1998），管道的考古宝藏，波兹南。

欧洲委员会（1992），欧洲考古遗址保护公约（修订版），瓦莱塔，16 卷 .1992 年，143 号欧洲条约汇编，https：//www.coe.int/en/web/conventions/full–list/–/conventions/rms/090000168007bd25。

国际古迹遗址理事会（1990），考古遗址的保护与管理宪章，https：//www.icomos.org/charters/arch_e.pdf。

克拉科夫，S.（2012），考古学 . 高速公路建设的考古研究——展览目录，华沙。

马西泽夫斯基 R.（2005），"保护考古遗址"，*Archeologia Żywa* 特刊，33—36 页。

奥尼茨祖克·A.（2014），公约在行动——波兰批准认可《瓦莱塔公约》的 20 年，《瓦莱塔公约》：伴随利益、问题、挑战的 20 年，东非共同体的临时文件 9，V.M. 万赫哈斯，P.A.C. 舒特编辑，布鲁塞尔，63—68 页。

奥尼茨祖克·A.（2018），"以问题为导向的实地考察是否重要？一个考古遗址管理者的观点"，网络考古学 49，http：//intarch.ac.uk/journal/issue49/9/index.html。

波兰（2003），2003 年 7 月 23 日，文物保护与管理，法律报，2003 年，第 162 期，第 1568 条，后期有修改。

波兰（2004），文化与国家遗产部 2004 年部长会议对文化遗产部门及组织机构的规定，法律报，2004 年，第 75 期，第 706 条。

波兰（2011），文化与国家遗产部 2011 年规定对登记在册的国家古迹和文物，由省级考古遗址保护负责记录国家文物被盗或非法运往国外的情况，法律报，2011 年，第 113 期，661 条。

波兰（2014），文化和国家遗产部 2014 年 1 月 10 日对考古研究补助金的规定，法律报，2014 年，第 110 条。

波兰（2018），文化和国家遗产部 2018 年 2 月关于文化遗产保护的部长会议，研究餐馆遗迹、文物保护、文化遗产登记及建筑工程的考古情况，建筑工程及其他活动中文化遗产的登记，以及考古文物的研究和勘测，法律报，2018 年，第 1609 条。

威廉姆斯·W·H.（2014），马尔他及其影响：喜忧参半，《瓦莱塔公约》：伴随利益、问题、挑战的 20 年，东非共同体的临时文件 9，V.M. 万赫哈斯，P.A.C. 舒特编辑，布鲁塞尔，151—156。

维斯纽斯基·M，科特洛夫斯基·L. 等 .（2013），高速公路考古研究，彼得哥什。

Preventive Archaeology in Poland

Agnieszka Oniszczuk[①]
National Heritage Board of Poland

Abstract:

Starting from the outlines of the organization of archaeological heritage management and its legal framework, the paper describes the system of development-led archaeological research in Poland. Referring mainly to motorway archaeology ongoing since the mid-1990s, the Author emphasises the advantages of systemic approach encompassing the entire archaeological process: from the planning stage through reconnaissance research and large-scale excavations, up to scientific analysis of the results and their dissemination. The latter should be diversified, using various means of communication, involving the scientific community and the wider public. In order to make rescue archaeology truly preventive, in terms of preventing the loss of information on destroyed sites, long-term preservation must pertain to all types of archaeological archives: material, documentary, and digital

Keywords: preventive archaeology, development-led archaeology, motorway archaeology, archaeological heritage management in Poland

INTRODUCTION

Archaeological heritage reflects the uniqueness of every location, from a small village to a big city. Almost everywhere, layers of the past bear the traces of people who did not make it to the pages of history books. Thus, the real value of archaeological sites lies in their original substance, which, quite ironically, gets destroyed during archaeological excavations. Archaeology can be truly preventive when non-intrusive methods are used to investigate sites and keep them intact for future generations. This term, however, is usually applied,

---

① Chief Specialist in archaeology in the Unit for expert studies and analysis of archaeological monuments of the National Heritage Board of Poland. Her professional interests include archaeological heritage management and heritage policies, resulting international and national regulations and standards, as well international cooperation in that scope. Board Member of European Archaeological Council and the Chair of the EAC Working Group for Archaeological Archives in Europe. Her research interests are post-medieval and urban archaeology.

also in this paper, to development-led research, in which case we prevent only the loss of information, as the destruction of the original archaeological substance has already been agreed upon. In this context, when we are faced with an ever-present development pressure, a comprehensive system is needed to manage archaeological heritage and preserve as much as we can for the future.

LEGAL BACKGROUND

In Poland the framework of that system is set by the Act of 23 July 2003 on the protection and guardianship of monuments (Poland 2003) . It defines, among others, a monument and an archaeological monument and differentiates administrative actions of monuments protection from the guardianship carried out by owners of monuments. Moreover, it regulates issues of various forms of legal protection, archaeological research, financing, and organisation of state heritage service specifying the roles of individual actors.

Significantly, individual provisions of the act correspond to the contents of European Convention on the Protection of the Archaeological Heritage, which was ratified by Poland in 1996 and henceforth has been a part of its legal system. Issues related to the protection of archaeological heritage are also dealt with in respective acts on spatial planning and motorway construction, as well as related ordinances and regulations. The issue of implementation of the Valletta Convention in Poland has already been discussed in more detail by the Author (Oniszczuk 2014) .

Regarding archaeological heritage, the most important regulations resulting from the act on the protection of monuments concern: organisation of state heritage service (Poland 2004) , archaeological research (Poland 2018) , state donations for carrying out archaeological research (Poland 2014) , as well as the register and inventory of monuments (Poland 2011) .

ARCHAEOLOGICAL HERITAGE IN LEGAL PROVISIONS

Archaeological monuments are legally defined as "immovable monuments constituting surface, underground or underwater remains of human existence or activity, composed of cultural layers and works or traces thereof contained in these layers, or movable monuments constituting such works". However, in order to be defined as such, they must first meet the general definition of a monument, which means that they have to be worthy of preservation for their historical, artistic or scientific value (Poland 2003, Art. 3) . Archaeological monuments are subject to protection regardless of their state of preservation (Poland 2003, Art. 6) .

Archaeological research is defined as actions aimed at discovery, identification, documentation, and securing an archaeological monument (Poland 2003, Art. 3) .

Archaeological objects belong to the State (Poland 2003, Art. 35) . They can be permanently stored in museums or "other organisational units", private or public, that ensure their permanent curation, cataloguing, and conservation, as well as accessibility for scientific purposes (Poland 2003, Art. 35) .

Fig. 1   Ostrów Lednicki, island on Lake Lednickie with relics of an early medieval residence of first Polish rulers. One of the first archaeological monuments protected by entry into the register of monuments, by W. Stępień.

SYSTEM OF ARCHAEOLOGICAL HERITAGE MANAGEMENT

Poland is a unitary state, divided into 16 provinces called voivodeships, each with its own Voivodeship Monuments Protection Office and its local branches (Fig.2) . They belong to the local level of state administration and the Voivodeship Monuments Protection Officers are financially and organizationally subordinate to the respective heads of provinces. On the national level, activities of provincial heritage services are coordinated and supervised by a deputy Minister of Culture and National Heritage having the function of the General Monuments Protection Officer. This kind of a dual subordination of provincial heritage service is the main determinant of heritage management in Poland.

With regard to archaeology, state heritage services carry out administrative and protective activities regarding ca.7750 registered archaeological monuments (i.e. protected sites of higher value) and over 450,000 archaeological sites known through fieldwalking or previous discoveries, included in the inventory of Polish Archaeological Record (Oniszczuk 2018) .

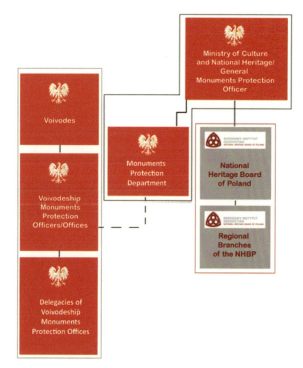

Fig. 2   Institutions charged with archaeological heritage management in Poland.

The National Heritage Board of Poland is not a part of state administration. It is an agency established by the Minister of Culture and National Heritage to implement the State's policy concerning the protection of cultural heritage and its supervision through assuring the best and most comprehensive conditions for preserving it for future generations. Its main tasks are to gather and disseminate information on heritage, set standards for its protection and conservation, and raise social awareness on cultural heritage of Poland in order to save it for future generations in accordance with the strategy for sustainable development.

ADMINISTRATIVE ASPECT OF ARCHAEOLOGICAL RESEARCH IN POLAND

Archaeological research is mostly funded by investors (developers, landowners etc.) according to the polluter pays principle introduced by the Valletta Convention and is subject to a clearly defined administrative procedure.

Anyone wanting to carry out works (construction, changing the way the land is used) that could lead to transformation or destruction of archaeological monuments is legally obliged to cover the cost of the necessary preventive archaeological research. The scope of that research is determined by the Voivodeship Monuments Protection Officer (Poland 2003, Art. 31) .

In order to carry out any archaeological fieldwork a permit from provincial heritage service is required. Any applicant, be it a person or an institution (researcher, landowner, developer) , has to justify the research, give its exact location as well as start and end dates. He/she is also obliged to submit a series of documents including: legal title to use the land or consent of the landowner, programme of the research, a written consent of a museum or other organisational unit to accept future finds, and a description of setting the research area in order after the fieldwork is completed (Poland 2018, Art. 9) .

The subsequent permit contains: the name and address of the applicant, location of the research, scope and manner of conducting the research, permit validity period, and the permit conditions. The latter regard, among others: the obligation to give the name and address of the head of the research to the Voivodeship Monuments Protection Officer at least 14 days before the beginning of fieldworks, the notification of the Voivodeship Monuments Protection Officer on any new circumstances that may influence the scope and duration of the research, securing the research area during the fieldwork and setting it order afterwards. Moreover, in the permit, the permanent storage place for the finds is specified, and the deadlines for transferring various elements of the archaeological archive to the Voivodeship Monuments Protection Office are given. These deadlines, counted from the date of completion of fieldwork, are usually as follows: 3 weeks for preparing the preliminary excavation report, 6 months for handing over the inventory of finds and field documentation, 3 years for full scientific study of the results and conservations of the finds that are then transferred to the appointed museum or storage facility (Poland 2018, Art. 18) .

DEVELOPMENT-LED ARCHAEOLOGY IN POLAND

General information

Luckily for archaeological heritage in Poland, investment boom, including massive infrastructure projects, came after formulation of the Valletta Convention in 1992. The document was to counteract the destruction of archaeological sites that had been caused in Western Europe by the outburst of large-scale infrastructure developments (Willems 2014, p. 152) . In Poland, however, it gave an impetus for creating the present system focused on development-led rescue excavations. Based on the data from the National Heritage Board of Poland, nowadays about 98% of all archaeological fieldworks (intrusive and non-intrusive) are development-led.

So far, major infrastructure projects preceded by systematic archaeological research have been the construction of the Yamal-Europe pipeline with archaeological research carried out in 1993-1998 (Adamczyk & Gierlach 1998, 18) , and motorway construction programme with archaeological fieldwork ongoing since 1996. The numbers can illustrate the scale of the latter. Until 2012 the area under research amounted to 1000 ha. The total of 2500 archaeological sites were excavated including: 2250 settlements, 200 burial grounds and 50 other sites, such as production sites, mines, and military relics (Kadrow 2012) .

Fig. 3   Excavations preceding construction of a motorway near Cracow in southern Poland, by M. Bugaj.

Systemic approach to motorway archaeology

Spectacular results of the pipeline excavations (Chłodnicki, Krzyżaniak 1998) demonstrated the advantages of systematic cooperation between industry and heritage sector. Thus, from the very start of the motorway construction programme it was clear that a comprehensive system must be created to handle the largest programme of preventive archaeological research that has ever been undertaken in Poland. In 1995 a dedicated state agency, the Archaeological Rescue Research Centre (one of the legal predecessors of the National Heritage Board of Poland) , was created. Its aim was to cooperate with the General Directorate of National Roads and Motorway (GDNRM) and create the framework of motorway archaeological research (Maciszewski 2005, p. 36) . This system, established in the 1990s, is still functioning with modifications reflecting legal changes and reorganisations of both cooperating agencies.

The entire process of archaeological research comprises reconnaissance research carried out with the use of various methods (fieldwalking, geophysical prospection, ALS data analysis, aerial prospection) , excavations, conservation of the finds, and scientific study of the results. The general rule is that all sites discovered during reconnaissance research must be excavated. Some construction projects are subject to archaeological surveillance, which means that an archaeologists is present on the construction site to report any discovery of previously unknown archaeological monuments to the heritage service. Afterwards, construction at the location of such discovery is stopped in order to carry out rescue excavations.

Archaeological contractors are chosen in public procurement procedure. The research is carried out according to precise guidelines that must be accepted by all archaeological contractors. The results are transferred to GDNRM in both paper and digital form. The latter is also standardised for the sake of future online publication.

The scope and type of necessary archaeological research on each stage of the process is determined by the respective Voivodeship Monuments Protection Officer (VMPO) . State heritage service is also legally charged with quality control of fieldwork and documentation and participates in transferring the finds to permanent storage.

The GDNRM finances the entire process of archaeological research. Reconnaissance research is financed according to the flat-rate or resultant cost estimate based on the length of the investigated route and test trenches, and the cost of the two remaining stages is calculated with the use of relative cost estimate with the use of a system of modifiers.

This system is based on the labour consumption of the so-called standard are and the modifiers describe conditions on a given site regarding: its function (modifier A) , number of settlement phases (modifier B) , number of features located on 1 are (modifier C) , average depth of these features (modifier D) , thickness of anthropogenic layers (modifier E) , and type of soil (modifier F) . Their values have been set based on the characteristics of prehistoric archaeological sites in Poland. In this system, 1 standard are is defined by modifiers with value 1 as a settlement or a cremation burial ground with one settlement phase, 0.2-3.9 features up to 0.8 m deep located on 1 are, without an anthropogenic layer, and located on sand. It has been initially assumed that 146 working hours are needed to excavate an area of this characteristics. The modifier values differ according to the amount of labour needed to excavate a given site, e.g. when the average depth of features exceeds 2 m value of modifier D increases to 1,6 instead of 1.

In practice, labour consumption of 1 are of each site is calculated on the basis of preceding reconnaissance research in such a way that modifiers adjusted to the site conditions are multiplied by 146 and the surface of the site in ares. The result is a number of the so-called normative units for the site, and during the tender archaeological contractors compete by offering the price for excavating one normative unit. If actual conditions on the site turn out to be different than expected the values of the modifiers are adjusted to the new situation in agreement with the GDNRM.

Another set of modifiers is used to calculate the labour consumption of scientific studies with regard to: the percentage of chronologically defined features, number of finds, number of analyses (their acceptable scope is defined in the GDNRM guidelines) .

In the above system, final cash settlement is accomplished after the research is completed. Because of the large-scale of motorway archaeological research, the practice of partial acceptances of fieldwork and partial financial settlements has been introduced.

On the basis of an agreement with the GDNRM, the National Heritage Board of Poland (NHBoP) appraises the reconnaissance prospection reports, takes part in partial acceptances of ongoing fieldwork, and, finally, deals with quality control of scientific studies of the results. The latter are peer-reviewed by two archaeologists - senior academic staff members, so the employees of the NHBoP focus on ensuring the internal coherence and the scientific character of these reports.

With regard to dissemination, the results are published by various research institutions and the unpublished studies are accessible at the Voivodeship Monuments Protection Offices and the NHBoP. So far, the GDNRM in cooperation with various bodies has prepared several exhibitions (e.g. Kadrow 2005) and richly illustrated popular science publications (e.g. Wiśniewski, Kotlewski 2013) and is working on new ones. Moreover, the issue of publishing complete scientific studies of motorway archaeological research on the website of the NHBoP is currently being addressed.

CONCLUSION

To conclude, the system employed over 20 years ago by the GDNRM seems complicated but has proved itself useful over the years. It has several qualities that seem crucial for systemic archaeological heritage management:

1. It has been prepared based on the experiences of Polish archaeology.

2. It is flexible and can be adjusted to changing legal provisions.

3. It resulted from and still requires cooperation of many stakeholders (the investor, state heritage service, archaeological contractors and the NHboP) .

4. It encompasses the entire archaeological process.

5. It has a clearly defined workflow and clear guidelines.

6. Finally, it addresses needs of the general public through exhibitions and publications.

Advantages of the large-scale development-led research in Poland, consistent with the rules set by the Valletta Convention and the Lausanne Charter (Council of Europe 1992, ICOMOS 1990) , are undeniable. Heritage managers get the data with the widest possible spatial and chronological coverage. Scale and repetitiveness of the works allows verification of existing methods (effectiveness of fieldwalking and test excavations) and standardisation. The research keeps changing our view of the past. Finally, by happening almost everywhere, it brings archaeology closer to the people; in this respect its potential is still to be explored and fully exploited.

BIBLIOGRAPHICAL REFERENCES

Adamczyk K., Gierlach M. (1998) , *The Archaeology of the Transit Gas Pipeline: - Idea - Conception - Practice*, in *Pipeline of Archaeological Treasures*, edited by M. Chłodnicki, L. Krzyżaniak, Pozna ń , pp.15-20.

Chłodnicki M., Krzyżaniak L. eds. (1998) , *Pipeline of Archaeological Treasures*, Pozna ń .

Council of Europe (1992) , European Convention on the Protection of the Archaeological Heritage (Revised) , Valetta, 16.I.1992, European Treaty Series No. 143, https://www.coe.int/en/web/conventions/full-list/-/conventions/rms/090000168007bd25

ICOMOS (1990) , Charter for the Protection and Management of the Archaeological Heritage, https://www.icomos.org/charters/arch_e.pdf

Kadrow, S. (2012) , *arche (o) typy. Archeologiczne badania ratunkowe w programie budowy autostrad* - text in the exhibition catalogue, Warszawa.

Maciszewski R. (2005) , "Preserving Archaeological Heritage", in *Archeologia Żywa* Special issue, pp. 33-36.

Oniszczuk A. (2014) , *The convention in action - Poland almost 20 years after the ratification of the Valletta Convention*, in *The Valletta Convention: Twenty Years After Benefits, Problems, Challenges*, EAC Occasional Paper 9, edited by V. M. van her Haas, P. A. C. Schut, Brussels, pp.63-68.

Oniszczuk A. (2018) , "Is Question-driven Fieldwork Vital or not? An Archaeological Heritage Manager's Perspective", in *Internet Archaeology* 49, http://intarch.ac.uk/journal/issue49/9/index.html

Poland (2003) , Ustawa z dnia 23 lipca 2003 r. o ochronie zabytków i opiece nad zabytkami, *Journal of Law* 2003, No 162, Item 1568, with further amendments.

Poland (2004) , Rozporządzenie Ministra Kultury z dnia 9 kwietnia 2004 r. w sprawie organizacji wojewódzkich urzędów ochrony zabytków, *Journal of Law* 2004, No. 75, Item 706.

Poland (2011) , Rozporządzenie Ministra Kultury i Dziedzictwa Narodowego z dnia 26 maja 2011 r. w sprawie prowadzenia rejestru zabytków, krajowej, wojewódzkiej i gminnej ewidencji zabytków oraz krajowego wykazu zabytków skradzionych lub wywiezionych za granicę niezgodnie z prawem, *Journal of Law* 2011, No. 113, Item 661.

Poland (2014) , Rozporządzenie Ministra Kultury i Dziedzictwa Narodowego z dnia 10 stycznia 2014 r. w sprawie dotacji na badania archeologiczne, *Journal of Law* 2014, Item 110.

Poland (2018) , Rozporządzenie Ministra Kultury i Dziedzictwa Narodowego z dnia 2 sierpnia 2018 r. w sprawie prowadzenia prac konserwatorskich, prac restauratorskich i badań konserwatorskich przy zabytku wpisanym do rejestru zabytków albo na Listę Skarbów Dziedzictwa oraz robót budowlanych, badań architektonicznych i innych działań przy zabytku wpisanym do rejestru zabytków, a także badań archeologicznych i poszukiwań zabytków, *Journal of Law* 2018, Item 1609.

Willems W. H. (2014) , *Malta and its consequences: a mixed blessing*, in *The Valletta Convention: Twenty Years After Benefits, Problems, Challenges*, EAC Occasional Paper 9, edited by V. M. van her Haas, P. A. C. Schut, Brussels, pp. 151-156.

Wiśniewski M., Kotlewski L. eds. (2013) , *Archeologia autostrady*, Bydgoszcz.

长城核心文化价值论

中国　西北大学　段清波[①]　刘　艳

摘要

　　中国文明主要是由农业文明和游牧文明互动共同构成的。历代长城的建造和以长城地带为中心的民族融合，在中国文明演进、尤其是帝国文明演进以及中华民族形成过程中具有重大的历史贡献和突出的核心文化价值；长城见证了帝国文明的全过程，是各个历史时期，不同政治实体社会治理理念、人们思维方式和行为处事方式、文化交流与民族融合理念、军事防御思想、科学技术水平等方面的综合体现。

　　关键词： 长城地带，农牧文明互动，长城核心文化价值

　　物质文化遗产承载着文化发展过程中的核心基因，是不同时期社会治理体系、宇宙观及核心文化价值观三者相互作用下的产物，也是不同时代社会成员在核心文化价值观约束下所形成的行为处世方式的物化表现[1]。长城遗产价值包括向来认知的历史、艺术和科学价值，具体表现为中国北方以农牧交错为主的生业交错地带丰富的历史演变、长城所承载的管理制度、建筑技艺、军事防御、商贸交流、交通体系和民族迁徙及地理文化景观等维度和侧面，还应通过对长城地带环境和社会文化等现象间规律性关系的探究，在认知中国文明演变机理的背景下，探讨蕴含在长城遗产中的核心文化价值[2]。

一、长城见证了帝国文明的全过程

　　从战国开始，中国古代社会的治理体系逐渐从夏商西周以来的以血缘宗法制为基础的分封制，向以地缘为基础的中央集权郡县制转变，列国间战争的目的，也转向为获取更多的土地和人口以增加财

---

① 　西北大学二级教授，"万人计划"领军人才、文化名家暨"四个一批"人才，中国考古学会理事。创建由"宇宙观、社会治理体系观、核心文化价值观"构成文明的"三观"理论体系，凝练出中国文明（中、对立、变通及礼、规矩）和汉文明（对立、变通及规矩）的主要特征。主持国家社科重大及教育部哲社重大课题；出版《秦始皇帝陵园考古报告》、《陕西省明长城资源调查报告》等10余部著作；发表学术论文近百篇。

富，这是长城出现的社会政治历史背景。长城出现在从分封制向中央集权郡县制转变的战国中期，作为中原农耕民族互防，到演变为主要防御草原游牧民族的军事防御工程，从战国历经秦汉、隋唐、明清等时期，长城主要是农业民族在修建防御北方游牧民族。长城内外因生产生活需要而产生的农牧间长期持续不断的互动，使得长城成为中国五千年文明中后半程的见证者，长城与帝国文明的兴衰相始终[3]。两千多年来一直横亘在农牧两大世界之间，长城是中国古代帝国时期最重要的文化遗产。

长城经历了农牧之间经济、政治、文化的对立统一和融合发展过程，见证了中原农耕政权北部边界的南来北往的演变。中原农耕民族对农牧交错带土地的争夺、开疆拓土的驱动时而有之。汉长城就是中原势力向外发展和农耕界线向北推移的具体表现之一[4]，也是农业民族修建的分布在最北部的长城。秦统一后，更是举全国之力对匈奴发动战争，夺取"河南地"，把阴山以南的地区统统纳入了农业生产区。历史上控制中原地区的历代统治者，多数都利用农业社会的强大组织力量不断修筑长城。从战国至清代两千多年间，12个朝代、24个政治实体先后修建了规模不等、长短不同、分布在今天404个县区的历代长城，长城是集墙体、壕、天险、障、道路、后勤等为一体的立体性防御工程体系[5]。

与此同时，因为经济形态的原因，与农业社会的常态化的贸易以及极端状态下南下的掠夺，也是古代游牧民族解决经济问题的两种手段。草原游牧民族对中原的威胁侵扰时有发生，匈奴南侵是修筑汉长城的主要原因。历史上还先后有十多个北方游牧民族政权，都不同程度地向西域和向中原王朝发动过武装侵略，基本上三百年左右为一个周期，有的政权如北魏、辽、金、元等，不仅打败了中原农业政权，甚至入主中原。

长城地带不仅仅是自然环境过度的敏感区，也常常是影响中原农业社会稳定的策源地，这里经常会出现频繁的冲突与融合[6]。在春秋战国、魏晋南北朝、五代宋辽金这三个分裂割据的时期，中原处于分裂状态，不仅中原与草原相互对峙，且草原地带也不统一，中原地区更是出现了诸如楚、齐、秦、魏、赵、燕、中山、北魏、东魏、北齐长城，长城地带出现了战国秦、赵、燕北长城、北魏北长城、北齐北长城、北周北长城，草原上则出现了辽长城和金长城，这些长城分布广，走向复杂，且规律性不明显[7]。长城是形成中华民族的主战场，诸如汉与匈奴、北魏与柔然、隋唐两代对突厥、宋辽金夏之间、明与蒙古和清等的民族对抗和战争都发生在长城地带。

二、长城是汉文明"对立"思维方式的物化表现

汉文明是自战国开始直至王莽时期形成的以汉字为交流的手段，以阴阳五行宇宙观，以对立、变通为思维方式，以规矩为核心文化价值观的行为处事方式的文化体系[8]。

从战国中期开始修建的历代长城，存在着从简单到复杂的发展过程，最终形成以土、石、砖材料构建的、以墙体为主、由点及线再到面的立体的防御体系，秦帝国"因地形，用制险塞，起临洮，至辽东，延袤万余里"；"及秦始皇攘郤夷狄，筑长城，界中国，然西不过临洮"。汉高祖刘邦下令修缮秦昭王所建长城，与匈奴于"故塞"为界；汉武帝时，为方便使者出使西域，同时隔绝西北部的匈奴

和西南部的南羌之间的联系，开始将疆域沿河西走廊向西北扩展；隋代曾七次修建长城；至明代，修筑长城边防更成为明朝北边防务的重大措施。由墙体、隘口、军堡、关城和军事重镇所形成的军防体系，具有战斗、指挥、观察、通讯、隐蔽等多种功能，关堡等同时也是边地居民聚集、贸易、南北交流的集散地。

中国南北地区经济形态、生业形式差异产生了文化价值取向的不同，冷兵器时期，定期性的南北冲突基本无解。自史前时期庙底沟文化后，北方民族几乎形成随气候环境周期性变化而纷纷南下的规律。尤其是自 4300 年前开始，游牧文化南下的压力成为中原农业民族持久的梦魇。战国中期，长城还主要修建在中原地区，是各农业国家之间相互防御的产物；齐、燕、韩、赵、魏、秦、中山等诸侯国先后修建长城，是由防御一方主持修建的。战国中后期，在新的兼并与反兼并形势下，南北冲突日益强烈，新的社会发展态势促成了新的防御方式，为了"障御[9]"周期性南下的北方游牧民族，遂将中原国家之间修建长长的墙体来防御对方的防御方式，移植在农牧交错的北部边境，在农牧交错交汇的地带的秦赵燕三国都开始修建防御北方牧人邻居的长城。自此之后，秦、汉、隋、明等中原王朝及南下后建立区域社会政权的北魏、北齐、金等时期，为防御纷纷南下的游牧政权，前赴后继地修筑了规模不等、体系繁简不一的长城。可以这么说，最早的长城是周朝属下诸侯之间征伐的产物，随后被长期持久性的应用在中华帝国的北部，是历史上农牧民族间矛盾与融合的直接体现。

从最初农业政权之间为维护自身利益而相继修建，到逐渐成为缓解农耕与游牧政权之间的冲突、维护了长城内外社会经济秩序的作用的转变，长城地带的发展演变使得长城的修建带来了多重的效应，这正是战国晚期开始形成的"阴阳五行相克相生"宇宙观下所形成的"对立"和"变通"思维方式的物化表现[10]。在中国古代社会，统治者幻想以一道长城为农业文明带来安全感的想法延续了两千多年，从此意义上讲，长城是农业民族的一道心理防线。历代长城是冷兵器时代规模最大、历时最久、体系最复杂的的军事防御体系，作为世界上规模、体量最大的人工构筑物，既是世界古代史上最伟大的军事防御工程，也是汉文明形成与发展演变过程的突出见证物。

三、长城是汉文明"变通"思维方式的体现

长城地带地处环境地貌和气候变化的敏感过渡带，由不同地质条件、气候特征所决定的经济地理的生态结构，在一定程度上造就了不同族群民俗民风文化等的迥然不同。在秦帝国建立之前，北部的游牧部族尤其是匈奴族，也是部落林立而互不相属，秦帝国建立十年后，前所未见的统一的草原游牧帝国横空出世。从此开始，直到近代热兵器流行结束，围绕长城所进行的农牧民族之间的互动，始终是中国文明演变过程中的主旋律[11]。这样的演进发展历程具有历史的必然性，因为在长城地带的生态环境、经济结构和民族构成格局之下，受农牧之间生活方式、经济和政治利益的驱使，为协调民族矛盾冲突，各族统治阶层必然要进行国家（民族）政治战略的变通选择，长城既是农牧冲突的标志，也是农牧矛盾的产物，还是农牧融合交流的平台。

客观地讲，从公元前 4 世纪开始，长城的修建逐渐转变成为缓解农牧政权冲突、维护长城内外社会经济秩序的目的。最初修筑长城是为在交通方面形成对北方草原民族南下形成阻障，此后的长城工程又导致了新的交通条件的形成。长城内侧沿线的道路、关堡、市等设施，客观上促进了"北边"交通体系的成熟[12]。在长城地带交通网络形成和经济文化发展的过程中，长城沿线也随之衍生发展了一批城镇和商业贸易、物资集散的中心地（张家口、大同等），最终使长城地带成为边疆与中心聚合与离心力量相互博弈的纽带，发挥了对内吸引和凝聚、对外融合的桥梁作用[13]。

两千多年来，中原农业民族通过屯垦移民和通商等方式，形成以长城沿线为中心的巨大网络，它的辐射作用把长城内外各民族紧密相连，通过为数不少的联通长城内外的关隘，也把农耕文明和游牧文明紧密相融。自史前时期长城地带农牧之间就进行着持续的、规模日益扩大的文化交流。战国秦汉时期，骑兵、长城、边郡互为支撑的防御体系形成后，中原文化与北方游牧经济文化之间的交流进入了快速融合时期[14]。秦汉至明，控制中原地区的历代统治者在不断修筑长城的同时，还采取大规模向长城一带沿线移民、修筑交通通道、开拓边疆新区域的举措；关市、榷场、绢马贸易、茶马互市贸易的开启与关闭，历代各民族的朝贡与馈遗、封赏的行与断[15]，其本质都是古代中原王朝许可的一种与边疆各民族的社会经济、政治关系和文化生活交流形式。

作为农牧文化交流最直接的方式，和亲及互市突出体现了汉文明变通的思维方式与特点。农业耕种和草原畜牧业主要是由自然环境的原因而决定的两种截然不同的生产方式，两者本质上的差异导致它们之间存在必需的交换关系，而游牧民族更是需要长期地获得农业民族提供的粮食、布匹、铁器、茶、盐等生活必需品，农业民族希望得到来自游牧地区的皮毛和奶制品等，这推动并维持了两大经济、文化类型的民族间二千余年持续不断的商品交换。可以说，农牧间不可分割的经济联系是互市的根本原因。明代，汉蒙之间于隆庆五年（1571 年）开始互市，一改长期坚持的闭关锁国政策，此后东起延永西抵嘉峪，"烽火不惊，三军晏眠，边圉之民，室家相保，弄狎于野，商贾夜行"。和亲也是农业文明不得已的一种策略，汉初匈奴"常往来盗边"，西汉政权被迫"约结和亲、赂遗单于，冀以救安边境"，并且"奉宗室女为单于阏氏，岁奉匈奴絮、缯、酒、实物各有数"。此后还有唐与吐蕃、回鹘、奚、契丹等民族的和亲。

四、长城地带是汉文明"规矩"核心文化价值观的集散地

中国文化在从氏族到部落、从古城到古国到王国到帝国、再从近代走向现代的发展过程，是一次次不断打破已有的或文化、或心理、或自然地理界限，学会和更大范围人群打交道的过程，也是不断地学会如何与不同文化背景下的人群和谐相处的过程，在这一过程中，不同时期形成的共识便是不同历史阶段的核心文化价值观[16]。长城地带各民族的起源地域各异，但在几千年相互打交道的过程中，通过交流与学习所进行的"民族融合"，已不再是简单的"汉化"或者"胡化"，而是全面深入到文化、制度、思想、精神的各个方面。不论是农业民族政权还是游牧民族政权，主导中原后都自觉不自觉地

希望能继续统一中国，这种思想的形成是长期以来民族融合的必然趋势。尤其是游牧民族政权入主中原后，想要稳定和谐发展就必须与农业民族的思想文化进行深度融合，在政治、经济、文化等方方面面与汉民族达到整合，这也正是汉族与各少数民族不断融合、最后形成多元一体的中华民族的重要过程。

长城地带经济文化交流，对中国文明的形成起到了极大的促进作用[17]。考古所见中原农耕文化和北方游牧文化交流的重要实物资料举不胜举。历史上农耕文化对游牧文化产生了极大的影响，汉族的语言文字、思想制度、礼仪风俗、文化艺术等深刻地影响着长城地带游牧民族的文化发展和文明进步，以长城地带为中心的农牧互动将汉文明的"规矩"核心文化价值观传播四方。例如《汉书》关于匈奴族与秦汉王朝之间的书信往来的记载，反映出匈奴族对汉文的理解和使用；党项族、契丹族和女真族还在汉字的基础上创造了本民族的文字；在长城以北的游牧区，出土了很多记载《论语》、《礼记》等儒家经典文献的木简[18]；在汉代的龟兹国，上层王室至平民百姓皆崇尚中原文化："乐汉衣服制度，归其国，治宫室，作徼道，周卫，出入传呼，撞钟鼓，如汉家仪"；乌桓时代的辽宁西丰县西岔沟墓地，发现了具有汉族风格的铁镢、铁斧、绳纹陶器、铜镜、货币等[19]；新疆罗布泊、辽宁西丰县的汉代墓葬大量出土了中原地区的铁斧、铁刀、铁镞、铁剑，说明冶铁技术在汉代已经流传至长城沿线[20]。同时，各少数民族文化也向中原汇聚，使得中原文化在发展中也受到各民族文化的强烈影响。比如从赵武灵王提倡胡服到清代的旗袍、马褂，带来汉族服饰的重大转变；魏晋时期大批北方游牧民族将"胡床"带入农耕区，引发汉族生活习俗的一场革命[21]；包括棉花、油菜、芝麻等粮食作物和相关种植技术，都是通过丝绸之路从西域地区传入中原，而大豆和板栗等五谷杂粮则是东北半农半牧经济类型下的产物。

民族融合发生发展的过程与统一的中华民族形成发展的过程具有同一性。中原王朝早在春秋时代已经有了郡的建置，"克敌者……下大夫受郡[22]"。战国时期，秦、赵、燕三国也在北部边疆设置行政机构"郡"以巩固边防。秦帝国在义渠故地设置三郡"筑长城以拒胡"。西汉中央政府设置职官"护乌桓校尉一人，比二千石"，兼管乌桓部落与周边农耕居民的产品交易行为"岁时互市焉"。这些对管理边疆的行政机构和管理游牧部落的职官的设置，使得两汉时期北方边郡一带出现了以不同生产方式进行生产生活的民族之间的交错杂居，客观上有利于农牧的深层次融合。此后还有宋朝的茶马司、元代的西蜀监、明朝的榷场使司和茶马使司等管理游牧部落的职官，唐时更建立了兼跨长城南北两种（或多种）迥然有别的地域及其族群为一体的政权，长城转而成为沟通南北东西的战略要地[23]。

在国家治理中，对农业、畜牧业民族采取双轨制形式的管理也是重要的制度创新。在农业区实行州、县制度，对畜牧业地区，中央机构和地区则设属国、大鸿胪、南北面官、理藩院，羁縻府州和都护府、都司、参赞大臣、办事大臣等，实行胡汉分治或因俗而治[24]。自秦汉在长城地带农业区建国，匈奴统一畜牧业地区而建立统一政权，至公元前五十一年呼韩邪单于归汉，两政权归于统一，中国国家政权始有农、牧政权合一的性质，直至明清，中国的国家基本制度一脉相承，文化传统从未被割断[25]。

此外，长城还发挥了重要的古代交通通道作用，交通网络既在长期的中外经济文化交流中形成，又对经济文化交流起过重要的作用。长城不仅仅是古代边疆的防御边界，同时也连接了中原文明与周边多种文明，是丝绸之路跨区域、跨文化交流、文明对话的重要纽带[26]，推动了东西南北区域思想意识、政治、文化、科技、经济的发展。在古代中国，长城地带各地区、各民族社会经济和文化发展水平差异极大，中原农业区相对比较进步和发达，长城的修筑使民族文化的差异以更直观的方式表现了出来。汉文明不仅对长城地带各少数民族的文化发展起着巨大影响，更通过长城沿线各少数民族传播到更远的区域，迄今在许多民族地区都发现和出土有《论语》、《孝经》，甚至《礼记》木简、帛书和纸抄汉文经、史、典籍，此外还有大量的汉文经、史、典籍被译成民族文字或口头传承而在长城地带各民族中广泛流传，并且有的儒家思想还演化成少数民族的民族习俗[27]，与此同时，一些游牧民族的文化习俗，如服装、坐具、饮食风俗等也融入到农业文明中。

五、结论

任何一种文明都是由社会治理体系、宇宙观、核心文化价值观共同构成，核心文化价值观是一种文明体系下人们行为处事方式的依据[28]。文化遗产价值是由一系列类型多样、彼此关联的子系统构成的价值体系，不同时代和不同民族的文化价值体系有着明显的差别[29]。在历史、艺术和科学价值为主导的认知体系下，从"合理利用"的技术层面认识长城的基本价值，首先回答了长城是什么及长城价值的具体表现形式[30]。进一步，在宇宙观、社会治理观、核心文化价值观（"三观"）的理论体系下，从中国文明形成发展演变的宏大历史背景看待长城的建造以及长城地带的农牧互动，可以探索和揭示考古学上所体现和反映的，蕴含汉文明思维方式和行为处事方式特点的长城的核心文化价值。具体而言，"有形"的长城是中国古代社会物质文明的产物，是汉文明"对立"思维方式的物化表现，具有突出的历史、科学、艺术、军事、建筑、文学、社会、景观、教育等价值；而"无形"的长城作为中国文明"礼"与"规矩"核心文化价值的集散地，见证了农牧民族从物质生活、到社会生活、再到精神生活的长期融合之路，体现汉文明变通的思维方式特点，是中华民族的精神象征和文化财富。

参考文献

[1] 段清波.考古学要发掘遗产的文化价值[N].光明日报，2015-07-22，第10版.

[2] 段清波、刘艳.重视研究文化遗产价值创新发展文物保护工作[N].中国文物报.2017-01-13.第003版：综合.

[3],[11] 段清波.长城——中华文明的见证[N].光明日报.2017-03-26，第07版.

[4] 白音查干.汉长城考察与研究[J].内蒙古师大学报（哲社版）.1987，（1）：95-104.

[5] 段清波、徐卫民.中国历代长城发现与研究[M].北京：科学出版社.2014年，第468页.

[6] 贺卫光.中国古代游牧民族与农耕民族在经济上的互补与非平衡需求[J].西北师大学报（社科

版）.2003，（1）：32–38.

[7] 董耀会 . 论长城与中华民族凝聚力的形成，第二届海峡两岸中华传统文化与现代化研讨会，江苏淮安，2004 年 .

[8] 段清波 . 考古学上汉文明论纲 [J]. 考古学集刊 .2018，（21）：189–217.

[9] 王国良 . 中国长城沿革考·自序 [M]. 北京：商务印书馆 .1935 年，第 1 页 .

[10] 段清波 . 从四方中心到阴阳五行的宇宙观：——中国文明的三观智慧（一）[N]. 学习时报，2018-08-08，A3：中外历史版 .

[12] 王子今 . 交通史视角的秦汉长城考察 [J]. 石家庄学院学报 .2013，（2）：14–25.

[13] 徐黎丽 . 通道地带理论——中国边疆治理理论初探 . 思想战线 [J].2017，（2）：67–75.

[14] 张晋 . 战国、秦汉时期中原骑兵、长城、边郡互为支撑的防御体系述论 . 内蒙古大学硕士论文，2015 年 .

[15]、[24]、[27] 李凤山 . 论长城带在中国民族关系发展中的地位 [J]. 中国史研究 .1998，（2）：140–153.

[16] 段清波 . 论文化遗产的核心价值 [J]. 中原文化研究，2018，（1）：102–110.

[17] 苏秉琦、殷玮璋 . 关于考古学文化的区系类型问题 [J]. 文物 .1981，（5）：10–18.

[18] 马利清 . 包头张龙圪旦一号墓的族属及部分南匈奴墓葬辨析 [J]. 复印报刊资料（先秦、秦汉史）.2014，（2）：86–93.

[19] 孙守道 . "匈奴西岔沟文化"古墓群发现 [J]. 文物 .1960，（8、9）：25.

[20] 邹厚本、韦正：徐州狮子山西汉墓的金扣腰带 [J]. 文物 .1998，（8）：37–43.

[21] 黄清敏 . 正史中的胡床及其变迁 [J]. 湖北民族学院学报（哲学社会科学版）.2010，（5）：200.

[22] 杨伯峻 . 春秋左传注 [M]. 北京：中华书局 .2009 年，第 1614 页 .

[23] 李鸿宾 . 中华正朔与内亚边疆——兼论唐朝北部长城地带的意涵 [J]. 学术月刊 .2017，（2）：13–19.

[25] 阴法鲁、许树安 . 中国古代文化史 1、2[M]. 北京：北京大学出版社 .1991 年，第 427、459 页 .

[26] 陈同滨、王琳峰、任洁 . 长城的文化遗产价值研究 . 中国文化遗产 [J].2018，（3）：4–14.

[28] 段清波 . 礼与规矩构成的文化价值观：——中国文明的三观智慧（三）[N]. 学习时报，2018-08-22，A3：中外历史版 .

[29] 刘艳、段清波 . 文化遗产价值体系研究 [J]. 西北大学学报（哲社版）.2016，（1）：23–27.

[30] 刘艳、段清波 . 长城世界文化遗产保护研究 [J]. 中国国情国力 .2016，（10）：42–44.

Core Cultural Values of the Great Wall[①]

Duan Qingbo[②③] and Liu Yan[④]
China Northwest University

Abstract

The Chinese civilization is a result of interaction between the agro civilization and the nomadic civilization. The construction of the Great Wall during the past dynasties and the ethnic integration with the Great Wall Zone as the center have made significant historic contributions and contributed prominent core cultural values to the evolution of the Chinese civilization, in particular to the evolution of the civilization of empires and the development of the Chinese nation. As a witness to the whole process of the civilization of empires, the Great Wall demonstrates the social governance concepts, the way of people's thinking and doing, the notions of cultural communication and ethnic integration, the thinking of military defense, as well as the development of science and technologies of different political entities in different historic periods.

Key words: The Great Wall Zone, the interaction between the agro civilization and the nomadic civilization, the core cultural values of the Great Wall

As the main carrier of cultural development, the material cultural heritage is not only a product of the

① Fund Project:2018 Key Project of the National Social Sciences Fund "Analysis and Study on Materials for the Ming Great Wall" (18ZDA223)

② He is second-tier professor of Northwest University, leading talent of the "10 Thousands Talents Plan", cultural master and talent for "Four Top Areas", council member of the Chinese Archaeological Society. He creates a "three-view" theoretical system that constitutes civilization from the "View of cosmology, social governance system and core cultural values", and condense main features of Chinese civilization (middle, opposite, flexible, rite, courtesy) and Han civilization (opposition, flexibility and rules) . He presides over major projects sponsored by the National Social Science Fund philosophy and sociology projects supported by the Ministry of Education, and has published more than 10 books including the *Archaeological Report of the Qin Shi Emperor's Mausoleum* and the *Investigation Report of the Ming Great Wall in Shanxi Province* and nearly 100 academic papers.

③ Duan Qingbo, Male,Born in Ruicheng of Shanxi province,Professor, Ph.D. advisor,engaged in archeological studies in Qin and Han Dynasties, and studies in the Great Walls of the past Chinese dynasties.

④ Liu Yan,Female,Born in Wenyang of Sichuan province,doctor of economics,engaged in cultural heritage protection and tourist economic researches.

interaction among social governance systems, the outlooks on universe, and the core cultural values of different historic periods, but also a reified demonstration of the ways of doing things by social members within the boundary of core cultural values in different times. [1] Undoubtedly, the Great Wall entails historical, artistic and scientific values, which are shown in the historic evolution of the interaction between the agro civilization and the nomadic civilization in northern China, as well as in the administration systems, architectural techniques, military defense notions, trade exchanges, transportation systems, ethnic migrations, and geographical and cultural landscapes. Besides, it's also necessary to explore the core cultural values entailed in the Great Wall by analyzing the regularity in the relationship between the environment and the social cultures in the Great Wall Zone, against the backdrop of the evolution of the Chinese civilization. [2]

I. The Great Wall witnessed the whole process of the civilization of empires.

Since the Warring States period, the social governance system of the ancient China made a gradual transition from the consanguinity-based system of enfeoffment dated back to the Xia, Shang and Western Zhou Dynasties to the centralized system of prefectures and counties based on geography. The purpose of wars between the States turned into increasing wealth by pursuing more land and populations. Such was the social, political and historic background of the birth of the Great Wall. First built in the mid of the Warring States period when the transition from the system of enfeoffment to the system of prefectures and counties occurred, the Great Wall at first was a way of defense among agro nationalities in the Central Plains of China, and then became a defense project against nomadic nationalities. From the Warring States period to the Qin and Han dynasties, the Sui and Tang Dynasties, and then to the Ming and Qing Dynasties, the Great Wall mainly acted as a way of defense against the nomadic nationalities in northern China. Just because of the continuous interaction between the agro and nomadic civilizations as a result of the needs for production and living, the Great Wall witnessed the ups and downs of the civilization of empires in the second half of the 5000-year Chinese civilization [3]. As a bridge which connected the agro and nomadic worlds, the Great Wall is the important cultural heritage of the ancient Empire period of China.

The Great Wall experienced the development of the contradiction and integration of the economies, politics and cultures of the agro and nomadic civilizations, and also witnessed the evolution of the changes in the northern boundary of the agro regimes in the Central Plains of China. The fight for the land in the agro-pastoral ecotone among agro nationalities occurred time to time. The Great Wall in the Han Dynasty is a manifesto of the expansion by the Central Plain regime towards the north [4], and it is also the Great Wall built by the agro nationality in the most northern part of China. After unification of China, the Qin Dynasty launched a war against the Hun and extended the agro zone to the whole region of the South of the Yinshan Mountains. Most of the rulers who controlled the Central Plains of China in history made great efforts to build and extend the Great Wall. In more than 2000 years from the Warring States period to the Ming and Qing Dynasties, 24 political entities in 12 dynasties built different sections of the Great Wall which nowadays covers 404 counties. The Great Wall is a defense project system which combines walls, trenches, natural barriers, blocks, roads and logistics [5].

At the same time, as a result of its economic pattern, the two main means for the ancient nomadic nationalities were the normal trading with the agro society and the extreme looting on the latter. The purpose of the Great Wall built in the Han Dynasty was just to tackle the threats and invasions by the nomadic nationalities to the Central Plains. There were more than 10 nomadic regimes in the North in Chinese history. All of them have evaded by force into the Western Regions and the Dynasties in the Central Plains to different extents. Some regimes such as the Northern Wei, Liao, Jin and Yuan have even conquered the Central Plains by beating the agro regimes in the Central Plains.

The Great Wall Zone is not only a sensitive zone of the change of natural environment, but also the source to affect the stability of the agro society in the Central Plains [6]. Frequent conflicts and integrations took place in that region. In the Spring and Autumn and Warring States period, the Wei, Jin, Southern and Northern Dynasties, as well as the Five Dynasties, the Song Dynasty, Liao Dynasty and Jin Dynasty, conflicts existed not only between the Central Plains and the nomadic region, but also within the Central Plains and within the nomadic region. In the Central Plains, the States of Chu, Qi, Qin, Wei, Zhao, Yan, and Zhongshan, as well as the Dynasties of the Northern Wei, the Eastern Wei, and the Northern Qi all built Great Walls; in the Great Wall Zone, the Warring States of Qin, Zhao, and Yan, as well as the Dynasties of the Northern Wei, the Northern Qi and the Northern Zhou all built Great Walls; in the nomadic region, there were the Great Wall of the Liao Dynasty and the Great Wall of the Jin Dynasty. Scattered widely, all these Great Walls had various directions without any rules [7]. As a major battlefield for the Chinese nation, the Great Wall witnessed the wars between the Han nationality and the Hun nationality, between the Northern Wei Dynasty and the Regime of Rouran Khaganate, between the Sui & Tang Dynasties and the Turk, among the Song, Liao, Jin and Xia Dynasties, as well as between the Ming Dynasty and the Qing Dynasty and between the Ming Dynasty and the Mongolian nationality.

II. The Great Wall is a reified demonstration of the way of thinking of "contradiction" in the Han civilization.

The Han Civilization is a cultural system with the Chinese characters which were formed between the Warring States period and the WANG Mang Era as its main communication means, yin-yang and five elements as its outlook on the universe, contradiction and flexibility as its way of thinking, and rules as its core cultural values [8].

The construction of the Great Wall since the mid of the Warring States period experienced development from simple to complex and finally turned the Great Wall into a 3-dimensional defense system with walls as its main skeleton built with soil, stones and bricks. During the Qin Empire, the Great Wall spread from Lintao to Liaodong; during the Han Dynasty, Liu Bang, founder of the Han Dynasty, built the Great Wall until the original frontier fortress with the Hun; in order to facilitate diplomatic missions and cut the connection between the Hun nationality in the Northwest and the Southern Qiang nationality in the Southwest, the Martial Emperor of the Han Dynasty extended the Great Wall toward the Northwest along the Gansu Corridor; the Sui Dynasty built the Great Wall seven times; till the Ming Dynasty, the construction of the Great Wall was a key defensive measure in the north for the dynasty. Combining walls, passes, military castles, and towns of military importance, the Great Wall has the multi-functions of fighting, commanding, observation, communication and hiding. The military camps and towns also acted as hubs for habitation, trading and exchanges between the South and the North.

The cultural values of the South and the North of China are different because of the different economic patterns and production ways. In the era of cold weapon, there was no way out for the frequent conflicts between the South and the North. Since the period of the Miaodigou Culture in Prehistoric Period, the northern nationalities explored southward periodically according to the changes in climate and environment. In particular after 4300 years ago, the evasion by the nomadic nationalities became a nightmare of the agro nationalities in the Central Plains. In the mid of the Warring States period, defensive walls were built in the Central Plains for the purpose of defense among agro states. The States of Qi, Yan, Han, Zhao, Wei, Qin and Zhongshan built the walls one after another. In the mid and late Warring States period, with the emerging conflicts between the South and the North and the new defense needs, in order to defend[9] the periodic evasion by the northern Nomadic nationalities, the states in the Central Plains copied the walls to the agro-pastoral ecotone in the northern border. The States of Qin, Zhao and Yan, which were located in that region, began to built defensive walls. Since then, the original Central Plains Dynasties of Qin, Han, Sui, Ming and the Dynasties of Northern Wei, Northern Qi, and Jin, which were established after southward evasions, all built defensive wall in order to defend the northern nomadic evasions. It's safe to say that the Great Wall was at first a product of wars among the different States during the Zhou Dynasty, and was then introduced to the north part of the ancient China. It is a direct demonstration of the conflicts and integration of the agro and nomadic nationalities.

From the purpose of safeguarding the self interests among agro regimes at the beginning, to easing the conflicts between agro and nomadic regimes and maintaining the economic and social orders inside and outside the Great Wall, the construction of the Great Wall has brought multi effects to the evolution of the Great Wall Zone. The Great Wall is the very reified demonstration of the way of thinking of "contradiction" and "flexibility", which was a product of the "yin-yang and five elements" outlook[10] on the universe. In ancient Chinese societies, the rulers had the illusion of securing the agro civilization by a defensive wall for more than 2000 years. In this sense, the Great Wall acted as a psychological line of defense for agro nationalities. The Great Walls in different times were the military defense systems with the largest scale, the longest building span and the most complex system in the cold weapon era. As the biggest manual architecture, the Great Wall is not only the greatest military defense system in the ancient history, but also a manifesto of the birth and development of the Han Civilization.

III. The Great Wall is an Embodiment of the Han Civilization's "Flexible" Way of Thinking

The area around the Great Wall is a sensitive transition zone in terms of environment and climate. The economic and geographical ecological structure, determined by the many environmental conditions and climatic characteristics, has to a certain extent created the vast difference in customs and cultures among different ethnic groups. Before the establishment of the Qin Empire, the nomadic tribes in the north, especially the Xiongnu, were also independent and unacquainted with one another. Ten years after the Qin Empire was established, an unprecedented empire made up of unified grassland tribes took shape. From then until the time when modern weapons became available, the interaction between the agricultural and pastoral people around the Great Wall had always been a main theme in the evolution of Chinese civilization[11]. This evolutionary development process was inevitable because given the ecological environment, economic structure and ethnic composition of the area around the Great Wall, in order to mediate conflicts between the lifestyles and economic and political interests between the two groups, the ruling classes of each tribe had to be flexible in their choices when it came to the nation's (or the tribe's) political strategy. The Great Wall is not only a symbol of the conflict between agricultural and pastoral people, but also a product of the contradiction between them, or even a platform for their integration.

Objectively speaking, from the 4th century BC, the construction of the Great Wall gradually changed to ease the conflict between the agricultural and pastoral people and maintain the social and economic order within and outside the Great Wall. The wall was initially constructed to form a barrier that could prevent the northern grassland people from travelling south. The Great Wall project has since led to the formation of new transportation conditions. The roads, military garrisons and cities along the inner side of the Great Wall, have objectively promoted the maturity of the "Northern" transportation system[12]. During the formation of the transportation network and economic and cultural development of the Great Wall, places along the wall have also seen the development of a number of centers for urban and commercial trade and material distribution (Zhangjiakou, Datong and so on) , and finally, the Great Wall area has become a hub for the interaction of forces of attraction and repulsion between the borderlands and the hinterlands, playing a bridging role of attraction and cohesion internally and of integration externally[13].

For more than two thousand years, the agricultural people of the Central Plains have formed a huge network centered around the Great Wall by means of stationing troops there, immigration, trade and so on. Its radiating effect has brought the various ethnic groups inside and outside the wall closer together, and has closely integrated the agricultural and pastoral civilizations by way of mountain passes along the inside and outside. Since prehistory, there have been continuous and ever-broadening cultural exchanges between the agricultural and pastoral peoples around the Great Wall. After the formation of defense systems supported by cavalry, the Great Wall and the border counties (buffer zones) in the Qin and Han Dynasties, exchanges between the Central Plains cultural area and the northern nomadic economic and cultural areas entered a period of rapid growth [14]. From the Qin and Han dynasties up until the Ming Dynasty, the rulers of the Central Plains throughout the ages who ruled the Central Plains, continued to build the Great Wall while allowing large-scale immigration, constructing transportation passages, and opening up new areas along its frontier; the essence of the opening and closing of trade in border towns, trading grounds, markets, as well as trade in tea and horses, and the state of vassalage or independence of the various ethnic groups in the past [15] was based on the kind of social, economic, political and cultural exchanges the ancient dynasties of the Central Plains allowed with the various ethnic groups around the frontiers.

As the most direct form of communication between the agricultural and pastoral cultures, attempts at pacifying the nomadic people by marrying off daughters of the imperial family to them and engaging in trade with them highlights the flexible way of thinking and characteristics of the Han civilization. Agricultural farming and grassland animal husbandry are two completely different production methods determined mainly by the natural environment. The essential differences between them have led to an inevitable relationship of exchange, with the nomadic people in particular needing to acquire the food, clothing, iron, tea, salt and other necessities produced by the agricultural people in the long term, while the agricultural people hoped to receive fur, dairy products and so on from the pastoral people; a situation which promoted and maintained trade between these two peoples with their own economic and cultural systems for more than two thousand years. It can be said that this inseparable economic link between agricultural and pastoral peoples is the root cause of mutual trade. In the fifth year of Emperor Longqing in the Ming Dynasty (1571), mutual trade began between the Han and Mongolian peoples. The long-term policy of keeping the country shut off was changed. After that, from Yanyong in the east to Jiayu in the west, "there was no threat of war, soldiers slept soundly, the people at the border married each other and looked after each other, and trade never ceased." Marrying off daughters of the empire was also a strategy that the agricultural civilization had no choice in adopting. In the early Han Dynasty, the Xiongnu "often used to come and rob and pillage the border areas", the Western Han regime was forced to "offer daughters up for marriage to those from the border areas and pay them off in order to maintain the security there". Since then, there were marriages between daughters of emperors in the Tang Dynasty and

those of the Tubo, Huigu, Xi, Qidan and other ethnic groups.

IV. The Great Wall Zone is the distribution center of the core cultural values of the "rules" of the Han civilization

The Chinese culture develops from clan to tribe, from ancient city to country, kingdom and empire, and from modern time to contemporary time. It is a process of constantly breaking existing cultural, psychological, or natural geographical boundaries, a process of learning how to get along with people in larger scope, and also a process of constantly learning how to to live with people with various cultural backgrounds in harmony. In this process, the consensus formed in different periods is the core cultural values in different historical stages [16]. The origins of different ethnic groups in the Great Wall area varies, but in the process of dealing with each other for thousands of years, the "People integration" through exchanges and learning is no longer a simple "Hanhua" (assimilation by Han people) or "Huhua" (assimilation by ethnic minorities) , but a comprehensive integration deeply rooted in all aspects including culture, system, ideology and spirit. After ruling the Central Plains in China, both the agricultural government and the nomadic power hope to continue to unify China consciously or not. The formation of this kind of thinking is an inevitable trend of people's integration for a long time. Especially after the nomadic regime entered the Central Plains, it was necessary to integrate deeply with the ideology and culture of the agricultural people in order to achieve stable and harmonious development, and to integrate with the Han people in politics, economy, culture, etc. It was also a process of integration between Han nationality and ethnic minorities and formation of a pluralistic Chinese nation.

The economic and cultural exchanges in the Great Wall area had significantly promoted the formation of Chinese civilization [17]. The important physical proof of the cultural exchange between the Central Plains and the Northern nomadic culture discovered in archaeological sites was innumerable. In history, farming culture had a great impact on nomadic culture. The Han language, ideology, etiquette, culture and art had profoundly influenced the cultural and civilization development of the nomadic people in the Great Wall area, and the interaction between agriculture and nomadic civilization centered on the Great Wall had spread greatly the core cultural values of the "Guiju (rules and principles) " of the Han civilization. For example, the records regarding letter correspondence between the Hun and the Qin and Han dynasties on the Han Shu reflected the Hun's understanding and use of Han language. The Dangxiang, the Qidan and the Jurchen also created characters of their own on the basis of Han characters. In the nomadic area north of the Great Wall, many Zhujian [18] (books made from bamboo strips) describing the Confucian classics such as Lunyu and Liji were unearthed. In the Kucha country in Han Dynasty, the Central Plains culture worshipers spread from the upper royal family to the civilians, who followed the music, system and clothes, build places and defending perimeters, did routine publication, tolled the bell under the Han influence. The tomb from Wuhuan period is located in Xichagou, Xifeng county, Liaoning Province, where iron shovel and axe, pottery with rope pattern, bronze mirror, currency with Han style were discovered [19]. Many iron axes, knives, shovels and swords from the Central Plains were unearthed in Han Dynasty tombs in Luobupo, Xinjiang and Xifeng, Liaoning, proving iron smelting technology had circulated to areas alongside the Great Wall [20]. At the same time, the culture of various ethnic minorities also gathered in the Central Plains, influencing its culture greatly. For example, from King Zhao Wulin's promotion of Hu clothing to the Qing Dynasty's cheongsam and Magua, the ethnic minorities had brought about a major transformation of the Han clothing. During the Wei and Jin Dynasties, a large number of northern nomads brought the "Hu bed (chair) " into the farming area, triggering a revolution in the living habits of the Han people [21]. Cotton, rapeseed, sesame and other food crops and related planting techniques were all introduced into the Central Plains from the Western Region through the Silk Road, while grains including soybeans and chestnuts were products of the semi-agricultural and semi-pastoral economy in the Northeast China.

The process of ethnic integration is in line with the process of the formation and development of the unified Chinese people. The Central Plains dynasties had already established the county system in the Spring and Autumn Period, with the records that Xiadafu (lower level officials) defeating enemies could be awarded counties as fief [22]. During the Warring States Period, Qin, Zhao and Yan kingdoms also set up counties as administrative agencies in the northern frontier to consolidate border defense. The Qin Empire set up three counties in the original place of Yiqu to build the Great Wall to reject Hu minorities. The Central Government of the Western Han Dynasty set up a governor well paid in Wuheng area, who also administrated occasional trade between the Wuhuan tribe and surrounding farmers. These administrative agencies for managing the frontiers and the officers for managing the nomadic tribes had made the inter-inhabited ethnic groups in the northern border areas of the Han dynasty with different living and producing habits, which benefited the deep integration between farming and animal husbandry. Since then, many government positions to manage the nomadic tribes were created including the Chamasi in the Song dynasty, the Xishujian in the Yuan dynasty, and the Quechangshisi and Chamashisi in the Ming dynasty. In Tang dynasty, regimes were established covering two or multiple areas and ethnic groups located south and north of the Great Wall, making it a strategic site for connection and communicaton between North, South, East and West China [23].

In the national governance, the management of the two-track system for agriculture and animal husbandry was also an important institutional innovation. In the agricultural area, the state and county system was implemented. For the animal husbandry area, affiliated country, Dahong lu North-South Double Systems, Lifanyuan, Jimifuzhou, Duhufu, Dusi, counselors, ministers and so on were established or appointed by the central and region governments, in order to implement divided administration between Hu and Han or divided administration on customs and living habits [24]. In the Qin and Han dynasties, kingdoms were established in the agricultural area of the Great Wall Zone, while Hun unified the animal husbandry area and established a unified political power. In the 51 BC, Hun King Huhanye chanyu returned to the Han Dynasty, unifying the two regimes and the Chinese state power began to combine both agriculture and animal husbandry civilization. Until the Ming and Qing dynasties, the general China national system was in the same vein, and cultural traditions were never cut [25]

In addition, the Great Wall had also played an important role as an ancient transportation channel. The transportation network was formed in the long-term economic and cultural exchanges between China and foreign countries, and played an important role in economic and cultural exchanges. The Great Wall was not only the defensive boundary of the ancient frontiers, but also connected the various civilizations of Central Plains and its surrounding area. It was an important link in the Silk Road for cross-regional, cross-cultural and cross-civilization communication [26], which promoted development of thoughts, politics, culture, technology and economy in the East, West, North and South regions. In ancient China, the development levels of society, economy and culture between different regions and ethnic groups in the Great Wall area varied greatly. The Central Plains agricultural area was relatively advanced and developed, and the construction of the Great Wall showcased the differences in ethnic culture in a more direct way. The Han civilization not only had a great influence on the cultural development of the ethnic minorities in the Great Wall area, but also spread to the further areas through the ethnic minorities alongside the Great Wall. Up to now, Lunyu, Xiaoiing, Liji and other Han language classics written on bamboo strips, silk and paper have been discovered and unearthed in many ethnic areas. Besides, many Han language classics were translated or orally passed through various ethnic groups in the Great Wall zone, and some Confucianism had also evolved into customs of ethnic minorities [27]. At the same time, cultural customs of some nomadic people, such as clothing, sitting, and eating, were also integrated into agricultural civilization.

V. Conclusion

All kinds of civilizations are composed of a social governance system, view of the universe and core cultural values. Core cultural values are the basis of people's behaviors in dealing with matters in a civilized system [28]. Cultural heritage value is a value system composed of a series of diverse and related subsystems. The cultural value systems of different eras and different nationalities have clear differences [29]. Under the cognitive system dominated by history, art and scientific values, the fundamental value of the Great Wall is understood from the technical level of "reasonable utilization". This first answers the specific forms of expression of what the Great Wall is and what its value is [27]. Moreover, under the theoretical system of views of the cosmos, social governance and core cultural values (the "three-view"), against the grand historical background of the formation and evolution of Chinese civilization, the construction of the Great Wall and the interaction of agricultural and pastoral peoples around it, the core cultural values of the Great Wall, embodied and reflected in archeology, can be explored and revealed, and found to contain the ways of thinking and ways of handling of affairs of the Han civilization. Specifically, the "tangible" Great Wall is the product of the material civilization of ancient Chinese society, and is the materialized expression of the "confrontational" thinking mode of the Han civilization. It has outstanding value in terms of history, science, art, military, architecture, literature, society, landscaping, education and so on. The "intangible" Great Wall, as the distribution center of the core cultural values of Chinese "etiquette" and "rules", witnessed the long-term integration of the agricultural and pastoral peoples in terms of material life, social life and spiritual life, showing the flexible way of thinking of the Han civilization. The Great Wall is a spiritual symbol and source of cultural wealth of the Chinese nation.

Reference

[1] Duan Qingbo. The culture value discovered and unearthed in archaeology[N].Guangming Daily, 2015-07-22, Page 10.

[2] Duan Qingbo, Liuyan. Attach huge importance to research on cultural heritage, innovate the cultural relic preservation[N]. 2017-01-13. Page 003: comprehensive part.

[3] [11] Duan Qingbo. The Great Wall-witness of the Chinese civilization. Guangming Daily. 2017-03-26, page 07.

[4] Baiyin Chagan. Survey and research on Han Great Wall[J]. Journal of Inner Mongolia Normal University (Philosophy and Sociology Edition) .1987, (1) :95-104.

[5] Duan Qingbo,Xu Weimin. Discovery and Research on Chinese Great Wall[M]. Beijing: Science Press. 2014, page 468.

[6] He Weiguang. The economic complementarity and non-equilibrium demand of nomadic people and farming people in ancient China[J]. Journal of Northwest Normal University (Sociology and Science Edition) . 2003, (1) :32-38.

[7] Dong Yaohui. On the formation of the Great Wall and the cohesion of the Chinese nation. The 2nd cross-strait Symposium on Chinese Traditional Culture and Modernization. Huaian, Jiangsu, 2004.

[8] Duan Qingbo. An Outline of Han Civilization in Archaeology. Papers on Chinese Archeology. 2018, (21) :189-217.

[9] Wang Guoliang. Research on the Great Wall of China. Preface[M]. Beijing: Commercial Press.1935, Page 1.

[10] Duan Qingbo. The cosmology from the center of the square to the five elements of yin and yang: Wisdom of Chinese culture (1) [N]. Study Times, 2018-08-08, A3: History of China and Foreign Countries Part.

[12] Wang Zijin, An Investigation of the Great Wall of Qin and Han Dynasty from the Perspective of Traffic History[J]. Journal of the Shijiazhuang academy. 2013, (2) :14-25.

[13] Xu Lili. Passage zone theory- A Primary Probe into China's Border Governance Theory. Study Frontline. 2017, (2) :67-75.

[14] Zhangjin. On the Defense System Supported by the Central Plains Cavalry, the Great Wall and the Border County during the Warring States Period and the Qin and Han Dynasties. Master essay in Inner Mongolia University, 2015.

[15], [24], [27] Li Fengshan, On the Position of the Great Wall Belt in the Development of Chinese National Relations. Journals of Chinese historical studies. 1998, (2) :140-153.

[16] Duan Qingbo. On the core value of cultural heritage [J]. The Central Plains Culture Research, 2018, (1) :102-110.

[17] Duan Bingqi, Yin Weizhang. Questions about the type of fauna of archaeological culture[J]. Cultural relic. 1981, (5) :10-18.

[18] Ma Liqing. An Analysis of the Ethnic Groups of the Tomb of Zhang Longdan and the Partial Tombs of the Southern Hun. [J]. Material in the Copy Press (Pre-Qin and Qin and Han Dynasty) . 2014, (2) :86-93.

[19] Sun Shoudao. Discovery of the ancient tombs of the Hun Xichagou Culture[J]. Cultural relic. 1960, (8,9) :25.

[20] Zou Houben, Weizheng. Golden buckle belt of the Western Han Dynasty Tomb of the Lion Mountain in Xuzhou. [J]. Cultural relic.1998, (8) :37-43.

[21] Huang Qingmin. Hu bed in the history and its changes[J]. Journals of Hubei Minority academy. (Philosophy and Social Science Edition) .2010, (5) :200.

[22] Yang Bojun. Annotations on Spring and Autumn Zuo Zhuan[M]. Beijing: Zhonghua Book Company.2009, Page 1614.

[23] Li Hongbin. China Frontier—on the meaning of the Great Wall in the Northern Tang Dynasty[J]. Academic Monthly. 2017, (2) :13-19.

[25] Yin Falu,Xu Shuan. Ancient Chinese cultural history. Book 1,2[M]. Beijing: Beijing University Press. 1991, Page 427,459.

[26] Chen Tongbin, Wang Linfeng, Renjie. The study of the cultural heritage value of the Great Wall. Chinese cultural heritage.[J].2018, (3) :4-14.

[28] Duan Qingbo. Cultural values of rites and rules: Wisdom of Chinese culture. Study Times,2018-08-22,A3:History of China and Foreign countries Edition.

[29] Liu Yan, Duan Qingbo. Research on the value system of cultural heritage[J]. Journals of Northwest University (Philosophy and Sociology Edition) 2016, (1) :23-27.

[30] Liu Yan, Duan Qingbo. Research on Great Wall World Cultural Heritage Protection. [J]. China National Conditions and Strength 2016, (10) :42-44.

隋代东都洛阳回洛仓遗址学术史回顾

中国国家博物馆　霍宏伟 [①]

摘要

　　回洛仓是隋代重要的国家大型粮库，位于隋东都洛阳城外北部，即今河南省洛阳市东北郊。2004 年，该遗址经考古钻探与发掘得到了进一步证实。2014 年，回洛仓遗址作为"中国大运河"核心组成部分，顺利入选世界文化遗产名录。本文从文献记载、考古钻探与发掘、学术文献的数据解析等不同角度，对回洛仓遗址考古发掘资料及研究成果做一简要梳理，总结出考古发掘的一些收获，体现在不仅初步掌握了该遗址的形制、布局及构成要素，而且积累了大量出土实物资料，对隋代仓窖的形制、结构及凿窖技术等问题均有了较为深入的认识。通过上述多方面的探讨，从而反映出回洛仓在"中国大运河"这一世界文化遗产中有着独具特色的重要地位。

　　关键词： 隋代东都洛阳城，回洛仓遗址，学术史，世界文化遗产

　　2014 年 6 月 22 日，在卡塔尔多哈召开的联合国教科文组织第 38 届世界遗产委员会会议上，回洛仓遗址作为中国申报"中国大运河"项目的核心组成部分（图 1），成功入选世界文化遗产名录。回洛

图 1　回洛仓遗址保护标识说明石碑

图 2　回洛仓遗址保护展示工程

　　① 霍宏伟，中国国家博物馆研究馆员，国博研究院副院长，历史学博士，主要研究方向为汉唐考古。著有《鉴若长河：中国古代铜镜的微观世界》《古钱极品》，合著《洛阳两汉彩画》《洛阳钱币发现与研究》《洛阳泉志》《中国钱币大辞典·考古资料编》。主编《洛镜铜华：洛阳铜镜发现与研究》。其中，《洛镜铜华》入选"2013 年度全国文化遗产十佳图书"，《鉴若长河》入选"2017 年度全国文化遗产优秀图书""三联书店 2017 年度十本好书"，入围"2017 中国好书"。

仓是隋代储藏粮食的国家大型粮库，该遗址发现于2004年，位于河南省洛阳市东北郊的瀍河乡。经过十余年的考古钻探与发掘，已基本掌握了该遗址的平面形制、布局及仓窖结构（图2），并得到了妥善保护与充分展示，建立了回洛仓遗址博物馆（图3）。今从文献记载、考古钻探与发掘、学术文献数据解析等三个方面，对回洛仓遗址的发现史与研究史做一简要回顾。

图3　回洛仓仓窖遗址保护展厅

一、文献记载中的回洛仓

回洛仓，最早见于史籍记载的是《隋书》，散见于《炀帝纪》《食货志》及《李密传》，"回洛仓"之"回"字，写作异体字"迴"或"廻"。在《资治通鉴》中也有一些记述。这两种史籍主要包括两方面内容，一方面是关于回洛仓创建及完工时间、地望、范围及仓窖数量等基本信息；另一方面，是涉及隋末农民起义军瓦岗军在李密的率领下与隋军在回洛仓一带作战的史料。

（一）关于回洛仓营建的史料

《隋书·食货志》："炀帝即位，……始建东都，以尚书令杨素为营作大监，每月役丁二百万人。……新置兴洛及廻洛仓。"[①]这条史料说明回洛仓的创建年代与隋炀帝营建东都洛阳城为同一时期，均为大业元年（605年）。2004—2005年，在回洛仓遗址仓窖C56内出土一块"大业元年"刻铭残砖，也充分印证了这一点[②]。

《资治通鉴》所记回洛仓内容较《隋书》略详，记录了仓城位置、范围及仓窖数量，所载日期有可能是仓城建成的时间节点。《资治通鉴》卷一八〇《隋纪四》：炀帝大业二年（606年），"十二月，置

---

①　（唐）魏征、令狐德棻撰.《隋书》[M].卷二四《食货志》.北京：中华书局，1973年：第686页。
②　洛阳市文物工作队.《河南洛阳市东北郊隋代仓窖遗址的发掘》[J].《考古》，2007年，第12期：第8—24页。

回洛仓于洛阳北七里，仓城周回十里，穿三百窖。"①

（二）关于隋末农民战争的史料

见于《隋书》者有两条资料。《隋书·炀帝纪下》：大业十三年（617年）夏四月，"己丑，贼帅孟让，夜入东都外郭，烧丰都市而去。癸巳，李密陷迴洛东仓。"②这条文献明确记述了回洛仓有"东仓"之说。

《隋书·李密传》：大业十三年，李密"因遣仁基与孟让率兵二万余人袭廻洛仓，破之，烧天津桥，遂纵兵大掠。东都出兵乘之，仁基等大败，仅以身免。密复亲率兵三万逼东都，将军段达、武贲郎将高毗、刘长恭等出兵七万拒之，战于故都，官军败走，密复下廻洛仓而据之。……会密为流矢所中，卧于营内，后数日，东都出兵击之。密众大溃，弃廻洛仓，归洛口。"③

有关大业末李密率领瓦岗军与隋军在回洛仓一带作战的史料，于《资治通鉴》中记载尤详。《资治通鉴》卷一八三《隋纪七》：恭帝义宁元年（617年），"癸巳，密遣裴仁基、孟让帅二万余人袭回洛东仓，破之。"元胡三省注："《新唐志》：孟州河阳有回洛故城。是地得名之由，见一百五十八卷梁武帝大同九年。"④

"东都出兵击，仁基等败走，密自帅众屯回洛仓。……乙未，还洛口。"⑤

"越王侗使人运回洛仓米入城，遣兵五千屯丰都市。"⑥

"己亥，密帅众三万复据回洛仓，大修营堑以逼东都；段达等出兵七万拒之。辛丑，战于仓北，隋兵败走。"⑦

"丁丑，越王侗使段达与庞玉等夜出兵，陈于回洛仓西北。密与裴仁基出战，达等大破之，杀伤太半，密乃弃回洛，奔洛口。"⑧

上述所引《资治通鉴》中的部分文献，紧紧围绕隋末农民战争与回洛仓的关系，披露了许多鲜为人知的历史细节。将今天沉睡地下的仓城，通过文字描述，立体地还原于当时错综复杂的社会环境之中，凸显出回洛仓控制着隋东都居民粮食命脉的重要性。

二、回洛仓遗址的考古钻探与发掘

回洛仓遗址的具体位置，曾经是一个未解难题。20世纪80年代，有学者根据《资治通鉴》记载"置回洛仓于洛阳北七里"推测，在今汉魏洛阳城北约6华里的朱仓村，周围地势平坦，地高干燥，传说为古代粮仓，可能为回洛仓遗址⑨。

---

① （宋）司马光.《资治通鉴》[M].卷一八〇《隋纪四》.北京：中华书局，1976年：第5626页。
② 《隋书》[M].卷四《炀帝纪下》.第92页。
③ 《隋书》[M].卷七〇《李密传》.第1628—1629页.
④ 《资治通鉴》[M].卷一八三《隋纪七》.第5726页.
⑤ 《资治通鉴》[M].卷一八三《隋纪七》.第5726页.
⑥ 《资治通鉴》[M].卷一八三《隋纪七》.第5727页.
⑦ 《资治通鉴》[M].卷一八三《隋纪七》.第5727页.
⑧ 《资治通鉴》[M].卷一八三《隋纪七》.第5735页.
⑨ 方孝廉.《洛阳附近的古代粮仓》[J].《中原文物》，1984年，第1期：26—29页.

回洛仓遗址的发现，源于 2004 年 6 月洛阳市第一拖拉机厂东方红轮胎有限公司整体搬迁改造工程启动。在位于洛阳市东北郊的瀍河乡马坡村和小李村征地两百亩，准备兴建厂房，先由洛阳市文物钻探管理办公室对这一片征地进行考古钻探，结果发现仓窖 71 座、道路 4 条。310 国道探区段南距隋唐洛阳城北墙约 1200 米。赵振华等先生认为，《资治通鉴》记述回洛仓位于洛阳北七里，说的是仓城与隋唐洛阳宫城之间的距离，并非仓城与隋唐洛阳外郭城北墙的距离。从 310 国道仓窖段向隋唐洛阳城中心大量七里，其位置恰好处于宫城之中[1]。

2004 年 9 月至 2005 年 6 月，洛阳市文物工作队对回洛仓遗址做了首次考古发掘。重点清理了编号为 C56、C63、C64 的 3 座仓窖与 1 条路土，在仓窖 C56 内还出土一块"大业元年"刻铭残砖。根据考古遗存及历史文献记载，推断该遗址为隋代回洛仓遗址[2]。

2012 年 1 至 10 月，洛阳市文物考古研究院等单位对回洛仓遗址进行了大面积的考古钻探，由此查明了回洛仓城的范围、总体布局及其与漕运相关情况。仓城平面呈长方形，东西长 1140 米、南北宽 355 米，共计 404700 平方米。墙宽 3 米、残存厚度 0.5 米。其整体布局是，在仓城东、西两部分区域，均为仓窖区，中央为管理区。东、西仓窖区的面积与平面布局基本相同，均由"十"字形道路将仓窖分为四个相对独立的储粮区。仓窖东西成行，南北成列。在计划发掘的 120 亩地范围内，钻探出 170 座仓窖，在其他区域钻探出 50 座仓窖，已确定的仓窖数量共计 220 座（图 4）。发掘者根据仓窖分布规律推测，整个仓城仓窖数量在 700 座左右[3]。

图 4　回洛仓遗址主要遗迹分布示意图

① 谢虎军、张敏、赵振华.《隋东都洛阳回洛仓的考古勘察》[J].《中原文物》，2005 年，第 4 期：26—29 页. 王璐.《一拖（洛阳）东方红轮胎有限责任公司整体搬迁改造工程文物钻探报告》[C]// 洛阳市文物钻探管理办公室编.《洛阳文物钻探报告》第一辑.北京：文物出版社，2008 年：第 203—215 页.
② 洛阳市文物工作队.《河南洛阳市东北郊隋代仓窖遗址的发掘》[J].《考古》，2007 年，第 12 期：8—24 页.
③ 洛阳市文物考古研究院.《洛阳隋代回洛仓遗址 2012—2013 年考古勘探发掘简报》[J].《洛阳考古》.2014 年，第 2 期：30—49 页.王炬.《洛阳市隋代回洛仓遗址》[C]// 中国考古学会编.《中国考古学年鉴（2013）》.北京：文物出版社，2014 年：第 307—308 页.

2013 年，回洛仓遗址发掘的工作重点是为同年 9 月京杭大运河申遗提供较为翔实的实物资料。主要清理了 C3、C46、C47、C143 等 4 座仓窖（图 5），了解了仓窖内部结构①。

2014 年 6 月至 2015 年 1 月，对回洛仓遗址的漕运渠道及仓城外南、北部的道路遗址进行了发掘。渠道位于仓城管理区南部，呈南北向（图 6），应该是为回洛仓运送粮食而开挖的人工渠道。在仓城北部储粮区的北墙外，发现 2 条早期路面，其中南北向路面应是仓城内南北向道路向北延伸的部分②。

图 5　回洛仓 46 号仓窖遗址俯瞰　　　　图 6　回洛仓漕运沟渠遗址

2015 年 5 月至 2016 年 1 月，发掘了位于回洛仓遗址西部的两座仓窖 C205、C206。由此可知，回洛仓遗址东、西两部分仓窖区在形制、规模、使用时间等方面基本相同，为全面掌握该仓城整体保存状况，提供了第一手的实物资料③。

2016 年，在清理的回洛仓遗址灰坑 H1 中，出土与回洛仓仓储有关的完整铭文砖 1 件、有铭文的残砖 6 件。铭文详细记载了管理仓窖的机构为"太仓署"，回洛仓名称为"新都仓"，以及储粮的数量，粮食的来源，仓窖在仓城中的具体位置，粮食入窖的年、月、日，各地与回洛仓粮食有关的官员姓名等。考古发掘证实，回洛仓使用时间短暂，隋亡后即遭废弃④。

通过对 2004—2016 年回洛仓遗址钻探与考古发掘资料的收集、整理，可以总结出以下五个方面的收获：第一，根据考古钻探与发掘结果，首次确定了文献中记载回洛仓的地理位置；第二，经过大面积的考古钻探，基本掌握了回洛仓遗址的形制、布局及功能分区，了解了该仓城的整体面貌与构成要素；第三，根据出土刻铭残砖，并结合历史文献资料，可以初步判断仓城的始建年代应是隋大业元年（605 年）；第四，近 10 多年来，相继清理了 9 座仓窖，积累了大量原始发掘资料，使今人对隋代

① 王炬、赵晓军.《洛阳市隋代回洛仓遗址》[C]// 中国考古学会编.《中国考古学年鉴（2014）》.北京：中国社会科学出版社，2015 年：第 332—333 页.
② 洛阳市文物考古研究院.《洛阳隋代回洛仓遗址 2014 年度考古发掘简报》[J].《洛阳考古》，2015 年，第 2 期：43—52 页.
③ 王炬、吕劲松、赵晓军.《洛阳市隋代回洛仓遗址》[C]// 中国考古学会编.《中国考古学年鉴（2016）》.北京：中国社会科学出版社，2017 年，第 320 页.
④ 王炬.《洛阳隋代回洛仓遗址 2015—2016 年发掘》[J].《大众考古》，2017 年，第 5 期.

单体仓窖的形制与结构、凿窖及防潮技术等问题都有了更为深入的了解；第五，在仓城灰坑中出土了一些刻铭砖，包含了大量文字信息，进一步丰富了当代学者对于隋代官仓管理制度的认识。

笔者建议，今后回洛仓遗址发掘应关注以下三个问题：第一，依据钻探、发掘及已知路土提供的线索，按图索骥，追踪仓城门址遗迹，弄清门址数量及分布位置；第二，在以往认为的"管理区"范围内，进一步查找、确认夯土台基，以证明晾晒谷物"场"的存在；第三，在仓墙与渠道交汇处，注意寻找水门或码头的遗迹现象。

三、有关回洛仓遗址学术文献的数据解析

借助于中国知网数据库的跨库检索功能，笔者对以"回洛仓"为主题的学术文献进行了计量可视化分析。文献总数为 134 篇；检索条件：主题 = 回洛仓，或者主题 = 回洛倉（模糊匹配）。

（一）总体趋势分析

1993 至 2018 年，在长达 25 年的时间内发表与回洛仓相关的学术文献数量趋势如下：1993 至 2005 年间，发表此类文章的趋势较为平缓，甚至有的年份还有空白。其中，1993、1994、1996、1998、2003、2004、2005 年均为 1 篇，2006 年为 2 篇，2007 年略有升高，达到 5 篇；2008—2010 年呈下降趋势，均为 3 篇；2011 年 5 篇，2012 年 4 篇，2013 年 10 篇，2014 年 17 篇，2015 年达到最高峰值，为 23 篇，2016 年 4 篇，2017 年 12 篇，2018 年 6 篇（图 7）。

与回洛仓相关的学术文献发表数量，自 2006 年开始逐渐呈上升态势，这是与 2004 年发现了回洛仓遗址有着密切关系。随着该遗址持续不断钻探与发掘成果的公布，相关的研究与报道文章也随之大量发表。2015 年刊发文献数量为 23 篇，达到顶点，这无疑是 2014 年回洛仓遗址作为"中国大运河"项目组成部分申报世界文化遗产成功之后带来的光环效应。

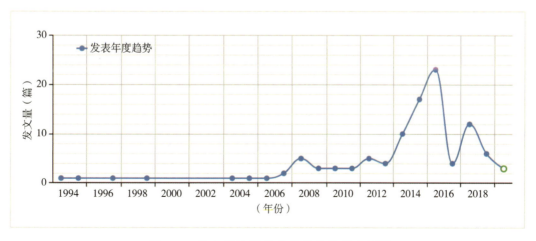

图 7　回洛仓遗址学术文献总体趋势分析图

（二）关键词分布

一是以"洛阳"为关键词的文献10篇，数量最多，以"回洛仓"为关键词者次之，为7篇。二是以"仓窖""隋代"为关键词者4篇，"仓储""隋唐""隋朝"者，均有3篇。三是以"古沉船""漕渠""含嘉仓""义仓""隋炀帝""整体搬迁""保护加固""武则天"为关键词者，均有2篇。以"社仓""单体仓窖""古代洛阳""国祚""科技"为关键词者，均有1篇。由此可以看出，关键词主要集中在"洛阳""回洛仓"这两个词上。

（三）学科分布

首先，属于考古学科的文献有77篇，占43.75%，接近一半的比例。其次，中国古代史33篇，旅游32篇。再次，文化9篇，档案及博物馆5篇。最后，农业经济、中国民族与地方史志、军事、领导学与决策学、地理均为2篇。中国通史、安全科学与灾害防治、文化经济、文艺理论、中国文学、人物传记、财政与税收、公路与水路运输、公安、行政法及地方法制，均为1篇（图8）。可以看出，对于回洛仓遗址的学术关注度较高，涉及到20个学科。

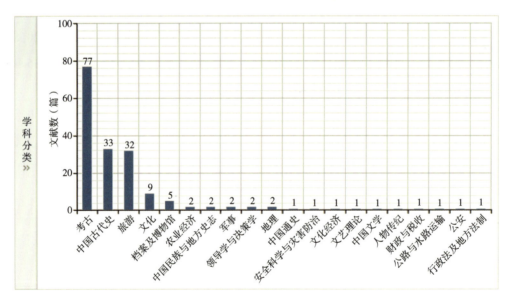

图8 回洛仓遗址学术文献学科分布图

（四）研究层次分布

属于基础研究（社科）者40篇，大众文化38篇，行业指导（社科）24篇，三者名列前茅。大众科普5篇，政策研究（社科）、文艺作品均为4篇，高级科普（社科）3篇，基础教育与中等职业教育2篇，行业技术指导（自科）、工程技术（自科）、职业指导（社科）均为1篇（图9）。由此分析，对回洛仓遗址的探讨，不仅成为学术界的热点问题，而且也成为社会大众关注度较高的考古议题。

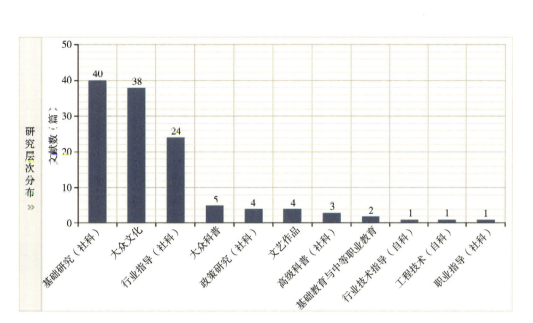

图 9　回洛仓遗址学术文献研究层次分布图

（五）文献来源分布

来自《洛阳日报》者 12 篇，刊发数量最多。《中国考古学年鉴》、《河南文化文物年鉴》、《洛阳考古》均为 7 篇，《中国文物报》6 篇。《光明日报》、《大众考古》、《黄河、黄土、黄种人》、《中国文化报》、《中原文物》、《洛阳年鉴》均为 3 篇，《中国国家博物馆馆刊》、《四川文物》、《农业考古》、《河南日报》、《人民政协报》、《世界遗产》、《武陵学刊》、《国学》、《学习时报》，均发表 2 篇（图 10）。

上述文献来源主要分为报纸、刊物及年鉴三类。报纸包括《洛阳日报》、《中国文物报》、《光明日报》、《中国文化报》、《河南日报》、《人民政协报》、《学习时报》，共计 7 种报纸。专业刊物主要有

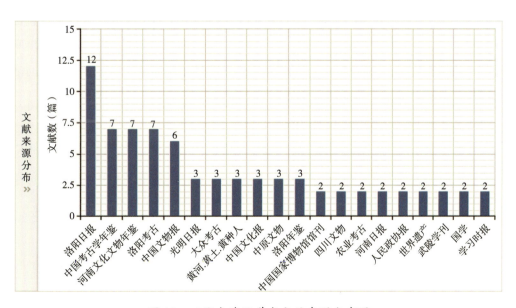

图 10　回洛仓遗址学术文献来源分布图

《洛阳考古》、《大众考古》、《中原文物》、《中国国家博物馆馆刊》、《四川文物》、《农业考古》等。年鉴有《中国考古学年鉴》、《河南文化文物年鉴》、《洛阳年鉴》。

（六）机构分布

有关回洛仓研究的学术机构，主要来自于文博考古机构、大专院校。属于前者的学术文献包括河南省洛阳市文物工作队 3 篇，河南省洛阳大遗址保护管理办公室 2 篇，洛阳古代艺术馆、河南省文物管理局、河南省文物考古研究所、中国文化遗产研究院均为 1 篇。

属于后者的主要有陕西师范大学、中国人民大学、西安建筑科技大学，均为 2 篇。湖南文理学院、苏州大学、湖南师范大学、湖南科技大学、江苏教育学院、广东工业大学、江苏师范大学、复旦大学，均为 1 篇。来自洛阳的作者数量最多。

（七）作者分布

作者包括 18 位，来自洛阳的作者数量最多。张晓东、余扶危、孟宪实发表与回洛仓相关学术文献均为 2 篇。梁克敏、王韬、李永强、谢虎军、叶万松、王阁、蔺俊伟、胡方、张敏、宫万琳、韩隆福、邱婕、曾谦、龚奭、王炬，均为 1 篇。

（八）基金分布

属于国家社会科学基金 2 项，河南省软科学研究计划 1 项。

四、结语

从宏观角度来看，回洛仓只是一个考古遗址点，"中国大运河"是一条纵贯南北的线。但是，应当看到东都洛阳城是隋大运河的中心枢纽，而回洛仓作为位于东都城北郊的一座国家大型粮库，汇聚了通过大运河输入的各地粮食。"民以食为天"，回洛仓的重要性不言而喻，由此亦反映出回洛仓遗址在"中国大运河"这一世界文化遗产中的独特地位。

附记：本文系国家社会科学基金项目"隋唐洛阳城空间体系研究"（项目批准号：18BKG031）阶段性成果。感谢中国文化遗产研究院党志刚先生、何正萱女士，洛阳市文物管理局李文初先生、洛阳市文物考古研究院王炬先生的支持与帮助，本文图一至图六由洛阳市文物考古研究院提供。

The Study in Huiluo Granary: An Historical Sketch

Huo Hongwei[①]
National Museum of China

Abstract:

Huiluo was a strategic state-run granary in the Sui dynasty. It was located in the northern part of Luoyang (then the capital) . The site of Huiluo granary was archaeologically confirmed in 2004. Ten years later, Huiluo, one of the key components of the Grand Canal of China, was inscribed on the World Heritage List. The present paper briefly discusses the history of the archaeological study in the site of Huiluo. It indicates that archaeologists have already shed revealing light on the site's shape, structure and composition. Digging into a large number of unearthed materials, researchers deeply examine the design and construction of granaries in Sui. Hopefully this paper will help readers understand better the Huiluo granary's significance to the Grand Canal.

Key words: Luoyang as Sui's capital, the site of Huiluo granary, World Heritage List, academic history

On June 22, 2014, the site of Huiluo (literally, returning to Luoyang) granary was inscribed on the World Heritage List (see Fig. 1) . Huiluo was a huge granary run by the central government of the Sui dynasty (581-618 AD) . The site was discovered in 2004. It is located in Chanhe, a small town northeast of present-day Luoyang city. The archaeologists have worked on this site for more than ten years and identified its shape, structure and composition (see Fig. 2) . The local government has built a special museum, whereby the Huiluo site can be well protected and fully displayed (see Fig. 3) . Having his research based on the ancient texts, the unearthed materials and recent research data, the author briefly discusses the history about the discovery and study of the

① Huo Hongwei, research fellow of the National Museum of China (NMC), and deputy director of NMC Instiute of Research, Ph.D. in history. His research interest is archaeology in Han and Tang dynasties. His publications include A Micro World of Bronze Mirrors in Ancient China and Masterpieces of Ancient Coins. His co-authored works include Colored Paintings of the Han Dynasty in Luoyang, Discovery and Research of Coins in Luoyang, A History of Luoyang Coins, and the Collection of Archaeological Documentations in the Chinese Dictionary of Coins. He was also the editor-in-chief of the book Discovery and Research of Bronze Mirrors in Luoyang, which was awarded one of the Ten Best Books of China in Cultural Heritage 2013. A Micro World of Bronze Mirrors in Ancient China won several national prizes, such as Excellent Books of China in Cultural Heritage 2017, Ten Best Books of Sanlian Bookstore 2017, and Good Books of China 2017.

Fig. 1 The stele describing the site of Huiluo granary

Fig. 2 The presentation and conservation project for the site of Huiluo granary

Fig. 3 The exhibition hall of the site of Huiluo granary

Huiluo granary.

I. A Textual Reexamination of the Huiluo Granary

The earliest extant written materials about the Huiluo granary (hereinafter referred to as the Huiluo) can be found in the *Book of Sui*. To be specific, several pieces of record ascribed to the "Annals of the Emperor Yang", "The Treatise on Economy" and "The Life of Li Mi" mentioned the Huiluo. The well-known *History in Aid of Governance* can also be included into this list. These records shed revealing light on the construction of the granary and the battles involving it in the peasant war in Sui's twilight years.

1. Primary sources about the construction of the Huiluo

"The Treatise on Economy" of *Book of Sui*. It reads: "When the Emperor Yang was enthroned, he appointed Yang Su, the head of the central secretariat, to the post supervising the construction of two state granary known as Xingluo and Huiluo. [In order to finish them,] two million laborers were mobilized every month." [1] This record demonstrated that the new emperor built the capital— Luoyang—and the Huiluo in the same year, that is, the firs year of Daye (605 AD) . One piece of 2004-2005 unearthed broken brick with the inscriptions reading "The First Year of Daye" corroborates this. [2]

History in Aid of Governance. It reads: "In the last month [of the second year of Daye (606 AD)], the Huiluo granary was finished at the site seven *li* north of Luoyang. This granary was ten *li* round and comprised of three hundred cellars." [3] Therein might lie the Huiluo's location, the number of Huiluo's cellars and the completion of the building work.

2. Primary sources about the battles involving the Huiluo in the peasant war

Book of Sui. Two pieces of record are available. One unambiguously indicated that the Huiluo was then known as the Eastern Granary. [4] The other showed that one of the leaders of the peasant army captured and then abandoned the Huiluo during the war. [5]

History in Aid of Governance. It provides more detailed records about the military campaigns around the Huiluo between the peasant and Sui armies. According to the present author's statistics, there are five pieces of concerned records. [6] These records unfolded the seldom-explored details regarding the relationship between the peasant war and the Huiluo before the readers. They reconstructed the history of the Huiluo against the complicated social background of the late Sui, revealing the true fact that the Huiluo was pivotal to the everyday life of the Luoyang residents.

II. The Archaeological Investigation of the Huiluo Granary

The exact site of the Huiluo had been not known to us. In light of the records in *History in Aid of Governance*, some in the 1980s inferred that the Huiluo should be seated at Zhucang, a village six *li* north of the Luoyang city. Taking into consideration the fact that the terrain of Zhuchang Village is high, flat and dry, a

---

① *Book of Sui* [隋书] (Beijing: Zhonghua shuju, 1973) , vol. 3, 686.
② The Luoyang Municipal Task Force of Cultural Relics (洛阳市文物工作队) , "The Archaeological Excavation of Sui Granaries in the Northeastern Outskirts of Luoyang" (河南洛阳市东北郊隋代仓窖遗址的发掘) , *The Archaeology* (考古) , no. 12 (2007) , 8-24.
③ *History in Aid of Governance* [资治通鉴] (Beijing: Zhonghua shuju, 1976) , vol. 12, 5626.
④ See: Vol. 1 of *Book of Sui*, 92.
⑤ See: Vol. 6 of *Book of Sui*, 1628-1629.
⑥ See: Vol. 13 of *History in Aid of Governance*, 5726, 5727, 5735.

scholar concluded that it was very probably the site of Huiluo granary.[①]

Archaeologists unraveled the mystery in June of 2004, when the China First Tractor Group was relocating. This industrial giant selected a new site, a two-hundred-*mu* land sitting between Mapo and Xiaoli villages in Luoyang's northeastern suburbs. According to the state regulation, an archaeological survey must be done before the construction work. When surveying, the archaeologists found 71 cellars and four interconnected roads. The distance between this site and the city wall of Luoyang as Sui's capital measures 1,200 meters. One piece of historical record asserted that the Huiluo was exactly built on the site seven *li* north of *Luoyang*. Some contend that Luoyang in this record refers to the imperial palace rather than to the capital's outer wall. Accordingly, the distance between the archaeological site and the midpoint of the Luoyang city is precisely seven *li*.[②]

In nine months (September 2004-June 2005) the Luoyang-based archaeologists made a groundbreaking excavation of the Huiluo. They worked particularly hard on three cellars (C56, C63 and C64) and one road. Most importantly, a broken brick on which there were the inscriptions reading The First Year of Daye was discovered in the fifty-sixth cellar. Textually and archaeologically, scholars conclude that it is exactly the site of Huiluo granary.[③]

Archaeologists in 2012 made a greater investigation lasting for ten months. In doing so, the Huiluo's size and layout and its relationship to the grain transportation by the Grand Canal were made clear. The Huiluo was a rectangular-shaped granary 1,140 meters long and 355 meters wide, covering in total 404,700 square meters. The width of its wall was three meters; and the (remaining) thickness, half a meter. The Huiluo was divided into three parts. The eastern and western parts were granaries; and the middle, the administrative area. The two granary areas was same in size and both were quatrochotomized by the cross-shaped road. The granaries were perfectly vertico-horizontally distributed. So far two hundred and twenty cellars have been detected (see Fig. 4) . In light of this, the archaeologists estimate that there should be, in total, seven hundred or so cellars in entire Huiluo.[④]

① Fang Xiaolian 方孝廉 , "The Ancient Granaries Located in Luoyang" (洛阳附近的古代粮仓) , *Cultural Relics in the Central Plains* (中原文物) , no. 1 (1984) , 26-29.

② See: Xie Hujun 谢虎军 , Zhang Min 张敏 , and Zhao Zhenhua 赵振华 , "An Archaeological Investigation of the Huiluo Granary in Luoyang, the Eastern Capital of Sui" (隋东都洛阳回洛仓的考古勘察) , *Cultural Relics in the Central Plains*, no. 4 (2005) , 26-29; The Luoyang Municipal Administration of Excavation of Cultural Relics (洛阳市文物钻探管理办公室) , *The Excavation of Cultural Relics in Luoyang: A Report* [洛阳文物钻探报告] (Beijing: Wenwu chubanshe, 2008) , no. 1, 203-215.

③ See: The Luoyang Municipal Task Force of Cultural Relics, "The Archaeological Excavation of Sui Granaries in the Northeastern Outskirts of Luoyang," *The Archaeology*, no. 12 (2007) , 8-24.

④ See: The Luoyang Institute of Archaeology (洛阳市文物考古研究院) , "The Annual Report (2012-2013) of the Excavation of Sui's Huiluo Granary in Luoyang" (洛阳隋代回洛仓遗址 2012—2013 年考古勘探发掘简报) , *The Luoyang Archaeology* (洛阳考古) , no. 2 (2014) , 30-49; The Chinese Archaeological Association (中国考古学会) ed., *The 2013 Yearbook of the Chinese Archaeology* [中国考古学年鉴 (2013)] (Beijing: Wenwu chubanshe, 2014) , 307-308.

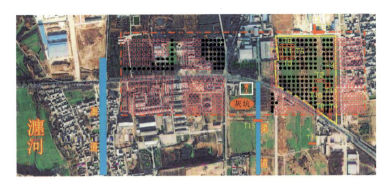

Fig. 4   The distribution map of the Huiluo site

Archaeologists in 2013 continued to work on the site of Huiluo, with a view to providing more convincing materials to the World Heritage Committee. They intensively investigated four cellars—C3, C46, C47 and C143 (see Fig. 5) , precisely figuring out the granary's inner structure.[①]

Archaeologists in 2014 and 2015 investigated Huiluo's canal and southern and northern roads outside the granary. The north-south canal was dug in the southern part of the administrative area and used exclusively to transport grain (see Fig. 6) . Two earlier roads were discovered outside the north wall of the northern area of granaries. Both should be the extension of the roads inside the Huiluo.[②]

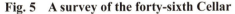

Fig. 5   A survey of the forty-sixth Cellar

Fig. 6: The Huiluo's canal

Archaeologists in 2015 and 2016 devoted themselves to the investigation of two cellars (C205 and C206), both of which were in the western part of the Huiluo. Their conclusion was that the eastern and western parts of the Huiluo were same in size, structure and date. This effort provides the first hand materials whereby the

---

① See: The Chinese Archaeological Association ed., *The 2014 Yearbook of the Chinese Archaeology* (Beijing: China Social Sciences Press, 2015) , 332-333.

② The Luoyang Institute of Archaeology, "The Annual Report (2014) of the Excavation of Sui's Huiluo Granary in Luoyang" (洛阳隋代回洛仓遗址 2014 年考古勘探发掘简报) , *The Luoyang Archaeology*, no. 2 (2015) , 43-52.

overall situation of the remaining Huiluo can be grasped.[①]

It is particularly worth mentioning that in 2016 an unbroken brick with inscriptions and six broken bricks engraved with characters were unearthed in one of the pits (H1) . Inscriptions indicated that the Huiluo's administrative organ was the Granary Authority and the Huiluo was also known as the New Capital Granary, as well as revealing the quantity and origin of the stored grain, the distribution of cellars, the storage time, and the names of concerned officials. According to the existing archaeological discoveries, it is safe to say that the Huiluo was abandoned as soon as the fall of Sui.[②]

Archaeologists made five achievements in the last twelve years (2004-2016) . First, the exact site of the Huiluo granary was confirmed. Second, the size, structure, composition, function and division of the Huiluo granary have been basically grasped. Third, the exact date of the construction of the Huiluo granary was the first year of Daye thanks to the inscriptions on the unearthed bricks. Fourth, nine cellars have been investigated with thoroughness and a great number of unearthed materials are greatly conducive to gaining an insight into the construction and use of the single granary in the Sui dynasty. Fifth, with the help of the unearthed inscriptions researchers obtain much better understanding of Sui's granary administration.

The archaeological investigation shall be furthered in the near future. In light of the known evidences, archaeologists shall try their best to find 1) where the gates were and how these gates were distributed, 2) the rammed earth on which the grain was aired in the sun, and 3) the water gate and wharf between the granary walls and the canal.

III. Data Analysis on the Academic Literature about the Huiluo Granary Site

The author conducted a quantitative visualization analysis of the academic literature on the subject of "Huiluo Granary Site" by using the cross-database search function of the CNKI (China National Knowledge Infrastructure) . 134 academic papers were searched under the criteria "subject = Huiluo Granary Site" (回洛仓 or 回洛倉 in Chinese; the latter is fuzzy matching) .

1. Analysis of the general trend

As shown in Fig. 7, the trend about the number of academic literature related to the Huiluo granary published in 25 years from 1993 to 2018 was as follows: from 1993 to 2005, the number of articles published

---

① See: The Chinese Archaeological Association ed., *The 2016 Yearbook of the Chinese Archaeology* (Beijing: China Social Sciences Press, 2017) , 320.

② Wang Ju 王炬 , "The Annual Report (2015-2016) of the Excavation of Sui's Huiluo Granary in Luoyang" (洛阳隋代回洛仓遗址 2015—2016 年发掘) , *The Popular Archaeology* (大众考古) , no. 5 (2017) , 14-15.

remained pretty much unchanged, and in some years no article was published. Among them, 1 paper was published in 1993, 1994, 1996, 1998, 2003, 2004 and 2005, 2 were published in 2006, and 5 were published in 2006, going up slightly; 2008-2010 witnessed a downward trend, with 3 papers being published each year; the number was 5, 4, 10, and 17 in 2011, 2012, 2013, and 2014 respectively; 23 were published in 2015, reaching a peak; and the number was 4, 12, and 6 in 2016, 2017, and 2018 respectively.

The number of academic literature published related to the Huiluo Granary has been on the rise since 2006, which could be attributed to the discovery of the Huiluo Granary Site in 2004. As the exploration of the site went on and more artefacts were unearthed, a large number of research papers and media reports were also published. The number of academic papers published in 2015 was 23, reaching a record high. It was because the Huiluo Granary Site joined the World Cultural Heritage in 2014 as part of the "China's Grand Canal" project.

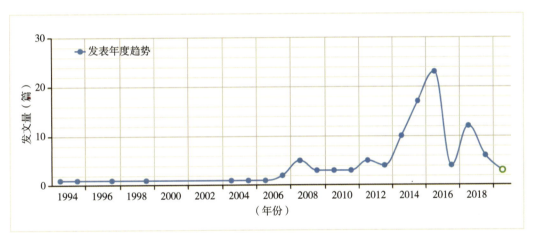

Fig. 7   General Trend of the Number of Academic Literature Published Related to the Huiluo Granary Site

2. Distribution of the key words

"Luoyang" is the key word of 10 papers, ranking the first, followed by "Huiluo Granary" (7 papers). What comes next is "Cellar" and "Sui Dynasty", the key words of 4 papers, and "Warehousing", "Sui and Tang Dynasties" and "Sui Era" (each appearing in 3 papers as a key word). Then comes "Ancient Shipwreck", "Drainage", "Hanjia Granary", "Spare Granary", "Emperor Yang of Sui Dynasty", "Overall Relocation", "Protection and Reinforcement" and "Empress Wu Zetian", each appearing in 2 papers as a key word. The last comes "Relief Granary", "Single Cellar", "Ancient Luoyang", "Fortune of the Nation" and "Technology", each appearing in 1 paper as a key word. It therefore can be deducted that the keywords are mainly concentrated on "Luoyang" and "Huiluo Granary".

3. Distribution of disciplines

First, 77 papers are about archaeology, accounting for 43.75% of the total. Then comes 33 papers about ancient Chinese history and 32 about tourism, followed by 9 about culture and 5 about archives and museums. Then comes 2 papers about agricultural economy, Chinese national and local history, military science, leadership and decision-making, and geography each. Finally comes 1 paper about China's general history, safety science and disaster prevention, cultural economy, literary theory, Chinese literature, biographies, finance and taxation, highway and waterway transportation, public security, administrative law and local legal system each (Fig. 8) . It can be seen that the much academic attention has been given to the Huiluo Granary Site, as 20 disciplines have been involved.

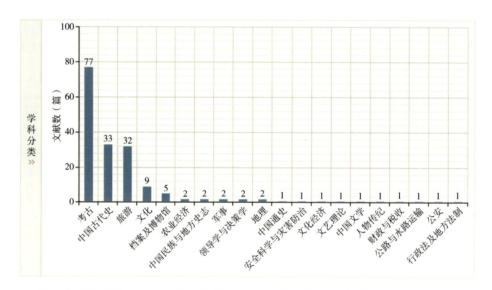

Fig. 8   Disciplines of academic literature related to the Huiluo granary site

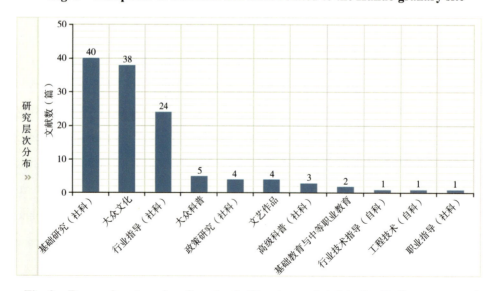

Fig. 9   Research categories of academic literature related to the Huiluo granary site

4. Distribution of Research Categories

The top three are as follows: 40 papers of basic research (social science), 38 of popular culture, and 24 of industry guidance (social science). Then comes 5 papers of popular science, 4 of policy research (social science), 4 of literary and artistic works, 3 of high level of popular science (social science), 2 of basic education and secondary vocational education, 1 of technical guidance for industry (natural science), 1 of engineering technology (natural science), and 1 of vocational guidance (social science) (Fig. 9). It can be seen that the exploration of the Huiluo Granary Site has not only become a popular subject in the academia, but also emerged as an archaeological topic attracting huge attention from the public.

5. Sources of academic literature

Twelve papers were published on the Luoyang Daily, ranking the first. Seven were published on China Archeology Yearbook, Henan Cultural Relics Yearbook, and Luoyang Archeology each, followed by 6 on China Cultural Relics News. Guangming Daily, Popular Archeology, Yellow River Yellow Earth Yellow Race, China Culture Daily, Cultural Relics of Central China, and Luoyang Yearbook each published 3 papers. Journal of National Museum of China, Sichuan Cultural Relics, Agricultural Archeology, Henan Daily, PPC Daily, World Heritages, Journal of Wuling, Chinese Traditional Culture, and Study Times each published 2 papers (Fig. 10).

The sources are categorized into newspapers, journals and yearbooks. There are 7 newspapers, including the Luoyang Daily, China Cultural Relics News, Guangming Daily, China Culture Daily, Henan Daily, PPC Daily, and Study Times. The journals include Luoyang Archeology, Popular Archeology, Cultural Relics of Central China, Journal of National Museum of China, Sichuan Cultural Relics, Agricultural Archeology, etc.

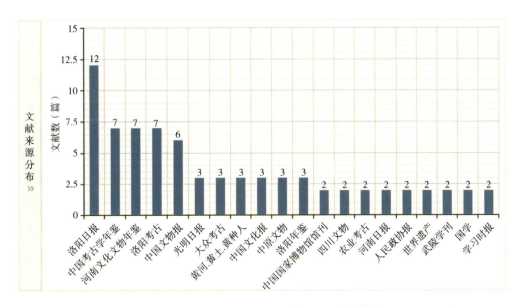

Fig. 10   Sources of academic literature related to the Huiluo granary site

The yearbooks include China Archeology Yearbook, Henan Cultural Relics Yearbook, and Luoyang Yearbook.

6. Distribution of institutions

The academic institutions conducting research on the Huiluo Granary are mainly archaeological institutions and universities. The former includes The Cultural Relics Team of Luoyang City, Henan Province (contributing 3 papers) , Luoyang Great Ruins Protection Management Office of Henan Province (contributing 2 papers) , and Luoyang Ancient Art Museum, Henan Provincial Cultural Relics Administration, Henan Provincial Institute of Cultural Relics and Archaeology, and Chinese Academy of Cultural Heritage (each contributing 1 paper) .

The latter includes Shaanxi Normal University, Renmin University of China, and Xi'an University of Architecture and Technology (each contributing 2 papers) , and Hunan University of Arts and Sciences, Suzhou University, Hunan Normal University, Hunan University of Science and Technology, Jiangsu Institute of Education, Guangdong University of Technology, Jiangsu Normal University, and Fudan University (each contributing 1 paper) .

7. Distribution of Authors

A total of 18 authors contributed the papers. Zhang Xiaodong, Yu Fuwei, and Meng Xianshi each published 2 papers about the Huiluo Granary. Liang Kemin, Wang Tao, Li Yongqiang, Xie Hujun, Ye Wansong, Wang Ge, Jian Junwei, Hu Fang, Zhang Min, Gong Wanlin, Han Longfu, Qiu Jie, Zeng Qian, Gong Yan, and Wang Ju each published 1 paper.

8. Distribution of funds financing the research

Two were financed by the National Social Science Fund of China, and one was financed by Henan Soft Science Research Program.

IV. Conclusion

From a macro perspective, the Huiluo Granary is just an archaeological site as part of the "China's Grand Canal", a stream that runs across the north and the south. However, it should be noted that as the eastern capital Luoyang City was the hub of the Grand Canal in Sui Dynasty, the Huiluo Granary was a major state food warehouse located in the northern suburb of the capital, gathering the grains transported there across different parts of the country through the Grand Canal. "Food is the paramount concern of the people". The importance of the Huiluo Granary was self-evident, suggesting it is quite unique in the world cultural heritage "China's Grand Canal".

Note: This article is an initial achievement of the project "Research on the Space System of Luoyang City in Sui and Tang Dynasties" financed by the National Social Science Fund of China (Project Approval Number: 18BKG031). The author would like to thank Mr. Dang Zhigang of Chinese Academy of Cultural Heritage, Mr. Li Wenchu of Luoyang Cultural Relics Administration, and Mr. Wang Ju of Luoyang Cultural Relics and Archaeology Institute, for their support and help. Figures 1 to 6 are provided by Luoyang Cultural Relics and Archaeology Institute.